2/98

NOTABLE U.S. AMBASSADORS SINCE 1775

NOTABLE U.S. AMBASSADORS SINCE 1775

A Biographical Dictionary

EDITED BY
Cathal J. Nolan

Greenwood Press
Westport, Connecticut • London

Library of Congress Cataloging-in-Publication Data

Notable U.S. ambassadors since 1775 : a biographical dictionary /
  edited by Cathal J. Nolan.
     p. cm.
  Includes bibliographical references and index.
  ISBN 0–313–29195–0 (alk. paper)
    1. Ambassadors—United States—Biography—Dictionaries. 2. United
States—Foreign relations—Dictionaries. I. Nolan, Cathal J.
E176.N895 1997
327.73'0092'2—dc21   96–50291
 [B]

British Library Cataloguing in Publication Data is available.

Library of Congress Catalog Card Number: 96–50291
ISBN: 0–313–29195–0

First published in 1997

Greenwood Press, 88 Post Road West, Westport, CT 06881
An imprint of Greenwood Publishing Group, Inc.

Printed in the United States of America

∞™

The paper used in this book complies with the
Permanent Paper Standard issued by the National
Information Standards Organization (Z39.48–1984).

10 9 8 7 6 5 4 3 2 1

In memoriam

Frank Sherman,
whose untimely death deprived this volume of a wise contributor,
its editor of a friend and colleague,
his students of a gifted and dedicated teacher,
and the world of a kind and decent man.

CONTENTS

CONTENTS

PREFACE

The purpose of this volume is to provide to the scholarly community, and to other interested readers, historical-biographical profiles of a select group of American ambassadors who had notable careers in the U.S. Foreign Service. Any work of this type demands that choices be made among a host of worthy possibilities. The period spanned by the volume is more than two hundred years, and the geographical scope is, ultimately, global. As America matured as a nation and expanded across a continent, perceptions of its commercial and security interests also widened. American diplomacy then had to take account of new issues and new regions that impinged on the national interest. This development is reflected in the choices made for this volume. Early ministers (as ambassadors were known throughout the nineteenth century) were chosen who were noteworthy in the founding of the diplomatic service and in elaborating its early principles, habits, and culture. Others were picked as representative of distinct periods in the history of the Foreign Service: the decades of gifted (and sometimes not-so-gifted) amateurism and broad foreign policy indifference during much of the nineteenth century; the founding of a permanent professional diplomatic service in the early twentieth century; and expansion of the Foreign Service into a truly global instrument of American foreign policy during two world wars, the Cold War, and after.

For the post–World War II period, special attention was given to ambassadors whose personal stories shed light on U.S. relations with the major powers of Europe and Asia, but without neglecting those whose careers dealt mainly with the emerging states of the Third World. Some selections were made owing to a particular ambassador's individual achievement or great influence on matters

of policy. On the other hand, several are included who did not necessarily out-
shine their peers in performance of their professional duties or enjoy careers
that kept them always near the center of events. Instead, they were included
because some aspect of their career or a specific appointment represented significant milestones in the evolution of the Foreign Service itself. Finally, one
nonambassador has an entry: Colonel Edward M. House warranted inclusion as
President Woodrow Wilson's key advisor during World War I, as an independent voice at the Paris Peace Conference, and because he served as Wilson's
personal envoy during times of enormous historical moment for the United
States and the world.

In addition to these considerations, the editor solicited specific expert opinion
from regional and historical experts, former or current State Department employees, and several retired U.S. ambassadors. Not all recommendations were
accepted, mainly for reasons of space, but the advice received was still invaluable in narrowing the field and in making hard, final choices. Of course, not
all who proffered advice or who read this book will agree with the final selections. Some readers no doubt will object that too few women or black or other
minority ambassadors made the list; others may complain that too many women
or blacks have been included for mere milestone or representative reasons at the
expense of some individuals whose careers were clearly more notable. Those
whose interests focus on Great Power relations may think that too many ambassadors to lesser powers have made the list, yet those who deal with smaller
countries will no doubt feel slighted, as usual, for considerations of power and
interest must retain the attention of most observers over and above the small
states or quiet historical periods on which some scholars concentrate scholarly
attention.

Of course, not all the numerous ambassadors who have represented the United
States deserve inclusion in this volume. Yet, many not selected did give service
to their country such that they truly deserve the accolade "notable ambassador."
Leaving aside errors of omission that may have been committed by this editor,
the fact that many deserving diplomats were left off the final list is itself a
testament to the exceptionally talented people the United States has usually sent
abroad as its ambassadors.

Numerous books and scholarly articles deal with individual ambassadors or
with a succession of U.S. ambassadors to a particular country. On shelves near
the one upon which this book is found, readers will easily locate tomes dealing
with America's ambassadorial relations with Russia, England, China, or the
Netherlands, among other nations. But there is no other volume that attempts,
as this one does, a sustained examination of the role played by individual personalities and the beliefs of key ambassadors in the diplomatic history of the
United States.

These profiles provide basic information and essential facts, such as birth and
death dates (where relevant), and the broad pattern of a given ambassador's
career and views. But they go beyond mere reporting to assess the relative in-

fluence, and success or failure, of each ambassador's effort to advance America's foreign policy goals. Many highlight the significance of personality and personal contacts in successful diplomacy. Some point instead to the intrusion and pursuit of personal or partisan political agendas as an intermittent and underappreciated feature of diplomacy. The profiles vary in length, but all authors were commissioned to write with the same focus: identify the salient biographical features of each subject, explore the evolution of political thinking and the influence of career decisions on political perspectives and influence, evaluate the methods each ambassador used to advance policy interests, and describe the results they obtained or the failures they suffered. Clearly, meeting these demands was more difficult for authors dealing with subjects who are still alive (or even still active) in the Foreign Service than for those who enjoy the historian's luxury of delivering prophecy in reverse.

A brief bibliography of "Works by" and "Works about" each ambassador closes most entries. A more general bibliographic list of works in English that might interest the general reader follows at the end of the book. An index is included for those who wish to cross-reference important events or specific ambassadors or countries. It also provides signposts useful in locating information about people, places, and events mentioned in the book that are not specifically profiled.

The editor would like to thank, first and foremost, all contributors to this volume. Those who submitted their entries on time and in good order deserve special thanks for their patience with the time it took to compile the volume as a whole; those whom The Fates caused to be late in submitting entries can be thanked for their cheerful patience with the editor's frequent queries and prodding. The original idea for the book was raised with the editor by Mildred Vasan, formerly Senior Reference Editor at Greenwood, now retired. As with three earlier books worked on together, her calm professionalism and deep, independent scholarly knowledge was of great aid and comfort. The editor is also grateful to Acquisitions Editor Nita H. Romer for her able assistance, and to Lynn Zelem and Charles Eberline for seeing the manuscript through the publication process at Greenwood Press.

Lastly, the editor wants to thank his children, Ryan Casey and Genevieve Michelle, not for any specific contribution that hastened completion of his task, but because they are still at that delightful age when seeing their "very own names" in a real book has a near-magical quality that elicits expressions of excitement and joy that are as priceless as they are fleeting and rare.

NOTABLE U.S. AMBASSADORS SINCE 1775

MADELEINE KORBEL ALBRIGHT (1937–) was

president of the Center for National Policy (1989–1993), professor of international affairs and director of the Women in Foreign Service Program, Georgetown University (1982–1993), and U.S. permanent representative to the United Nations (1993–1996); and is the first woman Secretary of State (1997–).

It is perhaps natural that some U.S. foreign policy observers would compare Madeleine Albright's tenure as U.N. ambassador with that of Jeane Kirkpatrick, who held the same post twelve years earlier. Both earned their M.A. and Ph.D. degrees from Columbia University, both were long-time members of the Democratic Party, and both lectured at Georgetown University before being selected for the U.N. post. Each was influential in formulating foreign policy in the administrations that they served, and both found their terms as U.N. ambassador dominated by human rights issues that played out in the shadow of the Cold War. In their diplomatic styles as well, there were a number of parallels between the two. Like Kirkpatrick, Albright also adopted a colorful and at times combative stance that was at odds with the stodginess more common in the corridors of the U.N. Kirkpatrick raised three sons, while Albright raised three daughters, and both women were approximately the same age when they were nominated. Finally, each served at the United Nations for only one full term. But in one important respect, their experiences as U.N. permanent representative were fundamentally different. While Kirkpatrick was appointed U.N. ambassador during a period when the credibility of the United Nations was being called into serious question by the United States, and Cold War tensions had markedly intensified, Albright served at the end of the Cold War and during a period of rising U.N. involvement and prestige in world affairs.

Madeleine Albright was born on May 15, 1937, in Prague, Czechoslovakia, to Josef and Anna Korbel. Her family escaped the Nazi occupation as refugees in England, although Albright—who had been raised as a Catholic—only later discovered that she was actually of Jewish descent, and that many family members, including three of her grandparents, were killed in the Holocaust. The Korbel family returned to postwar Czechoslovakia in 1945, only to see their country's independence lost as it was progressively incorporated into the Soviet sphere of domination after 1945. Madeleine Korbel was only eleven years old when her family defected to the democratic West in 1948. Her father was offered a post as Czechoslovakia's representative on a U.N. commission dealing with the Kashmir dispute. The family was based abroad when the Communist coup occurred in Prague. This experience left its mark: during her 1993 Senate confirmation hearings for the U.N. post, Albright described herself as a child of the Cold War, the hybrid product of an Eastern European childhood and heritage and an American upbringing and education.

Madeleine Korbel graduated from Wellesley College with a B.A. with honors in political science in 1959. That same year she married Joseph Medill Patterson Albright (they divorced in 1983), and the couple subsequently raised three daughters together. While her children were still growing up, Madeleine Albright attended the School of Advanced International Studies at Johns Hopkins University in 1962–1963 and earned an M.A. from the Department of Public Law and Government and a certificate from the Russian Institute, both at Columbia University in 1968. Making use of her impressive language skills—she speaks and reads fluently Czech and French, and also has a strong grasp of Russian and Polish—her M.A. thesis examined the Soviet diplomatic service. Her interest in Soviet and Eastern European affairs and international affairs was a natural outgrowth of her Czech and family background. Albright earned a Ph.D. from the Department of Public Law and Government at Columbia in 1976. Her doctoral dissertation examined the role of the press in Czechoslovakia's 1968 ''Prague Spring.''

Albright drifted away from academia into a long association with the Democratic Party. Her first political job was as a chief legislative assistant on the staff of U.S. Senator Edmund S. Muskie (1976–1978). Albright was subsequently assigned to the staff of the National Security Council and the White House, where she was responsible for foreign policy legislation during the final years of the Carter administration (1978–1980). There, she served under Zbigniew Brzezinski, the supervisor of her doctoral dissertation and a fellow intellectual of East European background. With the election of Ronald Reagan in the 1980 presidential elections, Albright returned to academia. Her departure from politics was not total, however, and she later served as a foreign policy coordinator in Walter Mondale's presidential campaign (1984) and as a senior foreign policy advisor in Michael Dukakis's presidential campaign (1988).

In the meantime, Albright accumulated additional academic credentials. She was awarded a fellowship at the Woodrow Wilson International Center for Scholars (1981–1982), and served as a Senior Fellow in Soviet and Eastern European Affairs at the Center for Strategic and International Studies where she conducted research in developments and trends in the Soviet Union and Eastern Europe. Subsequent positions to which Albright was appointed included professor of international affairs and director of the Women in Foreign Service Program at Georgetown University (1982–1993), vice chair of the National Democratic Institute for International Affairs in Washington, D.C. (1984–1993), and president of the Center for National Policy, an organization that promotes the study and discussion of various domestic and international issues (1989–).

Because of her academic credentials and long record of political service to the Democratic Party on foreign policy issues, Albright was selected for the position of U.S. permanent representative to the United Nations shortly after the Clinton administration was voted into office in 1992. At her confirmation hearings on January 21, 1993, the members of the U.S. Senate Committee on Foreign Relations demonstrated a high degree of bipartisan support for her appointment. During the hearings Albright outlined three policy choices that she believed faced the United States in the post–Cold War world: America could play the role of global policeman, with the overwhelming diplomatic and military burdens that would accompany such an independent stance; it could assume the stance of an ostrich and return to its isolationist past, as many Americans at the time were suggesting; or it could continue to pursue an activist foreign policy, but share the burden of that responsibility in partnership with other nations through such organizations as the United Nations. It was clear that Albright preferred the last course. Other concerns raised during Albright's confirmation hearings included the issue of U.S. financial arrears to the United Nations—which Albright felt should be paid—and the much more controversial question of whether or not American soldiers would be required to serve as peacekeepers under U.N. command.

Once her nomination as U.S. permanent representative to the United Nations was announced, it was clear that Albright would play a major role in the formulation of foreign policy in the Clinton White House. Like her Reagan administration predecessor, Jeane Kirkpatrick, Albright was made a full member of the cabinet and, much more important, of the National Security Council (NSC). Clinton and his foreign policy advisors declared as their aim a reinvigoration of idealism as a motivating factor in U.S. foreign policy, and continuance of America's traditional concern for promoting human rights, democracy, and free markets around the world. The incoming Clinton administration seemed set to return to the Carter years. Many of the major foreign policy advisors in the Clinton White House had served in the State Department and the National Security Council under Carter.

Albright was among the most influential and outspoken of the foreign policy advisors in the Clinton administration to publicly reject neoisolationism. Yet the Clinton administration in practice remained ambiguous about whether its preferred alternative to noninvolvement in global affairs was unilateralism or multilateral activism conducted through bodies such as the United Nations. This ambiguity about the U.S. role—as global leader or international partner—was evident in confusing reactions to crises in Bosnia and Haiti. With the collapse of communism in the Soviet Union and Eastern Europe and the end of the Cold War, there was less public interest in foreign policy, and many familiar formulas and signposts from the past decades of superpower rivalry had disappeared. Although many Americans seemed more receptive to the idea of a strengthened United Nations and a somewhat activist foreign policy agenda, this sentiment had to be tempered by a more sober assessment of the capabilities of that international body in the wake of failed ''peacemaking'' operations in Somalia and elsewhere.

Albright assumed her new responsibilities at a time when the United Nations strove to act as a global peacemaker. The United Nations became involved in more peacekeeping operations after 1990 than in all the previous years of its existence. By 1993 U.N. troops were committed to thirteen separate peacekeeping and observer missions around the world. Of that total, nine operations in-

volved humanitarian interventions in civil war situations, and the total level of
U.N. troop commitments rapidly expanded from 10,000 at the end of the Cold
War to 70,000–80,000 by 1995–1996. The annual U.N. peacekeeping budget
also underwent a tremendous expansion and now totaled $4 billion annually.
Meanwhile, the Security Council was meeting on security matters on a much
more regular basis than before.

Albright's appointment as U.S. permanent representative to the United
Nations in early 1993 came shortly after Boutros Boutros-Ghali's election as
secretary-general. Boutros-Ghali quickly issued a report entitled *An Agenda for
Peace* in which he called for a much more active role for the United Nations.
Not satisfied with merely keeping the peace, the secretary-general sought a more
proactive policy that would permit international forces under U.N. command to
intervene in situations of civil strife to make, and then to enforce, the peace.
Less than two years later, in May 1994, the Clinton administration issued Presidential Decision Directive 25, which established conditions for U.S. involvement in such peacekeeping operations. But many in the U.S. public and
Congress remained uneasy about ambitious plans for a growing international
role for the United Nations in the post–Cold War world. Despite an initial spate
of neo-Wilsonian sentiment that emerged in the United States in the wake of
the 1990 defeat of Iraqi forces by a U.S.-led military coalition, a number of
tactical retreats on U.N. peacekeeping missions since that time have damaged
the credibility of international activism on such a grand scale. This was particularly the case with a failure to carry through on public threats to bomb Serb
targets in May 1993, the deaths of eighteen U.S. servicemen in Somalia in
October 1993, and a long-drawn-out embargo of Haiti preceding the commitment of U.S. ground troops in October 1994.

Throughout her years as U.N. ambassador, Albright devoted a great deal of
her energy to ensuring Iraqi compliance with Security Council cease-fire resolutions and arms control undertakings that Saddam Hussein had committed to
after his defeat in 1990. Within months of Albright's arrival at the United
Nations, she helped lead the Security Council to impose sanctions and an oil
and arms embargo on Haiti in an effort to press its junta to permit the return of
elected President Jean-Bertrand Aristide, who had been ousted by a coup d'état
in 1991. On September 18, 1994, an agreement was brokered by a U.S. delegation led by former President Jimmy Carter. Under its terms, and under the
threat of imminent U.S. invasion, the Haitian junta stepped down in return for
amnesty. A U.S.-led military force assumed control of the country and aided its
transition to civilian rule. In Somalia, meanwhile, American forces were replaced
as scheduled in May 1993 by a U.N. force whose mission was to distribute
relief supplies, enforce the arms embargo, and help rebuild the country. But all
international peacekeeping troops were eventually withdrawn from Somalia, and
international relief efforts were suspended, as U.S. and U.N. casualties mounted
and discord set in among the member states of the international force. Albright's
job was to manage the diplomatic side of this phased withdrawal and to mitigate

the public relations disaster it incurred for the United Nations within the United States.

The ethnic strife in Bosnia and the systematic killings of hundreds of thousands of civilians in the region were probably the greatest concern of all for Albright and other members of the Security Council during the first Clinton administration. In October 1992 the Security Council had agreed to set up a war-crimes commission to collect information on atrocities in the newly independent Balkan states. The following month a naval blockade was imposed to enforce a U.N.-sanctioned embargo. In May 1993 the Security Council voted unanimously to declare a number of areas crowded with refugees "safe havens" under U.N. protection, and additional troops were requested. In another significant move, in November 1993 a U.N. War Crimes Tribunal in The Hague, established partly at U.S. urging, began to investigate allegations of genocide and other atrocities in that conflict. The United Nations was frustrated by Serb recalcitrance and mounting evidence of mass killings. Meanwhile, a growing American desire to pursue a policy that was more supportive of Bosnian Muslim forces and more active militarily was evident, but was complicated both by domestic opinion and a need to maintain close relations with more cautious European allies who already had troops committed on the ground. Finally, faced with congressional passage of a vote to end the arms embargo, President Clinton sponsored the Dayton Accord of November 1995, which led to a tenuous settlement of the conflict at the cost of U.S. deployment of ground forces. American leadership in pressing for the Dayton Accord was balanced by multilateral guarantees by European allies to commit troops to enforce the peace on the ground.

Madeleine Albright became increasingly visible during her term at the U.N. In fact, she probably ranks among the most influential U.N. ambassadors in actually helping to formulate U.S. foreign policy, and was particularly influential in pressing for a more assertive policy in war-torn Bosnia. She also actively and successfully represented the interests of the United States at the United Nations during a period when that organization was more influential than ever before in its history. Albright was instrumental, for instance, in denying a second term to U.N. Secretary-General Boutros Boutros-Ghali, and his replacement with the administration's choice, Kofi Annan of Ghana.

Her remarkable efforts at building bipartisan support during her four years as U.N. permanent representative also paid off when she was nominated to replace Warren Christopher as Secretary of State in the second term of the Clinton administration. The confirmation hearings before the Senate Foreign Relations Committee in January 1997 were described by some observers as a veritable "lovefest." Even powerful Clinton administration critics like Jesse Helms (R-NC) never doubted her appointment, allowing Albright to assume the most powerful cabinet post ever held by a woman in the United States. As Secretary of State, Albright has sought to use her position as a platform to educate the public on U.S. foreign policy issues. At the same time, Albright admitted during the 1997 hearings that the "assertive multilateralism" that she espoused four years earlier had now been downgraded to a more limited "doability doctrine," with the United States assuming the role neither of global policeman nor isolationist power.

Works by Madeleine K. Albright

Poland, the Role of the Press in Political Change. New York: Praeger; Washington, DC: Strategic and International Studies, Georgetown University, 1983.

Coauthor, with Barry E. Carter. "Foreign Policy in the 1984 Election: The Mondale Campaign." *Washington Quarterly*, 8, no. 3 (1985): 217–35.

"U.S. Foreign Policy after the Gulf Crisis." *Survival* (November–December 1990): 533–41.

"The Role of the United States in Central Europe." In *The New Europe: Revolution in East-West Relations*. Ed. Nils H. Wessell. New York: Academy of Political Science, 1991.

Works about Madeleine K. Albright

Cooper, Matthew and Melinda Liu. "Mad about Madeleine." *Newsweek*, February 10, 1997, 22–29.

Dobbs, Michael. "Remembrance of Things Past: Secretary of State Albright's Tragic Family History." *The Washington Post Magazine*, February 9, 1997, 8–13, 18–25.

U.S. Senate. Committee on Foreign Relations. *Nomination of Madeleine K. Albright to be United States Ambassador to the United Nations*. Washington, DC: U.S. Government Printing Office, 1993.

Who's Who in America 1995. New Providence, NJ: Marquis Who's Who, 1995, 39.

RICHARD D. WIGGERS

JOHN ALLISON (1905–1978) was a career Foreign Service
officer who became ambassador to Japan, Indonesia, and Czechoslovakia in the
1950s after serving as John Foster Dulles's assistant in the negotiation of the
Japanese Peace Treaty.

Allison was born on April 7, 1905, and graduated from the University of
Nebraska in 1927 with a B.A. in political science. Rejecting a scholarship for
graduate work at Nebraska and refusing to go to work with his father, he accepted a job in Japan teaching English. With this position, this bibliophile from
the American Midwest started a thirty-year career as an East Asia specialist.
After teaching for a year at a middle school, Allison accepted a similar position
at the Imperial Japanese Naval Engineer Officers' Academy. An astute observer,
he saw the signs of the nationalism and xenophobia that became more pervasive
in the 1930s. Tiring of Japan and of teaching, he moved to Shanghai in 1929
to become a branch advertising manager for General Motors. Following the
stock-market crash, Allison looked for a new job and found a clerk position in
the U.S. consulate in Shanghai. In 1931 he took and passed the U.S. Foreign
Service exam and was commissioned as a Foreign Service officer (FSO) in early
1932.

His first assignment in the Foreign Service was to the embassy in Tokyo as
a language student. While there, he quickly came under the influence of Ambassador Joseph Grew. Allison was one of the six FSOs Grew trained who later
became ambassadors. After two years of studying Japanese and a short stint as
vice-consul at the embassy, Allison returned to China. First in Manchuria, then
in Shangtung, he saw Japan's forced march into China firsthand. He arrived in
Nanking, then the Chinese capital, just ahead of the Japanese army and the
"rape" of the city, in which over 200,000 civilians were butchered. He was
one of the first American officials to return to Nanking after the occupation. The
city was a shambles. A Japanese soldier actually attacked Allison during his
investigation of the occupation. This incident and the diplomatic protests that
followed forced the Japanese army's high command to work to regain control
of its troops and field commanders, but it brought Allison criticism from Oswald
Garrison Villard in the pages of the *Nation*. Allison then returned to Japan as
the consul general in Osaka, just in time to close the office after the Japanese
attack on Pearl Harbor.

After being released from internment, Allison had a number of assignments
that touched on Japan to one degree or another. He spent the war years at the
U.S. embassy in London working on Far Eastern economic matters. The State
Department was reorganized several times during the late 1940s, and each time
Allison was made head of the administrative unit handling Japanese affairs. He
also served as an advisor to the U.S. delegation to the United Nations on Far
Eastern affairs. In 1949, during this service, he met John Foster Dulles, the

Republican foreign policy specialist who was a member of the U.S. delegation to the United Nations. Dulles asked Allison to write a speech for him on Korean unification. Dulles eventually used only a small portion of Allison's draft, but said that he kept more of Allison's text than was usual for him when dealing with speech writers.

This exchange marked the beginning of the most influential period in Allison's career and established a friendship that lasted until Dulles died in 1959. In 1951 Secretary of State Dean Acheson assigned Dulles the job of negotiating the Japanese Peace Treaty. Dulles sought out Allison and asked him to be his deputy and personal advisor. Although Allison opposed Dulles's efforts to pressure Japan into early rearmament, he considered work on the Japanese treaty the most rewarding experience of his Foreign Service career.

Dulles and Allison traveled to Japan and Korea in June 1950. They visited the thirty-eighth parallel, separating North and South Korea, just one week before the Korean War started. In Japan Dulles met with General of the Army Douglas MacArthur, Japanese Prime Minister Shigeru Yoshida, and a host of other dignitaries. MacArthur's unrestrained support for a peace treaty helped the State Department overcome military objections. The meeting with Yoshida was less productive, however. A cautious prime minister, Yoshida refused to engage in substantial dialogue with Dulles. After the meeting Dulles was frustrated and angry. Allison and MacArthur's political advisor William J. Sebald calmed him down by explaining that in Japanese culture a first meeting is designed for getting acquainted rather than for substantive negotiation.

Allison and Dulles saw MacArthur the day of the North Korean attack on South Korea. MacArthur initially dismissed reports of North Korean action as a minor border incident. But Dulles and Allison returned to the American embassy and drafted a message that they sent directly to Acheson. Both diplomats were stringently anti-Communist and recommended that U.S. troops be sent to Korea in the event the South Koreans could not withstand the invasion, even should this move provoke a strong Russian reaction. Acheson showed this message to President Harry S. Truman at a meeting at Blair House at which Truman decided to commit U.S. troops to the war in Korea.

After Dulles and Allison returned to Washington, the State Department and the Pentagon established an interagency committee to reach an accord on a Japanese peace treaty. Allison represented the State Department, while Gen. Carter B. Magruder negotiated for the military. The Allison-Magruder negotiations produced an agreement that called for bilateral treaty negotiations and U.S. bases in Japan after the occupation. The agreement also included a stipulation that the treaty not become operational until the end of the Korean War.

Truman approved this agreement. Dulles then wrote a two-page memo that established seven principles that would form the foundation of a treaty. The memo recommended stripping Japan of its empire and required U.S. troops to remain in Japan following the formal end of the occupation. It was quite temperate on other matters. It did not require reparations and, in fact, encouraged

Japan to rearm. When Yoshida saw the proposal, he was quite pleased. Australian Foreign Minister Percy Spender, however, lost his composure when he saw the memo. Australia, he said, would never sign a treaty that allowed Japan to rearm.

These differing reactions showed the need for some hard diplomatic bargaining. Allison and Dulles visited Japan, the Philippines, Australia, and New Zealand early in 1951. Through a series of bilateral negotiations they reached a general accord on the type of settlement the United States desired. Security treaties with the United States helped alleviate Allied concerns about allowing Japan to rearm. In Washington Dulles and his staff drafted an eight-page treaty. Allison was instrumental in rejecting an attempt by the military to insert a clause granting the United States rights of extraterritoriality in cases involving American servicemen accused of violating Japanese laws. Over the late spring and early summer Allison traveled to various foreign capitals to negotiate specific terms. Quite often his main effort amounted to rejecting demands for punitive damages. The most involved negotiations took place in London, where he had to merge a British draft treaty with the American one. His reception in Manila was more controversial and strained. Allison emerged from these meetings exhausted and eventually agreed to Filipino demands for limited reparations.

The peace conference, which was actually an elaborate signing ceremony, drew intense media attention. The meeting was televised live. *Newsweek* put Dulles on its front cover. Allison also became the subject of a full-page profile in the magazine and garnered fleeting fame as an answer to a *New York Times* crossword-puzzle question.

In late 1951, shortly after the conference, Assistant Secretary of State for Far Eastern Affairs Dean Rusk called Allison into his office and told him that he would be the new assistant secretary. Allison hesitated, knowing that it was unlikely that a Democrat would be elected in 1952 and afraid that he would be tagged as a political appointee. Dulles reassured him that he was known as a career Foreign Service officer and would not be treated as a regular political appointee. With that reassurance, Allison accepted the job. In this position he proved instrumental in developing a Truman administration policy tolerant of the neutralism of some of the newly independent nations in Asia. During the 1952 presidential election Dulles blasted the Truman administration's policies in East Asia. Acheson assigned Allison the task of countering these charges. Allison did so while avoiding any direct mention of his old companion Dulles or his specific charges. Despite this public spat, Dulles and Acheson remained on good terms personally. When Dulles became Secretary of State, he quickly reversed the U.S. policy on neutrality. However, he also appointed his friend to be ambassador to Japan a month after taking office.

Defense policy was a major issue between the United States and Japan in the early 1950s. Prime Minister Yoshida, who was beginning to lose political power, worried about rebuilding the military and about accusations in some quarters that he was an American puppet. Dulles wanted to quickly build a strong international military alliance system to contain the Soviet Union. He thus put pressure on the Japanese to rearm beyond an army of four divisions, but this pressure only weakened Yoshida's position and inflamed antimilitarist sentiment in Japan. Allison negotiated a vague agreement that committed the Japanese to rebuild without a specified figure. Dulles was not satisfied and rejected Allison's recommendation to revise the Mutual Security Treaty, which many Japanese found unequal.

Just as these defense negotiations wound down, another issue exploded, literally, that created the most serious breach between the United States and Japan since the end of the war. On March 1, 1954, the United States detonated a hydrogen bomb on Bikini Atoll. An unexpected change in high wind patterns caused radioactive dust to float down on the *Lucky Dragon #5*, a Japanese tuna trawler. Two weeks later the ship returned to Japan, and two crewmen sought medical attention. Under pressure from the Atomic Energy Commission, Dulles ordered Allison to have the Japanese government turn the ship over to the U.S. Navy. Allison knew that this incident could be damaging to U.S.-Japanese relations and sent multiple notes to Washington asking for permission to offer an official apology and compensation.

Antinuclear sentiment quickly developed in Japan. The *Lucky Dragon* incident led directly to the creation of a Japanese antinuclear movement and the League against Atomic and Hydrogen Bombs (*Gensuikyo*).

As diplomats began to lose control of the situation, Allison sent a note to Dulles warning that the crisis had the potential to undo the U.S.-Japanese alliance and the anti-Communist alliance system in the Pacific. Dulles endorsed the note and sent it to President Dwight Eisenhower. Allison traveled to Washington in early June and met with a number of high officials, including Eisenhower and Dulles. He was quickly instructed to offer up to one million dollars in direct compensation to resolve the matter. The Japanese, however, were not willing to settle so easily. Yoshida was fighting for his political life and assumed a tough public pose to counter charges that he was a U.S. puppet. A stalemate that neither side wanted, but preferred to ending the crisis on unfavorable terms, ensued throughout the summer. Allison became convinced that Yoshida's hold on power was weak, and that his commitment to the anti-Communist cause was suspect. He determined that Yoshida would soon leave the scene and persuaded Dulles to wait until a successor with a stronger hold on power was in place before negotiating an end to the episode. Allison even met with opposition figures, carefully building up their public stature (much to Yoshida's consternation). The prime minister's state visit to Washington that fall failed to resolve a number of issues and contributed to his fall from power. When Ichiro Hatoyama became Prime Minister, Allison entered into immediate negotiations and settled the issue for two million dollars in compensation.

The rest of Allison's three years in Tokyo were relatively uneventful compared to the first year. In 1956 he was given the choice of the embassy in

Pakistan or Indonesia. He chose Indonesia, but his stay there was brief and unpleasant. Allison himself called his eleven months in Indonesia a failure because he never persuaded the State Department to deviate from its punitive, anti-Communist policy toward one that offered inducements away from communism. He quickly saw that President Sukarno was neither a Communist nor an anti-Communist, but a nationalist and populist politician, seeking political support from various factions. Allison recommended that the United States support Indonesian claims against the Netherlands to West Irian Barat, the western half of the island of New Guinea. In November 1957 he proposed a six-point plan to resolve the issue and award the disputed territory to Indonesia. Dulles and the State Department responded with absolute silence. The secretary of state and his brother Allen Dulles, director of the Central Intelligence Agency, saw Sukarno as a dangerous dictator coming under ever-growing Russian and Chinese influence and routinely ignored Allison's advice and reports, which argued otherwise. In January 1958 Allison was transferred to Czechoslovakia.

Allison's experience at the Czech-German border was a warning of things to come. Despite his diplomatic passport and license plates, the border patrol delayed his entry into the country, and despite the luxurious physical comforts—the U.S. ambassador lived in a ninety-room mansion with an elevator, an indoor swimming pool, a train system, thirty-two phone lines, and nine domestic staff—Allison found his assignment gloomy and uninteresting. He was convinced that the phones were bugged and that his servants were agents of the secret police. Individual Czechs avoided contact with embassy personnel, but Allison also detected and accurately reported their widespread contempt for the Soviet Union. He noticed, for instance, that attendance at events and receptions for American and British athletes and musicians was much stronger and more enthusiastic than for those involving Soviets.

No longer enjoying his diplomatic duties, Allison considered retirement following the death of Dulles. In addition, Allison's wife was in ill health. In 1959 the University of Nebraska awarded him an honorary doctorate and asked him to give the commencement address. This experience encouraged him to retire from the Foreign Service a year later. He secured a teaching job at the University of Hawaii. He completed and published his memoirs in 1973 and died on October 28, 1978.

Work by John Allison

Ambassador from the Prairie; or, Allison Wonderland. Boston: Houghton Mifflin, 1973.

Works about John Allison

Cohen, Warren I., and Akira Iriye, eds. *The Great Powers in East Asia, 1953–1960.* New York: Columbia University Press, 1990.
Dunn, Frederick S. *Peace-making and the Settlement with Japan.* Princeton: Princeton University Press, 1963.

Immerman, Richard, ed. *John Foster Dulles and the Diplomacy of the Cold War*. Princeton: Princeton University Press, 1990.
Pruessen, Ronald. *John Foster Dulles: The Road to Power*. New York: Free Press, 1982.

NICHOLAS E. SARANTAKES

GEORGE BANCROFT (1800–1891),

one of the greatest American historians, was minister to Great Britain during the Mexican War and minister to Prussia and Germany during that nation's wars of unification. Bancroft's knack for cultivating important social relations, his cosmopolitan outlook, and his knowledge of European culture smoothed his way at the Court of St. James at a time when many English still considered the United States a minor power and an impertinent republican upstart. His experience in Germany—an assemblage of states on the verge of unification and interested in American neutrality—was quite different. There the New Englander's academic reputation and broad intellectual interests, coupled with his optimistic hope for a democratic use of Prussia's power on the world stage, brought Bancroft high accolades as the diplomatic representative of his country.

Bancroft's early failures hardly gave a hint that he would eventually belong to the exclusive community of a transatlantic elite, enjoy the acquaintance of Otto von Bismarck, the great German chancellor, and be the subject of one of Victor Hugo's poems. Born in Worcester, Massachusetts, on October 3, 1800, George Bancroft grew up in the white, Anglo-Saxon community of upper-class Massachusetts as the eighth of thirteen children. His father Aaron, a Congregational minister, and his mother Lucretia Chandler, the daughter of a judge, anticipated for George a career in the pulpit or on the bench.

His academic inclinations were fostered early at Phillips Exeter Academy of New Hampshire. At age thirteen he entered Harvard University to study theology and philology. After graduating in the class of 1817, with the help of his Harvard mentors he acquired a scholarship to study at Göttingen University in Germany. Thus he traveled to a Europe still struggling through the aftermath of the Napoleonic Wars. In the ensuing three years Bancroft gathered his first impressions on the German state system while reading Oriental languages, biblical studies, and ethnography. In 1820 he received the doctor of philosophy and master of arts degrees.

While his studies influenced his later historical writings, his travels and social connections contributed deeply to his understanding of European thought and politics and sowed the seeds of a strong interest in personal overseas relations. He made the most of his three years in Europe by meeting many of the famous men, and some well-connected women, of the time. He studied at Berlin with Hegel and Schleiermacher and met Baron Karl Wilhelm von Humboldt and Johann Wolfgang Goethe. He visited with Humboldt's brother in Paris, where he also met Marquis de Lafayette and Washington Irving. In Italy he met Lord Byron and Napoleon's sister, the Princess Pauline Borghese.

It was difficult to leave this glittering society for an offer to tutor Greek at Harvard, especially since in Bancroft's day Harvard resented foreign manners and views more than admired them. Simultaneously with college teaching, and while still unsure of his ultimate professional calling, Bancroft attempted preaching. Lecturing from the pulpit, however, satisfied neither his father nor the congregation nor himself. After an unsuccessful year at college-level teaching he tried the secondary level. Together with a friend, J. G. Cogswell, he founded Roundhill School for Boys, where he put his European experiences to use by employing teaching methods from Germany and Switzerland. This endeavor also proved unsatisfactory to him.

Three years into his teaching Bancroft stood out not as an innovative educator or school administrator but as a political speech writer and commentator. On July 4, 1826, on the fiftieth anniversary of the Declaration of Independence (and the day Thomas Jefferson died), Bancroft made a memorable speech in Springfield. He not only celebrated American history through its symbolic dates but also revealed himself as an outspoken advocate of the Democratic Party. Soon afterward he started writing for the *North American Review*. His writing proved popular, varied, and authoritative—characteristics that the Democratic politicians particularly liked from a man with a Whiggish pedigree. As he realized the satisfaction of writing, he began to embark on his magnum opus, ten volumes of the *History of the United States*, which he published over a forty-year span from 1834 to 1874.

In his thirties Bancroft seemed to have come into his own. He married Sarah H. Dwight of Springfield and soon enjoyed fatherhood. He left Roundhill School and teaching for academic and political writing and perhaps a career in government. In 1834 he ran for representative of the Northhampton (Massachusetts) General Court, but was unsuccessful. To this political defeat was added a personal tragedy when his young wife died in 1837. That year he found himself a widower with three children, but also achieved his first political appointment. Bancroft's talents as a speech writer for the Democrats (especially an 1837 Thanksgiving proclamation for New York State) had come to the attention of President Martin Van Buren, who rewarded the historian with the position of collector of the Port of Boston.

For the next seven years Bancroft lived as Brahmin Rebel—a Democrat in the Whig society of Massachusetts. Then his reputation and connections encouraged him to run for governor of his home state. Although this bid for office was also unsuccessful, Bancroft proved his worth as a delegate to the National Democratic Convention. His eloquent support for a hitherto-unknown Democrat helped secure the nomination and election of James K. Polk as president. From this point on, Bancroft's career thrived through political connections and appointments. For his endorsement, Polk rewarded Bancroft with the cabinet post of secretary of the navy and, later, minister to England. Bancroft's personal fortunes also turned when he married Elizabeth Bliss of Boston, a widow with two sons who remained his companion until her death in 1886.

The experiences Bancroft gathered as secretary of the navy provided a training ground for his diplomatic work but still left him unfulfilled. In the short period from March 1845 to September 1846 his accomplishments included the establishment of Annapolis Naval Academy and the Naval Observatory. As acting secretary of war in May 1845, Bancroft signed the order to Gen. Zachary Taylor to cross the Texas frontier with his troops, starting the Mexican War. He also issued orders to Commodore John Sloat on the Pacific coast that brought about the American occupation of San Francisco. His support for Polk in the Oregon boundary dispute sensitized him to the importance of historical maps and proved a most helpful education in geopolitics for his work a quarter-century later during another boundary dispute with England.

Despite these accomplishments, he felt better suited for the Foreign Service. When Polk offered him a choice of the ministerial post either in Paris or in London, for reasons of prestige he chose Great Britain. Bancroft's tenure as minister to the Court of St. James, from October 1846 to August 1849, saw the United States double its size while Europe struggled with the fallout of the revolutions of 1848.

In London his most pressing duty was to ensure England's neutrality in the Mexican War. Lord Palmerston, although not keen on seeing the United States embark on independent adventures, never gave Bancroft the impression that Britain would get involved on Mexico's behalf. Nevertheless, Bancroft kept close tabs on England's public opinion while participating in the rigorous social life of London's fashionable upper class.

With his polished demeanor and royal bearing, Bancroft fit into the aristocratic society of Britain, where he enjoyed its splendor and even its excesses while avoiding America's latest political dilemma, the extension of slavery into the newly acquired territories. Bancroft's own dilemma stemmed from his ideological unease about monarchy and his firm belief in the better success of republican government. He tried to assuage these feelings of conflict by a heavy schedule of research in archives and discussion with other great historians such as Thomas Macaulay of England and Adolphe Thiers of France. The subsequent upheavals of 1848, which had repercussions throughout Europe, strengthened his belief in the ultimate victory of government by the people.

Besides keeping Washington informed of British and French attitudes to the war with Mexico, as the American minister Bancroft had two other important charges: first, to have the duties on tobacco diminished, and second, to obtain a relaxation of trade regulations with the British West Indies. The first goal was achieved almost immediately since it had already been in the works before his arrival, and in the process he also accomplished a settlement of the postal rates between Great Britain and the United States. The more important goal of repealing certain trade restrictions along America's East Coast for a share of trade in the West Indies failed. The bill was under consideration by the British Parliament at the very time when America's new Whig president, Zachary Taylor, took office. Taylor's foreign policy team argued that Bancroft's work was unauthorized and that nobody needed the lifting of restrictions on U.S. coastal trade, throwing it open to the British. Bancroft, who saw his work of the previous two years disappear, deplored the loss of the British colonial trade and its direct and indirect benefits from the West Indies.

What incensed Bancroft, a man used to honoring traditional protocol, was his public dismissal by the Whigs before he had a chance to resign. The official record of his tenure in London during the time of the Mexican War and the European revolutions of 1848 seemed less impressive than his own self-evaluation. After all, "He had reported faithfully, in detail the effect of public opinion in Europe of the Mexican War, kept watch of the revolutions of 1848, negotiated a successful postal treaty with Great Britain and begun one with France, protested against British policy in Central America, worked for the ill fated but nearly successful tariff and trade agreements and had given full and constant information to the state department on the policies and problems of British internal and foreign affairs including British intentions on an Isthmian canal" (Nye, 1944, 183). This last point included a warning to the British not to fortify such a route—a move that indirectly led to the Clayton-Bulwer Treaty of 1850.

Bancroft counted among his greatest successes his rich collection of original source materials from both British and French archives with which he left England. Bancroft and his wife settled in New York City and bought a home in Newport, Rhode Island, where he indulged his hobbies of cultivating roses and horseback riding. Most of his time from 1849 to 1867, however, was spent in using the important primary material to write and publish his *History of the United States*. During this time Bancroft was a much-sought-after advisor and speech writer with fine international connections. He became the official eulogist of Andrew Jackson, a task that continued to keep him very unpopular in his home state. Bancroft also drafted Andrew Johnson's first annual presidential message in December 1865, and he wrote and delivered the famous "Memorial Address on the Life and Character of Abraham Lincoln" on February 12, 1866.

In recognition of his work for the Democratic Party and because of his intellect and abilities, President Johnson appointed him Minister to Prussia in 1867. Bancroft considered this the ideal appointment. While Bancroft the Democrat had gone to England with little sympathy for a governing aristocracy, he saw in Germany a country similar in interest, institutions, tendencies, and experiences to the United States. Besides, in Berlin he could visit with old friends, pursue historical research, delve into all kinds of new scholarly activities, and represent his country in an official capacity that kept him informed of both European and American politics.

Historians have largely seen Bancroft's tenure as the era of friendly understanding, peace, and goodwill between Germany and the United States. This was partly due to the fact that both America and Germany had domestic concerns that kept their international conflicts to a minimum. It was also due to Bancroft's personality, skills, and outlook. He had a keen interest in German scholarship and wanted to promote things German in the belief that Germany's excellence in intellectual endeavors reflected a naturally superior culture comparable to his own. Both countries seemed to him to strive for progress and a "more perfect union."

Such an attitude often led Bancroft to be unprofessional in his open admiration for Bismarck, whom he considered the "George Washington of a United States of Germany." Yet because of his great circle of friends on both sides of the Atlantic, and because of Germany's increasing international importance, such a biased stance by a diplomat did him and the United States little harm and some good.

The minister's bias was most visible in his open support for Germany during the Franco-Prussian War of 1870–1871. When writing dispatches, Bancroft clearly sided with his host country and put the responsibility for starting the conflict on Napoleon III of France. Even before the outbreak of war, as a Protestant American Bancroft showed his antipathy for the Catholic French and their ambitious, idiosyncratic emperor. But he correctly criticized French foreign policy as calculatedly hostile to the United States. At a dinner party, for example, he chided France for its anti-Union maneuvering during the American Civil War. Bancroft warned that Americans had not forgotten Napoleon III's scheming, and he reiterated similar warnings once the Franco-Prussian War began. Moreover, he went beyond his mandate in suggesting that the U.S. Navy would contribute to the defeat of France if this proved necessary. Such open partisanship by the representative of a formally neutral country created frictions with France that in turn caused the U.S. government to emphasize its official neutrality. Yet Secretary of State Hamilton Fish also proved the ineffectiveness of a French blockade of Prussia by sending U.S. warships to the Baltic.

Continental Europeans appreciated the historian's game of *Realpolitik* and Bancroft's outspokenness. The French and the Germans used his tactlessness for their own purposes: Bismarck published a personal letter in which Bancroft had congratulated the Iron Chancellor for "bringing the German hope of a thousand years to its fulfillment." When French officials read about such praise at their expense, they protested. The incident prompted Victor Hugo to pen Bancroft into a poem as the enemy of France. Scorning the close ties between the United States and Germany, Hugo remarked, "Ils sont plus Prussiens que les Prussiens." Generally these developments only enhanced Bancroft's stature as a major diplomatic player and endeared him to Bismarck, who made a show of asking Bancroft's advice both on expanding the war into the French colonies of the Far East and on possible mediation.

Bancroft and Bismarck discovered a mutual interest in opposing the dismemberment of China and in checking French naval power in the Baltic. At home the New Englander had close ties to East Coast commerce and shipbuilding interests. Bancroft's clear approval of the Prussian cause undoubtedly signaled to American firms that it was risky to side with France.

Bancroft knew where to draw the line, however, in his indulgence of Prussian power. In his reports to Washington he judiciously chose to say little about Prussia's war aims. When the Prussian envoy to Washington boasted that among his king's goals was the conquest and annihilation of France, Bancroft complained to the Prussian Foreign Office that its representative was doing his government great harm in American public opinion. It is a sign of Bancroft's influence with Bismarck and also of Bismarck's limited intentions toward France that the chancellor moved swiftly to recall the envoy from Washington.

At the start of his Berlin tenure Bancroft engaged in tedious but more typical foreign policy negotiations, concluding a naturalization treaty establishing, for the first time in international law, a right to expatriation. Such success was not enough for Republican Ulysses S. Grant, who won the 1868 election, to keep Bancroft at the post in Berlin, since Bancroft's mentor Andrew Johnson had been discredited after a failed impeachment. What convinced the Republicans of Bancroft's value was his personal relationship with Bismarck. The historian understood the value of a well-established reputation and the importance of influential friends. Giving much time to dinners, soirees, and festivities at which the internationally influential elite could be cultivated helped Bancroft convince Grant of his usefulness.

Bancroft adroitly negotiated the touchy issue of naturalization, which arose when Germans who had tried to avoid the draft by moving to the United States, acquiring its citizenship, then sought repatriation to Germany as American citizens ineligible for duty in a foreign war. Germany took the traditional view in claiming that even though these emigrants had become American citizens, they still had to fulfill their military duties in Germany. Americans, on the other hand, insisted on a liberal doctrine upholding a right of individual expatriation. Bancroft avoided haggling over legal definitions of citizenship and found a simpler solution. In his compromise he suggested that Germans with five uninterrupted years of residency in the United States could be naturalized. If these new American citizens, however, returned to Germany for more than two years, they could be viewed as having renounced their American citizenship.

In 1872 Bancroft turned to arbitration of the dispute between Britain and the United States over the boundary between British Columbia and the state of Washington. Bancroft, as the only remaining member of Polk's cabinet, advised the State Department not to agree to a compromise. Instead, he suggested Emperor Wilhelm I of Germany as arbiter, a choice he thought would have a positive outcome for the American side because of Bancroft's personal relationship with Bismarck. The emperor agreed to act as mediator in the negotiations. The case was further stacked in America's favor due to two other moves by Bancroft. In 1848, while minister to England, Bancroft had placed on record a description of the boundary according to his own map, and the representative of the State Department who participated in the negotiations was his nephew Bancroft Davis. Bancroft's diplomatic, personal, and scholarly skills thus came together to U.S. advantage, as the boundary claim was settled in Washington's favor.

At age seventy-four Bancroft decided to resign from diplomatic service. His nephew Bancroft Davis, who had served as assistant secretary of state with distinction and who had successfully prosecuted the Alabama claims[1] before an international court at Geneva, succeeded him. Bancroft spent his remaining years writing and revising his histories. He died on January 17, 1891, in Washington.

Note

1. The "Alabama Claims" were a series of disputes between the U.S. and Britain arising from the American Civil War, and named for damage done to Union shipping by the Confederate commerce raider, the C.S.S. Alabama.

Works by George Bancroft

History of the Colonization of the United States. Boston: C. C. Little and J. Brown, 1839.

Memorial address on the life and character of Abraham Lincoln delivered at the request of both houses of the Congress of America, before them, in the House of Representatives at Washington, on the 12th of February, 1866. 39th Congress, 1st sess., 1865–1866. Washington, D.C.: U.S. Government Printing Office, 1866.

History of the Formation of the Constitution of the United States of America. New York: D. Appleton, 1883.

History of the United States of America, from the Discovery of the Continent. New York: D. Appleton, 1895–1896.

Works about George Bancroft

Blumenthal, Henry. "George Bancroft in Berlin." *New England Quarterly* 37 (June 1964): 224–241.

Canary, Robert H. *George Bancroft.* New York: Twayne Publishers, 1974.

Handlin, Lilian. *George Bancroft, the Intellectual as Democrat.* New York: Harper and Row, 1984.

Howe, M. A. DeWolfe. *The Life and Letters of George Bancroft.* 2 vols. New York: Scribner's, 1908.

Nye, Russel B. *George Bancroft.* New York: Washington Square Press, 1964.

———. *George Bancroft, Brahmin Rebel.* New York: A. A. Knopf, 1944.

Sloane, William M. "George Bancroft—in Society, in Politics, in Letters." *Century Magazine* 33 (January 1887) : 473–487.

Williams, Mary W. *Anglo-American Isthmian Diplomacy, 1815–1915.* New York: Russell and Russell, 1965 (first published in 1916, reissued in 1965).

Willson, Beckles. *American Ambassadors to England, 1785–1929.* New York: Frederick A. Stokes & Co., 1929.

VERENA BOTZENHART-VIEHE

CHARLES EUSTIS BOHLEN (1904–1974), author

and diplomat, was born on Grindstone Island near Clayton, New York, one of three children born to Charles Bohlen, gentleman and sportsman, and Celestine Eustis Bohlen, New Orleans socialite and traveler. His maternal grandfather was the first American ambassador to France in 1892. Bohlen was educated at St. Paul's School and Harvard University.

St. Paul's School, Anglican and Anglophile like Groton, prepared its students for entry first into Harvard and Yale and then into the worlds of business, finance, and law. "Chip" (a nickname bestowed by his school chums that stayed with him all his life) was expelled from St. Paul's for demonstrating what was described as a bad attitude toward authority. This did not prevent his being accepted by Harvard, where he was tapped for the prestigious Porcellian Club. Handsome, gregarious, and charming, Bohlen excelled at those extracurricular activities much loved by undergraduates—talking, drinking, and making friends—but his academic record was not a strong one. He chose to major in modern European history, which reflected his cosmopolitan upbringing and lively interest in the world around him, but he had no clear career plans and only a limited income upon graduation from Harvard. He knew that he would be unhappy in such conventional careers as banking or business. On his return from a postgraduation trip, working his passage by boat to China and India, he found that a family friend had arranged an interview with Assistant Secretary William Castle of the State Department. It was this interview, Bohlen recalled, that decided him to become a diplomat.

What attracted Bohlen to a diplomatic career was the passage of the Rogers Act (1924), with the prospect that it offered of joining a professional Foreign Service and broadening his horizons. He applied for the program offered by Robert Kelley in the Division of East European Affairs that had been created to train specialists on the Soviet Union. Although the United States had still to recognize the Communist regime in Moscow, there was reason to believe that this recognition could not be delayed much longer. Only six applicants were accepted by Kelley into his demanding program, which combined practical experience in the field with years of university study of the Russian background (language, history, and politics) of the government in Moscow. Bohlen was delighted to be chosen as one of the six, who also included George Kennan.

After brief consular stints in Prague and Hamburg, Bohlen and Kennan found themselves working together in Riga, Latvia, which served as America's "window on Russia" during the years of nonrecognition. There these two young professionals began their long friendship. No two men whose professional lives would be so closely interconnected for the next twenty years were less alike in temperament. Each took on the anti-Communist coloring of Robert Kelley's division and life among the Russian émigrés in Riga, but Bohlen was surprisingly nonjudgmental compared with the intellectual and introspective Kennan. He wanted to talk like a Russian, drink like a Russian, and, if possible, think like a Russian. He had fallen under the spell of the land and its people.

Bohlen agreed with Kennan that Russia had been made wretched and then unrecognizable by the Bolshevik Revolution of November 1917. Would the new Communist regime in Moscow act like a conventional nation-state motivated by the balance of power or a revolutionary movement dedicated to overthrowing the capitalist order? Bohlen chided Kennan for being too darkly pessimistic about the prospect of coexistence with the Soviet Union. Kennan, who later confessed in his memoirs to personal doubts whether democracies and dictatorships contributed anything, singly or together, to a stable world order ("I sometimes felt," he said, "like a guest in my own century"), accepted this criticism from his best friend without protest. He knew that his intellectual anguish grated upon the nerves of others. He and Bohlen then resumed their debate—sometimes at white heat—on the nature of Stalin's regime and how to deal with it. No friendship ever meant more to him, Kennan recalled in his memoirs.

Late in 1933 word reached these two young specialists in Riga that Soviet Commissar for Foreign Affairs Maxim Litvinov had arrived in Washington to discuss recognition of his government in Moscow. Bohlen was delighted to be selected by President Franklin Roosevelt's new ambassador, William C. Bullitt, to go to Moscow. "You are not a typical Foreign Service officer," Bullitt told him, "and that is why I chose you." Bohlen lost no time in persuading the new ambassador that the embassy in Moscow needed Kennan as well.

Establishing "genuinely friendly relations" with the Soviet Union, as Roosevelt intended to do, would not be easy. In the same year that the new American embassy was opened in Moscow (1934), Stalin unleashed the purges on his country. Ambassador Bullitt quickly lost any illusion that the Soviet Union was a normal nation-state. The Russians were Asiatics and Stalin was the Caliph of communism, he wrote bitterly, whose subjects were committed to the liquidation of millions of nonbelievers. Kennan reeled under what he called the "hammer blows" of the purges, developed stomach ulcers, and took sick leave from Moscow. Another hammer blow fell in August 1939 when Stalin and Hitler signed their infamous pact of friendship and alliance. The Soviet Union, judged Kennan, was not a fit ally for any Western democratic nation.

In these troubled and tumultuous years of American-Soviet relations, Bohlen kept his own counsel. He refused to join with Kennan and others in denouncing FDR's efforts to woo Stalin away from Hitler as appeasement. Harry Hopkins, who became Lend-Lease administrator for FDR when Hitler invaded the Soviet Union in June 1941, fulminated against the anti-Stalin cabal in the State Department. He made an exception of Bohlen, who, like a good soldier, had demonstrated his loyalty to FDR's policy of working with Stalin. By 1944 Bohlen and Kennan were both back in Washington advising on policy toward the Soviet Union. One question was on everyone's mind as the Allies moved closer to victory: would national interest or the world Communist revolution determine

Stalin's actions in peacetime? (The Soviet Union, Ambassador Bullitt had predicted, was one of the greatest forces for good or evil in the world, and Western diplomats would have to deal with it.)

This was the question in late 1944 that Kennan raised with Bohlen, arguing somberly that it was "naïve" to expect that Stalin would continue to work within the Grand Alliance to make the world safe for democracy. Bohlen lost his temper and berated his friend for having no faith in FDR's plan to appeal to Stalin's national interest at the end of an exhausting war. All Stalin wanted was a clear acceptance by the West of a sphere of influence for the Soviet Union in Europe at the end of the fighting. Back on speaking terms, Kennan sent a simple proposal to Bohlen, who was advising FDR at the Yalta Conference in February 1945. "Why could we not make a decent and definitive compromise," he asked, "divide Europe frankly into spheres of influence—keep ourselves out of the Russian sphere and keep the Russians out of ours?" This sounded remarkably like the containment policy that Kennan would formulate one year later. Bohlen dashed off a reply framed in Rooseveltian language that he may have regretted later. He told Kennan that no democracy could make peace on such a stark balance-of-power basis. FDR hoped to tame the Russian bear and avoid dividing Europe into two hostile camps. Nevertheless, his own good sense compelled him to add that everything would depend on Stalin—"either our pals in the Kremlin intend to limit themselves or they don't."

In the end, it was Kennan who formulated the official response to Stalin's ambitions proclaimed by the Truman administration in July 1947 as containment policy (the "patient, long-term and vigilant containment of the expansive energies of the Soviet Union," in Kennan's words). Bohlen was quick to admit to Kennan that he had been naïve. For a brief time he had hoped for the balance-of-power peace that Kennan had advocated in Europe, but with each side maintaining an "open" atmosphere of influence. Stalin had destroyed this hope by his brutal actions in Poland, which made clear his contempt for free elections and other ("bourgeois") democratic conceits.

Those who knew communism at first hand, explained Ambassador Averell Harriman in Moscow, had come to understand that it was a disease. The conflict between the United States and the Soviet Union was not simply a power struggle between two nation-states but a life-and-death conflict between the forces of democracy and dictatorship. In Washington Bohlen was not happy with the apocalyptic language used by the ambassador, but the note of urgency sounded by Kennan in his containment message was compelling.

Bohlen fretted not about the necessity of containment but about the reaction of Congress. It was easy to demonize Stalin and "scare hell" out of Congress, but this was not a constructive approach. Containment in a military sense meant simply drawing a line and daring the Red Army to cross it. Much more was necessary. He advised the new president, Harry Truman, and Secretary of State George Marshall that hunger, poverty, and chaos were as much a threat to the war-torn nations of Europe as the Red Army. Containment demanded nothing less than the sending of massive American material aid and money to rebuild Europe. It called for a bold move that would reshape America's traditional role in the world (the "transformation of American foreign policy," as Bohlen called it in another context).

Bohlen, who wrote most of Secretary Marshall's address to the Harvard commencement class in June 1947 unveiling the Marshall Plan, added a personal coda to Kennan's containment policy. His own thinking had led him to identify what he called "Soviet" (as distinct from Russian) nationalism as the determinant force behind the Soviet Union's foreign policy. Stalin's intentions were intransigently hostile to the West. Ideology ("building socialism in one country") had been his justification for constructing his brutal regime at home. In the second stage ("protecting the socialist heartland") he had organized a protective bloc of satellite nations around the Soviet Union. In the third stage ("we will bury you") Stalin would launch the world Communist revolution, but this would not happen—Bohlen hastened to add—until what Lenin called the "correlation of forces" was absolutely favorable. Stalin would never deliberately jeopardize the power base that he had constructed and extended with so much effort. Intentions were one thing, capability was another thing, and there would always be a role for diplomacy in dealing with the Soviet Union.

Bohlen knew that Kennan valued his view of containment policy, but he worried about the hawks in Congress and around President Truman. Both he and Kennan worried about the militarization of the containment policy. Kennan, who never stopped regretting that the language of his original statement was too loose, bombarded the White House with warnings about the nuclearization of containment policy until Secretary of State Dean Acheson told him to take his moralizing about the H-bomb outside the department. In January 1950 Kennan was replaced as director of policy planning at the State Department by Paul Nitze, who was much closer to Acheson in outlook.

Acheson had more time for Bohlen, who was as careful as ever to make his objections on the grounds of strategy, not principle. In early 1949 Acheson had ordered a thorough review of containment policy that aimed at replacing Kennan's defensive doctrine applied to Europe with a global doctrine enforced by the United States as world policeman (this doctrine became known by its government classification number as NSC-68). This new version of containment, Acheson told Nitze, must "bludgeon" the mind of government and Congress into spending whatever was necessary to defend this global perimeter. Nitze was deputized by Acheson to listen to Bohlen's objections. Nitze listened politely, made some cosmetic changes to the language of NSC-68, and confessed afterwards that Bohlen seemed more concerned with the rhetoric than the substance of the new doctrine.

Bohlen did not press his objections. When North Korea invaded South Korea on June 25, 1950, he agreed with Acheson that the United States must intervene with military counterforce but warned against overreaction to what was an isolated exercise in "soft spot" probing by Stalin. Acheson was happy to indulge his colleague because Congress had decided at his urging to triple defense spending in the light of North Korea's attack. By this time Bohlen was much closer to Acheson in his outlook. He had abandoned FDR's optimism that Stalin was "get-at-able," had embraced Kennan's realism, and now admitted that Acheson was correct in preparing for the worst. It was "always better," Bohlen admitted when commenting on NSC-68, "to over-simplify in the direction of greater urgency rather than complacency" when dealing with the Soviet Union.

By 1950 Bohlen had reached the apex of his professional career. He was, after Kennan's marginalization in the department, the acknowledged expert on the Soviet Union. This was an exposed calling for a professional diplomat, but he had managed to survive every challenge from Harry Hopkins's fulminations against the "anti-Soviet cabal" in FDR's State Department to the campaign launched by Senator Joseph McCarthy to discover fellow travelers in the Truman administration. Bohlen was always "a partisan of the moment," commented George Kennan. All this (including Kennan's opinion of his colleague) was to change when the new Republican administration took office in 1952. Bohlen recalled in his memoirs that he found himself in the uncharacteristic role of defending his principles and his profession, and it was an exhilarating moment for him.

The news that he had been nominated by the Republican administration as ambassador to Moscow must have surprised as well as delighted Bohlen. President Dwight Eisenhower considered him to be simply the best-qualified man for the post, explained Secretary of State John Foster Dulles, who did not hide his own preference for sending a more passionate anti-Communist to the post. Bohlen warned the secretary that his name would be instantly identified by the McCarthyites in any Senate confirmation hearing with the Democratic Party's "betrayal" of America's allies at the Yalta Conference in 1945. "Well, tell them that you were there simply as an interpreter, not an advisor," responded Dulles, but Bohlen did not think that this was possible. He would speak his mind. "Do you have any other skeletons in your closet that might embarrass the Administration?" asked Dulles testily. No, replied Bohlen, who was told that his name would go forward.

On the day of his Senate hearing Bohlen met with Dulles for the ride to Capitol Hill to be informed by the secretary that it would be better if they took separate cars and were not photographed together. Bohlen managed to maintain his composure and even his sense of humor in this situation. These were days, he recalled afterwards, when the McCarthyite forces were cutting a swathe through the Foreign Service with their charge of twenty years of treason, and his colleagues went to sleep every night by forming their wagons into a circle.

As he expected, most of the hostile questions in the committee hearing were directed at the failings of containment policy under the Democrats. Bohlen answered forcefully that Poland and China and other nations at the time of the Yalta Conference were not American assets to "lose" to the Soviet Union. They were occupied by Red Armies, Japan had still to be defeated, Stalin's cooperation was vital, and his ambitions were still not known. Containment was a positive policy from Secretary Marshall to Secretary Acheson and did what the Republicans claimed to do with their "roll-back" policy—hold the line by every means possible against the Communist threat.

His answers must have been persuasive, because the Senate Foreign Relations Committee sent his nomination to the floor by unanimous vote. There was one last challenge from the McCarthyites, who claimed that there was a sixteen-page report in Bohlen's FBI file exposing his homosexual and philandering activities. At this stage President Eisenhower stepped in to assert his leadership and defend the man whom he had selected for Moscow. Bohlen was confirmed easily, the McCarthyites in the Senate were defeated, and Dulles began to regret the whole episode. ("No more Bohlens," pleaded Republican Senator Robert Taft.) Before Bohlen left for Moscow, Dulles learned that Avis and the children were traveling separately. Didn't he think it wise to travel together, asked Dulles, because of all the rumors about him? Bohlen, who had come to despise Dulles's moralizing and the kowtowing to the McCarthyites, replied that he would do no such thing.

In Moscow Bohlen found that not much had changed on the surface since his days as a junior secretary in the embassy at the end of the 1930s. The city, like the regime itself, was drab, gray, and unfriendly to foreigners. One small change was that now as ambassador he attracted the company, as soon as he set foot outside the embassy, of a quartet rather than a pair of plainclothes KGB policemen ("guardian angels," as embassy staffers called them) who went with him everywhere. Beneath this gray surface Bohlen sensed that dramatic changes were happening. It was rumored that Nikita Khrushchev had made a secret speech to the Twentieth Party Congress denouncing the crimes of the Stalin era. There were indications that the regime was softening in its attitude toward its own people and its bloc partners. It was blind flying in Moscow, reported Bohlen, and an ambassador had to rely, just as in Stalin's day, on pronouncements in *Pravda* and *Izvestia* and his fingertip feel for what was happening below the surface. Bohlen doubted that Khrushchev, who was emerging as the strongman in the Kremlin, was serious in his overtures to the West on such vital mutual concerns as the arms race and a divided Germany. Khrushchev wanted to look decisive in his dealings with the West, and he would do nothing to spark opposition in the Party itself or the Communist bloc with his proposals for détente.

When Bohlen left Moscow after five frustrating years, Khrushchev blasted him as a "shameless reactionary" who had helped to kill any chance of changing American-Soviet relations for the better. This was unfair. Afterwards, Bohlen asked himself whether he could have done more, but he was trapped between the hidebound Dulles and an essentially untutored president who knew little about his Soviet adversary. Eisenhower was open to dealing with Khrushchev, but Dulles, who still took his ideas about communism from Stalin's *Problems of Leninism* (the secretary called it an "atheistic tract"), resisted strongly. Dulles did not trust Bohlen, who was damaged goods after the Senate hearing. When

Sherman Adams, Eisenhower's chief of staff, suggested that Bohlen address the cabinet on the changes that were happening in the Soviet Union, Dulles objected that Bohlen was too "independent" and "not working with us." Bohlen might have gone behind Dulles's back and encouraged the president to seek an opening to Moscow, but he had too much respect for the office of the principal advisor of foreign policy. Dulles had no such scruples when it came to dealing with his subordinates in Moscow. (Perhaps he had heard the joke attributed to Bohlen that foreign policy under the Republicans was "dull, duller, Dulles.") In December 1956 he wrote Bohlen that he was relieving him of his duties because he knew of his desire to quit diplomacy and take up writing as a career. Bohlen, who hated to write, was amazed by this news. Encouraged by his friends, he resisted and accepted with as much grace as he could muster Dulles's reluctant offer to appoint him ambassador to the Philippines. He would not go quietly into the night at Dulles's bidding as his friend, George Kennan, had done.

This decision was timely, if nothing else, because Dulles was soon to die of cancer. In Manila Bohlen began to receive requests from Dulles's successor, Christian Herter, asking his advice in dealing with the Soviet Union. Much more welcome were the same requests from the new administration in Washington. Bohlen made no secret of his pleasure when John F. Kennedy won the presidency in November 1960. Kennedy admired Bohlen and in the month following his inauguration began assembling a team of experts (Bohlen, Kennan, Averell Harriman, and Llewellyn Thompson) who would help him deal with this most important adversary. Once again Bohlen was a member of the inner circle of decision makers in Washington.

Two irreverent spirits, despite their conventional eastern establishment background, Kennedy and Bohlen took an instant liking to each other. Bohlen was amused by the fact that the Kennedy men regarded him as an "elder statesman" where the Soviet Union was concerned. Presumably this was a tribute to his professional experience rather than his age. In any case, the new president devoted more time in one month to his Soviet specialist than Eisenhower had allocated over seven years, but there was a reason for this rush of attention.

In his first year of office Kennedy faced a series of challenges from Nikita Khrushchev, who was acting in his most belligerent and bellicose manner toward the young president. The first confrontation came just three months after Kennedy took office. In April 1961 a task force of Cuban exiles trained by the CIA was eagerly awaiting a signal from the White House to invade the island. Kennedy turned for advice to anyone who could tell him about the relationship between the new regimes (like Castro's Cuba) in the Third World and their champion in the Kremlin, but Bohlen—inexplicably—backed away. He told the president that he was not an expert on Cuba or covert operations. I acted "like an idiot," Bohlen confessed afterwards, when the invasion force came to grief at the Bay of Pigs.

Perhaps Bohlen was thrown off balance by Kennedy, who took advice wherever he could find it, but this unconventional style should not have surprised someone who had served in FDR's White House. Bohlen, who was a professional to his fingertips, saw no great virtue in such an informal decision-making process. Nevertheless, he was determined not to be overawed by the "action-intellectuals" (as Arthur Schlesinger called them) around Kennedy on the next occasion.

In June 1961 he accompanied Kennedy to the summit meeting with Khrushchev in Vienna where the two leaders tried to take the measure of each other. In a bruising encounter with Kennedy, Khrushchev served notice that wars of national liberation in the Third World together with the Soviet Union's triumphs in space signaled that the East-West balance of power was shifting dramatically. Nothing could stop these revolutionary forces, boasted Khrushchev, until the Western capitalist nations joined each other on the ash-heap of history. These were the toughest words ever said to him, a shaken Kennedy confessed later. Par for the course with Khrushchev, responded Bohlen. On this occasion the advice of Bohlen and the Soviet experts on what to do was listened to carefully and even deferentially by JFK.

The most pressing challenge made by Khrushchev at Vienna concerned the divided city of Berlin, whose fate would be decided, in Khrushchev's words, with the agreement of the Western powers in the next six months. He would act without them after this deadline passed. After his return to Washington Kennedy fretted over the delay in obtaining an answer from the State Department to this ultimatum. "What is wrong with your Department?" Kennedy asked Bohlen; "It can never give me an answer when I want one." "The trouble, sir," replied Bohlen, "is you, because you keep by-passing the professionals who know that decisions like this one cannot be made hastily." By building a wall to stop the exodus of thousands of refugees across Berlin, he explained, Khrushchev was simply looking for a way to repair his prestige, not a pretext to launch World War III. It was essentially a political move, not a decision for war on his part. Each side should back away from confrontation and give diplomacy a chance.

This was essentially the advice that Bohlen gave Kennedy one year later when Khrushchev took an even greater gamble and placed nuclear missiles in Cuba. Kennedy saw the photographic evidence of these missiles a few days after he had signed Bohlen's letters of accreditation as ambassador to France. Kennedy pressed Bohlen to stay and join his crisis-management team. Bohlen, who did not run from a personal challenge or a presidential request, was badly torn, but he advised Kennedy that keeping him in Washington would set alarm bells ringing in the war rooms of America's allies in Europe. He was convinced that Khrushchev was no more willing to go to war over Cuba than over Berlin. Again, this was primarily a political challenge. Reluctantly, Kennedy bowed to the judgment of this seasoned professional and told him to go as planned. Bohlen still fretted that his voice might not be heard and left a letter for the president explaining the role of diplomacy in talking the missiles out of Cuba, in one participant's description, rather than shooting them out. His advice was strongly supported by Llewellyn Thompson in the Ex-Comm's (Executive Committee) meetings. Afterwards, one advisor to Kennedy was convinced that these two Soviet experts were the unsung heroes of a crisis that ended on October 28, 1962, with an agreement reached without any dangerous resort to force.

Once in Paris, Bohlen was in a mood to enjoy what he and his colleagues considered to be a plum appointment for a professional diplomat at the end of his career. Practically bilingual, in love with France ever since his grand tours there as a child and his postgraduate studies in Paris, he was eager to display his ambassadorial skills. Moscow had been a hardship post for someone who believed that an ambassador served a useful purpose in the world of conventional diplomacy. These skills were called upon sooner than he expected. He had arrived at a difficult time in Franco-American relations when President Charles de Gaulle was about to embark on an independent course for his nation that would cause problems for his Atlantic Alliance partners, especially the United States. As a consequence, France left NATO, constructed an independent nuclear force, blocked Great Britain's entry into the Common Market, and pursued a Gallic version of *Ostpolitik* toward the Soviet Union. Dealing with "le grand Charles" was always difficult, admitted Bohlen, but he defended his country's position in Europe with skill and equanimity. In his opinion, these actions by de Gaulle presented no serious challenge to the policy of "flexible response" to communism that President Kennedy was putting in place.

Bohlen was winding down. Forty years in any profession is long enough, he commented when he finally retired from diplomacy in 1969. The hint of self-mockery in this remark was characteristic of the man. Never an ideologue or a conceptionalist, he was essentially a practitioner of diplomacy when it came to dealing with the Soviet Union. He understood from the beginning that the intentions of this adversary were intransigently hostile to Western democratic nations, but he insisted that no responsible leader in the Kremlin would ever jeopardize his power base at home or in the Communist bloc and launch World War III. The challenge to the West of Soviet nationalism, as he called it, had been captured by Trotsky's memorable phrase in 1919—"neither war nor peace." Patience and diplomacy were made to deal with this singular adversary, concluded Ambassador Bullitt after the United States had extended recognition to the Soviet Union. Bohlen never forgot this prescription.

Works about Charles E. Bohlen

Isaacson, Walter, and Evan Thomas. *The Wise Men: Six Friends and the World They Made*. New York: Simon and Schuster, 1986.

Ruddy, T. Michael. *The Cautious Diplomat: Charles E. Bohlen and the Soviet Union, 1929–1969*. Kent, OH: Kent State University Press, 1986.

Schlesinger, Arthur. "Origins of the Cold War." *Foreign Affairs* 46 (October 1967): 22–52.

Yergin, Daniel. *Shattered Peace: The Origins of the Cold War and the National Security State*. Boston: Houghton Mifflin, 1977.

KEITH EAGLES

CHESTER BOWLES (1901–1986), twice ambassador to

India (1951–1953 and 1963–1969), was an advocate in the United States for understanding Third World nationalism, in particular, India's nonaligned foreign policy position. At the same time, he believed in the universal applicability of American democratic institutions and values.

Bowles was born in Springfield, Massachusetts, to a prominent family. An indifferent student, he graduated from Yale University in 1924. In 1925 he married Julia Fisk. They had two children and were divorced in 1932. In 1934 he married Dorothy "Stebs" Stebbins, and they had three children. At an early stage he wanted to be a diplomat, but this goal was not reached until he turned forty. In the interim, he founded, with the future Senator William Benton (Democrat of Connecticut), an advertising firm and established himself in the advertising business. Later he used the public relations skills he learned in this business, one that actually grew during the Depression years, in promoting economic aid for India to the Truman, Eisenhower, Kennedy, and Johnson administrations and before a parsimonious Congress. A liberal, he broadly supported Roosevelt's various New Deal programs.

During World War II Bowles entered public service, first in 1942 as Connecticut director of the Office of Price Administration and from 1943 to 1946 as national price administrator and a member of the War Production Board. In 1946 he chaired the Economic Stabilization Board, where he alienated powerful members of Congress by vigorously trying to use its extensive regulatory powers to aid consumers.

In post–World War II terms Bowles was a liberal who wished to use government to achieve social justice. One of the enthusiastic founders of the Americans for Democratic Action (ADA), he shared the organization's anti-Soviet views. Although he was a Cold Warrior, his views were less narrow than most in his understanding of Third World nationalism. Eventually Bowles distanced himself from the ADA, which he considered an elite group removed from ordinary voters. Moreover, Republicans painted the ADA as soft on communism, and Bowles had political ambitions in Connecticut and at the national level. Bowles served one term as governor of Connecticut, from 1949 to 1951. In office he championed massive housing programs and civil rights guarantees of equality in housing, employment, and public facilities. As ambassador to India and as an advocate for economic aid to that nation, he would echo these earlier concerns.

When President Harry S. Truman offered an ambassadorship in 1951, Bowles requested India. He saw in India a historic opportunity and the political and economic key to transforming a newly independent Asian nation into a free and democratic society. Serving as ambassador to India was thus a challenge that Bowles welcomed. American leaders wanted this newly independent, strategically located nation to become part of the containment effort against the Soviet Union and communism in general. Tensions therefore heightened when India resolved instead to be neutral in its foreign policy and to follow a socialist economic model. More than most American political leaders, Bowles understood the complexities of a society still struggling to escape its colonial past that found itself caught in a power struggle between East and West. India refused to take part in the Japanese peace treaty negotiations because its prime minister was not consulted. The Indian government was also critical of the American decision to cross the thirty-eighth parallel in pursuit of North Korean troops. Indians saw continuing colonial domination—not international communism—as the principal threat to their national interest. As ambassador, Bowles was charged with repairing relations already badly strained by 1951. Some members of Congress advocated terminating all economic assistance to India. Questions arose over the reliability of any alliance with this new nation of close to 600 million people, fourteen major languages, six important religions, and an archaic caste system. Here was an opportunity for Bowles to conduct diplomacy in accordance with his long-held beliefs.

Bowles's enthusiasm for India endeared him to the Indian people in his first term as ambassador. Determined to meet Indians and to gather firsthand information, he traveled across the country several times to study village life and the fledgling nation's economic needs. He found ordinary Indians mostly friendly toward the United States. The Bowleses' informal family lifestyle endeared them to many. Bowles and his wife were often seen riding bicycles around New Delhi, and their children attended public schools. Prime Minister Jawaharlal Nehru's reception was equally warm, and the two men formed close personal ties, partly because of shared idealistic approaches to the international scene. Only privately did Bowles acknowledge that Nehru could be suspicious, impatient, and unwilling to appreciate another's viewpoint. American views, as mirrored in the press and among members of Congress, were not tolerant of India's neutrality. Bowles's views of Nehru, for instance, were not shared by others in the embassy or at the State Department, where the ambassador was thought to be naïve and gullible.

Bowles argued that leaders of Asian nations needed American financial assistance to prove domestically that they had not sold out their nations' newfound sovereignty. The United States could not prescribe economic systems for aid recipients. A democratic, freely elected government was the only standard Bowles insisted upon. India's collectivism, moreover, he saw as indigenous to its culture and society. Bowles took pains to distinguish between communism and democratic socialism. He was convinced that if economic modernization was not achieved within a reasonably short time, Indians would succumb to communism and become part of the Communist bloc. The economic assistance programs he proposed were substantially larger than those put forth by the administration. Bowles hoped, over the long term, to bring India within the U.S.

orbit. But Indian foreign policies, such as supporting U.N. membership for the Communist Chinese, were politically unpalatable to many in the United States.

An assessment of Bowles's first term as ambassador to India must recognize the new economic relationship he established between Washington and New Delhi, including $50 million in well-administered community-development projects. An indication of how quickly this influence waned was a Point Four grant that was raised to $200 million just before Bowles's departure and cut back again shortly after he left. More important, Ambassador Bowles raised the awareness of India as a nation of importance to the United States and shaped many Democratic Party foreign policy planks toward the subcontinent. By the time of his departure relations between the two nations were decidedly improved. This brief interval of cooperation would not last.

Bowles made known to the Eisenhower administration his willingness to remain at his post, but Eisenhower replaced him in 1953. He thereafter worked assiduously for the Democratic Party as a foreign policy advisor, especially on Third World issues. A prolific author, he wrote numerous articles and several books in the 1950s, most dealing with U.S. relations with underdeveloped countries. His main concern was foreign aid, which he believed the best deterrent against the spread of communism. But he displayed little recognition of the deeper roots of the appeal of communism, always attributing it to hunger and ignoring other factors.

Throughout the 1950s Bowles served as a strong advocate for Indian interests. However, the Cold War requirement in the 1950s of winning allies and votes in the U.N. General Assembly mattered more to the Eisenhower administration than Bowles's argument that the purpose of foreign assistance to developing countries should be to help a nation to speed the rate of its development. Partly because America's chief concern was European recovery, American aid to India developed in a somewhat piecemeal fashion, rather than as a process of deliberate planning. During the early postwar years much of the aid was for technical assistance and food. The outbreak of the Korean War in 1950 shifted the focus of this assistance primarily to security considerations to protect against Communist expansion. Despite Bowles's vigorous protests, in 1951 Congress delayed for four months wheat shipments, sorely needed because of famine caused by a lack of monsoon rains, while congressmen sharply chastised the Indian government for its foreign policy. India did not forget the incident and began its slow drift toward the Soviet Union. Bowles recognized the need, and justifiability, for newly freed nations to assert their independence from the Soviets and the West alike. He understood that India feared compromising its newly won sovereignty. Bowles took upon himself the task of explaining Indian nonalignment, which many American politicians interpreted as neutrality at best or naïve and pro-Communist at worst. At the same time, Bowles worked at getting the Indian government to temper its anti-Western rhetoric.

In light of India's recent colonial past and its severe internal problems, nonalignment seemed to the Indian government to be the preferable approach. Backing one side or the other in the Cold War would further divide a society already splintered by religious differences, language, and customs. India's preeminent position in South Asia meant that it did not need outside support to bolster its regional position. At the Asian-African Conference held in Bandung in 1955, India appeared as a leader of the newly emerging nonaligned nations. Neither the United States nor the Soviet Union held enough appeal for India to abandon its nonaligned stand. While intrigued with the Soviet attempt to use central economic planning to lift the nation from poverty, Indians recognized the harsher aspects of the Soviet dictatorship. India viewed the United States as more concerned with maintaining its Cold War alliances with its European allies than with promoting anticolonialism. Bowles believed that aid policies designed around the world Communist threat implied that once this threat ceased to exist, American interest in the underdeveloped nation would also cease.

Indian leaders could not easily read American intentions. Secretary of State John Foster Dulles publicly reproved nations that refused to be counted on the American side. But in the face of perceived Soviet incursions into South Asia, exceptions were made for India. Dulles's response to Bowles's criticism was vague and noncommittal. India's refusal to become part of the American-established military alliance, the Southeast Asia Treaty Organization (SEATO), antagonized Dulles. Because of SEATO's aim of preventing Communist Chinese expansion in Asia, India felt that its own influence in the region would be lessened if it aligned itself with these Western aims. Bowles believed that Asia perceived Western military alliances as interfering in Asian affairs. The ultimate solution for Bowles was for Asian nations to evolve their own independent associations.

Western security interests in South Asia exacerbated strains between India and Pakistan over religious and land claims. Anything the United States did to bolster the defense of one country against the Soviets or the Communist Chinese would be interpreted by the other as a threat to its security. Larger Cold War considerations outranked regional policies or American-Indian relations. Since India adhered to a policy of nonalignment, Pakistan was the obvious alternative in the region. Bowles adamantly opposed an arms deal with Pakistan in return for a military base not far from the Soviet border. The United States viewed aid as part of an anti-Communist alliance, but Pakistan accepted the assistance primarily to strengthen its political hand in South Asia. Bowles worried that building up Pakistan against Communists did not consider the broader implications for Asia. The United States risked forcing India to divert its funds of foreign currencies from economic development to purchase tanks and planes. Nehru regarded as meaningless the Eisenhower administration's assurances that the military assistance was not directed against India and that the United States would come to India's defense if it were used for such purposes. Bowles feared that U.S. meddling in South Asia might drive the Indians into the Communist camp.

Bowles sometimes exaggerated to sell his ideas to Congress and the Eisenhower administration. He was not above conjuring images of the loss of China in 1949 or describing India as Moscow's primary target in Asia. Much of the rhetoric was shaped to impress a State Department oriented toward Europe. His advice was not always heeded. Nevertheless, Bowles remained characteristically buoyant and optimistic.

Bowles remained in political life. Elected to Congress as a House Democrat in 1958, he served one term, in which he lobbied for foreign aid programs while a member of the House Foreign Affairs Committee. Once he decided that Adlai Stevenson and Hubert H. Humphrey could not win the 1960 Democratic Party presidential nomination, Bowles gave his support to Senator John F. Kennedy. In a bid to win liberal favor, Kennedy asked Bowles to be his campaign's foreign policy advisor. Bowles hoped to be named secretary of state, but Kennedy offered him only the position of under secretary of state. After disputing with the president's brother, Attorney General Robert F. Kennedy, and bristling under the direction of Secretary of State Dean Rusk, Bowles was forced to resign. Bowles was out of step with younger Kennedy administration policymakers, many of whom promoted a more activist, confrontational diplomacy toward the Soviet Union. Bowles's difficult relations with the Kennedy administration were partly due to differences in perspective between Kennedy, whose attention centered on Europe and the use of military power, and Bowles. Kennedy had little patience for Bowles's sometimes verbose, moralizing discussions of abstract principles. Bowles also failed to master the game of bureaucratic politics.

Late in 1961 Kennedy appointed Bowles special representative or ambassador-at-large for Asia, Africa, and Latin American affairs. The new job was designed to look like a key foreign policy position, but gave Bowles little real authority or influence. His recommendations reflected the same themes he had always promoted. On matters concerning India, he rejected the views of other foreign policy thinkers; he believed that liberal democratic solutions could be applied to all nations; and he was so associated with underdeveloped nations, in general, and India, in particular, that he diminished his credibility and effectiveness. Bowles had no feasible solution for the Vietnam War, only lofty, impractical concepts of neutrality. Over the military alliance with Pakistan, Bowles clashed with an administration that continued the Eisenhower containment alliance structure in SEATO. Bowles could not convince Kennedy officials to dismantle the relationship with Pakistan. Once he recognized the futility of his situation, he quit as special advisor.

In a concession to liberals, Kennedy sent Bowles back to India in July 1963 to replace Ambassador John Kenneth Galbraith. In the aftermath of the Sino-Indian War and Pakistani ties with China that aimed at protecting Pakistan against India, Bowles hoped to strengthen U.S.-Indian relations, but he soon became involved in the Kashmir dispute. The border state of Kashmir, which had been the scene of bloody warfare between India and Pakistan in 1948, evolved into an uneasy truce under U.N. auspices. The migration of over 10 million people and internal fighting that cost 500,000 lives was the traumatic result of the partition, as part of the independence decree, of predominantly Hindu India and predominantly Moslem Pakistan. India perceived the U.S. position as supportive of Pakistani claims. When Bowles advocated partitioning Kashmir as a means of achieving settlement, he found himself in conflict with the State Department, which suspected the Indian government of using the proposal to delay settlement of the dispute. Bowles's stand was probably a mistake, since it portrayed him as even more pro-Indian. In his second term Bowles repeatedly recommended against U.S. support of the Pakistani position in the United Nations. When war broke out over Kashmir in 1965, the United States suspended further economic assistance to both Pakistan and India. By this time Bowles's influence in Washington was rapidly waning.

Bowles remained at this post until 1969. He was usually unable to convince either Presidents Kennedy or Lyndon B. Johnson, who was preoccupied with the Vietnam War, of the efficacy of his recommendations. Administration concerns for both India and Pakistan were downgraded. Because Bowles was perceived as biased and pro-Indian, his recommendations were often dismissed. During his second term Bowles often became exasperated with Indian policies and attitudes, but he went no further than to confide these thoughts to his diary.

Chester Bowles was the leading American advocate for aiding the establishment of a liberal democratic state in India. His association with India for a quarter of a century is important because it highlights the contradictions and assumptions of American foreign policy toward underdeveloped Asian countries and because it illustrates the thinking of a prominent liberal foreign policy figure. Bowles believed in American exceptionalism, the notion that it was the purpose of the United States to promote liberal democracy in the wider world. He did not see Indians as unique. He did not question how Asians would perceive the export of American purpose, mission, and political ideology. He did not, however, believe that the American system could be exported wholesale and argued that in any case Indians must determine their own future. Bowles accepted America's paramount place in the postwar world. He saw dangers in Communist expansion, but thought that they could be met in the Third World with foreign aid programs and the encouragement of liberal democracy. While many of the economic development plans that Bowles proposed reflected his New Deal experiences and failed to take into account India's distinct economic, social, and political heritage, he recognized that rapid industrialization was not feasible without accompanying rural economic development and political stability. Bowles's contributions were his attention to broader long-term issues, his role as a visionary, and his insistence that the United States should abandon support for the status quo and become a force for social change in the Third World, albeit within a liberal democratic mode.

Works by Chester Bowles

Ambassador's Report. New York: Harper and Brothers, 1954.
The New Dimensions of Peace. New York: Harper and Brothers, 1955.

Ideas, People, and Peace. New York: Harper and Brothers, 1958.
The Conscience of a Liberal. Ed. Henry Steele Commager. New York: Harper and Row,
    1962.
Promises to Keep: My Years in Public Life, 1941–1969. New York: Harper and Row,
    1971.

Works about Chester Bowles

Barnds, William J. *India, Pakistan, and the Great Powers*. New York: Praeger Publishers,
    1972.
Brands, H. W. *India and the United States: The Cold Peace*. Boston: Twayne Publishers,
    1990.
Gupta, Surendra K. "Chester Bowles as U.S. Ambassador to India, 1951–1953." *Internationales Asienforum* 17, no. 1/2 (1986): 51–58.
Lazarowitz, Arlene. "Enlightened Cold Warrior: Chester Bowles as Advocate for Foreign
    Aid to India, 1953–1958." *Asian Profile* 14, no. 1 (February 1986): 49–60.
Schaffer, Howard B. *Chester Bowles: New Dealer in the Cold War*. Cambridge: Harvard
    University Press, 1993.

ARLENE LAZAROWITZ

WILLIAM CHRISTIAN BULLITT (1891–1967) was

U.S. ambassador to the Soviet Union and France.

Bullitt was born in Philadelphia on January 25, 1891. He was in the top echelon of society and had a distinguished lineage, being related in ancestry to Pocahontas, Patrick Henry, George Washington's father Augustine, and Fletcher Christian of *Bounty* fame. He was also descended from the Salomon and Horwitz Jewish banking family of Philadelphia. His parents wanted him to attend Groton, but he refused and instead attended the Philadelphia equivalent, the De Lancey School. He graduated from Yale University in 1912. He excelled in academics and was inducted into Phi Beta Kappa. Thee was no question that Bullitt intended to enter government service; early in life he told a friend that he intended to become governor of Pennsylvania, then secretary of state, and finally president. He attended Harvard Law School in 1913–1914, but quit to accept a position with the *Philadelphia Ledger* in 1915, where he served variously as an associate editor, foreign correspondent, and Washington correspondent. In 1917 he resigned to accept a position as an assistant secretary of state from 1917 to 1918 and then was assigned to the Division of Current Intelligence Summaries for the American Commission to the Paris Peace Conference. Bullitt was, in the words of Secretary of Labor Frances Perkins, a very ingratiating fellow. He made himself the news disseminator at Paris and chose to be an ally of Woodrow Wilson's special advisor, Colonel Edward M. House, who contested with Secretary of State Robert Lansing for primary influence over U.S. policy.

In this contest Bullitt wangled an appointment to go to Moscow to attempt to bring an end to the civil war in Russia and get the Bolsheviks to agree to an accommodation with the Allies. Lansing tried to restrict Bullitt's mission to pure fact finding, but Bullitt and House had discussed the mission with Prime Minister David Lloyd George's secretary, and their intent was to go beyond these limited instructions. Also, there was tacit approval from the president for Bullitt's version of the mission. He returned to Paris with an agreement that would have committed Lenin to pay the debts incurred to fight the war, divided territory in Russia between the White and Red armies followed by a cessation of hostilities between these forces, and granted amnesty for Russians who had aided the Allied cause. Leaks about the mission and Lansing's determination to scuttle it, along with aid from Winston Churchill and Georges Clemenceau, caused a failure to proceed on the foundation Bullitt established. He resented this reversal bitterly and blamed Wilson for not following through on what he had established. Shortly after this Bullitt called a press conference and announced his resignation from the Peace Commission, saying that he planned to go lie on the Riviera and watch the world go to hell in a wheelbarrow. Many Democrats later wished that he had done just that and perhaps that he might have accompanied the wheelbarrow; instead he went on a canoe trip in the wilds of Maine and on his return was subpoenaed to testify before Senator Henry Cabot Lodge's committee investigating the conduct of the American Commission at Paris. Bullitt stated that Lansing had told him that if the American people really knew what had happened at Paris, they would never accept the treaty. Thus for the next decade Bullitt was viewed as a pariah by Democrats and Republican supporters of the League of Nations, who believed that he helped sink American acceptance of the treaty and participation in the international organization.

This background is important in understanding Bullitt's subsequent career. That he could recover from this after a self-imposed exile, mostly in Europe, during the next twelve years was a miracle. He spent part of this time maintaining contacts with European political leaders and kept a correspondence with such American luminaries as Colonel House, who, along with Louis B. Whele, a prominent lawyer and Harvard classmate of Franklin D. Roosevelt, suggested to FDR that Bullitt would be useful as a foreign policy advisor if the Democrats won the 1932 election. Bullitt asked House to intercede for him, and thus began a new career in diplomacy after twelve years of abstention from active politics.

Bullitt made several trips to Europe in 1932–1933, first on his own, then as a secret representative of FDR to attempt to persuade the British and French not to loan money to the Japanese and in this way curtail their expansionism in Asia. He was also to examine the possible thwarting of Japan via resumption of relations with the Russians. He reported to FDR that recognition of the USSR would have a restrictive effect on Japan where there would be concern over possible collaboration between these two major powers with interests in the Far East. When Bullitt was in Britain, the Foreign Office warned that he was a dangerous man because he had ''pinko'' tendencies and had, after all, married the widow of the American Communist sympathizer John Reed. The Foreign Office went so far as to suggest that the British ambassador to the United States, Sir Ronald Lindsay, should work on President Roosevelt to restrict Bullitt's influence. Bullitt had married Anne Moen Louise Bryant Reed in 1923 after his divorce from Aimé Ernesta Drinker Bullitt. Anne and William had one daughter, Anne Moen Bullitt, who later married Nicholas Benjamin Duke Biddle. Anne Biddle was so disturbed over the reviews of her father's book attacking Woodrow Wilson, which was coauthored with Sigmund Freud based on notes that Freud had given to Bullitt, that she had the Bullitt papers, then deposited at the Sterling Library at Yale, removed so that historians could not use them.

Bullitt had a particular interest in the Russian Revolution. He had been in Russia with his mother during the revolution of 1905 and had a rudimentary knowledge of the language. Thus when FDR chose Bullitt as a special advisor on negotiations for resumption of relations in 1933 from Bullitt's post as an assistant secretary of state, he was excited and enthusiastic. He favored recognition as sensible and as an instrument to aid in curbing Japan and also giving the Nazi regime in Germany pause to consider what a close friendship between the Americans and the Russians might mean for Hitler's expansionist designs. In fact, Bullitt was chosen by FDR, along with Henry Morgenthau, Jr., to initiate the contact with the Soviets to explore the prospect for recognition. He was deeply involved in the negotiations and rightly expressed concern over the failure to obtain a debt-payment agreement before diplomatic relations with the USSR were consummated. The debt question remained a major factor in Soviet-American relations thereafter.

In the summer of 1933 Bullitt was assigned to the delegation representing the United States at the London Economic Conference, much to the chagrin of those in the British Foreign Office who considered him dangerous. When it came time to exchange ambassadors with the USSR, Bullitt seemed a logical choice as the first U.S. ambassador to the Soviet Union. He then undertook the task of trying to arrange a debt settlement that FDR, Hull, and Bullitt believed would clear the path for further cooperation to thwart the aggressor nations. In fact, Bullitt, in his opening remarks to President of the Soviet Republic Mikhail Kalinin, led the Russians to expect more in the way of cooperation than was really possible in the isolationist climate that prevailed in the United States because he promised a relationship that was not merely normal but genuinely friendly. He postulated a missionary role for himself in Russia and close collaboration by the two governments in their joint endeavor to ensure the peace. This foretold a host of difficulties if the relationship in some way failed to carry through on this ambitious program. This led the Russians to expect some subtle method of exerting pressure on both the Germans and the Japanese to halt their aggressive designs. Bullitt and Hull held out this carrot of cooperation thereafter as an enticement to pay the agreed-upon debt of some amount between 75 and 150 million dollars, promising and warning that further cooperation would be extended or withdrawn depending on such a settlement.

When Bullitt failed to gain a debt settlement, and the cooperation he expected from the Soviets did not materialize, his ego demanded a scapegoat, which he found in Soviet Commissar for Foreign Affairs Maxim Litvinov. The ambassador kept telling Hull and FDR that he was making progress in working with other Soviet leaders, but Litvinov stood in the way of a settlement. He never seemed to blame the real source of the problem, Joseph Stalin, who, as Litvinov noted later, could not resist the temptation of "doing" the Americans when there was no firm agreement on the method of payment. As the purges progressed and many of the Russian contacts the ambassador believed would aid in establishing closer relations with the United States met the executioner or went to Siberian exile, Bullitt became disillusioned with the Soviet experiment and wished to escape the icebox prison of Moscow. From welcoming the ambassador as an unbiased friend of the USSR when he arrived, the Soviet press turned to castigating him as a reactionary plotter against Russia when he left in 1936. However, his disappointment did not deter him from warning that the United States could not afford to break relations with the Soviets. In his last dispatch to the State Department Bullitt expressed his anger at Soviet duplicity, but this did not diminish the importance of Russia in future European and Asian troubles. He stated that one should not count on getting too much from the

Soviets, but also advised not to despair because at least minimal returns could be attained. Almost as a foreword to George Kennan's later famous Long Telegram and Mr. X article, Bullitt urged long-term patient pressure consistently applied and long-term contacts to help ameliorate the suspicious Russian psyche. Only in this fashion could a fruitful relationship be obtained.

On leaving Moscow in 1936, Bullitt returned to Washington and an assignment as a special assistant secretary of state until, on the death of Ambassador Louis Straus, the embassy in Paris became available. This was the assignment Bullitt had sought at the beginning of his service in the department in 1933. Fluent in the French language, as well as German, and a descendant of French immigrants to the United States, Bullitt seemed an ideal choice to send to the sophisticated French capital. Bullitt had been one of the émigrés in the 1920s, hobnobbing with the likes of Ernest Hemingway, and in addition had made sure that many important French government officials were confidants, including Clemenceau, Leon Blum, and Edouard Daladier. The first was premier during World War I and the latter two were to serve in that post during Bullitt's ambassadorship. It was during his assignment in Paris that Bullitt slowly shifted from a fundamentally isolationist orientation to being an advocate of intervention. Bright as he was, he could scarcely fail to perceive that a Nazi victory would destroy everything he believed in and that such a victory was probable unless the United States became actively involved. Thus he began to urge FDR to take a stand after years of suggesting that there was little that the United States could do except get itself involved in another European war that would not serve American interests. This campaign began in 1938 and reached fruition in 1941 when, after a tour around America, Bullitt wrote to FDR that people were in a mood to follow him even to war and that time was of the essence, as the hour of decision was nigh and more delay might be disastrous.

Roosevelt and Bullitt shared a close friendship for most of the period down to the war, but in the end the president did not forgive Bullitt for the role he played in getting rid of Under Secretary of State Sumner Welles. Though Welles was married several times and had a family, when he overdrank, latent homosexual tendencies surfaced and he was indiscreet in whom he propositioned. Such was the case when he attempted a liaison with a railroad porter on a train returning from the funeral of Speaker of the House William Bankhead. When Bullitt and Hull learned of this, they launched a joint campaign to get rid of Welles, and when the president finally gave in to the pressure after three years of urging and asked Welles to resign in September 1943, this spelled the end of Bullitt's association with FDR.

When Bullitt served in Paris, he was extremely close to the French government. Secretary of the Interior Harold Ickes said in jest that he was so close that he slept with the French cabinet. There is no question that Bullitt enjoyed the Paris post or that his contacts with leading French politicians were useful. This was in keeping with Bullitt's determination to know and cultivate the right people. In the Roosevelt administration and inner circle as well as in the Department of State he kept a host of people believing that they were very special to him. Harold Ickes was among those so chosen, as was Margaret "Missy" Le Hand, one of Roosevelt's personal secretaries. Through Judge R. Walton Moore, who had been a roommate of Bullitt's father in law school at the University of Virginia and thereafter his lifelong friend, Bullitt wooed Missy and made the romantic old judge his go-between in this distant courtship. Missy kept Bullitt's name before the president and was constantly handing on secondhand news about or from him emanating mostly from Moore, though Bullitt did occasionally write directly to her. Moore was an old congressional colleague and friend of Cordell Hull and served the State Department variously as an assistant secretary and counselor. This enabled Bullitt to escape Hull's wrath when he sometimes went over the secretary's head to the president. Through his correspondence with Moore, Bullitt bombarded the secretary of state and the president with his views of how the United States should respond to the European crises.

Bullitt was convinced that when it came time to actively oppose Hitler, the Chamberlain government in Great Britain would hang the French out to dry. Despite their long-standing mutual enmity, the ambassador saw Winston Churchill as the only source of real opposition to Hitler in England. The irony here was that as late as 1936 Bullitt was writing FDR that accommodation with Hitler was possible and that he had been working on an agreement that would provide economic security for Germany in return for ameliorating the arms race that was going full speed in Europe. The hope that Hitler could somehow be appeased prevailed in Bullitt's letters and dispatches through early 1938, and he even played a role in having the anti-Nazi U.S. ambassador in Germany, William E. Dodd, removed because he was a block to improved relations with the Nazis. This hope faded in Bullitt's correspondence after Munich, and he quickly became an advocate of American intervention in Europe and all-out aid to the French.

When Bullitt was informed by Premier Daladier that France was forced to accept Munich by Chamberlain and that if the French had had three thousand planes Munich would not have happened, Bullitt got on the *Normandie* and headed for Washington to expedite the sale of military aircraft to France. This was merely the first of numerous efforts on his part to provide the necessary military supplies to confront Germany. However, the president noticed that Bullitt's mercurial temperament caused considerable fluctuation in his reporting. FDR confided to Morgenthau that the trouble with his ambassador to France was that he would report in the morning that everything was rosy and by evening that one should abandon all hope. Thus Bullitt's influence was already beginning to wane before he angered Roosevelt via his role in destroying Welles's career.

During the remainder of the period before the war began Bullitt constantly bombarded Washington with reports of impending disaster if the United States did not take a stand against Germany. When the war actually did come on September 1, 1939, it was Bullitt who reported it by phone to the president. Shortly thereafter, in one of his moods of pessimism he told the president that all was probably lost and he might as well come home and be in the cabinet because there was not going to be anything left to do in Paris. Then he changed his mind and decided that he would stick it out no matter what. It was this mood that prevailed in the last days before the fall of France. When the other embassies were removing to Vichy, Bullitt refused to go. In fact, Bullitt remained as provisional mayor of Paris representing the diplomatic corps when it was declared an open city, and his fluency in German helped in this transfer of control. When he finally left Paris to follow the fleeing French government, Bullitt reported that the Vichy leaders were resigned to seeing France as a province of Germany and that they hoped by maintaining the Vichy government to be a favorite province of Germany. This was the point where Bullitt decided to give his allegiance to the Free French government in Algeria. He returned to the United States anticipating some important new post, but was disappointed, so he went to North Africa and accepted a commission in the Free French Army. A relative told Bullitt's biographers Will Brownell and Richard Billings that Bullitt had a fatal flaw. He would develop passionate devotions to a person whose leadership he could follow on the principles they represented; then, when they failed to live up to expectations, he would abandon them and consider them to be failures. Thus his relationship with FDR ended as had that with Wilson, in his becoming an outcast.

Works by William C. Bullitt

The Bullitt Mission to Russia: Testimony before the Committee on Foreign Relations, United States Senate, of William C. Bullitt. New York: B. W. Huebsch, 1919. Reprint. Westport, CT: Hyperion Press, 1977.

The Great Globe Itself: A Preface to World Affairs. New York: C. Scribner's Sons, 1946.

Coauthor with Sigmund Freud. *Thomas Woodrow Wilson, Twenty-eighth President of the United States: A Psychological Study*. Boston: Houghton-Mifflin, 1967.

Works about William C. Bullitt

Brownell, Will, and Richard Billings. *So Close to Greatness: A Biography of William C. Bullitt*. New York: Macmillan; London: Collier Macmillan, 1987.

Bullitt, Orville H., ed. *For the President, Personal and Secret: Correspondence between Franklin D. Roosevelt and William C. Bullitt*. Boston: Houghton Mifflin, 1972.

Craig, Gordon, and Felix Gilbert, eds. *The Diplomats: 1919–1939*. Princeton: Princeton University Press, 1953.

Farnsworth, Beatrice. *William C. Bullitt and the Soviet Union*. Bloomington: Indiana University Press, 1967.

EDWARD M. BENNETT

RALPH J. BUNCHE (1903–1971)

RALPH J. BUNCHE (1903–1971) was a noted diplomat who became the first African American to win the Nobel Peace Prize when he mediated the truce ending the Arab-Israeli War of 1948.

Born in Detroit, Michigan, on August 7, 1903, Bunch, as his name was then spelled, enjoyed the support of a close-knit family while enduring a series of childhood tragedies. His mother, Olive Johnson, had married Fred Bunch, an itinerant barber and circus barker, in 1901. The family moved frequently, first to Toledo, Ohio—where Olive gave birth to a daughter, Grace—then on to Knoxville, Tennessee, and then back to Toledo before returning to Detroit. In Michigan Olive entered a sanitarium for tuberculosis patients. For the next several years Lucy Johnson, Olive's mother, became the most important person in Ralph Bunch's life. Lucy, the widow of a teacher and elementary-school principal, took charge of him and ensured that he received a thorough education.

Hoping to restore Olive's health, the family, augmented by an aunt and uncle, moved to Albuquerque, New Mexico, in 1914. The New Mexico experience quickly turned to tragedy. Olive died, Fred abandoned the family, and Ralph's uncle committed suicide. As America entered World War I, Lucy moved the remnants of the family to Los Angeles, California, and added an ''e'' to Ralph's last name, as if to signify the start of a new life. In Los Angeles Bunche began to excel as a student and athlete. In 1922 he graduated from Jefferson High School as class valedictorian. Winning a scholarship to the University of California at Los Angeles, he played football, baseball, and basketball, worked on the school newspaper, and graduated summa cum laude. A young man of exceptional ability and wide-ranging interests, Bunche received a fellowship from Harvard University for graduate work in political science. With help from friends and family and a $1,000 contribution from a local black women's club, he set out for Harvard in 1927. At Cambridge the most decisive influence on Bunche may have been an outstanding group of fellow black students; they included Robert C. Weaver, who later became the first secretary of housing and urban development. Bunche received his master's degree in 1928.

Bunche accepted a faculty position at Howard University, where he organized the historically black college's first Department of Political Science. His scholarly interests foreshadowed the direction his diplomatic career would take. In 1932 a grant from the Julius Rosenwald Foundation allowed him to begin research for his dissertation, a comparative study of the French colony of Dahomey and Togoland, which France governed under a mandate from the League of Nations. Two years later Harvard awarded Bunche the Toppan Prize for outstanding research in the social sciences, and he became the first African American to earn a Ph.D. in political science. Bunche later studied at Northwestern University, the London School of Economics, and South Africa's Capetown University.

By 1936 it became clear that Bunche's professional life would combine a commitment to scholarship with a passion for racial justice and an interest in international affairs. In that year a grant from the Social Science Research Council allowed the young political scientist to visit Africa and Asia. At the same time, Bunche helped organize the National Negro Congress, an umbrella organization of civil rights leaders. Although he flirted with Marxism early in his career, Bunche abandoned the congress as it drifted leftward in the late 1930s. In 1936 he served as codirector of the Institute of Race Relations at Swarthmore College. He was a prolific writer who became an adroit diplomatic draftsman; his publications included *A World View of Race* (1936), which decried the worldwide exploitation of ethnic prejudices to obscure economic injustice.

From 1938 to 1940 Bunche assisted the Swedish sociologist Gunnar Myrdal in compiling his monumental work *An American Dilemma: The Negro Problem and American Democracy* (1944). Field research on racial conditions in the South found Myrdal and Bunche fleeing hostile sheriffs on more than one occasion, but *An American Dilemma* represented a pioneering study of black life. One of the massive memorandums that Bunche prepared for Myrdal was published posthumously as *The Political Status of the Negro in the Age of FDR* (1973).

Rejected for military service at the start of World War II because of phlebitis and poor hearing, Bunche joined the office of the Coordinator of Information— later the Office of Strategic Services, the forerunner of the Central Intelligence Agency—as an expert on Asian and African affairs in 1941. Among other duties, he wrote a training manual for U.S. troops scheduled to fight in North Africa. Soon made chief of the Research and Analysis Branch of the OSS's Africa Section, Bunche joined the State Department in 1944 as an expert on colonial issues. At the end of World War II he was head of the Division of Dependent Area Affairs, then the highest State Department post ever held by an African American.

Eager to promote decolonization under the supervision of the new United Nations, Bunche attended the Dumbarton Oaks Conference on the creation of the world body in August 1944. At the 1945 San Francisco Conference on the U.N. Charter, he served as secretary to the subcommittee of the U.S. delegation that drafted the American proposal for the trusteeship provision of the charter. As an advisor to Edward Stettinius, the U.S. representative to the London Conference of fall 1945, Bunche participated in the creation of the U.N. Secretariat and the U.N. Trusteeship Council. After serving as a member of the U.S. delegation to the first meeting of the U.N. General Assembly in London in January 1946, he seemed the obvious choice to direct the U.N. Trusteeship Division. He approached his new duties with relish, and if the process of dismantling the colonial empires did not proceed as rapidly as Bunche hoped, the trusteeship provision of the U.N. Charter gave legitimacy to the process of decolonization. By the end of 1946 he had negotiated eight trusteeship agreements with various Western powers, placing fourteen million people in six African and two Pacific nations on the path to political independence. From this relatively modest start, Bunche lived to see most of the Third World gain sovereignty.

In 1947 Bunche was appointed secretary of the U.N. Special Committee on Palestine, for which he ultimately wrote both the majority and minority reports. Both factions agreed that the British mandate in Palestine should end, but the majority report favored a partition of the territory between Arabs and Jews, while the minority report endorsed the creation of a federal state. The General Assembly approved the partition plan. Arabs opposed the division of Palestine, but the new state of Israel nevertheless declared its independence on May 14, 1948. Egypt, Jordan, Lebanon, Syria, Iraq, and Saudi Arabia immediately declared war. A week later the U.N. Security Council announced that it had appointed Count Folke Bernadotte of Sweden to mediate the crisis. Bunche, meanwhile, wasdispatched to the Middle East as the personal representative of Secretary-General Trygve Lie.

In June the warring parties agreed to a truce. Bunche helped organize the observer force that policed the cease-fire. Bernadotte's proposals for a permanent settlement angered Jewish extremists. He recommended, for example, that Jerusalem be placed under U.N. supervision, not Israeli control. On September 17, 1948, the Swedish diplomat was assassinated by the Stern Gang, a Jewish terrorist organization. Bunche narrowly escaped death himself. Flying back to the Middle East from Rhodes in the Mediterranean Sea, Bunche was to have met Bernadotte in Jerusalem, but his plane was late.

Appointed to replace Bernadotte, Bunche opened talks between Israel and Egypt on the island of Rhodes in January 1949. Firm, almost implacable, and endowed with a virtually inexhaustible reservoir of patience, he coaxed a formal armistice agreement from the parties by the end of February. Peace talks with Jordan began in March, and the other Arab powers soon fell in line as well. Although not a permanent settlement to the Arab-Israeli conflict, the Rhodes agreements helped bring almost a decade of relative stability to one of the world's most troubled areas.

Bunche's performance at Rhodes won him international acclaim. President Harry S. Truman offered him a position as assistant secretary of state. Unwilling to return to Washington and subject his family to the city's Jim Crow laws, Bunche declined. In 1950 he received the Nobel Peace Prize, becoming the first African American to win the award. He considered declining the honor—international civil servants, he believed, should not seek peace for personal recognition. But Trygve Lie thought that the prize would bolster the prestige of the United Nations and the Secretariat, and he persuaded Bunche to accept it. The National Association for the Advancement of Colored People (NAACP) gave Bunche its Springarn Medal for outstanding achievement by an American black. In 1953 he became the first black president of the American Political Science Association. The next year the new U.N. secretary-general, Dag Hammarskjöld, made Bunche under secretary-general, the highest U.N. post ever held by a U.S. citizen. Bunche was perhaps the most celebrated African-American public of-

ficial of his generation; his other accolades included sixty-nine honorary doctorates and a Presidential Medal of Freedom, awarded to him by Lyndon B.
Johnson in 1963.

This black American diplomat also attracted some unwelcome attention. As
a wave of anti-Communist sentiment swept the United States after World War
II, Bunche came under suspicion from Nevada Senator Pat McCarran of the
Senate Internal Security Subcommittee. McCarran, along with a federal grand
jury in New York, was investigating subversive activities at the United Nations.
Bunche was suspect mainly because of his associations with the National Negro
Congress in the 1930s. An informal meeting between Bunche and McCarran in
March 1953 seemed to reassure the Nevada Democrat, but Bunche still had to
satisfy the International Organizations Employees Loyalty Board, a Cold War
agency of the U.S. government with authority over Americans employed by the
United Nations. When Bunche left the National Negro Congress in 1940, one
of the leaders of the radical faction within the organization had been John P.
Davis. At a May 25, 1953, hearing before the Loyalty Board, Davis, by then a
prominent black publisher, magnanimously came to Bunche's defense, denying
that his former critic had any Communist sympathies.

On May 28 the board issued an order clearing Bunche of any charges of
disloyalty, but for years he remained a target of the far right and, as the civil
rights movement became more militant, of some black activists as well.
Bunche's position shielded him from the full brunt of American racism, but he
nonetheless spoke out frequently against discrimination. From 1931, when he
organized a protest against a segregated presentation of *Porgy and Bess* at Washington's National Theater, to 1965, when he went to Alabama to participate in
the Selma-to-Montgomery march for black voting rights, Bunche made clear his
hostility to all forms of segregation. His diplomatic achievements sometimes
seemed irrelevant to a younger generation of black militants, but he retained the
warm support of mainstream African-American leaders like Roy Wilkens of the
NAACP and Martin Luther King, Jr., of the Southern Christian Leadership Conference.

As U.N. under secretary-general, Bunche's primary responsibility was the
supervision of U.N. peacekeeping forces. The observer force he helped organize
to monitor the first Arab-Israeli cease-fire had been a pioneering effort in international peacekeeping. He was thus the most experienced official and the clear
choice to organize the first regular peacekeeping force, the U.N. Emergency
Force (UNEF), consisting of armed troops instead of unarmed observers. It was
sent to the Middle East as part of the settlement of the Suez crisis of 1956.
During Bunche's tenure major peacekeeping forces were also dispatched to Cyprus, where Turkish Cypriots chafed under a native Greek government, and
Kashmir, which India and Pakistan both claimed.

His greatest challenge came, however, in Zaire. Bunche went to the former
Belgian Congo in June 1960 to attend the ceremonies symbolizing the transfer
of power from Belgium to a new government led by Prime Minister Patrice

Lumumba. He found himself caught up almost immediately in the largest U.N. peacekeeping operation to that point in history. Within days of independence a power struggle developed between Lumumba and President Joseph Kasavubu, while Moise Tshombe led a secessionist movement in the province of Katanga. As a wave of disorder swept the nation, Bunche, operating virtually alone from a Leopoldville hotel room, faced what he later said was the most frightening experience of his career. For two months he supervised the deployment of peace-keeping forces as they flew into the Leopoldville airport. Ten thousand U.N. troops eventually suppressed the Katanga revolt and helped the central government consolidate its power under a new prime minister, Cyrille Adoula. Peace in Zaire came at great cost: Lumumba was assassinated by political rivals, and Dag Hammarskjöld died in a plane crash on his way to meet with Tshombe. No outside power was able to bring democracy to Zaire, but most contemporary observers gave the United Nations high marks for at least maintaining the territorial integrity of the huge central African nation.

Bunche enjoyed a few successes during his last years at the United Nations. In the late 1960s Great Britain wanted to withdraw from its Persian Gulf protectorate of Bahrain, which Iran had claimed for over a century, without abandoning the tiny sheikdom to the Iranians. Fortunately, the shah of Iran did not want to force a showdown with the British, and Bunche arranged a face-saving procedure by which Iran could honorably relinquish its claims: the secretary-general appointed a special representative to assess the political preferences of the Bahrainian public. The Iranian government accepted the mediator's conclusion that the majority of Bahrainians wanted full independence.

Yet as Bunche neared retirement, disappointments outweighed diplomatic victories. The UNEF—eighteen hundred soldiers stretched along the Egyptian side of a three-hundred-mile border with Israel—had been one of the United Nations' major apparent successes, but it proved unable to stop the Arab-Israeli War of 1967. Fighting began shortly after Secretary-General U Thant, at the demand of Egyptian ruler Gamal Abdel Nasser, removed the U.N. force. The Secretariat came under attack from all sides—even, ironically, from the Egyptians—for its conduct, but UNEF had entered Egypt only under a voluntary agreement between Dag Hammarskjöld and Nasser. U Thant and Bunche believed that they had no legal authority to keep U.N. soldiers in Egypt once Nasser formally requested their removal. Equally frustrating were efforts to end the American war in Vietnam. Bunche had opposed U.S. military involvement in Southeast Asia from its earliest days. In the fall of 1964 U Thant tried to arrange peace talks between the United States and North Vietnam in Rangoon, Burma. Fearful that negotiations might undercut the South Vietnamese government, the Johnson administration rebuffed U Thant's initiative. Later Bunche drafted a public appeal for a cease-fire and diplomatic talks, only to see that proposal rejected by Hanoi.

In addition to the frustrating limits on the power of the United Nations, Bunche labored under a host of physical ailments and personal problems. He suffered from phlebitis and diabetes, and his physical infirmities became apparent in the late 1950s. By the late 1960s he was almost blind. In 1930 he had married Ruth Ethel Harris, whose father was a politically prominent member of Montgomery, Alabama's black community. On balance the two enjoyed a happy marriage, but Ruth resented her husband's frequent absences from home. The two exchanged acrimonious letters over the years, and Ruth sometimes complained that Bunche preferred the company of white colleagues—who, she added, would never accept him as an equal—over his own family. The couple had two daughters, Joan and Jane, and one son, Ralph, Jr. Joan suffered from depression for years and committed suicide in October 1966.

His health failing, Bunche resigned from the United Nations on October 1, 1971. He died of kidney failure five weeks later, on December 9, 1971. Because the United Nations had no power to compel any nation to do what it did not want to do, Bunche's legacy appears to some as nebulous. But insofar as the United Nations was a clear advance over the international anarchy of the interwar years, Bunche may be regarded and commended as a man dedicated to the ideal of the international rule of law and the practice of multilateral diplomacy. Few other American diplomats worked as tirelessly for world peace, and perhaps no American life better embodied a commitment to international cooperation and an orderly community of nations.

Works by Ralph Bunche

"French Administration in Togoland and Dahomey." Ph.D. diss., Harvard University, 1934.

A World View of Race. Washington, DC: Associates in Negro Folk Education, 1936. Reprint. Port Washington, NY: Kennikat Press, 1968.

The Political Status of the Negro in the Age of FDR. Chicago: University of Chicago Press, 1973.

Works about Ralph Bunche

Halila, Souad. "The Intellectual Development and Diplomatic Career of Ralph J. Bunche: The Afro-American, Africanist, and Internationalist." Ph.D. diss., University of Southern California, 1988.

Haskins, Jim. *Ralph Bunche: A Most Reluctant Hero.* New York: Hawthorn Books, 1974.

Mann, Peggy. *Ralph Bunche: UN Peacemaker.* New York: Coward, McCann and Geoghegan, 1975.

Rivlin, Benjamin, ed. *Ralph Bunche: The Man and His Times.* New York: Holmes and Meier, 1990.

Touval, Saadia. *The Peace Brokers: Mediators in the Arab-Israeli Conflict, 1948–1979.* Princeton: Princeton University Press, 1982.

Urquhart, Brian. *Ralph Bunche: An American Life.* New York: W. W. Norton and Company, 1993.

JEFF BROADWATER

ELLSWORTH BUNKER (1894–1984) served as U.S. ambassador to South Vietnam during the height of the Vietnam War as well as during the American withdrawal.

Bunker was born in Yonkers, New York, on May 11, 1894, to a family of affluence. After graduation from Yale University in 1916, he worked for his father's National Sugar Refining Company. He did not enter the diplomatic corps until he was well into his middle fifties. Subsequently serving in a variety of posts throughout various regions in the world, Bunker was an unflappable patrician who was known as "The Refrigerator" for his icy composure.

In 1951 President Harry Truman appointed Bunker ambassador to Argentina. Relations between Washington and Buenos Aires had been poor since Juan Peron revealed fascist leanings during World War II. Bunker's appointment was the third in a series of businessmen-ambassadors selected in an attempt to harmonize U.S.-Argentinean relations by advocating goodwill and trade ties. Bunker served just over a year, primarily working to modernize the trade treaty that existed between the two nations. However, Peron continued to squander huge stocks of foreign capital in nationalization schemes that caused an acute depression and adverse trading conditions, and the ambassador made little progress as a consequence.

Bunker next became ambassador to Italy, a position he held until 1953. A political crisis had occurred when the Christian Democrats began losing political support. The ambassador, despite his short tenure, managed to play an important role with long-lasting results. Bunker advocated a policy of support for the retention of the moderate four-party coalition under the Christian Democrats in order to keep the extreme right and left out of government. Continued American aid to Italy became contingent upon a victory by the Christian Democrats and the moderates. Bunker helped convince the Christian Democrat leadership to end its efforts to reach out to the left as a way of broadening its support in order to stay in power, however, this action made the peaceful transfer of power to the left impossible for the near future in Italy. He also unsuccessfully attempted to chauffeur the European Defense Community agreement through the Italian parliament.

In 1956 President Dwight Eisenhower selected Bunker for an ambassadorial appointment to New Delhi. India under Prime Minister Jawaharlal Nehru had begun a turn from the West as America aligned itself more closely with Pakistan, its partner in the Baghdad Pact. Yet relations between the United States and India temporarily warmed due to Bunker's personal style of diplomacy, especially after the Soviet invasion of Hungary and the Suez crisis. This thaw developed even despite India's problems with Portugal over Goa and with Pakistan over Kashmir. Bunker successfully pushed for increased U.S. economic aid to India in order to overcome a serious foreign-exchange gap, a step he argued was necessary for vital American interests in the region. He also was responsible for the propitious visit of Eisenhower to India in 1959. However, Nehru rejected an approach by Bunker to resolve the subcontinent's problems in an integrated manner. Bunker also had a simultaneous appointment as ambassador to Nepal. Nepal had a consultative pact with India regarding external relations, and Nehru preferred to have all foreign ambassadors dually accredited. In Nepal Bunker helped to oversee the funding of a military force of Tibetan exiles based near Mustang.

Afterward, Bunker became a troubleshooter for the Kennedy administration. In 1962 he brokered the transfer of West New Guinea (West Irian) from Holland to Indonesia. After World War II the Netherlands government had insisted upon maintaining its presence in this remote region of the world, while Indonesia regarded the Dutch base as potentially destabilizing. Throughout the 1950s President Sukarno had campaigned against the Dutch presence. The issue of West New Guinea became a polarizing force in Indonesian politics that pushed Sukarno further toward anti-Western extremism and the Soviet orbit. In 1961 Sukarno publicly proclaimed that he would invade West New Guinea if his demands went unsatisfied. This put Washington in a bind, since the Netherlands was a key NATO ally and the Kennedy administration perceived that Indonesia was teetering on the brink of communism. In early 1962 Kennedy sent Bunker to mediate the dispute. After making clear that the United States would not go to war to preserve the position of the Dutch, Bunker persuaded Amsterdam to allow a U.N.-sponsored interim government to administer the territory and to oversee its ultimate transfer to Indonesia. In another diplomatic mission Bunker returned to Indonesia three years later when the Sukarno regime was in deep crisis. His report to President Johnson was pivotal in persuading the administration to adopt a posture of reduced visibility and involvement on the eve of Sukarno's overthrow by the military.

In 1963 Bunker attempted to mediate the situation in Yemen, where radical pan-Arabist army officers had overthrown the monarchy, proclaimed a republic, and laid claim to territory in Saudi Arabia and Aden. After failing to combat the Anglo-Saudi–financed rebellion of the former emir, the republicans turned to Egypt's Premier Gamal Abdel Nasser for support. Beginning in October 1962, Egypt sent a force of 70,000 men with tanks and planes into Yemen. Since the Kennedy administration was unwilling to jeopardize its rapprochement with Nasser, and since it believed that a republican Yemen would contribute to the stability of the region, it decided to recognize the Yemeni Arab Republic. Accordingly, it began mediation efforts, with Bunker as the point man. However, the crisis escalated after the Egyptians bombed Saudi bases early in 1963 and Saudi Arabia threatened to revoke American petroleum concessions if Nasser could not be restrained. In addition, Egypt was moving into a closer relationship with the Communist bloc, a fact underscored by Chou En-lai's visit to Cairo in December 1963. Kennedy responded by strengthening the American military commitment to Saudi Arabia. Given this hostile climate, Bunker not unexpectedly failed to obtain Egyptian agreement to his disengagement plan. He also failed to lessen Nasser's dependence upon Soviet weapons purchases. U.S.-Egyptian relations reached a nadir by 1964.

President Johnson appointed Bunker ambassador to the Organization of American States (OAS) in 1964. His principal assignment was to reestablish relations between the United States and Panama that had been severed following firing by U.S. troops upon Panamanian rioters. The riots had arisen out of a minor incident but had quickly extended to a generalized protest against the American presence in the Canal Zone, widely regarded as a colonial infringement upon Panama's territorial integrity. Bunker obtained agreement to restore friendly relations with the conservative Panamanian regime. Talks over the resolution of the Canal Zone crisis also began, for the Johnson administration concurred with Panamanian desires to replace the 1903 treaty with a new, more ameliorative arrangement.

In 1965 Bunker led an OAS peace mission to the Dominican Republic. In the aftermath of the death of long-time dictator Rafael Trujillo in 1961, the United States and its regional partners had established a transitional government. Juan Bosch, a progressive, won elections in December 1962, but was soon ousted. However, the new regime disintegrated after an attempted military coup in April 1965. Acting on fears in Washington relating to the possibility of a Communist takeover under the banner of a Bosch return to power, Bunker's mission brought about an immediate end to the civil war with the establishment of a coalition government and promises from Washington that it would not support a military takeover. American and other Western Hemisphere troops occupied the country to maintain stability. Free elections were held the next year. At the end of this assignment President Johnson again appointed Bunker ambassador-at-large.

In 1967 Bunker accepted assignment as ambassador to the Republic of South Vietnam, then the riskiest and most volatile post in the Foreign Service. He served as ambassador to South Vietnam from 1967 to 1973 and, although charged with responsibilities too grueling and demands too heavy for most men of his advanced age, adequately performed the duties of his post. Arriving in Saigon on April 25, 1967, he quickly achieved a reputation as one of the most ardent advocates of a continued strong military mission in Vietnam. Due to his prestige, he had direct access to the president. He persistently reported progress in the war effort, even during and after the Tet Offensive of 1968. As ambassador, Bunker was also chief of the U.S. Mission, helping to direct a war effort that was costing billions of dollars, and was the principal civilian American advisor to the Republic of South Vietnam. His optimistic nature made him overlook and underreport the failures of the American effort and in no small measure contributed to the continuance of the conflict.

Bunker was a wholehearted advocate of the policy of Vietnamization. He believed that the Vietnamese had to achieve their own victory. Accordingly, he supported the incursion into Cambodia in May 1970 as a means of strengthening the Saigon regime's forces. But the combined U.S.–South Vietnamese attack on Viet Cong and North Vietnamese bases in Cambodia had dismal results. Moreover, in America adverse public reaction was extensive. News reporting of the apparent extension and reescalation of the war set off a wave of demonstrations, including the fatal shooting of four students at Kent State University. In Vietnam Bunker had to assist President Nguyen Van Thieu in dealing with his own Cambodian-related riots by students, Buddhists, and veterans. Not even the infamous test of Vietnamization, Lam Son 719, a disastrous invasion of Laos in 1971, prevented the ambassador from indulging boosterism on behalf of the South Vietnamese government. Bunker argued that the enemy "Easter Offensive" in 1972 was an attempt by Hanoi to again demonstrate the failure of Vietnamization. After an initial Communist success in March 1972, the South Vietnamese successfully repelled the Communist attack with the help of American bombing. The ambassador firmly believed that Vietnamization could be successful in altering Hanoi's reliance on force as the primary means to a political goal before the end of his stay in Saigon and lauded the policy's achievements.

Another focus of Bunker's ambassadorship involved domestic Vietnamese matters. As America began its withdrawal, the military aspects of the war diminished in importance as they were overshadowed by internal politics and pacification. Bunker attempted to move the Thieu regime away from a military dictatorship to a government that was constitutionally based. But he strongly supported the interests of the Thieu regime despite its oppressiveness. He even acted to ensure Thieu's popular election in 1971, a move designed to garner broad-based support for America's Saigon ally. Thieu complicated things, however, by passing a law requiring each presidential candidate to get the signatures of a majority of provincial chiefs before he could run. Bunker was deeply concerned over the appearance of Thieu's running unopposed, which would be an embarrassment for the Saigon government. He attempted to persuade a weak challenger, either Duong Van Minh or Nguyen Cao Ky, to run against Thieu so that the election would have some legitimacy in the eyes of the world. When Minh and Ky both eventually refused out of realization that certain defeat was in the offing, Bunker acquiesced in Thieu's machinations so that at least the Communists could not manipulate the elections. Yet the ambassador did help to devise and strengthen a number of political institutions that arose in South Vietnam during his tenure.

During the Paris peace talks Bunker coordinated South Vietnamese support for the American negotiating position. In 1968 he was misled and reported prematurely to the White House on South Vietnamese conditional assent to a full American bombing halt. The resulting refusal of the Saigon regime to attend expanded talks caused a deep revulsion within America. By 1972 Bunker was the go-between from the White House to President Thieu regarding the Paris negotiations. He was again misled by Thieu, who at the last minute produced serious objections to leaving North Vietnamese troops in place in the South and

to Hanoi's failure to recognize the division of Vietnam at the seventeenth parallel. National Security Adviser Henry Kissinger also deceived Bunker by assuring him that the North Vietnamese had gone much farther than they actually
had in private discussions. Thieu only signed the peace agreement after explicit
pledges from President Richard Nixon that the continued presence of North
Vietnamese forces on southern soil would be recognized as violations of the
Paris accords and that Washington would react vigorously to any circumvention
of the agreement by Hanoi. Bunker also had told Thieu that the Nixon administration would regard his regime as sovereign no matter what the final agreement stated. However, before ending his tenure as ambassador in May 1973, he
recognized that neither side had kept to the Paris agreement. The lack of progress
toward political reconciliation dismayed him, although he believed that a chance
for peace still remained.

After six exhausting years Bunker left Saigon and the endgame of the war to
Graham Martin. He then returned to his duties as ambassador-at-large, where
he made important contributions regarding the Panama Canal treaty renegotia-
tion. The Ford administration wanted to establish a new relationship with its
Latin American allies and decided that renegotiating the canal treaty would
underscore its commitment to this new relationship. Secretary of State Henry
Kissinger worked out a tentative agreement with the Panamanian foreign minister in February 1974. The return of the Canal Zone to Panama would occur
within a specific period of time during which America would have the right to
operate and defend the canal. In accordance with this understanding, Bunker
began negotiations on the specifics and in late 1974 achieved a breakthrough.
He obtained agreement from the Panamanians that the United States would
operate and defend the canal throughout the life of the treaty, a three-year transition period for the transfer of jurisdiction would occur, and both sides would
support the canal's permanent neutrality.

However, the negotiations were shelved in 1975. Strong opposition in Congress to the end of the perpetual lease, and rioting in Panama, held up the
balance of the negotiating until President Gerald Ford left office. The Canal
Zone not only represented an important element in America's national security
policy, but also was a symbol of American heroic ingenuity from a bygone era.
The most effective critic was Governor Ronald Reagan of California, who believed that the canal's reversion to Panama marked another example of the
decline of American power in the world. His challenge to Ford undermined the
latter's candidacy in 1976.

The Carter administration was adamant on seeking a resolution to this obstacle
to better relations with Latin America. The United States, it was thought, could
not hope for improved relations with its neighbors in the Western Hemisphere
unless it worked out a fair settlement with Panama. In late 1976 the incoming
administration selected Sol Linowitz, ex-chairman of Xerox Corporation, to join
with Bunker in settling the issue. Secretary of State Cyrus Vance gave the
negotiators all the latitude that they needed in order to explore possible solutions.

The Carter White House had a base to build upon, but the key issues, namely, the duration of the treaty and the problem of maintaining America's right to defend the canal without continuing the appearance of infringement upon Panama's sovereignty after its expiration, remained outstanding. The American position rested firmly upon a perpetual right to keep the canal open, and it was difficult to get the Panamanians to accept this, since they considered that such an insistence implied a U.S. right to intervene in Panama's internal affairs. The Panamanian negotiator, Romulo Escobar Bethancourt, tested the American position by attempting to remove the U.S. role in protection altogether and by demanding a huge indemnity of over $3 billion in order to compensate for the years of American operation. In reality, though, the Panamanian government of President Omar Torrijos was waiting for an acceptable agreement to resolve the crisis.

The negotiators overcame the impasse with a brilliant diplomatic move. They divided the negotiations into two parts. One agreement on the American right of defense would be made in perpetuity, thereby undercutting domestic U.S. criticism. The other would deal with transferring the sovereignty of the zone to Panama. With this separation of issues, a timetable that was twenty years earlier than during the Ford-period negotiations, and the inclusion of an ambiguously worded nonintervention clause, Washington's insistence on guaranteeing the Canal Zone seemed less repugnant to Escobar. The negotiations in Washington moved into high gear, and the outstanding issues were quickly resolved, with Panama to receive a $10-million annual payment drawn from the canal's revenues instead of the huge remuneration. In the Carter administration's settlement with the Torrijos government, Panama received legal jurisdiction over the zone, although the United States would operate it until the end of 1999 and would have a permanent right to guarantee its neutrality thereafter.

With support from past Republican foreign policy experts like Kissinger and the skill of Under Secretary of State Warren Christopher, the treaty was approved. Although the agreements were signed on September 7, 1977, the formal treaty was not given consent by the Senate until the spring of 1978 with a vote tally of 68 to 32 in favor. Bunker had helped its passage by quietly lobbying for acceptance of the accords and by properly interpreting the wording of the agreements. He thus played a seminal role in paving the way for improved relations with Latin America. It was perhaps his greatest diplomatic achievement.

Bunker left the diplomatic service in 1978 at the age of eighty-four. He died on September 27, 1984, in Putney, Vermont. He was a statesman who now seems to have come from an era long bygone. He embodied the best of the American diplomatic tradition in his firm intent to resolve international disputes peacefully and according to the rule of law with patience and skill. He never rejected assignments that some might have seen as beneath his status and never complained about not being accorded the senior policy positions befitting one with so much experience and prestige. He was the quintessential, dedicated workhorse of American foreign policy who performed his duties with dignity. However, this reputation was somewhat tarnished by unrealistic reporting on the Vietnam War that sometimes ignored glaring policy failures.

Work by Ellsworth Bunker

The Bunker Papers: Reports to the President from Vietnam, 1967–1973. Ed. Douglas Pike Berkeley: Institute of East Asian Studies, 1990.

Works about Ellsworth Bunker

Burke, Lee H. *Ambassador at Large: Diplomat Extraordinary.* The Hague: Nijhoff, 1972.

Jorden, William J. *Panama Odyssey.* Austin: University of Texas Press, 1984.

LaFeber, Walter. *The Panama Canal: The Crisis in Historical Perspective.* Updated ed. New York: Oxford University Press, 1989.

McMahon, Robert J. *The Cold War on the Periphery: The United States, India, and Pakistan.* New York: Columbia University Press, 1994.

McMullen, Christopher J. *Mediation of the West New Guinea Dispute, 1962.* Washington, DC: Institute for the Study of Diplomacy, Edmund A. Walsh School of Foreign Service, Georgetown University, 1981.

Thies, Wallace J. "How We (Almost) Won the War in Vietnam: Ellsworth Bunker's Reports to the President." *Parameters* 13 (1979): 86–95.

KENT G. SIEG

JAMES BRYANT CONANT (1893–1978) was born on

March 16, 1893, in Dorchester, Massachusetts, the only son of James Scott Conant and Jennett Orr Conant (née Bryant). His family line on both sides was Yankee, going back at least as far as the founding of Salem, Massachusetts, by Roger Conant in 1626. He was educated at Harvard, later served for twenty years as one of its most distinguished presidents, and established a reputation as one of the nation's greatest educators and educational theorists. Though Conant is rightly remembered and revered for these achievements alone, his contributions to American security policy and diplomacy over a period of forty years were very significant.

At Roxbury Latin School, where he was enrolled in 1904 at the age of eleven, Conant revealed an innate understanding of chemistry and physics under the instruction of Newton Henry Black. Black also helped to cultivate Conant's appreciation of Europe, most particularly Germany, as a center both of science and of civilization. Thus at a remarkably early age Conant encountered his lifelong preoccupations: the application of science and knowledge to human progress and the place of modern Germany in world affairs. Conant excelled at his studies on the strength of intellect and precocious self-discipline. He entered Harvard with a scholarship at age seventeen.

In 1916 Conant left Harvard with a doctorate in chemistry. Thwarted by World War I in his plans to study in Germany, Conant lectured at Harvard and otherwise directed his energies toward a small-scale pharmaceutical-manufacturing venture in New York—an enterprise that literally went up in flames. A congressional declaration of war against Germany in 1917 inaugurated Conant's service to his government in the prosecution of a conflict in which the terrible depths to which science, especially chemistry, could stoop had in 1915 been revealed by German gas attacks on Allied trenches. Conant went to work in the American war effort on a variety of assignments, including research for a formula for a high-yield mustard gas suitable for large-scale plant production. The project produced a gas, lewisite, capable of producing death after hours of suffering, but the 1918 armistice came as the first shipment of the toxin was on its way to Europe. Still, the course of Conant's life had been set by his work for the Chemical Warfare Service: he was now a critical intellectual force in the alliance of science and the military in the development of weapons of mass destruction. He was to become a coauthor in the policies governing their development and also a diplomat struggling with the political consequences of their existence.

The decade of the 1920s was a period of boom for all the natural sciences. Despite the horror of and inevitable controversy surrounding chemical warfare, chemistry's importance to industry and medicine was beyond dispute. Returning to Harvard, Conant was in a position to advance both the maturation and the prestige of American chemical research, which at the time lagged behind that of Europe. During the 1920s Conant married Patty Thayer Richards, started a family, and rose to the rank of associate professor in 1924 and to full professor three years later. He crowned a reputation as one of the country's leading organic chemists with a host of peer awards and election to the American Academy of Sciences and the National Academy of Sciences. The U.S. government's Bureau of Chemistry consulted him on hiring practices, and the Rockefeller Institute for Medical Research made him a scientific advisor to its board of trustees. As his social and professional affiliations grew, Conant worked diligently to hone an acumen in philosophy, history, literature, and public affairs.

In 1933, the same year Adolf Hitler became chancellor of the German Reich and Franklin Roosevelt was inaugurated president of the United States, Conant was elected president of Harvard University. In the post he held for the next twenty years, Conant began his presidency by warning the Harvard faculty that he intended to run a tougher, more hands-on management regime at Harvard than they had become used to under his predecessor, Abbot Lawrence Lowell. Conant pruned Harvard of many of its more moth-eaten traditions and involved himself directly in faculty appointment and promotion, determined to replace "blue blood" with "new blood" and transform Harvard from a Brahmin gentleman's club into a meritocratic monument to high-performance academia on a Germanic model. Consistent with his reforms of hiring criteria, Conant also undertook to democratize admission procedures in order to facilitate the ambitions of promising scholars of modest means. Not until after 1945 and the passage of the GI Bill was Harvard open to a truly more socially diverse student body, but Conant was by 1936 chipping away at the university's most time-honored prejudices, such as its anti-Semitism and traditional preference for students of northwestern European descent.

The Great Depression and the deteriorating international situation of the 1930s, meanwhile, put Harvard through some of its most trying times. While the controversy of the New Deal inevitably elicited criticism of Harvard professors who openly supported the Roosevelt administration's domestic policies, Conant watched in horror as Hitler's regime strangled academic freedom in the German universities he had so long admired. Conant's ability to defend his faculty at home and to speak out against the abuse of academic freedom abroad was circumscribed not only by concessions to the constraints inherent in his position at the head of a prestigious institution but also by his own personality's blend of principle and pragmatism, a desire to do and say the right thing set against the need to avoid avoidable damage to Harvard and himself. On the occasion of a visit to Harvard in 1934 by Ernst Hanfstaengl, Hitler's press secretary, whose mother came from a prominent New England family, Conant equivocated over the degree of hospitality Harvard was obliged to extend to an official representative of the Third Reich and over the acceptance of an endowed Hanfstaengl Scholarship for Harvard students to study in Germany. He finally turned the scholarship down on the grounds that Harvard could not accept a gift from a regime currently engaged in a systematic debauch of higher education in some of the finest universities in the world, but not until after considerable soul-searching over the issue of whether university presidents could assume for themselves the right to openly criticize foreign governments. In essence, he decided that once Hanfstaengl had made his offer, he was under an obligation to turn it down and to elaborate fully on the reasons for his decision. This sensitivity to protocol was a recurring feature of Conant's academic and government career.

It was not until 1940 that Conant came to the personal decision that Hitler's Germany had to be stopped by any means, including American mobilization for war. Shocked by lightning German victories in the opening months of the war in Europe, Conant abandoned all efforts to remain aloof from organizations not directly related either to Harvard or to education. He joined the Committee to Defend America by Aiding the Allies and the Century Group, an informal group of well-connected, prointerventionist citizens promoting both aid to the Allied cause and a peacetime draft. Conant himself was recruited to the National Defense Research Committee by Vannevar Bush, head of the Carnegie Institution in Washington, and was made director of Division B for research into bombs, fuels, gases, and chemical warfare. By the autumn of 1940, however, Conant was increasingly impatient with the prevailing American policy of supporting besieged Britain by all means short of war. He believed not only that the United States should enter the war, but also that it should do so with more forthright self-interest than it had in 1917. After the defeat of Nazism American policy should be openly expansionist and committed to the reconstitution of global affairs through an international assembly in which the United States held more than 50 percent of the votes. He supported Lend-Lease and interventionism in testimony before the Senate Foreign Relations Committee and traveled in February 1941 to Britain on a mission from Roosevelt to exchange information on war-related science and to assess in what additional ways the United States could assist in the island's defense.

With American entry into the war after Pearl Harbor the following December, Conant's energies were refocused more narrowly on weapons research, more specifically on the project to create an American nuclear bomb. Though originally skeptical about the potential of nuclear energy, Conant was aware that German science had demonstrated as early as 1939 that a uranium atom could be split. As much as anything, the fear that Germany might develop a nuclear weapon and win the war led Conant to commit himself wholly to the creation of the world's first atomic bomb by American science. Concerned that work on the project begin immediately led Conant to recommend, over the objections of U.S. Army Intelligence, that the theoretical physicist J. Robert Oppenheimer be given security clearance to lead the Manhattan Project. Conant himself became critical to the progress of Oppenheimer's work. He intervened routinely to clear administrative roadblocks and to defuse conflicts between the scientific team and military staff. By the date of the successful Trinity test, July 16, 1945,

Conant embodied the union of government and science, the technocrat armed with scientific knowledge and administrative finesse.

After the war Conant served on an advisory committee to the Truman administration on the use of the nation's nuclear capacity, promoting in particular international control of atomic weapons. The year 1950 marked a turning point in his life. A failed bid for the presidency of the National Academy of Sciences marked a break with the American scientific establishment, and the sudden outbreak of the Korean conflict converted Conant to a Cold War view of international affairs. As founding chairman of the Committee on the Present Danger, Conant lobbied for a sharp increase in defense appropriations and a long-term commitment of U.S. troops to West European security, yet maintained that tactical nuclear weapons should be the core component of American security policy in Europe.

Conant had doubts about rearming Germany, but in 1952 these were not enough to dissuade the newly elected Eisenhower administration from offering him the post of high commissioner to Bonn. The appointment was made partly on the recommendation of the outgoing high commissioner, John McCloy, partly in response to the German government's express wish that an American of high prestige receive the post, but above all because of the president's confidence in Conant's sober judgment. In 1953 Conant inherited diplomatic duties in Germany at a particularly sensitive juncture. The Bonn government was in the midst of the struggle to secure domestic and European acceptance of German membership in the European Defense Community (EDC), while the McCarthy hearings in Washington demolished State Department morale with charges that the U.S. diplomatic corps was teeming with Communists. Conant also had difficulties initially in his relations with German Chancellor Konrad Adenauer, a seasoned politician fifteen years his senior who found Conant unduly professorial. In the face of predictions of American journalists that he would never measure up to the rigors of the Bonn posting, Conant applied himself to mastering his brief.

He was convinced that the Adenauer government was planning the creation of a national West German army, a development he considered dangerously premature in light of the fragility of the new German democracy. He fully appreciated German frustration at France's repeated delays in ratifying the EDC, but warned Secretary of State John Foster Dulles that Franco-German tensions might force Adenauer to play to the nationalist wing of his party in the name of political survival. Complicating the situation was the outstanding issue of the Saar region of southwest Germany, occupied by France after 1945. France sought to make the region semiautonomous and in 1953 was attempting to pry concessions from Adenauer by holding EDC ratification hostage to German flexibility on the Saar issue. Adenauer did not budge. In a meeting with the chancellor Conant underscored the fact that the United States considered Franco-German cooperation to be the very cornerstone of West European security. For his part, Adenauer believed that this role properly belonged with the United

States itself, and he expressed personal doubts about the reliability of the American commitment to Europe. Armed with a letter from Dulles, Conant again met with Adenauer to warn him that the United States could accept no unilateral defense initiatives from Germany and that if Adenauer were to let the Saar dispute keep France out of the EDC, Americans could only consider the resources they were already pouring into Europe to be a waste. Adenauer adjusted his demeanor appropriately. But Conant was not content to simply run messages between Washington and Bonn. In an address to American lawyers in Frankfurt he observed that if the EDC failed, the United States intended to get out of the occupation business altogether. The German press hailed the speech because of its implied threat to both London and Paris: they too had better get serious about the security issue if they did not want to be left alone in Europe with an untethered Germany.

By 1954 both Conant and Washington had concluded that the weakness of France's governing coalition had become the principal—and insurmountable—obstacle to EDC ratification. When the French parliament at last voted the EDC down, Washington's policy shifted with remarkable speed to integrating a German national army directly into NATO. An idea that had appeared nightmarish only months previously was now fast becoming a reality. Conant's perspective on the Germany-in-NATO alternative had changed above all because of the worry that security priorities back in the United States could shift decisively in favor of an "Asia First" policy unless a practicable European arrangement could be found right away. With a British commitment to post troops in West Germany for fifty years and a pledge from the Adenauer government never to produce atomic, biological, or chemical weapons, the way was cleared for German NATO membership. Conant suppressed his personal doubts concerning German rearmament in a campaign to secure American and European acceptance of the new Germany. The imperatives of the present danger trumped memories of the past.

When the Federal Republic of Germany joined NATO in May 1955, it became officially a sovereign state, and Conant's position changed from that of high commissioner to that of the first U.S. ambassador to West Germany. Yet even with the EDC issue now out of the way, Conant remained uncomfortable with his duties in Bonn. The Dulles State Department tended to cut him out of decision making on policy and even deprived him of information he considered essential to the more mundane aspects of representing American policy competently to the Adenauer government. This in turn may have hampered Conant's relations with Chancellor Adenauer, which never evolved beyond the strictly cordial. Conant considered Adenauer instinctively Machiavellian; Adenauer thought Conant a political sophomore. They were both right. Conant wanted to leave Bonn, but the Eisenhower administration kept him there until 1957.

Though consistently excluded from the most sensitive deliberations on the course of German-American relations, Conant soldiered on in his ambassadorial duties. In general terms he attempted on both sides of the Atlantic to express a fundamental optimism about the Federal Republic's political and economic future at every opportunity. This involved assuring the Adenauer government and the German populace of the continuing U.S. dedication to European security and telling the American public that their new ally had buried both Nazism and anti-Semitism. At the same time, Conant reacted to recurrent crises with what he considered the appropriate gesture of solidarity with the West German cause. When Moscow attempted to regulate road traffic through the Soviet zone of occupation to West Berlin and the East German police detained visiting U.S. congressmen, Conant rode through East Berlin in his ambassadorial limousine in a symbolic expression of defiance and contempt for the Soviet-sponsored German Democratic Republic. He failed, however, to get Washington to take what he considered to be appropriately stiff countermeasures against Soviet bullying, and his relations with the CIA in Berlin were governed by mutual suspicion. He tried unsuccessfully to halt the secret Operation Paperclip, in which scores of German scientists and engineers who had served the Nazis were being recruited to defense projects in the United States.

More substantively, Conant was the point man for Washington's efforts to get West Germany to live up to its commitments to NATO by proceeding quickly with the building of a West German army and introducing obligatory two-year military service. Possibly his most trying time as ambassador came in July 1956 when the *New York Times* announced that the Joint Chiefs of Staff (JCS) proposed to slash the U.S. armed forces by 800,000 men, thus cutting off at the knees the Adenauer government's efforts to sell the imperative of German military preparedness to a reluctant West German electorate based on the U.S. commitment to preparedness. Adenauer accused the United States of toying with German insecurities and notified Conant that his government would now have difficulty passing any form of national service legislation through the Bonn parliament. Adenauer also charged the United States with abandoning a "forward strategy" for the defense of Germany. The recent development of a tactical nuclear capacity in battlefield weapons—a technology about which Adenauer was altogether ignorant—inflamed the atmosphere of discussions even further. In fact, the rumored troop reductions existed only in the text of an unauthorized report written by JCS Chairman Admiral Arthur Radford, while "forward defense" (according to which NATO forces would meet a Soviet attack at the border between East and West Germany) was almost wholly a NATO tribute to German sensibilities and was widely considered militarily impracticable. The Eisenhower administration's new emphasis on strategic nuclear weapons, finally, made a large contingent of West German conventional forces more important than ever: they were to provide a forward defense formidable enough to make the Soviets organize their forces in concentrated formations that could then be obliterated by nuclear weapons. If Adenauer did not understand this, there is little evidence that Conant knew how to explain it to him. In any event, the emphasis on nuclear forces was unfortunate in its timing. The Adenauer government undertook to cut Germany's troop commitment from 500,000 to

325,000. A more politically astute U.S. ambassador could possibly have prevented this. Still, Conant himself was hardly responsible for circulating the news about revised U.S. security priorities at such a sensitive juncture in West German politics. Too often he heard of policy changes in Washington, or rumors thereof, no earlier than Adenauer.

In the end Conant was unable to make the Bonn government comfortable with Washington's plans for European security. In July 1956 Adenauer asked that Conant be replaced, and Conant was happy to go. He was offered the post of U.S. ambassador to India but turned it down in favor of a return to academic life. Even after his departure from Bonn in February 1957, Conant did not leave German politics behind. He publicly opposed recent proposals by George Kennan, the author of the policy of containment of the Soviet Union, that Germany be demilitarized, and spoke forcefully against any notion that the Federal Republic be made anything other than a full member of the Western alliance. His 1958 Godkin Lectures at Harvard, later published as *Germany and Freedom*, were dedicated to defending U.S. policy and to praising the achievements of the new German democracy to an American audience.

At the time Conant was sixty-five, yet he embarked almost immediately on a new career as educational theorist and prominent advocate of public school reform. He died in Hanover, New Hampshire, on February 11, 1978.

Works by James B. Conant

On Understanding Science. New Haven: Yale University Press, 1947.
Education in a Divided World. Cambridge: Harvard University Press, 1948.
Science and Common Sense. New Haven: Yale University Press, 1951.
Anglo-American Relations in the Atomic Age. Oxford: Oxford University Press, 1952.
Modern Science and Modern Man. New York: Columbia University Press, 1952.
Germany and Freedom. Cambridge: Harvard University Press, 1958.
Slums and Suburbs. New York: McGraw-Hill, 1961.
My Several Lives. New York: Harper and Row, 1970.

Work about James B. Conant

Hershberg, James G. *James B. Conant: Harvard to Hiroshima and the Making of the Nuclear Age*. New York: Alfred A. Knopf, 1993.

CARL CAVANAGH HODGE

FRANCIS DANA (1745–1811) was the American envoy to the

court of Catherine the Great of Russia during the American Revolution whose insights on the nature of European diplomacy helped to strengthen American isolationist tendencies following the Peace of Paris in 1783.

Born to an established Boston family, Francis Dana came of age during the early challenges to British colonial rule. His father, Judge Richard Dana, served as a magistrate in Boston. This high office admitted Richard Dana into the inner circle of the Bostonian legal establishment, where he associated with the leaders of colonial government. Richard Dana also maintained popularity among the citizenry of Boston through his judicial rulings and support of colonial rights. By no means a supporter of mob violence, he yet ruled against the troops involved in the Boston Massacre of 1770. From his father's words and deeds, Francis Dana learned much, and he furthered his education by gaining admittance to Harvard College's class of 1762.

During his years at Harvard Dana witnessed the early stirrings of resentment against British colonial policies following the favorable conclusion of the Seven Years' War. Boston was a center of dissent and criticism of the new taxes levied by the British government. Following his father's example, Dana studied law and became active in the defense of the patriot cause. His association with the patriot party brought him into a close friendship with John Adams that lasted a lifetime. His adherence to the patriot viewpoint damaged Dana's private law practice and caused him and others to enter into a more public political life. This turn to public life, along with his marriage in 1773 to Elizabeth Ellery, daughter of William Ellery of Rhode Island, brought Dana into the forefront of revolutionary politics in Boston.

On April 17, 1775, two days prior to the Battle of Lexington, Dana took his first step into the realm of diplomacy. Chosen by the Boston bar as its unofficial representative in London, Dana investigated public opinion in London regarding the impending controversy between the American colonies and the British government. He sought out the Wilkesite movement for support of the American cause. However, Dana soon realized the differing goals of the Wilkes party and the American revolutionaries, specifically the Wilkesites' continued attachment to the British Empire. Dana returned to America in May 1776 fully aware that the patriots could not look for support to any in England. Upon his return he traveled to Philadelphia to report to the Continental Congress on the state of affairs in England. There he met with Benjamin Franklin, who had returned earlier from London. The two leaders concurred that the patriots would find no friends in London.

In the summer of 1776 the Massachusetts Assembly selected Dana as a delegate to the Continental Congress. Dana journeyed with William Ellery to York, Pennsylvania, where Congress had retreated following the fall of Philadelphia.

The proximity of York to Valley Forge allowed Dana to experience firsthand the hardship faced by George Washington's army during the winter of 1777–1778 when Dana served as chairman of the Committee of Military Reorganization sent to investigate the conditions at Valley Forge and their cause. The privations that Dana witnessed and Washington's efforts to alleviate them influenced Dana to support fully the general and to counter the general's many naysayers in Congress. With Dana's support in Congress, the efforts to remove Washington from command were ended, and new means of procurement were established.

After a year of service in Congress, Dana sought to return to Boston to take on the duties of justice of the peace for Middlesex and to lead a private family life. However, his dreams of a sedate life in Boston were postponed by a call from Congress in September 1779 to serve as a secretary to Benjamin Franklin, the American ambassador to France. In his second venture into the realm of diplomacy, Dana was joined by John Adams. Sent by Congress to France, Adams was authorized to negotiate a peace and an alliance with England. Both Adams and Dana suspected France of attempting to control negotiations with England in order to influence the outcome in France's favor. The newly arrived diplomats feared that France's European interests would take precedence over the interests of the United States. To Adams and Dana, France's foreign minister, the Compte de Vergennes, appeared to have dominated Franklin's mission; Adams was determined that this would not happen to him. However, the undecided outcome of the American war and European politics prevented any movement toward peace negotiations.

In early 1780, shortly after the arrival of Adams and Dana in Paris, a propitious event occurred that altered Dana's mission in Europe. The creation of the "Armed Neutrality" by the nations of Russia, Prussia, Sweden, Denmark, and the Netherlands challenged British search and seizure of neutral shipping that had occurred throughout its war with the United States and France. The Baltic nations protested these acts and moved to secure the rights of neutral shipping of noncontraband cargo. Further British incursions were threatened with the combined naval forces of these five countries. Dana realized that this challenge pitted all the major European maritime powers against Great Britain. His understanding of the importance of sea rights to the United States and their military implications for the American Revolution led him to pursue an agreement with the nations of the Armed Neutrality, an object he vigorously discussed with his correspondents in Congress.

Dana believed correctly that Catherine the Great stood as the central figure in the Armed Neutrality. He saw this League of Neutrals as a step toward the universal emancipation of ocean commerce from the control of the British. Knowing that any reduction in British control of the seas would benefit the United States after the war, Dana pressed Congress to send a mission to Catherine to pursue recognition of the United States, an alliance, and a commercial treaty. Empress Catherine's statements regarding the freedom of the seas led Dana and Congress to believe that she had some sympathy toward their cause.

Empress Catherine's offer to mediate the war between France, Spain, and Great Britain in late 1780 furthered Dana's interest in establishing relations with Russia. He wanted to ensure that the United States would have equal representation at any peace conference and not be forced to rely on the French. His yearlong stay in Paris had acquainted him with the arts of European diplomacy; he realized that European political issues could easily dominate any peace conference. Dana's primary concerns in representing the United States focused on securing American independence and creating freedom of the seas. Connection with the League of Neutrals seemed an opportunity to gain additional recognition of American independence and neutral sea rights. He urged his colleagues in Congress to build an active foreign policy based on American interests. Dana supported an effort to gain admittance to the League of Neutrals or, at least, to receive the recognition of the United States from the five powers. Congress agreed with his position, and on December 19, 1780, Dana was appointed minister to the court of the Empress Catherine of Russia.

Before embarking on his journey, Dana discussed the proposed trip with Franklin and Vergennes. They decided that Dana should proceed as a private citizen and present his ministerial papers only at an appropriate time. This would prevent any difficulties resulting from the lack of diplomatic recognition of the United States by Russia. On this diplomatic mission Dana chose to bring John Quincy Adams, the fourteen-year-old son of John Adams, as his personal secretary. In the summer of 1781 the two traveled to St. Petersburg and established contact with Ambassador Manguis de Verac of France, who served as the interlocutor for Dana during the majority of his stay in Russia. However, Dana's continued suspicion of French diplomatic actions and his fear of their controlling American interests were only heightened by these interactions.

Soon Catherine's pretensions of neutral sea rights revealed themselves as efforts to secure her position in Europe. Actually, her court considered the American Revolution an unpleasant rebellion against monarchical rule. Dana's wise maintenance of his private personage allowed his continued presence in St. Petersburg to be tolerated by Catherine. Indeed, for nearly two years Dana remained in isolation from the court while he remained in contact with Verac, through whom he received information regarding the actions of Catherine's court. Although the lack of contact with officials from Catherine's court irked Dana, he agreed with Vergennes and Verac's decision to have him wait for an opportune moment to present his documents. While in St. Petersburg Dana showed tremendous patience and resolve to make gains for his country without bringing any disgrace upon it.

In addition to his lack of recognition from the court, Dana faced an additional burden, namely, the Russian court practice of purchasing ministerial signatures for all state treaties. Since at least four signatures needed to be placed upon any treaty, the total cost per treaty amounted to about five thousand pounds. This sum seemed outrageous both to Dana and to Congress; some members questioned Dana's veracity on the subject. Thus the value of a treaty of alliance and recognition became a subject of debate. As Dana's mission dragged on, Congress seemed less resolved to spend such a sum on a distant land. While Dana questioned the reasoning of Congress, he realized the need for caution in financial matters, for his earlier work in Congress had convinced him of the difficulties of gaining funding for any congressional actions.

After the success of John Adams's mission to secure Dutch recognition in 1782, Dana hoped to further American gains by securing similar recognition from Russia. However, Catherine strongly disapproved of the Dutch action, so the disillusioned Dana turned his efforts to gaining a commercial treaty. Dana hoped that the similarity of positions held by Catherine and the United States about the rights of neutral shipping would furnish a background for a commercial treaty. In his letters to Congress Dana suggested that the trade treaty would have more impact on the British after the war than any immediate material assistance given by Russia. Fortunately, the success of the Americans at Yorktown had created the essential ingredients for Dana's first goal of attaining American independence. He believed that it was equally important for the American diplomats to secure his second major concern, that of maintaining freedom of the seas. The importance of commerce to the United States led him to focus on writing a commercial treaty with Russia that embodied these principles.

As the American Revolution drew to a close in 1783, Dana greatly desired to return to his native Boston. Earlier, in October 1782, John Quincy Adams had left Dana to continue his education at Leyden. Despite the release of his trusted companion, the lonely Dana remained in Russia through 1783. The proximate conclusion of the war with England and the securing of British recognition of the sovereignty of the United States led Dana to believe that he might secure similar recognition from Catherine. He perceived that the British victories at sea in 1782 had once again placed them in control of the oceans. This control threatened American commercial interests and necessitated the securing of commercial treaties with other European nations to ensure the rights of American shipping. Consequently, Dana decided to use the changing circumstances to press his country's interests. Thus in March 1783 he presented his papers to the Foreign Ministry for certification.

Dana submitted his proposed commercial treaty in a memorandum to Empress Catherine. The British ambassador, James Howard Harris, thwarted the American emissary's efforts. Harris intimated that the independence of the United States had not been finalized and that premature recognition by Russia would not please Great Britain. Not wanting to upset Anglo-Russian relations, Catherine's court advisors delayed any further discussions with Dana by challenging his dated credentials. Realizing that the inaction of the Russians would not further his mission, Dana began to join with many in Congress who questioned the value of even a commercial treaty with Russia. Ultimately the Armed Neutrality proved a European diplomatic tool and not a true defense of neutral shipping rights. In addition, the Russian ministers expected compensation for their signatures. By May Dana and Congress concluded that the Russian mission must be abandoned.

These delays and inaction by the Russian court regarding Dana's proposed commercial treaty reinforced Dana's dislike of European diplomatic structures. Dana felt not only that Harris had interfered with his negotiations, but that Verac, the French ambassador, had sought to delay any treaty. The fear of domination by either the British or the French caused Dana to pursue independent diplomacy. This pursuit, however, was thwarted at every turn by European politics and diplomacy. Still, as Dana departed from St. Petersburg in late August 1783, he felt that his long stay had not been in vain. He prided himself on having maintained American independence of action. Prevented from gaining a commercial treaty that benefited the United States, he had equally avoided entangling alliances and had maintained a separate set of American interests.

Returning to the United States, Dana reported his conduct and travails to Congress, which approved of his efforts and believed that he had maintained the dignity of the United States despite demanding conditions. The Treaty of Paris had been accomplished without the assistance of Catherine's mediation, and the United States stood proudly independent of Europe. Throughout his stay in Russia Dana had maintained correspondence with John Adams and several other American leaders and thus had guaranteed his impact on important decisions from afar. His strong position on maintaining an independent American foreign policy had helped fortify Congress during its dealings with the French, who sought to channel American diplomacy through the halls of Versailles. A like-minded John Adams had pushed hard for independent American peace discussions with Great Britain and equality at the peace conference. These actions helped to set the United States on a course free from either British or French domination.

In the years following the end of the American Revolution, Dana remained active in local and national politics. He continued to influence American foreign affairs through his support of isolationist policies and his suspicions of French diplomatic efforts. Governor John Hancock appointed Dana chief justice of the Commonwealth of Massachusetts in 1791. From this position Dana supported the Alien and Sedition Acts in their efforts to quell Jacobin revolutionaries in the United States. Always wary of France, he defended American efforts to maintain neutrality during the European war. He supported efforts to reach accommodation with Great Britain regarding neutral shipping. His old fears of British domination were outweighed by fears of another war with Great Britain. At the turn of the century his health deteriorated rapidly. His constitution never fully recovered from a series of illnesses that struck him while he lived in Russia. By the time of his death in 1811, Dana had passed out of political life and political memory.

However, the impact of Dana's thought remained both during his lifetime and into the nineteenth century. Dana realized the importance of commerce to the

United States and the role of diplomacy in securing peaceful commerce through-out the world. His focus on the rights of neutral shipping and commerce became a central focus in American diplomatic efforts during the American Revolution and the early Republic. His New England background, which included his in-volvement in the earlier difficulties of the colonists with Great Britain, especially the Navigation Acts that restricted American cargo and destinations, made him conscious of the economic importance of ocean commerce and the need for freedom of trade. Throughout his public life Dana espoused these rights and actively sought to maintain them for the United States.

In his famous farewell address President George Washington advised his countrymen to beware of entangling alliances. For the preceding two decades Dana had held this very belief, and in his mission to Russia he had attempted to maintain America's distinct interests. He influenced the thinking of John Adams, John Quincy Adams, and scores of other American leaders. His delin-eation of specific American interests in trade and freedom of the seas helped to highlight how the interests of the United States differed from those of the various states of Europe. The illogical and convoluted methods of European diplomacy discouraged Dana and those with whom he corresponded. His disapproval of these tactics and policies led him to believe that the new republic would fare better standing alone. These sentiments were shared by the second American president, John Adams, who had returned from Europe with similar reservations about alliances with the European states. The general isolation of the United States from Europe during the early Republic met with Dana's approval.

Though Dana's mission to Russia had produced no tangible results, his po-sitions on commerce, freedom of the seas, and freedom from European entan-glements became the central points of American foreign policy. The choice of John Quincy Adams as ambassador to Russia in 1809 brought the original Dana mission full circle. Dana's former secretary and friend set forth to further Amer-ican interests in a manner becoming to his mentor. As one of the many founding fathers of the United States of America, Francis Dana influenced foreign affairs in order to maintain American liberties abroad and independence at home.

Works about Francis Dana

Bemis, Samuel F. *The Diplomacy of the American Revolution*. Bloomington: Indiana University Press, 1957.

Bolkhovitinov, Nikolai N. *The Beginnings of Russian-American Relations, 1775–1815*. Cambridge: Harvard University Press, 1975.

Cresson, William P. *Francis Dana: A Puritan Diplomat at the Court of Catherine the Great*. New York: Lincoln MacVeagh, The Dial Press, 1930.

Dana, Richard Henry. *Address on Francis Dana*. Cambridge: Harvard University Press, 1908.

Dull, Jonathan R. *A Diplomatic History of the American Revolution*. New Haven: Yale University Press, 1985.

Ferrell, Robert H., ed. *Foundations of American Diplomacy, 1775–1872*. Columbia: Uni-versity of South Carolina Press, 1968.

Kaplan, Lawrence S. *Colonies into Nation: American Diplomacy, 1763–1801.* New York: Macmillan, 1972.

U.S. Department of State. *The Diplomatic Correspondence of the American Revolution.* Boston: N. Hale and Gary and Bowen, 1829–1830.

DANIEL BYRNE

AUGUSTE DAVEZAC (1780–1851) was a Jacksonian

Democrat who twice represented the United States in the Netherlands as chargé d'affaires.

Davezac was born in May 1780 on the Caribbean island of Santo Domingo and baptized Auguste Geneviève Valentin D'Avezac. He was the third son of Jean Pierre Valentin Joseph D'Avezac de Castera and Marie Rose Valentine de Maragon D'Avezac de Castera, a rich French planters family. As children, Auguste and his sister Louise, who was two years his junior, had a private tutor. The large library their father had collected formed the basis for their lifelong interest in classical literature. Auguste continued his education in France at the Collège de Sorèze and the Military College of La Flèche. In 1791 the slaves on Santo Domingo revolted against the French planters with the support of the revolutionary government in Paris. Auguste's two eldest brothers were killed and his father fled to Virginia, where he died of yellow fever in Norfolk. The remaining members of the family escaped to the French- and Spanish-speaking city of New Orleans, which was still in Spanish hands. When Louisiana became American territory in 1803, the famed lawyer Edward Livingston settled in New Orleans, where he married Auguste's sister Louise in 1805.

Auguste himself eventually left France and, like the rest of his family, emigrated to the United States. At first he studied medicine at Edenton, North Carolina, and then practiced it in Accomac County, Virginia. Before long, however, he too moved to New Orleans. Having more interest in the legal than the medicine profession, he decided to study law under the supervision of his brother-in-law Edward Livingston. Admitted to the Louisiana bar, he commenced practice in New Orleans. Thanks to his eloquence and his affinity with the local Franco-Spanish population, Auguste Davezac—who, like the rest of the American branch of the family, no longer spelled his name D'Avezac— became one of the most successful criminal lawyers in Louisiana. It has been said that no client of his was ever sentenced to death.

When war with Great Britain broke out in 1812, he joined the local defense committee set up by Livingston. General Andrew Jackson arrived in New Orleans in December 1814 to defend the city against the British and was quickly befriended by Davezac, who became his aide-de-camp and judge advocate; for the rest of his life he was known as Major Davezac. During this period he developed a deep admiration for the general who in January 1815 defeated the British in the famous Battle of New Orleans and became a national hero.

After the war Davezac resumed his legal practice. When Andrew Jackson ran against John Quincy Adams in the presidential race of 1824, Davezac supported him energetically. Undaunted by his defeat, Jackson ran again in 1828, this time successfully. Once again Davezac placed his prodigious eloquence at the service of his hero. Nor did the general forget his former aide-de-camp, appointing him secretary of legation in The Hague. He was to assist the newly appointed envoy extraordinary and minister plenipotentiary of the United States to the Netherlands, William Pitt Preble. Davezac was happy to accept his new appointment, effective in August 1829.

As secretary of legation he corresponded privately with President Jackson and Secretary of State Martin Van Buren and kept them informed about Preble's negotiations with the Dutch government about the British-American northeastern boundary dispute, in which the Dutch king, William I, arbitrated. After Preble returned to the United States in May 1831, Davezac was temporarily responsible for the American legation, and in October of that year his brother-in-law Edward Livingston, the new secretary of state, wrote him that Jackson had appointed Davezac chargé d'affaires. Davezac promised to keep the State Department abreast of the political situation in Europe, which at that time was deeply disturbed by the July 1830 revolution in France, followed by a series of riots and revolutions elsewhere in Europe, and the secession of Belgium from the Netherlands.

The dispatches Davezac sent between 1831 and 1833 were largely devoted to the Belgian question. Painstakingly and comprehensively he wrote the State Department about the political developments and especially about the role Great Britain and France played in the negotiations, which were constantly delayed by King William I, who could not accept the political reality of the Belgian secession. In 1832 Livingston informed Davezac on two different occasions that the president was particularly satisfied with the accuracy of Davezac's dispatches and the important information they contained.

Conversely, the information that reached Davezac from the United States did not meet his expectations. In the summer of 1831 he complained repeatedly about this in his private correspondence with Livingston, pressing him for news about domestic politics. He also asked his brother-in-law to send newspapers regularly, as he had been without news for three months at that point. To remedy the problem, Livingston promised that newspapers henceforth would be sent by way of Liverpool instead of Le Havre.

As early as November 1830 William Pitt Preble had suggested that the State Department negotiate a trade agreement with Belgium. A year later Davezac reported that after the five Great Powers at the Conference of London had recognized Leopold of Saxony-Coburg as king of Belgium, he had tried to ascertain the Belgian monarch's thinking on the subject. The Belgian minister of foreign affairs informed Davezac that his government was eager to establish formal relations with the United States. To that end, King Leopold I would soon send a Belgian diplomat to Washington. To Secretary of State Livingston Davezac explained that he did not want the United States to lag behind other countries, who were eager to establish commercial relations with the new Kingdom of Belgium. Davezac played no part in the subsequent negotiations between the United States and Belgium, however; in January 1832 Livingston notified him that the president had appointed a chargé to Belgium.

Following his appointment as chargé d'affaires in October 1831, Davezac urged the Netherlands to place commercial relations between the two countries on a more equal footing. The United States was prepared to consider proposals for changing the trade agreement signed in 1782. Livingston authorized Davezac to start negotiating a new treaty according to strict guidelines. The principal goal of the United States was complete commercial reciprocity between the two countries, including the Dutch colonies. If the colonies were not included, the American government saw little point in altering the present agreement. Despite Davezac's lobbying with influential Dutch merchants, however, in the spring of 1833 he reluctantly informed Washington that the Dutch government had suspended the negotiations because William I preferred to control trade with Java himself.

Meanwhile the diplomat had received another commission from the State Department. In October 1832 the United States and the Kingdom of the Two Sicilies had agreed on the compensation the latter was to pay for plundering and confiscating American ships and their cargoes in the days of Joachim Murat, a reckless cavalry officer crowned king of Naples in 1808 by his brother-in-law Napoleon. The task of exchanging the ratified treaty and negotiating a bilateral trade agreement was assigned to Davezac, who was thus to inform the Dutch government that he would be away for some time.

Following his arrival in Naples in May 1833, Davezac and the Neapolitan minister of foreign affairs exchanged ratifications of the compensation agreement in early June. With a view to the negotiations of the trade agreement, Davezac sought to establish contact with prominent residents of the city and gathered information about American trade relations with Naples and any potential stumbling blocks. Despite the interest King Ferdinand II and his minister of foreign affairs expressed in a trade agreement with the United States, the negotiations proceeded very slowly. Time and again, just as the chargé was about to break off the negotiations, some ray of hope would encourage him to continue. In late December 1833 the State Department finally gave up and instructed Davezac to return to The Hague.

In reporting on the Netherlands, Davezac noted his impressions of the royal family, of the policies of William I, and of various ministers. In his dispatches on European affairs he began to include his own speculations. During his years in the Netherlands Davezac occasionally reported that developments in the United States were closely followed in Europe by admirers and worried statesmen alike. Naturally he swelled with pride whenever politicians spoke of the American experiment as the forerunner of improvements in their respective countries. The president's annual messages contributed not a little to the growing interest in America. Davezac did not doubt for a moment that America was predestined to play a great role on the world stage.

Davezac kept the State Department well informed, penning an average of twenty-eight dispatches every year. Yet his failure to carry out certain instructions hastened his return to the United States. Davezac ignored repeated requests from Secretary of State John Forsyth to send him a thorough account of his negotiations with the government of the Kingdom of the Two Sicilies and—not less serious—failed to report his expenditures to the Treasury Department every quarter. On two different occasions the Treasury had to remind the chargé to comply; the secretary of state even wrote him personally to this effect. None of this had the slightest result, however. Once it became clear that Davezac had no intention of obeying his instructions, the secretary of state had to inform the president. Davezac was given a last chance, but again he remained silent. Why he ignored even this generous offer remains a mystery. In May 1839 Davezac was therefore dismissed, and Harmanus Bleecker was chosen as his successor. Two months later Davezac took leave of King William I and the Dutch minister of foreign affairs, never suspecting that he would return six years later in the same capacity.

When Davezac returned to New Orleans in 1839, he was warmly welcomed by his Democratic friends. A banquet was organized in his honor, but obligations in Washington prevented him from attending. As an expression of gratitude he sent his fellow Democrats a sixteen-page letter about his impressions of the United States following his return. This published letter testifies to Davezac's deep admiration for his country.

Davezac was anxious to get to Washington to settle the financial problems that had precipitated his dismissal. Altogether unexpectedly, the Treasury Department's investigation showed that the government still owed him nearly $4,000. In not submitting quarterly financial reports while in the Netherlands, Davezac had neglected his duties, but now it seemed that the Treasury Department had been negligent as well.

The episode had no adverse effect on Davezac's faith in the government. Having settled in New York City in the meantime, he threw himself into Martin Van Buren's 1840 reelection campaign. When the results put not Van Buren but the Whig William Henry Harrison into the White House, Davezac sought to comfort the defeated president with the prospect of a Democratic victory four years hence. In February 1841 Davezac informed his hero Andrew Jackson of his intention to place himself at the disposal of the Democratic Party. His election to the New York State legislature in 1841 and 1843 enabled him to put his money where his mouth was. Between January and April 1842, and again between January and May 1844, Davezac represented New York City in Albany.

When the presidential elections of November 1844 approached, Davezac wanted to help Martin Van Buren have another crack at the White House. At the Democratic Convention held in May in Baltimore, however, it was already clear that the dark horse James K. Polk was the only candidate who could unite the party. Davezac soon discovered great qualities in this presidential contender, and in the course of the electoral campaign he delivered some 60 speeches in five different states and had his Democratic audiences on the edges of their seats. He became known far and wide for his eloquence and received no less than 166 invitations to speak in twenty different states. His speeches showed that he was not only an inspired demagogue, but also a fiery supporter of the 1840s American expansionist movement, Manifest Destiny.

There was no question that this militant Democrat would receive a political appointment following Polk's victory at the polls. Between November 1844 and March 1845 the newly elected president was inundated with letters, especially from the state of New York, about Davezac's efforts during the electoral campaign, recommending that he be awarded an important foreign mission. Andrew Jackson and Martin Van Buren were among those who wrote to Polk. In April Davezac received, again, an appointment as chargé d'affaires to the Netherlands.

During the years he spent in New York Davezac was apparently not practicing law but, beside his political activities, making a name for himself as a publicist. His efforts, which appeared in the *United States Magazine and Democratic Review*, attest to the author's knowledge of classical history and literature. In public speeches he seized every opportunity to express his admiration for Andrew Jackson, never failing to recall the glorious Battle of New Orleans of 1815. At times his boundless adoration for the former president became too much even for his countrymen. Needless to say, Davezac was stricken when he learned of Jackson's death in June 1845.

Immediately after arriving in the Netherlands in May 1845, Davezac wrote to Secretary of State James Buchanan of his desire to provide information not only about developments in that country but also about European opinions with regard to the Oregon and Texas controversies. President Polk personified America's passion for expansion. In his first annual message to Congress on December 2, 1845, in which he reaffirmed the principles of the Monroe Doctrine, he made incorporating these territories his goal. During his term of office he managed to do so, annexing Texas in 1845, Oregon in 1846, and California, New Mexico, and the area north of the Rio Grande in 1848, thus doubling the size of the United States. Davezac supported Polk's expansion policy wholeheartedly and can be considered as one of the most passionate exponents of the Monroe Doctrine and Manifest Destiny. In 1846 the chargé remarked with satisfaction that the rapid growth of the United States had made a deep impression in Europe. He wrote Buchanan that every American walked about Europe with head held high, confident that friend and foe now knew the true mettle of his countrymen.

Davezac even published a number of articles in the *Journal de la Haye* in support of the American cause in order to attack what he considered inaccurate reporting on the part of the British and French press about the American military operations in Mexico. He signed them *"un voyageur américain"* and sent copies to Washington together with his dispatches. This patriotic gesture was definitely not appreciated by the British minister plenipotentiary to The Hague, who complained to the Dutch government about what he saw as the bias of the *Journal de la Haye*.

Davezac reported extensively on the political situation in Europe leading to the revolution of 1848 and its aftermath during which conservative forces regained power. Like other American diplomats in the Old World in those years, he looked favorably on the revolutions of 1848 and hoped that it would lead to the adoption of constitutional forms of government throughout Europe modeled on the American example. His firm belief in the victory of democracy prompted him to overestimate the strength of the revolution and to underestimate the power of conservative elements. The democratic principles on which his own republic was founded proved to be premature for the Europe of the late 1840s.

Davezac also kept the State Department informed in detail about developments in the Netherlands, where the socioeconomic situation was appalling and where the middle classes strived for political reform. Influenced by the February Revolution in France, the Dutch king, William II, accepted a more liberal constitution in 1848. The author of the new constitution was the liberal leader J. R. Thorbecke, whom Davezac considered a great statesman. Secretary of State James Buchanan expressed his appreciation of Davezac's coverage of the Netherlands during this turbulent period on the European continent.

In May 1850 Secretary of State John M. Clayton informed Davezac that President Zachary Taylor had decided to appoint George Folsom as his successor in the Netherlands. It probably came as no surprise to Davezac that the Whig president wished to fill the post at The Hague with a member of his own party. After Davezac had already taken leave of the Dutch government, the minister of foreign affairs wrote his American colleague in September 1850 how much he regretted Davezac's departure, that everyone who had met the American chargé d'affaires had great respect for him, and that he had greatly contributed to the friendly relations between the Netherlands and the United States.

Just before returning to the United States, Davezac was rather pessimistic about the prospects for freedom in Europe and noticed the negative feelings of European monarchs toward his country, but he foresaw a brighter future for the Netherlands and wrote that the Netherlands cabinet presented a consoling spectacle to the friends of freedom throughout Europe.

Following his return to the United States, Davezac had little time to enjoy his leisure. After a short illness the seventy-year-old Democrat died in New York City on February 15, 1851. Davezac's death aggrieved his many friends. According to his obituary in the *New York Herald*, the Democrats at Tammany Hall would remember him "as one of their most zealous advocates."

Works by Auguste Davezac

"A Letter from Major Davezac to Mr. Wadsworth, a Member of the Louisiana State Legislature, in answer to an invitation to partake of a banquet offered by many of his fellow Democrats on his return to New Orleans, after his Missions to the Netherlands and Naples." December 29, 1839. Pamphlets C p.v. 1292 and AN p.v. 18 no. 5 in New York Public Library.

"Fragments of Unpublished Reminiscences of Edward Livingston." *United States Magazine and Democratic Review* 8 (October 1840): 366–84.

"Marius." *United States Magazine and Democratic Review* 8 (November 1840): 475–512.

"New Orleans." *United States Magazine and Democratic Review* 8 (December 1840): 537–38.

"The Conspiracy of Catiline." *United States Magazine and Democratic Review* 9 (August 1841): 144–62.

"A Chapter on Gardening." *United States Magazine and Democratic Review* 12 (February 1843): 122–28.

"The Literature of Fiction." *United States Magazine and Democratic Review* 16 (March 1845): 268–82.

"Le Général Jackson." A series of thirteen articles in the *Journal de la Haye* published October 1845 through April 1846.

Works about Auguste Davezac

[By editors of the periodical.] "Major Davezac." *United States Magazine and Democratic Review* 16 (February 1845): 109–11.

Foote, Henry S. *The Bench and Bar of the South and Southwest*. St. Louis: Soule, Thomas and Wentworth, 1876.

Hunt, Charles Havens. *Life of Edward Livingston*. New York: D. Appleton and Company, 1864.

Hunt, Louise Livingston. *Memoir of Mrs. Edward Livingston*. New York: Harper and Brothers, 1886.

James, Marquis. *Andrew Jackson: Portrait of a President*. New York: Grosset and Dunlap, 1961.

Marraro, Howard R. "Auguste Davezac's Mission to the Kingdom of the Two Sicilies, 1833–1834." *Louisiana Historical Quarterly* 32 (1949): 791–808.

van Minnen, Cornelis A. *American Diplomats in the Netherlands, 1815–1850*. New York: St. Martin's Press, 1993.

Weinberg, Albert K. *Manifest Destiny: A Study of Nationalist Expansionism in American History*. Baltimore: Johns Hopkins Press, 1935; Chicago: Quadrangle Books, 1963.

CORNELIS A. VAN MINNEN

JOHN WILLIAM DAVIS (1873–1955) earned the respect
and admiration of his country for contributions rendered as a distinguished lawyer, presidential candidate, and Woodrow Wilson's ambassador to Great Britain.
Throughout his career he was admired for his integrity, his sense of justice, and
his willingness to stand on principle, particularly when his personal convictions
were clearly at odds with popular opinion. As ambassador, he is remembered
most for his efforts to stabilize the decline in Anglo-American relations that
followed the end of World War I: disputes over oil interests, naval policy, the
Irish question, and European resentment engendered by Wilson's often moral-
istic attitude at the Paris Peace Conference severely tested the cooperative spirit
that characterized relations during the war.

Davis was born on April 13, 1873, in Clarksburg, West Virginia, to John
James Davis and Anna Kennedy Davis. He was the fifth of six children and the
only son. His renowned personal convictions and legal philosophy are attributable to the influence of his father. John James Davis possessed a forceful personality: he communicated his views with an unrivaled enthusiasm and
confidently believed in the truth of his philosophical assumptions. He considered
himself a Jeffersonian; however, his adamant support of states' rights located
the elder Davis closer to John C. Calhoun (although he did not share the South
Carolinian's secessionist views) than to Jefferson. This affinity for Calhoun
came into sharper relief during his three terms as a member of the West Virginia
House of Delegates. John James Davis vocally opposed constitutional amendments that accorded legal equality to former slaves and also stood firmly against
legislation that permitted the confiscation of rebel property. A life in politics,
however, did not suit John James Davis; rather, he dedicated most of his working
life to practicing law in Clarksburg, where he had established himself as a
passionate opponent of federal power and big business.

John W. Davis differed from his father insofar as he did not share his father's
rhetorical passion; in terms of personality he favored his mother's measured and
reasoned oratory and writing styles. Anna Davis taught young John to read and
write at a very young age: a regimen of Shakespeare, Poe, and Dickens in a
highly disciplined environment structured Davis's early years. At the age of ten
Davis enrolled in the Clarksburg Female Seminary, where he studied for two
years. From there he continued his studies at Pantops Academy, near Charlottesville, Virginia. In 1889, at the age of sixteen, Davis started college as a sophomore at Washington and Lee. Despite his unexceptional collegiate work, his
enthusiasm and sound judgment suggested to some of his professors that he
would make a good lawyer.

When Davis completed his degree, a lack of money hindered his desire to
continue his studies in law. To earn money for law school, he accepted a job
with the McDonald family of Charles Town, Virginia, and for nine months he

served as tutor for the nine McDonald children and six nephews and nieces. In the spring of 1893 he returned home, where he read law in his father's office for fourteen months. This short apprenticeship only intensified his resolve to attend law school, and with the help of his father he enrolled in the Washington and Lee School of Law in 1894. An intensive year of law school reinforced the principles Davis shared with his father: a strict constructionist interpretation of the Constitution and the belief that men possessed an immutable right to liberty and property dominated the course of study at Washington and Lee. Davis was, first and foremost, a Jeffersonian liberal and a natural rights lawyer.

Davis began honing his skills before the bar while practicing law with his father. A relatively uneventful year elapsed before Davis's alma mater asked him to replace a faculty member who had recently passed away. Although Davis enjoyed teaching, he returned to private practice after one year; he much preferred the challenges of private life. After arriving back in Clarksburg in 1897, Davis began to build an impressive career in and out of politics. He won the respect of labor organizers by adeptly representing the interests of striking miners during a time when the rights of workers were generally subsumed to the rights of property owners. He also represented railroad interests and eventually became regular counsel for the Short Line. Davis's involvement with the railroads eventually developed into an enduring relationship with big business and also opened a rift with his father. The elder Davis carried his suspicion of big business to his grave and resented his son's close ties with the railroads.

Davis's law skills also served him well in public life. In 1898 the voters of Harrison County elected him to the West Virginia House of Delegates. As chair of the Judiciary committee, Davis quickly established himself as an able lawmaker, and by the end of his only term in the state legislature he was being touted as a future governor. His political career resumed when he was elected to Congress as a Democrat in 1910. Davis's legal skills landed him on the Judiciary Committee, where his dim views of Republican protectionism and excessive profit taking figured prominently in several important bills. In addition to Davis's persistent opposition to protectionist legislation, even when such opposition harmed the interests of his own constituents, the most notable legacy of his congressional career was his anti-injunction legislation, which later became part of the landmark Clayton Anti-Trust Act. Esteemed for his integrity, compassion, and sense of justice, Davis impressed his colleagues during his two terms in Congress in much the same way he had captured the admiration of his colleagues in private practice and in state politics.

This exemplary reputation attracted the attention of Woodrow Wilson's attorney general, James C. McReynolds, who offered Davis the position of solicitor general at an important juncture in the history of the Supreme Court. After accepting the position in 1913, Davis assumed the responsibility of defending, in the nation's highest court, the most controversial legislative measures of the Roosevelt, Taft, and Wilson administrations. Davis argued cases that called for the regulation of private oil pipelines, the dissolution of International Harvester and United States Steel, the implementation of child-labor laws, and Congress's right to regulate working hours of railroad workers. Perhaps most significant are the two civil rights cases that Davis argued before the Supreme Court. In the first case, *United States v. Mosley*, Davis successfully argued that black suffrage included the right to have the ballots of black voters counted. In the second case, *Guinn v. United States*, he convinced the Supreme Court to strike down an Oklahoma law that prevented illiterate blacks from voting. Davis's success in advancing the cause of black civil rights would stand in stark contrast when, in the twilight of his career, he would appeal to the same body to uphold the segregationist policies of Southern states. During his five years as solicitor general Davis amassed an impressive record: he won forty-eight of the sixty-seven cases he argued before the Supreme Court, and members of the Court lauded him for his exceptional preparation and lucid presentation.

One year before Davis resigned his position as solicitor general, the United States entered the war in Europe. Germany's violation of Belgium's neutrality so repulsed Davis that he often found it difficult to countenance Wilson's early policy of neutrality. He considered American participation in the war as defending the sacred rights of law: America's participation in World War I was, for Davis, a righteous and just act.

Convinced of the justice of America's cause, Davis enthusiastically accepted an invitation in the spring of 1918 to become one of four members of the American High Commission to discuss with the Germans the possible exchange of prisoners of war. In late August he set sail for Berne, Switzerland, where the German-American Conference on Prisoners of War was scheduled to convene. While en route to Berne, Davis received a cable from Secretary of State Robert Lansing requesting, on behalf of the president, that he accept the ambassadorship to Great Britain. Initially reluctant, Davis expressed concern that he might be unable to meet the financial obligations of an ambassadorship. Lansing replied that despite the financial requirements of the position, duty demanded that he accept. Davis's wife, Nell, was equally adamant; she insisted that he accept the president's offer. After several days of reflection and consultation with members of the diplomatic community, Davis finally accepted.

Lansing instructed Davis, before presenting his credentials in London, to proceed to Berne for the prisoner-of-war conference. For two months Davis had to endure the commentary on his appointment. President Wilson's choice surprised the diplomatic community and met significant criticism in the media. While Davis's legal skills commanded great respect, critics charged that his lack of experience and name recognition outside of the legal profession made prominent figures, such as William Taft, Elihu Root, and Theodore Roosevelt, more sensible choices.

Davis arrived in London on December 18, 1918, at the high point of Anglo-American relations, and immediately won the hearts of his British hosts and dispelled the fears of his critics back home. Shortly thereafter a dispute over the Rhineland prompted Wilson to summon him to Paris, where the peace conference at Versailles had convened several months earlier. Deeply troubled by French demands concerning the Rhineland, Wilson called upon Davis to make every effort to soften the French position. For ten days during June 1919 Davis matched wits with France's Marshal Ferdinand Foch, who was determined that German power would remain in check. Davis was able to significantly dilute the French position while conceding relatively minor points in return. In the end, the treaty terms that pertained to the Rhineland occupation reflected most of Davis's suggestions.

Davis subsequently returned to his post in London, where he had to contend with the rapid deterioration of Anglo-American relations. One of the principal sources of friction was Woodrow Wilson himself. His idealistic moralizing at Versailles proved to be a constant source of irritation. Moreover, Wilson's refusal to accept changes to the League Covenant ensured its rejection by the Republican-controlled Senate and ultimately discredited the United States among its wartime allies. Davis responded to this humiliating situation by resolving to put his country in the best possible light given the circumstances. Davis, a committed internationalist, saw no alternative other than to accept the League of Nations, though he privately thought the text of the Covenant to be too specific. Despite his internationalist views and his disdain for the Republicans who engineered the treaty's defeat, he endeavored to explain to his British hosts the powers retained by the Senate and the Republicans' objection to Article Ten of the League Covenant, namely, that the political and territorial guarantees contained in the treaty violated long-standing tenets of American foreign policy.

In addition to Wilson's moralizing and America's failure to join the League of Nations, several other issues contributed to postwar Anglo-American turbulence. On the subject of oil, Davis found himself torn between the reality that strategic stability required British hegemony in Persia and Mesopotamia (the United States was unwilling and unable to provide such stability) and the realization that Britain intended to obtain the largest possible share of Near Eastern oil reserves. Davis explained to the British that the prospect of a British monopoly over the Persian and Mesopotamian oil fields would offend American sensibilities insofar as it would exclude American petroleum interests from fair competition in the region. A diplomatic rift opened when Britain, unmoved by the ambassador's argument, reaffirmed its privileged position in the Near East. Although Davis considered Britain's behavior in the Near East as patently self-serving, he continued to counsel U.S. support for British policy in the interest of promoting peace and stability.

America's naval objectives also heightened tension between Washington and London. Shortly after the end of the war Secretary of the Navy Josephus Daniels publicly called for a considerable expansion of American naval power. As well, some ranking officers in the U.S. Navy were known to have been rather ambivalent toward Britain during the war: they viewed Britain and Germany as moral equivalents. The revelation of these insensitive remarks evoked outrage and deep suspicion in a country whose power and empire rested on the strength of its navy: it was a matter of British policy that the Royal Navy be predominant in European waters. Through a series of speeches Davis assuaged British concerns by tactfully articulating American objectives while simultaneously paying respect to Britain's long-standing naval tradition and its global naval interests.

Throughout his tenure as ambassador Davis consistently earned accolades for his ability to faithfully represent and convey American interests without losing sight of the legitimate interests of his hosts. Only on the matter of Ireland did his personal views diverge significantly from the predominant sentiment of his country. America's own revolutionary heritage and the popular rhetoric of the idea of self-determination evoked enormous American sympathy for the plight of the Irish nationalists. Furthermore, the large Irish immigrant populations in New York and Boston transformed the Irish question into an important issue in American domestic politics: the Republican Party openly courted the Irish vote, and members of both parties repeatedly called for Irish independence on the floors of the House and Senate. Davis considered the pro-Irish attitudes of American politicians as demagoguery and as unwarranted interference in the affairs of another nation. More pronounced was his contempt for the Irish nationalist; Davis despised the political violence that was perpetrated by Sinn Fein to advance the cause of Irish independence. Although the repressive policies that continued after the war made supporting Britain immensely more difficult, Davis maintained his support for London's interpretation regarding the troubles in Ireland. During his tenure as ambassador Davis quietly worked to discourage the idea of Irish independence when given the opportunity.

In spite of the turbulence that characterized Anglo-American relations during Davis's time in London, he managed to establish a remarkably close rapport with his hosts. Commenting on Davis's many speeches, British newspapers spoke of his eloquence while the editorial pages were filled with barbs directed at American policy. It is ironic that an ambassador so well liked by his hosts received so little attention from the very man who appointed him. In fact, Davis recorded in his diary that he doubted whether he ever had the confidence of the president, and for the most part he was right; Wilson essentially ignored Davis by keeping him ill informed and by bypassing him on important policy issues. Wilson's behavior toward Davis speaks less of the ambassador's abilities than of the president's own preferences. At a time when Wilson could have usefully employed Davis, and when Anglo-American relations desperately needed attention, he chose to direct American foreign policy almost entirely by himself. Of course, Wilson's single-minded approach to the period that immediately followed World War I contributed significantly to the failure of his internationalist postwar agenda.

Wilson's preference for handling important foreign policy matters himself led Davis to frequently question his utility as ambassador and the value of his work in the position. These questions were only compounded by his concern over the personal expense he was incurring while in government service. Increasingly frustrated by his lack of input, Davis resolved to resign at the earliest opportunity less than one year after his posting. On December 23, 1920, two years after arriving in London, Davis tendered his resignation. Displeased with his timing, Wilson requested that Davis stay on until March 4, when the newly elected Harding administration would assume power. Davis reluctantly agreed. Three months later, on March 9, 1921, Davis boarded the *Olympic* and in a show of appreciation was honored by two squadrons of Royal Navy destroyers as he departed Southampton for New York.

Once back in the United States, Davis resumed his law practice by accepting a partnership with the prestigious New York law firm Stetson, Jennings, and Russell. Although Davis spent the rest of his career in private life, he did not stray far from politics and the most cogent issues of the day. He won the presidential nomination of a badly divided Democratic Party in 1924 but eventually lost to Calvin Coolidge due to what many described as a poorly run campaign. With the onset of the Depression and Franklin Roosevelt's subsequent election, Davis made a reputation for virulently opposing the New Deal, which he viewed as a dangerous expansion of federal power. During this period he gained even greater notoriety by defending his firm's most prestigious client, J. P. Morgan, from the congressional bank investigations that were initiated in the wake of the collapse of the stock market. In the twilight of his career, following the end of World War II, Davis publicly supported Alger Hiss and J. Robert Oppenheimer during the hysteria of the McCarthy hearings. Finally, in 1954 Davis argued unsuccessfully against Thurgood Marshall that states possess the right to enforce racial segregation in the landmark case *Brown v. Board of Education*. One year later, on March 24, 1955, John Davis died at his summer home, Yeamans Hall, just north of Charleston, South Carolina.

Friends and foes alike revered Davis for his integrity and concomitant sense of duty. Both in his private and public roles Davis was unafraid to take a stand on principle and support or oppose, as the case might be, controversial issues. This sense of duty was clearly evident during Davis's tenure as ambassador to Great Britain. Through the difficulties surrounding the disputes over oil, Ireland, and the League of Nations, Davis labored to put his country's interests and policies in the best light possible even though he questioned the wisdom of many of them. To be sure, Davis is notable not because he was intimately involved in important matters of policy formulation, but rather because he managed to stabilize Anglo-American relations during a time of precipitous decline. Most of his time was dedicated to repairing the damage caused by a parade of ill-chosen and ill-timed remarks uttered by his countrymen. That he accomplished this task without being accorded the full support of the Wilson administration is a credit to himself and to his country.

Works about John W. Davis

Harbaugh, William H. *Lawyer's Lawyer: The Life of John W. Davis*. New York: Oxford University Press, 1973.

Link, Arthur S. *Wilson the Diplomatist: A Look at His Major Foreign Policies*. Baltimore: Johns Hopkins Press, 1957.

McKercher, B. J. C., ed. *Anglo-American Relations in the 1920s: The Struggle for Supremacy*. London: Macmillan, 1991.

Walworth, Arthur. *America's Moment, 1918: American Diplomacy at the End of World War I*. New York: W. W. Norton and Company, 1977.

Willson, Beckles. *America's Ambassadors to England (1785–1928)*. Freeport, NY: Books for Libraries Press, 1969.

WILLIAM W. BAIN

WILLIAM E. DODD (1869–1940)

WILLIAM E. DODD (1869–1940) served as ambassador to Nazi Germany during the gathering storm of the early 1930s. Despite continuing intense interest in Nazi Germany and the eyewitness accounts by Americans who witnessed the Hitler regime, the diplomatic career of William E. Dodd and the diary he left behind of his four years in Germany have gone almost unnoticed. Dodd was a political appointee who did as well as a diplomat could under impossible conditions, with a few crucial exceptions. As an eyewitness observer of the Nazis, his knack for detail and his German contacts enabled him to write a diary that is a valuable historical legacy.

Dodd was born in Clayton, North Carolina, on October 27, 1869. He received bachelor's and master's degrees from Virginia Polytechnic University in Blacksburg and then went on to earn his Ph.D. in 1900 from the University of Leipzig in Germany. He returned to America and taught at Randolph-Macon College. He wrote prolifically about the Old South and then became a leading proponent of Wilsonian internationalism. Dodd was teaching at the University of Chicago when Franklin Delano Roosevelt offered him the position of ambassador to Germany. Dodd was not the first choice; Newton Baker, a Wilson stalwart and progressive-movement hero, was offered the position and turned it down.

The appointment of Dodd made sense for three reasons: (1) his identification with Woodrow Wilson, (2) his German academic contacts, and (3) his distrust of career diplomats. Unfortunately, Wilson's ideas had no answers for the international problems of the 1930s, academic contacts were almost useless in the stifling climate of Nazi Germany, and Dodd alienated the career diplomats he needed to be effective.

Dodd apparently believed that he could actually affect events in Germany by upholding the example of American republicanism. His main goal was the repayment of American debts, and his initial assessment of Hitler was that he had little chance of remaining in power. In early reports Dodd stressed strong opposition among church groups and monarchists and claimed that there was no organized opposition to the Nazis in the Wehrmacht.

A meeting between Hitler and Dodd on March 7, 1934, showed the American ambassador the difficult task ahead. Dodd tried to establish common ground by stressing how both nations could gain from better commercial relations and a resumption of the academic exchanges that had meant so much to Germany and America. When Hitler began complaining about Jews in Germany, Dodd suggested that the Nazis consider using a quota system for Jews in political and academic positions similar to the quotas in American government and universities. Hitler was not encouraged by Dodd's suggestion. Instead, the Führer used the occasion to blame Jews for Germany's internal problems and for all difficulties in German-American relations. Hitler maintained that the anti-Nazi propaganda circulating in America was actually generated by Jews. The interview ended without any indication that U.S.-German relations would improve.

A good example of the strengths and weaknesses of Dodd's diplomatic recording occurred during Hitler's purge of the Nazi SA, popularly referred to as the "Night of the Long Knives." On June 30, 1934, Dodd wrote to Washington after returning from a tour of the university towns of Heidelberg, Tübingen, and Marburg. He reported that the Wehrmacht and Heinrich Himmler's elite SS were both hostile to Ernst Roehm's SA, or Brownshirts. Two days later, when Roehm and other SA leaders had been executed without trial, Dodd predicted that the result would be "a more liberal domestic and foreign policy."

From July 1934 on, Dodd detached himself both from his duties as observer and from the social routine expected of diplomats in Berlin. His distaste for Nazi brutality led him to rely heavily on his old academic contacts for information. Dodd's reports on Nazi activities were sometimes long on metaphor and bereft of solid political analysis. He wavered between equating National Socialism with a return to medievalism and the "brown communism" analysis that held that only minor cosmetic differences separated the methods and goals of the leaders of Russia and Germany in the 1930s. Dodd kept plugging away at the topic of Germany's unpaid debts after Nazi actions proved how little they cared about international obligations. He did continue to collect extensive information concerning church-state relations.

Before Dodd left for Berlin, he made it very clear that he planned to support himself and his family on his meager salary. This left no money for elaborate entertaining. Dodd recorded frequently in his diary his disdain for social events, singling out Italian diplomats for especially bitter criticism. Although Dodd was entitled to his personal opinions, his behavior cut him off from the valuable information his fellow diplomats could share. His relationship with most American professional diplomats was equally frosty, with particularly strong animosity directed toward Summer Welles. During 1936 and 1937 a series of private and public incidents seriously reduced the ambassador's credibility. Part of the problem was his running feud with American diplomats who came from what Dodd believed were patrician backgrounds. Summer Welles was one colleague toward whom Dodd never concealed his animosity. In his diary Dodd fumed that William Bullitt, a wealthy lawyer with erratic political preferences and vicious ethnic prejudices whom FDR had sent to Soviet Russia, would jeopardize German-American relations.

A public problem that Dodd handled poorly was his frequent refusal after June 30, 1934, to attend Nazi Party functions. Although Dodd claimed in his diary that he was far from the only diplomat who avoided Nazi events, he gave the impression that he had allowed his personal distaste for what was happening in Germany to become more important than his obligations as a diplomat. After all, America had not severed relations with Germany, and diplomats usually do not boycott events to make a personal statement. Dodd's detractors back in the United States, mainly conservative members of Congress who hated Dodd's championship of Wilsonian idealism and liberal political causes, used the issue as proof that Dodd was an incompetent diplomat.

The biggest uproar occurred in May 1937 when Dodd wrote a letter expressing his political support for President Franklin Delano Roosevelt's plan to pack the U.S. Supreme Court in an effort to curb the Court's nullifications of New Deal legislation. In the letter Dodd attacked FDR's opponents and hinted that they were puppets of a billionaire Dodd left unnamed who was bent on establishing German-style fascism in the United States. An uproar immediately broke out, led by Senator William Borah of Idaho and other vocal foes of FDR, who demanded that Dodd both name the anonymous billionaire and resign as ambassador.

Dodd's reaction yields important insight into his political naïveté. He was indignant and felt that his main point (support for FDR) had been ignored, and that entirely too much discussion had focused on the question of the anonymous billionaire. Dodd was oblivious to the fact that a person in a highly public role, such as an ambassador, had to expect a major controversy when he made controversial remarks. Second, Dodd failed to realize that public discourse was very different from academic discourse. The rules of the game made it perfectly acceptable for opponents to exaggerate Dodd's remarks and quote them out of context. In any case, Dodd's enemies back home and in Germany now had powerful ammunition to use when urging his dismissal from the ambassadorship to Germany.

Dodd returned to America from August to October 1937. In September he wrote a letter to Secretary of State Cordell Hull urging a complete boycott of the Nazi Party rally held each year in Nuremberg. The letter was leaked to the press and aroused great indignation among German officials. A month before the letter was leaked, the Reich's ambassador to the United States, Hans Dieckhoff, had complained about Dodd's public criticisms of the Nazi regime. Hull informed Dieckhoff that Dodd was entitled to his personal opinions, but the secretary of state must have realized that Dodd's usefulness was limited in the face of German hostility. Department of State correspondence from 1937 indicates that Dodd left more and more of the burden of observation and analysis to subordinates at the embassy. After Dodd's letter to Hull was leaked in September, Dieckhoff met with Summer Welles to launch a formal protest and request that Dodd be replaced. The result was a classic case of Rooseveltian procrastination. Dodd was left in Berlin uncertain of his fate for weeks and was then informed by Cordell Hull on November 22, 1937, that in only three weeks Hugh Gibson would arrive to replace him. When he returned to private life, Dodd spent a year touring America speaking to liberal and left-wing antifascist groups and wrote an introduction to a translation of a Nazi children's book called *The Nazi Primer*. In December 1938 he killed a pedestrian while driving an automobile. The resulting trial and publicity ruined his health and left him mentally frail. Dodd died in 1940, his death largely unnoticed in the noisy debate over events in Europe.

Since his death William E. Dodd has not attracted the attention of many historians. A book of essays published in 1953, *The Diplomats*, edited by Gordon Craig and Felix Gilbert, devoted about ten pages to Dodd's time in Berlin. The theme of the book is that professional diplomats always are much more effective than political appointees; therefore, Dodd was bound to be portrayed in an unfavorable light. Dodd was criticized for his lofty goal of changing the Nazis by providing a democratic example and his tendency to withdraw and brood when the Nazis failed to respond. Great emphasis was placed on the domestic controversies that Dodd sparked; little analysis of his diplomatic reporting occurred.

A balanced assessment of Dodd's service should point out that from time to time he was capable of preparing very detailed reports on topics that were important in the 1930s and that continue to hold the interest of historians. His extensive reports on German churches under the Reich are a major source of information. Dodd tended to portray the churches as much more vigorous opponents of fascism than they actually were, but he nevertheless recorded events that otherwise might have been completely omitted from the historical record. His reporting of the June 30, 1934, "Night of the Long Knives" was accurate, even though his prediction that the Nazi leadership would pursue a more moderate path as a result was misplaced.

One area where Dodd seriously misled readers was in his analysis of German academics. Dodd had studied in Leipzig. He had achieved success because of the superior training he received in Germany, and it was inconceivable to him that professors and students would not oppose the anti-intellectual credo of Hitler. Unfortunately, the real story was different. German universities had always mixed in a heavy dose of elitism and ultranationalism with the liberal ideals Dodd had encountered as a student thirty years before. Instead of opposing the Nazis, most German students and academics were either indifferent or actively supported Hitler. It could be that by exaggerating the extent of opposition to the Nazis, Dodd minimized the threat Nazi Germany posed to the world.

A final evaluation of Dodd depends on one's point of view on whether political appointees should have a role in American diplomacy. Scholars like George F. Kennan and Norman Graebner, who favor a professional diplomatic corps, see Dodd as an example of everything that can go wrong with a diplomatic greenhorn. Dodd's few supporters, mostly liberal New Dealers, placed him in the pantheon of premature antifascists unfairly pilloried by domestic foes and Nazi propaganda. Which picture is accurate?

Dodd's mission was doomed before it began. He dealt with a regime that had nothing but contempt for diplomacy. He represented a president who constantly undermined his diplomats in the field. Dodd did his best to alert the world to the dangers of Nazism and record its horrors, and he performed this important task with admirable courage.

Works by William E. Dodd

Coauthor with Andrew C. McLaughlin, Marcus W. Jernegan, and Arthur P. Scott. *Source Problems in United States History*. New York and London: Harper and Brothers, 1918.

The Cotton Kingdom: A Chronicle of the Old South. New Haven: Yale University Press, 1919.

Expansion and Conflict. Boston: Houghton Mifflin, 1919.

Woodrow Wilson and His Work. Garden City, NY: Doubleday, Page and Company, 1920.

Coeditor, with Ray S. Baker. *The Public Papers of Woodrow Wilson*. New York and London: Harper and Brothers, 1925.

Lincoln or Lee: Comparison and Contrast of the Two Greatest Leaders in the War Between the States. New York and London: The Century Company, 1928.

Coauthor, with McKendree Llewellyn Raney, Lloyd Lewis, and Carl Sandburg. *If Lincoln Had Lived*. Chicago: The University of Chicago Press, 1935.

Ambassador Dodd's Diary, 1933–1938. Eds. William E. Dodd, Jr. and Martha Dodd. New York: Harcourt, Brace and Company, 1941.

Works about William E. Dodd

Craig, Gordon, and Felix Gilbert, eds. *The Diplomats: 1919–1939*. Princeton: Princeton University Press, 1953.

Craven, Avery, ed. *Essays in honor of William E. Dodd, by His Former Students at the University of Chicago*. Chicago: The University of Chicago Press, 1935.

Dallek, Robert. *Democrat and Diplomat: The Life of William E. Dodd*. New York: Oxford University Press, 1968.

MICHAEL J. POLLEY

EDWARD R. DUDLEY (1911–) was a noted New York jurist and the first black American to be appointed a U.S. ambassador.

Dudley was born on March 11, 1911, in South Boston, Virginia, the son of Edward and Nellie Dudley. Educated in the public school system of Roanoke, Dudley went on to earn his B.S. (majoring in predentistry) at Johnson C. Smith University in Charlotte, North Carolina. A career as a dentist never materialized, however. Following stints working in the public school system and in real estate, Dudley headed to New York, where he worked on a WPA theater project. While there, he returned to school and received his law degree from St. John's University in 1941. He spent the next year practicing law in New York City. It was during this time that he married Rae Elizabeth Olley and soon after had a son, Edward R. Dudley, Jr. During 1942–1943 Dudley served as New York State assistant attorney general.

In 1943 Dudley began a long and close working relationship with the NAACP. In that year he became assistant special counsel to the NAACP Legal Defense and Education Fund, serving under future Supreme Court justice Thurgood Marshall. Despite the gains made by black Americans during World War II, the United States remained a deeply segregated nation. The NAACP, through Marshall and Dudley, was at the forefront of the fight for civil rights, particularly in the field of voting. For the next two years Dudley was instrumental in filing suits in many Southern states on behalf of black Americans who were being denied their constitutional rights.

In addition to his strenuous efforts on behalf of the NAACP, Dudley was also a stalwart Democrat, and these two facts combined to bring him to the attention of the Truman administration in 1945. In that year he was appointed as legal counsel to the governor of the U.S. Virgin Islands. He remained in this post for two years, serving much of that time under an old NAACP associate, Governor William Hastie, but finally decided to return to his important work with the NAACP and Thurgood Marshall in 1947.

Dudley's second tour of duty with the NAACP was short-lived, however. In 1948 a combination of factors resulted in his selection as U.S. minister to Liberia. President Truman was confronted with an opening in Liberia when the current U.S. minister tendered his resignation (rumors circulated that the resignation was the minister's attempt to preempt his firing by an incoming Republican administration, since he—like many Americans—was sure that Truman would lose in 1948). Liberia had been for many years the traditional ''black'' post; twenty-three of the previous twenty-four U.S. ministers selected to serve in the African nation had been black, noncareer political appointees. (The sole exception—James G. Carter—was a black, career Foreign Service officer. He declined his 1927 appointment.) Most of the legation's staff was also made up of black Americans. Indeed, nearly all black Americans who had entered the

Foreign Service since the 1930s had begun their careers in Monrovia, had found that transfers were rare (and were usually to other African posts), and had quite often ended up spending most of their years with the State Department right where they began.

Thus in 1948 when the opening in Liberia occurred, the Truman administration began to cast about for an appropriate black appointee. Dudley had made a name for himself with his work for the Democratic Party and the NAACP. He was an obviously appealing candidate: he was young, vigorous, and professional. It certainly did not hurt in a tight election year, when the black vote might be particularly vital, that Dudley served with the most prestigious black civil rights organization in the country. Nevertheless, he was surprised by the offer. After mulling over what seemed to be a short-term job opportunity, Dudley decided that the experience would be interesting and educational and, at the relatively young age of thirty-seven, was appointed U.S. minister to Liberia in August 1948.

Despite the fact that Liberia was traditionally a "black" mission and that the appointment of an official of the NAACP was undoubtedly helpful to Truman's 1948 campaign, the selection of someone with Dudley's talents and initiative indicated that U.S. interest in Liberia was steadily increasing. World War II had been the catalyst in this newfound interest. During the war Liberia had acquired both economic and strategic significance. The former came from the production of natural rubber (approximately 25,000 tons annually) from the Firestone Company plantations operating in the country. Strategically, Liberia offered a base of operations for Allied troops during the war. The United States stationed a number of its own forces in Liberia, built the Roberts Field airport, and constructed the first modern harbor at Monrovia. These latter two projects represented a nearly $25-million investment. In addition, both a U.S. Economic Mission and Public Health Mission were also sent to Liberia.

With the conclusion of hostilities in 1945, U.S. interest did not wane. U.S. investments in the tiny nation increased. The Firestone Company had operated rubber plantations in Liberia for many years and by 1948 had approximately $25 million invested and held claims to one million square acres of land. Other U.S. companies were investing in the iron-ore–rich Bomi Hills. Standard Oil began preliminary investigations to determine Liberia's oil reserves. Liberia's hardwood timber, cocoa, and small deposits of industrial diamonds and gold also attracted U.S. investors. By 1948 it was estimated that total U.S. investment in Liberia exceeded $60 million.

Strategically, Liberia offered a useful "window on Africa" for U.S. policymakers. Though Africa was not of primary concern for U.S. diplomats in the years immediately following the war, there was apprehension and indecision concerning the fate of the European empires on that continent. Liberia was the only U.S. foothold in Africa and, as such, could serve as an outpost from which to measure and monitor the pulse of continental developments.

That Liberia had become a significant focal point for U.S. diplomacy in the postwar, colonial world was obvious in the 1949 decision to raise the status of the U.S. mission in that nation from a legation to an embassy, and to make Dudley the first black ambassador in U.S. history. Discussions took place in the Truman administration throughout late 1948 and early 1949, and the themes were always the same: Liberia had acquired new strategic and economic importance for the United States. An additional point to be considered was that such a move would strike a positive chord with the U.S. black population. Responding to these arguments, Truman announced the elevation of the legation to embassy status in March 1949 (the first U.S. embassy in Africa), and Dudley was promoted to ambassador. It was a significant achievement and received wide play in the U.S. press. However, Dudley had little time to consider the significance of his new title or its domestic impact. Four years of hard work lay before him.

Even before being elevated to ambassador, Dudley quickly perceived that he would have three major jobs to tackle. First, the U.S. mission—in terms of personnel, equipment, and housing—would have to be increased to deal with the steady demands of U.S. business and diplomatic interests. Prior to Dudley's arrival the mission had been run as something of a one-man show. The new minister, however, realized that those days were over and that he needed more staff, better equipment, and sufficient new buildings to house both. The raising of the legation to embassy level only exacerbated the problems. With the help of such veteran staffers as Rupert Lloyd, Dudley accomplished much of what he desired in this regard.

Second, the various U.S. business interests in Liberia had to be promoted, protected, and, on occasion, controlled as they attempted to push into this new market. Reports from the American mission indicated that Liberia had acquired something of a "boomtown" look and feel as U.S. businessmen, bankers, engineers, geologists, and speculators poured into Monrovia and out into the Liberian countryside. These reports also noted that British and French interests were active and often competed with the Americans. Dudley quickly realized that the key to protecting and promoting U.S. economic interests in Liberia was in cultivating a close working relationship with the ruler of Liberia, President William V. S. Tubman.

Tubman had been elected president of Liberia in 1944. From the beginning there had been charges of corruption and political repression leveled against his regime. Dudley's impression was that Tubman was a de facto dictator. He placed "his crowd of boys" in all important positions, generally ignored the Liberian legislature, and generally ran Liberia as he wanted. On the other hand, Dudley believed that both personally and pragmatically Tubman was a man with whom he could work. Personally, Dudley found the Liberian leader to be tough, but personable and almost overwhelmingly pro-American. While Tubman always made sure that he received some kind of financial remuneration from the various concessions and contracts he approved, Dudley felt that in general, the people of Liberia gained more than they lost with Tubman at the helm. In addition,

Tubman was also adamantly anti-Communist. While U.S. officials suspected Communist penetration of many other regions of Africa, Liberia was consistently considered to be in the pro-Western camp. Pragmatically, the U.S. ambassador believed that one either worked with Tubman or one did not work at all. Tubman and his group were in such absolute control of the political and economic institutions of Liberia that it made little sense to criticize a regime that was not going to collapse anytime in the foreseeable future. Finally, Dudley believed that even though Liberian elections were probably rife with fraud, Tubman had such popularity with the Liberian people that he would be elected anyway.

It should be noted that the Tubman regime was often harshly criticized by human rights groups in the United States, including Dudley's former employee, the NAACP. The association's president, Walter White, was particularly concerned with the political situation in Liberia. Dudley was obviously stung by some of the criticisms, considering them at best ineffective (Tubman was not overly concerned with such attacks) and at worst harmful (the United States needed the cooperation of the Liberian government in order to pursue its interests). In response to these criticisms, Dudley argued that a more constructive approach would be to try and work with the Tubman government through the sending of more black Americans as advisors in law, economics, and politics.

In any event, Dudley was extraordinarily successful in working with Tubman. Their relationship, though always professional, was relaxed and confidential. Dudley arranged weekly meetings between Tubman, himself, and the president of the Firestone Company works to deal with any problems. As often as possible, the U.S. ambassador met personally with the Liberian president to introduce the representatives of new and prospective U.S. business interests. Official business was often conducted in a cordial atmosphere, sometimes over drinks in the evening hours. American business concerns were nearly unanimous in their praise of Dudley's untiring, and usually successful, efforts on their behalf.

Third, Dudley and his staff were convinced that Liberia was in desperate need of economic and technical assistance from the United States. For years, stories had circulated that visitors to various parts of Africa were struck by the fact that the areas under colonial control, though undeniably backward in terms of development, were far more advanced than Liberia. Since World War II the United States had had both a Public Health Mission and an Economic Mission in Liberia, but Dudley pushed for more. In late 1950 he was successful, as the United States and Liberia signed a Point Four agreement. Under the terms of the agreement, the United States would provide over sixty technicians and their necessary equipment to Liberia. In purely monetary terms, the U.S. contribution would amount to about $850,000 a year, and the program would go on for five to ten years. Five major areas of need were targeted in Liberia: infrastructure (roads, power, water); public administration; public health; education; and agriculture. For Dudley and the United States, Liberia became a ''proving ground'' for Point Four aid to Africa. Prompted by the U.S. show of aid, the Export-

Import Bank granted Liberia two large loans in 1951 for road and sewage construction.

In addition to his official activities, Dudley also acted unofficially to try and increase the black presence in the U.S. State Department. He did so in two basic ways. First, he fought for—and was successful in securing—transfers for black employees at the Monrovia embassy to other, non-African posts. Dudley was certainly aware of the severely limited opportunities for blacks in the Foreign Service and saw these transfers to other posts as a way of breaking the cycle that saw black diplomats begin and end their careers in Liberia. Second, he argued that his groundbreaking appointment should be only the first, and that the Truman administration should move to appoint another black ambassador as soon as practicable. Though he was disappointed that this second suggestion was never carried out, he comprehended the domestic political realities facing the Truman administration in terms of any kind of desegregation activity, even in the field of foreign policy.

In 1953, with the taking of office by the administration of Dwight D. Eisenhower, Dudley tendered his resignation as U.S. ambassador to Liberia. More than a few people in the State Department pushed for his reassignment elsewhere, and both Eisenhower and Secretary of State John Foster Dulles wrote glowing letters to Dudley, praising him for his work in cementing U.S.-Liberian relations. For Dudley, however, his career in diplomacy was over. He enjoyed the experience, but desired to return to his important work with the NAACP and to get his family back to the United States. He was satisfied with the work he had done and felt that he had accomplished his major objectives during his nearly five years in Liberia.

Upon his return home Dudley rejoined the NAACP, becoming director of the organization's Freedom Fund. In 1955 he returned to the New York City legal system, becoming a justice in the city's Domestic Relations Court until 1961. With the advent of the John F. Kennedy administration in 1961, Dudley briefly returned to the diplomatic fold, serving as a consultant to Kennedy's Africa Task Force and, in 1962, chairing the State Department's Bureau of African Affairs' Advisory Council's Education and Social Division. His name was also discussed as a possible nominee for the ambassadorship to recently independent Nigeria. At the same time, Dudley devoted himself to New York politics, serving as the president of the Borough of Manhattan, becoming the first black to run for statewide office when he ran for state attorney general in 1962, and becoming the first black chairman of the New York County Democratic Committee. In 1965 he was elected a justice on the New York State Supreme Court and served in that capacity until his retirement in 1985.

Works about Edward R. Dudley

Anderson, R. Earle. *Liberia: America's African Friend*. Chapel Hill: University of North
        Carolina Press, 1952.
Krenn, Michael L. " 'Outstanding Negroes' and 'Appropriate Countries': Some Facts,

Figures, and Thoughts on Black U.S. Ambassadors, 1949–1988." *Diplomatic History* 14 (Winter 1990): 131–141.

Miller, Jake C. *The Black Presence in American Foreign Affairs*. Lanham, MD: University Press of America, 1978.

MICHAEL L. KRENN

HERMANN FREDERICK EILTS (1922–   ), career

diplomat and Middle East specialist, played a central role as U.S. ambassador to Egypt in negotiating the Camp David Accords and the Egyptian-Israeli Peace Treaty of the 1970s.

Eilts was born in Weissenfels/Saale, Germany. His father had been a pre–World War I diplomat, serving in England, France, and the Middle East, and a wartime army officer; his mother was a schoolteacher. Unable to survive economically in inflation-ridden postwar Germany, Eilts's father took the family to the United States in 1926, settling in Scranton, Pennsylvania, where he became a railroad employee. Eilts obtained U.S. citizenship in 1930 through the naturalization of his father.

Deciding as a teenager to follow in his father's footsteps as a diplomat, in 1942 Eilts earned a bachelor's degree in history at Ursinus College in Pennsylvania, finishing in three years with distinction. He became interested in Middle Eastern affairs in particular during a brief stint at the Fletcher School of Law and Diplomacy before entering the army. As a soldier he earned Bronze Star and Purple Heart medals and seven campaign ribbons for combat service in North Africa and Europe, part of the time in military intelligence. After discharge as a first lieutenant, in 1947 Eilts earned an M.A. with distinction at the School of Advanced International Studies, Johns Hopkins University, and almost immediately joined the Foreign Service as a career officer. His early assignments included tours of duty in the American embassies at Teheran, Jidda, and Baghdad and the American consulate at Aden, which also had responsibility for the Imamate of Aden. Appointed Secretary of State John Foster Dulles's special advisor on Baghdad Pact affairs in the Department of State in 1957, Eilts next assumed responsibility for Arabian peninsula and Near East regional affairs in Washington during 1960–1961, followed by a year of study at the National War College and an assignment to the American embassy in London as political officer concerned with Middle East issues. Next he served as deputy chief of mission at the American embassy at Tripoli. In 1965 he entered upon the first of two relatively extended ambassadorships in two important Middle Eastern countries—envoy to Saudi Arabia (1965–1970) and to Egypt (1973–1979)—with a three-year assignment (1970–1973) as deputy commandant of the U.S. Army War College sandwiched in between. Eilts retired from the Foreign Service with thirty-two years of service after his last assignment abroad to the Cairo embassy.

Among honors gained while in government service, he received the Arthur S. Fleming Award for Distinguished Government Service in 1953, the Department of the Army Distinguished Civilian Service Decoration in 1972, and the Department of State Distinguished Honor Award in 1979. Later he received a

U.S. Army War College Distinguished Fellowship in 1991 and the prestigious American Foreign Service Cup award in 1992.

Beginning a second career in education, in 1979 Eilts became Distinguished University Professor of International Relations at Boston University. He organized and chaired the Department of International Relations until 1993, in addition to holding the position of director of the Center for International Relations. He was also academic coordinator for military education. Since 1993 he has been professor emeritus. Eight academic institutions have awarded him honorary doctorates: Ursinus College (1959), Boston University (1978), Dickinson School of Law (1978), Cairo University (1979), Juniata College (1980), Baltimore Hebrew College (1983), Merrimack College (1986), and the American University in Cairo (1995).

While still on active duty in the Foreign Service, Ambassador Eilts wrote ground-breaking histories of early Arab-American relations and highly important essays on contemporary Middle Eastern politics and American foreign policy. His numerous and exceptionally influential publications drew from the deep wells of his scholarship and decades of personal experience in the region. Fluent in Arabic and several European languages, he wrote with a depth of knowledge and discerning cultural and political familiarity with Middle Eastern affairs that was remarkable for the breadth of its scholarship, even as it was highly valued at the highest policy levels for its insight and wisdom. It is no exaggeration to say that, through his publications, Ambassador Eilts educated a generation of diplomats, foreign as well as American, about the varying histories, religions and cultures of the key players in the Middle East.

Eilts wrote as incisively about major historical figures and crises as he did about contemporary diplomacy and military and economic security in the Middle East. Through his books, articles and teaching, he continued active instruction of U.S. and other diplomats and policymakers about the intricacies and rooted problems of the international relations of the Persian Gulf. He made professional diplomats aware, often for the first time, of that region's complex mosaic of competing factions, parties, sects, and divergent colonial and post-independence histories. His scholarship was, therefore, an integral part of his contribution to peace in the region. Without his singular contributions as diplomat, scholar and teacher, American diplomats and representatives of Middle Eastern countries would have encountered each other in direct negotiations without the full benefit of shared knowledge of each others' politics, history and national interests.

In addition to his academic duties, while at Boston University Ambassador Eilts continued to play an active diplomatic role behind the scenes, consulting with and advising the U.S. government on Middle Eastern affairs and on continuing peace negotiations concerning the region. He was frequently called upon to advise other governments involved in the peace process as well, so greatly valued was his counsel. He met often with high-level Arab delegations, diplomats and heads of state or government. His counsel was widely respected and influential, and always emphasized that regional peace, prosperity and security meant persevering on the path begun with the deep compromises of the Camp David Accords.

Eilts became known as perhaps the leading senior Arabist of his time in the American Foreign Service. He followed a career closely linked throughout with U.S. policies toward the Middle East. His wide contacts on the highest levels, his language ability in Arabic, and his long experience in the region enabled him more than once over the years to play a key diplomatic role. As far back as 1949 Eilts and his wife, Helen J. Brew, made a lasting impression on the late King Abdul Aziz and his family by traversing the still-roadless and largely desolate Saudi Arabia by Jeep, the first Americans to do so. While a junior officer in the embassy at Jidda, Eilts came to know one of Abdul Aziz's sons, Prince Faisal. During the 1967 Arab-Israeli War, with Faisal now king and Eilts now U.S. ambassador, their close relationship (Faisal called him, alone among American ambassadors, ''akhi,'' or brother) aided the envoy in persuading the king not to give in to the urging of the latter's military command to join the war against Israel. Partly because of this personal relationship, during this episode of strained relations, Eilts decided to hold the American community in place in the country—without serious mishap, it developed—despite nervousness among some Americans on the scene and on the part of official Washington; he thereby preserved U.S.–Saudi Arabian relations on an even keel. Earlier, in 1959, while on assignment in Washington, he wrote and took a leading role in negotiating bilateral defense agreements with Turkey, Pakistan, and Iran and a year later helped persuade Congress to fund, through the United Nations Relief and Works Agency (UNRWA), vocational schools for Palestinian refugees. In 1964 the Department of State chose Eilts, by this time an acknowledged authority on Arab affairs at the age of only forty-two, to take the post as deputy chief of mission in the embassy at Tripoli; Washington had need of his experience there due to the importance of pending air-base negotiations with Libya.

It is in connection with the settlement of the Egyptian-Israeli conflict, however, that Eilts made his most important contributions to U.S. diplomacy in the Middle East. Specially chosen by Secretary of State Henry Kissinger as the first American ambassador accredited to the government of Egypt after a six-year hiatus in diplomatic relations (1967–1973), he effectively reopened Washington's lines of communication with that critically important Arab state. He soon established a close working relationship with President Anwar Sadat that stood him in good stead when he was required to present U.S. positions to the Egyptian government and, probably more important, to interpret Sadat's reactions to Washington (Eilts had a direct telephone link with Sadat, requested by the latter, in the chancery and his residence in Cairo). His contacts with Saudi royalty also aided the cause. Almost thirty years after he had impressed Abdul Aziz with his trek across Saudi Arabia, another of the old ruler's sons, Fahd, long known to Eilts, was Saudi Arabian king during this period of delicate negotiations on peace between Israel and Egypt brokered by the United States. Thus, as the knowledgeable, trusted U.S. envoy to Egypt, Eilts actively participated—behind the scenes—in putting together the two agreements calling for Israel's withdrawal from the Sinai Peninsula in 1974 and 1975, an effort highlighted by Secretary Kissinger's shuttle diplomacy to and within the Middle East.

The peace process came to a head later during the administration of President Jimmy Carter, after Egyptian President Anwar Sadat's dramatic journey to Jerusalem in 1977. Eilts directly contributed to negotiating the two Camp David Accords signed in the United States in 1978. Although he was not present himself for the talks leading to the final Egyptian-Israeli peace treaty, he frequently received instructions in Cairo from Washington to persuade Sadat to overrule unhelpful stands taken by the Egyptian delegation in Washington, instructions that he succeeded in carrying out more often than not. The parties signed the resultant treaty in March 1979. It was the culmination of Ambassador Eilts's career; with the accord between two of the major armed antagonists, the Middle East peace process had received a major impetus toward a general solution. Later he adjudged the diplomatic advances of 1974–1979 in which he had a hand the most satisfying accomplishments of his professional life.

Hermann Fr. Eilts amply demonstrated his strengths during those years in Cairo. His American colleagues and embassy subordinates privately labeled him "Hermann the German" due to his meticulous attention to detail, Old World courtesy, and highly organized approach to diplomacy. Intense, energetic, and always serious minded, he personified the idea of a workaholic. Leading by example, as ambassador he routinely put in one-hundred-hour-plus work weeks at that critical time. Although he was described as "the quintessential Arabist" in the citation to his 1992 Foreign Service Cup award, Eilts did not have the attributes of an area specialist in the traditional, relatively narrowly focused sense. He maintained an independence of outlook and judgment equaled by few of his contemporaries in the Foreign Service; at once an experienced, trained professional attuned to the nuances of politics in the region and a member of the inner policy circles on Middle East affairs in turn of both Presidents Nixon and Carter, he also maintained good relations with Israel's Prime Minister Menachem Begin (an Israeli publication referred to him at that time as an "ambassador's ambassador"). He was a professional, but not a professional Arabist, in the field of diplomacy.

In 1994 Eilts held that the most disappointing aspect of his professional career related—like his proudest accomplishments—to the ups and downs of the peace process in the Middle East during the more than three decades following 1947. One of the setbacks was the newly installed Kennedy administration's lack of interest in following through on a hard-fought agreement, negotiated with Tel Aviv over a period of two years, to resettle 100,000 Palestinian refugees in Israel; another was the Reagan administration's failure to maintain the momentum toward an overall settlement in the region after Camp David and the Egyptian-Israeli treaty. Nonetheless, Eilts's contributions to finding peaceful solutions in the Middle East, a major achievement from the perspective of American national interests, will long be noted in any consideration of U.S. policies toward the region.

Works by Hermann F. Eilts

A Conversation with Ambassador Hermann F. Eilts: The Dilemma in the Persian Gulf. Washington, D.C.: American Enterprise Institute, 1980.

"Saudi Arabia: Traditionalism versus Modernism—A Royal Dilemma." In *Ideology and Power in the Middle East*, eds. P. J. Chelkowski and R. J. Pranger. Durham: Duke University Press, 1988.

Toward Arab-Israeli Peace: Report of a Study Group. Washington, DC: Brookings Institution, 1988.

"The U.S. and Egypt." In *The Middle East—Ten Years after Camp David*, ed. W. B. Quandt. Washington, DC: Brookings Institution, 1988.

"Egypt." In *The Middle East*, ed. M. Adams. New York: Facts on File, 1989.

"Reflections on the Suez Crisis: Security in the Middle East." In *Suez 1956: The Crisis and Its Consequences*, eds. W. Louis and R. Owen. Oxford: Clarendon Press, 1989.

Interviews with the author, September 18, 1994; October 16, 1994.

Works about Hermann Fr. Eilts

Kaplan, Robert D. *The Arabists: The Romance of an American Elite.* New York: Free Press, 1993.

Quandt, William B. *Camp David: Peacemaking and Politics.* Washington, DC: Brookings Institution, 1986.

HENRY E. MATTOX

ALEXANDER HILL EVERETT (1790–1847) was an

American diplomat to the Netherlands, Spain, and China who proved to be a keen observer of international politics, but lacked the requisite social skills to be a good diplomat.

Born in Boston on March 19, 1790, Everett was the eldest son of the preacher Oliver Everett and Lucy Hill Everett. His younger brother Edward was to have a brilliant career as governor of Massachusetts, minister to Great Britain, president of Harvard University, secretary of state, and U.S. senator. But Alexander himself was also promising. At sixteen he graduated from Harvard, the youngest and best member of his class, having already distinguished himself as a public speaker. It was at that point that his journal articles began to appear.

John Quincy Adams hired the gifted Alexander to work for his firm in Boston, where the young man received his legal training. This formed the basis for a lifelong friendship, as evidenced by their correspondence. Everett was first exposed to international diplomacy and European court life while his mentor was serving as minister plenipotentiary to Russia between 1809 and 1811. Adams took the nineteen-year-old along as his private secretary. After returning in early 1812, Everett practiced law for a few years in Boston. In 1815 he accompanied William Eustis, envoy extraordinary and minister plenipotentiary of the United States to the Netherlands, as his secretary of legation.

Diplomatic life in the Kingdom of the Netherlands was anything but dynamic and proved to be a bitter disappointment to Adams's protégé. While even for Eustis there was little to do, Everett spent his days copying letters, making translations into French, and performing various humdrum administrative tasks. He divided his copious free time between study in the Royal Library and composing letters to Lucretia Orne Peabody, his fiancée, who had stayed behind in New Hampshire. Social life in The Hague had little to offer diplomats seeking diversion. Yet for the retiring Everett this was not such a heavy cross to bear; he was even grateful for the lack of social stimulation, as he found it difficult to make contacts with other people. Eustis confirmed that Everett lacked the aplomb of a good diplomat. He described his secretary to President James Madison at an early stage as ''a man of the closet devoted to books, knowing very little of what passes around him,—capable of labor and research, but without the manners, habits and intercourse which are necessary to information and external business.''

Everett's sojourn in the Netherlands did not agree with him. By January 1816 he was wondering whether he would not do better to return to Boston and enter politics. John Quincy Adams, envoy extraordinary and minister plenipotentiary to Great Britain at that time, asked the secretary of state to make Everett his legation secretary, but another was appointed instead. The only advice he could give Everett was to return to Boston and find his way as a lawyer in American politics. He had no doubt that the young man would make something of himself and would be asked for a public office.

In the spring Everett decided to take Adam's advice, though he was not particularly interested in a legal career. The pressure normally associated with the profession would not leave him much time for literature, he feared. By September he was back in Boston, where he and Lucretia married.

The Netherlands' decision to staff the Washington legation with a chargé d'affaires and the subsequent recall of Eustis made it possible for Everett to succeed Eustis in that capacity. Only after Eustis had returned to New York in July 1818 did President James Monroe actually appoint Everett, who was Secretary of State John Quincy Adams's favorite candidate for the job. Not only did Adams send Everett his diplomatic instructions that summer, but he also enclosed some personal advice with respect to his required social behavior.

Armed with Adams's counsel and the best intentions, Everett set off for the Kingdom of the Netherlands, where he presented his credentials to the king in Brussels on January 4, 1819. Thanks to the good impression his predecessor had made, he was well received. The mutual respect would not last long, however.

One of Everett's first tasks was to prosecute the claims of American merchants against the Dutch government. The merchants had asked to be compensated for the merchandise seized in 1809 and 1810 by the Kingdom of Holland. However, the present government was unwilling to accept responsibility for acts committed by King Louis at the instigation of his brother, Emperor Napoleon. Everett rose to the challenge, undaunted by his predecessor's failure to vindicate the disgruntled merchants. In doing so, he apparently forgot the sage counsel of his mentor and offended the government in an unnecessarily sharp, supercilious manner.

Everett's closely reasoned arguments had no influence on the Dutch minister of foreign affairs. When in early 1820 it became clear that Everett did not know when to give up, the Netherlands instructed its chargé d'affaires in Washington to ask that the matter be dropped. The United States finally decided to try the French instead, who finally agreed to pay the American victims of Napoleon's policy the equivalent of half a million dollars in compensation in 1831.

Everett's *Sturm und Drang* diplomacy did not make him popular at court. On the contrary, King William did not invite him to dinner, while to other diplomatic festivities he was not permitted to bring his wife. Alexander and Lucretia lived in social isolation and made no friends among the resident diplomats of any country. Inevitably, Everett's seclusion colored his impression of the country in a negative sense.

While Everett may have failed to carve out a niche for himself in the Netherlands, he proved to be a keen observer of European politics. His thorough reports won the admiration of Adams. Gathering information about European politics in the Netherlands was not always as simple as one might expect. Everett complained that the Netherlands had lost its political importance and was no longer an important European listening post. He even suggested that the State Department move the legation to Prussia. Adams considered the proposal, but replied that in light of the American economy, Congress was reluctant to spend any more on the Foreign Service than it already did. That transferring the legation might well offend the Netherlands apparently did not occur to Everett. Tact was not his strongest suit.

Everett's dispatches to the State Department (totaling an average of twenty-six per year) formed the basis for a portrait he wrote of contemporary politics. *Europe; or, A General Survey of the Present Situation of the Principal Powers; with Conjectures on Their Future Prospects*, written by "a Citizen of the United States," was published in Boston in 1822. It was Everett's first and remains his best-known book.

Europe exudes its author's faith in progress. Everett was convinced that the rise of democratic and republican ideas was irreversible. In successive chapters he discussed the politics of the various European countries and then considered the balance of power between them. In the final chapter of *Europe* Everett sketched two opposing tendencies and their possible consequences. He summarized these tendencies as (1) the progress of civilization through the expansion of liberal principles throughout the Christian world and (2) the spread of Russia's conservative ideological influence, which could prepare the way for that nation's military domination of the rest of Europe. Everett believed that Russia's growing influence in Western Europe was the only way to draw those nations closer together. Once the nominal independence of and enmity between the various states had been brought to an end, the progress of civilization would exercise the same positive influence on the new, composite government that it had on the individual ones. Everett foresaw a united European commonwealth based on rational and liberal principles. He realized, however, that the final political unification of the continent under the banner of liberalism was a long way off, but comforted himself with the idea that the United States was already enjoying just such a progressive and republican form of government.

What Everett had to say in *Europe* about the Netherlands was very negative and undiplomatic. He considered the creation of the Kingdom of the Netherlands by the Congress of Vienna as an impotent measure to exert some control over France. In his opinion, unifying Belgium (the former Southern or Austrian Netherlands) and better still the whole territory of the Netherlands with France would have balanced power in Europe more effectively. In effect, the American diplomat doubted the right of the country to which he was accredited to exist. Not only that, he also doubted that the unification of the Southern and Northern Netherlands would last.

Although Everett was positive about King William I, he was of the opinion that the House of Orange had a fatal influence on the history of the country. He presented the Netherlands in his book as the sorry spectacle of a nation in decline and even expected the soil to return to the ocean. That Everett's views of the Netherlands and the House of Orange were not well received by the Dutch is hardly surprising. Being a diplomat, he published the book anonymously, but it was not long before he was identified. He had sent the manuscript to his brother Edward and asked him to pass it around his friends and acquaintances. On the other hand, the two-volume German translation of his brainchild, published at Bamberg in 1823, stated his name plainly: *Europa oder Uebersicht der Lage der Europäischen Hauptmächte im Jahre 1821. Von einem amerikanischen Diplomaten. (Mr. Alex. H. Everett, Chargé d'affaires der Vereinigten Staaten am Königl. Niederländ. Hofe.)*. Yet Everett was not worried about his reputation and doubted that anyone in the Netherlands had heard about the publication.

About the reception of his book in the Netherlands Everett was silent; it was his successor, Christopher Hughes, who had to face the consequences and reported about its negative effects. The rest of Europe, meanwhile, was very much interested in Everett's book. Besides German, it was also translated into French and Spanish and was admired by political scientists and economists alike. In the United States, too, *Europe* was well received. Among others, former President James Madison praised it. According to the *North American Review*, the book was so outstanding that English reviewers could not believe that it was written by an American.

Because his work for the legation was so undemanding, Everett could devote most of his time to study. He now turned his attention to the population theory of Malthus and wrote his *New Ideas on Population: With Remarks on the Theories of Malthus and Godwin* in the winter of 1822–1823. The book attempts to refute the theory that population growth depends on the means of survival and to prove the traditional view that such growth is the key to prosperity. The work's translation into French indicates that it, too, attracted international attention.

In the spring of 1824 Everett returned to the United States for a six-month furlough. He ultimately stayed much longer, however, since John Quincy Adams's election to the presidency raised his hopes of a higher diplomatic appointment. Indeed, the president decided to send Everett as envoy extraordinary and minister plenipotentiary to Madrid in order to convince the Spanish government to recognize the independence of its former colonies in Latin America. Despite Everett's best efforts, however, he was unsuccessful; a decade would pass before Spain was willing to negotiate, by which time Everett had long since returned to Boston following Andrew Jackson's electoral victory in 1828.

The diplomatic ambiance of the Spanish capital afforded Everett an exceptional view of events in Latin America, besides the new states' relations with one another and with Europe and the United States. He also recorded his observations during this time and published them as a kind of sequel to his *Europe*. The new book, a veritable ode to the United States, was entitled *America; or, A General Survey of the Political Situation of the Several Powers of the Western Continent, with Conjectures on Their Future Prospects* and was published at Philadelphia in 1827. Again Everett's name did not appear on the title page, but simply "By a Citizen of the United States, Author of 'Europe' &c." The following year a German translation was published.

In *America* Everett divided Christendom into three parts, each with its own political system: the United States, with a liberal form of government; the European continent, over which Russia with its despotic government held sway; and finally the British Empire, with a mixed political system in the homeland. Russia would soon unify the European continent as a single military state, while the British Empire would remain the scene of conflict between two irreconcilable principles, despotism and liberalism.

In Everett's opinion, there was no way of knowing whether President Monroe's message would effectively discourage European interference with Latin America. British policy was crucial, and it seemed to him that it was in favor of Latin America. The independence of the former Spanish colonies in that region and the prospect of trade with them was inevitably more attractive to the British than the restoration of Spanish power there. Britain's recognition of the colonies' independence had infuriated Spain and the Great Powers on the continent. On the other hand, the new Latin American regimes were thankful for British support, which, moreover, squared nicely with U.S. policy. Thus Great Britain and the United States, who had just been at war with one another, arrived at cooperation and friendship by coincidence. Being in the best interest of both, the new relationship would last, Everett predicted.

Everett foresaw that the importance of the United States for Great Britain would continue to grow, whereas Great Britain would gradually become less vital to the United States. While the latter would steadily expand as a result of its rapidly growing population, prosperity, and political power, Everett expected that Great Britain would lose its overseas colonies and therefore shrink, until finally the homeland would be all that remained.

The final chapter of *America* elaborated further on the inexorable rise of U.S. power and prosperity. As in his *New Ideas on Population*, Everett argued that population is the natural source of prosperity. The unprecedented growth of the U.S. population distinguished it from other powers and was the direct result of the nation's liberal form of government, which Everett considered the source of American prosperity. The author was convinced that the United States would soon become the most populous, most prosperous, and most powerful society the world had ever known, exceeding the combined power of the European states at the end of the nineteenth century.

Whereas *Europe* views Russian domination of the continent as a necessary step toward European unification, *America* sees the encroachment of Russia as a return of barbarism. Russian hegemony could be prevented, according to Everett, only if America would support the European continent. Everett thus foresaw a future European-American alliance against Russia. Thanks to his futuristic vision of Russia and America as the two superpowers, with Europe increasingly dependent on the latter, Everett has been numbered—with Tocqueville—among the largely forgotten prophets of the Cold War. Indeed, the Frenchman's views on the future roles of America and Russia may have been influenced by Alexander and Edward Everett, whom he met in the United States.

After returning from Spain, Everett was made editor of the Bostonian *North American Review* in 1830, a position he held for the next five years. Established in 1815, the journal mainly featured critical essays and book reviews. Everett published many articles in it before, during, and after his editorship; these were collected along with a number of other publications in his two-volume *Critical and Miscellaneous Essays*, which appeared in Boston in 1845 and 1846. His contributions to the *North American Review* dealt with literary, cultural, economic, and political affairs. In discussing European and American politics in connection with books that had appeared on these subjects, Everett elaborated on his boundless admiration for his homeland. Unlike Europe, burdened by interminable wars brought on by discord and rivalry, the Union was in an excellent position, he wrote, to guarantee the peace among the growing number of states.

Alongside his activities as editor of the *North American Review*, Everett threw himself into Massachusetts politics, for which he proved to be utterly unsuited. Though he had repeatedly served in the Senate of Massachusetts as a member of the National Republican Party, in 1834 his fellow party members decided that he could no longer run for office, whereupon he joined the Democrats. After moving to Norfolk, he twice ran unsuccessfully for the House of Representatives on the Democratic ticket. Not surprisingly, his change of party was held against him by his former political supporters, who accused him of opportunism. But the Democrats also had their doubts about the sincerity of their new comrade.

Only in 1840 did the Democrats seem to gain faith in Everett, when President Martin Van Buren appointed him special agent to investigate complaints against the American consul in Havana. When a Whig moved into the White House shortly thereafter, Everett accepted the presidency of Jefferson College in Louisiana, but was soon forced to leave the South for health reasons. When the Democrat James K. Polk was elected president, Everett's luck improved: In March 1845 he was appointed America's first commissioner to China. His instructions were to look after American interests in East Asia and to negotiate a treaty with Japan. But once again he was dogged by ill health. After breaking off his journey out, he tried again in 1846. This time he did reach China, but died not long afterward in Canton on June 29, 1847.

Works by Alexander Hill Everett

Alexander Hill Everett published a great number of articles in various American periodicals, especially the *North American Review* and the *United States Magazine and Democratic Review*. Also, a number of his addresses were published. See the bibliography in the work of Elizabeth Evans.

Europe; or, A General Survey of the Present Situation of the Principal Powers; with Conjectures on Their Future Prospects. Boston: Oliver Everett, Cummings and Hilliard, 1822.

New Ideas on Population: With Remarks on the Theories of Malthus and Godwin. Boston: Cummings, Hilliard and Co., 1823; 2nd ed., 1826. Reprint. New York: Augustus M. Kelley, 1970.

America; or, A General Survey of the Political Situation of the Several Powers of the Western Continent, with Conjectures on Their Future Prospects. Philadelphia: H. C. Carey and I. Lea, 1827.

Critical and Miscellaneous Essays. 2 vols. Boston: J. Monroe and Company, 1845–1846.

Works about Alexander Hill Everett

Draper, Theodore. ''The Idea of the 'Cold War' and Its Prophets: On Tocqueville and Others.'' *Encounter* 52, no. 2 (February 1979): 34–45.

Evans, Elizabeth, ed. ''Alexander Hill Everett: Prose Pieces and Correspondence.'' *John Colet Archive of American Literature, 1620–1920*, no. 2 (Summer 1974).

Gollwitzer, Heinz. *Geschichte des weltpolitischen Denkens.* 2 vols. Göttingen: Vandenhoeck und Ruprecht, 1972–1982. Vol. 1, 408–425.

Hoekstra, Peter. *Thirty-seven Years of Holland-American Relations, 1803 to 1840.* Grand Rapids, MI, and Paterson, NJ: Eerdmans-Sevensma Co., 1916.

Kohn, Hans. *American Nationalism: An Interpretative Essay.* New York: Macmillan, 1957.

McLaughlin, Andrew C., ed. ''Letters of John Quincy Adams to Alexander H. Everett, 1811–1837.'' *American Historical Review* 11 (1905–1906): 88–116, 332–54.

van Minnen, Cornelis A. *American Diplomats in the Netherlands, 1815–1850.* New York: St. Martin's Press, 1993.

Westermann, J. C. *The Netherlands and the United States: Their Relations in the Beginning of the Nineteenth Century.* The Hague: Martinus Nijhoff, 1935.

CORNELIS A. VAN MINNEN

BENJAMIN FRANKLIN (1706–1790), printer, philosopher, statesman, and diplomat, secured French aid for the American Revolution and helped negotiate the peace settlement with Great Britain.

Franklin was born in Boston in 1706, the youngest son of Peter and Abigail Folger Franklin. Franklin's father intended that Benjamin enter the clergy, but he could not afford the formal schooling. At age twelve Franklin apprenticed in his brother James's print shop. He left for Philadelphia in 1723 and set up his own shop in 1730.

Franklin devoted the next eighteen years to his printing business and became increasingly involved in public affairs. His most famous publication was *Poor Richard's Almanac*, an extended exposition on his philosophy of personal improvement, hard work, and pragmatism. This spirit led him into the study of science, where he gained fame for his experiments with electricity. He was active in philanthropy and education, helping to found the Library Company of Philadelphia, the American Philosophical Society, and the University of Pennsylvania. Franklin's local prominence also drew him into politics. He retired from the printing business in 1748 and spent most of the rest of his life in various public offices. Before the revolution he served as a member of the Pennsylvania Assembly (1751–1764), deputy postmaster for the colonies (1753–1774), and Pennsylvania's colonial agent in London (1757–1762 and 1765–1775). By 1775 Franklin represented Massachusetts, Georgia, and New Jersey as well.

Franklin's career in imperial and colonial politics formed the principles he later applied to American diplomacy. Franklin took an active part in preparing Pennsylvania's defenses during King George's War (1744–1748). The threat of French and Spanish privateers in Delaware Bay led him to write *Plain Truth; or, Serious Considerations on the Present State of the City of Philadelphia, and Province of Pennsylvania*, in which he called for unity and preparation to meet foreign danger. In 1754 he wrote the Albany Plan for colonial union. He laid out the theoretical basis for manifest destiny a century before the term was coined. In 1751 he wrote *Observations Concerning the Increase of Mankind*, arguing that the American population would double every twenty-five years, requiring westward expansion. He believed that colonial security and prosperity added to British wealth and power. He returned to this theme in his 1759 pamphlet, *The Interest of Great Britain Considered with Regard to Her Colonies and the Acquisitions of Canada and Guadaloupe*, which he wrote in response to the rumor that Great Britain intended to return recently conquered Canada to France in exchange for the sugar island of Guadeloupe. He argued that Canada was necessary for American security, and that American security would tie the colonies closer to Great Britain. National unity, westward expansion, and possession of Canada remained constant themes in Franklin's diplomacy.

Franklin's two tours in London as colonial agent constituted the beginning of his formal diplomatic career. His first tour served as his entrance into the intellectual circles of Europe. St. Andrews and Oxford offered him honorary degrees in 1759 and 1762, and from then on he was known as "Doctor." His second mission brought him to the center of the imperial crises that led to the American Revolution. For a time, the communications lag between London and the colonies prevented him from keeping pace with colonial positions on taxation. He offered no objection to the Stamp Act and even recommended a stamp distributor for Pennsylvania before learning of American objections. In 1766 he made the distinction between internal and external taxes that served as the rationale for the Townshend Duties. By 1768 he was fully opposed to imperial taxation and aided the American opposition wherever he could. In 1772 he received from a member of Parliament some letters written by Massachusetts Governor Thomas Hutchinson that supported parliamentary taxation, which he passed on to Massachusetts House Speaker Thomas Cushing. He was accused of tampering with the mail and was fired as deputy postmaster. He left for Philadelphia in March 1775, convinced that conflict was inevitable.

Franklin arrived home in May 1775 and was immediately elected to the Continental Congress. He served on the Committee of Secret Correspondence (later the Committee on Foreign Affairs), where he wrote the instructions for commercial agent Silas Deane. Franklin later served on the committees that drafted the Declaration of Independence and the Model Treaty.

Franklin's first diplomatic assignment under the Continental Congress was a mission to Canada. Two American forces invaded Canada in the fall of 1775. They captured Montreal but failed to take Quebec. In March 1776 Congress sent Franklin, Samuel Chase, Charles Carroll of Carrollton, and the Reverend John Carroll, S.J., to learn Canadian opinion. The commissioners arrived in Montreal in April and soon discovered that the political mission was as hopeless as the military effort had become. Franklin observed that the French Catholics were openly hostile to the Americans, and at least half of the few English Protestants were loyalists. He urged Congress to withdraw the army and fortify the border. Seeing no reason to continue, he left Canada on May 11.

The Canada mission was only a prelude to Franklin's most important post, commissioner and minister to France. In September 1776 Congress appointed Franklin, Arthur Lee, and Silas Deane commissioners to negotiate an alliance with France. Congress had hoped that the lure of American trade alone could bring French aid. However, military setbacks led Congress to instruct the commissioners to do whatever was needed to bring France into the war. France had offered secret aid through a dummy corporation administered by Pierre-Augustin Caron de Beaumarchais, but the Compte de Vergennes was unwilling to do anything more until France was better prepared for a confrontation with Great Britain. Instead, he waited for more explicit assurances that the United States would continue to fight.

Franklin's appointment was such an assurance. He was the most prominent

American of his day, and Congress clearly expected that he would take the lead in negotiations. Vergennes secretly received the commissioners on December 28, 1776, but could offer nothing more than the secret help already being provided. Franklin broadened his diplomacy to include French society as well as the French government. He may be seen as the father of public diplomacy. He brought his skills as a pamphleteer to bear in his contributions to the French government periodical *Affaires de l'Angleterre et de l'Amerique*. As Franklin moved through French society, he acted as the representative of an idea as well as a nation. He adroitly played on Parisian fascination with Quakers and allowed the French to believe that he himself was a Quaker. He affected a simple dress and manner, in deliberate contrast to the other diplomats and officials at Versailles, and portrayed himself as a rustic backwoods philosopher, despite the fact that he had spent much of his life at the center of British culture. Franklin's greatest achievement in the first year of his mission was to keep the French interested in and enthusiastic about the American cause, despite American failures on the battlefield.

Throughout 1777 France continued to grant loans to the United States (which would total thirty-five million livres by the end of the war), but refused to recognize American independence. Vergennes knew that such a move meant certain war with Great Britain and preferred to wait until the completion of the naval rearmament program. The Americans renewed their request for a treaty in September 1777, only to be refused. Silas Deane proposed to threaten reconciliation with Great Britain, but Franklin and Lee disagreed. By early 1778 the French navy was strong enough to risk war. The Americans, buoyed by news of the American victory at Saratoga, continued to seek an alliance. France and the United States concluded two treaties on February 6, 1778. The commercial treaty embodied the reciprocal trade policy laid out in the Model Treaty. The military treaty bound each power to protect the other's territory in the Western Hemisphere and forbade either from signing a separate peace.

Despite Franklin's successes, there were certain problems with his diplomacy. One was his age and periodic illness, combined with a heavy workload. Franklin acted as naval agent, admiralty judge, consul, and military recruiter in addition to commissioner. Another problem was his trusting nature, which made him ignorant of the network of British spies that surrounded the American mission. The most serious problem, according to his critics, was his personal style. Franklin flirted with the ladies at court and lavished public gratitude on the French king and nation. Some believed his activities to be at least undignified and at most unrepublican.

The problem of Franklin's style came to the forefront when Congress reorganized the mission in late 1777, recalling Silas Deane and replacing him with John Adams. Arthur Lee, who was always suspicious of Deane's commercial activities, accused Deane of using his office for private gain. Deane responded with a newspaper article accusing Lee and his family of disloyalty to the alliance and pro-British sympathies. Franklin did not believe Lee's charges and generally supported Deane. Adams was one of the Lee family's strongest allies. Adams also generally opposed Franklin's methods of diplomacy. Congress temporarily removed the conflict in September 1778 when it abolished the commission and named Franklin sole minister to France.

Franklin was the only real choice for minister plenipotentiary. Even John Adams, his harshest critic, believed that recalling the doctor would do more harm than good. Vergennes was comfortable with Franklin, more so than with any other American diplomat. When Adams returned to Paris as peace commissioner in 1780, Vergennes tried to ignore him, preferring to deal with Franklin. Franklin understood the working of the French court and knew how to approach Vergennes, whereas Adams spent much of his time telling Vergennes how to run the war. Franklin also opposed sending ministers abroad before knowing if they would be received, believing that no other nation could help the United States as much as France.

Franklin's duties as minister were largely the same as those as a member of the commission. His most important task was securing financial and military aid, and he negotiated a twelve-million-livre grant in 1779. He continued to commission privateers, both to raid British commerce and to take prisoners. Americans taken captive by the British were charged with treason and faced execution. Franklin urged the capture of British sailors as security for American lives. American-licensed ships operated in European seas throughout 1778, and Franklin oversaw the first British-American prisoner exchange in March 1779.

The harmony between Franklin and the French court did not always translate into harmony between the two nations or into success on the battlefield. The first Franco-American collaboration was the failed attempt to liberate Newport in the summer of 1778. For the first two years the French army brought no military victories. France's alliance with Spain complicated the military situation. Spain entered the war as an ally of France, but not of the United States, in April 1779. Spain had no interest in the American question, but hoped to regain Gibraltar and Minorca. Vergennes therefore could not commit resources to the American war as full as Congress wanted. Some in Congress began to resent both France and Franklin. The failure of American arms worsened the American mood. The British army captured Charleston in May 1780 and for the next year ran almost unchecked through the South. British success sent Congress into a panic, looking for a quick end to the war. Vergennes, fearful for French finances, also wanted to end the war.

In March 1781 Franklin asked Congress to recall him, pleading age and ill health. Congress ignored his request. In June Congress named Franklin, John Adams, John Jay, Henry Laurens, and Thomas Jefferson as peace commissioners. Both Congress and Vergennes feared that John Adams, acting as peace commissioner, would alienate France and prolong the war by making access to the Newfoundland fisheries a condition of peace. The panic preceded the revival of Franco-American arms. Lord Cornwallis surrendered his army at Yorktown in October, an act that led to the collapse of Lord North's government and the suspension of British offensive action.

The Marquis of Rockingham succeeded North as prime minister and hoped to separate the United States from the rest of Great Britain's enemies. Franklin himself sent the new government a note in March 1782 indicating a willingness to negotiate. The Rockingham ministry chose Richard Oswald, a Scottish slave trader with a reputation for reasonableness, to negotiate with the Americans. Oswald met with Franklin at the doctor's home at Passy in April. Franklin did not engage in official negotiations and reminded Oswald that no agreement could be made without France or the other American commissioners. However, Franklin did lay the groundwork for a settlement. He told Oswald that the quickest way to peace would be for Great Britain to cede all of Canada to the United States. If Great Britain wanted the United States to compensate loyalists for confiscated property, he argued, the money could come from the sale of Canadian lands. Franklin wrote these proposals into a letter, gambling that Oswald would not make it public, and did not reveal his proposals to Vergennes.

Formal negotiations waited on the assembly of the American mission and the reorganization of the British government. Rockingham died on July 1 and was replaced by Lord Shelburne, who favored a rapid settlement. John Jay arrived at Paris on June 23 and with Franklin conducted the bulk of the negotiations. John Adams did not arrive until late October. Henry Laurens arrived in late November, and Thomas Jefferson never left for Europe. On July 10 Franklin presented Oswald with "necessary" and "advisable" articles of peace. Franklin's "necessary" articles were British recognition of American independence, a boundary settlement, the reduction of Canada to its pre-1774 boundaries, and American access to the Newfoundland fisheries. The "advisable" articles were more ambitious. Franklin asked for reparations to Americans who had lost their property, an apology from Great Britain, a reciprocal trade agreement, and the cession of Canada. More cautious than before, he refused to write his proposals down, forcing Oswald to report them from memory. The two sets of articles served as the basis for negotiations.

Franklin's illnesses often left negotiations to John Jay. Jay's failed mission to Spain made him suspicious of French motives and eager to make a separate peace. The differences between Franklin and Jay were more formal than substantive. Franklin was already leaning in the direction of a separate peace, but would not risk a formal rupture with France. Franklin and Jay met with Vergennes and Joseph Matthias Gerard de Rayneval on August 10, and Vergennes told the Americans that their claims to the western territories were extravagant and hinted that France would not support them. In response, Jay favored breaking Congress's instructions. Franklin was apprehensive, but eventually agreed.

By late October the American and British negotiators broadly agreed on territorial limits. Fish, debts, and loyalists were the main sticking points. Franklin vehemently opposed any compensations to the leading loyalists, no doubt influenced by his son William's loyalism. He agreed to the payment of prewar debts and argued that such an agreement was payment for the fisheries. Oswald and the Americans signed the preliminary articles on November 30, 1782. Franklin had the task of explaining American actions to Vergennes. He wrote to Vergennes on December 17 and tried to convince the foreign minister that the Americans had tricked the British. He reminded Vergennes that the treaty was provisional, subject to a general agreement, and argued that despite British efforts, the alliance was not broken.

The American commissioners hoped to sign a commercial treaty, but the provisional treaty brought down the Shelburne ministry. The succeeding Fox-North coalition refused to make any further concessions. The Treaty of Paris, signed on September 3, 1783, read the provisional treaty into a general settlement. With the final treaty signed, Franklin again asked to be recalled. He returned home in 1785.

Retirement from the diplomatic corps did not mean retirement from public life. Franklin served as one of Pennsylvania's delegates to the Constitutional Convention. He contributed little to debate, although he did serve on the committee that drafted the Great Compromise, but rather lent his prestige to the convention and its final result. He left public office in October 1788 when he stepped down as president of the Supreme Executive Council of Pennsylvania, but remained interested in public affairs, serving as president of the Pennsylvania Abolition Society and signing the first petition against the slave trade presented to the new Congress. He died at his home in Philadelphia on April 17, 1790.

Franklin used his prestige as a scientist and philosopher and his experience as a colonial agent to keep French aid flowing despite political difficulties and military setbacks. This was his greatest achievement as a diplomat. He moved easily in intellectual circles and quickly mastered the art of European diplomacy. However, his personal style and implicit trust in the French court left him open to the charge that he was willing to accept French domination of the war. Although less confrontational than his colleagues, Jay and Adams, Franklin was just as willing to sign a separate peace when the situation demanded it. His role in securing French aid and an advantageous peace place him in the front rank of American ambassadors.

Work by Benjamin Franklin

The Papers of Benjamin Franklin. Ed. Leonard W. Labaree and William B. Wilcox. 31 vols. to date. New Haven: Yale University Press, 1959–   .

Works about Benjamin Franklin

Dull, Jonathan R. *Franklin the Diplomat*. Philadelphia: American Philosophical Association, 1982.

Morris, Richard B. *The Peacemakers: The Great Powers and American Independence*. New York: Harper and Row, 1965.

Stourzh, Gerald. *Benjamin Franklin and American Foreign Policy*. Chicago: University of Chicago Press, 1954.

Van Doren, Carl. *Benjamin Franklin*. New York: Viking Press, 1938.

ROBERT W. SMITH

JOHN KENNETH GALBRAITH (1908–) has been

an influential author, economist, economic historian, social critic, professor, and ambassador to India.

The son of Scottish immigrants, William and Catherine Galbraith, John Kenneth Galbraith was born and raised in Iona Station, an isolated town in rural Ontario, Canada. He grew up in the Calvinist tradition in a successful farming family that was interested in politics. At Ontario Agricultural College, then a branch of the University of Toronto, from which he graduated in 1931, he majored in agricultural economics. A research scholarship allowed him to attend the University of California at Berkeley, which granted him a Ph.D. in economics in 1934. His first teaching position was as an instructor at Harvard University, where he taught economics for five years. In 1937 he married Catherine (Kitty) Atwater, a graduate student at Radcliffe; they had four sons. After teaching at Princeton University for one year as an assistant professor, he turned to service for the U.S. government during World War II (during his teaching career, he had adopted U.S. citizenship). In 1949 he returned to Harvard as Paul H. Warburg Professor of Economics and remained there until his retirement in 1975.

Galbraith's government service began in 1940 as the economic advisor to Chester Davis, agricultural member of the National Defense Advisory Committee. The following year he moved to the Office of Price Administration, where he became deputy administrator in 1942. His blunt, vocal defense of comprehensive price controls, a hallmark of his economic views, failed to convince congressional and business leaders, whose criticisms led President Franklin D. Roosevelt to ask him to resign.

In 1945 Galbraith took a leave of absence from *Fortune Magazine*, where as a member of the editorial board he had developed a characteristic fluid writing style, to head the United States Strategic Bombing Survey, which evaluated the consequences of wartime bombing on the war-making capacity of the Axis powers. The report concluded that the bombing of Germany had been relatively ineffectual in hindering the German manufacturing of war materials. In the postwar period he directed the State Department's Office of Economic Security Policy, which helped design the economic recovery of Germany and Japan.

Galbraith was a lifelong liberal and "New Dealer" who favored government involvement in the economy. When Illinois Governor Adlai E. Stevenson campaigned for the presidency in 1952 and 1956, Galbraith served on the campaign staff as a speech writer. During the Eisenhower years he was a blunt critic of the administration's economic policies and chaired the domestic policy committee of the Democratic Advisory Council, which was formed in the late 1950s to provide alternatives and draft policies for a future Democratic administration. From 1956 to 1960 he chaired the council's economic panel.

Galbraith first met Senator John F. Kennedy when Kennedy was a student at Harvard. He became an early supporter of Kennedy's bid for the Democratic presidential nomination and actively and successfully solicited academic and liberal support for the Senator. During the 1960 campaign Galbraith served as Kennedy's agricultural advisor. During the administration Galbraith served on the foreign economic policy task force. Although he was an internationally recognized economist, he was also a controversial one, and Kennedy decided not to appoint him Secretary of the Treasury in order to avoid unduly agitating conservatives or even moderates during the Senate confirmation hearings.

In March 1961 Kennedy named Galbraith ambassador to India. India remained pivotal to American interests in Asia, and Kennedy was impressed with Galbraith's familiarity with its immense economic problems, his personal friendship with Indian Prime Minister Jawaharlal Nehru, and his stature as an economic and social observer. On a personal level, Kennedy admired Galbraith's intelligence and keen wit. Impatient with what he perceived as State Department inertia toward India, he looked to Galbraith to explore new policies. From a political perspective, however, too close an identification with Galbraith's liberal economic views could be damaging. Having Galbraith in his administration, but at the suitable distance of a post in New Delhi, served Kennedy's purposes.

With Galbraith as ambassador, Kennedy was kept informed about India. Invariably Galbraith balked at communicating with Washington through normal diplomatic channels, repeatedly bypassing the State Department to go directly to the president. Memos to the president were often filled with caustic barbs at the State Department bureaucracy. Secretary of State Dean Rusk, in particular, aggravated Galbraith, who considered him servile, passive, and unwilling to make waves. Whenever possible, he bypassed Rusk. When India sponsored the admission of the People's Republic of China to the United Nations, for example, Galbraith directly confronted Rusk, who opposed admitting the Communist state.

This issue of China was just one of several that strained U.S. relations with India. Even though the personal relationship between Nehru and Galbraith remained warm, Nehru was opposed to U.S. policies in South Asia. Nehru believed that whatever support was given to the region was for containment rather than development purposes. A case in point was the American policy of supplying military aid to Pakistan. Galbraith recommended a quiet detachment from military commitments to Pakistan to lessen tensions between the two South Asian nations. Although the United States viewed the arms shipments and alliance as part of its Cold War containment policies, Pakistan (and perhaps India as well) regarded them as support for Lahore's claims to Kashmir.

India was particularly sensitive about issues pertaining to colonialism. The immediate issue in the winter of 1961 was India's annexation of Goa, a Portuguese colony that formed an enclave within India proper. While Galbraith assured Nehru that the United States considered the Portuguese hold on the colony an anachronism and would work to persuade Lisbon to leave the region, the State Department offered only ambiguous promises that it would employ diplomatic pressures on Portugal. Additional tension resulted when the United States criticized India's actions during the U.N. debates without condemning colonialism, as Galbraith had advised.

In October 1962, during the Cuban missile crisis, Galbraith played a major role in helping the aged and ill Nehru plan India's response. He also assisted in organizing American military aid to India during the Sino-Indian border war. Galbraith used this opportunity to explain the U.S. position on the missile crisis to Nehru, and through him to other nonaligned nations that considered Nehru a leader.

Galbraith's 1969 work *Ambassador's Journal: A Personal Account of the Kennedy Years* is a diary of his twenty-seven months of diplomatic service. In it he detailed his myriad physical woes while in India even as he discussed his early attempts to keep the United States from involvement in Vietnam. An early critic of the Vietnam War, Galbraith advocated internal reforms in the weak and ineffectual Saigon government, which he believed lacked popular support. He strongly opposed any combat commitment and supported a neutral policy for South Vietnam. In November 1961 Galbraith visited South Vietnam to make an independent assessment for Kennedy. He told the president that until the Diem regime changed its ineffectual administrative, military, and political policies, the United States should measurably decrease its commitment and disassociate itself from the government's more controversial policies, such as the "strategic hamlet" practice of resettling large numbers of rural families. He argued that the United States should not oppose any coup attempt and he counseled somewhat vaguely a political rather than a military solution based upon a non-Communist government with a broad political base that fostered internal law and order. Galbraith shared these views with Nehru, who had also emphasized to Kennedy the prudence of not sending troops and thereby making the same mistake as France. In testimony before the Senate Foreign Relations Committee in 1966, Galbraith argued that Vietnam was not a testing ground for democracy and was not strategically important to the United States. The following year he called for a halt to bombing in the area.

After leaving the Kennedy administration, Galbraith immersed himself in liberal and Democratic Party politics. In 1967 he served as president of Americans for Democratic Action. In 1968 he worked on Senator Eugene McCarthy's presidential campaign, and he was an early supporter of Senator George McGovern's efforts in 1972 to win the presidency.

Galbraith's most significant contribution has been as an economist, albeit an unconventional one. His writings, which combine economic analysis with social observation and satire, are stinging critiques of the American economy. An important theme in his writings is the dominance of production, the affluence it produces, and the way to restore what he calls the social balance, the idea that the provision of public services must keep pace with the production of goods. Initially he intended to write for an academic audience. His 1952 book *A Theory of Price Control*, which he termed his best work, however, received such a limited reaction that he began aiming at a broader, general audience, which delighted in his skillful use of statistical evidence and biting expressions to debunk conventional economic wisdom.

The acclaim accorded him as a teacher and a popularizer by the general public for the clarity he brought to economic matters is not entirely shared by other economists. Nevertheless, as a tribute to his influence, Galbraith was elected president of the American Economic Association in 1972. Conservative economists were especially critical of his attacks on economic orthodoxy and on the statistical and technical side of economics and his willingness to levy higher taxes and institute wage and price controls. Radical political economists did not follow key Galbraith concepts either, such as "countervailing power" or the "techno-structure" and instead focused on class, hierarchy, control, and dominance. More specifically, Galbraith has been criticized for arguing that the endorsement of economic growth as a social goal corresponded closely with the rise to power of the mature corporation and the techno-structure.

Galbraith is a versatile, complex man of action as well as thought. Academic economists admire his use of language, wit, and intelligence even while they deplore his economic theories, which cannot be measured with precision. His lasting contribution to a popular, nonspecialized audience is to ask the society to reflect on public squalor amidst private affluence, to assess the power of big business and the inequalities in income, and to consider reordering national priorities and redefining goals to enhance the quality of life rather than the efficiency of production. He has adapted economics to social purposes to illuminate countervailing power and its effects, economic affluence in contrast with the quality of life in the United States, social imbalances and their implications, the functioning of the industrial state, and the techno-structure. Throughout his writings he has woven economics with culture and social institutions to provoke and persuade his audience. He has described himself as a nonviolent man who would like to see reform occur within a thoughtful and democratic system.

Works by John Kenneth Galbraith

A Theory of Price Control. Cambridge: Harvard University Press, 1952.
American Capitalism: The Concept of Countervailing Power. Boston: Houghton Mifflin, 1952.
The Affluent Society. Boston: Houghton Mifflin, 1958.
The New Industrial State. Boston: Houghton Mifflin, 1967.
Ambassador's Journal. Boston: Houghton Mifflin, 1969.
Economics and the Public Purpose. Boston: Houghton Mifflin, 1973.
A Life in Our Times. Boston: Houghton Mifflin, 1981.
The Culture of Contentment. Boston: Houghton Mifflin, 1992.

Works about John Kenneth Galbraith

Gambs, John S. *John Kenneth Galbraith*. Boston: Twayne Publishers, 1975.
Lamson, Peggy. *Speaking of Galbraith*. New York: Ticknor and Fields, 1991.

Munro, C. Lynn. *The Galbraithian Vision: The Cultural Criticism of John Kenneth Galbraith*. Washington, DC: University Press of America, 1977.
Pratson, Frederick J. *Perspectives on Galbraith*. Boston: CBI Publishing, 1978.

ARLENE LAZAROWITZ

MARSHALL GREEN (1916–   ) counseled Indonesia during its dramatic shift from anti-Americanism to close alliance with the West.

Green was born in Holyoke, Massachusetts, on January 27, 1916. He was an aide to Ambassador Joseph Grew in Tokyo after graduating from Yale University in 1939. In 1942 he joined the U.S. Navy and became a Japanese-language officer. At the close of the war he entered the Foreign Service, where one of his initial assignments was accompanying George Kennan, head of the policy-planning bureau, on a trip to Japan. The conclusions of Kennan and his aide Green brought about a reversal of course in Japanese occupation policy, an occurrence that Kennan considered his most important contribution in government after the Marshall Plan. In the early part of Green's career he saw service in New Zealand, Sweden, and the State Department headquarters in Washington (where he was Japanese desk officer), in addition to study at the National War College. By the mid-1950s he had become regional planning advisor in the Bureau of Far Eastern Affairs. In this capacity he wrote an important paper advocating counterinsurgency over conventional responses to Asian communism. Also, he notably assisted John Foster Dulles as action officer in the Offshore Islands crisis of 1958, at which time he suggested that bilateral discussions in Warsaw resolve the dispute instead of a further resort to force. He also originated the proposal for a new U.S.-Japanese Mutual Security Treaty, the signing of which occurred amidst violent demonstrations in Japan.

After serving as acting deputy assistant secretary of state for the Far East, in 1960 Green became deputy ambassador to South Korea. He assisted Ambassador Walter McConaughy in persuading Syngman Rhee to peacefully give up power in the face of popular dissatisfaction and student uprisings. He was also in charge of rescheduling the visit by President Dwight Eisenhower to Korea after cancellation by Japan of a planned visit there. In 1961 Green was acting ambassador in Seoul during the military coup masterminded by General Park Chung Hee. Without direction from Washington Green proclaimed support for the democratic government of Prime Minister Chang Myun against the coup forces, although he refused repeated requests for American military assistance to put down the uprising. When the military junta assumed control of the country, he acted to restrain repression in the aftermath. He later was consul general to Hong Kong and Macao, where he was information gatherer on events in China for Washington. He made several recommendations that Washington adopt a policy of restraint to abet change in the mainland. In 1963 he became deputy to Assistant Secretary for the Far East Roger Hilsman (who was succeeded in short order by William P. Bundy, Green's Yale classmate). In this capacity he specialized in developing policy toward the Communist areas of Asia.

Due to Green's wide experience and varied qualifications, President Lyndon Johnson appointed him as ambassador-designate to Indonesia in May 1965.

Green was thrust into a tough assignment. Indonesia was under the grip of President Achmad Sukarno, the man who had led the nation in its declaration of independence in 1945. He had gradually allied himself with the Indonesian Communist Party (PKI) in order to maintain his power and pursued close contacts with the major Communist nations in his leadership of the so-called non-aligned movement. He wound up mismanaging the nation's economy, with resulting massive dislocations. Relations between Washington and Jakarta had been in rapid decline since CIA involvement in a rebellion in Indonesia's outer islands during 1958. The deterioration was eased only by the Kennedy administration's attempt to mollify Sukarno with the transfer of Dutch New Guinea in 1963, although Sukarno soon began a scheme to crush the Malaysian Federation by force. In 1963 American aid to Jakarta had been cut back due to the sacking of the British embassy. Furthermore, Sukarno had withdrawn his nation from the United Nations in early 1965.

Green, however, took the situation in stride. His entry to Jakarta occurred in the midst of anti-American riots, including banners proclaiming "Green Go Home," that he believed Sukarno had staged. In addition, the Indonesian press accused the new ambassador of being a CIA agent. When Sukarno subjected him to a public haranguing on American foreign policy in the presidential palace, Green achieved retribution by saying to one of the president's mistresses that her beauty had prevented him from taking notice of Sukarno's remarks. But another incident demonstrated to those impressed by such things that Green might be a man of destiny: he had been told by an Indonesian mystic that a red-haired man would come to save Indonesia.

By 1965 the state of U.S.-Indonesian relations had reached its nadir, despite the warm association between Green's predecessor Howard Jones and Sukarno. Jones had advocated that the American government appease Sukarno as the only means by which to keep him out of Moscow's orbit, and he had strong backers for this position in Washington, including W. Averell Harriman, the outgoing under secretary of state for political affairs. Jones placated Sukarno by demonstrating little objection to his program of blending nationalism, communism, and religion known as NASAKOM. Yet Green meant to be different. He had no intention of subordinating American interests in Indonesia to the fawning game with Sukarno and opposed the policy of accommodation. While at the bureau, he had argued against a personal meeting between President Johnson and Sukarno and had recommended a reduction in the American presence in Indonesia in order to lessen it as a target of the radicals. He believed that the key to preventing Indonesia's leftist tilt lay with the anti-Communist officers in the Indonesian army. Since Indonesia and the United States appeared to be on a collision course, and since the situation in Indonesia jeopardized congressional support for other foreign assistance programs, Green's no-nonsense views had won the day.

Green arrived in Indonesia in July 1965. Sukarno had proclaimed 1965 "the year of living dangerously." After the recent burning of the Indian embassy and attacks on the American consulates at Medan and Surabaya, and in light of the fact that USIS libraries had been ransacked the previous winter, Green warned the Indonesian government that Washington would break off relations if a similar fate befell the American embassy. Surprisingly foreshadowing the future attitude of Indonesians toward the United States, the chief of police responded with vigorous assurances that American lives and property would receive the proper protection, and he notably even removed the pro-Communist guards that had been placed for some time in front of the American embassy.

At the end of September 1965 the PKI had as many as 3.5 million hard-core and associated members and had become the largest and most powerful political force in Indonesia, with considerable influence in the navy, air force, and national police. With the involvement of Sukarno and the logistical support of China, the PKI planned to overthrow the government bureaucracy in order to forestall the rising power of the army leaders. On the evening of September 30 the presidential bodyguard, acting on orders from the PKI, succeeded in murdering five of the top generals, but failed to eliminate two key officers, Generals Abdul Haris Nasution and Raden Suharto. Sukarno ensconced himself at a nearby air base with the chief of the air force.

The PKI succeeded in controlling Jakarta only for a day. Its revolt unraveled when Sukarno backed out. Suharto took firm control of the army and counterattacked. A massive and bloody reaction by the army, and by political groups that it had armed, led to the destruction of one of the largest Communist organizations in the world. Killings on a tremendous scale occurred, especially in rural parts of Java, Sumatra, and Bali. The embassy later estimated that as many as 300,000 persons were killed, although this figure may have been several times higher.

The U.S. government and its embassy had little forewarning of and involvement in precipitating the coup or the military reaction. Green's only important action in October was to suggest that American dependents not be evacuated in the coup's aftermath so as not to undermine confidence in the army, but Washington overruled him. He deliberately kept a low profile during the army's countercoup so as not to taint the army with too close an association with America. His policy was to let the Indonesians settle matters without outside influence, although in covert contacts with army officers American officials did encourage them to act against the PKI and eliminate it from Indonesian political life.

Sukarno, due to his prestige among the people, remained as president after the massacre, but the real power now fell into the hands of Suharto. Green acted to buttress the position of the general so that power would not slip back into Sukarno's hands. The ambassador established a close relationship with those who had been pro-Western: Suharto, his chief diplomatic aide, Adam Malik, Nasution, and the members of the Berkeley Mafia, Indonesian economic ministers trained in the United States, in the months following the coup. He found Suharto much less pretentious than Sukarno and gave the new government communications equipment and rifles for its internal security and also medicines, not for health, but to resell in order to garner foreign currency. The army funneled some of the money into (and used the walkie-talkies and small arms for) the eradication program against the Communists. Green did resist pressure from Washington, and from Canberra, for a full resumption of aid until the situation stabilized so as not to strengthen Sukarno. He told Washington not to send any aid until Suharto had formally requested it. But he did express his government's admiration for the Suharto regime's exuberance in pursuing the PKI.

By the spring of 1966 Suharto had achieved primacy in the new order by purging the military of unsympathetic elements and by preventing the nationalization of foreign companies, a step most welcome to the Americans. Nevertheless, in the waning days of Sukarno's influence during the spring of 1966, several American installations came under attack by leftist and pro-Sukarno demonstrators. They attempted to attack Green's wife in the ambassador's residence and even entered the premises of the American embassy, forcing the staff to begin burning sensitive diplomatic records. Yet Green personally reached out to student groups, the leadership of which was pro-Western, and they helped to lift the siege of the chancery. He also continued his policy of lying low until Sukarno could be brushed aside, but asked Suharto to prevent the carrying out of Sukarno's directive nationalizing American petroleum interests in Indonesia.

Matters came to a head in March 1966. Sukarno demanded that Green leave the country, and his supporters scaled the embassy walls and burned twenty-two American-owned automobiles. Sukarno also tried to prevent the execution of two prominent PKI members. On March 11 the army leadership forced Sukarno to hand over all power except the title of president to Suharto. This charade ended in 1967 when Indonesia's assembly stripped Sukarno of that office when it received an official report on his role in the PKI massacres.

Immediately after Suharto had established full control, Green had the flow of international aid to Indonesia reestablished with the full support of Washington. One important contributor that he arranged to join in the effort was Japan, which sent an amount equal to the American contribution. Before significant amounts of economic aid began to arrive in 1967, though, Green bolstered the Jakarta regime by obtaining $26 million in food available under the P.L. 480 program. He also cultivated foreign investment for Indonesia and encouraged it to join the World Bank and the IMF. Two other successes of his were to get Indonesia to establish a new method of reviewing bids that avoided corruption and graft and the removal of subsidies for state enterprises. Another achievement was ending Indonesia's policy of confrontation with Malaysia in mid-1966.

President Johnson regarded Green's management of the situation in Indonesia as one of his premier foreign policy successes. Green's most important contribution was in building up a bulwark of Southeast Asian anticommunism. His tenure occurred during a time when America was deeply involved in military action in Vietnam. He helped Indonesia avoid becoming a Communist nation, a development that would have jeopardized the American mission in Vietnam and would have encouraged Communist movements in other parts of Southeast

Asia and the Third World. Instead, Indonesia became a major player in the constructive regional system established under the Association of Southeast Asian Nations (ASEAN). Soviet and mainland Chinese influence in the region had been set back irrevocably. Green's low-profile posture in 1965, coupled with the American stand in Vietnam, had inspired the army to quash the Communist movement in Indonesia. Thereafter Indonesia had become such a staunch ally to the United States that Suharto even offered to commit training troops in support of the American effort in the Vietnam War, an offer that Green strongly discouraged the administration from accepting.

After his four-year tenure in Indonesia, Green temporarily joined the Vietnam peace negotiations occurring in Paris as the second to Ambassador Henry Cabot Lodge. He observed the tough stance that the North Vietnamese took in peace talks. Green participated in the key policy meetings at the end of February 1969 between Lodge, President Richard Nixon, Secretary of State William P. Rogers, and National Security Adviser Henry Kissinger in Paris. They decided upon the pace of Vietnamization (the turning over of fighting to the South Vietnamese) and that the formal talks would be downgraded since the administration would seek to discuss important issues outside of public scrutiny with the North Vietnamese. Kissinger proceeded to undertake his own private talks with Le Duc Tho that summer, demonstrating the unimportant role of the negotiating team in Paris.

This frustrating assignment for Green lasted only briefly. On May 6, 1969, President Nixon appointed Green as assistant secretary of state for East Asian and Pacific affairs. Green's top priority as head of the State Department's most embattled bureau was to assist the administration in achieving peace in Vietnam. After visiting eleven Asian capitals in the spring of 1969, Green argued that the excessive U.S. presence in Asia was a political liability at home and abroad, actually weakening governments that Washington wanted to strengthen. He advocated instead lowering the American profile in the rest of Asia as had been done in Indonesia, which would paradoxically strengthen the American position in various countries. America should not try to solve Asia's problems, but merely assist the Asians in doing so. The result was the Nixon Doctrine of July 1969, which shifted the burden of defense onto U.S. allies. Yet because of the limited success of Vietnamization, and knowing North Vietnamese intransigence firsthand, Green tried to persuade the administration to adopt a face-saving formula of a coalition government in Saigon, for this was the only area where common ground could be found. Nixon and Kissinger kept him ignorant of the Cambodian invasion in 1970. When it broke out, he had been working to preserve Cambodia's neutral status, if in name only. He was forced to defend the escalation policy with which he disagreed, but did manage to play a role in minimizing a renewed proliferation of the war. However, the administration did not fully trust Green because of his close ties to the Johnson administration and so wiretapped him for several years and kept him out of the Vietnam peace negotiations until mid-1972. Toward the end of that year the president tasked

Green to devise an aid package to bind up the war's wounds, of which three billion dollars was to go to Hanoi in an offer to encourage its observance of the Paris Accords.

Because Green did not want to be relegated to merely being Vietnam desk officer as his predecessor had been, he focused on other important regional issues, such as opening relations with China. Early on, he worked out various schemes to ease trade restrictions with Beijing. He also urged an overall cautious approach so as not to undermine relations with the Soviet Union and because he believed that the president needed Chinese assurances regarding important bilateral issues before any visit to China. With the announcement of the impending visit of the president to China, Green had to scramble to overcome the first of the so-called Nixon shocks that undercut relations with Japan by personally explaining the administration's secrecy to Prime Minister Eisaku Sato. Green did accompany Nixon on his momentous visit to China in 1972, although he and Rogers were excluded from major meetings by Kissinger, including the single conference between Nixon and Mao Zedong. Green helped to refine the Shanghai Communiqué produced by Kissinger and Zhou Enlai, which stated that both Nationalists and Communists regarded China as one and Taiwan as part of China. Other parts of the communiqué did serve as the basis for normalization of full diplomatic relations in 1979. Green noticed, though, that it did leave out America's commitment to its treaty obligations with Taiwan, a mistake the proportions of which approached Dean Acheson's gaffe over deleting mainland Asia from America's defensive perimeter in January 1950, and one that was soon corrected. Green's astute observation shocked the president, who instructed the furious Kissinger to iron out an understanding on this point with the Chinese deputy foreign minister. During this same time period Green also headed an interagency task force that worked out arrangements for the reversion of the Ryukyu Islands to Japan in 1972.

Green became the American ambassador to Australia and Nauru in June 1973. Australia was America's most important ally in the Pacific; more Americans lived there than in any other Asian country, and U.S. investment in Australia exceeded the combined total in all the other Pacific nations. However, relations had reached a low point after the election of the Australian Labor Party. In his role as ambassador Green ameliorated fallout from Nixon's unilateral opening toward China and the resumption of bombing in Vietnam that had occurred the previous year. One of his first acts was persuading President Nixon to receive Australian Prime Minister Gough Whitlam during a visit that became quite a success. Green's personal style of diplomacy, coupled with the denouement of the Vietnam War and an economic downturn in Australia, re-created an atmosphere of appreciation for the United States by Canberra.

At the twilight of his career Green moved into a broader range of issues. In 1975 he became the first coordinator of the National Security Council's (NSC's) Inter-Agency Task Force on World Population and made annual reports, approved by all seventeen member agencies, to the NSC on the issue. He traveled extensively, meeting with world leaders and others interested in population control and family planning, and attended international conferences to support population programs. In addition, he worked on advancing the rights of women and female literacy in the world, recognizing the close connection of these issues to lowering fertility rates. He was the Carter administration's chief delegate to U.N. population conferences in 1977 and 1979. He retired from active diplomatic service in 1979 but continued as a consultant to the State Department on population issues into the 1990s. He also established the government's policy regarding Indochinese refugees as chairman of the State Department's advisory board. He served as the director of the National Committee on U.S.-Chinese Relations and as cofounder, president, and honorary chairman of the Japan-America Society of Washington, D.C. He helped the society establish the Marshall Green Fund to promote Japanese studies, for which Emperor Hirohito awarded him the Order of the Rising Sun in 1986. He continued to give many speeches, especially relating to U.S. policy in the Asia-Pacific region.

Works by Marshall Green

The Silent Explosion. Washington, DC: U.S. Department of State, 1978.
New Imperatives in Socio-economic Development. Washington, DC: National Defense University, 1980.
Report on Indochinese Refugees. Washington, DC: U.S. Department of State, 1981.
Population Pressures: Threat to Democracy and Stability. Washington, DC: Population Crisis Committee, 1989.
Indonesia: Crisis and Transformation, 1965–1968. Washington, DC: Compass Press, 1990.
"The Evolution of U.S. International Population Policy, 1965–92." Population and Development Review, June 1993.

Works about Marshall Green

Brackman, Arnold C. The Communist Collapse in Indonesia. New York: Norton, 1969.
———. Indonesia: The Gestapu Affair. New York: Asian-American Educational Exchange, 1969.
Bunnell, Frederick. "American 'Low Posture' Policy toward Indonesia in the Months Leading Up to the 1965 'Coup.' " Indonesia 50 (October 1990): 21–60.
Kolko, Gabriel. Confronting the Third World: United States Foreign Policy, 1945–1980. New York: Pantheon, 1988.
Szulc, Tad. The Illusion of Peace: Foreign Policy in the Nixon Years. New York: Viking, 1978.

KENT G. SIEG

JOSEPH CLARK GREW (1880–1965) was a U.S. ambassador to Japan who set as his task in this assignment the avoidance of war between his country and Japan.

Grew was born in Boston on May 27, 1880. He graduated from Groton Academy in 1898 and from Harvard in 1902. Grew recorded in his diaries that he pursued the Gentleman's C in his classes and was more attuned to the Harvard baseball team than academic pursuits. He joined the Fly Club, the same social organization to which Franklin Delano Roosevelt belonged at Harvard; this, along with the Groton connection, served him well as ambassador. He was one of the few career diplomats who could address "Dear Frank" letters to the president and subtly present his views on foreign policy in personal correspondence.

Family connections and background gave Grew advantages in his career. Like most young men of his class, he was sent abroad by his parents after graduation; but Grew chose to go further afield than most. He went on to the Far East, where his exploit in shooting a tiger in a cave in Amoy, China, gained him the attention of President Theodore Roosevelt, who approved his appointment to the diplomatic service. He was a distant cousin of J. P. Morgan, but more important was his marriage to Alice de Vermendois Perry on October 7, 1905. She was a descendant of Commodore Oliver Hazard Perry, who, with his even more famous brother, Matthew, had opened Japan to the West in the nineteenth century. Alice Grew spent part of her youth in Japan and knew something of the language and customs and many of the leading families, which gave Grew entrée to decision makers and leaders in the society denied to many of his colleagues. The Grews had four daughters: Anita, Elizabeth (Elsie), Lilla, and Edith, who died in her teens. The other three married Foreign Service officers.

When Grew returned from his sojourn abroad, he tried to obtain a position with a Boston publishing house, but failed. The Reverend Endicott Peabody instilled in his boys at Groton the sense of noblesse oblige due to their position and wealth that enabled them to pay back to society what they gained from their privileged position. The same was true at Harvard. Thus Grew, imbued with this sense of public service obligation, plus a desire to see more of the world, decided to seek a position in the Foreign Service. Due to a childhood illness, he was partially deaf in one ear. When he first tried to enter the field of diplomacy, someone mistakenly reported that he was nearly deaf, and his application was denied. He tried again and secured an assignment to Cairo in 1904. When President Theodore Roosevelt introduced a new system of competitive examinations for the Foreign Service in 1906, Grew was one of the last to receive a transfer from the Consular Service to the Foreign Service.

After his marriage Grew returned for a short time to Egypt and then was assigned to Mexico City as a third secretary and to Moscow in 1907. He was promoted to second secretary and transferred to Berlin in 1908, then to first secretary at Vienna in 1911–1912, and back to Berlin in the latter year. He returned to the United States in 1912 and after Woodrow Wilson's election to the presidency called on Franklin Roosevelt and other old Groton and Harvard acquaintances to keep from being a victim of the spoils system. Grew suffered some embarrassment due to letters and speeches he gave defending Germany before U.S. entry into the war. This was a lesson in cautious reporting and speeches that he never forgot. During his assignment in Berlin Grew learned another lesson. During the absence of Ambassador James Gerard, Grew became acting ambassador. In this capacity he had a conversation with Chancellor Theobald von Bethmann-Hollweg, who brought up the subject of peace. Grew believed that this was a hint that the chancellor would welcome an American peace initiative and reported this to Washington, though he clearly stated that this was merely an impression rather than a firm request by the German leader.

Grew understood that if the United States then pursued this hint only to be rebuffed, he would receive the blame for embarrassing his government. Fortunately for the neophyte diplomat, the German chancellor wished to keep this option available and did not either accept or repudiate the concept of a negotiated peace. Though this incident was not forgotten as a lesson about how dangerous to his career an overstepping of the boundaries of reporting could be, it did illustrate an optimism about promoting peace that also remained with him. He later took every opportunity to predict a peaceful conclusion to American-Japanese antagonisms when he became ambassador to Japan. According to his biographer, Waldo Heinrichs, Grew made another error when he was in Germany, one he would repeat in Japan. He judged the temporary relief from the submarine danger to be more significant and permanent than it was and thereby caused the Wilson administration to delay its peace initiative until it was too late. His problem was that he underestimated the degree to which military imperatives directed policy decisions, which meant that he did not perceive what the course would be when military policy clashed with a more sensible approach to diplomacy. This was the error he was to make in Japan.

In 1918 Grew received an appointment that gained him a promotion that secured his career. He became secretary to the United States Commission to the Paris Peace Conference. He was in charge of arrangements for the Peace Commission, an assignment that carried with it the equivalent rank of minister. This proved a real test of his diplomatic skills as the various factions vying for control of the commission attempted to get the best accommodations, the most direct access to the president, and inside information concerning the agendas for the conference. By careful and judicious treatment of the various men who strove for position he gained a reputation for evenhandedness. After the conference concluded, Grew was promoted to the permanent rank of minister in an appointment as U.S. minister to Denmark in April 1920.

During his assignment to Copenhagen Grew received another lesson on how precarious the career of a diplomat serving the United States could be. He accidentally slighted a visiting delegation of congressmen, including Senator Joseph T. Robinson, who was a senior ranking member of the Senate and soon to become Democratic minority leader, and powerful House member Fred A. Britten. On return to the United States the congressmen tried to get Grew fired. Senator Lodge slipped through Grew's appointment to Switzerland when Robinson was absent, but this lesson in politics was not soon forgotten. Another incident that taught Grew to err on the side of caution occurred when he was under secretary of state during Frank Kellogg's tenure as secretary. During Kellogg's absence from Washington Grew as acting secretary authorized the use of American gunboats in a joint display of force with other powers to break a river blockade in China. When Kellogg returned, he gave his subordinate what Grew described as the dressing-down of his life when the secretary accused him of virtually declaring war on China.

Grew commented in his diary that these experiences were lessons in circumspection regarding relations with Congress, the public, and the Department of State. They caused him to hedge recommendations to the State Department by pointing out numerous contingencies and more often than not to make sure he did not go too far in recommending policies that might not be popular in the department. There were to be exceptions to this when he served in Japan, but his policy recommendations were still surrounded with "on the other hand" reporting. Grew came to give less than the measure of honest reporting that might be expected from a Foreign Service officer because rocking the boat was career threatening. This tendency was not altogether Grew's fault. American foreign policy in the 1920s and 1930s was based on long-term principles and short-term interests that were often contradictory. Grew was not an isolationist, but many of his superiors in the 1920s were. James Dunn and Jay Pierrepont Moffat saw their duty as careerists to keep the United States from any "entanglements," and these men occupied important positions in the department.

When Grew was U.S. minister to Switzerland, he recalled another incident that characterized the fear that the Foreign Service officers had to deal with constantly. Though the United States had refused to join the League of Nations, it had an observer at the League because there were issues that concerned American interests that the government could hardly ignore. Grew was seen by an American journalist speaking to the American observer on the street. Grew rushed over begging the reporter not to write that he had seen the minister speaking to the observer lest the limited cooperation with the League be curtailed. In the 1920s and 1930s American policy was reactive to each new crisis or problem. When Franklin D. Roosevelt could confide that he had no idea how to develop a long-range foreign policy and Secretary of State Cordell Hull could tell his ambassadors to read his and FDR's speeches to discover what American policy really was, it is not surprising that a Foreign Service officer whose position rested on a tenuous political relationship with the chiefs in Washington hesitated to expand on such a nebulous policy. That Grew should actually suggest policy decisions when he served in Japan speaks to his genuine concern for securing peace and his role in creating it.

Perhaps Grew's greatest success as a representative of U.S. interests came in his two assignments to Turkey. After his tour as minister to Switzerland Grew was sent to Lausanne as part of a team of American diplomats instructed to negotiate a Turkish treaty (later his first assignment as an ambassador was at Ankara). He advised Ismet Inonu, the Turkish foreign minister, on how to avoid being exploited by the French and British and then separately secured a treaty that would have made the United States the virtual lead embassy in Turkey, with oil-exploration and railroad-construction rights that would supplant British influence. Ironically, the Senate turned down the treaty that Grew arranged, and it was not until he went to Turkey as ambassador that he could get a second, less favorable treaty accepted by a voice vote in the Senate. The second treaty still gained more favored status for the United States than the Lausanne Treaty gained for the other allies of World War I.

Grew's ambassadorship to Turkey provided an escape from the hardship of serving as Kellogg's under secretary of state. Not only did Grew come to grief over China, but the secretary had the unfortunate habit of meeting with an unofficial "kitchen cabinet" of friends and cronies to discuss policy matters and then would call Grew in for special technical or other kinds of information. Grew would not be made privy to the points of discussion; he then would have questions fired at him from all directions, and the secretary would become irritated when there was no quick response. Part of the problem was that Grew could do very well in one-on-one conversations when he could turn his good ear to the discussant, but was lost in a crowd of questioners who sounded to him like a babbling brook. He stuck it out because he was in charge of implementing the reforms of the Rogers Act, which reorganized the Department of State and created for the first time a career Foreign Service structure that made for more secure posts outside of ambassadorships because the Foreign Service assignments were more or less guaranteed under the new structure. This achieved, Grew fled to the first available post, which was Turkey.

In 1932 Grew received the distinction of being the first career Foreign Service officer to be awarded an ambassadorship to a major country when he succeeded W. Cameron Forbes as the U.S. ambassador to Japan. Grew's own recollection of the assignment was that it was the one premier post he could afford because the ambassadors to such capitals as London and Paris had to pay for the entertainment obligations out of their own pockets thanks to the penurious attitude of Congress in allotting entertainment allowances to U.S. ambassadors. Tokyo was the cheapest major post available.

Grew arrived in Tokyo after the first diplomatic to-do over the Manchurian crisis had begun to subside and promptly began to stress a theme in his reports that would be fairly consistent during his long tenure in Japan. He emphasized the need for U.S. policy decisions that would encourage and support the moderate political faction in Japan. Grew made the mistake that had characterized his reporting from Germany in the early stages of World War I, namely, believing that the political parties were an important ingredient in Japanese policy and that they could overcome the military if given a chance. It was not that Grew misinterpreted the intent of the military, for he fairly well understood its objectives; rather, he misread how powerful that force was in determining policy and failed to note that any politician who did not cater to the military leaders' whims would be eliminated either physically by assassination or by removal from policy positions. The ambassador did see that there were also relatively moderate elements in the military leadership, but he overestimated their ability to resist the extremists in the Kwantung Army comprised of fanatics who had become disillusioned with Shidehara diplomacy (the diplomacy of accommodation that prevailed in the 1920s). Shidehara had rested Japanese policy on the assumption that Japan could achieve Great Power status and success by peaceful economic penetration of China and by a policy of cooperation with the other Great Powers. The worldwide depression doomed that policy to failure as European and American markets were closed to Japanese industrial output and the powers fought to maintain the lion's share of the China market as well. Force diplomacy was the response of Japanese military fanatics in the "Young Officer's Movement" to the restrictive policies of the powers.

During Grew's many years in Japan he rested his policy recommendations on two principles that he reported to the Department of State very early in his first year in Tokyo. He and his chargé d'affaires, Eugene Dooman, suggested that American policy should be developed on the understanding that national preparedness for the purpose of protecting legitimate interests in the Far East should be a given, but this should be accompanied by a sympathetic, cooperative, and helpful attitude toward Japan. He pleaded that there were only two ways Japan could solve its overpopulation problem—territorial and industrial expansion. He doubted that Japan's force diplomacy in China would ever be resolved to everyone's satisfaction and warned that restricting Japanese foreign trade would not be an acceptable route because it would only result in force diplomacy being the only remaining alternative in the view of Japan's leaders. He told his superiors in Washington that Japan's rationalization of policy was that economic imperatives dictated replacing the Western powers in China to accommodate a higher living standard for the Japanese, and that if that occurred at others' expense, that was unfortunate but necessary. He compared the Japanese attitude to the Manifest Destiny concept in American history.

Grew asked the policymakers in Washington to view the expansionist position taken by Japan as both reasonable and logical in its operation, based on irrepressible forces that rested on an underlying foundation of self-preservation. This was a telling dispatch because, like his predecessor, W. Cameron Forbes, he saw Japan's expansion in China as the result of a social Darwinist–style obsession with self-preservation. Weak China could not stop it, and the Western powers could not confront it without war. He believed that he could bring his country and Japan to some sort of agreement that would recognize basic American interests in the Far East while the United States would acknowledge Japan's more pressing need for markets and living space, hopefully by peaceable accommodation. He warned that if his government was determined to protect its interests unchanged and to continue to deny Japan Western markets, the only outcome would be war.

Cordell Hull did not, and probably could not, fathom Grew's sympathy for Japan's plight, and neither could Stanley K. Hornbeck, who was director of the Far East Division of the State Department and later in the 1930s special advisor to the secretary. When Hull forwarded Grew's dispatches to FDR, he cautioned that from the outset the administration had done everything possible to cooperate with Japan, to no avail. Grew did not understand how committed Hull was to the Wilsonian view of a world governed by American perceptions of the rule of law in international relations or how little the secretary understood Japanese culture. On one occasion Hull burst forth to a colleague that he had just given another sermon to the Japanese ambassador and that it had had no effect; he surmised that the trouble with the Japanese was that they did not behave like Christian gentlemen. That he expected them to do so was going to lead to trouble and to less and less credence being placed in Grew's pleadings as time went on because Hornbeck perceived the ambassador to be an appeaser and apologist for the Japanese.

Grew told friends that Washington was handling relations with Japan just right, but as the 1930s progressed, he became less convinced that this was so. He told the department in the late 1930s that the best course to follow was to take Teddy Roosevelt's advice to speak softly and carry a big stick. He was afraid that instead the government would speak loudly and carry a very small stick and that Japan would call the bluff. After the war began, he bemoaned Washington's failure to heed his advice. His last assignment was again as under secretary of state; he retired on August 15, 1945.

Works by Joseph C. Grew

Report from Tokyo. New York: Simon and Schuster, 1942.

Ten Years in Japan. New York: Simon and Schuster, 1944.

Turbulent Era: A Diplomatic Record of Forty Years, 1904–1945. 2 vols. Boston: Houghton Mifflin, 1952.

Works about Joseph C. Grew

Burns, Richard Dean, and Edward M. Bennett, eds. *Diplomats in Crisis: United States–Chinese–Japanese Relations, 1919–1941.* The chapter on Grew by Bennett is "The Diplomacy of Pacification: Joseph C. Grew." Santa Barbara: ABC-Clio, 1974.

Heinrichs, Waldo H., Jr. *American Ambassador: Joseph C. Grew and the Development of the United States Diplomatic Tradition.* New York: Garland, 1979.

EDWARD M. BENNETT

RAYMOND ARTHUR HARE (1901–1994) was U.S.
assistant secretary of state for Near East and African Affairs, director general of the Foreign Service, and a career ambassador.

Hare was one of the very few American ambassadors in the 1930s and 1940s who had been trained in Arabic and was a specialist in Middle East affairs. He was born in West Virginia and raised in Boothbay Harbor, Maine. He was educated at Grinnell College, where he was a member of Phi Beta Kappa. During his college years he developed an interest in foreign affairs and a yen for travel. He accepted an offer from the president of Grinnell to go to Constantinople as an instructor at Robert College between 1924 and 1926, where he taught students from all parts of the Middle East. In Constantinople he developed a lifelong interest in the study of Islamic architecture and began a collection of photographs and research notes that were presented to the Sackler Museum at the Smithsonian Institution.

Hare later worked for the American Chamber of Commerce for the Levant, and as he dealt with U.S.–Middle East trade, he came into continued contact with the American consulate. The consulate offered him a position in its commercial section. After taking the Department of State's Foreign Service examination in the field and the oral examination in Washington, he was appointed to the U.S. Foreign Service in 1927 and returned to the Istanbul consular staff.

After a brief tour in Constantinople Hare and a small, select handful of Foreign Service officers were assigned to a three-year program of Arabic and Turkish studies conducted under French government auspices at L'Ecole des Langues Orientales Vivantes in Paris. Although this period of study formed an initial foundation of Arabic, it was far from effective or comprehensive training. Hare later recalled that the French approach was more ''morte'' than ''vivante,'' and throughout his diplomatic career he continued his efforts. He became one of the few American diplomats of that era to reach a working level in Arabic. Such skill was very rare before a comprehensive training program was established by the U.S. Foreign Service Institute in 1946.

Hare emerged from his three years in Paris and was sent as vice consul to Beirut. He worked across the region at a number of Middle East consular posts and gradually rose through the diplomatic ranks. After a tour in Teheran he was assigned a regional desk in the Near East Affairs Bureau in Washington.

As World War II approached, Hare was sent to a critical wartime post at Cairo in 1939–1944 and was charged with overseeing the enormous influx of American Lend-Lease war materiel. By 1941 the staff of the Cairo legation were uncomfortably close to the conflict, and Hare's duties included military reporting and liaison work with the Middle East Supply Center and the Persian Gulf Command as the program expanded to supply both the British in Egypt and the Soviet military by shipping through the region and across Iran. During that time

Hare became convinced that the Middle East would become a pivotal area for American commercial and strategic interests in the postwar world and strenuously presented this argument to Washington.

After the war Hare returned to Washington, where he served as an advisor to the Dumbarton Oaks Conference on the United Nations. His background in dealing with Egyptian and British interests and his extensive regional experience led to his next assignment, to the U.S. embassy in London, where he established a liaison office to coordinate U.S. and British policy on Middle East affairs. A short time later, in 1944, he and British diplomat Michael Wright conducted secret British-American meetings in Washington on the postwar regional economic issues under the guise of trade talks.

In 1946 Hare was sent to the newly created National War College in an innovative program that served to foster cooperation between Department of State and armed-forces personnel and to acquaint the Department of State with the practical uses of the postwar navy. But before completing the program, he was abruptly reassigned to Nepal as deputy chief of mission for the newly established embassy as that nation moved toward independence. Over the next few years he traveled throughout the region, especially Pakistan and India, gathering background information on the swiftly changing situation. During this time he perceived that Mountbatten's haste to complete the British withdrawal would be very costly to India. His extensive field notes, which included interviews of regional political and religious leaders, were later donated to Columbia University.

Upon returning to Washington, he first headed the old subdivision on Middle Eastern and Indian Affairs and then served as deputy director of the Office of Near Eastern and African Affairs in 1948 (forerunner of the Bureau of Near Eastern and South African Affairs—NEA) as the State Department attempted to readjust its bureaucracy to cope with the changed political realities and ebbing British position. At this time NEA recognized the need for a new American policy on arms sales, and Hare was assigned to draft and negotiate an agreement with the British to limit arms sales to the Middle East. Known as the Tripartite Declaration of 1950, it declared that the British, the French, and the United States would limit arms sales to the region, and called upon the parties in the 1948 Arab-Israeli War to honor the armistice lines and find a solution to the conflict. It was to be severely weakened a few years later when France sold weapons to Israel, and it was effectively swept away by the 1956 Suez War. Although Hare had worked hard to limit the role of America as a supplier of arms to the Middle East, the Tripartite Declaration succeeded in halting arms transfers for half a decade, but only postponed the coming conflict.

Shortly afterward Hare achieved ambassadorial rank and was posted to Saudi Arabia in 1950, with responsibility for Yemen as well. On his second tour in Jidda Hare carefully built relations with the Saudi royal family just as the first large waves of revenue from the postwar oil development began to roll in. His objective was to stay out of the way of Aramco, the American consortium of oil producers, which handled its own relations with the Saudi royal family, but his goal was to secure the Saudi government's agreement on U.S. access to the military facilities at Dhahran. This required balancing the American interest in a long-term agreement with Saudi concerns over national sovereignty.

Rather than confront the knotty issues head-on, Hare quietly worked around them, assuring the Saudis that the agreement would not be publicized and offering a small contingent of fighter planes, which became the genesis of the Saudi air force. In 1952 they agreed on an extended-term agreement. Hare cabled the State Department to withhold all publicity and downplay terms, rather than risk jeopardizing the nascent deal. This lack of fanfare allowed the government of Saudi Arabia to present it as an advantageous bargain with a major power. In fact, it was a good deal for both sides and laid the groundwork for the developing U.S.-Saudi alliance in subsequent years.

Before completing his tour, Hare attempted to defuse the multisided conflict over the Buraimi Oasis in 1953. Although he did succeed in getting both the British and the Saudis to agree to sign a standstill agreement, his effort to resolve the conflict failed. Yet in presenting the case to Washington he clearly outlined that it was a problem to be solved between the states on the Arabian peninsula and not by the British and Americans, who were essentially outsiders.

In 1953 Hare returned to Beirut, Lebanon, as ambassador. During a brief posting he developed an understanding of the complexities of Lebanese politics, but was brought back to Washington within less than a year.

During the McCarthy era the State Department suffered from institutional paralysis under a series of political attacks and congressional budget slashings that were followed by an investigation of the personnel system. The Wriston Committee reported that the entire system of hiring, organizing, and promoting State Department personnel must be revised. Hare was assigned to oversee the implementation of the new policy as director general of the Foreign Service. ''Wristonization'' resulted in the combination of the two branches of the Foreign Service, its officers and its Washington staff, into one entity. These changes rotated long-time Washington staff into the field and overseas personnel to Washington. Throughout his career Hare emphasized the need to carefully select and mentor junior officers as vital to the department's effectiveness, and as director general, he oversaw the most widespread changes ever instituted.

In the spring of 1956 conflict in the Middle East reached crisis proportions as Secretary of State John Foster Dulles, who had canceled U.S. funding of the Aswan Dam project and assumed a confrontational stance toward the Egyptian regime, triggered the nationalization of the Suez Canal. During the Suez crisis Secretary Dulles proposed and attempted to organize an international authority to operate the canal and lost confidence in his ambassador at Cairo, Henry Byroade. In the middle of the summer Dulles launched a tremendous shake-up at NEA in which Byroade was ousted and diplomats in Washington and the Middle East were shifted around.

Hare was hastily returned to Cairo as ambassador and arrived shortly before the Suez War broke out. Taken by surprise at the Israeli attack, Hare spent the initial days evacuating U.S. civilians and State Department dependents while cabling London to avert any accidental British attack on the evacuation convoy. It was also Hare's task to deal with Nasser, then the chief promoter of Arab nationalism and the neutralist movement, which concerned Secretary Dulles, already resentful of Nasser's neutrality. Hare did not accept Dulles's view of neutralism as an evil in and of itself.

Hare carefully cultivated Nasser's confidence. Although Hare was skilled in reading Arabic, he found that Nasser spoke "good Army English." They established a good working relationship, meeting often and at great length. Hare's cables provide insight into the character of Nasser and American-Egyptian relations in those years. Most often Hare dealt directly with Nasser and took his own notes, which were then carefully reconstructed upon his return to the embassy. He also carefully cultivated additional sources of information in Egypt and in this manner made his reporting invaluable, since it coupled intimate detail with trenchant analysis. Perhaps his greatest skill was the ability to analyze his opposite number's reaction to events and his rejection of the conventional wisdom regarding the Nasser regime. Hare recalled many years later that he saw something in Nasser that others did not, but tempered that with the observation that since Nasser's power derived from a coup, he viewed American actions with suspicion, through a conspiratorial lens. The most critical issue came during the war itself when Nasser raised the issue of American assistance. Hare carefully dodged the question and was advised by Washington that the only assistance would be a promise to work through the United Nations.

In the shock of the collapse of the Iraqi monarchy and U.S. and British intervention to shore up the Jordanian and Lebanese governments in July 1958, Hare emerged as a strong voice in favor of reshaping American attitudes toward emergent nationalism. He recognized the need to deal with such crises not with a show of force by the Sixth Fleet, but rather through quiet diplomacy. While the ambassador at Beirut, Robert Murphy, launched a debate within the State Department to evaluate the success of the U.S. actions, which he argued had stabilized the situation and were applicable as a model for U.S. intervention elsewhere, Hare argued strenuously that events might have turned out very differently had even a single shot been fired as the American marines hit the Beirut beach, warning that something as insignificant as "one rifle shot" might have turned the entire landing into a fiasco. Furthermore, he weighed in heavily against the assumption that such an action could be repeated elsewhere. While he lauded Murphy's bold action in preventing a crisis, he warned that the landing was not a model for future operations. This suggestion was neither readily accepted nor adopted.

Hare also pointed out that the intervention had left a highly unfavorable image of the United States in the region. While Eisenhower had pressed for an Israeli withdrawal from Egyptian territory in 1956 and reaped a brief wave of pro-U.S. sentiment, subsequent American policy should be more conciliatory. Yet Secretary Dulles opposed any suggestions from the Near East Bureau that any forms of U.S. aid be sent to the region.

By late 1958, following Dulles's passing, the State Department began to recommend a program of food aid that was designed to reestablish good relations. As a strong initiator and supporter of this policy, Hare proposed that the United States begin a small-scale aid program, exchanging excess grain for Egyptian currency under Public Law 480 (known as P.L. 480 wheat), which aimed to restart stalled American-Egyptian relations. During his brief tenure Hare saw food aid as his particular pet project and lobbied Congress to defend the program as it had been originally designed, as a series of long-term, multiyear wheat contracts with Egypt. This had been conceived as a method of creating goodwill while at the same time undercutting Soviet influence in the Egyptian economy. Until the advent of P.L. 480 wheat shipments Egypt was economically interdependent with the Soviet Union, shipping large quantities of Egyptian cotton to the USSR in exchange for wheat and oil. In one deft move Hare's Christmas 1958 initiative sharply reduced Nasser's economic reliance on Moscow. As his son and biographer Paul Hare has pointed out, this aid program exchanged excess American grain at almost no expense for Egyptian goodwill and had the additional bonus of weaning the Egyptian economy away from its dependence upon commodity exchanges with the Soviet Union. Even Egypt's sharp critic of American policy, Mohamed Heikal, saw it as evidence of a new American attitude toward Egypt and an end to the punitive Dulles policy.

Known as "the Silent Ambassador" for his low-key manner and subtle style, Hare achieved much of his work with very little fanfare and avoided publicity, but was a skilled negotiator who could forcefully present his arguments within the bureaucracy. His particular diplomatic skill was as a subtle, nonconfrontational negotiator who slowly built lasting relationships and a deep understanding of those leaders with whom he worked. Hare's personal knowledge of the complexities of Beirut's political factions gave him an authoritatively strong voice in the ongoing "cable wars" within the Department of State, especially following the 1958 crisis.

In 1960 Hare was appointed under secretary of state for political affairs, but only served in the post briefly because he was assigned as ambassador to Turkey at the outbreak of the crisis in 1961. At Ankara he played a pivotal role in defusing the crisis and preventing a Turkish invasion of Cyprus. Hare built a reputation for quiet, effective diplomacy and for acting effectively and coolly in the crisis by contacting the Turkish minister only hours before the planned invasion. His efforts were nearly undone by a strongly worded letter sent to Ankara by President Lyndon Johnson. Yet Hare was at his best in those times. For his efforts during the crisis he received the Department of State's Distinguished Service Award in 1964.

Nearing the end of his career in 1965, Hare was appointed by President Johnson to the State Department's top geographical post, assistant secretary of state for Near Eastern and South Asian affairs, until his retirement a few months later.

As assistant secretary he pressed Congress to support the program of P.L. 480 wheat aid to the Middle East. However, the program increasingly became the victim of meddling as congressional and National Security Council personnel, in particular Robert Komer and Walter W. Rostow, sought to leverage the Nasser regime by shortening the terms of the agreements and appending onerous new requirements, including one that all shipments be made via U.S. vessels, adding considerable side costs to the once-inexpensive program. Hare, a long-time proponent of nonmilitary aid, was not, however, able to save the wheat program. Hare firmly maintained throughout his career that U.S. arms sales to the region created enormous difficulties, and in later years he mused that America had made a serious error in resuming them, only to become one of the largest suppliers to a volatile area.

In 1960 Hare was in only the second group of American diplomats to achieve the rank of career ambassador that included Charles Bohlen, Ellis Briggs, and Llewellyn Thompson. Following his brief stint as assistant secretary, he retired to become the head of the Middle East Institute in Washington, D.C., from 1966 to 1969 and served as its first full-time president. At that post he worked to put the institute on a sound financial footing and promoted greater understanding between the United States and the Middle East region by bringing young scholars into the organization.

In retirement he watched the Foreign Service career of his son Paul Hare, who followed his father in a series of posts and eventually to an ambassadorship as well. In later life Raymond Hare willingly consented to interviews, but steadfastly refused to write his memoirs. He lived quietly in Georgetown with his wife until his death at the age of ninety-two in 1994.

Works by Raymond Hare

Raymond Hare's diplomatic correspondence has been published in a number of volumes in the *Foreign Relations of the United States* series issued by the Department of State.
"Notes on South Asia, 1947." Sackler Library, Columbia University.
"Capability and Foreign Policy." *Department of State Bulletin*, July 1, 1957, 22–25.
"Charting the Future Course of US Foreign Aid in the Near East and South Asia." *Department of State Bulletin*, April 18, 1966, 668–71.
"The Great Divide: World War II." *Annals of the American Academy of Political and Social Science* 401 (May 1972): 23–30.
Oral history interviews with Raymond Hare, the Association for Diplomatic Studies, Arlington, Virginia, and Georgetown University Library, Washington, DC, interviewed by Dayton Mak, summer 1987.

Works about Raymond Hare

Hare, Paul J. *Diplomatic Chronicles of the Middle East: A Biography of Ambassador Raymond A. Hare*. Lanham, MD: Middle East Institute, University Press of America, 1993.
Kraft, Joseph. "Those Arabists in the State Department." *New York Times Magazine*, November 7, 1971.

"Raymond Hare." *Current Biography*, 1957.
"Raymond Hare: Ambassador to New Nation." *U.S. News and World Report*, March 7,
    1958, 19.
"Raymond Hare Remembered." *Middle East Institute Newsletter* 45, no. 3 (May 1994).
Winchester, J. "Foreign Service Man." *Scholastic*, November 29, 1956.

TERESA ANN THOMAS

WILLIAM AVERELL HARRIMAN (1891–1986)

served in critical diplomatic posts from 1941 through the Johnson administration and was one of a handful of key figures who guided American diplomacy from the isolationism of the 1930s through World War II, to the international liberalism of the Cold War period. He made a major contribution to the most important and successful period in the conduct of American foreign relations.

Averell Harriman was born in New York City on November 15, 1891, the son and fifth child of railway magnate Edward Henry Harriman and Mary Averell Harriman (née Averell). He attended Groton School, received a B.A. from Yale in 1913, and in 1915 became vice president of the Union Pacific Railroad. In 1916 he acquired the Roach shipbuilding yard near Philadelphia and formed W. A. Harriman and Company four years later. In the mid-1920s Harriman also had an interest in a manganese-mining concession in the Caucasus. He traveled to the Soviet Union and met with Trotsky and other Communist leaders, but was more forcefully struck by the incompetence and brutality of the Bolshevik regime than by the potential of doing profitable business with it.

The onset of the Great Depression destroyed Harriman's faith in the ability of the Republican Party to manage the U.S. economy. Although he was initially unconvinced that the Democratic administration of Franklin Roosevelt could do fundamentally better, he sensed the shift of power from Wall Street to Washington, became a constructive critic of the New Deal in the early 1930s, and eventually moved into an administrative position with the National Recovery Administration (NRA). He served with the U.S. Department of Commerce's Business Advisory Council from 1937 to 1940 and was given his first quasi-diplomatic post when Roosevelt sent him to London in the spring of 1941 to oversee U.S. Lend-Lease assistance to Britain during the critical phases of the German blitz.

Serving Roosevelt as an observer of conditions in Britain, while conveying both the urgency and nature of Britain's needs back to Washington, Harriman was in a position to influence both American perceptions of the unfolding conflict in Europe and the content of policy responses to it. At a point when neutrality remained the official but comparatively impotent U.S. position on the war, his forceful advocacy of Britain's cause often provoked annoyance among leaders of Washington's diplomatic and military circles critical of Britain's prosecution of the war. For his part, Harriman was impatient with congressional reluctance to identify American interests more forthrightly with those of beleaguered Britain. He was nevertheless so successful in winning the confidence of Prime Minister Winston Churchill that the British leader consulted with Harriman regularly during his first meeting with Roosevelt in Placentia Bay, Newfoundland, in August 1941. The meeting that produced the Atlantic Charter also led to an Anglo-American decision to appoint a high-level delegation to work out assistance to the Soviet Union, at war with Germany since the launch of Operation Barbarossa in June of the same year. Harriman was named co-chairman, alongside Lord Beaverbrook, of the mission to Moscow.

Their meetings with Stalin were extremely delicate, due as much to the Soviet leader's petulant behavior as to the substance of the discussions. It was Harriman, not Beaverbrook, who exhibited the requisite sangfroid in the face of Stalin's emotional theatrics. At the conclusion of negotiations Stalin was pleased that he had secured the best aid deal possible, and Harriman had learned a valuable lesson about the mood swings of the Soviet leader. Because the $1-billion aid package he had concluded with Stalin technically exceeded his brief, Harriman made it a personal mission to defend the U.S. commitment to Russia to a skeptical American public. With his own money he purchased time on CBS radio to explain Washington's policy in terms of enlightened self-interest, an argument that was suddenly easier to make after the Japanese attack on Pearl Harbor on December 7, 1941.

In the summer of 1942 Harriman accompanied Churchill to Moscow for more discussions with Stalin. Bearing the unwelcome news that there was to be no second Allied front in France that year, Churchill benefited enormously from Harriman's company, especially in explaining to the enraged Soviet dictator the strategic advantage of the Anglo-American North African campaign, Operation Torch. No prime minister, Churchill later observed, had been better supported by the representative of another country. Harriman's performance earned him appointment in October 1943 as U.S. ambassador to the Soviet Union. The Moscow mission gave Harriman an appreciation of the nature of the Soviet state and an opportunity to assess firsthand the probable direction of Soviet-American relations after the war. He was routinely under the surveillance of the Soviet secret survice and became so accustomed to its presence that he once stopped to offer a ride to agents whose car had slid into a ditch while tailing his own.

Harriman's overarching purpose in Moscow was to help create a positive atmosphere for Soviet-American relations in which Roosevelt could plot war plans and postwar settlements. In some respects this task became more complicated as the war progressed toward an Allied victory. At the summit conference of the Big Three in Teheran in November–December 1943, Harriman's job was to placate a suspicious Churchill while Roosevelt made a special effort to win the confidence of Stalin. Even excluding differences over the Soviet Union specifically, British and American visions of the postwar order were incompatible. Especially disturbing from the American viewpoint was the evidence of Churchill's preference for carving up Europe into spheres of influence in clear violation of the principle of national self-determination recorded in the Atlantic Charter. Harriman had to inform Churchill that such an approach would provoke a veto from Roosevelt while simultaneously disabusing the American president of any notion that Stalin could be trusted to respect the independence of the East European states.

Poland got special attention. Harriman threw himself into the problems of postwar borders and the composition of a postwar Warsaw government, returning again and again to the issues in his discussions with Stalin and Soviet Foreign Minister Vyacheslav Molotov. It was no mystery that Soviet resistance to the return of the exiled Polish government in London was based on Moscow's rejection of any regime not sufficiently "friendly" toward Russia, that is, Communist. Even Harriman, who had been as well placed as anyone to appreciate the true nature of the Kremlin regime, was taken aback by Stalin's cool brutality, not only in brushing aside diplomatic and financial incentives to accept the London Poles but also in halting the Red Army's offensive in Poland just long enough for the German army to crush the 1944 Warsaw uprising and exterminate the only Poles left in the city possibly capable of resisting Soviet authority. In the toughest talks he had ever conducted with Soviet officials, Harriman expressed Washington's fury at Stalin's abandonment of the Poles and pushed the State Department to upbraid Moscow for its murderous cynicism.

Convinced that Stalin's position on Poland foreshadowed aggressive intentions for Eastern Europe more generally, Harriman was now at the fore (along with George Kennan, the State Department's leading Sovietologist) of efforts to harden American policy toward Moscow. At the Yalta Conference of February 4–11, 1945, Harriman was not included in private talks of the Big Three on Poland. Instead, he helped draft a proposal that representatives of the exile government in London join the Soviet-backed provisional government in Warsaw in forming a temporary coalition of national unity pending free elections. The agreement amounted to tacit recognition of the Soviet puppet regime in exchange for Moscow's promise to broaden its political base. Upon his return to Moscow Harriman faced the most frustrating phase of his career in U.S. diplomacy. The Soviets not only betrayed the agreement on Polish elections and a new government, they also reneged on a promise for the speedy repatriation of American prisoners of war freed in Poland, lying to Washington all the while about the number of U.S. soldiers involved. Harriman retaliated. When Karl Wolff, the Nazi police chief of occupied Italy, surrendered to American OSS Director Allen Dulles in Switzerland, Harriman intervened to block any Soviet participation in Allied interrogation of Wolff. Moscow's reaction was openly to accuse the United States of bad faith and deception. It revealed, in combination with the Polish affair, a determination to exclude Washington from the postwar settlement in Eastern Europe while insisting on full Soviet participation in the future of Western Europe. The Wolff episode provoked the angriest communication Roosevelt ever sent to Stalin, but Harriman never thought it angry enough. Roosevelt died the night of its transmission.

Harriman viewed the swearing-in of Harry Truman as something of an opportunity to apprise the new president of the double standard of Soviet foreign policy. Harriman found Truman already in essential agreement with himself regarding Soviet duplicity and willing to express his views directly to the Soviets. During the San Francisco Conference of April–June 1945 Truman subjected Soviet Foreign Minister Molotov to a dressing-down over Moscow's violation of the Yalta agreement—demanding the scrapping of the Communist government in Warsaw in favor of one representative of the Polish people— while Harriman shocked the American press in what was supposed to be an off-the-record exchange with the observation that American and Soviet foreign policy goals had become irreconcilable. On the issue of Poland he was not exaggerating. He considered Moscow incapable of understanding that the United States did not seek to undermine the security of the Soviet Union by supporting a democratic government on Polish soil. Years later Harriman judged the San Francisco Conference to be the beginning of the Cold War.

At the Potsdam Conference of the Big Three on July 17–August 2, 1945, Harriman's participation was confined to the fringes of the U.S. delegation. James Byrnes, the new secretary of state, with whom Harriman had poor personal rapport, shared little privileged information and was equally prudish about delegating authority. Accustomed to the trust and personal discretion afforded him by Roosevelt, Harriman was now given the status of an adjutant at a conference the stakes of which he appreciated better than anyone else among the Western delegations. The conference proceeded in an atmosphere of mounting suspicion among the participants, but concluded a number of agreements. Germany was to be demilitarized and deindustrialized; a number of territorial issues were settled; and Russia reiterated its intention to enter the war against Japan. Compromises on the composition of the Polish government and temporary agreements on Poland's borders were also reached, but neither were to the satisfaction or in the interest of the Western powers. For Harriman, the stay in Germany was valuable in revealing to him two things: the tight control imposed by Soviet military personnel at the conference, and the extent to which war reparations claimed by Moscow were already stripping eastern Germany of its industrial infrastructure. There was also a revealing informal encounter with Stalin, in which Harriman ventured that it must be gratifying for the Soviet leader to find himself in Berlin. Stalin replied that Tsar Alexander, after all, had made it to Paris.

His wartime diplomatic duties essentially concluded, Harriman reluctantly decided after Potsdam to return to civilian life, leaving Moscow in January 1946 and arriving in Washington to the commendation of the Medal of Merit. But his stay was brief, and he continued to carry the message of Cold War to American business and professional circles. Most notably, he ensured that the famous Long Telegram, written by George Kennan at the Moscow embassy and warning of the inherently expansionist nature of Russian and Soviet foreign policy, received the widest possible circulation. Kennan's analysis, featuring policy conclusions much the same as Harriman's, promptly became the cornerstone of the Truman Doctrine and the first article of the U.S. policy of containment of Soviet geopolitical ambitions.

During the Iranian crisis in the spring of 1946 President Truman dispatched Harriman to London as ambassador. Because the crisis subsided before Harriman's arrival, he briefly joined Secretary of State Byrnes at treaty discussions in Paris before returning again to Washington with the cabinet brief of secretary of commerce. In this post Harriman was at the center of efforts to implement the European Recovery Program (ERP), announced to Congress by Secretary of State George Marshall in March 1947. As an advocate of free trade and a businessman with experience in Germany, Harriman understood that a German industrial rejuvenation was especially critical to the ERP's success. Truman made Harriman the chair of a committee composed of corporate, labor, and academic experts involved in assessing Europe's needs and planning the use of U.S. tax revenue to rebuild European markets. The only alternative to a U.S. investment in European recovery, Harriman warned Wall Street, was an isolationist foreign policy and a domestic economy staggering under the burden of much higher costs for military security. The committee's findings, *A Report on European Recovery and American Aid*, recommended that the United States provide between $12 billion and $17 billion for European economies over the next five years. In order to drum up support for congressional approval, Harriman put in eighteen-hour days on a speaking tour of the nation. His somnolent public speaking ability was more than compensated by the respect he commanded in corporate circles and his expertise in Soviet affairs. The ERP passed the Senate on March 14, 1948.

For his efforts Harriman wanted nothing so much as the reward of appointment to secretary of state. Truman instead called on Dean Acheson to replace the retiring George Marshall, and Harriman suffered one of his greatest disappointments, but he remained at the center of foreign policy. As special assistant to the president, his primary function was to coordinate policy and ease tensions between the State and Defense departments at a point when Communist revolution in China and the outbreak of the Korean War placed both departments under enormous pressure. Republican critics of the administration's foreign policy called for Acheson's resignation, and Washington was awash with rumors that Harriman would replace him. But Truman stood behind his secretary, and Harriman defended Acheson as one of the finest first ambassadors the country had ever known. Harriman stayed on as special assistant and as mutual security administrator until 1953. It was at Acheson's suggestion that Harriman was sent to Teheran in 1951 to help defuse the Anglo-Iranian oil crisis at a time when an American presence was needed to deter any Soviet gambit to replace the declining British influence there.

During the 1950s Harriman also ventured into electoral politics, but with limited success. He failed in a bid to win the Democratic presidential nomination in 1952, yet defeated Senator Irving Ives for the governorship of New York. Two years into an agenda of social reform in Albany, he tried again for the presidential nomination and failed again. In 1958 he lost his gubernatorial re-election campaign to Nelson Rockefeller, whom he had appointed chair of a minor state commission in 1956.

Under the Kennedy administration Harriman was at first ambassador-at-large and then was appointed assistant secretary of state for Far Eastern affairs. In both posts Harriman found himself at the center of extremely complex negotiations to end internal conflict in Laos and secure the neutrality to which that country had been supposedly committed since 1954. At the height of the crisis he called upon Kennedy to commit the U.S. Seventh Fleet to the Gulf of Siam and marine battalions to Thailand in order to deter the continuation of a Communist ground offensive, all the while alternately cajoling and threatening the rival Laotian princes toward the formation of a coalition government. Ultimately the major powers and the bordering countries signed an accord guaranteeing Laos's neutrality in Geneva in July 1962. Harriman accomplished his mission and erased Laos from the administration's list of crises. However, the long-term dividends of the agreement were limited because the neutrality was not honored and Laos became a principal conduit, via the Ho Chi Minh Trail, of military supplies to Communist guerrillas in South Vietnam.

Remustered to the position of under secretary of state for political affairs in April 1963, Harriman was sent two weeks later to Moscow to initiate three-corner discussions (the United Kingdom, the United States, and the USSR) on a nuclear test-ban treaty. Efforts toward limiting the spread of nuclear arms went back to 1958, but the Cuban missile crisis of October 1962 had given the issue new urgency. Over the ten days of direct negotiations with Soviet Premier Nikita Khrushchev and Foreign Minister Andrei Gromyko, Harriman was able to draw on his experience in similar situations with Stalin. He adopted a fairly hard-headed approach to the substance of the discussions and at one point was prepared to storm from the room in protest of Soviet petulance. On July 25, 1963, Harriman, along with his British and Soviet counterparts, put his signature on a partial test-ban treaty limiting the signatories to underground tests and banning outright detonation in the atmosphere, the oceans, and space.

Originally very firm on the U.S. commitment to the Republic of South Vietnam in its struggle against Communist insurgency from the North, by the early 1960s Harriman had come to a much more ambivalent position. Promoted to assistant secretary of state for Far Eastern affairs, he was determined that South Vietnam's territorial integrity be maintained, but was skeptical that there was any long-term solution for Vietnam attainable by military means. This attitude was in part the product of personal disdain for the military, but Harriman was also concerned that the United States had little to build upon politically in Vietnam. He was highly critical of the Saigon government of Ngo Dinh Diem, believing it folly to tie American goals in Vietnam too closely to the survival of Diem's corrupt regime. His prediction that Diem's government was ripe for a coup turned out to be accurate. Still, at the time of Kennedy's death Harriman could not be counted as a major influence on Vietnam policy, except perhaps that the president's ambivalence matched his own.

In March 1965 Harriman was reactivated as ambassador-at-large by the Johnson administration. Seeing Laos as his model, Harriman worked his way back into the inner circle of American diplomacy by suggesting that Moscow—and therefore his own expertise—could help broker a deal to extract the United States from the deepening conflict. Appropriately skeptical that the North Vietnamese would accept any agreement that did not guarantee them victory, in 1966 Johnson nonetheless gave Harriman permission to seek a diplomatic solution. Little power or support came with the job. Success was scarce as well. On the eve of Richard Nixon's inauguration to the Oval Office in 1969, secret negotiations in Paris had reached agreement only on the shape of the negotiating table. Harriman's diplomatic career was over.

Averell Harriman thus ranks as one of the last and greatest of a generation of citizen-diplomats, known to posterity as the Wise Men, who authored and implemented the Cold War doctrine of containment and influenced decisively the outcome of the American Century. He died in Yorktown Heights, New York, on July 26, 1986.

Works by Averell Harriman

America and Russia in a Changing World. Garden City, NY: Doubleday, 1971.
With Elie Abel. *Special Envoy to Churchill and Stalin, 1941–1946.* New York: Random House, 1975.

Works about Averell Harriman

Abramson, Rudy. *Spanning the Century: The Life of W. Averell Harriman, 1891–1986.* New York: William Morrow, 1992.
Isaacson, Walter, and Evan Thomas. *The Wise Men: Six Friends and the World They Made.* New York: Simon and Schuster, 1986.

CARL CAVANAGH HODGE

TOWNSEND HARRIS (1804–1878),

American consul at Ningpo and American minister to Japan, led the way in opening Japan to American trade and diplomatic relations.

Born in upstate New York, Harris operated a bookstore in Elmira and played a key role in the founding of Elmira College. After a series of reverses in the 1840s he relocated to New York City. Although he never attended college, he was a staunch advocate of education throughout his life. Harris was a highly successful merchant in the city and worked on the campaign to found the City College of New York, where a building is named after him. As a bachelor, he was free to pull up stakes in 1849 and begin trading throughout the Pacific. During the next five years he sailed to ports in Formosa, Hong Kong, Malaya, Manila, and India.

During 1854 Harris solicited influential friends in New York to secure a diplomatic post in the Far East. He was assigned the consular position at Ningpo, a post that he considered beneath his qualifications, with an unsatisfactory annual salary of one thousand dollars. After additional lobbying by Harris and his influential friends in the Democratic Party, he received appointment as first minister to Japan and began a long journey that included time in England, South Africa, and India and a stop in Siam to negotiate a commercial treaty. Harris began keeping a journal during the trip. Although the journal's literary quality is nothing special and the analyses are colored by the anti-British sentiments that Harris shared with many Americans who lived in the 1850s, Harris was a perceptive observer of the places he visited. In his observations concerning native societies Harris exhibited acute curiosity but very little tendency to cast moral judgments on the unfamiliar customs of India, Asia, or Japan. His reluctance to pass judgment would cause him some problems with other Americans in Japan from 1856 to 1862.

When Harris arrived in Japan on August 21, 1856, the difficulties he faced in establishing regular diplomatic relations were formidable. The jarring impact of Commodore Matthew Perry's two visits to Japan had left the leaders of the shogunate and the local *daimyo* leaders divided into two factions. The "expel the barbarians" faction urged an all-out effort to resist Western encroachment. The "open country" faction believed that resistance was futile, and that Japan would have to learn from the West in order to regain a strong position among nations. The shogunate reacted by avoiding both strong stands and tried to use delaying tactics. This was an approach of which Japanese customs and language were very supportive. For diplomats like Townsend Harris, negotiations with the Japanese became a waiting game instead of a chess game. The standard response to most of Harris's inquiries was "waiting for a response from [the shogunate] Yedo."

Japanese stalling tactics were not the only obstacle Harris faced in Japan.

Beginning in January 1857, he went through several serious bouts with diseases that he described on different occasions as Saint Anthony's fire, cholera morbus, and acid stomach. No Western medical doctors were available, and he tried his best to work his way back to health by walking 350 miles a month and giving up tobacco.

Harris's health problems were known to other Americans in Japan. Francis Hall, a merchant from Connecticut, noted in his diary that he believed that "age and infirmities sapped his [Harris's] vigor." Hall was also intensely religious and sensitive to rumors that Harris was living a life of sexual impropriety. According to Hall, Harris had asked the Japanese to send him a woman who could sew. When the woman arrived, Harris rejected her and indicated that what he really was seeking was a prostitute. In Harris's own account of the incident, it appeared that the Japanese officials took the lead in offering the services of a prostitute to Harris.

Hall continued to direct a steady stream of criticism toward Harris during the time they both resided in Japan. At one point he wrote that he believed that Harris was overcautious when he warned Americans in Japan not to go out after dark. Hall also faulted Harris for his excessive politeness and high estimate of himself. Sarcastically referring to Harris as "the treaty-king," Hall concluded that Harris was too uncritical of Japanese attempts to cast themselves in a favorable light.

While Hall's diary is valuable, a few factors must be taken into account when considering his portrayal of Townsend Harris. First, Hall's preoccupations were primarily religious. He spent time discussing whether any remnants remained in Japan from the first wave of Christian missions. He was not afraid to discuss prostitution, but he viewed it with an attitude of righteous voyeurism that was bound to clash with Harris's more detached view.

Another observer of Townsend Harris's diplomatic efforts was Henry Heusken, the Dutch translator whom Harris hired for the annual salary of fifteen hundred dollars. Heusken, who was killed by members of the antiforeign faction in Japan in January 1861, also left behind a diary with certain limitations. Its editors have noted that the dates in the diary are often unreliable, and that Heusken was often carried away by literary pretensions. Nevertheless, as the person who spent the most time with Harris in Japan, Heusken was able to relate in detail his diplomatic achievements. For instance, Heusken gave Harris high marks for his persistence throughout the difficult currency-exchange negotiations that began soon after his arrival in Japan. The Japanese wanted to keep commercial relations with the West to a minimum. One way to accomplish their goal was to insist on an unrealistic and unfavorable exchange rate. Harris never relented in his efforts to negotiate a rate that would work in favor of American commercial interests. His argument was direct and simple. Japan was faced with maritime powers whose commercial greed and expansionist policies had meant the downfall of many a ruler. The United States could be counted on to arrange the most equitable treaties the Japanese could possibly hope for. After the Opium

War in China, the Western nations had demanded the same privileges that England gained through its Unequal Treaties. If Japan dealt with America first, the other Western nations would be bound by America's generous example.

Heusken also documented Harris's constant vigilance against the many spies that Japanese officials attempted to place in his residence. These men were sent to the American residence under the pretense of providing security to Harris and Heusken. Harris rejected all such offers and insisted on selecting his own security guards from the available Japanese. As in any diplomatic situation, it is unlikely that Harris totally eliminated spying, but he made a point with the Japanese that he would not be bullied into accepting their terms for the conduct of the American mission.

The account by Heusken goes into great detail about the tenacity of Harris as a negotiator. The Dutch diarist included a lengthy narration of Harris's December 1857 audiences with the shogun. It is clear from this account that Harris was not intimidated by the elaborate protocol, and that he was not discouraged by the constant Japanese reliance on delay, couched in ceremonial language that reflected the Japanese priority on avoiding direct confrontation. Harris pressed on, remaining polite but never dropping any of the essential components of the American agenda for opening Japan.

Although Heusken's death at the hands of Japanese antiforeign fanatics robbed him of the chance to leave a general assessment of Harris's strengths and weaknesses, he left behind abundant anecdotes for future analysis. Based on Heusken's account, Harris should receive high marks for setting an agenda and pursuing it with very little support from the administration back home. Harris also succeeded in separating his official agenda from the American missionary agenda that played a major role in American policy in China during the same time. Harris viewed Japan as a market for American merchants and an empire whose cooperation was needed as the United States prepared for expansion in the Pacific. Promoting a missionary agenda would have brought America the problems a similar agenda created in Sino-American relations in the nineteenth century.

A final word on Heusken must address the question of how objective he was as an observer. Although many people in his role would be uncritical of their superiors, Heusken did not seem to fit that mold. He was critical of Harris's failure to arrange a better salary for him and of the security arrangements at the residence, and he was frank in recording the numerous times that health problems left Harris almost incapacitated. With all these factors in mind, Heusken is probably the most reliable eyewitness to Harris's accomplishments in Japan.

Added to the trials that Harris faced of being a diplomat in an unfamiliar land were the isolation and the long wait for instructions from which most nineteenth-century diplomats suffered. It was over thirteen months after Harris arrived in Japan before the next American ship, the USS *Portsmouth*, arrived. When it did, Harris was shocked to discover that an attempt had been under way in Washington to recall him from his post. Immediately after Harris had negotiated a commercial treaty in Siam the year before, he had sent a copy home to the administration. The text was somehow leaked to a New York newspaper that published it before any official announcement of the treaty occurred. Several administration officials were furious. Harris asserted that he had nothing to do with the premature announcement, and the issue blew over.

Perhaps the most difficult aspect of the situation in Japan was watching the United States drift toward civil war. Harris's July 4 journal entries are low-key testimonials to his passionate patriotism, and the concern he indicated as he heard of the calamitous events leading to secession was evident. Furthermore, the election of 1860 installed a Republican administration, and Harris had gained his position through Democratic Party patronage. By 1862 Harris was physically worn out, worried about events in America, and aware of his limits as a Democratic appointee. He returned home, became active in New York City politics and philanthropic activities, and died in 1878.

Townsend Harris left the diplomatic service and slipped very quickly into relative historical obscurity. Commodore Perry was the dramatic hero who was mentioned in connection with the opening of Japan; Harris was a footnote for historians, and a small one at that. He was an amateur diplomat for a country that would later develop a professional State Department. He was physically frail at a time when health and character were considered synonymous. Also, he pursued a commercial agenda at a time when military and missionary exploits seized the imagination of America. It was not until 1922 that the historian Tyler Dennett focused on Harris in his book *Americans in Eastern Asia*. Dennett gave high marks to Harris for "urbanity, character and ability" while noting that this policy in Japan was basically an extension of the American policy toward China. Dennett praised Harris for his efforts and compared his record with that of a more famous amateur diplomat of the previous century, Benjamin Franklin. Dennett's glowing recommendation did little to bolster Harris's historical reputation.

A later book by a lesser-known historian, Herbert H. Gowen, did little more than review the anecdotes and events from Harris's career that would appeal to general human interest, with very little to offer in the way of historical analysis. Gowen did include a five-line poem recited in 1931 by Baron Masuca, who had worked for Harris, who noted that the diplomat "argued vehemently, such was his sincerity." There is just enough ambiguity in the ceremonial poem to wish that more eyewitness accounts from the Japanese viewpoint had survived.

Based on this sparse record, what sort of assessment of the career of Townsend Harris is possible? First, it should be noted that in many ways Harris typified American aspirations of his era. He followed a successful career with a period of public service, he traveled widely, and he exuded the confidence in American expansion and prosperity that historians like Norman Graebner and William Appleman Williams chronicled in detail. Despite all this, Harris went against the American grain in some ways. He refrained from passing value judgments on the cultures he encountered. He never indulged in saber rattling and always worked for peaceful solutions to international problems. Last, Harris showed great personal courage by accomplishing a great deal in Japan despite frequent illness and constant isolation. Harris was ahead of his time in realizing how important Japan would become as America fulfilled its push toward Pacific expansion. He was definitely an amateur, but it is doubtful that a polished European diplomat would have accomplished any more than Harris did. Harris the man never will cast a long shadow; the events he set under way are a different story.

Work by Townsend Harris

The Complete Journal of Townsend Harris, First American Consul General and Minister to Japan. Garden City, NY: Doubleday, Doran & Company, Inc., 1930.

Works about Townsend Harris

Crow, Carl. He Opened the Door of Japan: Townsend Harris and the Story of His Amazing Adventures in Establishing American Relations with the Far East. New York: Harper, 1939.
Dennett, Tyler. Americans in Eastern Asia. New York: Macmillan, 1922.
Gowen, Herbert Henry. Asia: A Short History from the Earliest Times to the Present Day. Boston: Little, Brown, 1926.
Hall, Francis. Japan through American Eyes: The Journal of Francis Hall Kanagawa and Yokohama, 1859–1866. Ed. F. G. Notehelfer. Princeton, NJ: Princeton University Press, 1992.
Heusken, Henry C. J. Japan Journal, 1855–1861. Trans. and eds. Jeannette C. van der Corput and Robert A. Wilson. New Brunswick: Rutgers University Press, 1964.
Jones, Francis Clifford. Extraterritoriality in Japan and the Diplomatic Relations Resulting in Its Abolition, 1853–1899. New Haven: Yale University Press, 1931.

MICHAEL J. POLLEY

LOY WESLEY HENDERSON (1892–1986) was a career Foreign Service officer who exerted a profound influence on U.S. policy toward the Soviet Union and the Middle East and on the State Department.

Loy Henderson was born near Rogers, Arkansas, on June 28, 1892, and was the son of a Methodist minister. The family moved frequently around the Middle West as his father sought a church financially secure enough to enable him to raise his five children properly. Henderson graduated from Northwestern University with an A.B. degree in 1915 and then spent a year at Denver Law School and another in graduate school at New York University. He failed the physical exam for military service in World War I due to an early arm injury and instead joined the Red Cross. The misery he saw in Russia as a member of the Inter-Allied Commission to Germany for the Repatriation of Prisoners of War and in the Baltic states as a member of a relief commission impressed him deeply.

After directing American Red Cross operations in Germany in 1920–1921, he resigned in late 1921, took the consular service exam, and won an appointment as vice consul in May 1922. In his first post, Dublin, he issued visas and protected the rights of American citizens in difficulty there. In Queenstown in 1923, his next assignment, Henderson helped to reorganize the consulate in addition to doing commercial reporting.

In late 1924 he received a transfer to the Eastern Europe Division of the State Department under Robert Kelley. Kelley deeply distrusted the Soviet government and opposed recognition. He assigned Henderson to investigate the connection between the Comintern and left-wing political movements in the United States. Equipped with a solid foundation in Soviet affairs, Henderson set off in 1927 for Riga, a principal U.S. listening post for developments in the Soviet Union. Due to his reputation for management, however, he found himself assigned to reorganize the legation while trying to learn Russian and help the Red Cross on the side. He became ill from exhaustion, and only when he returned to duty in 1929 did he begin substantive reporting on Soviet developments.

The department called him back to Washington in 1930, where he again joined Robert Kelley. At the request of Secretary of State Cordell Hull, Henderson undertook a study of the implications of U.S. recognition of the Soviet Union, which was imminent by 1933. In addition to exploring the economic implications, he recommended obtaining a pledge from the Soviets not to interfere in internal U.S. politics, a pledge that would become a condition of recognition. In late 1930 he married Elise Heinrichson, the daughter of a former Latvian landowner, whom he had met in Riga.

The new U.S. mission in Moscow required the services of someone with recognized managerial skills, a need that brought Henderson to Moscow in 1934. As a senior officer, he enjoyed the services of George Kennan and Charles ("Chip") Bohlen as his right-hand men. He found most supplies in short supply and working space extremely restricted. Henderson relieved somewhat the space shortage by acquiring three fortuitously available apartments adjacent to the embassy—a silver lining to Stalin's purges.

An important event occurred in 1935. The Comintern met in Moscow, and American Communists attended the proceedings, thus breaking the formal Soviet pledge not to interfere in U.S. politics made at the time of recognition. Ambassador William Bullitt left Moscow in disgust, and Henderson remained in charge for about twenty months.

Joseph Davies, a friend of President Roosevelt without diplomatic experience, finally replaced Bullitt in 1937. He tended to take Soviet explanations of the purges at face value, and Henderson was forced to report contrary interpretations by personal letter. Henderson and his Foreign Service colleagues saw the purges as efforts to destroy the influence of academicians, the intelligentsia, the civil service, and the military in order to erase the influence of Trotsky and theoreticians generally. In spite of the fierce war of words and ideological differences between Moscow and Berlin in 1937 and 1938, Henderson reported with foresight that a rapprochement between the two nations was increasingly likely.

Henderson returned to Washington in the spring of 1938 and in October became the assistant chief of the Division of European Affairs with responsibility for Eastern Europe. When Western Europe fell to the Nazis in the spring of 1940, he realized that the United States would need to collaborate with the Soviet Union, but again with foresight, he feared that the White House would interpret Soviet cooperation as genuine friendship rather than a calculated judgment of its best interests.

Hitler's attack on Russia was not a surprise to Henderson. He and his staff believed that the Russians should receive Lend-Lease aid, but still did not want to see the administration go overboard in its assessment of the long-term future of Soviet-American relations. Even so, American left-wing groups began to accuse Henderson of dragging his feet on Lend-Lease.

After Pearl Harbor and Germany's declaration of war on the United States, Henderson saw clearly that the job of his office was to speed up delivery of aid to Russia to keep it in the war, even though the era of cooperation might last only until Soviet perceptions of its interests and peril changed. In Henderson's view, the USSR's ultimate aims still included territorial expansion, control of Europe, and even world revolution. He expected that these objectives would place the Soviets in ultimate conflict with the United States.

Even during the war Henderson spoke out, and his firm views became well known. He irritated leftist groups, Soviet government representatives, and circles close to the White House who wished closer relations with the USSR. While Henderson was on a temporary assignment in Moscow as chargé d'affaires in late 1942 and early 1943, Maxim Litvinov, the Soviet ambassador in Washington, warned that relations between Washington and Moscow would never improve as long as Henderson was in charge of Eastern European affairs. Although Henderson resumed that position upon his return, Secretary Hull received word from the White House that he should transfer Henderson. Consequently, the department arranged a posting for Henderson to Iraq as envoy extraordinary and minister plenipotentiary in July 1943. After twenty years of work devoted to Soviet affairs, Henderson believed that the intensity of the criticism of his views by left-wing and Soviet officials was a true measure of his success in trying to formulate a sensible policy.

Henderson arrived in Baghdad without particular knowledge of the Middle East, but he set about filling that gap with his usual energy. He judged developments in the area by their impact on the larger picture—the balance of power between the United States and the Soviet Union. Hence he became concerned over British imperial policy because it could alienate Arab nationalists, who, he correctly forecast, would become a major force in Middle East politics. He built a close relationship with Iraqi Prime Minister Nuri al-Said and regarded with misgivings the emergence of a Communist party in Iraq.

Henderson's grasp of Middle East developments earned him a transfer to the department as director of the Office of Near Eastern and African Affairs in April 1945. He knew that his Washington assignment would be active and probably stormy. In January 1946 he produced a long memo pointing out that the Soviets seemed determined to destroy the British structure of control in the Middle East so that their own forces could sweep across Turkey, through the Dardanelles, and to the Mediterranean. He believed that they would also sweep across Iran, through the Persian Gulf, and on to the Indian Ocean. In fact, the Soviets did move large forces toward Turkey, Iran, and Iraq. Alerted by Henderson, President Truman sent a cable to Moscow asking bluntly what the Kremlin's intentions were. Stalin pledged to withdraw his troops from the area within six weeks.

When, in the summer of 1946, the Soviets demanded the eastern provinces of Turkey and participation in control of the Turkish straits, Henderson warned that if they succeeded, the United States would find it extremely difficult to prevent the USSR from gaining control over all of Turkey, Greece, and the rest of the area. He and Under Secretary of State Dean Acheson persuaded President Truman to send a message of encouragement to Ankara and to order U.S. fleet units to the eastern Mediterranean. The Soviets backed down.

Meanwhile, conditions in Greece were approaching chaos as civil war with a large Communist input was raging. In February 1947 Henderson sent another memorandum to the secretary describing conditions there, stressing Greece's importance as a focal point in Middle East developments, and suggesting pressure on Greek leaders to form a coalition government and the institution of a U.S. aid program to help stave off leftist forces. The other shoe also dropped in the Middle East in February when the British embassy in Washington sent two diplomatic notes to Henderson stating that the United Kingdom could no longer afford to support Greece and Turkey and would have to pull out in six weeks. His Majesty's Government hoped that the United States could assume the burden. In the absence of Secretary Marshall, Under Secretary Acheson instructed Henderson, as chairman, and John Hickerson, deputy director of the

European Division, to start work that night on a paper presenting the facts of the situation and recommendations for U.S. actions in response.

President Truman accepted the necessity of strengthening Greece and Turkey in the face of Communist threats and agreed that the administration should request funds and authority to act from Congress. Henderson and his staff worked long hours with Acheson to prepare specific recommendations, including legislative proposals, plans for recruiting civilians to work in Greece, and projects with the Pentagon for military aid missions and arms supplies for both countries. As chairman of the Special Committee to Study Assistance to Greece and Turkey, Henderson coordinated the reports of the working groups and produced the final plan and related documents that became the basis for the Truman Doctrine. Henderson then made a rapid trip to Greece to implement his recommendation for a coalition government. By knocking heads together, he succeeded in setting up a government of national unity that managed to hold the guerrillas at bay until Marshall Tito's defection from the Soviet camp ended the insurgency.

The most controversial issue to confront Henderson during this departmental tour was the creation of a Jewish state in Palestine. Since his earlier experience involved the Soviet Union, he approached the Palestine problem from the angle of its impact on the conflict between the superpowers. He feared that an active U.S. role in establishing a Jewish state would cost the United States support and friendship among the Arabs and other Moslems whose help the United States would need in blocking Soviet inroads in the Middle East. He was also concerned about the possible loss of oil and communication routes in Arab countries needed to build a free Europe and stabilize conditions in Greece and Turkey. If the Zionists succeeded in establishing a Jewish state, Henderson foresaw increasing violence in the area and with it a growing U.S. commitment to Israel's protection. Although some Zionists accused Henderson of anti-Semitism, his reasons for opposing U.S. support for the establishment of Israel were perfectly consistent with his perception of U.S. interests in the Cold War.

A major controversy arose over the U.S. position on the report of the United Nations Special Committee on Palestine in 1947. The committee majority recommended the partition of Palestine, which was popular among Zionists because it would produce a Jewish state. Henderson warned, however, that if the partition plan were adopted, it would have to be implemented by force, the United States would have to support Israel, and the Palestine problem would return to the United Nations, like a festering sore, for many years to come. He also pointed out that an imposed partition ran counter to the principles of self-determination and majority rule since the population was preponderantly Arab. Henderson and his officers suggested a U.N. trusteeship for a long-enough period for emotions to cool and make a lasting solution possible.

Although Henderson stayed within bureaucratic channels and did not resort to the press to disseminate his views, his position, which Secretary Marshall firmly supported, became well known in the White House and among Jewish circles throughout the country. The White House and the State Department received tens of thousands of communications advocating partition and many criticizing Henderson. In September 1947 he attended a tense meeting in the White House during which David Niles, White House aide for contacts with minorities, and Clark Clifford, special counsel to the president, subjected him to an extremely rough cross-examination. Henderson held his own, but the president left the room in disgust at Henderson. Faced with unprecedented pressure from Zionists and others wishing to see the creation of a Jewish state, and in accordance with his own feelings in the matter, President Truman decided that the United States should support the partition plan, which won U.N. approval on November 29, 1947.

The last phase of Henderson's tussle with Israel concerned the timing of U.S. recognition. He warned that the Arab states would invade the new nation once it declared its independence and advised against taking the lead in recognition. White House aides with domestic politics in mind argued the opposite way. They won, and the United States accorded Israel de facto recognition eleven minutes after Israel's declaration of independence on May 14, 1948.

By this time Niles and others in the White House were more than fed up with Henderson. They demanded his removal. The president, weary of all the pressure, recognized that the outspoken State Department officer would be a liability in the election campaign of 1948. Consequently, Henderson received an appointment as ambassador to India and Nepal in July of that year, far away from Israel. Although he had failed to temper U.S. support for Israel's independence, he still considered his Washington tour a success on the whole because he had helped to alert government circles to the Soviet threat and had initiated the Truman Doctrine.

Upon his arrival in New Delhi, Henderson, true to his past record, recommended a more active policy. He proposed lifting the arms embargo imposed on India and Pakistan during their war over Kashmir, but this proved not to offer enough leverage to convert the existing cease-fire into a settlement. When the Communists won in China, Henderson tried in vain to persuade India to go slow in recognizing the new regime. However, he did help induce India to support U.N. action to halt the North Korean attack on the South in June 1950. He also supported vigorously and successfully the request from India for agricultural aid after a drought had ravaged the grain-producing areas.

In September of that year Henderson received a transfer as ambassador to troubled Iran. Under the leadership of Prime Minister Mohammed Mossadeq, the Iranian government had nationalized the assets of the Anglo-Iranian Oil Company, which held the petroleum concession in Iran and operated the huge Abadan refinery. The British government had blockaded oil shipments from Iran, and a tense confrontation existed. The U.S. government was anxious to find a compromise that would permit the oil to flow again and prevent conditions from arising that would allow the Communist Tudeh party to gain power.

Henderson became involved immediately in efforts to work toward a settlement, but obstacles, including the amount of compensation to be paid Anglo-Iranian Oil, prevented progress. When Henderson returned from consultation in Washington shortly after the 1952 election, he tried out a new U.S. proposal, but Mossadeq would not compromise with the British. At this point Henderson concluded that although he had admirable qualities, Mossadeq had to go in order to avoid an ultimate Communist takeover. In late June 1953 Henderson returned to Washington for consultation with the new administration and, as the expert on the scene, played a major role in reaching the decision to overthrow Mossadeq by covert means.

Henderson was on vacation in Austria when the shah called for Mossadeq's resignation, but he flew to Teheran when reports reached him that the coup attempt had failed. He was on the scene for the August 1953 riots, assisted by the CIA, that resulted in Mossadeq's replacement as prime minister by Fazlollah Zahedi and the successful negotiation of an agreement on oil production. Henderson considered the operation a disagreeable but necessary step to establish order and to protect Iran from Communist control.

When Henderson returned to Washington in October 1954 to receive a distinguished service award, Secretary of State John Foster Dulles mentioned that he needed him back in Washington to reorganize the State Department and Foreign Service, which were suffering from inefficient management and low morale. The administration believed that Henderson's reputation as an administrator, the respect he had earned as a career officer, and his conservative outlook, especially regarding the Soviet Union, made him an ideal choice to put things right. He accepted the post reluctantly under some pressure from President Dwight Eisenhower.

Henderson became deputy under secretary for administration in January 1955 and career ambassador, the highest Foreign Service rank, in March of the next year. He took measures needed to revitalize the department, including speeding up the centralization of most of its many operations in an enlarged building. He also made a six-week tour of the newly independent African nations in 1960 to plan the opening of new missions there.

Under Eisenhower, Henderson was again active in Middle East affairs. Secretary Dulles gave him responsibility for liaison with the Baghdad Pact organization, where he functioned as a very active observer. During the Suez crisis he became the top American member on the Suez Commission and an active participant in the first and second Suez conferences in 1956. In mid-1957, when the Syrian government appeared to be leaning far toward Moscow, Henderson made a Middle East tour and upon his return recommended speeding up arms deliveries to friendly countries in the area. The president acted positively on Henderson's recommendations.

Although Henderson, now known as "Mr. Foreign Service," turned sixty-five, the normal retirement age, in 1957, he remained on active duty until January 1961 at the request of the White House. The State Department named the auditorium in its new building after him as well. After an active retirement, much of it spent as director of the Center for Diplomacy and Foreign Policy at American University and at the Washington Institute of Foreign Affairs, Henderson died in 1986 at the age of ninety-three.

Work by Loy Henderson

A *Question of Trust: The Origins of U.S.-Soviet Diplomatic Relations: The Memoirs of Loy W. Henderson*. Stanford, CA: Stanford University, Hoover Institution Press, 1986.

Works about Loy Henderson

Acheson, Dean. *Present at the Creation: My Years in the State Department*. New York: W. W. Norton and Company, 1969.

Brands, H. W. *Inside the Cold War: Loy Henderson and the Rise of the American Empire, 1918–1961*. New York: Oxford University Press, 1991.

Kuniholm, Bruce R. *The Origins of the Cold War in the Near East: Great Power Conflict and Diplomacy in Iran, Turkey, and Greece*. Princeton: Princeton University Press, 1980.

Lytle, Mark Hamilton. *The Origins of the Iranian-American Alliance, 1941–1953*. New York: Holmes and Meier, 1987.

McCullough, David. *Truman*. New York: Rockefeller Center, Simon and Schuster, 1992.

Wilson, Evan M. *Decision on Palestine*. Stanford, CA: Stanford University, Hoover Institution Press, 1979.

WILLIAM N. DALE

MARTIN JOSEPH HILLENBRAND (1915–) was

ambassador to Hungary (October 1967 to January 1969), assistant secretary of state for European affairs (January 1969 to May 1972), and ambassador to the Federal Republic of Germany (May 1972 to October 1976) and witnessed major Cold War developments in Europe.

Born on August 1, 1915, in Youngstown, Ohio, of German-born parents, Hillenbrand graduated in 1937 from the University of Dayton in political science, received a master's degree in public law and jurisprudence in 1938, and earned a doctorate in international relations in 1948 from Columbia University. His first foreign service appointment came in 1939 as deputy consul in Zurich, Switzerland, where he processed the flow of refugees from Germany and France. After World War II Hillenbrand served exclusively in European affairs in the State Department and abroad, especially Germany.

In November 1958 Soviet Premier Nikita S. Khrushchev seemed to directly threaten the peace of Europe. The Federal Republic of Germany, or West Germany, had entered into the North Atlantic Treaty Organization (NATO) in May 1955, a fact the Soviet leader now claimed violated the Potsdam Agreement of 1945 on postwar Four Power control of Germany. Therefore, he demanded that the Western forces in Berlin leave that city, which was to become a "free city" law but would be Soviet dominated in practice. A peace treaty was said to be necessary to finalize the existing borders between East and West Germany. The access routes to Berlin were to be the responsibility not of the Soviet Union, but of East Germany, a political entity that neither France, Great Britain, nor the United States recognized as a sovereign state.

Soviet pressure on Berlin lasted from 1958 to 1962. As a State Department official, Hillenbrand was involved in producing various U.S. responses to Moscow's Berlin ultimatum. First as director of the Office of German Affairs, and then as director of the Berlin Task Force in the early 1960s, he drafted memorandums and cables that refined America's Berlin position. The Eisenhower administration had pursued a policy of firmness with Moscow, rejecting any idea of recognizing East Germany's desire to control access routes to Berlin. However, the administration of John F. Kennedy was not averse to seeking a modus vivendi with Khrushchev in Berlin. JFK displayed an early impatience with West German Chancellor Konrad Adenauer, who refused to endorse any notion of recognizing East German sovereignty, especially after the erection of the Berlin Wall in the days following August 13, 1961.

Hillenbrand, a leading voice in the Berlin Task Force, was the author or coauthor of a substantial number of working papers and analyses, recently declassified, that attempted to fashion a modus vivendi with Moscow. In April 1962 the Kennedy administration submitted to the West Germans a "Principles Paper" that the United States thought would be useful in its talks with Moscow.

One of the proposals envisioned joint East-West German committees; another was to discuss a nonaggression treaty between Warsaw Treaty Organization and NATO states. Adenauer refused to consider such proposals, which were then leaked to the German press. The ensuing shock, dismay, and recriminations in Washington and Bonn brought German-American relations to a new low point. It took the shock of the Cuban missile crisis of October 1962 to repair the diplomatic damage done to the German-American alliance.

Given his experience with Berlin and German affairs, Hillenbrand was next posted as deputy chief of mission in Bonn (1963–1967). There he helped Ambassador George McGhee (1963–1968) adjust to the political successors of Chancellor Adenauer (who had ruled West Germany from its founding in 1949 until his resignation in October 1963). Hillenbrand had proven himself an able Foreign Service officer in the administrations of Kennedy and Johnson. The latter appointed him the first American ambassador to Hungary in 1967, when it was agreed to raise both national missions to embassy level.

Prior to Hillenbrand's arrival in the Hungarian capital of Budapest in October 1967, a potentially damaging incident occurred. Cardinal József Mindzenty had been a leading figure in the failed Hungarian revolt against Soviet rule in 1956. Before the uprising he had spent nine years in prison under the Communist regime of Matyas Rakosi, who had had the priest physically and psychologically tortured. After only three weeks of freedom during the 1956 revolt, Mindzenty sought and was granted sanctuary in the American embassy. Rumors now had it that he was to leave the American embassy grounds owing to differences with the Vatican, which was negotiating with the Communist government for his release. It was no secret that the moment he left the U.S. building, his immediate arrest would follow. The international media gave maximum coverage to this situation.

On October 20, 1967, when Hillenbrand first approached the U.S. embassy structure on Szabadsag Ter, or Freedom Square, he did not know what to expect. In their initial meeting the cardinal apologized for the inconvenience the past uproar inflicted on the new American representative. Mindzenty told the new ambassador that he felt that the Vatican was blind to what it was dealing with: a government of atheists who despised Roman Catholicism and all religion. Hillenbrand assured the cardinal that his ambassadorship would in no way jeopardize the cardinal's position in the embassy. The ambassador was to develop an admiration for the patience and courage of this unusual houseguest.

Hungary was a Soviet satellite state, controlled internally by the Socialist (Communist) Workers Party. The U.S. ambassador had to interface with the Party leader Janos Kadar, who had been dispatched to Budapest by Soviet leader Khrushchev when Soviet forces crushed the 1956 revolution. In his talks with Kadar, Hillenbrand noticed that the Party leader was not at ease with his past. Kadar followed a policy of strict subservience to Soviet foreign policy priorities. Yet in doing so, he encouraged a group of reform-minded economists and liberal party officials to develop what was referred to as the New Economic Mechanism

(NEM). The idea was to give more discretion to the managers of Hungary's state-owned industries. This included permission to deal with non-Hungarian businesses. Hungary quickly emerged as the Eastern bloc's leading consumer of Western goods. The Soviets, who stationed large numbers of troops in Hungary, did not approve of this deviation from their command economy model. Khrushchev scornfully referred to the NEM as "goulash communism." But Hillenbrand observed that Kadar's unquestioned loyalty to Khrushchev's and Brezhnev's foreign policies translated into Moscow's acquiescence in Budapest's economic reforms.

The Hungarian capital was not at the center of East-West tensions in Europe. Still, it provided the ambassador the opportunity to report on two of communism's most pressing problems: the Sino-Soviet split and the Czech reform movement. Moscow's attempt to expel the Chinese Party from the world Communist movement was administratively centered in Budapest. Kadar saw to it that the preparatory meetings of the various Communist parties took place in Budapest. Hillenbrand discovered that the best source of information for the ongoing debate was the Italian embassy. The Italian Ambassador wined and dined the members of the visiting Italian Communist delegation, who freely spoke of their impression of the party debates. The Budapest conference of September 1968 gave the Kremlin what it wanted: the summoning of a world conference of Communist parties in Moscow for the purpose of expelling the Chinese Communists.

Unlike East Germany and Poland, Hungary did not react negatively to the political reforms advanced by the Dubček regime in neighboring Czechoslovakia. Hillenbrand reported to Washington that Hungarian Prime Minister Jeno Fock expressed support for the democratic programs introduced in Prague. Kadar, aware of Moscow's growing disenchantment with Dubček, asked the Kremlin for patience. Recalling their tragic fate in 1956, the Hungarians also tried to persuade Prague to go slow with its reform program as the Soviets publicly questioned the policies of the Czech liberals.

Brezhnev rejected Kadar's advice and sent over 200,000 Soviet and Eastern-bloc troops into Czechoslovakia, who destroyed the Prague Spring in August 1968. Budapest complied with its Soviet master's decision, as Hungarian forces occupied an area in the Hungarian-speaking portion of Slovakia just south of Prague. The American embassy reported that these troops had to be quickly replaced because they displayed an all-too-obvious sympathy with the embattled population. Hillenbrand conveyed to the government of Hungary President Johnson's statement of protest of the invasion. He noted the feeling of shock and despondency the Hungarians showed as the Brezhnev Doctrine suppressed yet another attempt at political pluralism.

Richard Nixon selected Hillenbrand as his assistant secretary of state, a post he held from 1969 to 1972. The two major issues of Hillenbrand's secretaryship were the *Ostpolitik* or "Eastern policy" of West Germany toward East Germany, and détente with the Soviet Union. West German Chancellor Willy Brandt sought to improve relations with Moscow and its Warsaw Pact allies via a policy of incremental adjustment. This represented a dramatic shift for the Federal Republic, which until Brandt's chancellorship had refused to recognize the existence of Communist East Germany. The West Germans also refused to accept the validity of the Oder-Neisse border separating East Germany from Poland. Finally, Bonn claimed to be the sole legal representative of all Germans, East and West. Now Bonn was prepared to amend these principles. Brandt, the first Social Democratic chancellor since the Weimar Republic, and his chief foreign policy advisor, Egon Bahr, initially found only doubt and suspicion in the White House. Previous German governments had sought Washington's approval before approaching Moscow on even minor matters, but now Bonn informed Nixon and National Security Adviser Henry Kissinger of its proposed actions. Yet Nixon and Brandt agreed that the situation in Europe had reached a turning point by the 1970s. Nixon, in his first trip abroad as president, asked in Berlin in February 1969 that the Soviets ease tensions in the divided city. In July Soviet Foreign Minister Andrei I. Gromyko said that his government was now ready to discuss the status of Berlin with the Western powers.

Hillenbrand knew that serious negotiations on Berlin and Nixon's desire for détente would require the input of the State Department's Bureau of European Affairs. Thus he brought back from the Bonn embassy James Sutterlin to be director of the Office of German Affairs. During the Four Power, or Quadripartite, Berlin talks of 1970–1971, the assistant secretary served as the State Department representative to the Senior Review Group of the National Security Council. He also chaired the Interdepartmental Task Force on Berlin, where he coordinated policy for the Berlin talks.

On September 3, 1971, the ambassadors of Great Britain, France, the United States, and the Soviet Union signed the Quadripartite agreement on Berlin. The keys to this document were *Zugang*, unimpeded civilian traffic between West Berlin and West Germany; *Zuordnung*, recognition of West Berlin's ties with West Germany; and *Zutritt*, that citizens of West Berlin be permitted to visit East Berlin and East Germany. This represented the first Four Power accord on Berlin since the end of the Berlin blockade of 1948.

On May 17, 1972, Nixon, accompanied by Kissinger and Hillenbrand, who was a senior member of the American delegation, met with Soviet leader Leonid Brezhnev in the Kremlin's St. Catherine Hall. Hillenbrand wanted a more open, direct diplomacy among the U.S. team, that is, White House and State Department officials working together to arrive at the limits of strategic arms. But Kissinger used his own back-channel approach of bypassing Secretary of State William Rogers, U.S. Ambassador to the USSR Jacob Bean, and the assistant secretary. The national security adviser and the Soviets drafted the crucial "Basic Principles on Relations" document without informing the State Department team. Furthermore, the president used the Soviet-supplied interpreter, Victor Sukhodrev, in his discussions with Brezhnev. Thus the American delegation was without any record of Nixon's private talks with the Soviet leader.

Hillenbrand attributed this form of diplomacy to Kissinger's desire to take credit for the Anti-Ballistic Missile and Strategic Arms Limitation treaties that were signed on May 26, 1972. Despite the White House methods of negotiating, the assistant secretary could not overlook what the president had helped to fashion: for the first time in the Cold War, ceilings were now placed on missile launchers and defensive missile systems.

After Moscow Hillenbrand accompanied Rogers to Berlin for the signing of the final Protocol of the Quadripartite agreement on Berlin, which rendered that document a legally binding agreement. Berlin, once the centerpiece of Cold War tensions, henceforth would experience as normal an existence as a walled, divided city could reasonably achieve.

Nixon named Hillenbrand U.S. ambassador to the Federal Republic of Germany prior to their trip to the Moscow summit. The U.S. Senate confirmed the appointment before the meeting in Moscow. The secretary of state asked Hillenbrand to remain in his assistant secretary post until the agreements in Moscow and Berlin were finalized, a request Hillenbrand honored. The Bonn ambassadorship came naturally to him. He was fluent in German, and his former position as deputy chief of mission in the West German capital helped to develop contacts with leading German political figures, such as Willy Brandt and Helmut Schmidt of the Social Democratic Party of Germany (SPD) and Rainer Barzel, leader of the opposition, the Christian Democratic Union (CDU).

As ambassador, Hillenbrand also held the position of U.S. chief of mission in Berlin. On November 7, 1972, a Basic Treaty was signed by the two Germanys that sought entry for both into the United Nations. Prior to the Basic Treaty, Hillenbrand met with British Ambassador Nicholas Henderson, French Ambassador Jean Sauvagnargues, and Ambassador Yuri Yefremov of the USSR to draft a declaration that approved the U.N. admittance while maintaining the Four Power rights in Berlin. However, the White House again bypassed the allied talks as Gromyko and Kissinger came up with their own draft declaration without informing Hillenbrand. The British and French representatives felt that the United States had cut them out of the Four Power process, a development that put the U.S. ambassador in a most embarrassing position. Kissinger's back-channel diplomacy undercut Allied cooperation. The final declaration allowed the Federal Republic to represent the interests of the Western sector of Berlin without affecting the rights of the Allies. In September 1973 the two German states became U.N. members.

The Yom Kippur War of October 1973 between Egypt and Israel tested Hillenbrand's diplomatic skills. During that conflict the Nixon administration sent massive amounts of military equipment to Israel from its stockpiles in the Federal Republic. The U.S. government failed to adequately inform its German ally of this use of its territory. On October 24, 1973, the German government through State Secretary Paul Frank asked Hillenbrand why Israeli ships were loading American cargo at the port of Bremerhaven. The U.S. ambassador had no answer because the White House did not advise the embassy. The Germans demanded that the loading cease immediately. Later the supplies were put on U.S. vessels for shipment to Israel. President Nixon and Henry Kissinger then expressed their public disgust with America's European allies. Hillenbrand believed that if traditional diplomatic channels of prior consultation had been utilized, allied tensions would have not developed.

Kissinger's go-it-alone style led to another controversy. On April 23, 1973, he gave a speech before the Associated Press in New York in which he proclaimed that 1973 was to be the Year of Europe. The message went forth that the Atlantic Alliance, now to be linked with Japan, needed a new charter to address the balance of forces in Europe and beyond. Reporter James Reston compared the speech to former Secretary of State George Marshall's talk at Harvard in June 1947 where the Marshall Plan was launched. But Nixon and Kissinger failed to first sound out the European Alliance states, who saw no need for a new charter. The noticeable lack of interest among the European chancelleries together with the Watergate scandal saw the Year of Europe end with a whimper. The U.S. ambassador in Bonn could only observe from the sidelines another failed diplomatic effort.

The year 1974 saw the fall of Nixon and Brandt. The Watergate affair should have come as no great surprise to Hillenbrand, who had witnessed an atmosphere of secrecy and conspiracy in the Nixon White House. In July 1974 Hillenbrand accompanied German Foreign Minister Hans Dietrich Genscher to the San Clemente White House for a *tour d'horizon* with the president. The ambassador found a president who had aged considerably owing to Watergate, but who still displayed, even in these last hectic days of his presidency, a clear vision of foreign policy realities.

The Federal Republic celebrated its twenty-fifth birthday in 1974. Hillenbrand informed U.S. policymakers that new SPD Chancellor Helmut Schmidt would give German policy two basic elements: predictability and stability. Although he worked well with Nixon's successor Gerald Ford, Schmidt, as Hillenbrand reported, believed that his American ally had been weakened by the Vietnam War and Watergate. Thus Schmidt turned more to France and its president, Valéry Giscard d'Estaing. The West German leader, a former finance and defense minister, defined security more in economic than ideological terms.

It is likewise interesting to note that Hillenbrand made U.S. officialdom aware of another German politician, the minister president of the Rhineland Pfalz, Helmut Kohl of the CDU. The ambassador visited Kohl periodically in his state's capital of Mainz, where he found a solid politician who mingled easily with the average voter. This ability to empathize would carry Kohl far beyond the confines of the Rhineland. Hillenbrand also reported that Schmidt's own SPD was coming under the control of the Young Socialists or the radical left wing. It would be this faction's refusal to follow Schmidt in 1982 over defense issues that would end his chancellorship.

In December 1976 Hillenbrand left the Foreign Service to become director general of the Atlantic Institute for International Affairs in Paris. American foreign policy during the Cold War was conceived inter alia as an act of containing Soviet aggression. Martin Hillenbrand did not invent this idea, but worked on its implementation in a Europe divided by the Iron Curtain. Containment did not become a sterile concept as it reacted to the shifting currents of European political, economic, and military developments. As one who was a part of the era of the Berlin Wall, the Prague Spring, and the SALT I treaties, Hillenbrand used his diplomatic talents to fine-tune U.S. containment policies. His Ph.D. dissertation researched the topic of power and morals and concluded that state policy will end in failure if power is not tempered by the constraints of morality. His thirty-five-year career in the State Department and two ambassadorships are best explained by the pursuit of that idea.

Works by Martin Joseph Hillenbrand

"The Future of the European Community as a Problem of American-European Relations." In *America and Western Europe: Problems and Prospects*, ed. Karl Kaiser and Hans-Peter Schwarz. Lexington, MA: Lexington Books, 1977.

"NATO and Western Security in an Era of Transition." *International Security*, Fall 1977, 3–4.

Editor. *The Future of Berlin*. An Atlantic Institute for International Affairs Research Volume. Montclair, NJ: Allanheld, Osmun Publishers, 1980.

Germany in an Era of Transition. Paris: Atlantic Institute for International Affairs, 1983.

"American Perceptions of NATO and the European Community." In *Shifting into Neutral?: Burden Sharing in the Western Alliance in the 1990s*, ed. Christopher Coker. London: Brassey's, 1990.

"America's Role in a European Peace Order." In *Europe in Transition: Political, Economic, and Security Prospects for the 1990s*, ed. J. J. Lee and Walter Korter. Austin: Lyndon B. Johnson School of Public Affairs, University of Texas, 1991.

Works about Martin Joseph Hillenbrand

Bark, Dennis. *Agreement on Berlin: A Study of the 1970–72 Quadripartite Negotiations*. Washington, DC: American Enterprise Institute, 1974.

Kissinger, Henry. *White House Years*. Boston: Little, Brown and Company, 1979.

———. *Years of Upheaval*. Boston: Little, Brown and Company, 1982.

McGhee, George. *At the Creation of a New Germany: From Adenauer to Brandt; An Ambassador's Account*. New Haven and London: Yale University Press, 1989.

Nitze, Paul H., with Ann M. Smith and Steven L. Rearden. *From Hiroshima to Glasnost: At the Center of Decision; A Memoir*. New York: Grove Weidenfeld, 1989.

Nixon, Richard. *RN: The Memoirs of Richard Nixon*. New York: Grosset and Dunlap, 1978.

Schertz, Adrian W. *Die Deutschlandpolitik Kennedys und Johnsons: Unterschiedliche Ansätze innerhalb der amerikanischen Regierung* [The Germany policy of Kennedy and Johnson: Different positions within the American government]. Köln, Weimar, Wien: Böhlan Verlag, 1992.

FRANK A. MAYER

STANLEY KUHL HORNBECK (1883–1966), U.S.

ambassador to the Netherlands from 1945 to 1947, was the most influential top State Department advisor on the Far East, representing the continuity of American policy between the two world wars. Hornbeck served successive administrations from Wilson through Roosevelt, leaving his imprint on all important decisions. Hornbeck's assignment in the Netherlands was only the anticlimax of his long and distinguished career, a preparation step for his retirement.

A son of a Methodist minister, Hornbeck grew up in Colorado and graduated from the University of Denver in 1903 with a B.A. in classics. The first Rhodes scholar from Colorado, he studied modern European history at Oxford from 1904 to 1906. It was a haphazard upbringing, as he recalled many years later. While he was in Oxford, Japan soundly defeated Russia in the Russo-Japanese War. The rise of Japan changed the balance of power in Asia. It also altered Hornbeck's interest. He returned to the United States to study Far Eastern politics with Paul Reinsch at the University of Wisconsin for the next two and one-half years.

A strong proponent of the Open Door, Reinsch taught his students the importance of China and America's Pacific future. In Reinsch's view, the American Open Door policy was a valuable achievement because it avoided conflicts among the powers in China by asking for international cooperation in keeping China open for trade and in maintaining China's integrity. Reinsch installed in Hornbeck's mind what later historians would call the Open Door *Weltanschauung*.

After finishing his Ph.D. program in 1909, Hornbeck went to China to teach in the Provincial College of Zhejiang in Hangzhou. This trip initiated Hornbeck's lifetime career association with China. As a foreigner, befriending only a few missionaries and diplomats, Hornbeck lived in isolation from the realities of Chinese society. He failed to learn the Chinese language and ignored deep-rooted social problems. Hornbeck lived through the Republican Revolution in 1911, which overthrew the Manchu dynasty, but he missed the actions in Hangzhou. A young Wilsonian progressive, Hornbeck enthusiastically supported the revolution and even became an advisor for Governor Zhu Rei of the revolutionary government on the prohibition of opium. In 1913 Hornbeck went to Mukden in Manchuria to teach in the Fengtian Law School. The light teaching load with handsome pay allowed Hornbeck to spend most of his time preparing a study of the Open Door policy for the Carnegie Endowment for International Peace, an assignment by Reinsch.

More than 840 pages long, Hornbeck's report to the Carnegie Endowment was the first major scholarly investigation of the Open Door policy and an illumination of his *Weltanschauung*, which viewed the Open Door as a representation of the traditional and fundamental principles of American diplomacy, not a modus vivendi. Like Reinsch, Hornbeck saw the China market as a great potential field for American commerce. By issuing the Open Door policy, the United States assumed the responsibility of leadership in the maintenance of the Open Door and in the defense of the integrity of China against the threat from Great Powers, especially Japan. This responsibility could neither be denied nor evaded, Hornbeck asserted. However, he insisted that the success of the Open Door first and last rested on China's efforts in maintaining its territorial integrity and enforcing treaty obligations. As for the powers, Britain, not the United States, should be the foremost champion of the Open Door, because America did not have vital interest in China. Hornbeck's opinion on the Open Door was not original. It was both idealistic and materialistic and sounded like both William Taft and Theodore Roosevelt. The report offered the key to understand his policy recommendations throughout most of the 1930s. Hornbeck in this report also suggested writing the Open Door policy into an international treaty. This suggestion forecasted his activities at the Paris Peace Conference of 1919 and the Washington Naval Conference of 1921–1922.

Hornbeck's apprenticeship in China ended in 1913 when Reinsch became Wilson's minister to China. Hornbeck returned to Madison to take over his mentor's teaching. During World War I Japan occupied the German-leased city of Qindao in Shandong and then took over the entire province. In January 1915 Japan presented to China the infamous Twenty-one Demands, in effect reducing China to a Japanese protectorate. The Japanese demands sparked a great public debate in the United States. Hornbeck condemned Japan in his speeches, articles, and the book *Contemporary Politics in the Far East*, which became a classic in the field. This book reprised his earlier report on the Open Door policy to the Carnegie Endowment. Hornbeck saw this ''Japanese Monroe Doctrine'' as a threat to the United States because the closing of the China market and the absorption of China's territory would not only diminish American trade in China but also proportionally increase competition in Latin America, menacing America's own Monroe Doctrine.

Hornbeck's activities and publications in the debate over the Twenty-one Demands made him a well-known expert in Far Eastern politics. Although he advocated an active policy against the Twenty-one Demands, the Wilson administration merely issued a note to deny recognition of any future treaty between China and Japan that might impair American interests in China.

In the summer of 1918 the Inquiry, Wilson's preparatory commission for peace, appointed Hornbeck, then a captain in the Ordinance Department, as the chief of its Far Eastern Division. When the peace conference opened in Paris in 1919, Hornbeck, working closely with E. T. Williams, the State Department's own Far Eastern expert, pushed hard to transform the Open Door doctrine from an American policy into an international agreement. Reinsch from Beijing supported Hornbeck's effort. But the Shandong issue destroyed the opportunity. Bowing to the Japanese threat to introduce a racial-equality clause in the League of Nations Covenant and to walk out of the conference as the Italians already had done, Wilson broke his promise to China and awarded Shandong to Japan. Hornbeck, like most members of the American delegation, felt disappointed with Wilson's decision. Williams and Reinsch both resigned in protest. Hornbeck remained.

Having failed in Paris, Hornbeck tried again at the Washington Naval Conference. This time he was successful. The Open Door policy entered the Nine Power Treaty, and China recovered Shandong with some minor concessions on the railroad issue. But the conference failed to meet the Chinese demands for tariff autonomy and the end of extraterritoriality, two major legacies of nineteenth-century imperialism in China. Chinese dissatisfaction helped the rise of the Chinese Nationalists. Their leader, Dr. Sun Yat-sen, set as the goal of diplomacy the full restoration of Chinese sovereignty. Subsequently the extraterritoriality issue in particular became the breaking point between China and Hornbeck. Hornbeck's support of the Open Door had stressed equal opportunity in trade and the territorial integrity of China without supporting Chinese administrative integrity, also mentioned in John Hay's Open Door Notes. In Hornbeck's view territorial integrity of China was a necessary condition for equal opportunity to trade in China. He did not resist Chinese tariff autonomy, but resolutely defended extraterritoriality in the public debate over China policy in 1927, citing Chinese political instability, alleged weakness in Chinese culture, and benefits of the treaty system. But in articles, booklets, and debates Hornbeck also opposed military intervention in China. His articulation won the approval of new Assistant Secretary of State Nelson T. Johnson, who recruited Hornbeck as the chief of the Far Eastern Division (FE), a position opened by Johnson's promotion.

Opposed to China on the treaty-revision issue, the new chief of FE was no longer anxious to defend the Open Door policy when the Japanese army assassinated Zhang Zoulin, premier of the warlord government in Beijing, and attempted to prevent or delay the Nationalist Northern Expedition by manufacturing the Jinan Incident of 1928, in which the Japanese attacked the Nationalist army and massacred the civilians in that city. Hornbeck acknowledged in a memorandum that such actions were violations of the Nine Power Treaty, but advised against a strong reaction by the United States.

Between 1928 and 1931 Hornbeck's main duty was negotiating the end of American extraterritoriality in China. Public opinion in the United States generally supported that end. Chinese negotiator Wu Chaoshu wanted a quick, short, and general agreement on principle, leaving the details for further discussion. This approach followed the model of the new Sino-American tariff treaty, fitted the Chinese communication style, and would serve the political expedience of the Nationalist government. Hornbeck believed that the United States should not give up extraterritoriality before Britain, because that would put the Americans in an inferior position. He engaged in delay tactics by insisting on working out all details. On September 18, 1931, when Secretary of State Henry Stimson warned Hornbeck not to place more obstacles in the way of the negotiations and not to avoid action, it was too late.

During that night the Japanese army manufactured the Mukden Incident and quickly took over Manchuria. Having failed to foresee the event, Hornbeck initially reacted by blaming both China and Japan. While public opinion showed little consensus, Hornbeck suggested avoiding American leadership and letting the League and Britain take initiatives. Hornbeck argued that the powers could not reverse the de facto situation in Manchuria; therefore, they had to allow the Japanese army to remain there. When Stimson drafted a nonrecognition note, Hornbeck insisted on changing the phrase "will never recognize" to "does not intend to recognize" in order to leave the door open for future recognition. The outraged Stimson almost fired Hornbeck but eventually accepted his new definition of the nonrecognition doctrine.

During the Manchuria crisis Franklin D. Roosevelt's secretary of state, Cordell Hull, was inexperienced in diplomacy. Hornbeck's influence greatly increased. Handicapped by the Great Depression and isolationism, the administration did little to influence the Far Eastern situation. Hornbeck also came under the spell of isolationism. When the Japanese army moved inside the Great Wall in 1935 and attacked Beijing, China pleaded for American mediation. Hornbeck argued that the Open Door policy might be further scratched and dented, but from the point of view of material interest there was nothing vital to the United States. He advocated a policy of letting the Japanese invasion take its own course. He acknowledged that his policy was inhumane and might cause serious political consequences in the Nationalist government, but he believed that in the long run American interests would be best served. Failing to enlist American support, China capitulated by signing the Tanggu Truce on May 31, 1935, giving Japan a charter for aggression in North China.

From 1932 to 1938 Hornbeck formed a three-dimensional policy: avoiding protest against Japanese aggression, steering away from any involvement in China, and building up the American navy. In pursuing a hands-off-China policy, he had opposed in 1933 the $50-million Cotton and Wheat Loan to China, but the president overrode Hornbeck. When Japan announced its Amau Doctrine to oppose any Western aid to China in 1934, Hornbeck attempted to resurrect the China Consortium to coordinate foreign investment and competition in China. When the American Silver Purchase Act of 1934 destroyed the Chinese monetary basis by draining Chinese silver out to the international market, he fought fiercely against Secretary of the Treasury Henry Morgenthau and rejected the Chinese plea for help. Eventually Hornbeck lost to Morgenthau, but he successfully resisted pressure from America's China lobby, the American Asiatic Association, to alter the U.S. policy in China for active participation in the Nationalist economic reconstruction.

One major reason Hornbeck insisted on such a passive China policy was his understanding of the relation between diplomacy and force. Hornbeck firmly believed in Theodore Roosevelt's maxim "Speak softly and carry a big stick."

After the Japanese attack at Shanghai in 1932, Hornbeck started to argue for building up American naval strength. Whether the United States wished to enforce its views or to safeguard the peace, Hornbeck said, the soundest course to pursue was a great American navy serving as a backup for diplomacy and a deterrent against war.

In July 1937 the Sino-Japanese War erupted. On October 5 Roosevelt responded to the renewed crisis in China by making his famous "Quarantine Speech." FDR sent Hornbeck with Norman Davis and J. P. Moffat to attend the Brussels Conference on the Far East (November 3–24, 1937), but the meeting ended in total failure. The fall of Shanghai and the Japanese rape of Nanking at the end of the year marked the beginning of a slow transformation of American policy in Asia, although the United States chose to downplay the Japanese sinking of the naval gunboat USS *Panay* near Nanking in December of that year.

Shortly after the war started, Hornbeck became the special political advisor to the secretary of state. He began to abandon his hands-off-China policy after the Quarantine Speech, which he found inadequate, and suggested taking more forceful actions. He opposed the withdrawal of American troops and the navy from China and the Pacific in order to appease Japan. Hornbeck applauded the persistent Chinese resistance and concluded that it was better to have Chinese soldiers continuing to fight the Japanese than to take the risk of a stronger Japan that would dominate and use the resources and manpower of China for its march of conquest in Asia and the Pacific. Hornbeck therefore battled against applying the neutrality laws in Asia, because China needed American weapons. He preferred to have the laws repealed.

After occupying most of the important cities in eastern and central China, Japan formally announced the death of the Open Door by proclaiming the New Order in Asia in November 1938. Hornbeck's position hardened. He protested the Japanese closure of the Open Door, supported a $25-million American loan to China, and pressed economic sanctions against Japan while continuing his advocacy of American naval construction, which gained approval at the end of 1938. Finally, in July 1939 Hornbeck's suggestion to end the commercial treaty of 1911 became American official policy, and in December 1939 the Roosevelt administration approved a moral embargo against Japan.

In 1939 and 1940 the situation in both Europe and Asia deteriorated quickly. Japan took over the Spratly Islands in the South China Sea, spreading war outside the continent. War broke out in Europe in September 1939. German occupation of the Netherlands and the defeat of France in June 1940 provided Japan an opportunity to occupy French Indochina and Dutch Indonesia, threatening British Burma, Malaysia and Singapore, and the American colony, the Philippines. The Japanese southward thrust would achieve two strategic goals— to secure oil and other war materials in South Asia and to cut off supplies to China via Vietnam and Burma. The fall of European colonies in Asia would also severely undermine the Allied war effort in Europe. Hornbeck never failed to see the connection between Europe and Asia, but he criticized the American military's inclination to abandon Asia in favor of concentration on Europe. During World War II Hornbeck's argument for supporting China neither succeeded nor failed completely. His "and China" argument worked. The American "Europe first" strategy slighted, but did not abandon, China.

Hornbeck also won in July 1940 a partial American embargo of strategic materials such as oil and scrap iron against Japan. Hornbeck continued to push for a full embargo and saw more and more items added to the list by the end of the year. The embargo prompted Japan to seek a summit meeting with Roosevelt. Fearful of a Far Eastern Munich, Hornbeck opposed the summit meeting. His position against Japan became so strong that some of his colleagues accused him of being anti-Japanese. Subsequently, Hornbeck was not present at the Hull-Nomura Talks in 1941, remaining behind the scene to cut any ambiguity of the Japanese proposals into pieces and to destroy any compromise.

While Hornbeck won all the important policy recommendations, his underestimation of the Japanese military led to his major blunder. Throughout this period Hornbeck consistently viewed Japanese politics in a rational way. He insisted that failure in conquering China would diminish the Japanese military's influence, and that rational men in Japan would see the odds against Japan in the event of a war with the United States. Therefore, more pressure on Japan meant that the Japanese leaders would come to their senses more quickly. An embargo would crumble Japanese war capability, and the bold display of American willingness to use force would compel Japan to back off. As late as November 27, 1941, Hornbeck still argued that Japan would not attack the United States. He bet in a memo five-to-one odds that the United States and Japan would not be at war on or before December 15, 1941, three-to-one odds that they would not be at war on or before 15 January 1942, and even money that they would not be at war on or before March 1, 1942. To forestall a Japanese attack, Hornbeck wrote another amazing memo on December 4, just three days before the Japanese attack on Pearl Harbor. In this memo he urged an American initiative to "Destroy the Navy of Japan!"

When the war in the Pacific broke out, Hornbeck regretted his indulgence in wishful thinking that the Japanese would not dare to attack the United States before March 1942. He might also have regretted that the U.S. Navy did not destroy the Japanese fleet first. In any case, after the outbreak of the war, as the White House directly handled important decisions relating to the war, Hornbeck's influence declined, but his support for Chiang Kai-shek never wavered. Whereas many in America and in England saw little contribution of China to the Allied cause, Hornbeck insisted that pinning down in China over one million Japanese soldiers (about two-thirds of the total Japanese forces) itself was of great significance, for which China deserved more than a mere 5 percent of the Lend-Lease materials. He was never able to convince the administration or the American military on this matter. Failing to deliver the promised materials and troops, Hornbeck turned to moral support for China. Because the nominal existence of extraterritoriality in the war against a common enemy did not justify the allied status of China, Hornbeck proposed reopening negotiations to end extraterritoriality in China. Britain also agreed. On January 11, 1943, the Sino-American treaty terminated American extraterritorial rights, finally freeing China from a century of the unequal treaty system.

While supporting the Nationalist government against Japan, Hornbeck also lost sight of an important political development in China—the rise of the Chinese Communist Party (CCP). Since the late 1920s the Far Eastern Division (FE) had lacked a clear understanding of the nature of the Chinese Communist movement. Rather than seeing in the CCP a true Communist movement, most FE officials viewed its members as common brigands who used the "hammer and sickle" symbol only to gain respectability, as Minister in China Nelson Johnson put it. Hampered by shortage of hands and overwhelmed by the day-to-day development of crises caused by Japanese imperialism in China, the FE and Hornbeck simply chose to ignore the CCP. Hornbeck did not see Edgar Snow's report on his visit with the CCP leader Mao Tse-tung in an English newspaper published in China on the eve of the Xian Incident at the end of 1936, because Johnson did not bother to dispatch it to the FE. During the war Hornbeck often dismissed as "irresponsible" reports on the CCP and the corruption of the Nationalists from field diplomats.

Wartime Sino-American relations were also complicated by the conflicts between Chiang Kai-shek and his chief of staff, American general Joseph Stilwell, and between Stilwell and his air force officer, General Claire Chennault. Stilwell wanted a political reform in China and emphasized a land offensive to reopen the Burma Road, whereas Chennault stressed the effectiveness of his air campaign. Hornbeck listened to the two generals arguing their differences in Washington in May 1943 and recommended in favor of Chennault. In 1944, as complaints in Chongqing mounted against Stilwell, Hornbeck repeatedly questioned whether the United States was contradicting its stated principle of supporting Chiang's government by demanding political reforms in China. Although Hornbeck did not make the decision, his attitude contributed to Stilwell's final recall in October of that year. The end of the Stilwell mission symbolized a failure of American policy in China. A month later Hornbeck himself also finished his Far Eastern career and left for the Netherlands as the American ambassador.

Works by Stanley Hornbeck

The Most-Favored-Nation Clause in Commercial Treaties. Bulletin of the University of Wisconsin, no. 343, Economics and Political Science Series 6, no. 2. Madison: University of Wisconsin, 1910.

Contemporary Politics in the Far East. New York: D. Appleton and Company, 1916.

China To-day: Political. World Peace Foundation Pamphlets 10, no. 5. Boston: World Peace Foundation, 1927.

The United States and the Far East: Certain Fundamentals of Policy. Boston: World Peace Foundation, 1942.

The Diplomacy of Frustration: The Manchurian Crisis of 1931–1933 as Revealed in the Papers of Stanley K. Hornbeck. Compiled by Justus D. Doenecke. Stanford, CA: Hoover Institution Press, 1981.

Works about Stanley Hornbeck

Buhite, D. Russell. "The Open Door in Perspective." In *Makers of American Diplomacy*, ed. Frank J. Merli and Theodore A. Wilson. New York: Charles Scribner's Sons, 1974.

Burns, Richard Dean. "Stanley K. Hornbeck: The Diplomacy of the Open Door." In *Diplomats in Crisis*, ed. Richard Dean Burns and Edward M. Bennett. Santa Barbara, CA: ABC-Clio, 1974.

Hu, Shizhang. *Stanley K. Hornbeck and the Open Door Policy, 1919–1937.* Westport, CT: Greenwood Press, 1995.

Leonard, Thomas M. "Stanley K. Hornbeck: Major Deterrent to American-Japanese Summitry, 1941." *Towson State Journal of International Affairs* 8, no. 2 (Spring 1974): 113–21.

Thomas, James C., Jr. "The Role of the Department of State." In *Pearl Harbor as History*, ed. Dorothy Borg and Shumpei Okamoto. New York: Columbia University Press, 1973.

SHIZHANG HU

EDWARD MANDELL HOUSE (1858–1938) was an

intimate advisor to President Woodrow Wilson who influenced U.S. foreign policy in the crucial period of World War 1 and its aftermath. His influence was second only to that of Wilson himself.

The son of T. W. House, a leading, wealthy Texas citizen, Edward House had a privileged youth. He met many prominent people who visited the family homes in Galveston and Houston and enjoyed the colorful life of the vast Gulf of Mexico coastal plain near Houston. In the autumn of 1877 House entered Cornell University, but left at the beginning of his third year when his father became ill. After his father's death in January 1880, House undertook the management of the family properties. In the late 1880s and early 1890s he became a prominent member of Texas society while pursuing farming and land speculation. House was drawn into state politics through his friendship with Governor James Stephen Hogg, whom House helped gain reelection in 1892. Hogg rewarded House with the title of colonel.

Concerned more with the process of politics than its substance, House proceeded to build his own faction—"our crowd," as he called it—into a powerful force in Texas politics. An ambitious political operator, skilled in organizing and inspiring others, he worked largely behind the scenes, developing ties of loyalty with his close associates and using patronage to rally party workers behind his candidates. Every governor of Texas who served from 1894 to 1906 was a protégé of Colonel House.

At the turn of the century House became bored with his role in Texas politics and restlessly searched for broader horizons. He sought further wealth through investments in oil and railroads and felt the pull of the East. For years he had summered on Boston's North Shore, and gradually he began to winter in New York, severing most of his ties with Texas and only occasionally visiting the state. A conservative, sound-money Democrat, he disliked the platform of William Jennings Bryan and in 1904 gave his support to Alton B. Parker, who won the Democratic nomination. Discouraged by the prospects of the Democratic Party after Parker's defeat in 1904 and Bryan's in 1908, House found solace in leisurely tours of Europe and in spiritualism, believing that he would have another chance in a life after death.

House continued his search for a Democratic presidential candidate amenable to his advice. In November 1911 he met Woodrow Wilson, with whom he quickly formed a close and long-lasting friendship. He advised Wilson on political matters during the latter's 1912 campaign for the Democratic nomination and the presidency. After Wilson's election House played a key role in patronage decisions, eventually placing five friends in the cabinet, although he refused any cabinet position for himself. During the winter of 1912–1913 House joined a circle of presidential intimates dedicated to advancing Wilson's political career and to maintaining Wilson's physical and emotional well-being. House was a shrewd political infighter who liked people and understood how to move them. He performed all sorts of political tasks, such as mediating quarrels within the Democratic Party, that the president found distasteful. He also catered to many of Wilson's personal needs, recognizing his yearning for male companionship and his vulnerability to emotional stress. House's gently deferential manner, his lack of assertiveness, and his assurances of affection and support soon made him Wilson's most trusted confidant.

House developed a deep and genuine admiration for Wilson. He believed that inspired leadership could solve the nation's problems and bring its spiritual regeneration, and in Wilson he found an effective political leader who embodied his own moral and political values. The president's first wife, Ellen Axson Wilson, had a keen insight into her husband's emotional makeup and a wise tolerance of his political associates. She welcomed House into her family, seeking his advice on both personal and political matters. Her death in August 1914 left Wilson in despair and caused him to lean even more heavily on House for companionship and emotional support.

Wilson's second wife, Edith Bolling Galt, whom he met in March 1915 and married in December, was a different sort of person. She was lively and attractive, but was poorly educated and underestimated House's value as a personal and political advisor. Wilson imprudently drew her into his work, showing her House's letters and many important state papers; he encouraged her to believe that her judgment was as good as that of his experienced advisors. House resented Wilson's transfer of affection to Edith and the extent to which she changed his relationship with the president. After Wilson's remarriage the remarkable intimacy between the two men lessened. They remained dependent on one another, but the closeness of their early years faded.

In 1913 and 1914, as Wilson pushed his New Freedom agenda through Congress, House served as a high-level political intermediary, quieting Democratic factional squabbles and helping fuse the needs of many special-interest groups into a coherent, moderate legislative program. He collaborated with Wilson in moving the Democratic Party away from its traditional advocacy of states' rights and limited government toward an extension of federal authority over the nation. House's visits to the White House excited much speculation, as journalists labeled him a taciturn man of mystery and exaggerated his influence with the president.

In May 1914 House traveled to Europe, where he stopped in Berlin, Paris, and London to talk with government leaders. Sensing the tension in the air, he warned Wilson of the danger of a major crisis. When World War I broke out in August, House was the first member of the administration to inform himself about the complexities of the struggle and to grapple seriously with the dangers and opportunities the war poised for the United States. As Wilson began to appreciate the magnitude of the conflict and the difficulties of U.S. neutrality, he turned to House for advice and sent him as his personal emissary to European capitals to talk with belligerent leaders. Wilson failed to inform his secretary of state, William Jennings Bryan, of House's activities. A long-time Anglophile who identified with the Allied cause, House saw no prospect for peace until the belligerents had lost their hope for total victory.

Wilson's choice of House gave a strange quality to U.S. attempts to end the war. A curious combination of shrewdness and naïveté, House was driven by the spur of fame to seek a prominent place in the history of his era. From Europe House sent back vivid, detailed letters of every aspect of the war. He also dramatized these missions, exaggerating the possibilities for peace and his influence on European leaders. He often misjudged British and French leaders and assumed that in the end, reason, calmness, and idealism would triumph over the passions generated by the war.

Prior to American entry into the war in 1917, House undertook two missions to Europe. During the first, from January to June 1915, he visited London, Paris, and Berlin and learned that the Allies were not prepared to think seriously about ending the conflict. He sympathized with their position and sought to cultivate their goodwill. After the sinking of the *Lusitania* on May 7, 1915, with the loss of American lives, tension heightened between the United States and Germany. House now viewed the war as a struggle between democracy and autocracy and became convinced that U.S. intervention was inevitable. One way or another, House wanted to guarantee an Allied victory. On the other hand, Wilson viewed U.S. mediation as a way to end the war. The president still believed that the United States could remain aloof, and he was not yet willing to use U.S. military power to ensure an Allied triumph.

From January to March 1916 Wilson sent House on another mission to Europe, although it is clear that the two men had different notions of what was to be achieved. During his second trip House negotiated a memorandum with British Foreign Secretary Sir Edward Grey in which the two conferees agreed that on a signal from the Allies, Wilson would propose a peace conference to put an end to the war. If Germany refused to attend the conference or, once there, insisted on unreasonable terms, the United States "would probably enter the war against Germany." Because the Allies refused to invoke the House-Grey Memorandum, this scheme was never tested, and the differences between House and Wilson did not rise to the surface. On January 31, 1917, Germany announced resumption of unrestricted submarine warfare: all vessels, enemy and neutral, found near British waters would be attacked. On February 3 Washington severed diplomatic relations with Berlin. On February 25 Wilson learned of a telegram sent to Mexico by German Under Secretary of State Arthur Zimmermann proposing a military alliance. These events, along with the sinking of American ships by German U-boats, ended all hopes for peace and led directly to the U.S. declaration of war against Germany on April 6, 1917.

After U.S. intervention House continued to be Wilson's closest foreign policy advisor. In June 1915 Bryan had resigned, and his successor, Robert Lansing, never won the president's confidence. House consulted with the president over his plans for peace and served as his special diplomatic emissary to the Allied governments. He formed a closer relationship with British leaders than Wilson realized, working directly with Sir William Wiseman, head of British secret intelligence in the United States, to minimize friction between the two governments.

In September 1917 Wilson directed House to assemble a group of experts, eventually known as "the Inquiry," to study American war aims and to plan for peace negotiations. In late October House traveled to Europe to participate in inter-Allied military discussions and to seek their agreement on war aims. He returned to the United States empty-handed and helped draft Wilson's unilateral statement of aims—the famous Fourteen Points of January 8, 1918. In the summer of 1918 Wilson assigned House the responsibility for preparing a covenant for a League of Nations, and he and the president exchanged drafts in the ensuing months. In October, when Germany sought peace on the basis of the Fourteen Points, Wilson again dispatched House to Europe to engage in pre-armistice negotiations with the Allies. The success of these efforts led Wilson and House to overestimate U.S. influence and to remain convinced that out of the chaos of war a new community of nations would emerge, based on a League of Nations and a sweeping reconstruction of the international order.

When the Paris Peace Conference opened on January 18, 1919, House, for the first time in Wilson's presidency, held an official position as a member of the American Peace Commission. As the conference unfolded, differences emerged between Wilson and House on basic issues of the peace. The latter had grown impatient, eager to dominate the deliberations and bring about his version of a peace settlement. He was more willing than the president to make concessions on key questions such as reparations and Allied territorial demands. House lost touch with the direction of Wilson's thought, and his arrogance and ambition gradually became apparent to Wilson and other members of the U.S. delegation. At first, during the drafting of the covenant, House and Wilson worked together, but a gap became obvious when Wilson returned to the United States in mid-February and House took his place with other leaders of the chief wartime powers. House lacked the president's deep commitment to the Fourteen Points, as well as his distrust of the Allies. He was far more willing to concede to British, French, and Italian demands. During Wilson's absence he accepted, despite the president's clear instructions to the contrary, French plans to occupy the left bank of the Rhine and the separation of the covenant of the League from a preliminary treaty with Germany.

In mid-March, when Wilson returned to Paris and became aware of House's concessions, he lost confidence in his intimate advisor. While an open break did not occur, House's influence waned. On June 28, 1919—when the Versailles Treaty was signed—the two men parted, never to meet again. Wilson returned to the United States, where he confronted critics of the peace treaty, while House remained in Paris and London, where he sought to speed up the formation of the League of Nations and to encourage Anglo-American cooperation. When

House returned to the United States in October, Wilson was seriously ill and critics of the peace treaty were dominant in the Senate. House urged Wilson to compromise with his opponents, but the president rejected his old friend's advice. House never understood why he had lost the confidence of the president.

During the 1920s House made frequent trips to Europe as a private citizen and energetically urged American membership in the League of Nations and the World Court. He also sought to mediate bitter quarrels within the Democratic Party and to strengthen the party's organization. In 1932 he supported Franklin D. Roosevelt for the presidential nomination. After Roosevelt's election House attempted to reestablish his role as a presidential confidant. Although House influenced some diplomatic appointments, the president seldom consulted him, and he became increasingly critical of the New Deal. His unique career as a confidential advisor ended in frustration.

Works by Edward M. House

Philip Dru: Administrator, A Story of Tomorrow, 1920–1935. New York: B. W. Huebsch, 1912.

Coeditor, with Charles Seymour. *What Really Happened at Paris: The Story of the Peace Conference, 1918–1919*. New York: Charles Scribner's Sons, 1921.

Works about Edward M. House

Floto, Inga. *Colonel House in Paris: A Study of American Policy at the Paris Peace Conference 1919*. Princeton: Princeton University Press, 1980.

Fowler, Wilton B. *British-American Relations, 1917–1918: The Role of Sir William Wiseman*. Princeton: Princeton University Press, 1969.

George, Alexander L., and Juliette L. George. *Woodrow Wilson and Colonel House: A Personality Study*. New York: John Day Company, 1956.

Heckscher, August. *Woodrow Wilson: A Biography*. New York: Charles Scribner's Sons, 1991.

Link, Arthur S. *Wilson*. 5 vols. Princeton: Princeton University Press, 1947–1965.

Neu, Charles E. "Woodrow Wilson and Colonel House: The Early Years, 1911–1915." In *The Wilson Era: Essays in Honor of Arthur S. Link*, ed. John Milton Cooper, Jr., and Charles E. Neu, 248–78. Arlington Heights, IL: Harlan Davidson, 1991.

Seymour, Charles. *The Intimate Papers of Colonel House*. 4 vols. Boston: Houghton Mifflin, 1926–1928.

Walworth, Arthur. *Wilson and His Peacemakers: American Diplomacy at the Paris Peace Conference, 1919*. New York: W. W. Norton and Company, 1986.

Weinstein, Edwin A. *Woodrow Wilson: A Medical and Psychological Biography*. Princeton: Princeton University Press, 1981.

CHARLES E. NEU

CHRISTOPHER HUGHES (1786–1849), one of

America's first career diplomats, represented his country in Europe for some thirty years and won goodwill wherever he went, but never received a higher rank than that of chargé d'affaires. John Quincy Adams believed that Hughes had all the requisite qualities of a diplomat, and Henry Clay claimed that during his term of office as secretary of state, the information Hughes sent him was more copious and significant than that of all the other diplomatic representatives in Europe combined.

Christopher Hughes was born in Baltimore on February 11, 1786, the son of the merchant Christopher Hughes, Sr.—an Irish immigrant who made his fortune in the United States—and Margaret Sanderson Hughes. Of their fourteen children, only six reached adulthood. His twin sister, Peggy, and her husband, Colonel Samuel Moore, were the only relatives Christopher was close to during his diplomatic career. After finishing preparatory school at Annapolis, Christopher entered the College of New Jersey at Princeton as a sophomore in 1803 and completed his legal studies six years later. He had no interest in a legal career but found politics exciting and spent some time as the speech writer, bodyguard, and favorite companion of Samuel Smith, a senator from Maryland whose daughter Laura he married in 1811.

A meeting with President James Madison in the summer of 1813 led to Hughes's appointment as secretary of the American delegation that was to negotiate a peace and trade agreement with Great Britain in the Belgian town of Ghent. Hughes impressed his superiors favorably while they were in the Flemish city. After the British and American delegations had signed the so-called Treaty of Ghent in December 1814, the young Hughes was commissioned to take one of the three exemplars to Washington. Upon arrival in the United States he had the opportunity to discuss the negotiations with President Madison and Secretary of State James Monroe. The Ghent episode provided Hughes with the basis for a diplomatic career and a lifelong friendship with John Quincy Adams and Henry Clay.

Since Monroe could not yet promise him another diplomatic appointment, Hughes took his father-in-law's advice and announced his intention to represent Baltimore in the Maryland state legislature. Following his victory in October 1815, he attended the legislative session in Annapolis that lasted from early December until late January 1816. Toward the end of the session he deferred an unexpected chance to run for the House of Representatives to his father-in-law, who was duly elected.

Several weeks after the Annapolis session had ended, Hughes received a special assignment from Monroe. In New Granada, now known as Colombia, the Spanish authorities had seized a number of American ships at Cartagena, confiscated the cargo, and peremptorily imprisoned the crews. Hughes's task was to secure the release of all three. He was only partly successful: Fifteen of the more than fifty prisoners were permitted to return with him to the United States; the others had already died of natural causes, escaped, or been freed previously. The ships and cargo were out of the question, however, since the Spanish authorities had already sold everything. By July Hughes was back in Baltimore and reported his findings to Monroe.

That same month the secretary of state offered to appoint Hughes secretary of the American legation in Sweden. The American minister plenipotentiary in Stockholm, Jonathan Russell, had asked for permission to leave and had suggested reducing the level of American representation to that of chargé d'affaires, with which his superiors in Washington had agreed. Following Russell's departure, Hughes would thus assume the rank of chargé. Hughes decided to accept the appointment, and after making the necessary preparations, he and his wife reached the Swedish capital in late April 1817.

Between April and December of that year Hughes represented the United States in the Kingdom of Sweden and Norway—united in one monarchy in the nineteenth century—as chargé d'affaires. Russell had gone home in the fall of 1816, but the Senate amended the trade agreement he had reached with the Swedish government and therefore sent him back to Stockholm to defend the amendments. His return meant that Hughes became legation secretary once again, involving a considerable sacrifice in terms of status and income. Fortunately for him, Russell was able to reach an agreement with the Swedish government in January 1818. Owing to the slow postal service, however, he received no word of the treaty's approval by the United States, or orders to leave Sweden, until the summer. When the diplomat finally left in October 1818, Hughes resumed the rank of chargé d'affaires.

Hughes was well liked by the rest of the diplomatic corps. His friendly relations with the French, British, and Russian envoys enabled him to gather valuable information about the foreign policy of their respective countries. Because various of these colleagues corresponded with Hughes even after they were transferred from Stockholm to other posts, he received political news from a number of European capitals. He reported this to Secretary of State John Quincy Adams, who was particularly pleased with Hughes's letters. Besides his political reporting, Hughes's attempts to promote American trade with Sweden and Norway were also applauded by his government. During the years he represented American interests in the kingdom he managed to solve a number of trade-related problems.

After Adams was inaugurated president in March 1825, he promptly granted Hughes's requests for transfer to a more southerly European capital and for a leave of absence in the United States. In early June the diplomat received word of his assignment to the Kingdom of the Netherlands as chargé d'affaires. In July he took leave of Stockholm to carry out a special assignment in Copenhagen. The object of his mission to Denmark was twofold: settling insurance claims against the Danish government made by American merchants and convincing Denmark finally to admit an American consul to the Caribbean island of St. Thomas. Hughes made no headway with the claims, but did with the matter of the consul. He then left for Brussels, where he arrived in early September. After he had presented his credentials to the Dutch minister of foreign affairs, he had an audience with the king. He subsequently left for the United States, where he stayed till May 1826. The next month he was back in the Netherlands.

In dealing with the Dutch, Hughes was forced to confront the legacy of his predecessor Alexander Hill Everett, whose negative remarks on the Netherlands in his book *Europe* had been poorly received in the kingdom. Fortunately, Hughes was ultimately successful in repairing the damage caused by Everett. In the years that followed, his popularity at court and among his colleagues continued to grow.

As a representative of his country, it was not always easy for Hughes to stay abreast of developments in the United States. The State Department and Hughes's friends did keep him informed to a certain extent, but the chargé found it impossible to stay really au courant without the benefit of American newspapers. To his exasperation, however, newspapers arrived very irregularly indeed. Though Hughes asked the State Department repeatedly to supply him with information on a regular basis, the situation did not improve.

For his part, Hughes did his best to keep the State Department informed of developments in the Netherlands and Europe as a whole. The receptions and dinners where the diplomatic corps regularly met provided an exceptionally good opportunity to gather information. Hughes also had correspondents in various European capitals. In the course of the three and one-half years he spent in the Netherlands, the chargé sent fifty-four dispatches to Washington, averaging fifteen per year.

His years of loyal service did not earn him a promotion. Hughes felt oppressed by the humble rank of chargé. Particularly galling was the fact that it barred him from the royal table. Though the king treated him with deference, it was clear to the chargé that the Netherlands wanted the United States to reciprocate its delegation of a minister plenipotentiary to Washington. His steadfast hopes for promotion were in vain, however. Another of Hughes's constant aggravations was the exorbitant cost of living in the Kingdom of the Netherlands. His complaints on the subject run through his letters like a leitmotif.

From the fall of 1828 until the spring of 1830 Hughes's career became entangled with the northeastern boundary dispute between Great Britain and the United States, which centered on the state of Maine. In the fifth article of the Treaty of Ghent, signed in 1814, the two nations agreed that the border in that region, contested since 1783, would definitely be drawn by a bilateral commission. If the negotiations failed to resolve the dispute satisfactorily, the same article called for the designation of an arbiter. The lengthy negotiations were indeed inconclusive, so Great Britain and the United States in 1827 agreed to settle the matter by arbitration. In June of the next year the two parties unanimously settled on William 1 of the Netherlands as arbiter, and the following October Secretary of State Henry Clay instructed Hughes to approach the king on behalf of President John Quincy Adams, who relied on Hughes's diplomatic skills. This was finally a matter of substance for the long-suffering diplomat.

Long before Hughes was informed of the proposed arbitration, the matter had been thoroughly prepared by Albert Gallatin and William Pitt Preble, a prominent lawyer from Maine. The two men studied the documents relevant to the long history of the dispute and prepared their defense of the United States, reaching a unique understanding of the legal and political ramifications. Meanwhile, Adams and Clay had come to the conclusion that it was in the interest of the United States to send a minister plenipotentiary to the Netherlands. The matter was considered at length. Hughes was a seasoned diplomat well acquainted with the court of William I, but knew little about the boundary dispute or, for that matter, Maine politics. Preble, on the other hand, was fully informed of the legal aspects of the problem but had no diplomatic experience, nor could he hope to earn quickly the good reputation in the Netherlands Hughes enjoyed. In December 1828 the president and secretary of state finally decided to appoint Hughes envoy extraordinary and minister plenipotentiary and to make Preble his expert advisor. Hughes's promotion was put before the Senate, while the *National Intelligencer* broadcast it across Europe. Assuming that he would be approved, Hughes's friends even began sending him letters of congratulation. In January 1829 it seemed that the promotion he had craved for so long was imminent.

In Washington, meanwhile, there was a lame-duck president in the White House, and in anticipation of Jackson's inauguration the Senate decided to postpone discussion of the outgoing administration's appointments. At the same time, opposition to Hughes's promotion arose on various fronts. Following President Jackson's inauguration, he and the new secretary of state had no objection to submitting the proposed appointment to the Senate—until, that is, they took stock of the political opposition in Maine. Many Maine residents believed that their state would be served better by Preble.

In February 1829 Hughes learned of the opposition to his appointment. The final decision was taken in May. Secretary of State Martin Van Buren notified Hughes that owing to the political situation in Maine, the president had chosen Preble to become envoy extraordinary and minister plenipotentiary, but asked Hughes to remain at his post until Preble's arrival. To sweeten the pill, Van Buren assured Hughes that the president was planning to give him another appointment in the near future.

In September Hughes sent Van Buren several letters elaborating on his feelings regarding Preble's appointment, which he had had to read about in the press. He quoted unequivocal statements by John Quincy Adams and Henry Clay to the effect that he was best suited to carry out his task in the Netherlands. After years of loyal service he felt betrayed and for the duration of 1829 and the first few months of 1830 was utterly despondent.

Preble arrived in the Netherlands in January 1830, and in March Hughes received word that President Jackson had appointed him chargé d'affaires in Sweden. Of course, he was not really delighted, but he could console himself with the fact that he was still in the Foreign Service and could remain in Europe. Official notice of his appointment as chargé to the Kingdom of Sweden and Norway reached him in early June. With the long period of hope and despair now behind him, Hughes began, albeit with mixed feelings, to prepare for the trip north.

Hughes represented the United States in Sweden for twelve years, longer than he spent at any other post in the course of his career. There was little excitement to report from the periphery, but whenever he could, Hughes sought to promote American commercial interests in Sweden and Norway. He was generally healthy and content and enjoyed good relations with the successive Swedish ministers of foreign affairs, the rest of the diplomatic corps, and a number of prominent Swedish families.

Hughes attached great importance to maintaining contact with his many friends in both Europe and the United States. During this period he took two home leaves, staying with his sister and brother-in-law in Baltimore and visiting many friends and acquaintances, including John Quincy Adams. Naturally he also met with his superiors in Washington. His wife Laura's death of tuberculosis in 1832 was a terrible loss, followed successively by the deaths in 1839 of his father-in-law Samuel Smith and his son Charles. The absence of his daughter Margaret, who had settled in Baltimore in 1833, and the lack of any challenge in Sweden made the diplomat want to leave.

In 1841 Hughes repeatedly petitioned the State Department for a more prestigious European assignment, but to no avail. Disconsolate, he turned to Adams for help. There seemed to be little chance of success at first, but during another visit to the United States his luck improved in April 1842. John Quincy Adams and other politically influential friends managed to convince President John Tyler to grant Hughes another assignment. Once again he was made chargé d'affaires to the Netherlands. Though this was no promotion, at least it spared him having to return to Stockholm.

Shortly after his arrival in The Hague in August 1842, Hughes presented his credentials to the Dutch minister of foreign affairs and was warmly welcomed by the royal family. He soon learned that American prestige in Europe had been seriously tarnished. Debt-ridden states, the national deficit, and immoral politicians had all helped to create a negative image of the United States in the Old World. Hughes was obviously very troubled by the situation. The delight with which conservative, aristocratic circles reacted to the decline of American prestige was a thorn in his side. That, and the dismal news he received from home, eroded the chargé's interest in public affairs.

Aside from lamenting his country's fall from its pedestal, there was little the diplomat could do in The Hague by way of gathering information. On several occasions Hughes confessed that there was nothing of even the slightest interest to tell his superiors. The little about which Hughes did inform the State Department—he sent an average of ten dispatches per year—included such inconsequential matters as the formal opening of the States General, royal weddings and births, and the unexpected appointment in October 1843 of a new minister of foreign affairs. He also described the great financial difficulties that afflicted the Netherlands following the Belgian secession; indeed, he considered the state of the Dutch economy no less deplorable than that of the American.

The focus of social life in The Hague was the court, where, according to Hughes, one ball was followed by another. Protocol demanded the chargé's presence there. Besides the royal family, several envoys—primarily British and Russian—helped keep The Hague's night life going. Except for a few official dinners, the chargé was almost never invited anywhere by the Dutch, about whom he had not a good word to say.

Hughes obviously felt very ill at ease in The Hague. Not only did he find his diplomatic duties trying and most of the people bores, but he also complained of listlessness and depressions. From the moment of his arrival he never did feel really fit. Having lost all interest in his surroundings, he was given to long walks by himself. So bored was he that he felt more dead than alive and longed to leave behind him the torpidity of The Hague.

As during his first assignment to the Netherlands, the exceptionally high cost of living was a constant aggravation. Hughes complained about it repeatedly. Everything was two or three times more expensive than it had been in Sweden. All Hughes could do under the circumstances was to try to live as cheaply as possible in order to avoid debts before returning to the United States.

Inevitably, Hughes was not in The Hague for long before he longed to return to his relatives in Baltimore. He blamed himself for not foreseeing his unhappiness, given his previous experience in the Netherlands. Although he would continue to fulfill his obligations as long as duty and decency demanded, more than anything else he wanted to leave Europe and be back in the United States. He wrote his sister that he was tired of princes and aristocrats who hated his country; an American, in his opinion, did not belong in such circles anyway. The Hague had convinced him how senseless it was for an American to live on the European continent.

Following the inauguration of James K. Polk in March 1845 and James Buchanan's subsequent appointment as secretary of state, Hughes was relieved of his duties and succeeded by Auguste Davezac. In June 1845 Hughes took leave of the Dutch government and returned to Baltimore. But the retired diplomat had not been back for a year before he began dreaming of another diplomatic appointment. Evidently he soon forgot the homesickness that had so plagued him in the Netherlands, for in June 1846 he told President Polk that he wished to reenter the Foreign Service. The president took no heed of Hughes's request, however, just as Secretary of State James Buchanan ignored his plea to be sent to Naples in 1847. While Hughes hoped in vain for another diplomatic appointment, his health began to decline. Following a long illness, he died in his hometown on September 18, 1849, at the age of sixty-three.

Works about Christopher Hughes

Dunham, Chester Gray. "The Diplomatic Career of Christopher Hughes." Ph.D. diss., Ohio State University, 1968; Ann Arbor, MI: University Microfilms International, 1969.

Reeves, Jesse S. "Coke of Norfolk and Lafayette: The Correspondence of Two Great Liberals with Christopher Hughes of Baltimore." *Michigan Alumnus Quarterly Review* 45 (1938): 1–11.

———. "A Diplomat Glimpses Parnassus: Excerpts from the Correspondence of Christopher Hughes." *Michigan Alumnus Quarterly Review* 41 (1934): 189–201.

———. "Washington's Autographs and Some Others: Further Excerpts from the Correspondence of Christopher Hughes of Maryland." *Michigan Alumnus Quarterly Review* 42 (1936): 168–78.

van Minnen, Cornelis A. *American Diplomats in the Netherlands, 1815–1850.* New York: St. Martin's Press, 1993.

Whiteley, Emily Stone. "Christopher Hughes, Wit and Diplomatist." *Baltimore Sun*, January 13, 1929.

CORNELIS A. VAN MINNEN

JOHN JAY (1745–1829), diplomat and jurist, served as minister to Spain and negotiated two treaties with Great Britain.

Jay was born in New York City in 1745, the sixth son of Peter and Mary Van Cortlandt Jay. His ancestry was Huguenot, which helps explain some of his later hostility to France and lingering sympathy toward Great Britain. Jay graduated from King's College in 1764 and was admitted to the New York bar in 1768.

Jay entered the Continental Congress in 1774 and over the next two years established a reputation as a conservative Whig. He advocated reconciliation with Great Britain as long as possible, supporting both Joseph Galloway's Plan of Union and the Olive Branch Petition. Jay was serving in New York's Provincial Congress when the final vote on independence came. Like many leaders from the middle colonies, Jay did not advocate independence, but accepted it as an accomplished fact. Jay drafted the New York constitution of 1777 and served as chief justice until 1779.

Jay returned to the Continental Congress in December 1778. He owed his rapid advancement to the Silas Deane affair. Deane was one of the original commissioners to France and was primarily responsible for administering the flow of supplies. Congress recalled Deane in late 1777, mainly because he had issued too many commissions to French officers, many of whom did not speak English. Deane's colleague, Arthur Lee, accused Deane of using his office for personal profit. Deane responded with a newspaper article that accused Lee and his family of pro-British sympathies. The dispute between Lee and Deane revived the political divisions that preceded independence. Moderate members supported Deane, while radicals supported Lee. Debate raged throughout 1778. When Congress failed to censure Deane for his attacks on the Lees, Henry Laurens resigned the presidency in disgust. Jay, a moderate and Deane supporter, replaced him.

The Silas Deane affair shaped American diplomacy throughout the war and launched Jay's career as a diplomat. Conrad Alexandre Gerard, the French minister, openly sided with congressional moderates and lobbied for Jay's election as peace commissioner and minister to Spain. Lee's allies abandoned Lee himself and rallied behind John Adams. Congress remained deadlocked until the two sides agreed to divide the two jobs. On September 27, 1779, Congress elected Adams peace commissioner and Jay minister to Spain.

Spain entered the war as a French (but not American) ally on April 12, 1779. Spain had little interest in the United States itself, but saw the war with Great Britain as an opportunity to take back Gibraltar and Minorca. Jay arrived at Cadiz on January 22, 1780, with several goals in mind. First, he sought Spanish recognition and an alliance. Second, he hoped to convince Spain to accept American territorial claims. Third, he sought a loan of five million dollars. Jay remained at Madrid until May 1782, but reached none of his goals. Count Floridablanca received Jay unofficially on May 11, 1780, but never offered recognition. Spain was skeptical of American territorial claims and was not convinced that the United States could win on the battlefield. The fall of Charleston in May 1780 further cooled Spain's attitude.

Jay all but gave up on the mission by September. He believed navigation of the Mississippi to be the critical point of contention and asked Congress for further instructions. On October 4, 1780, Congress voted to instruct Jay to insist on the right to navigate the Mississippi to its mouth. Jay received the message on January 30, 1781. However, military events overtook his new instructions. British victories in the south prompted Congress, led by the Virginia delegation, to instruct Jay to give up Mississippi navigation if it would bring Spain into the war. Jay received the second set of instructions in May. Despite Spanish assurances, he did not believe that a complete surrender would improve relations. Jay offered a compromise on September 19 in which the United States would give up the right of navigation south of the American claim at thirty-one degrees north latitude if Spain would agree to a mutual guarantee of territory. He would consider the United States bound by his proposal if the war ended first. Floridablanca stalled in responding. Even the American victory at Yorktown did not alter Spanish policy.

In June 1781, near the lowest point of the American war effort, Congress elected Jay, Benjamin Franklin, John Adams, Henry Laurens, and Thomas Jefferson peace commissioners and abolished the commission to John Adams. Congress further instructed the commissioners not to negotiate without first consulting France. Both France and the Continental Congress feared that John Adams's anti-French attitude and insistence on American access to the Newfoundland fisheries would unnecessarily prolong the war. Jay left Spain in May 1782 and arrived in Paris in June, ready to take up his new mission. His diplomatic career brought a revolution in his thought. He had been considered pro-French in 1779. However, he came to believe that France, from fear of the growth of American power, had dictated Spanish policy. His time in Paris deepened his suspicions. Jay and Franklin met with the Compte de Vergennes and his aide, Joseph Matthias Gerard de Rayneval, on August 10. Vergennes and Rayneval told the Americans that their western claims were extravagant, and that the United States should accept a border closer to the Appalachians. Jay did not share Franklin's implicit trust in Vergennes and believed that the Americans should openly violate their instructions and sign a separate peace. Jay family legend has it that after the meeting Franklin asked Jay if he meant to break Congress's instructions. Jay then smashed his clay pipe and told Franklin that he would as easily break the instructions. When Jay learned of Rayneval's trip to London in September, he feared that Great Britain and France were approaching an agreement.

The British governments that succeeded the North ministry wanted to split the alliance by reaching an agreement with the United States. Richard Oswald negotiated with Franklin throughout the spring and summer. When Franklin fell ill, Jay took over and objected to the fact that Oswald's commission did not recognize American independence. Franklin attributed Jay's concerns to his legal training. Jay also differed with Franklin over the exact goals of the peace. Franklin concentrated on acquiring Canada. Jay feared Spanish and French designs on the Mississippi and concentrated on the west. Jay preferred to have Great Britain on the southern border and was prepared to allow Great Britain to retain the Floridas.

Jay took the lead when official negotiations began in October. He submitted a draft treaty on October 5 that incorporated many of the proposals Franklin had made in July. Jay's draft set the American boundaries at the Mississippi on the west, thirty-one degrees north latitude on the south, the St. Lawrence River and forty-five degrees north latitude to Lake Nipissing on the northwest, and the St. John's River to the Bay of Fundy on the northeast. Jay's draft gave the United States the right to catch and dry fish off Newfoundland, granted both powers the right to navigate the Mississippi, and established reciprocal trade between Great Britain and the United States. Jay restated his offer to let the British keep the Floridas and urged Great Britain to withdraw its troops from New York and Charleston and instead attack Pensacola. With the draft, Jay and Franklin abandoned Canada to concentrate on the west. Oswald accepted the draft and sent it on to London, hoping that it would mean a quick end to his labors. The cabinet rejected the treaty on October 17, demanding a better Maine boundary, some provision for the loyalists, and American exclusion from the fisheries.

The next round of negotiations included John Adams, who arrived from the Netherlands on October 26. Adams fully approved of Jay's conduct and was pleasantly surprised to find that Jay shared his suspicions of the French. Jay began reworking the treaty in early November, writing the provision giving Great Britain more territory if it held West Florida as a separate article. The new draft reset the northern boundary at a line dividing the Great Lakes. The Americans refused to restore confiscated property to prominent loyalists, and Jay insisted that instead the British should compensate American property losses. The British government was prepared to accept the new boundaries only if the Americans made some provision for the Tories.

Fish and Tories dominated the final days of the peace negotiations. The Americans agreed to ask Congress and the states to provide for restitution of property to those who lived in British-occupied areas and those who did not take up arms against the United States. John Adams spent three days defending the American right to the fisheries and announced that he would not sign a treaty without them. Jay agreed, and the Americans accepted the "liberty" rather than the "right" to the fisheries. The two sides signed the provisional articles on November 30, 1782. Both Jay's allies and critics gave him primary credit for the treaty. Adams wrote that the title "the Washington of Negotiation" belonged to Jay rather than himself. Congressional critics approved the treaty, but blamed

Jay for taking the lead in violating the instructions and demanded that the commissioners inform the French of the secret West Florida article.

The European powers signed preliminary peace articles on January 20, 1783. The American commissioners had hoped to sign a commercial treaty as well. However, the provisional treaty toppled the Shelburne ministry, and the Fox-North coalition that followed took a harder line with the United States and refused to make any further concessions. The American commissioners signed the Treaty of Paris on September 3, 1783, reading the provisional articles into the general settlement. Jay declined other diplomatic offices and returned home in 1784.

Upon his return Jay found that Congress had elected him secretary of foreign affairs, replacing his brother-in-law, Robert R. Livingston. Jay was reluctant to accept and did so on the condition that Congress would remain in New York City. As foreign secretary, Jay faced many of the problems left unresolved after the revolution. To make matters worse, Congress had little or no power. According to the peace treaty, Great Britain agreed to withdraw all of its forces from American territory. The United States was to allow some restitution of loyalist property and the collection of prewar debts. The state governments routinely interfered with the execution of the treaty, giving Great Britain an excuse to retain the forts in the Northwest. The treaty also gave the United States the right to navigate the Mississippi, but the Spanish refused to allow American ships where the Mississippi flowed between Spanish banks.

Jay supported every attempt to give Congress more power in order to carry out an effective foreign policy. However, the states twice rejected an impost that would have given Congress an independent revenue. The French alliance was of little help. The French signed a commercial treaty with Great Britain in 1786. When forced to choose between Spain and the United States on any issue, France routinely supported Spain.

Jay turned to Spain for a commercial treaty and a potential military alliance. Don Diego de Gardoqui, the Spanish minister, negotiated with Jay for two years. Once again, the Mississippi proved to be the main stumbling block. Gardoqui had no authority to make concessions on the lower Mississippi, but was willing to abandon Spanish territorial claims east of the Mississippi and offer reciprocal trade. By 1786 Jay gave up on the absolute right to the Mississippi and agreed to forbear the use of the lower Mississippi for twenty-five years, enough time for the United States to gain strength. Jay's final offer was similar to the offer he had made to the Spanish government in September 1781. The South was willing to give up the Mississippi in wartime, but not in peace. Congress refused to accept the Jay-Gardoqui Treaty, and many Southern members were convinced that the treaty was part of a plot to divide the Union.

Jay saw firsthand how a weak government harmed American foreign policy and fully supported the new Constitution. In the fall of 1787 he joined with Alexander Hamilton and James Madison to write the *Federalist* essays. Illness limited Jay to four contributions, in which he concentrated on foreign policy.

In *Federalist* 2 Jay warned against the dangers of disunion and argued that the stature of the delegates to the Constitutional Convention itself spoke well of the Constitution. Jay addressed specific foreign policy problems in *Federalist* 3 and 4 and argued that the Constitution would strengthen the government and allow the United States to force commercial concessions from Great Britain and enforce its claim to the Mississippi. In *Federalist* 64 Jay defended the Senate's role in treaty ratification.

Jay served as the first Chief Justice of the Supreme Court under the Constitution and continued to serve as secretary of state until Thomas Jefferson took office in 1790. The international impact of the French Revolution brought Jay back into American diplomacy. The revolution that broke out in 1789 soon burst out of its constitutional and territorial bounds. The revolutionary government executed Louis XVI and declared war on Great Britain in January 1793. An Anglo-French war fought on the high seas would inevitably affect the United States. Throughout 1793 Edmund Genet recruited Americans and outfitted privateers in American ports to fight on the French side. Great Britain hoped to prevent French colonial goods from reaching European ports and passed a series of orders-in-council designed to strike at neutral shippers in the West Indian trade. The orders fell hardest on the United States.

Domestic debate over foreign policy deepened the political divisions that emerged with Alexander Hamilton's fiscal program. In January 1794 James Madison called for commercial retaliation against Great Britain. Hamilton feared that any action against Great Britain would bring war or at least cut off trade. Either result would ruin the nation's finances. Hamilton pressed George Washington to send Jay as a special envoy, both to reach a settlement and blunt republican action in Congress. Washington agreed, appointing Jay in April 1794.

Jay left for Great Britain on May 12 and arrived a month later. His general goal was to prevent war, and his specific goals were to sign a commercial treaty and evict the British from the Northwest. Jay was eager to reach a settlement. He preferred Great Britain to revolutionary France, and he knew that the United States would be negotiating from a position of weakness. The United States had few cards to play. Once the British agreed to withdraw from the Northwest, Jay moved on to commercial issues. He did not share the republicans' faith in the coercive power of American commerce and merely hoped to restore normal relations. On November 19, 1794, Jay and Baron Grenville signed a treaty that established reciprocal trade and accepted the British interpretation of neutral rights, renouncing the idea that free ships make free goods. Above all, Jay had kept the peace, which was his main object all along.

The Senate barely consented to the Jay Treaty in July 1795 in the face of republican opposition. The House of Representatives approved the necessary appropriations by one vote in April 1796. Upon his return Jay took office as governor of New York, serving until 1800. That year he retired from public life, turning down John Adams's request that he serve as secretary of state. Jay devoted much of the rest of his life to church affairs and served as president of the American Bible Society in 1821. He died at his home in Bedford, New York, on May 17, 1829.

Jay's greatest triumph was the Treaty of Paris. The Jay Treaty was at best a limited success, and the Spanish mission was defeated by circumstances beyond Jay's control. Several themes link Jay's three missions. One was his steady defense of American expansion. He refused to give up the Mississippi to gain a Spanish alliance, despite the fact that he was authorized to do so. The most he would do was to give up rights where the United States could not enforce them. Jay sought a separate peace largely because France did not recognize U.S. western claims. In 1794 Jay refused to redraw the border to allow Great Britain access to the source of the Mississippi. Another theme was Jay's suspicion of France. Jay blamed France for the failure of his Spanish mission. Revolutionary France was no better than royal France. If Jay's diplomacy changed at all between 1783 and 1794, it may be said that the older Jay was a far more cautious diplomat.

Works by John Jay

The Correspondence and Public Papers of John Jay. Ed. Henry P. Johnston. 4 vols. New York: G. P. Putnam's Sons, 1890–1893.

The Federalist. Ed. Jacob E. Cooke. Middletown, CT: Wesleyan University Press, 1961.

John Jay: Unpublished Papers. Ed. Richard B. Morris. 2 vols. New York: Harper and Row, 1975–1980.

Works about John Jay

Bemis, Samuel Flagg. *Jay's Treaty: A Study in Commerce and Diplomacy.* Rev. ed. New Haven: Yale University Press, 1962.

Monaghan, Frank. *John Jay, Defender of Liberty against Kings and Peoples.* New York and Indianapolis: Bobbs-Merrill Co., 1935.

Morris, Richard B. *The Peacemakers: The Great Powers and American Independence.* New York: Harper and Row, 1965.

Pellew, George. *John Jay.* Boston: Houghton Mifflin, 1898.

ROBERT W. SMITH

THOMAS JEFFERSON (1743–1826), author of the Declaration of Independence, third president of the United States, and father of the University of Virginia, served as minister to France from 1785 to 1789.

Jefferson was born at Shadwell, Goochland County, Virginia, in 1743, the third child of Peter and Jane Randolph Jefferson. He attended the College of William and Mary from 1760 to 1762 and read law in the office of George Wythe.

Jefferson's legal career soon gave way to his political career, which coincided with the coming of the American Revolution. He entered the House of Burgesses in 1769, in the midst of the nonimportation movement, and remained until 1775. His most important contribution to the resistance movement was his 1774 pamphlet *A Summary View of the Rights of British America*, which denied any parliamentary authority over the American colonies. He succeeded Peyton Randolph as a member of the Virginia delegation to the Continental Congress in 1775. He was not an active debater, but his pen and place of birth won him the job of writing the Declaration of Independence.

Jefferson returned to the Virginia legislature in 1776, where he concentrated on the revision of Virginia's law code. He was elected governor in June 1779 and served during the two darkest years of the war. A British raiding party nearly captured Jefferson and the legislature in June 1781. Jefferson left office soon after, intending to return to private life. Congress elected him a peace commissioner in June 1781, but Jefferson never assumed the office. The death of his wife in November 1782 probably led to his return to public life. He returned to Congress in 1783 and wrote his famous reports establishing the monetary system of the United States and the government of the western territories.

After a decade at the center of American politics, Jefferson entered the center of American diplomacy. On May 7, 1784, Congress elected Jefferson a commissioner to negotiate commercial treaties, replacing John Jay, who returned home to become secretary of foreign affairs. Jefferson arrived in Paris on August 6 and soon after met with John Adams and Benjamin Franklin, his old colleagues on the committee drafting the Declaration of Independence. By all accounts relations between the Americans were cordial. Relations between the United States and Europe were not as fortunate. Peace brought its own diplomatic problems, stemming from American weakness and relative European indifference to the new nation.

One of Jefferson's biggest obstacles was that official Europe held the new republic in low regard and did not expect the United States to last. Congress did not help matters by cutting the salary for ministers in half and disallowing spending for outfits. European trade systems remained closed. Great Britain barred American ships from the West Indian trade on July 2, 1783. France offered less trade than the United States hoped. France opened Dunkirk, L'Orient, Bayonne, and Marseilles to all shipping in 1784 and allowed a limited amount of trade in the French West Indies, but reversed course with an *arrêt* of August 30, 1784, and prohibited the United States from bringing wheat and flour to the West Indies and from carrying out sugar, coffee, cotton, and cocoa. Other decrees imposed duties on fish shipped in American bottoms and paid bounties to French shippers. Custom as well as policy worked against Franco-American trade. French manufacturers did not produce the ordinary goods that Americans wanted. In addition, the French system of royal monopolies made French commerce difficult to penetrate, and American merchants slid back into the more familiar patterns of prewar British trade. The French government tended to view the growth of Anglo-American trade as a betrayal.

French trade was one of the problems Jefferson took on when he succeeded Benjamin Franklin as minister to France on May 17, 1785. Jefferson thought that replacing Franklin was a singularly humbling experience. He did not have Franklin's prestige, but he did share Franklin's interests in philosophy and science and eventually traveled in the same intellectual circles. Like Franklin, Jefferson came to act as the minister of an idea as well as a nation. Jefferson expected to use one particular idea, free trade, to his advantage. Jefferson believed that American agricultural production could break down European trade barriers and expand freedom and opportunity. Despite frequent setbacks, Jefferson held this belief for the rest of his career.

Jefferson had one main goal as minister, to open French ports as wide as possible. Two products, tobacco and whale oil, were to be the main objects of trade. Jefferson had the aid of the Marquis de Lafayette, who served as intermediary with the French government and supported American commerce with a zeal equal to that of any American. Jefferson negotiated with the Compte de Vergennes for a larger share of the West Indian trade, but was careful not to push too hard. Jefferson's main obstacle was not Vergennes but the Farmers-General, which controlled the collection of many customs duties and held a monopoly on the importation of tobacco. In 1785 the Farmers-General granted Robert Morris a three-year exclusive contract to supply tobacco. While Morris profited, Chesapeake tobacco prices dropped. Lafayette suggested that Jefferson ask Vergennes to establish a committee to study Franco-American commerce. Jefferson approved the idea, but asked Lafayette to make the proposal himself. Vergennes created the American Committee in January 1786. In May the committee agreed to purchase tobacco above the Morris contract and not to make another such contract after Morris's expired. In October the committee waived duties on various American goods, but the decision did not take effect until December 1787.

Like tobacco, whale oil was a staple of Franco-American trade, which Jefferson hoped to use to replace the British trade. Nantucket was the center of the American whale-oil trade, and that trade was virtually cut off by the American Revolution. The British government encouraged American whalers who were locked out of the British trade to move to Nova Scotia. In 1785 Lafayette negotiated a contract granting Nantucket whalers exclusive supply privileges with a French company. Jefferson took a different approach, hoping to throw all French ports open to American whale oil. Two things stood in Jefferson's way. First, the Anglo-French commercial treaty of 1786 opened the French market to British goods, which flooded the market. The second was the *arrêt* of September 1788, which barred the importation of foreign whale oil. Jefferson responded with his brief essay *Observations on the Whale-Fishery*, in which he argued that the United States should be exempt from the prohibition on foreign whale oil. If France barred American whale oil, Jefferson argued, it would drive what was left of the American maritime industry to Great Britain to find work. The result would be to strengthen the maritime power of France's greatest rival. Jefferson's pamphlet was a typical mix of goodwill and vague threats of dire consequences. Jefferson's work paid off with the *arrêt* of December 7, 1788, which exempted American whale oil from the ban.

After three years of tending to commercial relations, Jefferson moved on to a piece of unfinished business, the making of a consular convention. The treaty of 1778 provided for consular establishments, but Congress rejected Franklin's 1784 project for fear of French influence in American politics. Jefferson's draft limited the activities of consuls in both nations, allowing them to handle the commercial and military affairs of their own nation. Jefferson did not directly present American fears of French influence, but rather told the Compte de Montmorin that the United States did not need consuls, but he realized that the French did. Jefferson stated that he merely wished to bring diplomatic practice into accord with American law. Jefferson and Montmorin signed the convention on November 14, 1788, and the Senate approved it the next year.

The duties of the French mission did not consume all of Jefferson's time, and he took the opportunity to travel and pursue other interests. Like Franklin, Jefferson took an interest in science and philosophy and defended American accomplishments at every turn. He went so far as to have an American moose sent to France to rebut Buffon's charges that American animals were inferior to their European counterparts. Jefferson met with the explorer James Ledyard and encouraged him to explore northwestern North America. In his studies and travels Jefferson acted as a filter between European and American culture. He spent much of his time searching bookstores and sending his discoveries to friends back home, particularly James Madison. Jefferson's tour through Hesse inspired his redesign of the moldboard, and the Maison Carrée in Nîmes served as the model for the Virginia Capitol at Richmond.

Jefferson's tour of Europe convinced him of the superior condition of the United States. Despite certain setbacks, such as the failure to stand up to the Barbary pirates and continuing difficulties with Dutch bankers, Jefferson was generally optimistic. He did not believe that Shays's Rebellion signaled the collapse of the Republic. Although he supported the Constitution, he criticized the lack of a bill of rights and hoped that once nine states ratified the Constitution, the last four would demand amendments.

As the Americans framed and debated their Constitution, France began the sequence of events that ultimately led to the French Revolution. French participation in the American Revolution badly strained French finances, and problems persisted throughout the 1780s. The king summoned the Assembly of Notables in February 1787. The last such meeting had taken place in 1626. The comptroller, Charles-Alexandre de Calonne, informed the Assembly of the size of the national debt and advised that the tax burden be spread more evenly over the population. Calonne also recommended that the provincial assemblies, or *parlements*, be popularly elected and meet together without regard to estate. The nobles rejected these proposals as attacks on their ancient privileges and replaced Calonne with the Comte de Brienne, who organized the provincial assemblies along traditional lines. Notwithstanding, the nobles did tend to oppose the royal prerogative and appeared as champions of freedom. The nobles kept the upper hand in French politics throughout the spring and summer of 1788. Political affairs seemed calmer in the fall, when the king appointed Jacques Necker to head the government and called for a meeting of the Estates-General in May 1789. A cold winter and a bread shortage added to the political uncertainties that greeted the Estates-General. The Estates had not met in 175 years and had no clear idea of how to proceed. The members of the Third Estate, representing about 96 percent of the population, wanted to meet without regard to estate. The king opposed such a move, but some members of the clergy and nobility met with the Third Estate in a self-styled National Assembly.

The coming of the French Revolution was the most important event of Jefferson's ministry, less for any role Jefferson might have played than for the way it would shape the rest of his career. At each stage Jefferson was hopeful that some form of liberty would triumph over royal tyranny. With the rise of the nobles, Jefferson wondered if the French were merely exchanging one form of tyranny for another. Jefferson believed that if the French government changed at all, it would evolve into a constitutional monarchy on the British model rather than a republic. When the Estates-General met, many of the emerging revolutionaries looked to Jefferson, as the representative of a successful revolution, for guidance. In June 1789 Jefferson, Lafayette, and William Short, Jefferson's secretary, drafted a charter of rights. The draft transferred many of the royal powers to the National Assembly, including all legislative and financial powers. The draft also called for freedom of the press, due process of law, civilian control of the military, and the abolition of the fiscal privileges of the nobility. Lafayette introduced the charter into the National Assembly, and some of its provisions became part of the Declaration of the Rights of Man and Citizen. By the time Jefferson left Paris in September, he believed that the French were well on the way to establishing a republic. He had observed that the American Revolution held an almost biblical authority over the French and believed that the French Revolution would only strengthen Franco-American friendship. However, Jefferson was in contact with only a small part of French revolutionary opinion. Jefferson had based his faith on the presumption that men like Lafayette and Pierre du Pont de Nemours would control future events. Jefferson's faith was disastrously misplaced.

After Jefferson took office as secretary of state in 1790, he brought with him the two core beliefs that had guided his mission to France. First, he firmly believed in the strategic and reformative power of American commerce. Second, and more recently, Jefferson fully approved of the French Revolution and believed that it would strengthen the alliance. In both of these beliefs Alexander Hamilton opposed Jefferson. Jefferson supported James Madison's efforts to raise tonnage duties on British shipping in order to force Great Britain into a commercial treaty. Hamilton opposed such measures on the grounds that his fiscal plans needed the revenue from British trade. Jefferson sympathized with France, even when the revolutionaries turned bloodier, executed the king, and made war on all of Europe. Jefferson never advocated entering the war, but did hope for a French victory. Jefferson believed that the 1778 treaties survived the death of the monarchy, including the mutual guarantee of territory. Edmond Genet's conduct as French minister and Hamilton's relationship with President Washington combined to undermine Jefferson's position. By 1793 Jefferson was tired of cabinet battles and retired at the end of the year.

Jefferson fully intended to retire to his farm, but events led him back into national politics and to the leadership of the Republican Party. He ran for president in 1796, finished three electoral votes behind John Adams, and took office as vice president. He viewed the Adams administration with increasing horror, seeing the Quasi-War and the Alien and Sedition Acts as the culmination of a Federalist plot against republican government at home and abroad. Jefferson ran again in 1800 and, aided by a divided Federalist Party, defeated John Adams. Jefferson finished in a tie with his running mate, Aaron Burr, and was elected by the House of Representatives.

The rise of Napoleon Bonaparte drained Jefferson's enthusiasm for the French Revolution, or at least for its outcome. French ownership of New Orleans made France a natural enemy in Jefferson's mind and made an alliance with Great Britain thinkable. In 1803 Jefferson dispatched James Monroe and Robert R. Livingston to purchase the port city. Bonaparte had no intention of selling until his plans for a revived French empire in North America collapsed. After the revolt in Santo Domingo Bonaparte offered to sell all of Louisiana. The Americans quickly agreed, and Jefferson brushed aside his constitutional objections. However, Jefferson believed that the Louisiana Purchase was incomplete without the Floridas.

If Jefferson abandoned his faith in the French Revolution, he held fast to his belief in the coercive power of American commerce. This belief was central to his reaction to French and British trade restrictions and remained so twenty years later. With the mounting British outrages against American shipping, Jefferson intended to use the commercial weapon to obtain redress. After the *Chesapeake* affair Jefferson called not for war, but for an embargo on American trade with other nations. The Embargo Act operated under the assumption that Europe depended on American trade for its survival. However, the embargo punished Americans most severely, nearly driving New England from the Union and leading Jefferson into the sort of executive actions he had once denounced as tyrannical.

After Jefferson left office in 1809, he never returned to public life, claiming to prefer reading the Greek classics to the newspapers. Jefferson confined his politics to letters of advice written to his successors. Two projects occupied Jefferson's final years. One was the University of Virginia, which obtained its charter in 1819. Jefferson intended it to be a modern university and an alternative to what he saw as the hidebound William and Mary. Jefferson also repaired his friendship with John Adams, which had been one of the many casualties of the French Revolution. Jefferson died at Monticello on July 4, 1826, preceding John Adam's death by a few hours.

Work by Thomas Jefferson

The Papers of Thomas Jefferson. Ed. Julian P. Boyd with Lyman H. Battlefield, associate editor. 26 vols. to date. Princeton: Princeton University Press, 1950–   .

Works about Thomas Jefferson

Cunningham, Noble E., Jr. *In Pursuit of Reason: The Life of Thomas Jefferson.* Baton Rouge: Louisiana State University Press, 1987.

Malone, Dumas. *Jefferson and His Time.* 6 vols. Boston: Little, Brown and Company, 1948–1981.

Peterson, Merrill D. *Thomas Jefferson and the New Nation: A Biography.* New York: Oxford University Press, 1970.

ROBERT W. SMITH

PHILIP CARYL JESSUP (1897–1986) was an international lawyer, the first ambassador-at-large, a member of the U.S. delegation to the United Nations, a judge on the World Court, and an educator. He was involved with all important international organizations during World War II and the immediate postwar period.

Jessup was born in New York City, one of five sons of Henry Wynans Jessup, a professor of law at New York University and a lay leader in the Presbyterian church, and the former Mary Hay Stotesbury. His college education was interrupted by infantry service in Belgium and France during World War I, and he graduated from Hamilton College in 1919. He later wrote that his experiences on the wartime front led him to devote his life to measures calculated to promote peace and avoid war. In 1924 he received a law degree from Yale University. On the basis of his thesis about the law of international waters and maritime jurisdiction, Columbia University granted him a Ph.D. in international law in 1927. He married Lois Walcott Kellogg in 1921, and they had one son, Philip, Jr., born in 1926.

From 1925 to 1926 Jessup advised Senator Irvine Lenroot (Republican of Wisconsin) and former Secretary of State Elihu Root on the question of the United States joining the Permanent Court of International Justice (the World Court). He credited Root, whom he met when Root was a scholar-in-residence at Hamilton College, and John Bassett Moore, an American jurist and historian, for stirring his interest in international law. In 1930 he served as legal advisor to Ambassador Harry S. Guggenheim in Cuba. Except for these brief assignments, Jessup spent most of the time between 1925 and 1942 practicing law in New York City and lecturing in international law and diplomacy at Columbia University Law School, where he was a well-liked figure on campus and where he eventually became a respected expert on international law and the Far East and published extensively in his field.

Prior to American involvement in World War II Jessup favored a neutral position for the United States and was a prominent spokesman for the powerful isolationist lobby America First, a position he held until the Japanese attack on Pearl Harbor. At the outset of the war he even opposed sending aid to Great Britain. American entry into the war changed his position, and in 1942 he was appointed associate director of the Naval School of Military Government and Administration at Columbia University, which prepared naval officers and civilians for military administration and civilian relief work in conquered countries. In 1943 he was chief of training and personnel in the Office for Foreign Relief and Rehabilitation, a State Department agency. In 1944 he served as assistant secretary general of the Bretton Woods Conference, which established the World Bank and the International Monetary Fund.

After the war Jessup became a liberal internationalist dedicated to world peace. He played important diplomatic roles, especially in the United Nations, during the formative Cold War years from 1947 to 1953. From 1947 to 1949 he served on the United Nations Committee on International Law, a body charged with formulating into a set of laws the issues raised by the Nuremberg war-crimes trials. He later wrote with optimism that he viewed the trials as evidence of the changing attitude toward international law, toward crimes against peace, and toward the individuals responsible for Nazi war crimes. In 1947 he became deputy to U.N. Ambassador Warren R. Austin and often filled in for the ailing ambassador in debates over the preservation of a cease-fire between Israel and the Arab states. In this series of discussions he held that an Arab refusal to prolong the truce in the Middle East was a threat to world peace. The Arabs capitulated and continued the truce. He presented the U.S. proposal for admitting Israel to membership in the United Nations. In 1950 he was U.S. deputy representative to the Interim Committee of the U.N. General Assembly. His work as a skilled diplomat, a conciliator who attempted to see the other point of view, and a draftsman enhanced the role of the United Nations. The protracted U.N. debates did not tax Jessup, who viewed the organization as helpful in current conflicts, especially those relating to wars of national liberation. He remarked that this friction got headlines and recognition for the organization. He impressed Secretary of State Dean Acheson with his diplomatic skill, good judgment, and infectious sense of humor. Acheson credited Jessup's leadership role with helping to inspire and create a confidence and trust in American integrity by nations in the North Atlantic Treaty Organization and the United Nations.

From 1949 to 1952 Jessup was the first ambassador-at-large, a post created by Secretary of State Acheson to permit the secretary of state to remain in Washington as the president's principal advisor on foreign affairs, yet still have distinguished representatives and negotiators at important meetings and conferences. He was a close advisor to Acheson, who so admired Jessup that he agreed to his condition that he be permitted to continue to teach as the Hamilton Fish Professor of International Law at Columbia University. As ambassador-at-large, Jessup engaged in lengthy secret diplomatic maneuverings with Soviet Ambassador Jacob Malik over lifting the Berlin Blockade in 1949, and he deserves much of the credit for ending the blockade. Jessup also participated in the deliberations leading to U.S. entry into the Korean War in June 1950 and helped formulate strategy. He accompanied President Harry S. Truman when he flew to Wake Island in the Pacific to consult with General Douglas MacArthur about the future of the war.

Jessup also helped review U.S. policy toward China and served as editor-in-chief of the controversial *White Paper* on China, a compilation of the diplomatic correspondence between the United States and China over the previous decade. The two-volume work concluded that despite the U.S. warnings to Chiang Kai-shek about corruption, some military aid to the Nationalist Chinese, and attempts to negotiate a coalition between the Nationalists and the Communists, the United

States had little or no control in the area and that corruption and inefficiency in Chiang's regime, as well as its unpopularity and reluctance to fight, were responsible for the fall of China to the Communists in 1949. The civil war in China, Jessup argued, was a product of internal Chinese forces beyond the control of the United States, and that nothing it could have done would have changed the results. The Chinese Nationalists themselves lost the war to Mao Tse-tung and the Communists.

While remaining ambassador-at-large, Jessup was also appointed a member of the U.S. delegation to the United Nations, an assignment that gave Senator Joseph R. McCarthy (Republican of Wisconsin) the opportunity to publicly attack Jessup in 1950. McCarthy alleged that Jessup's involvement in the Truman administration's China policy and testimony as a character witness for Alger Hiss, a once-respected State Department official accused of passing government secrets to the Soviet Union, revealed his Communist sympathies. McCarthy pointed to Jessup's role as principal author of the China *White Paper* as evidence of his attempt to discredit Chiang Kai-shek and the Nationalists and to favor recognition of the People's Republic of China. McCarthy and his supporters attributed the American failure to provide more support for Chiang and the fall of China to the Communists to betrayal in high places in the U.S. government. Amidst the tensions of the Cold War, many saw McCarthy's charges as an accusation of treasonous acts by Jessup. Jessup proved that he had supported the Truman administration's position against recognition of Communist China and had played an active part in successful efforts to prevent its recognition by the United Nations.

McCarthy elaborated his case against Jessup by claiming that he belonged to six Communist-front organizations, in particular, the Institute of Pacific Relations. Jessup had not been affiliated with two of the organizations and had left two before they were cited as Communist fronts, and two were never designated as fronts. On the Alger Hiss matter, Jessup argued that he testified as to Hiss's reputation and had not given his opinion, a stand that held little sway with McCarthy, who pointed to Jessup's noninterventionist stand as subversive, although he continued in this stance after the Nazi invasion of the Soviet Union, in contrast to the Communist Party position. McCarthy even depicted Jessup's frequent statements against the Soviets in the United Nations as a cover to hide pro-Soviet conspiracies. Jessup responded with a vigorous counterattack. After examining over a thousand pages of testimony and exhibits, a Senate committee cleared him of allegations of disloyalty in 1950. Nevertheless, the allegations continued to trouble his career. The Senate committee charged with approving the U.N. appointment voted against confirmation on the grounds that the McCarthy hearings lessened his effectiveness, but President Truman gave Jessup a recess appointment that did not require confirmation.

After the election of President Dwight D. Eisenhower in 1952, Jessup left government service to return to teaching at Columbia University, where he attracted students from all parts of the world, and where he remained until 1961.

That year he took one of the most prestigious judicial positions in the world, that of a judge on the International Court of Justice in Geneva, a post he held until 1970. In 1966 he issued an important dissent when the Court dismissed a complaint that Ethiopia and Liberia filed against the imposition of apartheid in South-West Africa, also known as Namibia. When the Court argued that Ethiopia and Liberia did not have a legal interest in the region, Jessup countered that states can have legal interests in matters that do not concern their material or tangible interests or those of their nationals but that are of general concern to all states, especially on general humanitarian grounds. Apartheid was not just a political issue for Jessup. These interests of the international community did not mean that all such interests were universal, but should be joined by common interest, geography, or shared values. When the public peace was violated, the community should bring its combined powers to bear. Jessup considered the Court underutilized, especially by the United States. Indeed, he argued, contrary to the American position, that the United States should adhere to the compulsory jurisdiction of the Court. Jessup believed in an international judiciary, an affirmation of his trust in the peaceful cooperation of nations deeply rooted in law. Although favored in academic and professional circles, these ideas won little support from major governments jealous of their autonomy.

Jessup's broad liberal, humanistic, and idealistic thoughts about international concepts were tempered by pragmatism. He refuted skeptics who questioned the actuality of international law and the nationalists who interpreted the country's interests in a narrow way. Disorder and conflict would result from the absence of rules for the day-to-day business of world affairs. In concrete terms he was able to illustrate how the rules and concepts bore on the issues of the governments and the peoples concerned. To rid international law of old concepts rooted in the conditions of the past, he coined a new phrase, "transnational law," to denote the body of law concerning relations among individuals, corporations, and governments when the arrangements crossed national boundaries. His pragmatic emphasis on experience over theory attracted him to political leaders such as Dean Acheson. Acheson was also sympathetic toward Jessup's appeal for a restoration of the traditional system of American foreign policy directed by the State Department under a secretary of state who was actually in charge of the formulation and execution of foreign policy, a situation that was not always the case in the post–World War II era.

Jessup envisioned a more organized and effective legal order that recognized the interest of the international community, protected the basic rights of individuals, prohibited armed force except in self-defense, employed judicial procedures or conciliation for settling disputes, and extended international regulation and administration to global and regional areas of interdependence. Broadly stated policies in legal instruments must be construed with regard to the consensus of the community on which their authority ultimately depended. While Jessup recognized that diversity and special conditions create many different kinds of international communities with their own special interests and laws, he called for order, responsibility, and justice. Meanwhile, he attempted to find common goals and interests with which to unite nations.

In a lucid literary style he set forth these views in his book *A Modern Law of Nations*, published in 1948. International law, like national law, must be directly relevant to the individual person. International law was not a closed or artificial system of academic thought, but a living force in practical international affairs that derived its authority from contemporary consent and widespread endorsement. The United Nations had a role to play. Perhaps idealistically, he proposed an international bill of rights that would deny the cloak of national sovereignty to a nation that denied human rights to its citizens. On the question of choosing between the freedom of the state to do anything it pleases with its citizens and the notion that all human beings are granted rights that the state is bound to respect, he argued that the fundamental rights of people were inherent in the individual and not derived from the state. In this mode the United Nations ought to forbid terrorist activities, the assassination of heads of state, counterfeiting of foreign currencies, the slave trade, traffic in narcotics, and unauthorized manufacturing of atomic or other weapons.

Jessup published *The Birth of Nations*, his principal book concerning his diplomatic role, in 1974. A personal memoir, it describes the frenzied activity, trials, and frustrations of American diplomats coping with postwar conditions over which they had little control. As an active executor of State Department policy in several critical incidents involving the breakup of the European colonial empires, Jessup was in a unique position to recount the events preceding the birth of such nations as South Korea, Indonesia, Morocco, Tunisia, Libya, Somalia, and Israel. While he focused on the birth of ten nations, he also considered the explosion of national births that inflated U.N. membership from 50 nations in 1945 to 132 in 1972. Painstakingly he described how policies toward these new nations were formed and how negotiations were conducted. Washington's attitude toward colonial independence often vacillated. Sometimes, as in the case of Indonesia, differences over policy developed within separate factions in the State Department. On another occasion the American delegates to the United Nations, including Jessup, were not consulted and were acutely embarrassed by an abrupt shift in Washington over U.S. recognition of Israel. Such changes, flagrant violations of the basic rules of diplomacy that U.N. diplomats be kept fully and constantly informed of national policy and actions, according to Jessup, created a lack of trust in the integrity of U.S. purposes and a skepticism about statements of future intentions and policies. Regardless, he remained passionately committed to the use of law and diplomacy for the peaceful settlement of international disputes, in general, and to the use of the United Nations, in particular. Unlike Dean Acheson and George Kennan, who thought the United Nations boring, Jessup had faith in the organization's usefulness. For support, he pointed out how American dominance and economic pressure on the Dutch worked with U.N. mechanisms to gain independence for Indonesia. President Truman was praised for his commitment to U.N. involvement in U.S.

policies in the Korean War, while President Richard M. Nixon was rebuked for not relying on the organization during the Vietnam War.

In later years Jessup became critical of American foreign policy, especially that toward Indochina. Presidents Franklin D. Roosevelt and Truman should not have been persuaded to deter the French from returning to Indochina. He criticized U.S. unilateralism in Vietnam and became an active and influential foe of the Vietnam War. In 1970 he wrote to individual senators urging them to suspend funding for the war.

As a prominent diplomat during the early Cold War years and an influential scholar of international law, Philip C. Jessup made constructive contributions. His patient negotiating skills were critical to ending the Berlin Blockade. He held to his international convictions and his sense, despite his earlier isolationist position, that the United States had an obligation to play a significant role in world affairs. In the face of narrow nationalist views, he held for international laws and organizations.

Works by Philip C. Jessup

A Modern Law of Nations. New York: Macmillan, 1948.
Transnational Law. New Haven: Yale University Press, 1956.
The Price of International Justice. New York: Columbia University Press, 1971.
The Birth of Nations. New York: Columbia University Press, 1974.

Works about Philip C. Jessup

Friedmann, Wolfgang, Louis Henkin, and Oliver Lissitzyn, eds. Transnational Law in a Changing Society: Essays in Honor of Philip C. Jessup. New York: Columbia University Press, 1972.
Schacter, Oscar. "Philip Jessup's Life and Ideas." American Journal of International Law 80 (October 1986): 878–95.

ARLENE LAZAROWITZ

NELSON TRUSLER JOHNSON (1887–1954), chief

American minister to China from 1930 to 1935 and American ambassador to China from 1935 to 1941, argued unsuccessfully for greater resistance by the United States to Japanese aggression in China during the 1930s and for the abolition of Western treaty rights and extraterritoriality. Called by historians a "benevolent pragmatist," Johnson believed deeply in the ideals of American democracy but argued that a sober understanding of national interest was necessary for the successful conduct of American foreign policy. A man of deep integrity, Johnson also possessed a gregarious personality, a well-developed sense of humor, and an understanding of human nature that enabled him to become an effective administrator.

Nelson Trusler Johnson was born on April 3, 1887, in Washington, D.C. His father, a lawyer, moved the family to Oklahoma when he was nine years old. At the age of thirteen he enrolled in Sidwell Friends School in Washington and lived with his grandmother, whose independent mind and humane outlook on life imprinted themselves on her young charge and influenced the development of his own personality. After graduating from the Friends School he attended George Washington University from 1906 to 1907. Upon passing the Foreign Service examination, he left in 1907 for two years of Chinese-language study in Peking. For the next few years he received a number of postings in China, first as vice consul in Mukden from 1909 to 1910, in Harbin from 1910 to 1911, and as deputy consul-general and assessor attached to the Mixed Court in Shanghai from 1911 to 1915. In 1915 he served as consul in Chungking, moving in the same year to Changsha, where he served as consul from 1915 to 1918, after which he returned to Washington, D.C., as a member of the Division of Far Eastern Affairs in the Department of State. After two more years as consul general-at-large, Johnson became chief of the Division of Far Eastern Affairs in 1925, rising to assistant secretary of state from 1927 to 1929. In 1930 he was appointed minister to China, and in 1931 he married Jane Beck. In 1935 the status of the ministry was raised to that of an embassy, and his title changed to ambassador. In 1941 he asked to be posted to Australia as minister, where he could be reunited with his wife and two children. In 1945 he returned to the United States, and in 1946 he became secretary general of the Far Eastern Commission until he retired in 1952. He died of a sudden heart attack on September 3, 1954, in Washington, D.C., at the age of sixty-seven.

Over the course of his long career in the State Department, Nelson Johnson spent thirty-four years specializing in China. He was the U.S. minister and then ambassador to China during some of the most critical years of the twentieth century. His success in that post was due in part to his own interest in and respect for the Chinese heritage. During the years in which he lived and worked in China, he read widely in Chinese history, literature, and philosophy and became familiar with the main body of Western scholarship on the Chinese heritage. In addition, he acquired an impressive command of the spoken Chinese language, although he never learned how to read Chinese characters at more than a rudimentary level. This skill with the spoken language, together with his natural curiosity and open personality, enabled him to communicate easily with Chinese from all walks of life. When he traveled, he made special efforts to meet as many people as possible in order to understand more fully the Chinese point of view on world events. Partly as a result of these qualities, Johnson was able to convey to his superiors in Washington an accurate appraisal of the situation on the ground in China and was equally adept at explaining the American government's views in a way that Chinese leaders could readily understand.

Ambassador Johnson's greatest disappointment arose over his failure to convince Washington of the dangers of Japanese militarism in the 1930s, beginning with the occupation of Manchuria in 1931 and then the attack on China proper in 1937. By the middle of the decade he was certain that appeasement of Japan by the Western powers would lead to a wider war that would eventually involve the United States. He worried, in dispatch after dispatch, that failure to stand up to the younger officers who were coming to dominate not only the military but also the civilian government would encourage them to believe that the Western powers would not interfere to prevent Japan from dominating East Asia. Much as Winston Churchill did in Europe, Johnson accurately foresaw the main forces that would ultimately lead to war, but was unable to make government leaders understand the seriousness of the situation. American foreign policy, in the 1930s as in most times, was a reflection primarily of domestic politics, of which Johnson had less appreciation than did his counterparts in Washington, and over which he had no control. The mood of the country was isolationist, and no politician who desired to keep his job could afford to support a policy of military intervention in far-off parts of the world. The days when America would willingly accept global responsibilities lay in the future.

Among his other disappointments was the failure of the international system to deal effectively with Japanese aggression. Once a strong supporter of the Kellogg-Briand Pact of 1928 outlawing war as an instrument of foreign policy, and of the League of Nations, Johnson reluctantly concluded that the Kellogg-Briand Pact was useless without a credible means of enforcement, and that the League would play no significant role in international affairs for much the same reason. Its inability to compel member states to implement sanctions against the Japanese government after the Japanese occupation of Manchuria in 1931 convinced Johnson that the League was little more than a paper tiger.

Johnson's alarm over the direction of Japanese policy in Asia arose as a result of direct observation. His vantage point in China provided a unique opportunity to observe the disparity between pronouncements made in Tokyo by the Japanese government and actual conditions on the ground. This perspective thus provided Johnson with a much more accurate assessment of the true nature of Japanese foreign policy than diplomats and journalists in Tokyo or Washington, who were inclined to take the Japanese government at its word. The incident that first opened his eyes to the fact that events were being driven not by government officials in Tokyo but by lower-ranking officers in the field occurred in 1932 in Shanghai. Japanese naval officers, emboldened by the occupation of Manchuria and the formation of the puppet government of Manchukuo, fired at point-blank range on Chapei, the Chinese section of the city, killing large numbers of civilians and creating an international incident. For months the Japanese refused to cease their periodic bombardment of the city despite surprisingly effective resistance by Nationalist Army forces and despite vigorous protests by other powers concerned over the protection of foreign nationals in Shanghai. During the negotiations to bring about a settlement of the dispute, it became clear to Johnson that the government in Tokyo was not fully in command of the situation. From that point on, he began seriously to doubt the reliability of any statements made by the civilian government in Tokyo. Although he may have influenced some leaders, including Secretary of State Cordell Hull and President Franklin Roosevelt, to avoid implementing the provisions of the neutrality laws that would have made it difficult to provide weapons and supplies to China in the late 1930s, Johnson believed that Washington was too slow to see the gathering storm clouds.

Johnson's efforts to convince Washington to abolish the unequal treaty rights and the privilege of extraterritoriality, conferred on European powers as a result of the Opium and Arrow wars in the nineteenth century, were similarly unsuccessful. Through them foreign powers had been given a number of special powers. Among them was the authority to set low tariff rates for all goods imported into China from abroad, so that the Chinese could not protect their own domestic industries from foreign competition (or use tariff revenue as more than a modest source of government income). Extraterritoriality, for its part, enabled Europeans to be subject to their own laws whenever a dispute arose between Europeans and Chinese nationals. Both arrangements constituted violation of Chinese sovereignty. In the early 1930s there was some hope that they might be revoked. Negotiations between the United States and China, led by Johnson, were reaching a promising point when the Japanese occupation of Manchuria caused them to be set aside in 1931. They were not resumed. Washington dithered until 1943, long after Johnson had left China and after the United States itself had entered the war against Japan. The 1943 revocation came also, as Johnson later noted with some irony, after Japan had occupied all the treaty ports and therefore rendered the American declaration superfluous. Had it been done earlier, repudiation of the special privileges might have lent Chiang Kai-shek's Nationalist government greater legitimacy at a time, particularly after the Japanese invasion of China proper in 1937 when the government needed public support the most. What might have been done, in other words, at little cost to American interests but with great benefit to Sino-American relations was accomplished only after it had ceased to have any practical effect whatsoever.

Nelson Johnson's main contribution as the chief diplomatic representative of the United States in China from 1930 to 1941 was to steer Sino-American relations through one of the most momentous decades in the twentieth century. Dominated from almost the beginning of the decade to the end by the rising power of Japan in East Asian affairs, Nelson's tenure was marked by smooth relations and substantial cooperation between China and the United States. This foundation of mutual understanding aided materially in the eventual outcome of World War II. A lesser diplomat might well have made mistakes undermining this partnership with consequences that could only have benefited the Japanese war effort. Johnson's greatest success, however, was in his eyes his greatest failure, since he believed that the rise of Japanese militarism might have been thwarted earlier and at much lower cost in human life had there been stronger resolve on the part of Western powers to take a stand. Like Cassandra, condemned by Apollo to have her predictions of the future disbelieved by the very people she warned of imminent catastrophe, Johnson foresaw the likely outcome of appeasement in Asia but could not persuade Washington leaders who, understandably in a democratic polity, were guided primarily by considerations of domestic politics.

Works by Nelson Trusler Johnson

Nelson T. Johnson Papers, Manuscripts Division, Library of Congress, Washington, DC.

Works about Nelson Trusler Johnson

Buhite, Russell D. *Nelson T. Johnson and American Policy toward China, 1925–1941.* East Lansing: Michigan State University Press, 1968.
Starr, Daniel P. "Nelson Trusler Johnson: The United States and the Rise of Nationalist China, 1925–1937." Ph.D. diss., Rutgers University, 1967.
Vincent, John Carter. *The Extraterritorial System in China: Final Phase.* Harvard University East Asian Monograph no. 30. Cambridge: Harvard University Press, 1970.
Wood, Herbert J. "Nelson Trusler Johnson, the Diplomacy of Benevolent Pragmatism." In *Diplomats in Crisis: United States–Chinese–Japanese Relations, 1919–1941,* ed. Richard Dean Burns and Edward M. Bennett, 7–26. Santa Barbara, CA: ABC-Clio, 1974.

ALAN T. WOOD

ROBERT FRANCIS KELLEY (1894–1976), director

of the State Department's Division of Eastern European Affairs, 1926–1937, is viewed by many as responsible for much of the hard-line anti-Soviet attitude of the State Department in the period before and after the recognition of Russia in 1933.

Kelley was born on February 13, 1894, in Somerville, Massachusetts, and was educated in the Boston public schools. In 1911 he entered Harvard University, where he studied modern European history. With the intention of researching the origins of the Crimean War, he took courses in Russian and eventually became fluent in the language. After receiving his A.B. magna cum laude in 1915, he spent a year at the University of Paris on a Sheldon Traveling Fellowship. He intended to continue his studies in St. Petersburg, but the course of World War I prevented him from doing so. Instead, Kelley returned to Harvard as a graduate student and received his A.M. in 1917 while also serving as an instructor in the History Department. While he was able to complete his course work and comprehensive examinations for his Ph.D., his continued studies were interrupted by American entry into the war.

Kelley joined the army in October 1917 and spent most of the war in the United States, but in late 1918 he was sent first to Silesia and then to join the American Army of Occupation in Germany. He spent a year in Aldernach as a liaison officer between the army and local German authorities. In early 1920 he was detailed as assistant military attaché to Denmark and Finland and military observer in the Baltic Provinces, serving first in Copenhagen and then proceeding to Riga, Latvia. Kelley remained there for the next three years, making frequent trips to the other Baltic states and gathering information on events occurring in the nearby Soviet Union. This period of service and his contact with exiled Russian citizens helped to solidify his attitudes toward the Soviet Union and would govern his later actions in the Eastern European Division.

In mid-1922, faced with the decreasing size of the American army and with the encouragement of the commissioner to the Baltics, Evan Young, Kelley took the examination for the Consular Service. Passing the exam, he resigned from the army in December 1922 and was assigned as vice consul in Calcutta, India. After less than a year, however, perhaps at the urging of Evan Young, who had been appointed as chief of the newly created Eastern European Division of the State Department, Kelley was transferred to Washington, where he remained until the dissolution of the division in 1937. Kelley's early tenure included testimony before Congress on the threat of Bolshevik propaganda in the United States and a progressively greater role in the leadership of the division. His testimony before the Senate Foreign Relations Committee and its chairman William Borah helped to end congressional attempts to change American policy toward the Soviet Union and earned Kelley a personal letter of commendation from Secretary of State Charles Evans Hughes. He became assistant chief of the division in March 1925, acting chief in October 1925, and chief in 1926. Kelley led the division until it was disbanded in 1937.

One of the first steps Kelley took upon his elevation to the position of chief of the Eastern European Division was the creation of a new protocol governing the selection, training, and promotion of officers in his division. Working in concert with Allen Dulles, head of the Near Eastern Division, he developed a set of regulations in June 1927 that stressed the need for a more complete understanding of the languages, histories, and cultures of the countries of Eastern Europe, Russia, and the Near East. After a probationary period of eighteen months in a consular position in the region and an examination by officials within the particular divisions, an officer would be assigned to a period of formal study at an institution chosen by the department. This program was to last three years, and the successful completion of these programs would mark the final stage in the process of preparing officers for postings to the Near East or Eastern Europe.

During the period Kelley headed the division, seven officers were assigned to the Eastern European language-training program, which ended with the dissolution of the division in 1937. Six of these, William M. Gwynn, Norris Chipman, B. Eric Kuniholm, Charles E. Bohlen, Edward Page, Jr., and Francis B. Stevens, underwent their language training at the University of Paris, studying with the same professors with whom Kelley had worked during his advanced training more than ten years earlier. Only one, George Kennan, studied elsewhere, at the University of Berlin, due to his posting in Germany. There has been some criticism of Kelley's selection of Paris as the main training site for his officers; it has been argued that Kelley was attempting to instill in his officers the same "anti-Soviet" bias that supposedly influenced his own conduct in directing American policy toward the Soviet Union. It is more likely that Kelley's familiarity with the program in Paris led to its selection, not to mention that Paris was one of only a few sites in the world that offered the sort of intensive instruction he felt was necessary to properly prepare his officers to carry out their functions within the division.

During the period 1927–1933 Kelley and his division supported the stated government policy of nonrecognition of the Soviet Union. Kelley gave speeches and wrote memorandums that promoted and more clearly defined this practice. Indeed, prior to 1933 there was only one instance when Kelley offered an endorsement of recognizing Russia. It is unclear whether this document, written in 1924, before he assumed any leadership role in the division, reflected Kelley's own beliefs at the time or was an assignment from his superiors to thoroughly prepare him for the sorts of attacks the nonrecognition policy faced from its critics. Whatever the case, it was the only time Kelley showed any support for the cause of Soviet recognition.

With the election of Franklin Roosevelt, nonrecognition came to an abrupt end. What bothered Kelley the most about the new policy was not specifically the change itself, but the speed with which it occurred. He urged Secretary of State Cordell Hull, and by implication President Roosevelt, not to take Soviet promises about future negotiations to resolve outstanding questions in Soviet-American relations at face value. He was most concerned about the resolution of three issues: noninterference in the United States by agents of the Soviet Union; compensation for property lost by Americans after the Bolshevik government nationalized many foreign assets in the country; and, perhaps most important, the repayment of debts incurred by various Russian governments prior to the Russian Revolution in 1917. The Soviet government promised that these matters would be satisfactorily dealt with once recognition had been granted. Kelley argued that this approach had not worked for Great Britain in the 1920s and would not work at this time. His prediction was later borne out; none of the three issues were ever resolved to the satisfaction of the United States.

In the years after recognition the Eastern European Division came to be viewed by many within the administration as causing difficulties between the United States and the Soviet Union. As head of the division, Kelley came under the most scrutiny. After Roosevelt's reelection in 1936 proponents of a more conciliatory line toward Russia moved against Kelley and the division. In June 1937 the State Department reorganized its geographical divisions, and the Eastern European section was abolished entirely, its duties being folded in with the Western European Division to create a single European Division. Kelley and many of his officers felt that this action was politically motivated, an attempt to get rid of a troublesome group that attempted to slow the process of reconciliation with the Soviet Union. Indeed, Kelley, Kennan, Loy Henderson, and Bohlen all referred to this action as a "purge" and felt that perhaps the Russian government had a hand in the dissolution of the division.

Under this new system there was no room for Robert Kelley. Instead of a new post within the department, he was made counselor of the American embassy in Ankara, Turkey, where he remained until near the end of World War II. During this period Turkey was a focal point of struggle between the Allied and Axis powers. Kelley's tasks included first keeping Turkey out of the war and later helping to bring the country into the conflict on the Allied side. He was also involved in helping interned American pilots escape, limiting Turkish exports to Germany, controlling Turkish imports from Allied countries, and espionage and counterespionage. In early 1945 Kelley was quietly forced to retire from the Foreign Service for minor currency violations. This action occurred without the department first informing Ambassador Laurence Steinhardt of its decision. Kelley believed that his coerced departure came as a result of actions by those in the department who were looking for any excuse to remove him from the Foreign Service. He remained very bitter about this action, complaining in letters to Steinhardt about other embassy officials who had also participated in black-market currency transactions. Not only had these officers not been compelled to leave the service, but one had even been promoted. From the actions of the State Department, it could be argued that Kelley's suspicions had some merit, and that perhaps there were those who wished to remove his perceived anti-Soviet influence from the department entirely at a time when the United States hoped desperately to come to lasting agreements with the Soviet Union.

According to his own autobiographical sketch, Kelley spent the next few years "traveling in the United States getting acquainted with the West and South." In 1949 he may have joined the newly created Central Intelligence Agency, though the only record of this in his papers is a letter to Kelley from the CIA Personnel Office saying that he was under active consideration for a position and requesting that he complete a medical history form. What is known is that Kelley became active in efforts to help Soviet refugees fleeing from Stalinist Russia. In 1951 he participated in the establishment of Radio Liberty, which began broadcasting in March 1953.

In the period from 1953 to 1967 Kelley served first as deputy to the president and later as vice president of Radio Liberty, residing in Munich, West Germany. Upon his retirement he returned to Washington and died on June 2, 1976. He was a member of the American Historical Association, the American Society of International Law, Phi Beta Kappa, the Catholic Club, the Washington Institute for Foreign Affairs, and Diplomatic and Consular Officers Retired.

Robert Kelley has been credited by some historians as being the leading anti-Soviet influence in the State Department during the 1920s and 1930s and as greatly shaping the attitudes of certain of his officers, including Charles Bohlen, Loy Henderson, and George Kennan, who would go on to help direct American policy during the Cold War. These authors see a direct line from Kelley's ideas to the hard-line approaches adopted by the United States during the darkest days of Soviet-American antagonism from the late 1940s well into the 1960s. Looking at Kelley's memorandums and other documents from his tenure in the Eastern European Division, however, one could argue that he was not anti-Soviet but rather "pro-American." His policy recommendations regarding Russia aimed more at protecting American interests than at isolating the Soviet Union. For example, during the period in which he was the main State Department spokesman for nonrecognition, Soviet-American trade grew tremendously, reaching levels even greater than before World War I. While he may have supported the policy against Russia, it must also be remembered that Kelley ultimately carried out orders from his superiors, and in the period prior to 1933 the presidents and secretaries of state generally supported nonrecognition as the best way in which to deal with the Soviet Union.

Furthermore, while Kelley seemed reluctant to support Roosevelt's unconditional recognition of Russia in 1933, the most he was guilty of was trying to slow down what he perceived as a "rush to recognition" and to protect what he viewed as America's best interests. Indeed, in 1937 Kelley wrote memorandums supporting attempts by the Roosevelt administration to sell battleships to the Soviet Union, actions that were later derailed by the Navy Department. In supporting this plan, Kelley argued that strengthening the Soviet navy would not run counter to American national interests, which in 1937 ran more to limiting the ambitions of Germany and Japan than to anti-Soviet posturing. With this statement Kelley showed most clearly that his decisions relating to Russia were most influenced by his perceptions of what would best serve America.

As to Kelley's lasting influence during the Cold War, it is instructive to look at the attitudes of his subordinates who went on to positions of authority after World War II. Loy Henderson had perhaps the most hard-line attitude toward the Soviet Union of these men, yet he did not participate in the language-training program and actually received most of his training before he met Kelley; it could be said that at most the two men shared certain attitudes about the Soviets, rather than one influencing the other to any great extent. George Kennan's views may have been most influenced by Kelley, to whom he expressed gratitude for the training that he received about the Soviet Union. Yet he was the only division officer not trained at the University of Paris, and it can be argued that his views and later actions were not particularly anti-Soviet; instead, he operated most like Kelley, arguing from a more academic background than other officers. Finally, Charles Bohlen, who was accepted by the more pro-Soviet officials in the State Department after the dissolution of the Eastern European Division, was so deeply influenced by Kelley that in his memoirs he could not even spell Kelley's name correctly. Bohlen trained in Paris and yet managed to remain the objective diplomat who was the professed goal of Kelley's language-training program.

Robert Kelley was not a raging anti-Communist or anti-Soviet. While his background and training produced a man more in tune with imperial Russia, he also dealt with the successor Soviet Union from a position of understanding, and his policymaking decisions were most influenced by his commitment to protecting what he saw as the best interests of the United States. His academic background provided a new direction for Foreign Service officers, and the training program that he helped establish allowed for the further professionalization of the department. Education and academic objectivism were the trademarks of Robert Kelley and his officers, and this may be his lasting legacy, more so than his supposed ideological influence on those who trained under him.

Works by Robert F. Kelley

"Soviet Policy on the Europe Border." *Foreign Affairs* 3, no. 1 (September 15, 1924): 90–98.

"The Territorial Organization of the Soviet Power." *Geographical Review* 14, no. 4 (October 1924): 615–21.

"The Politburo." *Foreign Affairs* 7, no. 2 (January 1929): 255–58.

"The International Aims and Polices of the Soviet Union." *Review of Politics* 24, no. 2 (April 1962): 183–211.

Works about Robert F. Kelley

There are no works that focus exclusively on Kelley, though many studies of the first years of American-Soviet relations deal with that important part of his career. Some examples are given here.

Bennett, Edward M. *Recognition of Russia: An American Foreign Policy Dilemma*. Waltham, MA: Blaisdell Publishing Company, 1970.

Henderson, Loy. *A Question of Trust: The Origins of U.S.-Soviet Diplomatic Relations: The Memoirs Loy W. Henderson*. Ed. George W. Baer. Stanford, CA: Stanford University, Hoover Institution Press, 1986.

Peterson, Jody L. "Ideology and Influence: Robert F. Kelley and the State Department." Ph.D. diss., Washington State University, 1996.

Propas, Frederic L. "The State Department, Bureaucratic Politics, and Soviet-American Relations, 1918–1938." Ph.D. diss., University of California, Los Angeles, 1982.

Richman, John. *The United States and the Soviet Union: The Decision to Recognize*. Raleigh, NC: Camberleigh and Hall, 1980.

Yergin, Daniel. *Shattered Peace: The Origins of the Cold War and the National Security State*. Boston: Houghton Mifflin, 1977.

JODY L. PETERSON

GEORGE FROST KENNAN (1904–   ) has enjoyed four

different careers, as diplomat, policymaker, historian, and critic. In three of these he attained undeniable distinction. While he directed the State Department's Policy Planning Staff (1947–1949), he helped devise West European recovery and Japanese rehabilitation, thereby giving palpable shape to the concept of containment. As a historian, he has won recognition (including a Pulitzer Prize) for his work on early Soviet-U.S. relations and on the origins of World War I. Though by no means everywhere endorsed, he has also been respected as an impassioned observer of the contemporary scene, offering critiques on subjects ranging from the Cold War arms race and the Vietnam War to social-environmental degradation.

Kennan's performance in diplomacy was considerably more ambiguous than in his other fields. Admittedly, he was an able Foreign Service officer who produced reliable reportage during the 1930s and in World War II from such posts as Moscow, Prague, and Berlin. As Ambassador Averell Harriman's deputy in 1944–1946, he wrote lucid analyses of Soviet politics and international aims, exemplified by his influential Long Telegram. Ironically, however, given his testimonials on the primacy of diplomacy, Kennan proved unlucky on the two occasions when he assumed ambassadorships. His blundering in 1952 caused Stalin's government to declare him persona non grata. During his residency in Belgrade (1961–1963) he was unable to reverse the deterioration in Yugoslav-U.S. relations. These lackluster ambassadorial performances raise hard questions about Kennan and—by extension—for U.S. diplomacy, even in its post–Cold War phase.

As evident from the record of missions abroad where he served as a subaltern (1930s–1940s), Kennan displayed those properties common to the U.S. Foreign Service officer. At the same time, his main accomplishments stemmed from his own determination—not from playing bit parts in a team effort.

Like other recruits who entered the Foreign Service in the immediate wake of the Rogers Act (1924), Kennan took pride in acquiring the habits of mind needed for success in professional diplomacy. In his case these entailed the application of energy and intellect to become an area specialist. Along with other graduates of Robert Kelley's Soviet immersion course (notably Charles Bohlen), he became conversant with pre-1917 czarist cultural-political history, mastered not only the rudiments of the Russian tongue but also its subtlety, and developed a discernment for the hidden meaning in Soviet pronouncements. Early exposure to the victims of Stalinist misrule and Kelley's conservative preferences also fortified Kennan against the siren call of Bolshevik socialism.

This combination of experience and scholarship enabled him to play a useful part in William Bullitt's Moscow ambassadorship (1933–1936). His linguistic skills advanced the cause of negotiations—from the rental of embassy office space to the rescue of compatriots who had fallen foul of Stalinist law—and gained for him deep appreciation for the texture of Soviet life. His command of Russian also allowed him to study the purge trials as they unfolded. Consequently, Kennan was able to tutor Bullitt on the nature of Soviet reality and composed some of the ambassador's better reports for Washington. During 1944–1946, while Kennan directed the embassy's day-to-day operations, he again played a key role in the education of an ambassador (then Harriman), spelling out for him the implications of the Grand Alliance's unraveling.

Kennan's shortcomings belonged to those of the interwar diplomatic caste. Loyalty to the Foreign Service (above all to its Soviet hands) made him impatient with outsiders whenever they presumed to venture an opinion on the USSR or pursue a policy contrary to his viewpoint. The most obvious example is Kennan's harsh condemnation of Ambassador Joseph Davies. Obsequious in the presence of power and irresponsible in his public statements in support of Soviet legality, Davies nevertheless dutifully promoted Franklin Roosevelt's conciliatory policy toward Stalin, which helped lead to Soviet-U.S. cooperation in the emergency of 1941–1945.

Kennan's bland response to the entreaties of a terrified Jewish acquaintance in Prague as the Germans marched in, his unfeeling account of Jewish refugees fleeing through Lisbon to the United States in 1941, and his reservations about Americans whose origins resided outside of northern Europe were expressions of a genteel anti-Semitism and nativist outlook that afflicted the State Department. Kennan's inadequate response to the plight of persecuted Jewry also highlights the following: Even in the ethically circumscribed routine of the bureaucratic office, there is such a thing as dereliction of duty to conscience. Moreover, his skepticism about the New Deal was compatible with that of many in the Foreign Service, where, despite the introduction of reforms, an ethos of social elitism still clung.

If Kennan can be understood in the 1930s and 1940s as a product of the Foreign Service, assessment of him must also incorporate his particular tenacity and perspicacity. These traits, with his sturdy prose, later made it possible to sustain a scholarly career at a time in life when most people's thoughts turn to retirement. In 1946 these qualities gave the verve to his analysis in the Long Telegram. Queries originating in the Treasury Department about the Soviet attitude toward international financial machinery (the World Bank and the International Monetary Fund) required no more than another, rather ordinary, appraisal of Stalin's near-term aims. Instead, despite his qualms about the intellectual capacity of the U.S. government and his frustration at having previous warnings about the USSR ignored, he let fly a detailed analysis of Soviet ideology, practice, and ambitions. Viewed in the context of his overall literary corpus, the resultant document was unexceptional, a by-product of the telegraphic medium in which it was composed. But its impact on the Truman administration's thinking would have secured Kennan, had he never been heard of again, a snug place in Foreign Service lore and appreciative, if brief, mention by diplomatic historians.

Kennan's careful interpretation of things Soviet did not always translate well in Washington, however. The most important case in point is his reporting of 1945–1946, when he tried to advance propositions about the ambiguous nature of postwar Soviet power (a large army but battered cities and economy). These were not fully assimilated by a White House unsettled by the actions of the NKVD and Communist faithful in Eastern Europe. Kennan advocated a tactical change of emphasis in contending with the Soviets, not an unrelenting Cold War. Similarly, his emphasis on the USSR as a conventional great state motivated primarily by shifts in the balance of power, not a revolutionary experiment working to overthrow the entire capitalist order, was lost in the gathering din of Cold War hyperbole. The ascendant view in Truman's circle in 1946 was expressed by Clark Clifford, who urged that the United States prepare for all contingencies, including a ''total'' and ''horrible'' war against the Marxist-Leninist USSR.

Of the more than sixty ambassadors sent by the United States since 1809 to Russian territory, only Kennan was forbidden by his hosts from continuing to reside there. Of course, a number of other ambassadors were also deemed odious or otherwise objectionable to czarist and Communist officialdom. John Randolph of Virginia addressed the august Nicholas I in the familiar *tu* form; Randolph's eccentricities caused hilarity in the court, where opinion held that the poor man was half-insane. Cassius M. Clay scandalized St. Petersburg society as a braggart, pugilist, and reckless ladies' man. David Francis was clueless about Bolshevik ambitions; Lenin thought him a pathetic representative of the capitalist world conspiracy. Laurence Steinhardt was damned by Stalin as craven and a defeatist. William Standley's grousing about Moscow's ingratitude for Lend-Lease aid won him vilification in the Soviet press. There are other illustrations in what is an impressively long list of defeated ambassadorships. In fairness, it should also be noted that Kennan was not the only envoy to embarrass his government, nor was he alone in not establishing common ground with his suspicious-minded hosts. Still, his 1952 ministry stands out by virtue of its comprehensive dismalness.

There are several reasons that help to explain Kennan's clumsy misstep (making comparisons in public between Nazi Germany and the USSR). He was not in sympathy with the main thrust of Dean Acheson's Soviet policy and felt estranged from the administration. He was upset by the mistreatment inflicted on honorable members of the Foreign Service in the McCarthy season of hysteria, particularly by charges brought against John Paton Davies. In the embassy itself Kennan failed to build rapport with his subordinates despite the goodwill waiting for him when he arrived. He was alternately aloof and temperamental, always exacting. His relations with the young Malcolm Toon were particularly atrocious and resulted in his writing a damaging fitness report that almost derailed the future ambassador's career. Moreover, risky intelligence operations, over which Kennan had no control or sympathy, were mounted by military attachés assigned to the embassy. As for the larger Moscow environment, it was sublimely malevolent in the last days of Stalin. The anti-American war of words waged by *Pravda* and *Izvestia* was at its height; spying on and harassment of embassy personnel were unrelenting; normal contact with high ministers or ordinary citizens was forbidden; fear saturated Soviet society. Once a Soviet sentry chased off children who had the temerity to approach the ambassador's two-year-old son in the garden of Spaso House.

These considerations suggest that the man who misspoke at Tempelhof Airport had ample reason to feel dispirited and doubtful about the efficacy of ambassadorial diplomacy. Yet, as he has freely admitted, Kennan himself bears major blame for the ignominy that overtook him in September 1952. It was he who was unable to command the internal calm necessary to all successful missions. Disaster struck only when he departed from Talleyrand's commandment, "Et surtout pas trop de zèle."

This episode was all the more unfortunate because it occurred at a time when Acheson was groping for a solution to the Korean fighting. He expected to involve the Soviets in producing an armistice, achievement of which was hampered when his ambassador sparked an unnecessary crisis with Moscow. Judgment here is best passed in Kennan's own words: "I was not wholly fitted for the task I had been given" (*Memoirs*, vol. II).

The fault with Kennan's second ambassadorship did not lie in his relations with the executive branch in Washington, or with his captaining an embassy, or with the country of his posting. On the contrary, matters proceeded satisfactorily in each of these categories. He approved of President Kennedy. He and the Foreign Service officers in the embassy in Belgrade cooperated well; feelings were warm. He respected Tito and enjoyed contact with his subjects. In this last connection, Kennan skillfully used his position to argue against Yugoslav complaints concerning NATO, Western rearmament of the German Federal Republic, and U.S. policies in Southeast Asia and against Cuba. As for the level of Kennan's reporting from Belgrade, it was first-rate and grounded in the idea that the United States should help bolster Yugoslavia's independence from the Soviet bloc. To this end, he argued with seniors in Washington that the United States should be cool in the face of Tito's periodic anti-Western outbursts, tolerate his posturing in the nonaligned movement, and continue those policies demonstrating to non-Soviet East Europeans that fruitful collaboration was possible between Communist and capitalist states.

Sadly for Kennan's second ambassadorship, he was helpless against the tidal wave of congressional interference and anti-Tito sentiment that swamped Yugoslav-U.S. relations in the early 1960s. Pressures generated by Croatian exiles, angry reaction in Congress to Tito's rhetoric at meetings among the nonaligned, and attempts by Soviet and Yugoslav leaders to improve their dealings overwhelmed thoughtful diplomacy. Kennedy's decision in June 1961 to retain observance of Captive Nations Week, which included justification for the overthrow ("liberation") of the Communist regime in Belgrade, was an augury of things to come. Against Kennan's strenuously voiced advice, Congress—led by Senator William Proxmire and Representative Wilbur Mills—eventually adopted punitive economic measures against Yugoslavia. These not only proscribed future programs of financial-technical assistance to Yugoslavia (of the type that had aided Tito in countering Stalin), but also nullified Yugoslavia's most-favored-nation status and interdicted the sale of electronic parts for warplanes previously bought by Belgrade.

Though sympathetic to Kennan's ideas about Yugoslavia, Kennedy did not speak publicly on their behalf. The president was unwilling to risk his narrow margin of goodwill in Congress on a "fuzzy" issue that could easily develop into a serious conflict with the House and Senate majorities. Kennedy's entire legislative agenda, Kennan later acknowledged, might have been jeopardized if it appeared that he appeased communism and was unwilling to defend freedom everywhere, including the Balkans. Still, Kennan brooded about a president unwilling to educate the American public on world politics, and about congressional willfulness in rejecting counsel from one who had for decades been intimately involved with East European affairs. The denouement in Yugoslav-U.S. relations occurred in 1963, the year when Kennan quit Belgrade. American stevedores refused to service ships bound to or arriving from Yugoslavia. A spontaneous boycott of Yugoslav goods gained strength in the United States; merchants publicly destroyed items made in Yugoslavia and canceled additional orders. In Tito's American visit in the autumn of 1963, for which Kennan acted as part-time host, the Yugoslav delegation was harassed by threatening demonstrators, some of whom wore Nazi uniforms. Melees in Washington and New York resulted in injuries to three Yugoslav officials. Female members of the entourage, including Tito's wife, were subjected to spitting, obscenities, and lewd gestures. The spectacle of Croat Americans riding roughshod over the national interest and yet another instance of congressional obtuseness confirmed Kennan's misgivings over democratic diplomacy.

As an element in America's policy establishment and practice, the diplomatic vocation has not enjoyed universal appreciation. To many observers, both within the United States and without, the diplomatic corps has been hobbled by amateurism and a lack of high standards. This condition is exemplified by the presidential practice of appointing favorites from outside the Foreign Service to distant capitals—a tradition deplored by Kennan. Moreover, as various analysts have decried, the U.S. diplomat is rarely esteemed by his compatriots. They occasionally question his political loyalty, attribute exotic tastes and habits to him, and are likely to charge him with harboring antidemocratic notions. Not only is the diplomat an object of caricature in popular American culture, depicted as a "cookie pusher" in pinstripes and not very manly, but the art of diplomacy is often disparaged. This trend has been reinforced as diplomacy has been superseded in the twentieth century by eruptions of vast international violence and tension (for example, World Wars I and II and the Cold War) and

as national leaders have bypassed classical diplomacy's form in favor of direct
negotiations with other heads of state.

Notwithstanding the emergence of mass democratic politics and of new negotiating habits made possible by advances in transportation and communication, ambassadorial diplomacy has remained a distinctive feature of international
life. In the context of Soviet-U.S. history, the embassy in Moscow helped shape
views in Washington about the nature of Communist society, economy, and
external policy—to which cause Kennan made important contributions in the
1930s and 1940s.

As illustrated by his career, diplomacy has no epiphanies. Its world is not
occupied by angels and devils, but by imperfect, frightened people trying to
preserve their security and that of their children. Giving way as it must to
compromise in the arid zone of estrangement, this situation leaves little room
for heroism in the grand manner. Diplomacy after the Cold War perforce still
belongs to the politics of amelioration. Meticulous study of the other—be it
Russia or the Ukraine, to say nothing of Japan or the Middle East and elsewhere—continues to have its place, without which the formation of U.S. policy
is handicapped. Realism still requires the cultivation of foreign leaders (as Kennan cultivated Tito) and peoples by Americans attuned to others' history. Furthermore, as taught by Kennan in his theorizing, successful diplomacy requires
taking the long view of problems and solutions. As the frenzy in 1963 about
Yugoslavia also highlights, diplomacy is best aided by the example of a self-
possessed and decent United States. In the words of the Long Telegram, "Every
courageous and incisive measure to solve internal problems of our own society,
to improve self-confidence, discipline, morale and community of spirit of our
own people, is a diplomatic victory . . . worth a thousand diplomatic notes and
joint communiques."

Two more lessons for the future of U.S. diplomacy can be drawn from Kennan's experience. First, there is no ready formula for success. The unexpected
will always occur. Coups, invasions, provocations, and other turmoil are recurrent phenomena in the lives of nations. Sibyls, not fallible diplomats, can perfectly predict the initiation and finale of such events. The ambassador's
obligation, then, is to stay abreast of the main political currents running through
the country of his assignment. Knowing the direction of their flow, not their
ultimate destination, is the envoy's responsibility. Kennan, the protégé of Kelley,
was exactly right for his time and since in declaring that modern diplomacy
requires the in-depth study of entire societies (history, culture, economics, politics, language) and of the relationships among them.

The second consideration is that diplomacy will continue to reflect the peculiar blend of U.S. political habits and institutions. Kennan's career was en-
twined with national vices and strengths. Ignorance of larger political realities
abetted congressional nonsense in the case of Yugoslavia. Casualness of approach and the vicissitudes of domestic politics explain Joseph Davies. Yet

attempts to transcend America's intellectually indolent self have produced felic-
itous results, as evidenced by the saga of the Long Telegram.

The immense sterility of the Cold War obscured the fact that the sovereign
state is inadequate for dealing with many contemporary emergencies: the population explosion, the North-South cleft, AIDS, and cultural clashes. The supposedly self-reliant state and present international system may indeed be
obsolete and on their way to extinction—arguably to be superseded by multi-
national companies, permeable borders, and regional units such as the European
Union. Yet the state is tenacious of life and likely to inhabit any of the brave
new worlds posited by theorists. The functional need of the ambassadorial office,
with its emphasis on patience and perseverance, will not soon perish. Kennan's
diplomatic career alternates as a cautionary tale and an example of what is
required to avoid disaster.

Works by George F. Kennan

George Kennan has published three autobiographical volumes, for one of which he
was awarded the Pulitzer Prize. The literary value of his work is extremely high. His
published historical scholarship and political analysis are also important to students of
international relations. Students of Soviet diplomatic history and of Russian intellectual-
political history, in particular, should consult Kennan's writings.

American Diplomacy, 1900–1950. Chicago: University of Chicago Press, 1951.
Soviet-American Relations, 1917–1920. 2 vols. Princeton: Princeton University Press,
    1956, 1958.
Soviet Foreign Policy 1917–1941. Princeton: Princeton University Press, 1960.
Russia and the West under Lenin and Stalin. Boston: Little, Brown, 1961.
From Prague to Munich: Diplomatic Papers, 1938–1940. Princeton: Princeton University
    Press, 1968.
Memoirs. 2 vols. Boston: Little, Brown, 1967, 1983.
The Decline of Bismarck's European Order. Princeton: Princeton University Press, 1979.
At a Century's Ending: Reflections, 1982–1995. New York: W.W. Norton, 1996.

Works about George F. Kennan

Five book-length studies of George Kennan have been published or are currently being
written. Virtually every student of twentieth-century U.S. foreign policy tries to come to
grips with Kennan's intellectual and practical position in policymaking. Listed here is a
sampling of some of these works.

Hixson, Walter. *George F. Kennan: Cold War Iconoclast.* New York: Columbia Uni-
    versity Press, 1989.
Jensen, Kenneth, ed. *Origins of the Cold War: The Novikov, Kennan, and Roberts "Long
    Telegrams" of 1946.* Washington, DC: United States Institute of Peace, 1991.
Mayers, David. *George Kennan and the Dilemmas of U.S. Foreign Policy.* New York:
    Oxford University Press, 1988.
Miscamble, Wilson. *George F. Kennan and the Making of American Foreign Policy,
    1947–1950.* Princeton: Princeton University Press, 1992.
Polley, Michael. *A Biography of George F. Kennan: The Education of a Realist.* Lew-
    iston, NY: E. Mellen Press, 1990.

Smith, Michael Joseph. *Realist Thought from Weber to Kissinger*. Baton Rouge: Louisiana State University Press, 1986.
Stephanson, Anders. *Kennan and the Art of Foreign Policy*. Cambridge: Harvard University Press, 1989.

DAVID MAYERS

JEANE JORDAN KIRKPATRICK (1926–) is resident

scholar at the American Enterprise Institute for Public Policy Research (1977–) and Thomas and Dorothy Leavey University Professor of Political Science at Georgetown University (1978–) and was U.S. permanent representative to the United Nations (1981–1985).

For the past two decades Jeane Kirkpatrick has been the most visible woman working in the U.S. foreign policy arena. She was the first female to serve as permanent representative for the United States—or any other major power—at the United Nations, and during her tenure she probably exercised greater influence over the formulation and articulation of U.S. foreign policy than any of her predecessors or successors. She was also one of the most controversial figures to ever hold that post. With a long list of impressive scholarly credentials, Kirkpatrick has gained a deserved reputation for hard work, plain talking, and creative thinking. She is the author of numerous books and monographs on a wide range of U.S. political and foreign policy issues, the recipient of a number of honorary degrees, and the holder of at least a dozen academic and other awards. Kirkpatrick has been hailed for years as a potential candidate for national political office, and her four years at the United Nations during the early 1980s seemed to shed as much light on the shifting nature of national politics in the United States as they did on the evolving role of foreign policy and Cold War concerns in American national opinion. Continuing an association with Georgetown University and the American Enterprise Institute that has lasted for nearly two decades, Kirkpatrick has focused her expertise on the study of U.S. foreign policy, with a particular emphasis on American relations with Europe and the United Nations.

Born in Duncan, Oklahoma, on November 19, 1926, Jeane Jordan spent most of her childhood in Oklahoma and Illinois. Her father, Welcher F. Jordan, was an oil-drilling contractor, and it was her mother, Leona Kile Jordan, who most encouraged her studies and career aspirations. After completing high school, Jeane Jordan attended Stephens College in Columbia, Missouri, during World War II, where she earned an A.A. in 1946 before transferring to Barnard College in New York City, where she earned her B.A. in 1948. This was soon followed by an M.A. in political science from Columbia University in 1950 and post-graduate studies at Johns Hopkins University (1950–1951) and the University of Paris (1952–1953). Concurrent with her studies, Jeane Jordan worked as a research analyst with the State Department (1950–1952), an assistant to one of the directors at the Governmental Affairs Institute (1953–1954), and a research associate at George Washington University (1954–1956).

In 1955 Jeane Jordan married Evron M. Kirkpatrick, a State Department official and later executive director of the American Political Science Association. While raising a family of three sons, Jeane Kirkpatrick continued to work as a research associate with the Fund for the Republic (1956–1957) and at the American Council of Learned Societies (1958–1959) and became assistant professor of political science at Trinity College in Washington, D.C. in 1962. She was hired as an associate professor of political science at nearby Georgetown University in 1967 and completed her Ph.D. dissertation on Peronist politics in Argentina the following year at Columbia University. In 1973 Kirkpatrick became a full professor at Georgetown University, and she was subsequently appointed Thomas and Dorothy Leavey University Professor of Political Science at the same institution in 1978. The previous year Kirkpatrick also became resident scholar at the American Enterprise Institute for Public Policy Research in Washington, D.C. Throughout her career she repeatedly acted as a consultant to the federal Departments of State, Defense, and Health, Education, and Welfare and published a number of monographs on various domestic political issues.

A lifelong Democrat, Kirkpatrick held a number of prominent positions in that party throughout the 1970s and supported many of the ideals of the welfare state, organized labor, and women's rights. But her growing interest in politics was also a reaction to the counterculture and protest movements of the 1960s. Like many with liberal political backgrounds who would later be labeled neoconservatives, Kirkpatrick was disturbed by what she perceived to be the excesses of national self-criticism. During 1972 she responded to this growing sense of estrangement by helping to found the Coalition for a Democratic Majority. This organization was a political vehicle for prominent Democrats who continued to hold liberal views on domestic issues, but were concerned by the apparent abandonment by their party of its traditional foreign policy platforms of liberal internationalism and anticommunism. In particular, coalition members sought a tougher stance in America's dealings with the Soviet Union in the wake of the apparent failure of détente in improving superpower relations and reducing the two nations' global rivalry. Their views were expressed most effectively through the publications of the American Enterprise Institute—which Kirkpatrick officially joined in 1977—and the public affairs journal *Commentary*. Kirkpatrick was also one of a group of coalition members who met with President Carter in January 1980 to express in person their concern with the apparent loss of U.S. influence in Africa and Latin America, and the failure to maintain their nation's power and resolve in the face of a perceived Soviet military buildup and its recent invasion of Afghanistan.

Several months before the White House meeting, in November 1979, an article written by Kirkpatrick appeared in the journal *Commentary*. Entitled "Dictatorships and Double Standards," it marked her first major foray into the foreign policy field and became a seminal work in her career, garnering national attention that would help to propel her into the post of U.N. permanent representative one year later. In the *Commentary* article Kirkpatrick criticized what she considered to be the unilateral moral and political disarmament of the United States that took place during and after the détente period. She opposed a Carter administration foreign policy that she considered weak and a failure, and that appeared to include a double standard on human rights that operated against U.S. strategic and economic interests in countries such as Nicaragua and Iran. Kirkpatrick was convinced that pro-American dictatorships such as those of the Somoza family and the shah were less repressive and more likely to liberalize and democratize themselves than the totalitarian regimes of the left that often succeeded them. The implications were clear. Kirkpatrick believed that in its pursuit of human rights compliance, the United States should distinguish between non-Communist states that were merely authoritarian and Communist regimes that were totalitarian. Furthermore, she believed that Washington should avoid undermining legitimate authority in states that lacked the requisite democratic substructure to undergo liberal reform, particularly in cases where they were friends and important allies of the United States.

As it happened, Kirkpatrick's *Commentary* article caught the attention of the Republican presidential campaign team. Ronald Reagan was determined to reinvigorate U.S. foreign policy and pursue a much more adversarial stance against the Soviet Union if he were elected, and her article and approach seemed to fit the bill perfectly. Kirkpatrick also offered the opportunity to bridge the remaining divide between Reagan Republicans and disenchanted Democrats, particularly on foreign policy issues. Kirkpatrick decided to back the Reagan candidacy in the fall of 1980 in the hope that a Reagan presidency would end the Vietnam era of U.S. circumspection and foreign policy retreat and restore the consensus and self-confidence in U.S. foreign policy that she believed had deteriorated during the past decade. Within weeks of winning the presidential election, and in spite of Kirkpatrick's Democratic Party pedigree—she did not officially switch parties until April 1985—Reagan nominated Kirkpatrick for the position of permanent representative to the United Nations.

Like Henry Kissinger and Zbigniew Brzezinski in prior administrations, Kirkpatrick was destined to play an important intellectual role in the formulation of U.S. foreign policy during this period. Other analysts have compared Kirkpatrick to Daniel Patrick Moynihan, another Democrat, academic, and one-time U.S. permanent representative to the United Nations. Both were considered idealists in the face of pervasive cynicism about the international body, and both had a reputation for being somewhat confrontational in their approach. The combativeness for which Kirkpatrick later became known at the United Nations was noticeably absent, however, when she appeared before the U.S. Senate Committee on Foreign Relations on January 15, 1981, for her confirmation hearings. In addition to fleshing out her views on human rights, Kirkpatrick reminded the committee that if she could survive the bitter factional politics of a university department, she could probably survive anything that could be thrown at her during a term as U.S. ambassador at the United Nations. The nomination was quickly approved.

During her four years at the U.S. Mission, Kirkpatrick was noted for crafting her public statements with great care, and her speeches were as eloquent as they were ideological at times. But to many, Kirkpatrick remained an outsider to the

regular life of U.N. routine and protocol. In keeping with her scholarly background, Kirkpatrick had a tendency to be somewhat dogmatic in her approach,
and she would often lecture foreign diplomats rather than discuss issues. Ignoring U.N. tradition, she also responded to each and every attack on the United
States from whichever source it emanated. This provoked a great deal of reaction
from State Department officials and others in the U.S. foreign policy establishment and the media who felt that she was being overly combative. As the sole
female in a profession dominated by males, Kirkpatrick also faced a negative
response because of her gender, especially from many of her U.N. counterparts.
Although she was fluent in French and Spanish and had some knowledge of
Italian and Portuguese, Kirkpatrick was also not a devout social mingler, a clear
disadvantage in an environment such as that of the United Nations. She did
succeed in establishing a close working relationship with the new secretary-
general, Javier Perez de Cuellar, but for the most part she was an outsider to
the various aspects of regular U.N. routine and protocol.

Kirkpatrick was the first U.N. permanent representative to sit on the White
House's National Security Council and often reported directly to the secretary
of state (the mercurial Alexander M. Haig, Jr., during 1981–1982 and the more
soft-spoken George P. Shultz from 1982 to 1989) and to President Reagan, with
whom she rapidly developed close personal ties. But this meant that she was
often bypassing the traditional channel for U.N. decisions, the State Department's Bureau of International Organization Affairs, thus creating growing resentment within that bureaucracy. Secretary of State Haig seemed particularly
resentful of the influence wielded by Kirkpatrick in the making of U.S. foreign
policy. He often failed to support her on foreign policy initiatives and at times
even seemed to be trying to deliberately undermine her influence. Tensions
between the two peaked during the Falklands crisis in early 1982, and Haig
finally resigned that June.

In addition to the bureaucratic problems that it created, Kirkpatrick's prominent foreign policy role in the Reagan White House also meant that she had to
attend many NSC and White House meetings in Washington. Combined with
numerous speaking appearances throughout the United States and abroad, this
led to frequent absences from New York. Kirkpatrick was able to recruit her
own team at the U.S. Mission, and it turned out to be a relatively stable one.
Kenneth Adelman played a prominent role as deputy permanent representative
until April 1983, when he became head of the Arms Control and Disarmament
Agency, while Ambassador Charles Lichenstein sat in the Security Council and
was an old family friend. All of Kirkpatrick's staff had strong bonds of personal
loyalty and shared her neoconservative views on foreign policy issues. But most
had little experience in multilateral diplomacy, and those who were veteran staff
members of the U.N. Mission from previous years were largely left out of the
inner circle of Kirkpatrick loyalists. Within months several career FSOs left,
only adding to the inexperience of those who remained. Like Kirkpatrick, most
members of the U.S. delegation were further handicapped by the fact that they

spent little time on the informal contacts that are so important to the successful functioning of the United Nations.

In assuming the role of U.S. permanent representative to the United Nations, Kirkpatrick sought to ensure that the international organization was taken seriously, particularly as a venue of U.S. foreign policy, and that it pursued policies and initiatives that were credible, consistent, and in the U.S. national interest. Kirkpatrick complained about U.S. impotence at the United Nations, which she believed had intensified during the Carter years, and was determined to use her position to restore American influence and end years of apparent retreat and apology. She believed that the decline of U.N. credibility and of U.S. prestige within the organization was the fault of the individual member states and their delegates. She was also disturbed by the fact that Third World ideologies, many of them anti-Western, appeared to dominate the thinking of many at the United Nations. With a two-thirds majority, the nations of the Third World could control the agenda and the flow of resolutions in the General Assembly, and their delegates had a tendency to focus on Israeli-Arab issues, Namibia, South Africa, and the New International Economic Order, all issues that would leave the United States voting in the minority.

Ensuring the accountability of foreign delegates was one of Kirkpatrick's first initiatives. Beginning in 1981, copies of any anti-U.S. speeches that were made at the United Nations were forwarded to the U.S. embassy in that state. The voting records of each of the U.N. member states were also regularly recorded and passed on to Congress. The implicit threat was clear: should a nation decide to use the U.N. forum to vote against the United States, it should be prepared to accept the possible consequences. In the case of developing states that received large amounts of American economic or military aid, this linkage was a real concern.

Kirkpatrick believed that decolonization and development were both issues in which the United States should have common cause with the emerging nations of the Third World. Believing that the Soviet Union rather than the United States was historically the imperial power, Kirkpatrick was convinced that the decline of American and the growth of Soviet influence at the international body reflected Americans' own previous incompetence in the arena of multilateral politics. Little changed during her tenure, however, and to some extent Kirkpatrick seemed to be pursuing a strategy of simply ignoring the North-South dialogue. The United States cast the only "no" vote in a U.N. resolution intended to restrict the sale of baby formula in the Third World. It refused to sign the 1982 Law of the Sea Treaty and was also in an isolated position on a number of other consensus positions such as Israel, South Africa, and disarmament. In December 1984 the United States withdrew from UNESCO over its policies and alleged waste and mismanagement. In other cases Kirkpatrick supported a reduction in U.S. financial support for U.N. organizations whose policies ran contrary to perceived American interests, such as the Environmental Program and the Food and Agricultural Organization.

The focal point of U.S. foreign policy during the first term of the Reagan administration was clearly the Soviet Union and the renewed Cold War. Both the president and Kirkpatrick believed that after the 1950s many in the Western democracies in Europe and North America progressively lost sight of the inherently adversarial nature of the Soviet regime and became far too involved in self-criticism of their own societies and systems. Even during the recent era of superpower détente, Kirkpatrick believed that the Soviets continued to pursue ideological aggression around the globe through the promotion of subversion and terrorism, most recently in the direct invasion and occupation of Afghanistan in 1979. In a speech entitled "We and They" that was given soon after her appointment as U.N. ambassador in 1981, Kirkpatrick officially signaled a renewed intensification of the ideological rivalry between the two superpowers, although the resurgence of Cold War antagonisms had actually already been initiated during the final years of the Carter presidency. Kirkpatrick soon set out to garner large majorities for U.N. resolutions calling for the withdrawal of Soviet forces from Afghanistan and Vietnamese forces from Cambodia. But the high point of superpower confrontation at the United Nations took place in 1983 when Kirkpatrick played a very public role in condemning the Soviet government for the shootdown of a Korean airliner, KAL-007, that had wandered into Soviet airspace. Tapes of the conversation between the Soviet pilot and the ground control station that had been obtained by American authorities were played before the Security Council to dramatic effect. Kirkpatrick was frustrated, however, when the United States still had difficulty mustering sufficient votes to condemn the Soviet Union for this incident and the accompanying deaths of 269 civilians.

As usual, another focal point of U.S. attention at the United Nations during this period was the Middle East. Under Kirkpatrick's leadership the United States continued to be a firm supporter of the state of Israel. This culminated in the fall of 1982 in an American-led defeat of efforts to expel Israel from the United Nations by rejecting its credentials (as had been done with South Africa since 1974). During November 1983 the U.S. Congress also came to Israel's defense by passing Public Law 98–164, whose provisions obliged the U.S. government to suspend participation in the U.N. General Assembly if Israel were ever denied credentials in the future. The United States also found itself having to defend the Israeli bombing of the Iraqi nuclear reactor in 1981 and the U.S. extradition of suspected terrorist Ziyad Abu Eain to Israeli that same year, which also saw the invasion of Lebanon, with the Israeli army simply brushing aside the UNIFIL force that was already in place to monitor the border. The final result was the evacuation of Beirut by the Palestine Liberation Organization (PLO) under the protection of an international force that included U.S. troops, and the 1983 bombing of the U.S. Marine barracks and embassy in Lebanon.

Another major foreign policy concern during the Kirkpatrick years involved the regions of Central and South America. During the same month that she was being confirmed by the Senate as U.N. permanent representative, another Kirkpatrick article appeared in the journal *Commentary* on the subject of U.S. security interests and Latin America. In its pages Kirkpatrick criticized the Carter administration for the Panama Canal Treaties, drastic reductions in economic and military assistance to many states in Latin America, and its role in bringing down the Somoza regime in Nicaragua. Now, within months of arriving at the United Nations, Kirkpatrick found herself defending the sale of U.S. arms to El Salvador and playing a major role in engineering the much tougher stance that was taken by the United States toward the Soviet-backed regime in Nicaragua, including the decisions to back the contra forces and defend the U.S. role in the mining of Nicaraguan waters. As it turned out, Kirkpatrick remained an active and vocal supporter of the contras even after she resigned her U.N. post in 1985. Although she tried to maintain the U.S. policy of dealing with regional issues within the Organization of American States (OAS) rather than the United Nations, in 1982 she was unable to prevent Nicaragua from being elected to the Security Council. Kirkpatrick was also torn during the 1982 Falklands (Malvinas) dispute between her concerns for relations with America's British and Latin American allies. The culmination of the crisis was a bureaucratic feud with Secretary of State Haig about whether or not the United States should veto a Security Council vote calling for a cease-fire in the conflict. The Americans found themselves isolated yet again in 1983 when the Security Council voted unanimously to criticize the United States for its invasion of Grenada in the wake of the overthrow and execution of that nation's leader, Maurice Bishop, in a Marxist coup. The United States had to use its veto, but an overwhelming majority of members voted for a similar resolution in the General Assembly.

By the time of the 1984 presidential elections, much had changed in Kirkpatrick's world. Many members of her original U.N. team began to leave for various jobs, shake-ups were taking place in Reagan's White House staff, and the emergence of Mikhail Gorbachev in the Soviet Union was leading to warming U.S. relations with that country. After four years as permanent representative to the United Nations, and without clear indications that she would be made secretary of state or national security adviser, Kirkpatrick finally decided that it was time to leave the United Nations and return to academia. Nonetheless, the diplomatic achievements that have been attributed to her during her four-year tenure are numerous. Kirkpatrick reasserted American authority and strengthened the visibility—if not the influence—of the United States at the United Nations. She also got free-market strategies of Third World development placed back onto the international agenda and pressed for a more evenhanded consideration of human rights issues. On the other hand, many have criticized Kirkpatrick for offering an almost blanket moral rationale for all U.S. foreign policy actions in the name of the national interest. Kirkpatrick's critics have charged that conservative idealism as expressed through prominent Reagan administration officials like her became blind to the excesses of anti-Communist regimes. None of this takes away from the fact that Kirkpatrick was one of the most visible and forceful U.S. permanent representatives in U.N. history. As so often in her career, she did not hesitate to take an unpopular position, trusting in history to vindicate her condemnation of well-meaning but misguided reformism.

Works by Jeane Kirkpatrick

Editor. *The Strategy of Deception: A Study in World-Wide Communist Tactics.* New York: Farrar, Straus, 1963.

Political Woman. New York: Basic Books, 1974.

Co-author, with Warren E. Miller. *The New Presidential Elite: Men and Women in National Politics.* New York: Russell Sage Foundation, 1976.

Dismantling the Parties: Reflections on Party Reform and Party Decomposition. Washington, DC: American Enterprise Institute for Public Policy Research, 1978.

Dictatorships and Double Standards: A Critique of U.S. Policy. Washington, DC: Ethics and Public Policy Center, Georgetown University, 1979.

"U.S. Security and Latin America." *Commentary* 71, no. 1 (January 1981): 29–40.

The Reagan Phenomenon, and Other Speeches on Foreign Policy. Washington, DC: American Enterprise Institute for Public Policy Research, 1983.

We and They: Understanding Ourselves and Our Adversary. Washington, DC: Ethics and Public Policy Center, 1983.

The Reagan Doctrine and U.S. Foreign Policy. Washington, DC: Heritage Foundation, 1985.

Legitimacy and Force: State Papers and Current Perspectives. 2 vols. New Brunswick, NJ: Transaction Books, 1988.

Works about Jeane Kirkpatrick

Arms, Thomas S.*Encyclopedia of the Cold War.* New York: Facts on File, 1994, 333–34.

Fasulo, Linda M. *Representing America: Experiences of U.S. Diplomats at the UN.* New York: Facts on File Publications, 1984, 284–91.

Finger, Seymour Maxwell. "The Reagan-Kirkpatrick Policies and the United Nations." *Foreign Affairs*, Winter 1983/1984, 436–57.

Hoeveler, J. David, Jr. "Jeane Kirkpatrick: America and the World." In *Watch on the Right: Conservative Intellectuals in the Reagan Era.* Madison: University of Wisconsin Press, 1991, 143–76.

Lynn, Naomi B. "Jeane Kirkpatrick: From the University to the United Nations." In *Women Leaders in Contemporary U.S. Politics*, ed. Frank P. Le Veness and Jane P. Sweeney, 91–104. Boulder, CO: Lynne Rienner Publishers, 1987.

Moritz, Charles, ed. *Current Biography Yearbook 1981.* New York: H. W. Wilson Company, 1981, 255–59.

Rosen, Jane. "The Kirkpatrick Factor." *New York Times Magazine*, April 28, 1985, 48–51, 68–73.

Urban, George. "American Foreign Policy in a Cold Climate." *Encounter* 61, no. 3 (November 1983): 9–33.

U.S. Congress. Senate Committee on Foreign Relations. *Nomination of Jeane J. Kirkpatrick.* Washington, DC: U.S. Government Printing Office, 1981.

Whelan, James R. "Jeane Kirkpatrick: Ideals Come First." *Saturday Evening Post*, December 1984, 50–55, 102–3, 108.

RICHARD D. WIGGERS

SOL M. LINOWITZ (1913–   ) was a devoted public servant

who utilized in diplomacy the skills he acquired in law and business to improve significantly U.S. relations with Latin America, negotiate the Panama Canal Treaties, and further the Middle East peace process.

Linowitz grew up in modest circumstances in Trenton, New Jersey, the son of Jewish immigrant parents. Through the efforts of one of his teachers, he attended Hamilton College in upper New York State. He worked his way through college, waiting tables and depending heavily on a National Youth Administration job but helped also by the college community, which recognized his potential.

Among his many jobs, Linowitz read to Elihu Root, an elderly man by that time, who resided part of the year at Hamilton. Root had been a highly successful corporation lawyer who subsequently became secretary of war under President William McKinley, secretary of state under President Theodore Roosevelt, and finally U.S. senator from New York. Significantly, Linowitz made the same transition from a career in law to one in public life. In spite of the time spent making a living, Linowitz earned his A.B. degree, graduating Phi Beta Kappa and salutatorian of his class in 1935.

He also waited tables and relied on a National Youth Administration job at Cornell Law School. Yet he found time to become editor-in-chief of the *Cornell Law Quarterly* and to graduate at the top of his class. Linowitz's ability to handle several challenging tasks at the same time with skill and dispatch had already become evident.

He preferred to start his law practice in a town of moderate size and, accordingly, accepted an offer from the firm of Sutherland and Sutherland in Rochester, New York, after graduation from law school in 1938. The next year Linowitz married Toni Zimmerman, a bacteriology student whom he had met at Cornell, and the young couple settled down to the life of an upwardly mobile professional family in Rochester.

However, Pearl Harbor interrupted his progress there, as it did that of most young Americans at that period. Linowitz tried his best to join the armed forces, but poor eyesight and a knee injury forced him to find another way to serve. He became chief of the Rent Control Review Branch of the Office of Price Administration in Washington. Two years later he obtained a commission in the navy after all. Assigned to the general counsel's office, he spent the bulk of his time renegotiating contracts with navy suppliers.

After the war Linowitz returned to the practice of law in Rochester. During this period he became a close friend of Joseph C. Wilson, son of the founder of the Haloid Company, which manufactured photographic paper. Wilson became president of Haloid, and Linowitz joined the board. The two men began development of the copying machine company that they later named Xerox, one

of the major firms in the United States. Linowitz's role involved many phases
of company development, but since its success depended on patents arising from
a basic invention of Chester Carlson, he concentrated on the crucial legal, patent,
and licensing aspects. Later he added international activities and contacts with
the government to his responsibilities.

Linowitz participated to an unusual degree in the civic life of Rochester, often
in the company of his friend Joe Wilson. Among his many activities, he became
president of the Rochester branch of the United Nations Association, thus coming into ongoing contact with foreign affairs issues. He maintained an enviable
independence of spirit throughout his career. In his relationship with Xerox,
whether as vice president, general counsel, chairman of the executive committee,
or chairman of the board, he kept his law practice and worked out of his law
office as much as possible.

In time, through his association with Xerox and his civic activities, Linowitz
achieved a national reputation for ability, hard work, and integrity. He developed
a close, easy relationship with President Lyndon Johnson, who frequently included Linowitz in group meetings in the White House and sought his advice
on general questions of domestic and foreign policy. In 1964 Linowitz accepted
the president's request to establish and chair the National Committee for International Development, a high-level group designed to encourage public understanding of American aid programs. At the same time, he helped the White
House prepare legislation promoting higher education. He also became vice-
chairman of the John F. Kennedy Center for the Performing Arts in 1965, being
a lover of music and a violin player himself.

Linowitz believed that men who had been successful in law or business had
an obligation to make their talents available to the nation. His experience in
opening Xerox subsidiaries in Latin America had left him with the strong impression that North Americans had too long neglected their neighbors to the
south, so when the president offered him the ambassadorship to the Organization
of American States in October 1966, he accepted on the understanding that his
responsibilities would include representation of the Alliance for Progress, originated by President John F. Kennedy, with its multiple aid programs for Latin
American states. He already knew that President Johnson was thinking in terms
of rejuvenating the alliance and, in that connection, of a major conference of
all Western Hemisphere chiefs of state. Hence the preparations for such a conference became Linowitz's first major diplomatic task.

These preparations boiled down to two substantial projects, which he performed in tandem with Lincoln Gordon, the assistant secretary for American
Republic affairs in the State Department. The two men and their consultants had
to decide exactly what the United States wanted to achieve through such a
summit, and they had to establish contact with the many chiefs of state involved.
The president's schedule afforded time for the conference in April 1967, which
gave Linowitz and Gordon less than five months to complete all the arrangements.

By dint of hard and effective work by its organizers, the conference, held at Punta del Este, Uruguay, passed off without a hitch. The twenty-three-page Action Program contained in the final communiqué principally promised action to develop commodity agreements, setting minimum prices for Latin American products, progress toward a Latin American common market, and restraint in arms purchases. But in Linowitz's opinion a new sense of hope and a perception of the value of hemispheric cooperation among equals surpassed the concrete achievements in importance. He pointed out that 1967 was the first time in more than twenty-five years that no government was overthrown by force in Latin America.

In his capacity as ambassador to the Organization of American States, he had to bear the burden of resentment created by U.S. intervention in the Dominican Republic in 1965. However, the reputation of the Xerox subsidiaries Linowitz had established in Mexico, Brazil, and Venezuela and his own candor and friendliness helped to mollify the prevailing distrust.

As representative of the Alliance for Progress, Linowitz concentrated on maintaining a substantial level of economic aid for Latin America. However, in spite of his efforts, which included many hours of congressional hearings, the legislators reduced drastically the 1969 aid appropriation, disregarding Linowitz's warning against the dangers of frustrating expectations that the United States itself had raised.

Linowitz returned to private life in early 1969. This time he did not return to Rochester, but instead joined the Washington office of the Coudert Brothers law firm, where he could concentrate on international legal matters. But America's own problems claimed much of his time. He served as president of the Federal City Council, which focused on Washington's economic and social problems, and became chairman of the National Urban Coalition.

Continuing his interest in Latin America, he became chairman of the United States–Latin American Commission, an organization established under the aegis of the Center for Inter-American Relations in New York at the instigation of David Rockefeller. The commission published a significant report in 1976 covering major hemispheric issues. It stressed in particular the urgency of negotiating a new Panama Canal treaty. By the 1970s top political circles in Washington realized that the Hay-Bunau-Varilla Treaty of 1903 was becoming a major irritant in U.S. relations with Latin America. The treaty's terms gave the United States control over a ten-mile-wide zone, effectively cutting Panama in two. The United States paid only $2.3 million a year to Panama for its rights there, which were to endure in perpetuity. Presidents Lyndon Johnson, Richard Nixon, and Gerald Ford had all endeavored, without notable success, to negotiate a new treaty. Vociferous opposition from conservative and nationalist groups, as well as uncooperative attitudes in Panama, caused their efforts to fail.

In 1977 President Jimmy Carter, urged on by Cyrus Vance, his secretary of state, gave top priority at the beginning of his term to the negotiation of a new Panama Canal treaty. Vance, at the president's suggestion, asked Linowitz to take on the job of chief negotiator, which had been held for several years by Ambassador Ellsworth Bunker. Linowitz declined on the grounds that Bunker, a good friend, could do the job as well as he, but he did agree to join Bunker as conegotiator if the latter thought that the idea had merit. Bunker did, and Linowitz accepted the post with the understanding that he could continue his law practice and board memberships unless there was a possibility of conflict of interest. The arrangement took effect in February 1977 and produced a team in which Bunker provided necessary continuity and Linowitz furnished added energy and determination to succeed. The appointment was for only six months, the maximum time he could serve without Senate confirmation, since Carter wished to avoid a Senate fight over confirmation on so explosive an issue. The limitation in effect placed an August 10, 1977, deadline for completing the negotiations.

The first session with the Panamanians, held in Panama in February, failed to make headway. Nor did the next session in Washington in March produce progress. The Panamanians, led by Romulo Escobar Bethancourt, operating under the keen eye of Panamanian strong man General Omar Torrijos, would not agree to the right in perpetuity of the United States to defend the canal nor to U.S. control over a part of their territory. The Americans, for their part, did not address seriously enough Panamanian desires for transfer to Panama of facilities and territories in the Canal Zone.

In May 1977 Linowitz produced a new approach, namely, to divide the ground hitherto covered by one treaty into two treaties. One would establish enduring authority for the United States to protect the canal and enforce its neutrality. The second would deal with Panamanian sovereignty over the Canal Zone area, establish an authority to operate the canal, designate payment in return for its use, and deal with rights of Americans working there. The dual approach broke the stalemate, and the negotiators were finally able to work on treaty substance in a positive way.

Linowitz introduced a tactic of identifying the areas of most concern to the Panamanians, chiefly concerning territory, rights to facilities, and financial return. He yielded on these items to the extent he could while retaining the support of the U.S. military, which was concerned to retain facilities necessary to maintain its forces. In return, Linowitz asked the Panamanian negotiators for their help in achieving U.S. objectives. On numerous occasions he found means to break the impasses that bedeviled the talks. He suggested, for instance, Panamanian representation on the authority to be established for operating the canal in order to reconcile them to initial U.S. control of its administration.

However, Linowitz did not give an inch when, late in the negotiations, the Panamanians asked for over a billion dollars to recompense them for the alleged inadequacy of the annual sums paid by the United States over the years. Bunker and Linowitz responded that a request for any such payment would doom the treaties in the Senate, where opposition to surrendering "our canal" was already fierce. Linowitz made it clear on many occasions that compensation to Panama for utilities and services would have to come from revenues earned from canal tolls and not from the U.S. Treasury.

By the end of June 1977 the main features of the canal treaties were clear, although progress was slow. The Panamanians changed their minds frequently, even in agreed treaty texts. One night in early August Linowitz stayed up till one in the morning comparing the U.S. text with a translation of the Panamanian counterpart. He found numerous changes of substance not agreed upon in the latter just before his commission was to expire. At the meeting the next morning, Linowitz, who was normally optimistic, told the Panamanian negotiators that he believed that the usefulness of the negotiations had ended, and he and the rest of the U.S. delegation announced their readiness to depart. Such a strong reaction caught the Panamanians off guard. Faced with Linowitz's imminent departure and with him the loss of opportunity to complete the treaties, they speedily regrouped, and by the next day their attitude became one of cooperation. The negotiators quickly resolved the problems raised by the altered text. At six that evening the negotiating teams announced that they had reached agreement on the outlines of the two treaties, leaving the detailed wording to be worked out by legal experts.

Although Linowitz's commission expired at that point, his work on the treaties continued during the ratification process. Opposition was mounting throughout the United States to the level that he thought that violence could erupt. Emotional opponents repeatedly accused him of giving away America's canal to a "tin-horn dictator." Linowitz and Bunker held educational seminars, usually in Senator Robert Byrd's office, for about seventy senators in all. The two men were the leadoff witnesses before the Senate Foreign Relations Committee in hearings that continued for three controversy-filled weeks. Linowitz also traveled around the country giving speeches and interviews in a huge effort to sway the Senate in favor of the treaties. Finally, on March 16, 1978, the Senate approved the first treaty and on April 18 the second one with a single vote to spare in one of the longest and most bitter ratification battles in U.S. history.

Even before the ratification debate ended, the Carter administration called for Linowitz's services in a foreign policy area far from Latin America. Secretary Vance sounded him out on his willingness to take over the thankless task of special representative for the president in the Middle East. But before that project could ripen, Carter asked Linowitz to chair the Presidential Commission on World Hunger. Prominent political scientists, nutritionists, and college presidents composed this distinguished body. It took very seriously its task of analyzing the root causes of world hunger and what the United States could do about it. The commission's report, released in late 1979, recommended that the United States make the elimination of hunger the main focus in its relationships with developing countries and outlined the policies required to reach this objective.

In October 1979 Vice President Walter Mondale, on behalf of President Carter, offered Linowitz the post of secretary of commerce, but he declined on the grounds that he believed that he could be of greater use in an assignment related to foreign policy. Within three weeks the president asked Linowitz to replace Robert Strauss as personal representative of the president for the Middle East Peace Negotiations. Linowitz hesitated because of his deep involvement in Jewish affairs, including chairmanship of the board of the Jewish Theological Seminary and previously of the executive committee of the American Jewish Committee. However, President Carter's insistent urging overcame this objection, and the announcement of his appointment came on November 6, 1979, followed by Senate confirmation early the following year.

With Carter's term drawing toward its end, Linowitz had only a short time to devote to the mountainous negotiating problems ahead. Although the Egyptian-Israeli peace treaty resulting from the Camp David Accords had been signed in March 1979, the section of the accords concerning Palestinian autonomy and the ultimate status of the West Bank and Gaza still remained unimplemented.

President Anwar Sadat of Egypt, Prime Minister Menachem Begin of Israel, and the representative of the American president were conducting long-drawn-out negotiations on this subject. The Israelis refused to deal with the Palestine Liberation Organization, which they considered a terrorist group dedicated to the destruction of Israel. Since no other competent Palestinian organization existed, the Palestinians, the objects of all this negotiating attention, were not directly represented at the table.

A sharp division existed between the Israelis and the Egyptians, representing Palestinian interests, over the nature and powers of the self-governing authority called for in the Camp David Accords. The Palestinians wished the authority to resemble a legislature with broad powers and substantial membership, while the Israelis wanted it to be a small administrative council with limited powers. They were most worried over the security situation during the transition period, while President Sadat, on the other hand, was increasingly irritated by Israel's continued construction of settlements on the West Bank and went so far as to delay negotiations in protest.

Linowitz reacted to the confrontation by obtaining a promise from the Israelis to limit the number of settlements and a joint statement calling for recommitment by Israel and Egypt to the principles of Camp David and the resumption of negotiations. In succeeding months Linowitz succeeded in working out many details with the other negotiators. In spite of deep emotional differences between the parties, he was able in January 1981 to give President Carter a list of twenty-five topics on which Egypt and Israel agreed the Palestinian self-governing authority should exercise control.

But time worked against completion of this painful and painstaking exercise. After defeating Carter in the 1980 election, President Ronald Reagan failed to appoint a negotiator to replace Linowitz. The latter, still an optimist, believed that if Reagan had done so, the two countries could have reached full agreement on the autonomy provisions of the accords, which were still not fully implemented a generation later.

With the Middle East assignment, Linowitz completed his service to the U.S.

government in the foreign affairs field, although he continued to play an advisory role. If anyone deserves the appellation of distinguished public servant, it is Sol Linowitz—a pragmatic idealist with tremendous energy who over an outstanding career did not shrink from taking on the hardest diplomatic tasks.

Works by Sol M. Linowitz

Campus Tensions: Analysis and Recommendations. (Special Committee on Campus Tensions, Report). Washington, DC: American Council on Education, 1970.

International Business-Government Relations. Washington, DC: American University, Center for the Study of Private Enterprise, 1970.

World Hunger, a Challenge to American Policy. New York: American Foreign Policy Association, 1980.

The Making of a Public Man: A Memoir. Boston: Little, Brown and Co., 1985.

The Betrayed Profession: Lawyering at the End of the Twentieth Century. New York: C. Scribner's Sons, 1994.

Works about Sol M. Linowitz

Jorden, William J. *Panama Odyssey.* Austin: University of Texas Press, 1984.

Moffett, George D. *The Limits of Victory: The Ratification of the Panama Canal Treaties.* Ithaca, NY: Cornell University Press, 1985.

WILLIAM N. DALE

HENRY CABOT LODGE, JR. (1902–1985) was the

elder statesman of Republican diplomats during the Cold War, serving as ambassador to the United Nations in the 1950s and to South Vietnam throughout the escalation of the conflict.

Lodge was born in Nahant, Massachusetts, on July 5, 1902. A man well acquainted with privilege, Lodge followed his illustrious ancestors into public affairs after graduation from Harvard University in 1921 and a brief career in journalism. His first elective office was as a Massachusetts state representative; he was elected U.S. senator from Massachusetts in 1936. Although he was reelected in 1942, he became the first senator since the Civil War to resign in order to continue on active service in the army. After seeing action in North Africa (where he led the first American unit to engage the Germans in combat during the war), Italy, and France, he won reelection to the Senate in 1946.

As the scion of the declining moderate eastern establishment wing of the Republican Party, Lodge mounted numerous challenges to the power of conservative Robert Taft in the Senate. In 1951 Lodge organized a campaign committee to push for the nomination of Dwight D. Eisenhower as the Republican candidate for president to head off Taft's own aspirations. By running Eisenhower's 1952 bid, however, Lodge failed to campaign for himself and narrowly lost his seat to Democratic challenger John F. Kennedy. President-elect Eisenhower rewarded Lodge with an appointment as American representative to the United Nations. In the 1960s he was ambassador to Saigon twice as well as ambassador to West Germany. After heading the delegation to the Paris peace negotiations on Vietnam, Lodge became President Richard Nixon's special envoy to the Vatican.

In order to entice Lodge into his first ambassadorship, Eisenhower designated the chief of missions to the United Nations as cabinet rank, second only in seniority to the secretary of state. Eisenhower selected Lodge because he wanted to make the United Nations a principal forum of maintaining peace and also desired to improve the image of the United Nations in the esteem of the American people. Lodge fulfilled his charge successfully. He quickly became one of Eisenhower's closest advisors on foreign affairs and even undertook actions within the Security Council without prior direction from the State Department. He persuaded the president to make his 1953 "Atoms for Peace" speech at the United Nations in order to lend the body credence. The speech eventually led to an agreement on the peaceful uses of atomic energy. For most of his tenure at the United Nations, however, Lodge was an ardent Cold Warrior, maintained a consistently hostile attitude toward the Soviets, and rejected any effort by the Communist Chinese to gain a seat in the world body.

The most difficult problems that he faced at the United Nations occurred in October 1956. The moderate premier of Hungary appealed to the United Nations for help after being besieged by the Russians. Accordingly, Lodge mobilized a meeting of the Security Council in order to rally world opinion. Yet another major crisis overshadowed the situation in Hungary and prevented success there. When the Israelis invaded Egypt in late October, Lodge called for a cessation of their actions. Soon both France and Britain also attacked to retake the nationalized Suez Canal. Lodge opposed their actions in open forum at the Security Council by surprisingly joining the Soviet delegate in condemnation of the Anglo-French attack. Ironically, he received the brunt of public criticism for the administration's failure to support the Hungarian freedom fighters and for so strongly indicting the closest of America's allies.

Lodge contributed to several other important foreign policies of the Eisenhower administration. After civil war broke out in Lebanon during 1958, the embattled president of that country appealed to President Eisenhower for support. The president immediately ordered military forces to intervene directly. Lodge steered the matter directly into the responsibility of the U.N. secretary-general in order to ease superpower confrontation over the intervention. In addition, Lodge accompanied Soviet Premier Nikita Khrushchev on his visit to the United States in 1959, introducing him to prominent American financiers as well as common citizens. He seconded Eisenhower in his meeting with Khrushchev at Camp David, and they planned a major summit conference for 1960. When the summit was canceled due to the Soviet shooting down of an American surveillance aircraft, Lodge had to defend the U-2 affair in the Security Council, a difficult task, especially after the administration had denied that it was a spy plane. He tried to reestablish American credibility by asserting that both sides had conducted espionage. At the United Nations he exhibited a goodwill gift from Soviet children to former Ambassador to the Soviet Union W. Averell Harriman that, since it had a radio transmitter hidden inside, had allowed the KGB to eavesdrop for years.

Because of the crisis in the Congo, Lodge continued to function in the U.N. post when Richard Nixon named him his vice presidential running mate in the 1960 presidential election. He campaigned unenthusiastically in the fall after resigning from the administration, notably making a principal mistake in proclaiming at Harlem that he would include an African American in the cabinet. After defeat at the polls Lodge became director of the Atlantic Institute, an organization dedicated to fostering unity among the nations of the North Atlantic.

In a bipartisan move President Kennedy selected Lodge as ambassador to the Republic of Vietnam in June 1963. Kennedy needed a representative in Saigon who would analyze objectively and report honestly and an ambassador who could communicate in French, the language of the elite Vietnamese. Lodge played a prominent role in the development of American policy toward Vietnam throughout the rest of the 1960s. He helped to orchestrate the overthrow of the Ngo Dinh Diem regime, beginning with his arrival in August. A crisis begun by Buddhists' protests against the Diem government's repression, conducted primarily by the president's brother, Ngo Dinh Nhu, had brought matters to a head. Lodge realized that the demise of the Diem regime was a mere matter of time. He had concluded that the government's unpopularity destabilized the country and harmed the military effort against the Viet Cong. He and others in the administration advocated the replacement of the Diem regime with a more compliant one that would prosecute the war against the Communists more vigorously. On August 25 Lodge received a cable from Washington stating that Diem's government could not be preserved. He was authorized to support alternate leadership. Lodge then sought out the leaders of South Vietnam's military and encouraged them to launch a coup against Diem.

When the coup failed to occur due to the timidity of the Vietnamese generals, Washington instructed Lodge instead to pursue a policy of persuading Diem to reform his regime. Although he later received word from the State Department that the August 25 cable had been a mistake, Lodge recognized that the situation was worsening. In September, since he was unsuccessful in forcing Diem to reform, Lodge proposed that American pressure be brought to bear against Diem. Not possessing faith in Diem, the ambassador contended that America would have to withdraw if the Saigon regime did not change. To further his campaign against Diem, he also undercut the American military mission's optimistic reporting to Washington in private meetings with Secretary of Defense Robert McNamara in September. In October Lodge threatened to cease all aid to Diem if he did not remove his brother. He also demanded that Diem transfer his private guard into combat and cut off the funding for this unit until Diem complied. Under direction from Washington, Lodge informed a group of South Vietnamese generals led by Duong Van Minh that the embassy would not thwart any attempt to remove Diem and his brother. Lodge supported coup planning and took no measures to make a last rapprochement with Diem.

The coup successfully transpired on November 1. When it started, Lodge firmly believed that he could have saved Diem from his death, but a directive from the White House had prevented him from doing so. Following the coup, Lodge attempted to stabilize the successor regimes of Minh and Nguyen Khanh. He remained a staunch supporter of the ensuing governments in Saigon, although the continual changes of administration worsened the effectiveness of the military effort.

A potential presidential candidate in 1964, Lodge refused to campaign for the nomination after liberal Republicans started a Lodge write-in draft to block conservative Barry Goldwater. He only left Saigon after his wife's illness became pronounced. Back home, he then campaigned solely for another moderate Republican candidate. After Goldwater's nomination he assured Lyndon Johnson that he would not work for the conservative challenger's election in the fall.

Lodge continued his involvement with Vietnam during the Johnson administration's debates over intervention. In July 1965, after the decision to massively escalate the war, Lodge was reappointed to the Saigon post. During his second term as ambassador to the Republic of Vietnam, Lodge was an early proponent of what later became known as pacification. He realized that America's Vietnam policy rested on a psychological foundation that was crumbling at both the American and Vietnamese ends. The war had to be turned over to the Vietnamese, and American casualties had to be reduced. He railed against the policy of search-and-destroy, since high numbers of American deaths would create a violent public reaction. Instead, Lodge proposed shifting American emphasis to the creation of durable local political institutions in South Vietnam. He urged the president to win over the South Vietnamese people's loyalty by not using self-defeating military tactics such as bombing, napalm, and other measures that sustained and even generated support for the Viet Cong cause. He believed that the South Vietnamese had to carry on their own struggle, and he suggested that American troops should secure the ports and airfields while freeing the South Vietnamese army to join the battle in the countryside.

The Saigon government had to gain the political support of its people before it could achieve success in the military struggle. One outcome of Lodge's efforts was the creation of the Revolutionary Development Cadres (RDC), an organization that ostensibly would carry out appropriate social and economic reforms to raise the population's living standards. The RDC was a paramilitary force that fanned into rural South Vietnam not only to train the peasants to defend themselves against Viet Cong raids but to organize development projects in the hamlets. This effort did have limited success in improving the living conditions of the rural population. However, the results of pacification bore little correlation to the tremendous amount of money invested in the effort. As for the war in South Vietnam, Lodge left military decisions to the generals in the field. He generally supported the intensive bombing campaign and its continuance despite several bombing halts by the administration.

He also meddled in internal South Vietnamese politics. He personally berated Prime Minister Phan Huy Quat for failing to show determination in prosecuting the war and for not forcefully putting down internal protests. In 1966 the Struggle Movement, a militant Buddhist political organization, began massive protests against the dismissal of a prominent Buddhist general by Quat's successor, Nguyen Cao Ky. With the assistance of several army units, the Struggle Movement was able to seize control in the cities of Hue and Da Nang. Initially Lodge supported Ky's decision to restore his authority by force because he considered preservation of Saigon's governing military junta vital. American transport planes airlifted Ky's troops from Saigon to quell the rebellion. After the failure of Ky's first operation, Lodge appeared to become more neutral in the squabble and attempted to mediate with the monk Tri Quang and other Buddhist leaders. When Ky launched a second attempt to put down the Struggle Movement, though, the ambassador allowed Ky's units, some with their American advisors in accompaniment, to come through American bases. Lodge acquiesced to the repression of the militant Buddhist movement throughout the country and looked the other way as the military continued in power after supposedly free elections.

Lodge also dabbled in the search for a peaceful settlement to end the war. His thinking became heavily influenced by Professor Henry Kissinger, who came to South Vietnam as a special consultant in 1965 at Lodge's request. Kissinger told him that the administration's emphasis on unconditional negotiations and bombing pauses limited the risks for the North Vietnamese and undermined the morale of the Saigon regime. He reinforced Lodge's belief that both the political and the military efforts had to be coordinated. Lodge was convinced and reported to Washington that it had to link a bombing halt and negotiations to the end of North Vietnamese infiltration southward. He opposed public negotiations, though, since they would allow the Communists to make up for military failure by bargaining for what they could not achieve on the battlefield. He suggested that any such negotiations be conducted secretly.

In 1966 Lodge met with Polish diplomat Januscz Lewandowski through Italian Ambassador to Saigon Giovanni D'Orlandi and began the MARIGOLD talks. Lewandowski had told D'Orlandi that the Hanoi Politburo was transmitting through him a specific peace offer: Hanoi would enter into talks if the National Liberation Front (NLF) was included and if the United States ceased its bombing campaign. As a result of this contact, Lodge believed that the North Vietnamese were ready to begin talks for a settlement. The sticking point remaining was that Hanoi refused to undertake reciprocal action in decreasing its hostilities. Lodge and Lewandowski did come up with a formula that allowed Hanoi to enter into talks without publicly agreeing to restrain its infiltration southward. Yet on the very next day after Lewandowski agreed to set up a meeting between a North Vietnamese diplomat and American Ambassador to Poland John Gronouski, American bombings occurred in North Vietnam, and the fragile MARIGOLD discussions became stillborn. Secretary McNamara later told Lodge that this talks with Lewandowski might have shortened the war by two years if the American attack had not effected a change in Hanoi's attitude.

Lodge left Saigon in April 1967, after being unanimously thanked by the U.S. Senate for his Vietnam service, to become an ambassador-at-large for President Johnson. He was involved in the post–Tet Offensive reassessment discussions as a member of the Wise Men group that considered the request of the general in charge of American forces in Vietnam, William Westmoreland, for an additional 206,000 soldiers. He praised the unity that the South Vietnamese had maintained in the attack's aftermath and reluctantly supported the decision of this group to recommend deescalation of the war. Lodge did not favor disengagement, but preferred a renewed emphasis focusing more on pacification than attrition. He believed that if the effort in Vietnam had been focused on population organization rather than on destroying the enemy, the results of Tet would have spelled victory rather than defeat.

In February 1968, Lodge became ambassador to West Germany, a post he held until 1969. At that time in Germany, Kurt Kiesinger had replaced Konrad Adenauer, and difficulties had arisen over the German contribution to NATO. With Lodge's experience and fluent German, he was the logical choice for the position. While he was in Germany, he also became a member of the Allied Commission that controlled West Berlin and resided there at least once a month to show the flag. Nevertheless, the recurring problem of Vietnam interrupted this assignment.

In January 1969 President-elect Richard Nixon appointed Lodge as the chief negotiator (with ambassadorial rank) for the Vietnam peace negotiations in Paris, replacing Averell Harriman, because of Lodge's long experience with this difficult situation. Lodge's credentials signified that he would be a hard-line negotiator. His delegation included New York attorney Lawrence E. Walsh and Ambassador Marshall Green. Early on he thought that President Nixon would make him the "czar" of Vietnam policy. Yet despite assurances to the contrary, he was not given authority to discuss substantive issues in Paris. His hands were tied by the administration, since National Security Adviser Kissinger entered into private discussions with the North Vietnamese personally. Lodge tried to make his Paris role meaningful. Repeatedly he asked for permission to meet with his North Vietnamese counterparts in secret sessions, as Harriman had done and which had proved so useful in advancing the talks forward in 1968.

Nixon and Kissinger came to Paris in the spring of 1969 to set forth a new policy. At a crucial meeting of March 2 they agreed with Lodge that the negotiations would split into two parts. The United States and North Vietnam would discuss the military issues, while South Vietnam and the NLF would concentrate on internal political matters. Lodge soon was given permission to begin these talks. Yet this permission came too late, since both sides had become intransigent. The North Vietnamese had dug in their heels due to the Nixon administration's delay in moving forward in Paris. Hanoi would not budge despite Lodge's offer of mutual withdrawal, free and supervised elections, and a cease-fire. By late summer the disillusioned Lodge asked to be relieved from the Paris post, although Kissinger persuaded him to remain until November. The official end of his tenure occurred on December 8, 1969. No replacement was named until July 1970 in order to demonstrate American frustration over the lack of movement by the North Vietnamese. The real reason Lodge never accomplished anything substantial at Paris, however, was that his effort had been a charade to cover for secret contacts carried out simultaneously by Kissinger with Le Duc Tho.

In 1970 President Nixon appointed Lodge American envoy to the Vatican. The position did not have remuneration, nor did it require residence in Rome, but it was an important venue where matters of world peace were taken up. Lodge tried to remain involved with Vietnam policy after his departure from Paris. He believed that his position at the Vatican would be useful in the Vietnam negotiations. He also tried to restart the D'Orlandi channel. Yet the administration refused to let Lodge pursue any initiative beyond Kissinger's purview. However, Lodge did succeed through Vatican auspices in increasing the amount of mail exchanged between American POWs in Hanoi and their families.

During the Nixon years Lodge tried to keep active on other issues. In 1970 he unsuccessfully attempted to arrange private contacts with the regime in Peking with the goal of normalizing relations. In 1971 he was chairman of a presidential commission that recommended allowing the admission of mainland China into the United Nations while retaining membership for the Chinese government on Taiwan. However, his star had been eclipsed. He retired from government service in 1977 and died on February 27, 1985.

Works by Henry Cabot Lodge, Jr.

The Storm Has Many Eyes: A Personal Narrative. New York: Norton, 1973.
As It Was. New York: Norton, 1976.

Works about Henry Cabot Lodge, Jr.

Bereton, Charles. "1964: A Yankee Surprise." *Historical New Hampshire* 42 (1987): 253–82.
Hatch, Alden. *The Lodges of Massachusetts.* New York: Hawthorn Books, 1973.
Kahin, George McT. *Intervention: How America Became Involved in Vietnam.* Garden City, NY: Anchor Books, 1987.
Miller, William J. *Henry Cabot Lodge.* New York: Heineman, 1967.

KENT G. SIEG

LINCOLN MACVEAGH (1890–1972)

LINCOLN MACVEAGH (1890–1972) was a classical scholar and publisher whose long service (1933–1952) as U.S. envoy to six nations was briefly but dramatically linked with the rise of the Cold War and the inception of the policy of containment. A political appointee, he was the scion of prominent families and of two generations of diplomats. His father had been Coolidge's ambassador to Japan, and his grandfather had served as minister to Ottoman Turkey and to Italy. A great-uncle had been Taft's secretary of the treasury, his great-grandmother was the cousin of President Lincoln, and his mother was a direct descendant of Thomas Rogers, a signer of the Mayflower Pact.

Born in October 1890 in Narragansett Pier, Rhode Island, MacVeagh went to the Groton School in Massachusetts (class of 1909), where his schoolmates included Dean G. Acheson, W. Averell Harriman, and G. Hall Roosevelt, Eleanor Roosevelt's younger brother and MacVeagh's lifelong friend. After Harvard (magna cum laude, Phi Beta Kappa), where he majored in philosophy, he spent a year at the Sorbonne studying French, German, and Italian. In 1915 he joined the Henry Holt Publishing Company as textbook salesman and two years later married Margaret Charlton Lewis, daughter of a distinguished Latin scholar and herself an accomplished student of Latin and Greek. Their only child, Margaret Ewen, was born in 1920.

In May 1917 MacVeagh enlisted and the following year saw action in France with the 80th Infantry Division, rising to the rank of major. Following his discharge, he returned briefly to Henry Holt, where he became a director, but resigned in 1923 to found the Dial Press in New York. Making his home in nearby New Canaan, Connecticut, he spent the next ten years building up his publishing company, cultivating clients and taking occasional trips through Europe with his family. His broad literary pursuits, refined taste, and meticulous ways, as well as his work as editor, helped him develop a writing style that combined clarity of thought and precision with elegance. In years to come his diplomatic reports would be widely read in the Department of State for their language as much as for their substance.

In the fall of 1932, following Franklin Roosevelt's electoral victory, prominent Connecticut Democrats suggested to the new president that MacVeagh was especially well suited to be U.S. envoy to Greece. In January 1933, in the first of what was to become a long series of "Dear Franklin" letters, MacVeagh offered "to put special knowledge, which I have gathered through years, at your personal disposal. . . . You would have another pair of your own eyes in Greece, if I were there, at the same time that you would please some hard-working party friends at home." Roosevelt agreed, and in September 1933 MacVeagh arrived in Athens as the U.S. minister to the Hellenic Republic.

In Greece, where he remained until June 1941, MacVeagh was welcomed as a philhellene and a serious student of the classics. Government officials treated him with respect and cordiality, and prominent Athenians sought his company and his views on Greek and Balkan issues. His frequent travels by car took him to virtually every corner of that small country, and he took special interest in economic conditions, regional problems, and signs of social and labor unrest. As a result, his numerous dispatches and letters to Roosevelt provide a continuous and remarkably solid chronicle of Greek domestic and international developments: the political upheavals of the early 1930s, the collapse of the republic and the return of King George II (whom MacVeagh came to know well), the establishment of the Metaxas dictatorship in 1936, the gathering war clouds, Mussolini's attack on Greece in October 1940, the Albanian war, and the German invasion and occupation in April 1941. In the absence of significant American political interests in interwar Greece, MacVeagh's role in Athens was largely that of a well-informed observer. Other than periodic attempts to get the Greek government to honor its foreign debt obligations to the United States and accept more American goods, his major encounter with the authorities concerned the extradition of Samuel Insull, Sr., the Chicago tycoon who in 1932 had fled to Greece to escape arrest and trial on charges of larceny and embezzlement. Despite Insull's lavish cultivation of Greek political supporters and problems over the U.S.-Greek extradition treaty, MacVeagh succeeded in having the fugitive forced to leave the country so that he could be apprehended by U.S. authorities. (He was tried and acquitted.)

With Greece under enemy occupation, MacVeagh was recalled to Washington, leaving Athens on June 5, 1941. Almost immediately he was named the first U.S. minister to Iceland, where he arrived in October. At his new post virtually all his official activities were related to the war effort. He negotiated agreements for the construction of the large American airbase at Keflavik and for the operation of the Northern Ferry Command, whose convoys carried supplies to Murmansk. He also helped defuse countless problems involving American and British military officials and their Icelandic hosts. In late May 1942 MacVeagh had as his house guest V. M. Molotov, the Soviet foreign minister (on his way to London and Washington), and learned firsthand of the urgency with which Stalin's government expected the Western Allies to open a second front against the Germans in Europe. At the conclusion of his brief appointment in April 1942 MacVeagh was awarded the Order of the Icelandic Falcon.

In June 1942, following his formal confirmation as the U.S. minister to the Union of South Africa, MacVeagh left Iceland and returned to the United States to prepare for his new assignment. On September 21, in the company of British troops heading for the Middle East to face Rommel's advance toward Egypt, he sailed from New York for Capetown, arriving there on October 13; four days later he took charge of the American legation in Pretoria and assumed his duties as the American representative on the South African Supply Council. It was not an easy task. Although in principle the government of Gen. Jan Smuts was fully committed to the Allied war effort, the crusty Boer soldier viewed American involvement in his country as evidence of economic and cultural imperialism to be resisted at every turn. Not the least of MacVeagh's challenges was developing an effective relationship with Smuts. Moreover, South Africa's business community, in which pro-German sentiments were common, was less than enthusiastic in its desire to supply the Allies with much-needed strategic materials. It became MacVeagh's responsibility to gently pressure the authorities in Pretoria to switch from the lucrative gold market to the production of such less profitable but much more vital raw materials as coal, asbestos, chrome, copper, and vanadium. He also supervised the coordination of numerous American wartime agencies scattered across that vast country. As in his previous posts, he took time to study the country and its various peoples and to report extensively on its many and complex problems. By all accounts he was successful in his work and received the president's personal thanks and the department's commendation. Before long, however, he was given a new and more daunting assignment: in late September 1943, as Rommel's defeat in North Africa and Allied operations in the Mediterranean suggested (falsely, as it turned out) that the Balkans might soon be liberated, MacVeagh was informed that Roosevelt had chosen him to become U.S. ambassador "near the Greek and Yugoslav Governments [in exile] in Cairo."

In South Africa the MacVeaghs had been the guests of honor of the many prosperous Greek communities in that part of the world. At the same time, prominent Greeks in the United States with ties to the Roosevelt administration apparently sought to have MacVeagh posted to Cairo in the hope that he might counter what they perceived to be Britain's domineering involvement in Greek affairs, including support for the unpopular King George. Already in December 1942, in a Christmas message, the head of the Greek government in exile had written to MacVeagh, "May God grant that my fellow countrymen before long may be able to show you in freedom all their gratitude for your unfailing sympathy toward them and faith in Greece's future."

In Cairo MacVeagh's main role was that of Washington's liaison with British authorities who had overall direction of the Allied effort in the Middle East, the eastern Mediterranean, and the Balkans. Since the future of Yugoslavia was being discussed in London and in the mountains of that divided land, where Tito was the rising star, MacVeagh had little to do with that portion of his formal assignment but report to Washington on developments that he was following from afar. On the other hand, he established close ties with the Greek government and with the various prominent Greek personalities in Cairo, most of whom he knew well from his years in Athens. He followed closely the growing tensions in Greek politics, which led to mutinies among the Greek troops in Egypt, and advised his superiors to distance U.S. policy from British efforts to dictate to the unruly Greeks. With the help of information gathered in Yugoslavia and Greece by the Office of Strategic Services (OSS), he reported extensively on the powerful resistance movements in those states and warned that they were being dominated by radical elements with strong political ambitions. He took part in the secret talks in which Romanian representatives sought unsuccessfully to surrender their country to the Anglo-Americans rather than to the advancing Soviet forces. In June 1944 he informed the department that an Anglo-Soviet agreement concerning Greece and Romania was already in place. Worried that British weakness and the growing Soviet influence in Eastern Europe would bring these two allies on a collision course after the war and spark civil wars across the Balkans, MacVeagh urged Roosevelt to have Southeastern Europe liberated under U.S. military authority. However, Roosevelt would not be drawn into the morass of Balkan problems. A discouraged MacVeagh recorded in his diary (August 24, 1944), "So, as far as the Balkans are concerned, he [Roosevelt] has told Mr. Churchill to go right ahead and run the show."

In September 1944, as the liberation of the Balkans finally appeared imminent, the naming of a new U.S. ambassador to Yugoslavia permitted MacVeagh to devote all his attention to his Greek assignment. On his recommendation, and to signal that the United States did not endorse Britain's handling of Greek affairs, he did not follow the rump Greek cabinet to Italy, where it was moved by the British authorities in preparation for the voyage home. On October 27, having avoided the flurry of ceremonies and celebrations, he arrived in the Greek capital and quietly set out to reopen his understaffed and poorly equipped embassy. In the ensuing weeks, as tension mounted between the British-backed government of George Papandreou and the leftist resistance movement, MacVeagh kept himself aloof from political developments, making it clear that the Roosevelt administration would not become involved in Greek internal affairs. At the same time, he warned his superiors that in Greece Allied relief efforts were totally inadequate and predicted that the approaching winter would bring to the war-ravaged country starvation and anarchy. He was concerned about the growth of Communist influence and the potential for Soviet trouble-making in Greece. However, he blamed the political crisis in Athens largely on the human suffering caused by the lack of effective governmental authority and the collapse of the economy. In addition, he blamed the British for making a bad situation worse through their well-intentioned but haughty and rigid tactics.

In December 1944, when serious fighting broke out in Athens, MacVeagh sent the president an elaborate analysis of the crisis and concluded that "at bottom, the handling of this fanatically freedom-loving country . . . as if it were composed of natives under the British Raj, is what is the trouble." Following a private meeting with Prime Minister Winston Churchill, who was in Athens during December 26–28, MacVeagh reported to Roosevelt that the British leader was "deeply disappointed over what he feels to be our Government's lack of understanding of his attitude and its failure to support him." MacVeagh told Churchill that he had already recommended to the president the creation of an international commission to deal with Greece's problems. For a brief moment in the months ahead MacVeagh's idea seemed destined to bear fruit. In March 1945 Roosevelt proposed to Churchill that a team of American, British, and

Soviet officials be sent to Athens to study the economic situation and recommend remedies. However, when Churchill vetoed Soviet involvement in the undertaking and counterproposed a purely Anglo-American effort in Greece, Roosevelt dropped the idea on the grounds that such a bilateral approach might be viewed in Moscow as a violation of the Yalta agreement on tripartite cooperation in liberated Europe.

All through 1945–1946 MacVeagh could do little more than report on Greece's continuing drift toward polarization and full-scale civil war and on Britain's inability to bring the political and economic situation under control. He was disheartened by his superiors' apparent indifference to his post and by the total lack of instructions from Washington on which to base his relations with the Greek government and the British embassy in Athens. To make matters far worse, the sudden death of Roosevelt deprived him of that special relationship that MacVeagh had treasured and left him anxious and dispirited. "For me," he wrote in his diary on April 13, 1945, "the personal side of my job is gone, the vitalizing element. The ship will sail on, and I may still be for a while a part of the crew, but *my* captain is gone." Nor was his sense of isolation unfounded. In June 1945 the department made no attempt to consult MacVeagh when, in response to British urging, it decided to take part in the Allied supervision of the all-important Greek national elections, which were finally held on March 31, 1946. Nor was he kept informed of the long deliberations in Washington and London about the timing of the plebiscite on the monarchy (King George returned to Greece in September 1946). Nevertheless, in late November 1945, still uninstructed and acting on his own as an "old friend of Greece," MacVeagh managed to avert a new governmental crisis in Athens when he persuaded the regent, Archbishop Damaskinos, not to step down.

In January 1946 MacVeagh returned to the United States because his wife was seriously ill and needed the kind of care she could not get in Athens; they went back in late June. While he was in Washington, he called on President Truman and had long meetings at the department not only on Greek issues but also on the growing tension between the United States and the Soviet Union. Once back in Athens he tried to communicate to Greek politicians (and later to King George) his government's hope that moderation, peaceful discourse, and democratic solutions would be sought by all sides in the Greek crisis. But in the absence of any clear American commitment he had little but words to offer. By the summer of 1946 fighting between Communist-led guerrilla bands and government security forces was escalating, and MacVeagh's prognostications became increasingly gloomy. By year's end he was reporting that insurgent activity across northern Greece represented a systematic effort to seize control of the countryside and bring down the government. Writing to a colleague on October 14, 1946, he warned that unless Britain succeeded in establishing a democratic regime in Greece, the country could "go down the Soviet drain,— unless, of course, we wish to take the primary responsibility for Greece ourselves."

To his delight, his efforts to persuade his superiors that the United States should help to avert collapse in Greece suddenly appeared destined to succeed. By mid-October the Truman administration was coming around to the view that the victory of the Greek insurgents would be a victory for the Soviet Union's expansionist policies. An American economic mission arrived to investigate and make recommendations, and under pressure from the United States and Britain the United Nations launched its own inquiry into charges that the Greek insurgents were being supplied by the neighboring Communist regimes. In a letter to a superior MacVeagh exclaimed, "I feel now as Cassandra might, had anyone suddenly agreed with her!" In a major departure from his earlier interpretations, by January 1947 MacVeagh was blaming the Greek civil war largely on external factors. On February 20, aware that the department was following developments in Greece with growing concern, he telegraphed Washington that the situation had become critical and urged that the United States make clear "to everyone, including [the] Soviet Union, our determination not rpt [repeat] not to permit foreign encroachment, either from without or within, on [the] independence and integrity of Greece."

MacVeagh's bold and alarmist message, accompanied by a long background memorandum endorsed by Under Secretary Dean Acheson, reached the desk of Secretary of State George Marshall hours before the department was notified that Britain intended to terminate soon its support to Greece and Turkey. In years to come MacVeagh took pleasure in the knowledge that his many reports from Athens, and in particular his telegram of February 20, 1947, had played a significant role in the drafting of the Truman Doctrine. In mid-March he was recalled for consultations and gave testimony in the Senate hearings on the proposed program of assistance to Greece and Turkey. Hoping to deflect criticism that the Greek government was undemocratic and therefore undeserving of U.S. support, in his presentation he stressed the importance of foreign involvement in the Greek civil war. Moreover, he argued that defeating the insurgents would not be especially difficult if their movement could be "beaten at the top." As he put it, "The fellow to blame was the fellow who controls the little countries to the north of Greece, the fellow who is backing them, right square back to the Moscow Government."

Following the enactment of the Truman Doctrine, MacVeagh signed in Athens the U.S.-Greek agreements on assistance and its implementation (June 20, 1947). His influence dramatically increased; he masterminded a crucial restructuring of the Greek cabinet (August 1947) and secured the acquiescence of King Paul (King George had died on April 1, 1947), enabling the coalition government to function until the defeat of the insurgents in 1949.

He was not destined to enjoy the fruits of his labor. The death of his wife in Athens (September 9, 1947) left him emotionally devastated, and his own health began to fail. But what upset him the most and precipitated his departure from Greece were his problems with the growing number of U.S. agencies, civilian and military, now operating all around him, and in particular his personal clash with the chief of the American Mission for Aid to Greece, Dwight P. Griswold. MacVeagh, the old-fashioned ambassador, fell victim to the new and brash "shirt-sleeve" diplomats.

No American official was more enthusiastic in his support of Washington's involvement in Greece than MacVeagh. However, he believed that it was important to preserve the image of Greece as a sovereign state, that there should be no foreign interference in the operations of the Greek bureaucracy, and that overall supervision of American policy in Greece should remain the exclusive responsibility of his embassy. Griswold, on the other hand, viewed MacVeagh's principles and style as outmoded and ineffective. A former Republican governor of Nebraska who was believed to have presidential aspirations, he made no secret of his conviction that direct and persistent American intervention in Greek public affairs at all levels of government was necessary for the success of his mission. Within weeks following his arrival in Athens he was dealing directly with the Greek government and its officials and was complaining to Washington that MacVeagh lacked the firmness to be effective with the unruly Greeks. American journalists labeled Griswold the most powerful man in Greece.

Concerned that press accounts of the MacVeagh-Griswold quarrels might weaken congressional support for the aid program, especially among Republicans, the department attempted to divide in some detail the authority of the two top officials in Athens. However, Griswold refused to yield and threatened to resign, while his supporters in Washington demanded that MacVeagh be recalled and Griswold be named ambassador. It became clear that MacVeagh had lost out when the House of Representatives assigned the task of investigating the MacVeagh-Griswold controversy to a Nebraskan who had already asked for MacVeagh's withdrawal from Greece. On November 19, acting on options presented to him by the department, President Truman decided to recall MacVeagh (he had been in Washington since early October for surgery) and to keep Griswold as chief of the aid mission but not as ambassador (Griswold retired in August 1948). At the same time Truman approved the department's recommendation that MacVeagh be named U.S. ambassador to Portugal, a decision that was not made public until February 1948. MacVeagh received the news in the hospital and at first refused the new post, but his friends in the department finally persuaded him to accept. In a letter dated March 9, 1948, Truman praised MacVeagh for his "scholarly statesmanship and diplomatic judgment" and for "laying an indispensable groundwork for our common efforts to preserve Greek independence." For his part, MacVeagh felt betrayed and humiliated. He wrote to his brother that what he had tried to do in Athens was unite all Greeks "without siding with any, . . . and not to have to wave the big stick and thus both endanger that cooperation and give support to the communist charge that our 'imperialism' is making slaves of the local inhabitants." He concluded, "One does learn something about dealing with alien independent peoples after years of experience at the game, and if we subordinate our experts all around

Europe to the interruption and interference and dictation of politically ambitious amateurs, we certainly are heading for disaster.''

After the turbulence of postliberation Greece, Portugal (where MacVeagh arrived in June 1948) was an oasis of stability, order, and decorum. Kept out of the United Nations by a Soviet veto, the corporate regime of President Antonio Carmona was eager to strengthen its ties to the United States and secure for itself a place in the anti-Soviet camp being built in the late 1940s. The Portuguese authorities, as well as Lisbon's large expatriate community, welcomed MacVeagh as the cultured representative of the Western world's dominant power, and he received every courtesy and consideration. He devoted his energies to the busy work of the embassy, traveled extensively across the country, and kept his social engagements to a minimum. He handled much of the groundwork for Portugal's inclusion in the North Atlantic Treaty (signed in Washington on April 4, 1949), which the United States and Britain strongly supported. He also negotiated and singed the agreement for Portugal's participation in the Marshall Plan, the U.S.-Portugal Mutual Defense Assistance Program, and the Azores Defense Agreement. Following his retirement he was awarded the Portuguese Grand Cross of the Military Order of Christ.

In January 1952, in what appeared to be a routine reassignment, MacVeagh was named ambassador to Spain and on March 27 presented his credentials to Generalissimo Francisco Franco. At his new post his duties and routine changed little from what they had been in neighboring Portugal, and he received all the attention and honors reserved in the West for the representatives of American power. His principal task was to negotiate the establishment of U.S. military bases in Spain and the allocation of some $100 million in American economic, technical, and military assistance. His work was disrupted in the fall of 1952 by the presidential elections at home. The Republicans attacked Truman's foreign policy, and there was every reason to expect that Eisenhower's victory would result in a shake-up of diplomatic personnel. In early 1953, a few months before MacVeagh could complete twenty years in service (which would have made him eligible for a much more substantial government pension), he was retired by the new administration, bringing to an abrupt end his stay in Spain and his diplomatic career.

MacVeagh decided not to return to the United States but to make his home in Estoril, the fashionable town outside Lisbon. In 1955 he married Mrs. Virginia Ferrante Coats, the daughter of Marchese and Marchesa Ferrante di Ruffano of Naples, Italy, and adopted her children. In 1971, following a long illness, he was brought to the Washington, D.C., area, where he died in January 1972.

MacVeagh's friendship with the Roosevelts was too tenuous to land him a major embassy or to give him influence among policymakers, and he had no other powerful supporters in Washington. Moreover, he was too introverted and dignified to engage in self-promotion. Once he was appointed to his first post, his strengths were all of his own making: the skills and qualities of an effective diplomat came to him naturally, and he acquitted himself exceptionally well.

To be sure, he was too principled and old-fashioned to adjust to the demands of the hyperactive and interventionist policies unleashed by the Cold War. Yet it can be argued that the long-term interests of the United States would have been better served by MacVeagh's style of diplomacy than by that of his detractors.

Works by Lincoln MacVeagh

Editor. *Poetry from the Bible*. New York: Dial Press, 1925.

Greek Journey. New York: Dodd, Mead, and Company, 1937.

"Dear Franklin . . ." Letters to President Roosevelt from Lincoln MacVeagh, U.S. Minister to South Africa, 1942–1943. Pasadena: Munger Africana Library, 1972.

Ambassador MacVeagh Reports: Greece, 1933–1947. Ed. John O. Iatrides. Princeton, NJ: Princeton University Press, 1980.

JOHN O. IATRIDES

JOHN JAY McCLOY (1895–1989) had a career as an ambassador and advisor to presidents that spanned more than five decades. The personification of effective discretion, McCloy belonged to a select elite of corporate lawyers and investment bankers who from the 1920s to the 1980s gave American diplomacy the hard edge of pragmatism so critical to the emergence of the United States as the *primus inter pares* among nations.

McCloy's comparatively humble origins influenced his personal philosophy of public service. He was born on March 31, 1895, in north Philadelphia, the second son of John Jay McCloy and Anna McCloy (née Snader). McCloy's father rose to a supervisory position and a middle-class income with the Penn Mutual Life Insurance Company but died of a heart attack in 1901, leaving Anna McCloy with modest financial means to support herself and her six-year-old son (McCloy's older brother perished of diphtheria in 1899). Ploughing the savings of her work into McCloy's enrollment in the Peddie Institute, she was able to buy him solid academic instruction, a spartan athletic program, and the self-assurance of a prep-school background.

McCloy's academic and athletic performance at Peddie earned him a scholarship to Amherst College. In 1916 McCloy moved on to study corporate and commercial law at Harvard and, after brief service as a second lieutenant in the army reserve in France, graduated in 1921 with the intention of seeking employment with a firm in Philadelphia. Instead, he accepted a position with the Manhattan firm of Cadwalader, Wickersham, and Taft, an astute decision from two perspectives: Manhattan's broader horizons enabled him to view the practice of law as a project in the public as well as corporate interest, and McCloy's boss, George W. Wickersham, was chairman of the newly created Council on Foreign Relations. After three years at Cadwalader McCloy switched firms and joined Cravath, Henderson, and de Gersdorff. It was at Cravath in 1930 that McCloy was given the responsibility of investigating the viability of a possible suit to be brought against the German government by American firms damaged financially by the "Black Tom" munitions explosion of 1916, widely thought to be the work of saboteurs. The experience convinced McCloy that the United States ought to create its own intelligence apparatus and accept the possibility that some of its activities would inevitably offend constitutional scruple. In the early months of World War II McCloy was critical to the establishment of the first civilian intelligence organization in American history, the Office of Strategic Services, forerunner of the Central Intelligence Agency.

By the late 1930s McCloy had become something of a legend on Wall Street, noted for his patient persistence, a talent for negotiating deals out of court, and his ability to avoid making enemies. Particularly impressed was Henry Stimson, the past and future U.S. secretary of war. Stimson, to whom he was appointed as special assistant in December 1940, used McCloy as an all-purpose troubleshooter, a role that suited McCloy's appetite for discreet service as a "legman" who could attend to tasks best kept from the spotlight of publicity. McCloy testified to Congress on behalf of the Roosevelt administration's Lend-Lease initiative and the new powers it gave to the executive branch to aid the British war effort against Hitler's Germany.

After the Japanese attack on Pearl Harbor on December 7, 1941, McCloy was responsible more than any other official in Washington for the advocacy and implementation of Executive Order 9066, the internment of Japanese Americans. Despite criticism of internment as a violation of the Constitution, McCloy never doubted that the president had to be given whatever powers were necessary to meet a perceived threat to the security of the United States. The policy withstood criticism in no small part because of McCloy's skilled legal defense of it. Mc-Cloy was also privy to decisions at the highest level on the American prosecution of war against the Axis powers. In many instances his influence was significant, especially with regard to political considerations. At General Dwight Eisenhower's request, he argued on behalf of American recognition of postliberation political authority for General Charles de Gaulle in France, so that Eisenhower's strained relations with de Gaulle could be overcome and coordination of Allied invasion plans with Free French sabotage activity could proceed smoothly.

McCloy's major contribution to American policy in Europe, however, was made in Germany. Indeed, it involves no exaggeration to say that his role in Germany's postwar reconstitution and rehabilitation is among the most remarkable successes in the history of American foreign relations. He aided Stimson in opposing the proposal of Treasury Secretary Henry Morgenthau that defeated Germany be stripped of its industrial assets and pastoralized. At the same time, he opposed summary execution of German war criminals and advocated internationally sanctioned trials of the surviving Nazi leadership. McCloy thought that the Nuremberg tribunals, imperfect though they were, had the merit of testifying to the world on the nature of Nazi atrocities while diverting moral outrage away from a vengeful peace and toward an approximation of justice.

On a visit to Germany in April 1945, McCloy was so shaken by the scale of the destruction wrought by Allied bombing that he doubted that Germany could ever fully recover, yet came to the conclusion that the United States should do what it could to advance German economic revival. Appointed in February 1947 to the presidency of the newly founded International Bank for Reconstruction and Development, better known as the World Bank, McCloy was able to bring American power to bear on the problems of the German and European economies. Combining political experience with Wall Street credentials, McCloy was able to win respect for the bank's mandate while imposing his aggressive pragmatism on its board of directors in pursuit of tangible results. He rejected criticism from European leaders that the bank's lending ambitions were too modest, pointing out that it would never become a reliable source of investment capital until its commercial practices won the confidence of the financial community.

Although he was not averse in principle to loans to Eastern European states, McCloy was convinced that Western investment there would redound more directly to the industrial vitality and war-making capacity of the Soviet Union than to anyone else. At a point when relations between Washington and Moscow over Europe were becoming progressively more strained, he also recognized that vigorous economic diplomacy in Western Europe was vital to the credibility of the Truman administration's policy of "containment" of Communist influence. He therefore lobbied Congress for a forthright commitment to the European Recovery Program (the official name of the Marshall Plan) in the substance of appropriations sufficient to bring Western Europe into an American-led international monetary and trading system.

Because McCloy believed that Germany was to be the "cockpit" of all U.S. policy in Europe, his appointment by the Truman administration as the first American high commissioner to occupied Germany was especially astute. Experience as the assistant secretary of war gave McCloy the confidence of the U.S. Army; his bipartisan politics meant that he had few enemies in Congress; and his frequent defense of French interests and personal friendship with Jean Monnet, head of the French National Planning Commission, made him acceptable to Germany's traditional rival. As early as 1944 President Roosevelt had asked McCloy to head a civilian High Commission to reestablish democratic government in Germany immediately after surrender, but McCloy advised that a temporary occupation administration would be more appropriate and recommended General Lucius Clay as military governor, a position Clay filled brilliantly from 1945 to 1949. As high commissioner, McCloy's own administrative brief, especially pertaining to the use of Marshall Plan funds, gave him sweeping powers.

Employing a practice he had first developed at the World Bank, he appointed a cabinet of administrative aides to run the High Commission's various departments and entrusted each with wide discretion. From the outset McCloy's understanding of his task was that he should direct his mission toward the German populace as one of fundamental friendship and goodwill while seeing that German political life underwent a comprehensive reconstitution such as would make it difficult for a democracy to be debauched in the manner of the ill-fated Weimar Republic. To some extent that process had already begun with the Allied implementation of "denazification," the removal of active members of the Hitler regime from positions of authority and influence in German society, for which McCloy had been responsible while still with the War Department. Ever the pragmatist, however, McCloy was among the first to recognize that the systematic rooting out of Germans with valuable administrative experience was in too many instances at cross-purposes with the aim of rehabilitating Germany's economy and public affairs.

In January 1951 he chose for the latter priority by announcing a series of clemency decisions for German citizens convicted of war crimes. The most notable involved the use of his authority as high commissioner to commute many of the death sentences handed down to Nazi war criminals at Nuremberg and to reduce the sentences of others. In coming to the decisions, McCloy was subject to pressures from German government and opposition parties—which in some instances breached all conventions of etiquette—on behalf of clemency. Once announced, the decisions cost McCloy immediate condemnation in the press and public opinion in France, Britain, and the United States. McCloy's reasoning was in part based on the recommendations of an Advisory Board on Clemency for War Criminals he appointed in response to Chancellor Konrad Adenauer's protest that many of the Nuremberg sentences passed on lesser Nazis had been too severe, especially insofar as the new West German constitution banned capital punishment. Both the Nuremberg procedures and the deliberations of the Clemency Board were designed to give some formal recognition to the fact that the Third Reich had violated the conventions of war, German civil and military codes, and elementary laws of humanity. The release of Alfried Krupp, chairman and sole proprietor of the infamous Krupp arms manufacture, provoked the loudest protest, due less to the Krupp firm's involvement in Nazi war production and use of slave labor than to the fact that he was a walking symbol of German industry's collusion with military aggression going back to the 1890s and beyond. To McCloy, Krupp's lineage was precisely the wrong reason to put him in jail, and at the time there were compelling political reasons to extend leniency wherever it could be justified. Symbolic gestures to German national pride, however distasteful with Nazi tyranny still fresh in the memory, could broaden the electoral support for the Adenauer government, the only co-alition then available that combined democratic credentials and a parliamentary majority with unqualified support for American Cold War diplomacy in Europe. Yet McCloy did not simply capitulate to political expediency, as so many of his critics charged. He agonized over every decision, weighing the historic gravity of Nazi brutality in the recent past against the imperative that the infant Federal Republic of Germany, formally constituted in May 1949, survive the challenges of present and future.

Of greater long-term consequence was McCloy's remarkable success in influencing the formative years of democratic Germany's struggle to find its feet politically and inaugurate a new relationship with its neighbors. In late September 1949 he applied a combination of American economic pressure and shuttle diplomacy between London, Paris, and Bonn to arrive at an agreement over potentially disastrous currency devaluations. His dealings with West German Chancellor Adenauer over the issue were tense. Adenauer accused McCloy of dictating a solution in a way that could only damage the popular legitimacy of the new German government, its cabinet having been appointed only days before. While McCloy later conceded that his procedure in the affair had at times been brusque, it is equally true that in discussions with the French government he integrated Adenauer's insistence that a solution to exchange rates and export pricing could only work if it were viewed as part of a whole new order for European commerce. In response to protests of both government and opposition parties against the dismantling of German heavy industry, McCloy was particularly creative. He warned Chancellor Adenauer and opposition leader Kurt Schumacher that testing the strength of the Allies over the issue would be foolhardy, yet he encouraged debate over possible alternatives to what he too deemed an aimless policy. In the process he got ahead of Washington by suggesting that German war reparations might be met through current production, and by proposing further that the "war-making" potential of German industry might be brought under the control of an authority responsible for all West European heavy industry. In essence his statements conceded that the International Authority for the Ruhr, established in December 1948 to direct production and prices of the heavy industries of the Ruhr Valley, discriminated against Germany, but equally they suggested that international control of the war potential of all the West European states represented a just alternative so long as other measures were taken to ensure that European industry generally conformed to the principles of competitive free enterprise. In the face of clashes between British troops and German workers refusing to take part in the dismantling, McCloy then prepared proposals for his government to take to a Paris meeting of Allied foreign ministers in November 1949. McCloy advised U.S. Secretary of State Dean Acheson that the meeting should produce something that contributed substantially to the development and popular acceptance of the new West German republic but that could not be construed as Allied surrender to German agitation against dismantling. The meeting achieved a compromise deal on German steel production and plant closings while holding out to Bonn the possibility of further concessions if the Germans would undertake a program of industrial decartelization and reform of their civil service. McCloy's position in Germany and the United States was enhanced enormously by this outcome. After a meeting with Adenauer in Bonn, Acheson announced that the voice of U.S. foreign policy in Germany was indisputably that of John McCloy.

Initially opposed to the idea of rearmament as a danger to the project of nurturing a liberal German state, McCloy later became a supporter of a German contribution to West European security. More than any other American he appreciated the disturbing impact of the outbreak of the Korean War on West Germans' public confidence in the American ability to defend the Federal Republic. Discussions with Chancellor Adenauer led him further to the conviction that popular German support—both for American political aims in Europe generally and for the legitimacy of their own fledgling democracy specifically— could be lost unless a vehicle were found for Germans to contribute to their own defense. McCloy also feared that a long-term commitment to West German security without German troops would be politically unsustainable with public opinion in the United States. Through Acheson he helped to focus Washington's attention on the political imperative of a multilateral European structure force with a German component at its very core. A European Defense Force (EDF) had the additional merit of offering France a real buttress to its own security without reviving fear of a national German army.

McCloy had simultaneously to assure the Adenauer government that a Soviet attack on Germany was actually unlikely so long as the United States had nuclear superiority. Last, he understood that the long-term vitality of a democratic republic in Germany depended on Adenauer's ability to guarantee the security of the Federal Republic while gaining small measures of sovereignty for the Bonn government. He often found Adenauer querulous and unnecessarily difficult, yet appreciated that the chancellor was both an extremely capable politician and utterly committed both to Germany's democratic revival and its membership in a Western alliance. This measure of Adenauer's ability and Germany's situation, combined with McCloy's ability to win the trust of the two sides of any issue, was critical to building confidence between Bonn and Washington. When General Dwight Eisenhower was appointed Supreme Allied Commander in Europe (SACEUR), McCloy invited several German generals to a cocktail party in Eisenhower's honor. Though Eisenhower had once vowed never to shake the hand of the German military, he understood the enormous diplomatic capital to gained by going along with the event as McCloy had orchestrated it. The rearmament issue itself was not settled until 1955. The EDF concept fell to the veto of the French parliament, and the Federal Republic joined the North Atlantic Treaty Organization (NATO) with a national army at the disposal of the SACEUR. Though this arrangement was altogether different from that promoted by McCloy, there is no doubt that his early diplomacy on the rearmament issue was critical to the trust extended to the Bonn government by both the Truman and Eisenhower administrations and hence to West Germany's vital contribution to West European security.

With the election of the Eisenhower administration in 1952, McCloy returned to private life as the head of the Chase Bank. Despite the promise of a "new look" for American foreign policy from the first Republican administration since the Depression, Eisenhower and his secretary of state, John Foster Dulles, achieved a good deal of continuity in American relations with West Germany. McCloy's advice was a good part of the reason for this. Dulles took McCloy's cue in appointing James Conant, the president of Harvard University, his successor in Bonn and used the former high commissioner to convey messages to Adenauer during the first years of the new administration. In fact, McCloy never really retired from public service altogether. Though his official diplomatic services for the United States came to an end in 1952, he remained an invaluable consultant to successive administrations on arms control and was a member of the Warren Commission appointed by President Lyndon Johnson to investigate the assassination of President John F. Kennedy in 1963.

It is for his outstanding service as the first high commissioner to the Federal Republic of Germany that McCloy is rightly remembered as among the finest diplomats the United States has ever produced. At the most difficult of times McCloy was the principal liaison between the American superpower and the Bonn republic. The unique powers enjoyed by a high commissioner during Germany's transition from occupied territory to sovereign state meant that McCloy was able to make a lasting impact on postwar Europe. He helped to engage the United States in European affairs as never before and cemented the most important bilateral relationship in the Western alliance. For this he was rightly praised by President Kennedy as the "Godfather to German freedom" whose legacy to the Federal Republic was in many ways as profound as that of Konrad Adenauer himself. When McCloy died on March 11, 1989, he was remembered in the Federal Republic as one of Germany's best friends.

Work by John J. McCloy

The Atlantic Alliance: Its Origin and Its Future. New York: Columbia University Press, 1969.

Works about John J. McCloy

Bird, Kai. *The Chairman: John J. McCloy, the Making of the American Establishment.* New York: Simon and Schuster, 1992.

Isaacson, Walter, and Evan Thomas. *The Wise Men: Six Friends and the World They Made.* New York: Touchstone, 1986.

Schwartz, Thomas Alan. *America's Germany: John J. McCloy and the Federal Republic of Germany.* Cambridge: Harvard University Press, 1991.

                                                          CARL CAVANAGH HODGE

GEORGE CREWS McGHEE (1912–), U.S. ambassador to Turkey (December 1951 to June 1953) and Germany (May 1963 to May 1968), implemented the Truman Doctrine in Greece and Turkey and in the mid- and late 1960s helped the administration of Lyndon Johnson adjust to the post-Adenauer era in German politics.

Born in Waco, Texas, on March 10, 1912, McGhee attended Southern Methodist University and the University of Oklahoma, where he received his B.S. degree in geology and physics in 1933. As a Rhodes scholar, he then went to Oxford University and there took his Ph.D. in the physical sciences in 1937. These Oxford years had a profound impact on the young Texas geology student. His fellow students came from that class of English patricians that supplied the British Empire with its administrators and policymakers, a world then unknown to McGhee. He quickly became a self-professed Anglophile, an attitude that later influenced his diplomatic judgment.

McGhee next established himself as a geologist and oil producer and by 1940 became the sole owner of the McGhee Production Company. During World War II he served on the War Production Board and later as a naval liaison officer for Major General Curtis LeMay, Commander of the 21st Bomber Command, which conducted the Allied air war against Japan.

McGhee's diplomatic career began in 1946 when he applied for entry into the State Department. Another Texan, William S. Clayton, assistant secretary of state for economic affairs, chose McGhee as his special assistant. Clayton, a self-made millionaire who had organized the world's largest cotton-trading firm, Anderson Clayton, imbued McGhee with a sense of America's mission of containing communism in the period following the defeat of the Axis powers in 1945.

The years immediately following World War II witnessed the creation of a foreign policy consensus of anticommunism in the United States. The Truman Doctrine of March 1947, the Marshall Plan of June 1947, and the NATO alliance of 1949 were crucial events that conditioned America's response to what was perceived as a dangerous Soviet drive for imperial expansion. By 1947 England could no longer financially support those forces battling the Communist-led guerrillas in Greece. When London asked the American government for military and financial relief, President Truman responded with a predominantly military aid program for Greece and Turkey to prevent what Washington saw as Soviet probes into the Mediterranean and Middle East. McGhee's apprenticeship under the politically powerful Clayton led to his appointment as coordinator for aid to Greece and Turkey in 1947. He monitored the flow of $250 million in arms and economic aid to the weakened Greek government. U.S. military advisors were dispatched to Greece, but the coordinator scrupulously enforced a policy that no American personnel would take part in combat operations. Consequently, there were no U.S. casualties in what was to be a successful program that defeated the Moscow-backed Greek guerrillas. The $150-million aid package to Turkey allowed that nation to counter Moscow's aggressive demands to revise the Montreaux Convention to place the Turkish Straits under the control of all Black Sea powers (mostly Soviet-bloc states) and ratify joint Turkish-Soviet defense of the straits. McGhee's frequent visits to the Turkish cities of Ankara and Istanbul helped him to cultivate linkages to such prominent political figures as Kasim Gülek, leader of the then-governing Republican Peoples Party, and Celal Bayar, founder of the opposition Democratic Party. McGhee soon became an advocate of larger military aid to Turkey, whose sizable land army and anti-Communist philosophy appealed to the coordinator's geopolitical perceptions. Bayar's efforts to allow American corporations easier access to Turkish markets following the Democratic Party's successful national election victory in May 1950 cemented McGhee's perception of Turkey as a solid, probusiness, anti-Communist frontline state.

In February 1949 McGhee was appointed by Deputy Under Secretary of State Dean Rusk as special coordinator for Palestine refugee affairs. He recommended a $250-million aid program for the 700,000 Arab refugees displaced in the war following the creation of the state of Israel. In June 1949 Truman named McGhee assistant secretary of state for Near Eastern, South Asian, and African affairs (NEA). His area of jurisdiction included all of Africa except the Union of South Africa, the Middle East, and South Asia, an area comprising around 600 million people. Except for Greece, Turkey, Iran, and Saudi Arabia, European colonialism dominated the fate of these peoples. McGhee's tenure saw the appearance of societies emerging from the effects of Europe's imperial experience. The memoirs of his assistant secretaryship, *Envoy to the Middle World*, document his exposure to the postcolonial era: Jawaharlal Nehru of India, Mohammed V of Morocco, Mohammed Mossadeq of Iran, and Kwame Nkrumah of Ghana. McGhee spoke to these statesmen of his priority of thwarting Moscow's attempt to influence their nations via subversion. In doing so, he was not averse to working directly with the former colonial powers, especially with the much-admired British, in developing regional defense efforts. But given the heritage of empire, McGhee's idea failed to generate enthusiasm for such security structures. Only Turkey offered support.

The Korean War of 1950 dramatically changed U.S. political and military strategy. Until Korea the Joint Chiefs of Staff opposed any NATO role for Greece and Turkey, but the trauma of Korea redefined and expanded the concept of containing communism. McGhee advanced the idea of Turkish NATO membership, a position helped by that nation's support for America's Korean commitment. He used the image of a solid Turkish ally to overcome the Joint Chiefs' opposition to its admittance into NATO. When Britain asked that any Turkish NATO contingent be placed under its commander in case of conflict with Moscow, Ankara objected. McGhee's support of that objection increased his credibility in Turkish political circles. It came as no surprise that Truman appointed him U.S. ambassador to Turkey in December 1951 following the retirement of George Wadsworth from that post.

McGhee's ambassadorship was characterized by the attempt to convince Turkish leaders to create a Middle East defense organization to offset Soviet influence in this oil-rich area. In February 1952 Turkey joined NATO, and in his talks with President Bayar and Foreign Minister Mehmet Fuad Koprülü the ambassador compared Turkey's regional role to that of the United States with Latin America. This defense concept included Britain and France, which the Turkish leaders told McGhee could only arouse opposition from Arab nationalist parties. The Turks welcomed large-scale injections of American military and economic aid but refused to pursue a policy that gave any appearance of Turkey acting as a stand-in for Western interests. Bayar and other politicians were grateful to McGhee, whose White House connection helped to offset criticism of aid to Turkey from the well-organized Greek-American lobby in the U.S. Congress. Also, the ambassador asked the American public for understanding of the Turkish response to its Armenian minority during World War I. Thousands of Armenians had been executed (or, as others claimed, massacred) by the Turkish sultanate. But McGhee asserted that the Armenians were collaborating with the Russians, with whom Turkey was at war. Such advocacy attempted to offset the Armenian-American lobby that sought to condemn Turkey for its policy of reprisals.

McGhee's support for Turkish interests paid dividends when Communist dictator Joseph Stalin died on March 5, 1953. The Soviets offered to renew the 1925 Treaty of Friendship with Ankara, one they had denounced in 1945. Moscow also abandoned its claim to the Turkish provinces of Kars and Ardahan. Soviet diplomats even told Turkish officials that Stalin's past policy of confrontation was misguided. Still, Ankara balked at pursuing an opening to Moscow.

During the last months of his ambassadorship McGhee participated in Secretary of State John Foster Dulles's initial discussions with Turkish Prime Minister Adnan Menderes. Dulles, the foreign policy spokesman for the new Republican administration, stressed Washington's recognition of Turkey's crucial role as NATO's southern anchor. The new U.S. government would continue to bolster Turkey's armed forces.

McGhee's concept of a Middle Eastern security pact bore fruit in 1955. Turkey, Iraq, Iran, Pakistan, and Great Britain formed the Baghdad Pact. Given Israeli objections, the United States offered only verbal support. However, the pact quickly unraveled after Arab nationalists assassinated the pro-British prime minister of Iraq, Nuri as-Said. The pact's failure mirrored McGhee's inability to convince these nations, who had experienced European colonialism, to see a greater danger in Soviet communism than in the influence of their former imperial rulers.

With Dwight Eisenhower's election as president, McGhee left government service and again became an independent oil producer. When John F. Kennedy entered the White House in January 1961, he asked former Truman Secretary of State Dean Acheson to review the necessity of maintaining U.S. Jupiter missiles in Turkey. Acheson, aware of McGhee's expertise with Turkish affairs, asked the former ambassador to sound out Ankara for a possible removal of the missiles. McGhee advised JFK that Turkey would oppose such a withdrawal. Kennedy appointed McGhee counselor of the Department of State and then chairman of the Policy Planning Council. On December 4, 1961, he became under secretary of state for political affairs. When in May 1963 the U.S. ambassador to the Federal Republic of Germany (West Germany) required serious surgery, McGhee, who made no secret of his desire for his own mission, was picked by JFK as American ambassador to Bonn, a position he held for the next five years.

McGhee's opinion of Germany was greatly influenced by his academic training in geology and physics, where German achievements were pronounced. He was also a member of the exclusive Bilderberg Group founded by Prince Bernhard of the Netherlands to strengthen American-European ties. McGhee's membership allowed him to interface with such German leaders as Helmut Schmidt, a future chancellor, Fritz Berg, leading spokesman for German business interests, and Carlo Schmidt, deputy speaker of the German Bundestag (parliament).

McGhee's ambassadorship in Bonn began during the last days of the Adenauer chancellorship (1949–1963). This period of German history was characterized by Adenauer's *Westbindung* policy of German membership in NATO and the Common Market. West Germany, divided from East Germany by the Iron Curtain, readily followed America's lead in the initial Cold War years.

American-German relations had been characterized by tension and distrust during the presidency of John F. Kennedy. Unlike Presidents Truman and Eisenhower, JFK found Chancellor Adenauer a difficult ally. Specifically, Kennedy's policy of seeking discussions with Moscow over the future of Berlin in the months following the building of the Berlin Wall in August 1961 raised fears in the German capital of a possible U.S.-Soviet agreement at the expense of German interests. McGhee's reports to Washington reflected JFK's dislike of Adenauer, who was described as overly suspicious, arrogant, and authoritarian.

The Vietnam War tarnished the American image as Free World leader, especially among young Germans. The conflict in Southeast Asia also intensified the U.S. balance-of-payments problem. JFK's successor, Lyndon B. Johnson, looked to West Germany to increase its payments for stationing American troops on German soil. Other themes such as Franco-German relations and the closely related question of European unity occupied McGhee's time as ambassador, but none was more important than the issue of paying for U.S. troops.

McGhee developed a close working relationship with Ludwig Erhard, who succeeded Adenauer as chancellor. He believed Erhard, who spoke of smoothing out U.S.-German relations, which had been bruised by JFK's relationship with Adenauer. However, Johnson demanded from Erhard a definite commitment to increase German support payments. Such assistance would reduce LBJ's need to raise taxes to fight the war in Vietnam. But Erhard had been weakened po-litically by West Germany's first postwar recession, which left the chancellor with no financial room to maneuver. McGhee was aware of Erhard's difficult position and even sympathized with his plight, but did not confront LBJ with the idea that Erhard would jeopardize his pro-American policy if he submitted to Johnson's demands for higher payments. Johnson did overcome the chancel-lor's objections and received the pledge for more payments, but the adverse reaction in Germany destroyed Erhard politically.

The chancellor was a member of the Christian Democratic Union (CDU), a party that had dominated German politics since the creation of the Federal Re-public in 1949. The collapse of Erhard's government gave the opposition Social Democratic Party of Germany (SPD) a chance to rule in Bonn. Led by Willy Brandt, the mayor of embattled West Berlin, the SPD formed a Grand Coalition with the CDU on December 1, 1966. Brandt, who become foreign minister, made no secret of the fact that German reunification, a goal of all parties, could best be achieved if Bonn began its own policy of rapprochement with Moscow and its Eastern-bloc satellites. But would Germany now downplay its ties to the West? As Americans increasingly became entangled in Vietnam, would the new government in Bonn use this U.S. focus in Asia to undermine or avoid the anti-Communist policies built up by Washington and its European allies since 1947?

McGhee discussed such questions openly with Brandt and the new CDU chancellor and leader of the Grand Coalition, Kurt Georg Kiesinger. McGhee found Brandt, unlike Adenauer, a good listener and welcomed his new look toward the East. The ambassador found much to admire in Kiesinger. His dis-patches portrayed the new chancellor as a thoughtful, open statesman who sought to understand America's Vietnam dilemma. Both assured the ambassador that the change in Bonn from Erhard to Kiesinger would not mean a rejection of *Westbindung*. The Europe of the late 1960s had recovered from the ravages of World War II. Germany had to adjust its foreign policy to the new political landscape. Membership in NATO and the firm tie to Washington would remain the two pillars of German policy. In his meetings with LBJ and his cables to Secretary of State Dean Rusk, McGhee took the position that it was in America's interest to encourage the West German attempt to develop its own response to the new European political scene, even if this meant more German-Soviet dis-cussions over reunification and relations with the Eastern bloc. Johnson's ac-quiescence did much to solidify German-American relations.

The Nuclear Non-Proliferation Treaty (NPT), signed on July 1, 1968, by the United States, Great Britain, and the Soviet Union, was seen by these nuclear signatory powers as an important step to limit and control the use of such weaponry, while the nuclear powers agreed to share nuclear technology. West Germany had entered the NATO alliance in May 1955 by pledging never to manufacture nuclear weapons, but Bonn raised various questions about the NPT as its contents took shape in the fifteen months prior to its signing.

Foreign Minister Brandt and Chancellor Kiesinger voiced their concerns to

McGhee that if the Federal Republic signed the treaty, this might prevent the creation of a possible European nuclear force in the event of European political integration. Also, Bonn found a danger of exposure to industrial espionage through the treaty's proposed inspection procedures. The American ambassador articulated the U.S. position that if and when Europe was to achieve that degree of political integration requisite for a unified military structure and command, the NPT would not hinder the transfer of either French or British nuclear weapons to such a command.

Likewise, McGhee argued that the inspection contemplated under the treaty did not permit the inspectors access to information of a commercial value. The current U.S.-German nuclear-supply agreement made use of the NPT's proposed safeguards. America did not require information or knowledge of Germany's nuclear research and development. Although McGhee was not able to overcome Kiesinger's doubts, in November 1969 the Federal Republic signed the NPT. By that time Brandt was chancellor.

Two schools of thought have dominated the historiography of the Cold War: the traditionalists, who defend the policy containing communism, and the revisionists, who condemn containment as an attempt to protect a capitalistic world order, camouflaged in a language of freedom and democracy. Both can be applied to McGhee's early diplomatic career. His tenure as coordinator of aid to Greece and Turkey, assistant secretary of NEA, and ambassador to Turkey was shaped by President Truman's response to blunt what was then believed to be a worldwide Communist offensive. He was not a trained diplomat and wrote in *Envoy to the Middle World* that foreign policy is nothing more than adjusting a nation's interests to a world undergoing change. Hence containment came easily to this Cold Warrior. His views assumed that those societies in the process of liberation from British or French colonialism should adopt American-like economic structures. Here the revisionist critique has validity. But McGhee's legacy is that of a Cold Warrior in transition. His ambassadorship to Germany gives evidence of a diplomat more open to change, one who would not oppose new approaches that sought to operate beyond the narrow restrictions of Cold War concepts.

Works by George C. McGhee

Envoy to the Middle World: Adventures in Diplomacy. New York: Harper and Row, 1983.

Editor. *Diplomacy for the Future.* Lanham, MD: University Press of America, 1987.

At the Creation of a New Germany: From Adenauer to Brandt; An Ambassador's Account. New Haven and London: Yale University Press, 1989.

Coauthor, with Cecilia McGhee. *Life in Alanya: Turkish Delight.* Benson, VT: Chalidze Publications, 1992.

Works about George C. McGhee

Acheson, Dean. *Present at the Creation: My Years in the State Department.* New York: W. W. Norton and Company, 1969.

Feroz, Ahmad. *The Turkish Experiment in Democracy, 1950–1975*. London: C. Hurst and Co., published for the Royal Institute of International Affairs, 1977.

Gaddis, John L. *Strategies of Containment: A Critical Appraisal of Postwar American National Security Policy*. New York: Oxford University Press, 1982.

Hunt, Michael H. *Ideology and U.S. Foreign Policy*. New Haven and London: Yale University Press, 1987.

Jonas, Manfred. *The United States and Germany: A Diplomatic History*. Ithaca, NY: Cornell University Press, 1984.

Kuniholm, Bruce R. *The Origins of the Cold War in the Near East: Great Power Conflict and Diplomacy in Iran, Turkey, and Greece*. Princeton: Princeton University Press, 1980.

Morgan, Roger P. *The United States and West Germany, 1945–1973: A Study in Alliance Politics*. London: Oxford University Press, 1974.

FRANK A. MAYER

EDWIN MORGAN (1865–1934) spent most of his diplomatic
career as ambassador to Brazil.

Morgan was born on February 22, 1865, at Aurora, New York. He studied history at Harvard and was awarded a B.A. in 1890 and an M.A. in 1891 before going on to study for a year in Germany. In 1895 he became an instructor in history at Adelbert College in Cleveland, which was later incorporated into Case Western Reserve University. In 1900 Morgan joined the Foreign Service and held various junior diplomatic posts in Korea and Russia until his appointment as minister to Cuba in 1905. He became minister to Uruguay in 1909 and was transferred to Portugal in 1911. In 1912 he was promoted to the post of ambassador to Brazil and held this appointment continuously for twenty-one years until his resignation in 1933. No American diplomat has served longer at a single ambassadorial post.

Edwin Morgan was typical of late nineteenth-century diplomats in that his entry into the Foreign Service was aided by political connections. His family background was staunchly Republican, and though Morgan did not personally seek elective office, he could boast a grandfather who had been elected to the House of Representatives in 1852 and a cousin who had served as governor of New York during the Civil War. The Morgans of Aurora were also wealthy and socially influential. They were a well-established family that could trace its background directly to an ancestor who had settled in Boston in 1636. Though the family was not related to the celebrated Morgan banking dynasty, it had acquired a substantial fortune from merchant express companies, including an involvement in the founding of American Express. Edwin Morgan therefore possessed a private income to supplement the relatively meager salary paid to employees of the State Department. Wealth proved to be an advantage in Brazil, where Morgan became renowned for lavish official receptions and also for generous patronage of the arts.

Morgan was, however, neither a political hack nor a wealthy socialite seeking a temporary job overseas. In fact, he exemplified the professional career diplomat who was emerging at the beginning of the twentieth century. Such officials typically joined the Foreign Service in their mid-thirties. While they might lack specific diplomatic experience, this was often compensated for by education at one of the Ivy League colleges and, in the case of Morgan, a further period of study and travel in Europe. Working up from junior positions, they acquired the skills and experience that were expected to lead eventually to an ambassadorship at a major European capital. Edwin Morgan's early career faithfully followed this pattern as he rose from secretary of legation in Korea to ambassador to Brazil. His initial service in Korea earned him the reputation of an expert on Far Eastern affairs. Morgan's transfer to Cuba in 1905, however, resulted in him becoming associated in the minds of his superiors with Latin countries. His experience of the Far East was forgotten as the Taft administration assigned him to a succession of Latin capitals beginning with Montevideo in 1909 and continuing with Lisbon in 1911 and finally Rio de Janeiro in May 1912.

The vacancy in Brazil was caused by the serious illness of Ambassador Irving Dudley. Indeed, the threat of tropical disease and especially yellow fever had long made Brazil an unattractive posting for Americans. Nevertheless, the country had acquired a new degree of prominence in inter-American affairs at the beginning of the twentieth century. This was underlined in 1905 by the raising of diplomatic relations to ambassadorial level—Brazil was the first South American country to be given this honor by the United States—and the choice of Rio de Janeiro as the venue of the third Pan-American conference in 1906. There was also the well-publicized success of the Brazilian foreign minister, Rio Branco, and the Brazilian ambassador at Washington, Joaquim Nabuco, in giving Brazil the image of the leading country of South America and advocating a policy of rapprochement or, as it was called at the time, "approximation" with the United States. The appointment of Edwin Morgan in 1912 indicated the desire of the Taft administration to place an experienced career diplomat in charge of the Brazilian mission.

Morgan arrived at Rio in June 1912. At first he made no secret of his personal ambitions and that he regarded Brazil as just another step on the ladder to a prestigious European appointment. Foreign diplomatic colleagues, however, were impressed by Morgan's seriousness of purpose and evident determination to work hard to earn promotion. For example, the new ambassador was dismayed to discover that the American embassy was actually located not in Rio but in the pleasant spa city of Petrópolis in the mountains to the north of the capital. This comfortable state of affairs was abruptly brought to an end by Morgan, who immediately ordered the transfer of the embassy to Rio. The European legations reluctantly followed suit, thereby acknowledging the leading diplomatic role enjoyed by the United States in Brazil.

Reflecting a century of rivalry for hemispheric preeminence, American diplomats in Latin America preferred to remain aloof from their European colleagues. Morgan was no exception. But the new ambassador was different from the majority of Americans in Brazil in his display of genuine sensitivity to Brazilian opinion and local customs. From the very beginning of his ambassadorship he demonstrated political astuteness by flattering Brazil's achievements and sense of international status. One of his first and most appreciated public acts was to place a wreath at Rio Branco's tomb. Moreover, Morgan consciously sought to cultivate close personal relations with the Brazilian ruling elite. In this he was aided by his considerable personal wealth and cultured background. Indeed, his bachelor status, gregarious personality, lavish hospitality, and love of the arts soon endeared him to Brazilian society and earned him the tribute of being described as the "most Brazilian of Americans" and even as an "honorary Brazilian."

Morgan's tactful diplomatic approach proved invaluable during the first months of his ambassadorship. He arrived in Rio at a time when a major controversy was developing between his government and Brazil. A succession of bumper coffee crops had led the state of São Paulo in 1908 to devise a policy known as "valorization," in which the damaging effects of massive overproduction and falling prices were alleviated by holding back coffee supplies from the world market. However, the resulting steep rise in the price of coffee aroused criticism, especially in the United States, where the Justice Department proceeded to investigate the activities of what was alleged to be a "coffee trust" acting against the interests of American consumers. The Brazilian ambassador at Washington publicly condemned American policy as insulting to his country. This merely stung American leaders into a high-handed and unsympathetic response. The crucial voice of conciliation came from Edwin Morgan, who constantly reminded both sides of their mutual desire to maintain and develop friendly relations. Morgan worked closely with Brazilian Foreign Minister Lauro Müller and willingly adopted the role of conciliator because he believed that a continuation of the dispute could only be harmful to American interests. The election of a new American president in 1912 provided a welcome opportunity to reach a compromise. Largely on Morgan's advice, the Wilson administration invited Müller to visit the United States during the summer of 1913. The visit underlined the improvement in relations between the two governments. Another pleasing development for Morgan was the decision of the new administration to keep him on as ambassador to Brazil. In fact, Morgan was the only ambassador held over from the Taft administration. While this may have reflected satisfaction with his conduct during the valorization dispute, more significant perhaps was the fact that Morgan possessed influential supporters in the White House. These included Colonel Edward House, who was President Wilson's friend and closest confidant. In retrospect, however, staying in Brazil proved to be a mixed blessing for Morgan's subsequent diplomatic career.

A prominent feature of American diplomacy at the beginning of the twentieth century was an emphasis on expanding trade and investment with Latin America. Indeed, an increase in exports to Brazil had long been considered desirable in order to rectify the adverse trade balance that had existed with that country for several decades. But Morgan was not a forceful advocate of "dollar diplomacy." Like the majority of his diplomatic colleagues, he believed that there were limits to what governments could achieve for private business interests. He did seek, however, to redress the imbalance of trade by pressing the Brazilian government to grant special tariff concessions so that imports of American goods would be cheaper than those of their European rivals. Such diplomatic activity produced relatively small changes in customs duties and had only a slight impact on well-established patterns of trade. Much more significant for the extension of American commercial influence in Brazil was the sudden decline of European economic competition caused by the outbreak of war in Europe in 1914. Nevertheless, progress in winning markets was disappointingly slow. American merchants wished to sell, but Brazilians lacked the funds to buy. Moreover, while

Morgan urged his countrymen to seize economic opportunities, he was well aware of Brazil's economic deficiencies and warned American bankers to exercise great care in granting loans to Brazil. The ambassador's cautious approach was sensible, but it did arouse criticism from American businessmen that he was indifferent to the promotion of American interests in Brazil. Critics were disarmed, however, by the fact that during the 1920s the United States successfully displaced Britain as the leading exporter to and major source of new capital investment in Brazil.

After resolving the valorization dispute in 1913, the Wilson administration showed little interest in Brazil. The idea of approximation was simply ignored. Morgan was viewed by officials in Washington as the expert on Brazil whose principal function was to report events rather than to make policy. Following the outbreak of war in Europe in 1914, Morgan reassured the State Department that Brazil would imitate the United States and pursue a policy of neutrality. He also dismissed rumors of Foreign Minister Müller's allegedly pro-German bias and observed that German propaganda was having little impact in Brazil. These reports merely served to reinforce the belief held in Washington that Brazil possessed only marginal importance for the United States. Brazil's entry into the war in October 1917 prompted a brief reawakening of American diplomatic interest, but subsequent decisions on the war effort and the peace settlement were made by the Wilson administration with scant reference either to Morgan or the Brazilian government.

Morgan was particularly frustrated by the apathy of the State Department toward Brazil's desire to contract foreign military missions to modernize its army and navy. Although Morgan saw these missions primarily as an opportunity to gain profitable orders for American military equipment, he also recognized the long-term strategic value to the United States of developing closer military cooperation between the two countries. In 1919 the Brazilian government contracted a French mission to modernize its army. A naval mission was proposed two years later. Britain was the strong favorite for the contract because Brazilians had traditionally maintained a close association with the British navy. World War I, however, had created an opening for American influence when the shortage of British naval instructors had forced Brazil to turn to the United States. American instructors were sent to Brazil and made an excellent impression. Morgan skillfully exploited this good feeling and utilized his influential contacts to win the naval contract for the United States in 1922. The resulting mission was small in numbers and survived only until 1930. Nevertheless, the winning of the naval contract represented a notable diplomatic success for Morgan and the United States and established a crucial foundation for future extension of American influence over the training, operational procedures, and strategy of the Brazilian navy.

After Morgan's arrival in Brazil with such high personal ambitions in 1912, his diplomatic career had become effectively stalled. The return of the Republicans to the White House in 1921 raised hopes of a transfer to the embassy at

Rome. The Harding administration preferred, however, that Morgan remain in Brazil. Ironically, Morgan's long tenure of office and his acknowledged success in gaining the confidence of the Brazilian ruling elite had become major obstacles to his career advancement. State Department officials had come to consider his name as virtually synonymous with Brazil. In effect, Morgan was regarded as irreplaceable. In 1929, despite being only a year away from the retirement age of sixty-five, he was asked to stay on as ambassador at Rio for a further five years.

Morgan's remarkable reputation provided an excuse for American diplomatic indifference and inertia toward Brazil. As long as he presided over the embassy in Rio, State Department officials concluded that American interests were secure and safe. In Brazil Morgan's influence assumed almost legendary proportions. European colleagues called him "the king of Rio" and greatly envied his ability to bypass official channels and transact diplomatic business by personal contact, but this required Morgan to be regularly engaged in social activity and forever attentive to his vast network of personal relationships. Such activities could not be easily delegated to subordinates, so that over the years Morgan gradually took on almost all the diplomatic work of the embassy by himself. What appeared as a strength, however, was transformed into a distinct liability whenever the ambassador was away from his post. This problem surfaced during the abortive São Paulo revolt of July 1924, but had more serious consequences for American diplomacy during the 1930 revolution. In October 1930 a military revolt broke out in Brazil while Morgan was on vacation in Europe. On his departure in September Morgan had reported that conditions were delicate, but he did not predict serious disturbances or that the government of President Washington Luís might be overthrown. Consequently, officials in Washington were quite unprepared for the turn of events. Their confusion was increased by the fact that an inexperienced and ill-informed diplomatic secretary was in charge of the embassy in Rio. The automatic response in Washington was to locate Morgan and instruct him to return immediately to Brazil. The complete victory achieved by the rebels proved to be an embarrassment for the State Department, which had acted on the assumption that Washington Luís would hold on to power. Morgan's reports were mostly responsible for this belief, but he was not blamed or held to account. By keeping him in office for so many years, State Department officials had effectively deprived themselves of alternative sources of information about Brazil. Morgan's experience and wisdom in the unsettled state of Brazilian political affairs following the 1930 revolution were regarded as more important than ever.

The electoral victory of Franklin D. Roosevelt in 1932 signified the end of more than a decade of Republican control of the White House. The new Democratic president seized the opportunity to terminate several diplomatic appointments, including that of Edwin Morgan, who duly resigned in April 1933. Morgan's identification with Brazil had become so complete that he preferred to reside in that country rather than return to the United States. He died suddenly from angina on April 14, 1934, and was buried in Petrópolis with a ceremony in which the Brazilian government accorded him full honors. As a further mark of tribute to his memory, a street in one of the most affluent residential sections of Rio was given the name Rua Embaixador Morgan. During an era in which anti-American feeling was very pronounced in Latin America, it was remarkable for an American diplomat to be shown so much respect and affection. This demonstrated that Morgan had achieved that most elusive goal for an ambassador of quietly and effectively representing the interests of his own country while still appearing sympathetic and evenhanded to the country in which he served. Morgan was so successful that he was prevailed upon to remain as ambassador in Brazil for more than two decades. In the process, however, his hopes of a prestigious European posting were gradually abandoned, and he became reconciled to ending his career in Brazil.

JOSEPH SMITH

Work by Edwin Morgan

Slavery in New York. New York, London: G. P. Putnam's Sons, 1898.

RICHARD WILLIAM MURPHY (1929–   ) was U.S.

assistant secretary of state for Near East and African affairs during the Reagan administration and a specialist in Middle East affairs.

Richard Murphy was born in Boston and educated at Harvard University, where he majored in history and literature and graduated in 1951, and at Cambridge University in 1953, where he studied anthropology. After university he served in the U.S. Army (1953–1955) and during that time took the written examination for the Foreign Service. Upon completion of army duty in 1955, he was admitted to the first State Department class following the two-year hiring freeze during the McCarthy era. While at his first post in Salisbury, Zimbabwe (then Rhodesia), he volunteered for a new program designed to train diplomats as specialists in Arabic-language and area studies. After a year of study under State Department auspices at the Center for Strategic and International Studies of the Johns Hopkins University, Murphy spent another year of specialized language training in the Middle East.

He emerged fluent in Arabic and was posted to a small consulate in Aleppo, Syria, followed by another small consulate in Iraq and then one in Jidda, Saudi Arabia. In Jidda he served as a translator and interpreter as well as a political reporting officer and began accumulating area expertise at a time when the Yemen Civil War raged, with Saudi Arabia and Egypt pitted in conflict over the southwest corner of the Arabian peninsula. Murphy worked with Lyndon Johnson's envoy, Ellsworth Bunker, as liaison to the U.N. peacekeeping team. During this time he developed an impression of Gamal Abdel Nasser as an imperious leader who presented a variety of challenges to American interests in the region.

This negative image of Nasser was further reinforced during a subsequent tour in Jordan. Murphy arrived in Amman a year before the outbreak of the Six-Day War as head political reporting officer, a post he held throughout the Six-Day War as well. He was selected to remain as a key member of the reduced embassy staff after the evacuation of most embassy personnel during the hostilities, which occurred when Nasser forced an abrupt showdown with Israel that drew Jordan and Syria into the devastating conflict as well. He remained as an assistant to Ambassador Findley Burns during the crisis and as a result was awarded the Department of State's Superior Honor Award in 1968.

After a total of thirteen years of Middle East posts, and broad experience, Murphy returned to Washington and was eventually assigned the position of country director for Arabian peninsula affairs. Following the abrupt British announcement that it was ending its commitment "east of Suez," there was a broad reevaluation of the American commitment in the Arabian peninsula. The decision was made to broaden American representation among the emerging emirates of the Persian Gulf and the southern Arabian peninsula. The British withdrawal came at a time when America's vital national interest was to maintain access to a stable and secure oil supply, and Murphy directed the expansion of the American presence as five new missions opened in the region.

In 1971 Murphy was offered his first ambassadorial appointment to what was then America's smallest foreign embassy, Nouakchott, Mauritania, a decade after its independence from the French but in the midst of a tragic drought. He oversaw an expanded program of food aid that airlifted emergency grain shipments to remote nomadic tribes facing starvation. This operation gained goodwill for the United States at a time when African nationalism was increasingly a force to be reckoned with. Because Murphy had done well in his first ambassadorship, his position at Nouakchott was followed by a series of increasingly important posts.

Murphy arrived in Syria in 1974 as the first ambassador after diplomatic relations were broken after the Six-Day War, as a major effort was undertaken to normalize relations after the October 1973 war. There was little to build on, as a U.S. Interests Section had been reestablished only a month prior to his arrival. In August 1974 Secretary of State Henry Kissinger conducted high-level meetings with the Syrian Foreign Minister in Washington, while the Ford administration pushed a Middle East foreign aid package through Congress. At the same time, Murphy laid the groundwork for reopening the U.S. AID program, and a grain sales agreement was signed in late November 1974. Perhaps as a result, a visit by Soviet leader Leonid Brezhnev was canceled.

During his four years in Damascus Murphy was also occupied with serious human rights issues, in particular, the plight of Syrian Jews and their access to the West, an issue that both the Ford and Carter administrations continually pressed on President Hafez al-Assad. After much effort by Murphy, Assad reluctantly allowed the emigration of a few Syrian Jewish women.

Although the Kissinger shuttle diplomacy was in full operation during these years, discussions between Assad and Murphy over a demilitarized zone between Syrian and Israeli troops on the Golan Heights dragged on. An effort to promote Israeli-Syrian disengagement was overtaken by events when Egyptian leader Anwar Sadat arrived in Jerusalem and American diplomacy focused increasingly on bilateral Egyptian-Israeli issues. Assad's escalating criticism of Sadat significantly reduced congressional support for subsequent aid packages, and U.S.-Syrian relations descended to a chilly level.

In an abrupt career shift Murphy was next given an out-of-area assignment to the Philippines. Ambassador Murphy arrived at Manila in 1978, when the Philippines had been under martial law for eight years and the aging regime of Ferdinand Marcos was in difficulty. At the time tensions between Marcos and various leftist or Communist liberation groups were high. Murphy arrived with instructions to support U.S.-Marcos ties and to maintain the fundamental U.S. interest, access to military and naval bases on the islands. At the same time, he was under pressure from Marcos to continue the close relationship with the United States.

Within a few months of his arrival terrorism escalated against the Marcos regime. In October 1980 a convention of 3,500 American travel agents at Manila was threatened by the April 6 Liberation Movement. The convention opened with Marcos and Ambassador Murphy present, but was disrupted when a bomb exploded inside the convention center, injuring ten Americans and eighteen Filipinos. Subsequently Marcos rounded up and jailed a number of opposition leaders, including Benigno Aquino. In spite of these events, Marcos continued to press for U.S. support for his faltering regime.

In July 1981 the ambassador to Saudi Arabia abruptly resigned, and Murphy was called back to Washington to replace him. Secretary of State Alexander Haig offered Murphy the post at a time of crisis in U.S.–Saudi Arabian relations, with the sale of AWACS (Airborne Warning and Control System) aircraft to Saudi Arabia in jeopardy. Secretary of State Haig assigned Murphy to work with the Saudi government, which was deeply concerned over the possible failure of the effort, while the Reagan administration mustered congressional support. The transfer of AWACS aircraft to Saudi Arabia was strenuously opposed by Israeli Prime Minister Menachem Begin. Israel saw the sale to Saudi Arabia as a threat to its security and argued that AWACS was a defensive system but had offensive potential. Murphy argued that it was needed by an American ally in the Persian Gulf, and the contract was revised to include conditions: Israel was assured that limits would be placed on the aircrafts' range, and the Saudi Arabian government agreed to the presence of some American crew members.

Following the approval of the AWACS sale by the Senate, Murphy remained in Saudi Arabia, negotiating with the Saudi government for its support as the United States attempted to extricate the Palestine Liberation Organization (PLO) from Beirut, Lebanon. As the U.S. position in Lebanon deteriorated, the U.S. embassy in Beirut was bombed and Murphy was dispatched to lead the investigation and evacuation effort for the Department of State.

In 1983 Secretary of State George Shultz appointed Murphy to the top geographical post for Middle East affairs, assistant secretary of state for Near Eastern and South Asian affairs (NEA), spanning a broad region from India to Morocco. Murphy became the first of the new generation of Middle East area specialists to serve in that post and worked with a secretary of state who had knowledge of the region and was focused on its problems. He served in that position from 1983 through January 1989.

As assistant secretary, he was immediately confronted with a number of serious foreign policy problems, including the bombing of the U.S. embassy at Beirut, the Iran-Iraq War, and the war in Afghanistan. Linked with these issues were the problems of Pakistan's nuclear capability, the Lebanese civil war, the Arab-Israeli conflict, and the Palestinian Intifada. His professional and personal goal was to work with Secretary Shultz to open negotiations on a comprehensive peace settlement for the Arab-Israeli conflict, and he often traveled with two portfolios, as assistant secretary and as Shultz's personal envoy. The hallmark of his diplomatic style was a low-key, even wry, approach that Shultz appreciated.

The most serious concern focused on the Persian Gulf, where the Iran-Iraq War had raged since 1980 and would continue until 1988. The war was in the background of every policy decision, and the continued hostilities had increasingly raised questions about the potential scope of the war and the security of nations friendly to the United States as well as the security of the oil supply as tankers traversed the Persian gulf.

A particularly vexing dilemma was what U.S. position to take between the two combatants during their long conflict, and how to protect America's vital interest. Murphy and others in the Department of State attempted to devise a strategy that balanced both sides while honoring the security requests of a number of Arab states concerned over the spread of a conflict in which over a million combatants eventually died. The department ultimately tilted to support of Iraq as Secretary Shultz, along with Secretary of Defense Caspar Weinberger and Murphy, opposed arms sales to Iran. For many in the Reagan administration, it was particularly important to prevent the revolutionary Iranian regime of the Ayatollah Khomeini from emerging triumphant.

Others, particularly in the National Security Council staff, opposed this policy and promoted increasingly close military and political ties with Iran. Many Gulf nations that had formerly feared Saddam Hussein argued that he had changed and encouraged the United States to aid the Iraqis rather than allow an Iranian victory. Murphy viewed Hussein with some distrust, but increasingly heeded the Arab Gulf states that argued that the Iraqi regime was less of a threat than Iran.

Over time, the Reagan administration was more deeply fractured as Robert McFarlane, Oliver North, and other NSC staffers conducted their own ad hoc policies exterior to normal lines of policy. When secret contacts were undertaken to provide arms as part of the Iran-Contra effort, McFarlane, North, and Howard Teicher secretly requested and received funding for the Nicaraguan contras from Saudi Arabia, without the knowledge of either Secretary Shultz or Assistant Secretary Murphy. Secretary Shultz was kept in the dark until McFarlane was forced by events to inform him, although he then kept Murphy in the dark on U.S. involvement. The Reagan administration promoted a policy of supporting its long-time allies in the Gulf, Saudi Arabia and Kuwait, and Murphy was assigned to organize the reflagging of Kuwaiti oil tankers to protect the supply of oil during the conflict in the Persian Gulf, a policy that he was called upon to repeatedly defend under heavy congressional criticism.

Murphy was sent on a number of diplomatic missions as Shultz's personal envoy, both in the peace process and following the Israeli invasion of Lebanon. In 1985 Secretary Shultz dispatched him on a series of regional shuttles to arrange what Shultz referred to as "the Murphy meeting" to be the first step to implement the Reagan peace initiative. In his memoirs, *Turmoil and Triumph*, Secretary Shultz recalled the importance of Murphy's task to arrange a high-level meeting to pave the way for peace talks. This process continued for months as Assistant Secretary Murphy and his team forged ahead to bring Israeli and Jordanian teams together as a precursor to direct negotiations. This was an attempt to draw the Jordanians into Shultz's peace effort and open a new level of negotiations in which Shultz could then perhaps achieve a breakthrough.

Although Murphy did succeed in getting qualified support from King Hussein, the Jordanian terms included a PLO component and other reservations that Israel viewed with pessimism. Ultimately the effort failed to bring the major regional parties to the peace table because Israeli Prime Minister Shimon Peres regarded the Palestinian members of the delegation as too closely linked with the PLO and Reagan remained determined to stick closely to the letter of the U.S. agreement not to negotiate with the PLO until it formally recognized U.N. Resolution 242 and Israel's right to exist. Shultz then abandoned the idea. The final event that torpedoed Murphy's efforts was a congressional resolution banning arms sales to Jordan until it began direct negotiations with Israel.

As the Iran-Iraq War dragged on, the State Department and the NSC remained at loggerheads over the U.S. position, and NSC aides McFarlane, North, and Teicher designed a plan to gain release of American hostages taken in Lebanon, promote closer ties with Iran, and undercut Iraq, while funneling profits from covert arms sales to the anti-Sandinista rebels of Nicaragua, known as the contras. Throughout this period Murphy had argued against arms sales to Iran.

The Lebanese government faced a crisis in 1988 when tensions threatened to explode into renewed civil war over the 1988 presidential elections. Disagreement had broken out between the numerous Lebanese factions and the Syrians over the slate of candidates. Murphy launched a series of diplomatic shuttles between Damascus and Beirut in an attempt to stave off the collapse of the Lebanese government as Maronite Christian candidates overwhelmed the fragile system and Syrian president Hafez al-Assad emerged as the power broker. The Assad regime finally insisted on limiting the number of candidates to one, and in spite of Murphy's efforts, Lebanon once more sank into conflict.

Arabic-language specialists within the State Department, referred to by some as Arabists, have been criticized for having an unrealistically pro-Arab bias. In fact, Murphy's diplomatic efforts on behalf of the AWACS sale and his advice have proven accurate: the Saudis proved to be valued allies during the Gulf War. The ''Murphy meetings'' did succeed in drawing the Jordanian-Palestinian parties into the peace process and might have achieved some results if Secretary Shultz had agreed to go forward with the Jordanians' reserved consent to his proposal. Murphy's efforts to draw Syria into the peace process after the October 1973 war had the potential for resolving problems that have since festered into the intractable dilemma over the Golan Heights.

Murphy correctly predicted in a secret study written in 1985 that any U.S. operations in the region ''will likely depend on Saudi cooperation and support'' and argued in favor of arms sales to Jordan as a way to avert their resorting to Soviet weaponry. American aid, military and nonmilitary, did succeed in limiting Soviet influence in the Middle East, particularly in Jordan and to a lesser extent in Syria.

Throughout his career Murphy emphasized the need for American policy to work toward a comprehensive solution for the Arab-Israeli conflict, and it is ironic that it was only in 1989, as his term as assistant secretary of state drew to a close, that the United States appeared ready to make a breakthrough in the Middle East. In part, the Palestinian Intifada forced a change in the status quo. For Murphy, in the aftermath of rising resistance Israel had to rethink its position on the Occupied Territories, Palestinians took a new look at their society, and there was a change in the peace process. But despite Murphy's having finally succeeded in getting the Palestine Liberation Organization to meet Israeli conditions for recognition and to accept Israel's right to exist in 1988, a breakthrough in the peace process was not achieved during his time as assistant secretary for Near East and South Asian affairs.

In 1985 Murphy was awarded the rank of career ambassador. Retiring from the Foreign Service in 1989, he briefly headed the Middle East Institute. Over the years he has published a number of opposite-editorial pieces. In the aftermath of the Persian Gulf War he proposed a postwar plan for the Middle East in the hope of achieving a breakthrough between Arabs and Israelis. In recent years he has held the position of senior fellow for the Middle East at the Council on Foreign Relations in New York. From that post he has worked to promote economic progress under the 1993 Arab-Israeli Declaration of Peace and at the Casablanca Conference on regional economic cooperation.

Works by Richard W. Murphy

Many of Murphy's major addresses and interviews as assistant secretary of state for NEA, 1983–1989, were reprinted in the *Department of State Bulletin*.

"Sell the Saudis Defense Equipment." Op-Ed, *New York Times*, May 20, 1986.
"What Now in the Middle East? Can a Superpower Help Solve the Arab-Israeli Puzzle?" *World Monitor*, February 1989, 38–45.
"Mideast: Strategies for Stability." *World Monitor*, October 1990, 66–68.
"Remaking the Mideast . . . His Blueprint for Seizing Postwar Momentum to Build Political Stability." *World Monitor*, April 1991, 28–33.
"Give Mideast Talks a Boost." Op-Ed, *New York Times*, February 21, 1992.
"Sitting Down with Syria." Op-Ed, *New York Times*, January 12, 1994, 21.

Works about Richard W. Murphy

Kaplan, Robert, *The Arabists: The Romance of an American Elite*. New York: Free Press, 1993.
———. "Tales from the Bazaar." *Atlantic*, August 1992.
Kraft, Joseph. "Those Arabists in the State Department." *New York Times Magazine*, November 7, 1971.
Sciolino, Elaine. "A Departing Envoy's Grim Afghan View." *New York Times*, January 30, 1989.
Shultz, George P. *Turmoil and Triumph: My Years as Secretary of State*. New York: Maxwell Macmillan International, 1993.

Solecki, John. "Arabists and the Myth." *Middle East Journal*, 44, no. 3 (Summer 1990), 446–57.
Waas, Murray, and Craig Unger. "Annals of Government: In the Loop: Bush's Secret Mission." *New Yorker*, November 2, 1992.

TERESA ANN THOMAS

WALTER HINES PAGE (1855–1918) served as Woodrow Wilson's ambassador to the United Kingdom during World War I. Noted for his staunch support for the British war effort, Page spent most of his time in London desperately trying to convince the American foreign policy establishment that the United States must join the Allied side in World War I (which he believed to be a righteous crusade) in order to destroy German militarism and to save the world for the English-speaking peoples. This millenarian view of World War I and an unrelenting effort to stay the decline of Anglo-American relations during the early years of the war ultimately compromised his credibility with Woodrow Wilson and undermined his effectiveness as ambassador.

Before Page developed his belief that world order depended upon Anglo-American cooperation, a desire to reform the backwardness of the American South dominated his life. From the time of his birth on August 15, 1855, in Cary, North Carolina, the ever-growing divide that separated the industrial North and the agrarian South profoundly conditioned how Page viewed the world. The physical destruction of the Civil War, the massive loss of life, and the humiliation of Reconstruction imbued him with a suspicion of Northerners. Notwithstanding this suspicion, Page never identified with the Confederacy nor with the institution of slavery; his overriding interest was to restore the South's standing in national life.

Page's antisecessionist sentiment and his aversion to Confederate romanticism are attributable to the lasting influence of his father, Allison Francis Page. Although Allison Page owned four slaves, he also held a dim view of Southern secessionist aspirations. As a moderate Whig, he very much favored the nationalist views of Henry Clay over John C. Calhoun's states' rights perspective, which dominated Southern political thought at the time. Allison Page's political views were not unusual in a state where plantation farming did not take hold as it did in the lower South. His nationalist views were rather typical of a hardworking businessman whose occupation rested in the lumber and turpentine-distilling businesses. He evidently considered the "peculiar institution" as an available system of labor rather than a foundational institution of the Southern way of life, and the idea of secession as a manifestly foolish ambition.

Notwithstanding the influence Allison Page had on his son's political outlook, Walter Page spent most of his childhood with his mother, Katherine Raboteau Page. Katherine Page, a devout Methodist who despised alcohol, tobacco, and strong language, had the greatest influence on Walter's childhood. He enjoyed a remarkably close relationship with his mother on account of the fact that he was often sick as a child and that he was also the firstborn child after Katherine Page had suffered two miscarriages. Educated to a level that most women of her day did not enjoy, Katherine Page taught Walter how to read and write and instilled in him a love for learning, particularly reading. He readily took to his mother's love for literature and began to read books at a voracious rate before the age of ten. During these early years he often spent hours reading in his grandfather's small musty library.

At the age of thirteen Page traveled to Mebane, North Carolina, to attend the Bingham School, a military school that was considered one of the state's finest. Two years at Bingham left a lasting impression on him. As the son of a man who did little to advance the Confederate cause, he drew scorn from other students, many of whom had fathers who were high-ranking members of the Confederate officer corps. Nevertheless, Page excelled in his studies and eventually won the affection of his classmates. In 1870 he returned home to attend a coeducational school his father had helped to establish.

One year later, at the age of sixteen, Page began his collegiate education by enrolling at Trinity College, the state's only Methodist institution. An underfunded institution with a less-than-challenging course of study, Trinity did little to inspire Page's intellectual growth. Dissatisfied with Trinity, he transferred to Randolph-Macon College in January 1873. At Randolph-Macon Page found the intellectual challenge that Trinity lacked. He won distinctions in most of his subjects and began to favor a career in journalism rather than one in the Methodist ministry. His declining interest in the ministry became a major point of contention with his father, who had sent him to college with the expectation that he would enter the ministry upon graduation. Despite his father's disappointment, Page continued his education as a graduate student at the newly opened Johns Hopkins University in Baltimore.

Page's arrival in Baltimore in 1876, at the age of twenty, marked an important point in the young man's life. He discovered in Baltimore—a city much larger than any place he had lived—a vibrant intellectual atmosphere that was both exciting and intimidating. Page found his program of classical studies to be difficult and began to question the quality of his preparation for the program. He withdrew from Johns Hopkins halfway through his second year on the ground of illness; however, his lack of commitment to the rigorous course of study also figured prominently in his decision. Although Page did not earn a degree, his two years in Baltimore precipitated a substantial shift in values: his religious beliefs were significantly eroded as a result of his training in critical scientific method. Religion ceased to play an important role in his life thereafter.

Shortly after returning home in February 1878 to recuperate, Page accepted an appointment to teach English literature at the University of North Carolina. Later that year he accepted a professorship in English at the Boys' School in Louisville, Kentucky. Despite the fact that he was well suited to teaching—indeed, he performed admirably in both positions—the profession did not satisfy Page's greater aspirations. In 1879 he resigned his teaching position and set out to launch his literary career.

Page's first foray into the literary world left him half-owner of a small Southern cultural magazine, *The Age*. When this first venture failed one year later, Page secured a position as an editor of a small newspaper in St. Joseph's,

Missouri. Page's daily tasks were rather ordinary; however, editing the *St. Joseph's Gazette* provided valuable experience for a young man trying to break into the publishing world. In 1881 he landed a job with a well-respected newspaper, the *New York World*. Two years later he quit as a result of a dispute over journalistic philosophy with the newspaper's new owner, Joseph Pulitzer. Jobless, Page moved back to Raleigh, North Carolina, in 1883 and founded his own newspaper, the *State Chronicle*. Page used the new newspaper to advance his New South agenda: greater sympathy toward blacks and a critical view of the war, Southern politicians, and sectionalism were hallmarks of the *State Chronicle*. Not surprisingly, Page's New South convictions were a constant source of tension in Raleigh. In February 1885 he resigned his position, apparently out of frustration with the deeply entrenched sectionalism of Southern life. Page's resignation from the *State Chronicle* precipitated another journey north to New York.

Although Page left North Carolina frustrated by Southern backwardness, he continued his New South campaign by sending a series of letters to the *State Chronicle* that extolled the necessity of educational and agricultural reform and, to a lesser extent, industrialization. At the same time, he quickly built an esteemed reputation in New York for his editing skills, which led to a long and successful career in the newspaper and magazine business. Starting as the business manager and continuing later as the editor, Page transformed a new journal, *The Forum*, into a widely read and respected publication. After eight years with *The Forum*, Page joined the *Atlantic Monthly*—the country's premier literary magazine—and became its editor in 1898. Late in 1899 he left the magazine and after an unsuccessful publishing venture announced the formation of a publishing company with Frank Doubleday. Page remained at Doubleday, Page, and Company until Woodrow Wilson appointed him ambassador to Great Britain in 1913.

Page first met Wilson while working for the *New York World* in September 1882. The two men took a liking to one another at the outset; they shared similar views on politics and government, and they both, being from the South, despised Southern provincialism. Wilson immediately impressed Page, who later remarked that the future president had one of the finest minds in America. Over the years Page maintained his ties with Wilson insofar as his role in the publishing world led him to frequently seek out Wilson for interesting manuscripts. Page's high opinion of Wilson prompted him to enthusiastically assist his drive for the presidency. Page became a central figure early in the presidential campaign as he skillfully used the pages of *World's Work* to promote Wilson's virtues. Once Wilson captured the White House, Page was one of many supporters who benefited from the spoils of victory.

Page almost became a member of Wilson's cabinet as secretary of the interior; however, complaints about a Southerner heading the department responsible for administering pensions of Union army veterans provoked Wilson to abandon the idea. On the advice of Wilson's closest advisor, Colonel Edward House, the president appointed Page to be ambassador to Great Britain on March 26, 1913. Page's appointment drew little attention except from himself: reflecting on his lack of experience, the ambassador-to-be questioned his own qualifications. Nonetheless, he accepted the job with unbridled enthusiasm since he was eager to serve the new president.

Page's first year in London passed without much fanfare. After presenting his credentials to King George V on May 30, 1913, Page set out to find a home and to reorganize his staff. During the busy summer social season the new ambassador spent most of his time attending banquets and delivering speeches. On the diplomatic front the only significant matters of concern were Britain's recognition of a military government in Mexico and its protest over Panama Canal tolls. London resolved the Mexican problem by withdrawing its support for the new Mexican government out of respect for U.S. interests in the Western Hemisphere. On the issue of Panama, Wilson quietly worked toward repealing the toll legislation that disadvantaged British merchant shipping. Perhaps the greatest difficulty during the ambassador's first year in London was his personal expenses. Once Page conveyed to the president that his ambassadorial financial commitments were out of all proportion with his official salary, Wilson quickly arranged for private sources to cover the shortfall.

The onset of World War I the following year shattered Page's socially dominated routine and placed burdens upon him that surely hastened his death. Page simultaneously considered the war as a dispiriting madness and as a righteous crusade. He initially approved of Wilson's policy of neutrality; he viewed neutrality as a way for the United States to assume a position of international leadership by avoiding the destruction and expense of war. However, a more accurate picture of Page's conception of the war is revealed in how he viewed the belligerents. In addition to his well-known disposition toward Britain, Page regarded France with ambivalence and Russia with plain distrust. Page's belief that English-speaking peoples were destined to rule the world and that Anglo-American cooperation presupposed global peace and order dominated his thinking for the duration of the war. Promoting the cause of Anglo-American unity ultimately replaced Southern reform as Page's most passionate objective in life. This resolute and rather pedantic world view also compromised Page's usefulness as an agent of the American government; his diplomatic assessments and advice were all hopelessly colored by his grand view of Anglo-American destiny.

After the outbreak of the war Page's most immediate task was to assist in repatriating American citizens caught in the war. The ambassador is credited with doing a remarkable job in marshaling the resources required to return sixty thousand people to the United States. As ambassador of the leading neutral country, Page also performed diplomatic duties for Britain's opponents; shortly after the outbreak of hostilities, Germany and Austria-Hungary transferred to the American ambassador responsibility for their diplomatic missions. As well, Britain's burgeoning requests for war materials dramatically increased the ambassador's work. Despite the sudden increase in responsibility and a paucity of staff and resources, Page's admirable performance during the early months of the war won Wilson's appreciation and gratitude.

A series of disputes, all related to British naval policy, German submarine warfare, and American neutrality, tarnished Page's early successes and undermined his credibility with his superiors in Washington. The first source of tension concerned an American request that Britain comply with the Declaration of London of 1909, which governed the seizure of neutral cargoes during times of war. Britain refused persistent American requests that it accede to the declaration out of fear that neutral-country commerce would decisively favor the German war effort. Page sent several messages to the president and to the State Department explaining that the American request was futile and ill advised. He also expressed in frank terms his disregard for Secretary of State William Jennings Bryan and his counsel, Robert Lansing. Page believed that Bryan and Lansing did not fully understand the nature of the war and that they were collectively responsible for subverting what the ambassador believed to be the important objective of American foreign policy, namely, the preservation of Anglo-American cooperation. In spite of Page's desperate and rather undiplomatic pleas, the United States continued for some time to press Britain to accept the Declaration of London, and the Royal Navy continued to seize American merchant ships.

The content and tenor of Page's messages irreversibly harmed his standing throughout Washington. Obviously Page's conception of neutrality did not correspond with official American policy, and the substance of his remarks led Lansing, House, and Wilson to believe that Page sympathized too closely with Britain. Among members of the State Department, Page's reputation declined in proportion to the intensity of his denunciations of Bryan and Lansing. Wilson expressed in a letter his concern with Page's behavior by reminding the ambassador that the president must account for public opinion in making foreign policy decisions. At the request of the president, House asked Page to refrain from expressing further unneutral sentiment. It is evident that Page's messages had some effect on Wilson's decision to soften his position regarding the Declaration of London, but this influence was purchased at a substantial cost to his credibility. The damage had been done: Page's seemingly uncritical support of Britain steadily reduced the ambassador's influence as the war progressed.

As the war dragged on, Wilson's commitment to a policy of neutrality hardened Page's support for the British cause and provoked a stream of ever more terse correspondence to the president and his advisors. Wilson's failure to sever diplomatic relations with Germany after the sinking of the Cunard liner *Lusitania* on May 7, 1915, set off another series of strongly worded messages that further diminished his reputation. Page desperately tried to convince Wilson to enter the war on the side of the Allies and even went so far as to suggest to House that such a decision would be good for the Democratic Party and for Wilson's chances of reelection. Wilson's preference for relying on strongly

worded diplomatic notes to protest the sinking of the *Lusitania* disappointed
Page; he believed anything short of the use of military force to be a waste of
time.

Page's sense of dejection that followed the *Lusitania* incident worsened when
Anglo-American relations continued to deteriorate and his standing with Wilson
underwent a sharp decline. Believing that Page identified too closely with British
interests, Wilson stopped reading the ambassador's frequent dispatches by the
end of 1915. In addition to Page's troubles with the president, a series of events
on the diplomatic front exacerbated his depression and isolation. He began to
question Wilson's leadership after Lansing delivered to London a curtly worded
note protesting the impact Britain's blockade had on American commerce. Page
responded to the note by advising Washington that only an immediate break of
relations with Germany and Austria would salvage British respect for the United
States. Four months later, in February 1916, a confrontation with House ended
with Page declining to participate in an initiative that might have secured peace
through mediation and uttering an angry denunciation of American policy in
general and of Wilson in particular.

After the confrontation with House, Wilson decided to bring Page home so
that he could observe public opinion firsthand. This, the president thought,
would restore Page's sense of perspective with regard to American foreign policy objectives. Unfortunately, Page misinterpreted Wilson's intent; he arrived in
Washington in August 1916 under the mistaken impression that he would be
consulting with the president. Page did have one opportunity to express his well-
known views to Wilson; however, the president and his advisors ignored the
ambassador for most of his visit. In the end the trip was a failure: Page did not
moderate his pro-British views, his ever-passionate pleas for intervention convinced no one, and he returned to London more disillusioned than before his
departure. The visit only reinforced Page's belief that Wilson and House did
not understand war.

When Page arrived back in London in October, he faced more diplomatic
friction with his hosts. By late 1916 the British blockade had become a major
source of difficulty. In an effort to protect American commerce, Congress passed
legislation—with Wilson's support—that empowered the president to retaliate
against the British blockade. Undeterred, Britain hardened its position by tight-
ening the blockade; it began intercepting U.S. mail bound for neutral ports and
began withholding coal from American captains who refused to provide assurances that they were bound for friendly ports. As expected, Page responded with
a flurry of messages in which he expressed the futility of pressing the blockade
issue; he also advised patience and understanding for the British position.

Page's depression did not last much longer. The United States broke relations
with Germany in February 1917 and declared war the following April. America's entry into the war vindicated Page with the British public, but his standing
with Wilson and the State Department never recovered. By this time Wilson
routinely bypassed Page in favor of House in the conduct of Anglo-American

diplomacy. Moreover, Page himself had lost much of his appetite for the job; after his disappointing visit to Washington six months earlier, he decided to resign after the presidential election in 1916. Only America's declaration of war and, ironically, a request from Wilson convinced him to stay on. The remainder of the war proved to be relatively uneventful for Page as he became an increasingly unimportant figure. Washington automatically discounted his dispatches because he was perceived to be overly pro-British, and Britain's ambassador in Washington warned London not to take Page's statements as being representative of American policy.

Page's declining health also reduced his role after the United States entered the war. He was forced to take a substantial amount of time off and on August 1, 1918, notified the president that he was unable to continue as ambassador. Near death, Page arrived in New York on October 12; two months later, on December 21, he died in North Carolina with his family by his side.

Page won enormous respect from his hosts, and British newspapers declared him to be a great ambassador. However, a more critical examination of his role during the war reveals that he actually had very little influence with the Wilson administration. His greatest influence came early in the war, before he alienated the president with his rather ill-tempered correspondence that pleaded for U.S. intervention on the side of the Allies. His failure to win greater influence is attributable to his proclivity toward identifying more closely with Britain than with the stated interests of his own government. Page believed that he was acting in the best interest of humanity and consequently grew rather unsympathetic to the American policies that he was supposed to be representing. Thus Walter Page's ambassadorship is best remembered for his desperate attempts to promote Anglo-American cooperation, his conviction that the United States must help destroy German militarism, and his millenarian view of the Anglo-American destiny that depended upon the successful prosecution of the war.

Works about Walter Hines Page

Cooper, John Milton. *Walter Hines Page: The Southerner as American, 1855–1918.* Chapel Hill: University of North Carolina Press, 1977.

Gregory, Ross. *Walter Hines Page: Ambassador to the Court of St. James.* Lexington: University Press of Kentucky, 1970.

Hendrick, Burton J. *The Life and Letters of Walter H. Page.* 3 vols. Garden City, NY: Doubleday, Page, and Company, 1924.

Safford, Jeffrey J. *Wilsonian Maritime Diplomacy, 1913–1921.* New Brunswick, NJ: Rutgers University Press, 1978.

Willson, Beckles. *America's Ambassadors to England (1785–1928).* Freeport, NY: Books for Libraries Press, 1969.

Woodward, David R. *Trial by Friendship: Anglo-American Relations, 1917–1918.* Lexington: University Press of Kentucky, 1993.

WILLIAM W. BAIN

THOMAS R. PICKERING (1931–   ) is a senior career

ambassador considered by many to be the finest U.S. diplomat of his generation and one whose postings reflect some of the most important concerns of American foreign policy since the 1970s.

Pickering was born on November 5, 1931, in Orange, New Jersey. His educational training included an A.B. in medieval European history from Bowdoin College in Maine in 1953 and a master's degree from the Fletcher School of Law and Diplomacy in 1954. Attending on a Fulbright Scholarship, he earned a second M.A. in British Commonwealth history from the University of Melbourne in 1956. Following three years in the navy, Pickering joined the Foreign Service in 1959. He was involved in disarmament issues until 1964, when he became principal officer in Zanzibar and then deputy chief of mission in Tanzania between 1967 and 1969. Returning to Washington, Pickering served as deputy director of the Bureau of Political-Military Affairs until 1973, when Secretary of State William Rogers appointed him executive secretary of the department. He continued to hold this post under Rogers's successor, Henry Kissinger. As Kissinger's special assistant, Pickering accompanied the secretary on his early forays into Middle East diplomacy. This service in part earned Pickering his first ambassadorship to Jordan in February 1974.

Pickering began his duties in Amman in the midst of a U.S. diplomatic whirlwind. Following the October 1973 Arab-Israeli War and the subsequent oil embargo, Kissinger sought to alleviate tensions in the region. While he successfully brokered agreements between Israel and two of its neighbors, Egypt and Syria, progress on the Israeli-Jordanian front remained elusive. This lack of progress was due to the deeper Israeli attachment to the occupied Jordanian territory (the West Bank and East Jerusalem) as well as the territories' linkage with the Palestinian question. Yet to the United States, the Jordanian component of the process was vital to the success of the larger peace plan. Even with the continued rise of Palestinian nationalism and the designation of the Palestine Liberation Organization (PLO) as the ''sole legitimate representative of the Palestinian people,'' the United States preferred Jordan as the spokesman for the Palestinians. Known as the ''Jordanian option,'' this attitude remained a hallmark of U.S. policy despite initial Carter administration endeavors in 1977 to provide a measure of PLO participation at a reconstructed Geneva peace conference. Much of Pickering's efforts therefore centered on reconciling Jordanian efforts to regain the territories with some measure of Palestinian control over their own affairs, perhaps within a Jordanian-dominated confederation.

During the 1977–1978 period other issues posed difficulties to Pickering's tenure in Amman. In February 1977 the ambassador was occupied with the fallout over revelations that King Hussein had received CIA funds for the past two decades. In exchange, the king and other Jordanian officials provided intelligence information to Washington. Pickering also devoted the latter part of his Amman service to negotiating the details of Jordanian access to U.S. missile air defense systems, a deal opposed by Israel. Both the disclosure of the CIA payments and the difficulties surrounding the weapons transfer strained the traditionally close U.S.-Jordanian relationship. However, as Pickering in 1978 moved to his next assignment, Hussein touted him as "the best American ambassador I have ever dealt with."

Pickering returned to Washington in September 1978 as assistant secretary of state for oceans and international environmental and scientific affairs. During his term as assistant secretary, Pickering was engaged in issues as varied as international whaling, nuclear nonproliferation programs, and the final negotiations for the controversial Law of the Sea Convention (UNCLOS III). With the change in presidential administrations, Pickering was reassigned overseas to Nigeria in 1981.

During Pickering's tenure Nigeria was viewed more as an opportunity for U.S. foreign policy than as a problem. His service coincided with that country's Second Republic. Nigeria had moved from thirteen years of military rule to elected civilian control in 1979. The ambassador's twin challenges were to deepen the roots of these democratic processes and institutions as well as to encourage American business opportunities in Nigeria. In large part due to the U.S. reliance on Nigerian oil, Washington had a $10-billion balance-of-trade deficit with Lagos. Consequently, Pickering was behind efforts to launch the Nigerian-U.S. Business Council, which brought together businessmen from the two countries. Yet while the United States sought to promote American products, the world recession of the early 1980s hit Nigeria hard, especially with revenues from oil declining over 50 percent by 1983. Among the political issues handled by Pickering was a joint U.S.-Nigerian effort regarding the civil war in Chad. Both governments opposed the Libyan-backed forces as well as Libyan attempts to annex the Auzou Strip. Nigeria was the main architect of a 4,800-member Organization of African Unity peacekeeping force dispatched to Chad in December 1981 to help Hissene Habre consolidate power. Otherwise, the Reagan administration's preoccupation with problems in the Horn and in southern Africa—largely tied to the Cold War—left little room for a nuanced Nigerian policy.

Pickering's confirmation hearings for his next post in El Salvador were delayed at the request of Senator Jesse Helms (Republican of North Carolina). Helms sought to question Pickering on his role in the Law of the Sea Conference and on family-planning programs in the developing world in which he had been involved during the Carter administration. The nomination was also seemingly part of the larger ideological tug-of-war between conservatives such as Helms and Representative Jack Kemp (Republican of New York) and George Shultz's State Department over the general direction of foreign relations, particularly with regard to Central America. The congressional conservatives argued that political appointees rather than career diplomats were needed to carry out President Reagan's foreign policy. The Senate eventually confirmed Pickering, and he began his duties as ambassador in September 1983.

U.S. attitudes toward the situation in El Salvador were in flux at the time of his posting. A four-year left-wing rebel insurgency—led by the Farabundo Marti National Liberation Front (FMLN) and supported by Nicaragua—coupled with a right-wing–dominated government linked to paramilitary squads responsible for the deaths of thousands, complicated U.S. efforts to encourage a democratic transition in that country. This democratic transition was a chief focus of Reagan's Central American policy. Pickering's two immediate predecessors (Robert White and Deane Hinton) ran afoul of the Reagan administration with outspoken condemnation of the death-squad activity. However, as the abuses increased, Shultz signaled a shift in U.S. policy and gave Pickering wide latitude, which included issuing anti–death-squad statements and working to discover who was responsible for the deaths of American nuns and labor leaders in El Salvador. The ambassador's actions were bolstered by a late 1983 visit from Vice President George Bush. Bush forcefully took on the death-squad activity associated with the interim government and threatened the withdrawal of U.S. military support if this activity did not cease. Despite continuation of the civil war, presidential elections were held as scheduled in two rounds of voting in March and May 1984. Moderate Christian Democrat Jose Napoleon Duarte defeated the Nationalist Republican Alliance (ARENA) candidate Roberto D'Aubuisson, reputedly the principal architect of death-squad activities. Duarte was his country's first civilian president in fifty-three years. The avidly anti-Communist D'Aubuisson and his American supporters such as Helms questioned the validity of the electoral results and implied that the United States had fixed them in favor of Duarte. Between the two rounds of voting Helms wrote a scathing letter to Reagan urging the president to dismiss Pickering and labeled the ambassador "the purchasing agent" for covertly funneling CIA monies to Duarte (reportedly $1.4 million). It was later revealed that in fact the U.S. government had provided funds to Duarte and other candidates in order to offset ARENA's large financial advantage and thus to level the political playing field. A copy of Helms's letter was leaked to D'Aubuisson, and shortly thereafter Pickering experienced death threats. In May 1984 Washington sent Ambassador-at-Large General Vernon Walters to warn D'Aubuisson that he would be held personally responsible if Pickering was murdered. Walters also lectured the ARENA leader about the proper role of loyal opposition. Meanwhile, back in Washington, Helms was called on the carpet by the White House and hastily appointed as part of the official delegation to Duarte's inauguration to underscore support for the electoral outcome. The senator also privately reiterated Walters's warnings to D'Aubuisson while in El Salvador. Not surprisingly, Pickering remained under heavy guard throughout his tenure as ambassador. In January 1985 the ambassador cabled Washington that D'Aubuisson was plotting against Duarte. He cautioned against giving the ARENA leader a U.S. visa, fearing that this would allow D'Aubuisson an opportunity to meet with supporters in Miami and launch his plans. Because of the continued threat of assassination, Pickering's tour of duty was cut short. He was reposted to Israel in June 1985.

A by-product of Pickering's time as ambassador to El Salvador surfaced in July 1987 during the congressional Iran-Contra hearings. He testified that in December 1984 a Salvadorian diplomat had given him a document listing $1 million worth of military equipment that the contras were going to receive from unnamed foreign sources. The diplomat asked Pickering to pass this information to officials in the U.S. government working with the contras, who might be able to facilitate delivery of these donations. Pickering passed this list directly to the person he thought was dealing with contra affairs, Oliver North at the National Security Council, without contacting the State Department. Pickering testified that he viewed his role as ambassador to forward information and not to make judgments regarding the information. He delivered this document to North because he believed that North was legally working within the framework of the Boland Amendment, which prohibited U.S. government assistance to the contras. In retrospect, he said that the list should have been given to the State Department first. Pickering also acknowledged reading intelligence reports weeks after meeting North that suggested that the contras had indeed received the materials contained on the list.

A national unity government was in place when Pickering arrived in Israel. Elections in 1984 had produced a political stalemate that forced the left-of-center Labor Party and the right-of-center Likud Bloc into an uneasy coalition. Traditionally the United States had favored Labor's view of the Middle East. The ambassador's dilemma was to encourage the Labor positions without ignoring Likud views and being accused of interfering in Israeli domestic affairs. This task proved even more difficult because the coalition agreement provided that the prime ministership would rotate between the two parties.

In late 1985 Labor Prime Minister Shimon Peres spoke positively about some form of international sponsorship for the Arab-Israeli peace process. The Arab states had long advocated this idea, but it had long been opposed by Israel, especially Peres's coalition partner. A series of clandestine meetings between Israelis and Jordanians were held throughout 1985 and 1986. Their intensity increased as Amman severed ties with the PLO in February 1986 and introduced, with Israeli support, a $1.3-billion development plan for the West Bank and Gaza. Within the region Pickering encouraged these meetings, but the United States was skeptical of their success because of internal Israeli politics. Peres and Hussein met secretly in London in April 1987 and worked out details for an international conference that would include some measure of Palestinian participation. Despite this agreement, further progress was hampered by Likud's Yitzhak Shamir, who was now prime minister. Shamir continued to insist on direct negotiations without international involvement, an idea that was anathema to the Arab states.

Pickering's tenure as ambassador also coincided with numerous cleavages in the usually close relationship between the United States and Israel. In November

1985 a Jewish American, Jonathan Pollard, was arrested in Washington on charges of spying for Israel. Pickering was part of the effort to determine what information had been passed to the Israelis and to secure Tel Aviv's cooperation in recovering stolen documents. After a brief stalling period Israel cooperated and provided much of the information used to convict Pollard. A year later the Israeli-U.S. alliance was further strained with revelations of what became known as the Iran-Contra affair. Tel Aviv's role in the shipment of military equipment to Iran and the initial blame placed on it by the Reagan administration soured ties for some time.

Perhaps the deepest tensions between Washington and Tel Aviv occurred with the outbreak of the Palestinian uprising (Intifada) in December 1987. The scope of the unrest, coupled with media scenes of Israeli brutality regarding the Palestinian demonstrators, severely damaged Israel's image in the United States. Pickering both privately and publicly expressed concern over the human rights abuses. He gave a number of speeches that angered many among the Israeli right. The unrelenting Intifada forced Shultz to address the neglected peace process. He made a series of visits to the region in 1988 in a failed attempt to jump-start negotiations. However, by late 1988 the Intifada, Jordan's renunciation of claims to the West Bank, and the PLO's recognition of Israel prompted a dramatic shift in U.S. policy. In December Washington announced that it was opening a direct dialogue with the long-shunned PLO. It was one of Pickering's last duties as ambassador to inform the Israeli government of this policy change. Shamir denounced the U.S.-PLO dialogue as a dangerous blunder. Pickering left Israel with mixed reviews. While most Israelis viewed him favorably, in the words of a Likud ally, those on the right tended to see Pickering as ''a hostile ambassador of a friendly state.''

Rumors circulated throughout 1988 that Shultz was considering a shake-up in ambassadorial postings that would bring Pickering back to Washington as under secretary of state for management. The Reagan administration had already forwarded his replacement's name to the Senate for confirmation when Shultz changed his mind and decided to leave staffing decisions to the new president. President-elect George Bush in December 1988 tapped Pickering to be the U.S. ambassador to the United Nations, passing over possible conservative political appointees like Maureen Reagan, who was lobbying hard for the position. Pickering became only the second career officer (after Charles Yost) to be named U.N. ambassador. Unlike most of his predecessors, he would not have cabinet rank, raising speculation that he was there not to make policy but mainly to implement it.

Unlike his previous positions, the role of U.N. envoy thrust Pickering into a more prestigious and visible post. The job required contacts with 160 foreign governments at once, often under a press spotlight. At the time of his assignment the United Nations was just emerging from Cold War paralysis that stymied its usefulness. The Security Council, a captive of the superpower rivalry, began to function by 1989 as a more collegial body and offered the promise of making real contributions to international peace and security. In addition, Bush, himself a former U.N. ambassador, sought to reverse the Reagan administration's lack of commitment to, and funding of, the international organization.

During the early period of his posting Pickering dealt with numerous issues and conflicts. Israel's response to the Intifada and other Middle East problems continued to appear frequently on the Security Council agenda. Pickering also waged battles within the administration regarding the wisdom of certain U.S. policies—many times emerging on the losing side. Vice President Dan Quayle, for example, pressed hard for repeal of the 1975 General Assembly resolution equating Zionism with racism. Pickering argued that this would be difficult without movement on the Middle East peace process. However, the administration persisted in pressing the issue. While Pickering was an effective ambassador, the first eighteen months seemed to suggest that the lack of cabinet rank and direct access to the president and secretary of state had diminished the position within policymaking circles. Yet this changed dramatically with Iraq's August 2, 1990, invasion of Kuwait.

Once the Gulf crisis began, the U.N. Security Council became the focal point of international action against the Iraqi aggressor. The council responded swiftly and within hours of the invasion passed a series of increasingly harsh resolutions in a bid to reverse the Iraqi aggression. Concurrently with these events in New York, the U.S. government initiated its own policies to deal with the crisis and protect its interests and Gulf allies, chiefly Saudi Arabia. Pickering emerged as the point man to preserve international solidarity. Throughout August this responsibility proved difficult as the United Nations and Washington moved in different directions. For instance, Secretary of State James Baker's comment on August 12 that the United States would unilaterally interdict Iraqi commerce at sea threatened to undermine multilateral efforts. Pickering urged the administration to seek a measure of U.N. cover in order to keep the Security Council united against Iraq. Intensive diplomacy, with Bush and Baker working the phones to bring the Soviets and the Chinese on board and Pickering and the British U.N. ambassador in New York securing the support of other council members, produced Resolution 665. It charged member states with naval forces in the Gulf to enforce the trade embargo enacted against Iraq. Such authorization was the first of its kind outside of U.N. control and legitimized previous unilateral U.S. policy.

The unprecedented unity of the Security Council was forged first with agreement among the other permanent members: Britain, France, China, and the USSR. The permanent five scrutinized draft resolutions word by word. Following this consensus, Pickering made sure that the temporary European and Western states on the council, such as Canada and Finland, were on board before approaching those members representing the developing world. Through use of this method all resolutions during the crisis passed with no fewer than thirteen of the fifteen members voting yes.

During the fall Israeli violence in the Occupied Territories threatened to unravel the council's unity. Members found it difficult to punish Iraq for invading Kuwait without addressing the harsh Israeli measures used against the Palestinians. Pickering skillfully directed resolutions condemning the Israeli actions while at the same time securing U.N. approval for the all-important Resolution 678. This resolution set a January 15, 1991, deadline for Iraqi withdrawal and authorized states "to use all necessary means" to gain Baghdad's compliance. The Bush administration utilized the dozen U.N. resolutions, particularly 678, to gain congressional approval for the war that began in January 1991. In the end the Security Council passed fourteen resolutions during the 1990–1991 period dealing with the crisis. Resolution 687 of April 1991, the longest in U.N. history, set the terms for Iraqi surrender. Throughout 1991 and 1992 Pickering successfully preserved this U.N. solidarity to keep sanctions in place until Iraq fully complied with the pertinent Security Council resolutions.

Outside of the Gulf conflict, Pickering took the lead in a number of other pressing issues facing the Security Council. During his tenure the United Nations launched the largest peacekeeping operation in its history in Cambodia to help end that country's protracted civil war. Also, the United Nations assisted in mediation efforts to end another civil war with which Pickering was very familiar, the long-running conflict in El Salvador. By nearly all accounts Pickering was considered to be the most able and successful of U.S. ambassadors to serve at the United Nations. His professionalism, mastery of languages (he speaks French, Spanish, Swahili, Arabic, and Hebrew), and quiet diplomatic style successfully wedded Security Council actions with the broad dictates of U.S. foreign policy.

In February 1992 the Bush administration announced that Pickering would leave the United Nations to become ambassador to India. There was speculation that Baker was displeased with the publicity surrounding the enhanced role of the U.N. envoy. In many ways Pickering was the victim of his own success. His tenure in New York was central to revitalizing the role of the organization in international affairs. While he hoped to continue at the United Nations for another year, he accepted the posting in New Delhi and arrived in India in May 1992. His service was short-lived. When newly inaugurated President Bill Clinton announced his first ambassadorial appointments in January 1993, Pickering was moved from India to Russia.

When he arrived in Moscow in May 1993, the United States and Russia were engaged in an era of unprecedented cooperation. On issues as varied as nuclear disarmament and the Middle East peace process, Russia and the United States seemed to be working hand in hand. Pickering added Russian to his list of language skills and continued encouraging business opportunities for American companies initiated by his predecessor, Robert Strauss. Fostering the democratic transition in Russia was also high on the ambassador's agenda. Friendship with Moscow and an almost uncritical approach to Boris Yeltsin's rule were top priorities of the Clinton administration. Following parliamentary elections in December 1993 in which pro-reform parties did not fare well, cracks began to appear in the post–Cold War friendship. By 1995 Russian fears regarding the proposed eastward expansion of NATO, differences over resolving the war in Bosnia, Moscow's military response to the breakaway republic of Chechnya, and U.S. objections to the sale of Russian nuclear reactors to Iran sank relations to their lowest point since the collapse of the Soviet Union. As had been the case in most of his previous postings, Pickering's ambassadorial skills were once again put to the test in repositioning U.S. policy within a rapidly changing diplomatic environment.

Pickering left his Moscow posting—and the Foreign Service—in November 1996 to become president of the Washington-based Eurasia Foundation. His name soon appeared on numerous short-lists as a possible replacement for the retiring Warren Christopher as Secretary of State. In early 1997, Christopher's successor, Madeleine Albright, tapped Pickering as Undersecretary for Political Affairs—the number three position at the State Department.

Works by Thomas R. Pickering

"Elections in El Salvador." *Department of State Bulletin*, April 1984, 77–79.
"The Post–Cold War Security Council: Forging an International Consensus." *Arms Control Today*, June 1992, 7–10.
"Russia and America at Mid-Transition." *SAIS Review*, Winter/Spring 1995, 81–92.

ROBERT J. BOOKMILLER

WHITELAW REID (1837–1912),

long-time editor and principal owner of the *New York Tribune*, served as U.S. minister to France (1889–1892), ambassador extraordinary on special mission to Queen Victoria's Diamond Jubilee (1897), member of the Peace Commission following the Spanish-American War (1898), and ambassador to Great Britain (1905–1912) and made significant contributions to the adoption of an imperial foreign policy and to Theodore Roosevelt's successful promotion and cultivation of an Anglo-American special relationship.

The second of three children, Whitelaw Reid was born in Xenia, Ohio, and grew up there in a religious Reformed Presbyterian family of modest means. An avid reader even as a youth, Reid entered Miami University at age fifteen, graduating three years later with an outstanding academic record, a knowledge of French, and several newspaper articles to his credit. After working for a year as the principal of a grade school in South Charleston, Ohio, where he taught as well as supervised, Reid became editor of the *Xenia News* in 1858. Already connected to the young Republican Party, having supported the Fremont campaign in 1856, Reid was a strong advocate for Abraham Lincoln in 1860.

It was during the Civil War that Reid first achieved national prominence as a journalist. Writing for the *Cincinnati Gazette* as he accompanied Union forces, Reid proved to be a perceptive observer and critic, crafting penetrating eyewitness accounts of such crucial battles as Fort Donelson, Shiloh, and Gettysburg. Based primarily in Washington after April 1862, Reid was a valuable asset to the *Gazette*, and his growing reputation as a devoted Republican possessing integrity as well as insight was reflected in his appointments as librarian of the House of Representatives and clerk of the House Committee on Military Affairs. The war years also saw Reid become a *Gazette* stockholder and generally strengthen his financial position.

During the period 1865–1867 Reid toured the former Confederacy, invested without much success in Southern plantations, wrote two books (the second, *Ohio in the War*, was a particularly impressive production whose interpretations of Grant, McClellan, and others have stood the test of time), and returned to the *Gazette*'s headquarters in Cincinnati. In 1868 he joined the staff of Horace Greeley's *New York Tribune*, where he was soon named managing editor. During Greeley's Liberal Republican campaign to defeat President Ulysses Grant in the election of 1872 (with which Reid sided out of conviction as well as expediency), Reid assumed complete control of the *Tribune*. When Greeley died shortly after Grant's victory, Reid succeeded through a combination of skill and good fortune (and much to his own surprise) in becoming proprietor and editor of the newspaper, positions he never relinquished.

During his decades in charge of the *Tribune*, Reid emphasized operational efficiency, financial stability, and high-quality journalism. This last issue was of genuine importance; even when confronted with declining circulation and financial losses (which he and his family subsidized) during and after the 1890s, Reid never ceased to view his journal as a dignified guardian of the conscience of the Republican Party and as "a paper written by gentlemen for gentlemen."

The nomination and election to the presidency of Ohio's Rutherford Hayes in 1876 reunited Reid with the regular Republican Party, from which he never again strayed. In 1878 Reid himself emerged as a major figure in the party when his newspaper provided a devastating reply to Democratic accusations that the Republicans had been guilty of fraud in 1876; the *Tribune* deciphered a large quantity of coded telegrams and then exposed extensive fraud on the part of the Democrats. Afterwards, the nomination and victory in 1880 of his close Ohio friend James Garfield brought Reid a very high degree of influence within the national Republican Party—the apogee of his career in this regard. In addition, Reid's marriage to Lizzie Mills in April 1881 turned the editor from the person of substantial means that he had become through his own efforts during the 1870s into a person of truly great wealth. Before many years had passed, Whitelaw, Lizzie, their son Ogden, and their daughter Jean were enjoying magnificent residences in New York City and Westchester County along with a fine retreat in the Adirondacks.

The death in September 1881 of President Garfield, victim of an assassin's bullet, constituted a blow from which Reid's political career never completely recovered. While Reid, Secretary of State James Blaine, and Garfield had managed to destroy the power in New York Republican politics of the corrupt Roscoe Conkling, Conkling's lieutenant Thomas Platt survived to fight another day, an outcome for which at times Reid paid a heavy price.

Reid's shifting political fortunes after 1881 brought the ambitious editor substantial measures of both fulfillment and frustration. After more than three years in the Republican wilderness during the Chester Arthur administration, Reid's hopes of resuming a pivotal role in party and national affairs were dashed when his good friend Blaine met with defeat in the presidential election of 1884. In 1889 his strong editorial and financial support during the recent presidential campaign of Benjamin Harrison combined with his closeness to Blaine, once again secretary of state, to win Reid an appointment as minister to France, where he served until 1892. That year he sought and gained the Republican nomination for vice president and campaigned vigorously for his ticket, but unable to overcome a public perception that the Republican tariff bill of 1890 had been extreme, he and Harrison were beaten by the Democrats.

Inactive politically during 1893–1896 as he attempted to get the upper hand on the asthma and bronchitis that were severely troubling him, Reid returned to the fray during the presidential campaign of 1896. Following William McKinley's victory, Reid endeavored to be appointed secretary of state or ambassador to Great Britain. Unfortunately for the editor, the reinvigorated Senator Platt was adamant in his opposition to either appointment, and McKinley therefore declined to select Reid, citing the journalist's illnesses as the face-saving explanation. But responding to the urgings of Max Seckendorff, head of the *Tribune*'s Washington bureau, and John Hay, McKinley's ambassador to Britain and Reid's very close friend, McKinley did appoint Reid in 1897 to lead the American mission to Queen Victoria's Diamond Jubilee. The next year McKinley named Reid to the Peace Commission that negotiated the Treaty of Paris with Spain following the U.S. victory in the Spanish-American War. Platt again weighed in vehemently, however, to prevent Reid from becoming either secretary of state or ambassador to Britain when these coveted positions opened up at different points in 1898.

The owner of the *Tribune* had battled the New York Republican machine for three decades and had plenty of scars to show for it. In 1901 Reid agreed to a truce with Platt (initiated by the latter) on the condition that Platt would cease obstructing Reid's political career. More important, by the beginning of the new century Reid had won the affection and respect of Theodore Roosevelt. Alone among the major New York papers, the *Tribune* was a consistent and strong backer of President Roosevelt's domestic and foreign policies. Aware of Reid's talents and desires and appreciative of his support, Roosevelt appointed Reid ambassador to Great Britain, a position Reid held with distinction from June 1905 until his death from bronchitis in December 1912.

As minister to France during 1889–1892, Reid proved to be a diligent and skillful diplomat who served his country well and was highly esteemed both by his hosts (with whom he communicated in French) and by the ambassadors and ministers to France from other nations. Reid's three most significant accomplishments as minister were winning the French government's repeal of a ban on imports of American pork, negotiating a commercial reciprocity agreement between the United States and France, and working out a new Franco-American extradition treaty. Each of these matters was complex, requiring attention to detail, flexibility, imagination, and hard work, and Reid's performance was thoroughly commendable.

Of his experiences in France, it was actually a rather extraordinary encounter with the government of Portugal that was to have the greatest impact on Reid's ultimate contributions to American foreign policy. Reid had carried with him to France a negative outlook on any U.S. involvement in European affairs, an opposition to American expansion in the Pacific or the Caribbean (despite an affinity for the Monroe Doctrine), and, in general, a narrow, small-navy concept of the role of the United States in the world. But when Portugal—in an effort to improve its position in a dispute with Great Britain concerning these two countries' African territories—transmitted to the United States directly through Reid in 1891 a stunning proposal that included the establishment of U.S. naval bases in the Azores and in Portuguese Africa, Reid was surprisingly receptive. (Harrison and Blaine were not, so the offer went nowhere.) Beginning with this unlikely episode, Reid's thinking on American foreign policy evolved gradually during the 1890s. The overwhelming U.S. triumph in the Spanish-American War completed the transformation of Reid into an articulate proponent of an overseas American empire and a modern and powerful American navy.

Serving on the five-member U.S. Peace Commission in Paris during the autumn of 1898, Reid (whose facility in French made him the only member able to communicate with the Spanish delegation without an interpreter) was one of three American commissioners favoring a U.S. takeover of the entire Philippine archipelago. When this position gained the support of McKinley, the Americans imposed it (along with other hard-line demands) on their dismayed Spanish counterparts. In the months following the completion of the treaty, through the *Tribune* and other outlets and in a number of major speeches, Reid argued forcefully for ratification (narrowly accomplished in February 1899) and skillfully defended the constitutional, historical, and moral legitimacy of the new American imperialism. Reid unreservedly endorsed President Roosevelt's policy of suppressing the Filipino rebellion and then shepherding the islanders along the difficult path to self-government. Bingham Duncan, the author of a very fine biography of Reid published in 1975, considered Reid's efforts during both the peace negotiations and the ensuing debate over imperialism "his most important positive contributions to his country's foreign policy."

The Republican editor of the *New York Tribune* also made important contributions in another area—the building of a solid friendship and informal alliance between the British Empire and the United States, particularly during the presidency of Theodore Roosevelt. In the 1880s Reid had readily engaged in the politically remunerative nineteenth-century American sport of "twisting the lion's tail," harshly condemning and helping to prevent ratification of the Cleveland administration's fisheries treaty with Britain in 1888 (an ironic action in light of Reid's own later work) and eagerly publicizing the Sackville-West letter (engendered by clever Republican trickery and identifying President Cleveland as Britain's preferred candidate) during the presidential campaign of that same year. (Also ironically, the *Tribune*'s anti-British record may have been decisive in Harrison's unwillingness to appoint Reid minister to Great Britain—the editor's strong preference over France—in 1889.) But just as had happened on American expansionism, Reid was putting forward a sharply altered perspective on Anglo-American relations by the late 1890s—a perspective he retained for the rest of his days.

Reid publicly announced his affection for Britain without ambiguity or embarrassment when he remained in England for three weeks following the expiration in early July 1897 of his commission as ambassador extraordinary on special mission to Queen Victoria's Diamond Jubilee. (Reid had been reveling in the exciting social scene he had found in Britain and was in no hurry to leave.) In two widely reported short addresses delivered the week of the Fourth of July, Reid spoke of Anglo-American solidarity and the cultural unity of the people of the United States, Britain, Canada, and Australia. The unabashedly pro-British tone of these talks did not deter the speaker from distributing them, printed and bound, to various notables, including President McKinley.

Regarding the Spanish-American War and its aftermath, Reid's *Tribune* emphasized the sharp contrast between British support for and continental European hostility toward the United States. Reid also defended the unpopular British side during the Boer War of 1899–1902. In speeches, *Tribune* columns, and private correspondence he consistently professed the desirability and even the inevitability of an Anglo-American partnership. Thus it was natural for President Roosevelt to select Reid to head a special American embassy to the coronation of Edward VII in June 1902 (the king's illness caused the postponement of the coronation and the closing of the special embassy). Late in 1904 Roosevelt decided to appoint Reid ambassador to Britain, making clear to any doubters that he considered Reid "entitled to that position" on account of the journalist's "service to the party" and "fitness for the place."

Theodore Roosevelt considered the forging of a durable bond of friendship and an informal alliance between the United States and the British Empire one of his foremost foreign policy priorities. A special Anglo-American relationship, Roosevelt was convinced, would contribute mightily to the peace of the world and the progress of civilization and would establish an international balance of power highly favorable to the long-term protection of vital American interests.

Reid's "fitness for the place" went beyond the standard ambassadorial attributes and the similarity of his and the president's perspectives on Anglo-American relations. Roosevelt was an adroit hands-on diplomatist who dominated his administration's foreign policy and who preferred to conduct diplomacy outside standard channels in an informal, personal manner. Therefore, the ideal Rooseveltian ambassador to the Court of St. James—in addition to being a champion of Anglo-American harmony, in addition to being a man of wealth, a gracious host, and a gifted speaker, and in addition to possessing the diligence, intelligence, good judgment, and discretion that have always been essential to the effective handling of challenging diplomatic assignments—would need to be a keen observer of the British scene who had the president's affection and trust and who was willing and able to correspond directly with Roosevelt with regularity and insight.

Whitelaw Reid was just such an ambassador. Between his assumption of the ambassadorship in June 1905 and the end of Roosevelt's presidency in March 1909, Reid sent well over one hundred letters directly to Roosevelt and received about ninety from the president. This interaction between Reid and Roosevelt was enormously helpful (and pleasing) to the president as he successfully guided Anglo-American relations in the direction of ever-increasing amity and cooperation.

Roosevelt availed himself of Reid's services while carrying out the two most complex and important negotiations of his presidency, the arrangement of the Treaty of Portsmouth ending the Russo-Japanese War in the summer of 1905 and the risky American diplomatic intervention during the two stages of the dangerous Franco-German crisis over Morocco in 1905 and 1906. While Reid's role in these two matters was not central, he provided Roosevelt with a dependable line of communication with the British government and source of information about its thinking.

Moreover, Roosevelt's selection of Reid as the recipient of his long and accurate letter of April 28, 1906, reviewing and documenting the course of the Moroccan crisis indicated the very high degree of confidence he had in his ambassador. Indeed, Roosevelt and Reid confided in each other about a large number of matters, including Roosevelt's frank perspectives on Britain (usually, but not always, complimentary), Japan, and Germany (usually not complimentary in these last two cases). For his part, the acutely observant Reid regularly updated Roosevelt on the shifting fortunes of various British political figures.

Roosevelt's great confidence in Reid's discretion and tact is most apparent in the president's engagement of Reid in a delicate campaign to persuade the British government to replace its ambassador to the United States, Sir Mortimer Durand, with someone better suited to the position and more to Roosevelt's liking. In June 1906 Roosevelt asked Reid to convey to the British leadership (diplomatically, of course) Durand's "utter worthlessness" as ambassador and "how strongly I feel" about the problem. Having been unable as a consequence of this ambassadorial handicap to keep abreast of Roosevelt's thinking and actions during the Moroccan crisis—as Reid made clear—the British government recognized the imperative of acceding to the president's wishes. Reid was pleased to inform Roosevelt in October that Durand would be relieved soon, which he was.

The issue that absorbed Reid's time and attention as ambassador to Britain more than any other was the long-standing and seemingly intractable Anglo-American disagreement over the Newfoundland fisheries. Here Reid played an important role in support of the efforts of Secretary of State Elihu Root to find a solution. During these negotiations, largely conducted through regular diplomatic channels, Reid's conferences with Foreign Secretary Sir Edward Grey and his communications with Root helped the United States and Britain make temporary arrangements when necessary and eventually arrive at a permanent settlement. President Roosevelt, as usual, marked out the American position in these negotiations. He and Reid did correspond directly about the fisheries matter on numerous occasions and were in complete accord about the need for American flexibility while working toward a treaty. When the ambassador expressed doubts about "the importance to the United States of this Newfoundland fishery question," the president fully concurred. The American proposal for arbitration by the Hague Tribunal, ultimately accepted by Britain as the basis for an agreement, reflected the president's determination to eliminate the fisheries issue as a recurring threat to harmonious Anglo-American relations.

Finally, Ambassador Reid could count among his significant contributions to Roosevelt's diplomacy the assistance he rendered as Roosevelt labored behind the scenes to quash a nasty and prolonged dispute between American and British athletic officials stemming from the 1908 summer Olympic Games in London. Here Reid brought to bear his finely honed journalistic skills as he reported on and offered his analysis of the controversy in a letter of August 11. While finding fault primarily with the British, Reid assigned some blame to the Americans as well and lamented that "there has been bitterness enough developed over these races to come near counterbalancing the diplomacy of years." Roosevelt praised Reid's "full and convincing statement," agreeing "with every word," and proceeded to employ the ambassador's account as he dealt with the matter successfully over the next several months. As the diplomacy of the Olympics squabble reached its climax in late November, the president noted with satisfaction that Reid's "view of the course to follow" coincided "exactly" with his own. Injecting a bit of humor, Roosevelt suggested to Reid that the irritating Olympics affair was "a case for the application of one of my favorite anecdotes—that of the New Bedford whaling captain who told one of his men that all he wished from him was 'silence, and damn little of that.' "

In a letter to the president of January 22, 1909, Reid characterized "my service under you" as "intimate." The adjective was apt. The appointment of Reid as ambassador to Great Britain had worked out extremely well for Roosevelt, in whose statecraft personal relationships played such an integral part.

Although the Taft administration's approach to Anglo-American relations (and to foreign policy in general) was rather ill conceived and far less coherent than Roosevelt's, Reid continued to perform the duties of ambassador with skill and grace. In 1909 and 1910 he was an effective messenger between Secretary of State Philander Knox and Foreign Secretary Grey during awkward negotiations over an American demand to join a consortium of powers financing railroad construction in China. Reid again performed well as a messenger during the negotiations in 1911 for a general arbitration treaty (later blocked by the Senate) between Britain and the United States. During Anglo-American discussions in 1912 regarding U.S. legislation exempting American coastwise vessels from Panama Canal tolls (in apparent violation of the Hay-Pauncefote Treaty of 1901), Reid ably defended an American stance with which he privately strongly disagreed.

Between 1889 and 1912 Whitelaw Reid achieved a very laudable record as a diplomat in the service of his country. One of the most distinguished and successful journalists in American history, he was also, without question, a notable U.S. ambassador.

Works by Whitelaw Reid

After the War: A Southern Tour. Cincinnati: Moore, Wilstach and Baldwin, 1866.

Ohio in the War: Her Statesmen, Her Generals, and Soldiers. 2 vols. Cincinnati: Moore, Wilstach and Baldwin, 1868.

Two Speeches at the Queen's Jubilee, London, 1897. New York: DeVinne Press, 1897.

Problems of Expansion. New York: Century, 1900.

American and English Studies. 2 vols. New York: Charles Scribner's Sons, 1913.

Careers for the Coming Men. New York: Tribune Association, 1902; New York and Chicago: Saalfield Publishing, 1916.

Making Peace with Spain: The Diary of Whitelaw Reid, September–December, 1898. Ed.
　　H. Wayne Morgan. Austin: University of Texas Press, 1965.

Works about Whitelaw Reid

Baehr, Harry W. *The New York Tribune Since the Civil War.* New York: Dodd, Mead,
　　1936.
Beale, Howard K. *Theodore Roosevelt and the Rise of America to World Power.* Balti-
　　more: Johns Hopkins University Press, 1956.
Cortissoz, Royal. *The Life of Whitelaw Reid.* 2 vols. New York: Charles Scribner's Sons,
　　1921.
Duncan, Bingham. *Whitelaw Reid: Journalist, Politician, Diplomat.* Athens: University
　　of Georgia Press, 1975.
Smart, James G. "Whitelaw Reid: A Biographical Study." Ph.D. diss., University of
　　Maryland, 1964.
Tilchin, William N. *Theodore Roosevelt and the British Empire: A Study in Presidential
　　Statecraft.* New York: St. Martin's Press, 1997.

WILLIAM N. TILCHIN

PAUL SAMUEL REINSCH (1869–1923), American minister to China during the Wilson years, fought to maintain the Open Door in China to advance American economic interests and forestall the expansion of Japanese influence on the Asian continent.

Reinsch was born on June 10, 1869, in Milwaukee as the only son of German immigrant parents, George J. Reinsch, formerly a Lutheran minister and later a federal government employee, and Clara Witte Reinsch, a well-educated and ambitious member of a Schleswig-Holstein family. His parents provided him with a religious environment with emphasis on education.

Upon completing his bachelor of arts degree at the University of Wisconsin at Madison in 1892 with a 95 average, Reinsch moved on to the law school and was admitted to the Wisconsin bar in 1894. His disappointment with law practice in Milwaukee prompted him to return to Madison in the fall of 1895 to enroll in the Ph.D. program in history and political science. Under the guidance of Frederick Jackson Turner, Reinsch learned to analyze social and economic forces behind historical developments and international relations. He received his Ph.D. in 1898, thereafter remained at the University of Wisconsin as assistant professor, and was promoted to full professor in 1901.

Reinsch's academic career at the University of Wisconsin prior to his appointment as minister to China in 1913 coincided with the surge of progressive movement in that state. As the chairman of the newly created Political Science Department and advisor to Governor Robert M. La Follette, Reinsch contributed to the reform movement. His scholarship, however, mostly concentrated on international relations and imperialism. His major work, *World Politics at the End of the Nineteenth Century, as Influenced by the Oriental Situation*, published in 1900, and numerous other writings established his national reputation as an expert on international relations and imperialism in East Asia. His popular courses on Oriental politics and contemporary international politics at Wisconsin attracted able students such as Stanley K. Hornbeck and Horatio Bates Hawkins, who would later work closely with the Chinese.

Reinsch developed a set of familiar but somewhat contradictory ideas labeled by his biographer, Noel H. Pugach, as "progressive expansionism" or "progressive imperialism." Reinsch tied progressivism and economic/cultural expansion together through the concept of the globalization of the American system. He believed that the primary force behind modern imperialism was economic. While he strongly opposed predatory imperialism and colonialism driven by excessive nationalism, he justified economic expansion on grounds that industrialized nations needed foreign markets to prevent economic depression at home and therefore had the right to insist on the security of overseas trade and investment. As a proponent of the universality of American institutions and values, Reinsch argued that America's peaceful Open Door economic expansion would also bring material improvement and moral regeneration to backward countries and provide a model for a democratic federal commonwealth. The world, therefore, must be open to American goods and capital as well as ideas. Reinsch particularly emphasized China's importance to the future of American trade, and in doing so, he apparently accepted the myth of the "China market." The principles of the Open Door in China were to allow the United States to protect China from other imperialist powers' attempts to partition it and at the same time to expand American economic, and consequently cultural, influence.

Like many university professors during the Progressive Era, Reinsch relished the opportunity to participate in policymaking and test the power of ideas in the real world. He actively pursued a regular diplomatic appointment, particularly in East Asia, while Theodore Roosevelt and William H. Taft were in office. After serving as a delegate to the Third and Fourth Pan-American Conferences in 1906 and 1910 and to the First Pan-American Scientific Congress at Santiago in 1909, Reinsch was finally chosen by President Woodrow Wilson as American minister to China in 1913. Although Reinsch was not Wilson's first choice (Charles Eliot and John R. Mott both declined the offer), the president could not have found a more enthusiastic advocate of the Wilsonian mission in China. Both cherished humanitarianism, Christian ethics, democracy, and international peace, and both were against formal imperialism or colonialism. Both men shared a general conviction that the United States alone must serve as the model for China's deeply troubled path to modernization. They also shared an independent and competitive approach to the Open Door policy in China as opposed to cooperation with the Great Powers who had their spheres of influence.

The scholar-diplomat sailed for China in October 1913, determined to put his ideals into practice. Reinsch brought to China a reinvigorated version of the Open Door policy and held fast to it as his fundamental guide to action. He believed that the central idea of the Open Door was vigorous but fair economic competition free from the special privileges and political influence guaranteed by the spheres of influence. Upon his arrival in China, therefore, Minister Reinsch launched a two-pronged campaign to expand American business enterprise in China and to abolish the practice of spheres of influence.

Reinsch's assiduous efforts to bring American investment into China, however, failed to produce the desired results. Most of the business deals the minister negotiated fell through—the Standard Oil Company's oil deal in Shaanxi and Hebei, the Huai River conservation program, and the contracts for the Chinchou-Aigun Railway and the Huguang Railways, just to name a few. In fact, the amount of American exports to China between 1913 and 1915 declined. Reinsch criticized American businessmen for their reluctance, ignorance, shortsightedness, backward techniques, and indifference to American national interests. He also legitimately blamed foreign interference and opposition, particularly by the Japanese, and the problems of Chinese internal politics. Although the American minister never admitted his own mistakes, he was clearly too ambitious and hasty. He was so eager to attain his goals that he often failed to assess the situation objectively, often misjudged the other parties' intentions, and sometimes even acted without authorization from the State Department. Undaunted by the disappointing results, Reinsch continued to search for a means to expand American economic operations in China. He saw a great need for the establishment of American banking facilities in East Asia to carry out America's independent long-range investment. Reinsch worked hard to organize such an American financial syndicate, the American International Corporation, established in November 1915, for instance, only to find it lured into cooperation with Japanese investors, which the minister considered as a betrayal of both Chinese and American interests.

Reinsch increasingly came to identify two forces as the major obstacles to his efforts to broaden American economic opportunity in China. First, when Japan took advantage of the European powers' preoccupation with World War I and threatened to break the existing delicate balance of power among the Great Powers' interests in China, Reinsch quickly singled out Japan as the chief enemy of the Open Door and American interests. Japan took a bold diplomatic step by presenting the so-called Twenty-One Demands to China in January 1915. Japan's intention was not only to establish its predominant position in Manchuria, Inner Mongolia, and the German leasehold in Shandong, which Japan had recently occupied, but also to extend its economic, political, and military influence throughout China. Calling it the greatest crisis yet experienced in China, Reinsch vigorously assisted the Chinese in arousing world opinion against Japanese aggression and duplicity and encouraged the Chinese to keep resisting the Japanese pressure. He also played a crucial role in alerting the policymakers in Washington, D.C., to the seriousness of the crisis. As a result, Washington warned Japan not to infringe upon American treaty rights or Chinese political and administrative integrity. When Japan extracted substantial concessions from China by sending an ultimatum, the United States refused to recognize any new arrangement that violated the Open Door principles. Thus Minister Reinsch played an instrumental role in preventing Japan from scoring a sweeping victory through the infamous demands. After this incident Reinsch opposed any American enterprise's attempt to cooperate with Japanese investors in China and tried to block any Japanese efforts to expand their economic operations.

The other obstacle to Reinsch's Open Door expansion was China's internal political instability. Although Reinsch desired to transform the young republic into an American-style democracy, he was persuaded that the centralization of power in the hands of Yuan Shikai, permanent president of the Chinese republic, would facilitate China's orderly transformation and development. Yuan's attempt to establish a new dynasty caught Reinsch by surprise, but he continued to support the monarchist effort until Yuan's sudden death in June 1916. When it became obvious that Yuan's failed monarchical attempt had driven China into civil war, had invited Japanese interference, and had further discouraged American investments in China, Reinsch, who was eager to save China's unity, resorted to the very practice that President Wilson and he himself had once denounced: intervention in Chinese internal affairs by the use of political loans. However, Reinsch soon realized that Japan had already gained the upper hand over any other competitors in extending a series of stabilization and reform loans known as the Nishihara Loans to the Beijing government under Prime Minister Duan Qirui.

The prospect of America's entry into the war against Germany in early 1917 provided Reinsch with another opportunity to stop the Chinese government from further collaboration with Japan. Upon Washington's invitation to China to associate itself with the United States in severing diplomatic relations with Germany, Reinsch was determined to persuade Beijing to follow American leadership on this matter. To secure Beijing's compliance, he suggested America's financial and other assistance to China without authorization from the State Department.

Reinsch's hasty action, however, precipitated the developments that the United States wanted to avoid. His action provoked Japan into demanding the leadership role in China's foreign and military affairs, and at the same time, the issue of war participation caused further internal division and chaos within the Chinese government. The Japanese-American rivalry over who should guide and assist China's entry into the war led to the controversy as to whether Japan had "paramount" political and economic interests in China. The upshot of the controversy was the conclusion of the Lansing-Ishii agreement of November 1917, in which the Japanese special envoy, Kikujiro Ishii, and Secretary of State Robert Lansing reaffirmed the Open Door principles, but at the same time the United States recognized Japan's "special interests in China." Japan immediately claimed the agreement as its diplomatic victory. Reinsch, who had been kept in the dark about the Lansing-Ishii negotiations, was furious, but there was little that he could do to reverse the impression that the United States had made a concession to Japan.

By the end of 1917 Reinsch came close to the verge of a complete physical and mental breakdown, partly because of the growth of a brain tumor but mainly because of the exhaustion and stress from overwork and the overwhelming impression that Japan's domination over a disintegrating China seemed unavoidable. In the following year he was forced to rest on the diplomatic front, but he never gave up the hope that the American standards would prevail in Chinese markets and continued to search for a formula for a comprehensive plan for Chinese economic development. He explored an idea of a new consortium, which was to consist of the leading powers acting as trustees for China and to assist China's economic development by providing political and industrial loans. Although this idea eventually evolved into the so-called Second Chinese Consortium, Reinsch's major scheme to neutralize all the Chinese railways in the spheres of influence displeased both the Japanese and the Chinese, made the Europeans reluctant, and failed to obtain the State Department's support.

In the meantime, the collapse of the Eastern front in the Great War in Europe by the Bolsheviks' peace with Germany in March 1918 led to the Allied military venture in Siberia. Reinsch supported the proposed Japanese-American joint expedition in the summer of the same year primarily to prevent Japan from taking independent military actions in Siberia. Through a series of secret agreements extracted from the Beijing government, Japan was virtually allowed to control the Chinese Eastern Railway and part of North Manchuria (a former Russian sphere of influence) in the disguise of Sino-Japanese joint occupation. Japan also sent to Siberia a far larger number of Japanese troops than President Wilson had been led to believe. Considering these Japanese actions as further evidence of their aggression, Reinsch was fully convinced that Japan had become the enemy of liberal democracy who was bent on East Asian domination. On the eve of the Paris Peace Conference in 1919, Reinsch warned the State Department that should the United States fail to contain Japanese expansion, Japan would create in East Asia ''the greatest engine of military oppression and dominance that the world has yet seen.''

The Paris Peace Conference, Reinsch's last hope to make the Open Door a reality, turned out to be the final discouraging event that prompted his resignation. At the outset of the conference, Reinsch knew that China's case for Shandong had been undermined by both the Sino-Japanese treaties of 1915 and the secret agreements of 1918, in which China granted Japan not only the right to succeed to the German rights in Shandong but also joint control of the Shandong Railway. Reinsch, however, hoped to use the occasion to carry out sweeping reforms in China as part of the Wilsonian peace program and proposed the abolition of spheres of influence and the creation of an international trusteeship in China. Although he did his best to educate the American delegation at Paris, especially President Wilson, about the importance of the China question, there were limitations to his influence in Beijing.

Despite his sympathy for the Chinese claims, President Wilson was forced to yield to Japanese and Allied pressures on the Shandong question in order to save the League of Nations—the centerpiece of his new peace program. Reinsch was stunned by the decision and felt that the president had betrayed China. He therefore supported China's refusal to sign the Treaty of Versailles and welcomed the anti-Japanese and nationalist tone of the May Fourth Movement. Although he did not complain specifically about the decision in Paris in his letter of resignation dated June 7, 1919, he later expressed his vexation with President Wilson's neglect of ''carefully considered expressions'' of his views and those of other East Asian experts at Paris. Breckinridge Long, Reinsch's confidant in the State Department, observed that the American minister was overworked, tired out, and discouraged at the physical impossibility of achieving what was too much for any one man to do. President Wilson accepted Reinsch's resignation on August 18, but kept him in China until the Senate completed the hearings on the Shandong issue in the peace treaty in mid-September.

After returning to the United States, Reinsch moved to Washington, D.C., and devoted his life to promoting a closer relationship between China and his country. He obtained a position as counselor to the Chinese government and advised the policymakers in Beijing on legal, political, and economic matters. He also joined the law firm of Davies and Jones in Washington, D.C., where he offered legal services to businessmen and companies that had business with or were interested in China. Overall, the results of Reinsch's efforts in Washington were disappointing. The advocate of China soon found himself unable to influence Chinese government leaders, who simply ignored his advice, like that from all the other foreign advisors. He could not even collect his salary from the bankrupt government in Beijing. The Washington Conference sponsored by the Harding administration in 1921–1922 brought back Reinsch's enthusiasm and encouraged him to lobby on behalf of China. The conference indeed produced agreements favorable to China—the Nine Power Treaty endorsing the Open Door principles in China and the Sino-Japanese settlement on Shandong. The irony is that Reinsch, who had no connection or influence with the Chinese delegation, which had its own American advisors, played virtually no part in the negotiations in Washington.

Reinsch went to Beijing in July 1922 to collect his salary and renegotiate his contract with the Chinese government. While he was traveling in southern China, he became ill and started to suffer from hallucinations. His doctors in Shanghai discovered a brain tumor and later diagnosed the malady as encephalitis and pneumonia. Reinsch died on January 26, 1923, in Shanghai at the age of fifty-three.

Minister Paul S. Reinsch was one of the most passionate representatives that the United States had ever sent to China. He went there with a mission to advance American interests by turning the Open Door ideals into a reality. He was determined to abolish the foreign spheres of influence and to guide China's economic and political modernization following American standards. Faced with insurmountable problems, such as the constant internal strife in China, the hostile international environment, and the reluctance of American investors, however, Reinsch was unable to find effective means to realize his goals. Curiously, he never questioned or reevaluated the workability of his goals and the assumptions used for their rationale; instead, he blamed obvious villains like Japan and her Chinese collaborators. By turning America's rivalry with Japan over China into a crusade against an evil empire, Reinsch made it impossible to work out a cooperation or a realistic compromise with Japan, thereby making his mission an unattainable one.

Works by Paul S. Reinsch

Colonial Autonomy. Chicago: n.p., 1904.

Colonial Administration. New York: The Macmillan Company, 1905.

American Legislatures and Legislative Methods. New York: The Century Co., 1907.

Intellectual and Political Currents in the Far East. Boston and New York: Houghton Mifflin Company, 1911.

Public International Unions; Their Work and Organization: A Study in International Administrative Law. Boston, London: Ginn and Company, 1911.

American Love of Peace and European Skepticism. New York: American Association
for International Conciliation, 1913.

Precedent and Codification in International Law. Baltimore: American Society for Judicial Settlement of International Disputes, 1913.

An American Diplomat in China. Garden City, NY: Doubleday, Page, and Company,
1922.

Secret Diplomacy, How Far Can It Be Eliminated? New York: Harcourt, Brace and
Company; London: G. Allen and Unwin, 1922.

*World Politics at the End of the Nineteenth Century, as Influenced by the Oriental Sit-
uation.* New York: Macmillan, 1900. Reprint. Wilmington, DE: Scholarly Resources, 1972.

Works about Paul S. Reinsch

Chi, Madeleine. *China Diplomacy, 1914–1918.* Cambridge: Harvard University Press,
1970.

Curry, Roy W. *Woodrow Wilson and Far Eastern Policy, 1913–1921.* New York: Bookman Associates, 1957.

Israel, Jerry. *Progressivism and the Open Door: America and China, 1905–1921.* Pittsburgh: University of Pittsburgh Press, 1971.

Pugach, Noel H. *Paul S. Reinsch: Open Door Diplomat in Action.* Millwood, NY: KTO
Press, 1979.

NORIKO KAWAMURA

WILLIAM EVERETT SCHAUFELE, JR. (1923–),

was U.S. ambassador to Upper Volta/Burkina Faso (1969–1971), U.S. ambassador, senior advisor, and deputy U.S. representative to the U.N. Security Council (1971–1975), assistant secretary of state for African affairs, (1975–1977), and U.S. ambassador to Poland (1978–1980).

During the summer of 1950 William E. Schaufele, Jr., began an illustrious career with the U.S. State Department that would span the next three decades. Starting out as a Foreign Service officer (FSO) in postwar Germany, Schaufele rapidly rose to the rank of ambassador, serving in that capacity in Upper Volta/Burkina Faso, in Poland, and at the U.S. Mission to the United Nations. He subsequently retired with the rank of career minister in 1980 at the relatively young age of fifty-six. Almost by chance, U.S. relations with the emerging states of Africa became the focus of much of Schaufele's diplomatic career, culminating in his work as assistant secretary of state for African affairs during the mid-1970s. His role in the region included extensive involvement in the Congo crisis of 1964 and the coordination of famine relief efforts during the early 1980s following his retirement from the Foreign Service. As a senior member of America's U.N. Mission, and then as assistant secretary of state for African affairs, he worked closely with Secretary of State Henry Kissinger on a number of diplomatic issues involving the states of southern Africa. Schaufele also played an important role in the U.S. Mission to the United Nations during a period of incredible upheaval brought on by numerous international armed conflicts and a vastly expanded membership, particularly in the Third World. Finally, during his last overseas posting as U.S. ambassador to Poland, Schaufele witnessed the emergence of the Solidarity trade-union movement and the beginnings of the eventual collapse of communism in Eastern Europe. By the time he retired at the end of three decades of service, Schaufele had developed a well-deserved reputation as a troubleshooter and crisis manager, and his effective but low-key approach endeared him to many of his State Department colleagues.

William E. Schaufele was born on December 7, 1923, in a suburb of Cleveland, Ohio. Both of his parents were descended from German immigrants, and like many of his generation, his life was deeply marked by both the Depression and World War II. Schaufele entered Yale University with a scholarship at the height of the war in July 1942 and was enrolled as a premed student until he was inducted into the U.S. Army after only one year of study. Upon completing basic training, he landed with the 10th Armored Division in France in the fall of 1944. His unit fought in the Battle of the Bulge at Bastogne and elsewhere in France and Germany, and after V-E Day Schaufele remained in Europe until January 1946, when he was finally discharged from the army. He returned to the United States to resume his studies, switched his major field of study from medicine to international relations, and graduated with a B.A. from Yale University in 1948. Schaufele then pursued graduate studies at Columbia University, where he earned a master's degree from the School of International Affairs in 1950. That same year Schaufele met and married his wife and passed the Foreign Service exam, and later in the summer of 1950 he accepted his first State Department appointment when he was selected to return to Germany as a Kreis resident officer in the Munich area.

In 1952 Schaufele was transferred to a new post as labor affairs officer at the U.S. consulate in Düsseldorf, and the following year he returned to Munich as a visa and then an economic reporting officer. Schaufele and his family were transferred back to Washington, D.C., in the midst of the 1956 presidential election, and after his arrival he briefly served on the staffs of the Foreign Service Institute and the Foreign Reporting Staff. He was then assigned to the State Department's Morocco desk in preparation for his 1959 transfer to the U.S. consulate general in Casablanca. It was this first overseas posting in Morocco that provided the seed for Schaufele's two decades of concentration on African affairs.

In 1963 Schaufele was transferred from Morocco to open a new U.S. consulate in the newly independent African state of Zaire (the Republic of the Congo). He arrived in the regional capital of Bukavu just prior to the outbreak of the brutal Simba rebellion of 1964. Schaufele was recalled to Washington before the worst of the fighting reached Bukavu, and he subsequently assumed responsibility for the Congo Working Group at the State Department. The strife in Zaire became bloody and protracted and eventually involved anti-Castro Cuban pilots and a mercenary force led by Mike Hoare in addition to the various local factions. The impetus for the rebellion was finally broken when a Belgian paratroop battalion was dropped on the provincial capital of Stanleyville by U.S. transport aircraft. As a result of his years of work on African issues, Schaufele was promoted in 1965 to the position of deputy director of Central African affairs, and in 1967 he became the State Department's director of Central West African affairs. In 1969 Schaufele returned to Africa as U.S. ambassador to Upper Volta.

After two years overseas Schaufele was ordered to return to the United States in October 1971 to take up new responsibilities at the U.N. Mission in New York City. The Nixon administration had been elected in 1968, and the turnover of U.S. permanent representatives during these years was remarkable. Charles Yost (1969–1971) was soon succeeded by future President George Bush (1971–1973), whose own short stay in the U.N. post was followed in quick succession by the brief terms of Associated Press correspondent John Scali (1973–1975), future U.S. Senator Daniel Patrick Moynihan (1975–1976), and Republican politician William Scranton (1976–1977). Under these circumstances, continuity in representation and policy at the U.N. Mission had to be provided by the other senior members of the U.S. delegation, which included Christopher Phillips (deputy permanent representative to the United Nations, 1970–1973) and W. Tapley Bennett, Jr. (deputy permanent representative on the Security Council,

1971–1972, and deputy permanent representative to the United Nations, 1973–1976). Schaufele himself served as senior adviser to the permanent U.S. representative on the Security Council (1971–1973) and then as deputy permanent representative on the Security Council (1973–1975). He also assumed the increasingly important role of operational head of the American delegation and strove to coordinate its activities and issue clear and consistent assignments to representatives on each of the separate committees. As a measure of his personal dedication and his importance to the U.N. Mission, Schaufele took only sixteen days of leave during the next four years.

Schaufele discovered that America's U.N. Mission was often plagued by instructions from Washington that were either too vague or too specific. Furthermore, during the early 1970s the attitude of the American public toward the United Nations was beginning to transform from one of neutrality or even mild approval to growing hostility and skepticism. Senior officials in the Nixon administration seemed to be equally unenthusiastic about the role of the United Nations in U.S. foreign policy, an attitude that only further complicated the already-difficult tasks of the mission. Multilateral diplomacy was also very different from the bilateral diplomacy to which Schaufele had become accustomed during his earlier assignments in Africa and Washington. Based on his own observations, Schaufele believed that international organizations like the United Nations were more effective in functional areas such as development assistance than on security issues. But dating back to his experience in the Congo crisis, Schaufele was also a strong proponent of U.N. peacekeeping operations, and while he was serving at the mission he even published a 1973 article to that effect. This faith in peacekeeping persisted throughout his career and compelled him during 1995–1996 to defend in print the use of U.S. ground troops in Bosnia to enforce the precarious peace there.

The issues that faced Schaufele and the other members of the American U.N. Mission during these tumultuous years were many and varied. During 1971 international attention was focused on the contentious issue of Communist Chinese membership in the United Nations—a decision that Schaufele and the remainder of the U.S. delegation opposed and eventually lost in the General Assembly, interrupted as it was by Kissinger's path-breaking visit to China and the war between India and Pakistan over the secession of Bangladesh. The attention of the 1973 General Assembly was dominated by the Yom Kippur War between Israel and the Arab states. When negotiations to resolve that conflict finally began in Washington and Moscow, the United Nations played a supporting but no less important role. The peacekeeping efforts in that conflict culminated in the passage of Security Council Resolution 340, which established the Second United Nations Emergency Force (UNEF II) in the Sinai. During 1974 Turkey invaded the Mediterranean island of Cyprus, and the U.N. peacekeeping force that was already in place there, the United Nations Peace-keeping Force in Cyprus (UNFICYP), became embroiled in the conflict and the subsequent truce negotiations. That same year the chairman of the Palestine

Liberation Organization (PLO), Yasir Arafat, was invited to participate in a General Assembly debate on Palestine, and the PLO was granted nonvoting observer status at the United Nations.

Another important development that faced Schaufele and his colleagues at the U.N. Mission during this period was the growing power of the Third World and the nonaligned movement. It was during the late 1960s and early 1970s that the Group of 77 nonaligned states began to grow in numbers and influence in the General Assembly. By the time Schaufele arrived in 1971 to assume his new responsibilities, there had already been a massive injection of newly independent U.N. member states from the Third World. They now comprised a bloc of votes that could easily strangle or initiate almost any issue in the General Assembly. The year 1974 was particularly important because it marked the first serious manifestation of the increasingly confrontational North-South conflict. The defining moment seemed to come with the passage of the Charter of Economic Rights and Duties of States, which was adopted by a majority vote in the General Assembly in December. Among other provisions, this controversial resolution facilitated the nationalization and expropriation of foreign-owned property and recommended the creation of producer associations similar to the Organization of Petroleum Exporting Countries (OPEC) for the marketing of raw materials to the developed world. Not surprisingly, the United States and its allies opposed the passage of this resolution, but they were soundly defeated.

During Schaufele's term at the U.S. Mission a great deal of pressure was exerted by African states and other Third World nations to end white rule in Rhodesia and South Africa, expel South Africa from the General Assembly, and enforce the 1963 international arms embargo against the apartheid regime. In apparent recognition of the growing importance of African issues on the U.S. foreign policy agenda, Schaufele was finally moved from the U.N. Mission back to the State Department headquarters in Washington in early 1975. After being temporarily appointed inspector-general of the Foreign Service, later in the year he was sworn in by Henry Kissinger as assistant secretary of state for African affairs. Extensive visits by Kissinger and Schaufele to Africa during 1976 demonstrated the growing importance of that continent to perceived U.S. global interests.

The first major issue to be addressed by Schaufele was the situation in Angola and the controversial presence of Soviet, Cuban, and South African troops and advisors there. He attempted to win both African support for a negotiated withdrawal of all foreign troops from Angola and continued congressional support for covert U.S. funding of opposition movements in that country. Despite Schaufele's efforts, the Organization of African Unity (OAU) recognized the Soviet-backed Popular Movement for the Liberation of Angola (MPLA) government in February 1976, and Congress banned any further American funding for the antigovernment forces. As for the remainder of the region of southern Africa, the official U.S. position was to promote majority black rule in Rhodesia and independence for Namibia. But while Schaufele and Kissinger opposed apartheid in principle, they also believed that confrontation with the South African regime should be minimized since the cooperation of the white minority government was needed to secure permanent peace in other conflicts in southern Africa. Working with the notoriously secretive Kissinger to resolve the issues of Angola, Rhodesia, and the remainder of the volatile region, Schaufele was now forced to operate in an atmosphere of private diplomacy to a greater degree than he was accustomed to in the Foreign Service. The pace was grueling, with Schaufele logging approximately 30,000 miles of air travel in one four-day period alone.

The shuttle diplomacy continued throughout the summer and fall of 1976, and Schaufele eventually found himself working closely with British diplomats to set up talks in Geneva over the Rhodesia issue. By late fall Kissinger decided to send Schaufele to observe the progress of the talks in the belief that only an American official of his rank could prevent their breakdown. Unfortunately, the victory of Jimmy Carter in the 1976 presidential elections indirectly led to a stall in the Geneva talks. The negotiations over the future of Rhodesia/Zimbabwe dragged on for several more years before an agreement was finally reached by all parties in 1980, leading to the election of the black-led government of former rebel leader Robert Mugabe.

By the spring of 1977 Schaufele was back in Washington testifying before the Senate in favor of a proposed $100-million economic development package for Rhodesia to assist in the anticipated transition to majority rule and heading a State Department group that had been appointed to arrange for the evacuation of U.S. personnel and their dependents from Ethiopia. Unfortunately, Schaufele was considered suspect by the incoming Carter administration because of the intimacy of his earlier working relationship with Nixon appointee Henry Kissinger. Although he had been asked by the new secretary of state, Cyrus Vance, to stay on as assistant secretary of state for African affairs, it was apparent that Andrew Young, Carter's choice for the post of permanent representative to the United Nations, wanted to run African affairs directly out of the American U.N. Mission in New York City rather than through the State Department in Washington. Eventually Schaufele was displaced, and a more compliant successor was chosen in his stead.

In search of a new role in the State Department, in June 1977 Schaufele was nominated to the vacant post of U.S. ambassador to Greece. Unfortunately, during his confirmation hearings before the Senate Foreign Relations Committee, Schaufele made the mistake of stating that the proximity of some of the Greek islands to the coast of Turkey was "unusual." Although his confirmation unanimously passed the Senate, there was a bitter press campaign in Greece against his appointment based on reaction to that single, seemingly innocuous phrase. Faced with growing opposition from the Greek government and some members of the Greek-American community, the State Department had to withdraw Schaufele's name from consideration to avoid a diplomatic incident.

Schaufele subsequently turned down vacant U.S. embassy posts in Portugal and the Netherlands, claiming that both positions were too dull for his liking, and was instead nominated in December 1977 and confirmed in early 1978 as U.S. ambassador to Poland. As it turned out, his timing for assuming this post was impeccable from a diplomatic standpoint because Schaufele was serving at the U.S. embassy in Poland when Cardinal Karol Woytyla was elected pope. He was also present during the pope's first state visit to that country, an event that strengthened the hand of the Jaruzelski regime in dealing with the Soviet Union and the position of Solidarity and the Catholic church within Poland. Schaufele also witnessed the birth and attempted suppression by the Communist government of the Solidarity trade-union movement and the beginning of the tumultuous chain of events that eventually led to the collapse of communism in Eastern Europe. With the culmination of the 1980 U.S. presidential elections nearing, however, Schaufele found himself reluctant to serve under either of the candidates for president, and he subsequently announced his retirement from the State Department.

At only fifty-six years of age Schaufele still had incredible energy, and he was not content merely to reflect on his many years of past service. Soon after his departure from the State Department in 1980, he was appointed president of the Foreign Policy Association, a nonpartisan organization that stimulates discussion among public officials and private citizens about America's role in foreign affairs. After he left the Foreign Policy Association in 1983, he was hired to reorganize and direct the African operations of Catholic Relief Services, an overseas relief agency that at the time was playing the largest role in sending food and other aid to the victims of the Ethiopian famine. Other jobs for Catholic Relief Services brought Schaufele, acting as a consultant, back to two of his former embassy posts, Morocco and Poland, to survey and report on international aid operations in these two countries as well.

Schaufele was an acute observer of human nature and an insightful judge of the caliber of his colleagues. In interviews about his three decades of State Department experience conducted after his retirement, Schaufele assessed some of the individuals with whom he had worked previously. During the Congo crisis Schaufele developed the highest respect for the professionalism of Secretary of State Dean Rusk. He found George Bush gregarious and active as U.N. permanent representative and even admired the occasional sharpness and combativeness of Daniel Patrick Moynihan in the same role. But he was critical of U.N. Secretary-General Kurt Waldheim, whom he thought weak and unprincipled, with an obvious ambition for the Austrian presidency. As for Kissinger, with whom he worked closely for several years, Schaufele noted that the controversial secretary of state lost respect for subordinates who did not challenge him at times, as Schaufele surely did. State interests and not morality were Kissinger's primary concern in diplomacy, according to Schaufele. He also observed that his former boss was occasionally able to show compassion for others, and though he was demanding of his subordinates, Schaufele enjoyed working with Kissinger.

Reflecting on other aspects of his career in more recent years, Schaufele regretted not having taken at least a year's sabbatical at some point in order to reflect more fully on his profession. Like many career diplomats, he and his wife and two sons also paid the heavy prices of dislocation and personal separation. Schaufele continues to believe that the United Nations remains an important instrument of U.S. foreign policy. He also remains a strong—and vocal—supporter of peacekeeping operations and of a professional Foreign Service. He is firmly convinced that most American presidents and secretaries of state who enter office with skepticism about the role of the Foreign Service eventually leave with high praise and an improved understanding and appreciation of its role. In numerous speeches and editorials that he has given since his retirement, Schaufele continues to promote the tradition of diplomatic expertise that he first entered and dedicated his adult life to as a young man in 1950.

Works by William E. Schaufele, Jr.

"United Nations Peacekeeping Forces: The United States Perspective." In *The United Nations: A Reassessment: Sanctions, Peacekeeping, and Humanitarian Assistance,* ed. John M. Paxman and George T. Boggs, 67–78. Charlottesville: University Press of Virginia, 1973.

Polish Paradox: Communism and National Renewal. New York: Foreign Policy Association, 1981.

Works about William E. Schaufele, Jr.

Fasulo, Linda M., ed. *Representing America: Experiences of U.S. Diplomats at the U.N.* New York: Facts on File Publications, 1984, 177–92.

Political Profiles: The Nixon/Ford Years. New York: Facts on File, 1979, 571–72.

Who's Who in America 1982–1983. Chicago, IL: Marquis Who's Who, 1982, 2949.

RICHARD D. WIGGERS

WILLIAM JOSEPH SEBALD (1901–1980) was a naval

officer turned lawyer and diplomat who served as General Douglas MacArthur's
political advisor during the occupation of Japan.

Sebald was born on November 5, 1901, and graduated from the U.S. Naval
Academy in 1922. In 1925 he volunteered for assignment in Japan as a language
officer. While he was in Japan, he met and married Edith de Becker, a child of
English and Japanese parents. Dr. Joseph de Becker, Sebald's father-in-law and
a lawyer practicing in Japan, helped Sebald learn Japanese as they translated
legal codes. After becoming competent in Japanese, Sebald traveled throughout
the country with the U.S. naval attaché on inspection tours of Japanese naval
bases. He became convinced that the Japanese were violating the Washington
Conference Treaty on naval disarmament.

After Sebald returned to the United States, he decided to leave the navy. In
1930 de Becker's law firm offered him a partnership. He resigned his commission and entered law school at the University of Maryland, graduating in 1933.
Sebald practiced law in Japan for six years, during which time he translated a
number of Japanese laws and codes. Under constant surveillance in the late
1930s and then accused of being an American spy, Sebald left Japan in 1939.
He practiced law in Washington, D.C., for two years, until the attack on Pearl
Harbor.

Sebald rejoined the navy as a civilian a week after the attack, working in
naval intelligence. In March 1942 he was recommissioned as a lieutenant commander. With his Japanese background, he headed the combat intelligence section for the Pacific.

After the war came to an end, friends in the State Department asked Sebald
to enter the Foreign Service and join MacArthur's headquarters as a specialist
in Japanese law. Not ready to return to private life and aware that the navy was
about to shrink, he accepted the offer and traveled to Japan in January 1946.
The intense devastation of the Tokyo-Yokohama area impressed him the most
when he returned. He also found the Japanese people totally broken in will and
spirit.

Sebald's job was undefined when he arrived, which reflected the State Department's position in Japan. MacArthur never fully incorporated George Atcheson, the Foreign Service officer the State Department assigned to him as
political advisor, into a policymaking role. Sebald quickly became Atcheson's
main assistant following changes in mission and personnel. Atcheson became
chief of the Diplomatic Section, a division in MacArthur's headquarters, and
the U.S. representative on the Allied Council for Japan. This body of the victorious powers in the Pacific theater was an advisory committee to MacArthur.
Since the meetings were open, the group quickly became a Cold War battlefield
for the Soviet Union and the United States on the subject of Japan. Sebald's

work soon focused on this group. He helped devise rules of procedure, which limited the committee's propaganda value to the Soviet Union.

Sebald met MacArthur only briefly during his first year and a half in Japan, but events conspired again to promote Sebald. In mid-August 1947 Atcheson died in a plane crash, and MacArthur had Sebald replace him without consulting the State Department. In essence, Sebald acted as both the U.S. ambassador in Japan and MacArthur's own foreign minister. During the next three and a half years Sebald had unlimited access to MacArthur and developed a solid working relationship with the general. Sebald's naval background gave him a status Atcheson never enjoyed with MacArthur, and his understanding of the general's likes and moods helped him build on this foundation. He met with MacArthur more than any other person during the general's entire stay in Japan. MacArthur trusted him and often tempered his anti–State Department tirades, knowing that Sebald was caught in the middle. The general also had Sebald do most of the entertaining of important dignitaries visiting Japan, since he disliked formal dinners and functions. Still, Sebald faced a number of problems in Japan. He often never saw telegrams addressed to him, and as a civilian, he and his staff never received the same accommodations accorded to their military peers. The State Department also withheld his official promotion to Atcheson's job for two years.

Fighting the spread of communism was Sebald's main concern. He found that MacArthur worried little about this issue, saying that communism was not a factor in Japanese life. Sebald's clashes with the Soviet representative on the Allied Council for Japan convinced him otherwise. Sebald believed that the continual attacks the Soviets made on American reforms helped undermine their standing in Japan. His patient, but persistent work for the repatriation of Soviet-held Japanese prisoners of war undercut communism in Japan. At one meeting he brought 106 bales of letters from families of the missing men. Sebald admitted that the issue did not grab headlines on a regular basis, but it attracted wide attention and, in his opinion, forced the Soviets to make more than token efforts.

For twelve months in 1948 and 1949 Sebald worked to resolve the legal and diplomatic issues stemming from the sinking of the *Awa Maru*, a Japanese ship carrying civilians and traveling under diplomatic immunity and a guaranty of safe-conduct from the U.S. government. An American submarine torpedoed the ship, and the United States quickly accepted liability for the sinking. At MacArthur's recommendation, Sebald argued that Japan's surrender absolved the United States of any obligation, and the hundreds of millions of dollars worth of aid the United States had provided during the occupation more than compensated for the sinking of this ship. Japan eventually agreed to this view and gave up its claim for reparations.

MacArthur's assignment to witness the execution of Japanese war criminals was an unwelcome break for Sebald from his negotiations on the *Awa Maru*. Despite his negative experiences in prewar Japan, Sebald questioned the wisdom of the International Tribunal for the Far East. He avoided attending the hearings after the first day, finding the whole proceeding unseemly and gaudy. After the defendants were found guilty, MacArthur asked the representatives of the victorious Allied powers for their views on his reducing the verdicts. In his capacity as the U.S. representative, Sebald recommended that no change take place. MacArthur eventually decided to leave the verdicts as they were and instructed Sebald to have the four members of the Allied Council witness the executions. On December 23, 1948, a reluctant Sebald witnessed the deaths of the seven sentenced to hang. He and the other witnesses drank heavily before and after the hangings.

Sebald's influence started to grow in 1950, when the United States began preparing to negotiate a peace treaty with Japan. Secretary of State Dean Acheson appointed John Foster Dulles, a former U.S. senator and a foreign policy consultant to former Republican presidential candidate Thomas E. Dewey, to determine the feasibility of negotiating a peace treaty. Sebald arranged for Dulles to meet Japanese Prime Minister Shigeru Yoshida when he visited in June 1950. Yoshida refused to talk on substantive issues, leaving Dulles flabbergasted and frustrated. Sebald and John Allison, Dulles's assistant, explained that a first meeting in Japanese culture is for getting acquainted rather than conducting business. In January 1951 President Harry S. Truman instructed Dulles to begin negotiations on the treaty. When Dulles returned to Japan in February, Sebald arranged for him to meet with a broad spectrum of Japanese leaders. The meetings were held at Sebald's home, and his staff provided the translators. After another unproductive meeting with Yoshida, Sebald warned the prime minister that Dulles was losing patience. The following meetings between Dulles and Yoshida were more productive.

President Truman's dismissal of MacArthur from his commands in April increased Sebald's influence, but almost undid the work on the peace treaty. Although Sebald never became part of MacArthur's inner circle, a group that had ties with the general going back to the prewar days in Manila, he had become the most important member of the general's second tier of advisors. Yet MacArthur excluded Sebald from his entourage when he visited Taiwan to talk with Chiang Kai-shek in August 1950 and Wake Island to confer with Truman in October 1950. In both instances MacArthur said that it was better for Sebald if he was not present. When Sebald called on MacArthur after his dismissal, the general warned him that he would probably be dismissed since he was closely identified as a MacArthur man. Sebald also called on Yoshida, telling him of the dismissal and explaining that U.S. policy toward Japan had not changed. He also asked Yoshida, on his own authority, not to resign from office as was the custom in Japan in these situations, since the United States dearly desired political stability. When Lt. Gen. Matthew B. Ridgway arrived in Japan to replace MacArthur, he brought no personal clique with him. This fact, plus Ridgway's willingness to consult all sides in an issue, increased Sebald's influence in Tokyo. Dulles returned to Japan a few hours after MacArthur's departure to reassure the Japanese that U.S. policy had not changed. In a meeting Sebald, Dulles, and Ridgway agreed that reducing occupation controls and reversing the purge of prewar leaders was the best way to reassure the Japanese.

When the occupation formally ended in 1952, Sebald went to Burma as U.S. ambassador. His stay in Rangoon was uneventful. Burma chose a policy of neutrality in the Cold War, refusing to join the Southeast Asia Treaty Organization (SEATO). Nevertheless, Sebald attended the Manila Conference of 1954, where he witnessed the creation of SEATO.

Later that year Sebald returned to the United States to become deputy assistant secretary of state for Far Eastern affairs. Ironically, his first duty in Washington was overseeing the implementation of the SEATO alliance. Dulles, now secretary of state, began consulting Sebald on Japanese issues. Despite his work on the Japanese Peace Treaty, Dulles had little knowledge of the Japanese point of view. This fact allowed Sebald to influence policy toward Japan. Although there were a number of unresolved issues between the United States and Japan, including the status of Okinawa and the revision of the security treaty, the United States took no action. Given the political weakness of the government of Prime Minister Ichiro Hatoyama, Sebald recommended waiting until either Hatoyama solidified his position or a stronger prime minister replaced him. The secretary of state followed this advice, rejecting the recommendations for action of his old friend Allison, now the ambassador in Tokyo.

In 1957 President Dwight Eisenhower appointed Sebald U.S. ambassador to Australia. His assignment in Canberra was uneventful. There were no major issues outstanding between the United States and Australia. Sebald's main task was reassuring the Australians about Japanese intentions in seeking revision of the security treaty.

In 1961 Sebald retired from government service and joined a Washington, D.C., law firm. He wrote his memoirs and a policy-oriented study on Japan in the 1960s. There was a brief flurry of rumors following the election of Richard Nixon to the presidency that Sebald might be named U.S. ambassador to Japan. Nothing came of these rumors, despite Sebald's best efforts to capitalize on them. He lived out his retirement in Naples, Florida, and died on August 10, 1980.

Works by William Sebald

Editor and translator. *The Civil Code of Japan*. Kobe: J. L. Thompson and Co., 1934.

Editor and translator. *The Criminal Code of Japan*. Kobe: Japan Chronicle Press, 1936.

Editor and translator. *The North China Affair Special Tax Law and Regulations for the Enforcement of Same*. Kobe: Japan Chronicle Press, 1937.

Editor and translator. *The China Emergency Special Tax Law and Enforcement Regulations*. Kobe: Japan Chronicle Press, 1938.

Editor and translator. *The Foreign Exchange Control Law and Enforcement Regulations*. Kobe: Japan Chronicle Press, 1938.

Editor and translator. *The Principal Tax Laws of Japan*. Kobe: Japan Chronicle Press, 1938.

With MacArthur in Japan: A Personal History of the Occupation. New York: W. W.
  Norton, 1965.
Coauthor, with C. Nelson Spinks. *Japan: Prospects, Options, and Opportunities.* Wash-
  ington, DC: American Enterprise Institute for Public Policy Research, 1967.

NICHOLAS E. SARANTAKES

HUGH HEYNE SMYTHE (1913–1977) was an educator
and the first black American to serve as a U.S. ambassador in the Middle East.

MABEL MURPHY SMYTHE-HAITH (1918–   ) is
an educator and the first black American woman to serve as a U.S. ambassador in Africa.

Hugh Smythe was born in Pittsburgh, Pennsylvania, on August 19, 1913, the son of William Henry and Mary Elizabeth Smythe. His father died just a few years after his birth, and so from an early age Smythe was working, both to help support his family and to save for his college education. In 1932 he enrolled at Virginia State College, an all-black institution. There he acquired his interest in sociology, eventually majoring in that subject and receiving his B.A. in 1936. He also developed an interest in foreign affairs and shortly after his graduation applied for work with the Department of State, but was rebuffed. The following year he received his M.A. from Atlanta University. From 1938 through 1940 he did postgraduate work at Fisk University and the University of Chicago and some teaching at the former institution. While he was at Fisk University, he met and married Mabel Murphy, who had attended Spelman College. In 1942 he served as a research associate at Atlanta University.

In 1941 Smythe began his doctoral studies in anthropology at Northwestern University, which were interrupted by military service during World War II (1942–1944). He received his Ph.D. in 1945, completing his dissertation on "Patterns of Kinship Structure in West Africa." During the years after his military service Smythe remained busy with a number of positions, including assistant director of research for the Negro Land Grant College Cooperative Social Studies Project (1944) and teaching jobs at Morris Brown University in Atlanta (1944) and the Tennessee State Agricultural and Industrial University (1945–1946).

In 1947 Smythe became deputy director of special research for the NAACP, working with the world-famous W.E.B. DuBois. He continued this work until 1949, and it was during this time that he had his second experience with the Department of State. Encouraged by the NAACP to apply for a Foreign Service position, Smythe did so in 1949. Although his written application piqued the State Department's interest, when he had his personal interview before the examining board, he ran into what he felt to be a formidable wall of racism and was turned away.

After a brief period of employment with a New York public relations and advertising firm during the years 1949–1950, during which time he also was taking courses at Columbia University's East Asia Institute, both Smythe and his wife received appointments to teach in Japan, he at Yamaguchi National University, and she as the first woman professor at Shiga University. Smythe found the Japanese people and culture to be fascinating. He was particularly struck by the absence of racism displayed toward himself as a black American. Following his return to the United States in 1953, he joined the Sociology Department at Brooklyn College, City University of New York, and remained in this position until his death in 1977.

By the early 1960s Smythe's intellectual breadth, international experience, and work in U.S. civil rights problems (in addition to his work with DuBois, he had helped Gunnar Myrdal collect data for the groundbreaking work *An American Dilemma*) brought him to the attention of the incoming administration of John F. Kennedy, and he began perhaps the busiest eight years of his life. The Kennedy administration made as one of its first goals the "desegregation" of the State Department and the U.S. United Nations Mission. Between 1961 and 1962 Smythe served as a U.S. representative to a dizzying array of U.N. committees and conferences, including ECOSOC, the Sub-Commission on Prevention of Discrimination and Protection of Minorities, the Human Rights Committee, the Status of Women Committee, the U.N. Social Committee, the U.N. Statistical Committee, the UNICEF Program Committee and Executive Board Meeting, and the First International Conference of Africanists, held in Accra, Ghana, in 1962. During this same time he was a frequent lecturer at the U.S. Foreign Service Institute.

Between 1963 and 1965 Smythe returned to nongovernment work. He was a Fulbright Professor at Chulalongkorn University in Thailand from 1963 to 1964. Upon his return he did some lecturing to U.S. Special Forces troops at Fort Bragg about his experiences in Southeast Asia. In 1965 he served as chief consultant to the Youth in Action poverty program established in Brooklyn.

In 1965 Smythe received an appointment as U.S. ambassador to Syria, becoming just the tenth black American to hold such a position and the first to be assigned to a post in the Middle East. It was hardly a choice assignment, and the next two years were filled with tension and, on occasion, even danger for the new U.S. ambassador and his family. (Mabel Smythe accompanied her husband to Syria; their teenage daughter Pamela, a student at Brandeis University, visited during breaks in school.) Smythe's tenure in Syria was marked by political volatility, at least one very bloody coup, growing animosity between the United States and Syria, and, eventually, the complete severance of diplomatic relations in 1967.

At first glance, Smythe's appointment was surprising. Although his name had come up often in discussions in the Johnson administration concerning notable and qualified black Americans to appoint to ambassadorial positions, it was usually linked to an appointment in the Far East or Africa. These were Smythe's areas of expertise, and he seemed a natural choice for a post in one of these regions. In addition, ever since the late 1940s the idea of appointing a black American as an ambassador to a Middle East nation had been debated, and the conclusion always seemed the same: the nations of the Middle East would consider the selection of a black ambassador as an insult.

In hindsight, however, Smythe's appointment makes more sense. Even more so than the Kennedy administration, Johnson's was committed to the appointment of more black Americans to high diplomatic positions. Furthermore, Johnson was determined to appoint blacks to positions outside the "traditional" assignments: Liberia and other black African nations. Smythe had a number of desirable qualities for holding such a position in an acknowledged hotspot. His interest in the international ramifications of race, religion, and ethnicity could certainly find any number of direct applications in the cauldron of Middle East politics and intrigue. His color was merely an added bonus. Syria was undoubtedly one of the most anti-Western, pro-Soviet states in the Middle East, and its anti-imperialist rhetoric usually included potshots at U.S. racism. Perhaps Smythe's appointment could take some of the steam out of such arguments. Finally, while his appointment was something of a gamble, the reality was that U.S.-Syrian relations could hardly get any worse than they already were in 1965.

The history of U.S.-Syrian relations up to the time of Smythe's arrival in October 1965 was one plagued by increasing animosity. Since its independence from France during World War II, Syria had demonstrated both tremendous amounts of Arab nationalism and political instability. Both were of concern to the United States, and Syria's growing ties to Nasser's Egypt during the 1950s only heightened that concern. There is considerable evidence to suggest that the Eisenhower administration, acting through the CIA, plotted to overthrow the Syrian government in 1958. The repercussions of this meddling, together with Syria's increasingly close relations with Moscow and condemnations of U.S. support for Israel, pushed the two nations farther and farther apart during the early 1960s. U.S. intelligence analyses consistently portrayed Syria as the most unstable, radical, and anti-American state in the Middle East. Syria responded with vitriolic attacks against U.S. imperialism in the region and charges of U.S. espionage in Syria itself. Indeed, just a few months before Smythe's arrival Syria had expelled Walter Snowden, the U.S. embassy's second secretary, and another embassy employee for being part of an alleged spy ring. A number of Syrians, charged with being coconspirators, were sentenced to death.

All in all, it was not a promising posting. Smythe might have simply isolated himself in the U.S. embassy. Syrian leftist groups organized protests against the U.S. embassy, specifically singling out Smythe as an agent of U.S. imperialism and as a "traitor" to his race. Just four months after his arrival the bloodiest coup in Syria up to that time occurred, and Smythe had to make his way to work around the carnage and destruction. Syrian security officers trailed his every step, and even the simple task of meeting with a Syrian government official was an exercise in patience and stamina.

Instead, however, Smythe concentrated on the fundamentals of his job: protecting the small U.S. business interests in Syria, keeping the U.S. government informed of Syrian developments, and the rather thankless task of trying to improve U.S. relations with his host nation. He also intensified U.S. efforts at what he called "people-to-people diplomacy." This involved visits to each of the twelve states in Syria, increasing USIS programs, setting up local welfare programs (such as training programs for the blind), and other health and economic aid projects. Despite the limitations under which he was forced to operate, Smythe was widely cited as the hardest-working ambassador in Damascus.

All of Smythe's work, however, could not prevent a final rupture of U.S.-Syrian relations. In June 1967 Israel launched preemptive strikes against Egypt, Jordan, and Syria. Claiming that the United States was behind the attacks, Syria officially broke relations just a few days after the Israeli strikes. Smythe handled the potentially dangerous situation with style and forcefulness. Faced with screaming, rock-throwing, anti-American mobs and a forty-eight-hour evacuation order from the Syrian government, he stood his ground and demanded—and got—an extension of the evacuation order from the Syrians.

Following his departure from Syria, Smythe was almost immediately offered the ambassadorship in Malta. Though this was a far less exciting and demanding posting than Syria, Smythe accepted and stayed on until 1969. Compared with the tumultuous period in Syria, Malta was a sea of tranquillity, and Smythe's main problems revolved around staffing, repairs to the embassy and ambassadorial residence, and a degree of isolation.

During both his academic and governmental careers Smythe remained a consistent and vociferous critic of the misuse and nonuse of black Americans by the Department of State. His often scathing denunciations of what he perceived as undercurrents of racism in the department often provoked heated rejoinders from State Department officials, but his wide correspondence with other black Americans in the diplomatic service revealed a great deal of support for his position.

Following his retirement from his post in Malta, Smythe returned to his teaching duties at Brooklyn College, but also remained active in international affairs. He served as a special consultant to the Department of State and the Congressional Black Caucus. He also worked with the Ford Foundation, the Phelps Stokes Fund, and various organizations concerned with Africa and the Middle East. He died on June 22, 1977.

Mabel Murphy Smythe-Haith was born on April 3, 1918, in Montgomery, Alabama, the daughter of Harry Saunders and Josephine Dibble Murphy. She attended Spelman College in Atlanta from 1933 to 1936, where she met and later married Hugh Smythe. In 1937 she obtained her B.A. from Mount Holyoke College. She earned her M.A. from Northwestern University in 1940 and went on to gain her Ph.D. at the University of Wisconsin in 1942 in economics. From 1942 through 1947 she taught at Lincoln University, Tennessee State Agricultural and Industrial University, and Brooklyn College. In 1951 she accompanied her husband to Japan, where she taught at Shiga University. Upon her return to the United States she worked for the NAACP's Legal Defense and Education Fund for School Desegregation Cases. In 1954 she became a teacher and eventually principal at New Lincoln High School in New York City, where she continued to work (with time-outs for teaching at other institutions and accompanying her husband to his ambassadorial postings) until 1969. In 1970 she began a long association with the Phelps Stokes Fund, serving as director of research and publications until 1972 and as vice president until 1977. During that same period she was scholar-in-residence with the U.S. Commission on Civil Rights in 1973–1974.

Like her husband, Mabel Smythe also evidenced a tremendous interest in international affairs, and she served on a number of committees and advisory boards concerned with U.S. foreign policy. From 1962 through 1969 she served on the Department of State's Advisory Council on African Affairs. She also worked on the U.S. Advisory Commission on Educational and Cultural Affairs from 1962 to 1965. In 1964 she was part of the U.S. delegation to UNESCO, and from 1965 through 1970 she was a member of the U.S. National Committee for UNESCO.

In 1977, the same year that Hugh Smythe died, she was selected by the incoming Carter administration to serve as U.S. ambassador to Cameroon, becoming only the second black woman to be selected for such a position (Patricia Roberts Harris had been the first) and the first black woman to serve as a U.S. ambassador to an African nation. Neither the selection nor the posting were particularly surprising, however. Her name had been discussed a good deal during the Johnson administration in regard to openings in the Department of State. The fact that her husband was an ambassador during most of that time, however, probably hurt her chances for a position then. The Carter administration made a concerted effort to recruit and appoint highly qualified black candidates for foreign policy positions. Indeed, Carter appointed fifteen black Americans as ambassadors, just one less than the Nixon-Ford administrations had appointed in eight years, and just one less than the combined appointments of the Truman, Eisenhower, Kennedy, and Johnson administrations.

Mabel Smythe's knowledge of and interest in African affairs made her an attractive candidate. Her appointment to Cameroon was a reflection of the Carter administration's commitment to human rights as a part of the nation's foreign policy. During the late 1960s and 1970s Cameroon had been one of the more socially progressive African states, seeking international assistance in the promotion of women in national affairs and taking a sympathetic and enlightened view of the refugee crisis the nation faced during that period. Mabel Smythe's appointment was undoubtedly an acknowledgment and appreciation by the Carter administration of these positive steps.

Nevertheless, the new ambassador's job was not merely symbolic. U.S. interests were pouring into western Africa, eagerly trying to displace the older European entrepreneurial activities left over from the days of colonialism. Cameroon was an attractive area of investment. It had known but virtually untapped oil resources and also contained various other raw materials. Protecting, monitoring, and promoting these interests were parts of Smythe's job. In addition, the U.S. embassy in Cameroon served as a listening post to one of that nation's neighbors, Equatorial Guinea.

The small nation of Equatorial Guinea had been a problem for U.S. foreign policy since the late 1960s and early 1970s. In 1968 the murderously repressive regime of Francisco Macías Nguema Biyogo had taken power. The horrifying brutality of his rule resulted in the deaths of an estimated 20,000 people and the flow of thousands of refugees into neighboring countries, such as Cameroon. Perhaps more troubling to U.S. policymakers was the increasingly pro-Communist orientation of the Macías government. Soviet and Chinese aid poured into the country, and thousands of Cubans traveled there to teach and train Equatorial Guineans. Adding to the concern engendered by this Communist penetration of this western African nation was the fact that it was rumored that there were large deposits of uranium in the country. With the overthrow of the Macías dictatorship in 1979, relations with the United States—which had been terminated in 1975—were reestablished. As had been a traditional practice, the U.S. ambassador to Cameroon was also accredited to Equatorial Guinea, and Mabel Smythe took the position in December 1979.

Mabel Smythe left her posts in Africa in February 1980, called back to Washington by the Carter administration to serve as deputy assistant secretary of state for African affairs. With the coming to office of the Reagan administration in 1981, Smythe left government service to return to academia. She was Melville J. Herskovits Professor of African Studies at Northwestern University from 1981 to 1983 and Distinguished Professor until 1985, at which time she became professor emerita. She married Robert Haith, Jr., in that same year. Mabel Smythe lives in Washington, D.C., where she remains actively interested in foreign affairs, particularly those related to Africa and refugee problems.

Works by Hugh Smythe and Mabel Smythe-Haith

Both of these scholars were prolific writers. The following is but a brief selection, accentuating their coauthored works.

Smythe, Hugh, and Mabel Smythe. "Report from Japan: Comments on the Race Question." *The Crisis* 59, no. 3 (March 1952): 159–64.
———. *The New Nigerian Elite*. Stanford, CA: Stanford University Press, 1960.
Smythe, Mabel M., ed. *The Black American Reference Book*. Englewood Cliffs, NJ: Prentice-Hall, 1976.

Works about Hugh Smythe and Mabel Smythe-Haith

Miller, Jake C. *The Black Presence in American Foreign Policy Affairs*. Lanham, MD: University Press of America, 1978.

MICHAEL L. KRENN

LAURENCE ADOLPHE STEINHARDT (1892–1950), lawyer and diplomat, was born in New York City, the second of three children and the only son of Adolphe Max Steinhardt, cofounder of a steel-enameling and stamping company, and Addie (Untermyer) Steinhardt. Both parents were of German-Jewish ancestry. His uncle was Samuel Untermyer, a prominent New York attorney active in state and national Democratic Party politics. Steinhardt took his B.A., M.A. and LL.B. degrees at Columbia University and was admitted to the New York bar in 1916. During World War I he enlisted in the army field artillery as a private and rose to sergeant on the provost marshal's general staff. In 1920 he joined his uncle's law firm, Guggenheimer, Untermyer, and Marshall. He married Dulcie Yates Hoffman in 1917; they had one daughter, Dulcie Ann.

As a rising young attorney, Steinhardt gave the impression of setting aside his Jewishness in an effort to become an exemplar of the Protestant work ethic in his professional life. There was something almost ruthless about his dedication to the competitive character of the American free-enterprise system and his own ambition. Conservative and hardworking, he became suspicious of the frenzy for speculation and quick profits that gripped Wall Street in the 1920s. Well before the market crashed in October 1929, he moved his personal stocks and securities to a safer haven. Commanding a six-figure income, he had no sympathy for those who had lost everything—"They still refused to give up the movies and the flivver and the lights of Broadway for the farm," he noted coldly of the unemployed in his own New York State.

Attracted to the fiscal orthodoxy and conservatism of the Democratic Party candidate for president in the election campaign of 1932, Steinhardt signed up as a Roosevelt-before-Chicago man. He had been bitten by the political bug. A heavy contributor to FDR's campaign chest, Steinhardt knew that his stock stood high with the new president after the election and debated with friends and relatives privately whether a subcabinet position or a state attorney's job were within his grasp. As always, he was a realist about these things, and when a diplomatic appointment was offered to him, he accepted with good grace. He expected to be "quite an opportunist about it," he confided to his sister, and "stay in the post the shortest period of time to make an impression and gain some useful connections."

Talk of this kind would not have gained Steinhardt any friends among the professionals in the State Department, but in other ways he was an admirable choice for the post of minister to Sweden in 1933. Sweden had been identified by Secretary of State Cordell Hull as one of the most likely candidates to sign a reciprocal trade agreement with the United States. At a time when the nations of Europe were turning increasingly toward protectionism in an attempt to combat the ravages of the Depression, Secretary Hull, with FDR's blessing, was ready to launch a personal crusade to bring tariff barriers down by means of bilateral trade agreements. Negotiating these agreements preoccupied Hull, who was a devout Wilsonian entrapped by a fiercely isolationist Congress. Why not send to Stockholm a young New York lawyer experienced in commercial law and with all kinds of reasons to work hard for the secretary?

Arriving in Stockholm in May 1933, Steinhardt moved quickly to establish contacts in business and government circles. His capacity for hard work and attention to detail enabled him to resolve in a matter of months a dispute between an American company and the Swedish State Railroad that had been languishing in the courts for eleven years. His hosts were duly impressed by his hard-driving approach. What impressed Steinhardt about his hosts, and Europeans generally, was their selfishness when dealing with American businessmen abroad. The only way to deal with these Europeans who gave nothing away, he confided to a friend, was to respond in kind with a policy of "nothing for nothing." They took advantage of American idealism and generosity and "laugh[ed] at [us] as suckers." It was high time for the "American Santa Claus" to "close up shop." These were harsh words, although Steinhardt was careful to keep what were his personal views to private correspondence. His words reflected the growing feeling on both sides of the Atlantic, especially after the failure of the London Conference in November 1933, that the global trading community envisioned by Woodrow Wilson was a dream in full retreat before the reality of hard economic times. In Stockholm Steinhardt worked hard to keep this dream alive out of loyalty to Secretary Hull, impressing on American and Swedish export firms that there was more to be gained over the long term by cooperation than by competition. He did his work well, because when the principals took over the final stage of negotiations in May 1935, a trade agreement quickly emerged with no delays or last-moment objections. Steinhardt's role, a delighted Hull told him, was a pivotal one.

Steinhardt deserved this praise by the secretary, but what was strangely missing for someone who had immersed himself in economic issues for a full year was any extended commentary on Sweden's "middle way." This was the name bestowed by the American journalist Marquis Childe in his best-selling account of Prime Minister Per Albin Hannson's remarkably successful program to combat hard economic times in Sweden. The parallel between this Social Democratic program and the direction being taken by the New Deal was so striking that FDR sent a committee to observe and report, but Steinhardt remained oddly unaffected. He called himself a New Dealer, but he remained a fiscal conservative and someone who could never be accused of having a large social conscience.

Pleased with his representative's work for him in Stockholm, Secretary Hull promoted Steinhardt and appointed him ambassador to Peru in April 1937. On this occasion his mission for Hull was to prepare the way for the Eighth Pan-American Conference scheduled to be held in Lima in 1938 and to mark the next stage in FDR's "good neighbor" policy in Latin America. Before he turned to his Pan-American agenda, the new ambassador had to deal with a delicate professional matter closer to home. On his arrival in Lima, Steinhardt discovered to his dismay that he had inherited from his predecessor a dilapidated embassy building whose staff was demoralized and apathetic. Much of the staff's unhappiness was caused by the landlord, Mme. Benavides (the wife of the president of Peru), who was unhappy in her turn because she was compelled to pay a kickback on the monthly rent. This money had been going into the personal account of the previous ambassador, who had another lucrative arrangement with an embassy employee to import liquor under ambassadorial privilege and then sell it for a profit. Steinhardt, who believed in the highest standards of probity in personal and professional dealings, was horrified. After a brief internal investigation, his predecessor, who had spent twenty years in the American Foreign Service, was persuaded to retire early and without fanfare.

Steinhardt was delighted when the department wrote to commend him on his diligent inquiries and concern for the ethical standards of the diplomatic profession. It was these professionals whose good opinion mattered more than anything else to him. In Lima the embassy building was quickly restored and renovated, and the ambassador turned to the more important task of rebuilding his government's influence in the country.

By 1937 the "good neighbor" policy launched by the New Deal had made significant progress. Designed by FDR to erase the stigma of dollar diplomacy and to promote economic recovery under democratic governments in Latin America, this program faced a stern challenge in Peru. Peru was a desperately poor country ruled by a military dictator, President Oscar Benavides, who did not bother to hide his profascist sympathies. Italy and Germany were Benavides's preferred investment and trading partners, and Steinhardt fought to protect American business interests and his government's influence. Just as threatening to the political equilibrium in the country was an emergent nationalist movement, the Allianza Popular Revolucionara Americana (APRA), whose leaders demanded an end to all foreign influence.

In this situation the Eighth Pan-American Conference, which opened its sessions in December 1938, looked certain to be disrupted by angry protests from the left or the right. Secretary Hull, who was elected president of the conference, did not hide his anxiety. Behind the scenes Steinhardt worked frantically to preserve the appearance of pan-American unity. The conference itself shortened its sessions and proclaimed no convention or treaty, but did manage to issue more than one hundred proclamations and declarations of hemispheric unity. More important, there were no political incidents. Secretary Hull declared himself well pleased. In particular, he praised the work of his ambassador in Lima, who had kept a cool head in some difficult situations.

It was just these qualities of professionalism and poise that prompted Secretary Hull to offer Steinhardt his greatest challenge to date. In a letter to a friend Steinhardt confided that unlike other political appointees, he had achieved a particular position with the career officers in the State Department, who now thought of him as one of their own. He was also convinced that FDR was delighted to find someone who could do the job better than the career officers (''white-spats boys'') in the State Department. Occasionally his thoughts returned to his original ambition for a career in public life, but, as one colleague shrewdly observed, an ambassador was always in the center of things, and Moscow was a pivotal post in Europe.

In the summer of 1939 war seemed a matter of weeks away in Europe, and one focal point was Moscow, where an Anglo-French delegation and a German delegation were vying desperately to win an alliance with Stalin. It was blind flying there, Loy Henderson (assistant chief for European affairs) warned Steinhardt. Henderson was the most experienced and respected specialist on the Soviet Union in the department. There had been one break for the American embassy amidst all the rumor and speculation in Moscow. For several months several members of the German embassy who were anti-Nazi in outlook had been feeding their American counterparts information about the strengthening rapprochement between Stalin and Hitler. Arriving in Moscow in the early days of August 1939, Steinhardt brought with him a carefully worded letter from President Roosevelt advertising the danger of any pact with Hitler. To his dismay, Steinhardt found that information about this secret letter had already been leaked to the newspapers. A few weeks after his arrival the Nazi-Soviet Pact was proclaimed on August 23, 1939, and days later Hitler invaded Poland.

Steinhardt was incensed. What angered him was not simply this betrayal of confidence but the poisonous atmosphere of intrigue and suspicion that filled every aspect of life for a Western diplomat in Moscow. Diplomats lived under virtual house and office arrest, surrounded by secret police agents. They were spies with passports, in *Pravda*'s description, to be harassed beyond endurance. ''Everything is forbidden, everything is watched,'' Steinhardt wrote a friend, ''and everyone lives under a fear complex.'' Diplomats possessed personal immunity when they lives in Stalin's police state, but their emotions were cruelly exposed.

In a series of dispatches written during his first nine months in Moscow, Steinhardt came to the conclusion that the Nazi-Soviet Pact was a full-blooded alliance between two predatory leaders who were determined to divide Europe between them. He told Loy Henderson that things had changed since Henderson had been in Moscow; Stalin had become an old-fashioned Russian imperialist. The United States must deal with him on a basis of strict retaliation (''blow for blow'' and ''tit-for-tat''). Everyone in Washington seemed to agree.

In the summer of 1940 news that President Roosevelt had changed signals and ordered direct talks to remove long-standing differences between the two countries caught Steinhardt off guard. He had not been consulted. He asked Loy Henderson what was happening, because ''I have grave doubts that our policy of . . . appeasement will get us anyplace.'' Henderson confessed that he too was mystified, but that ''as long as that is our policy I am endeavoring loyally to cooperate.''

What explained FDR's action was the end of the phony war in Europe. The dramatic invasion of the Low Countries and Scandinavia by the German armies and the surrender of France in the summer of 1940 shocked Stalin into an active defense of his country's interests in the Baltic states and the Balkans. There were signs of a rift between the two allies. Steinhardt would have none of it. To think that Stalin would do anything to invite Hitler to attack him, he told a friend, was "childish beyond belief." In Washington Secretary Hull tried to caution his ambassador that the president was treading a fine line between Hitler and Stalin. The "higher-ups" were playing games of "international policies" instead of getting results there in Moscow, Steinhardt told Henderson, and it would not work. The men in the Kremlin did not respond to "ethical and moral considerations . . . customary between individuals of culture and breeding." Sent to Moscow to "keep the lid from blowing off things" (his own words), Steinhardt was coming to the boil himself.

In March 1941 Secretary Hull sent a secret cable to Steinhardt informing him that the department was in possession of an "authentic" document containing details of Hitler's invasion plan for the Soviet Union scheduled for the "near or not distant future" and telling him to inform Moscow. No, responded Steinhardt, because the Kremlin would treat what Hull said as either disinformation or provocation. No good could come of passing this document along.

This was a remarkable response by an ambassador charged with executing his government's policy. It was all the more shocking when, two months later, Hitler launched his long-planned invasion of the Soviet Union on June 22, 1941. Immediately FDR ordered all aid possible under Lend-Lease arrangements to be sent to this new ally against the Axis powers and sent his personal representative, Harry Hopkins, to set up the arrangements in Moscow. Steinhardt was not invited to the Hopkins-Stalin meetings. In November 1941 Henderson wrote Steinhardt to come home and that he was not under a shadow, but Steinhardt knew better. He had "overreached" himself, he told his wife on his return to Washington.

A few years earlier another American ambassador, William C. Bullitt, had lost his temper in this most difficult post and had made every effort to "devil the Russians." Steinhardt had also destroyed his usefulness in Moscow, but his experience and skills were simply too valuable not to be used in Europe at war. Late in 1941 he was sent to Ankara, Turkey, where he rediscovered his old coolness under pressure and played a key role in keeping this country neutral and vital Turkish exports of chrome metal out of German hands. For Steinhardt, this victory in the economic war against Germany was his "most useful job." Late in 1944 FDR named Steinhardt ambassador to Czechoslovakia. In this sensitive post Steinhardt advised Washington not to extend the Marshall Plan to the Communist-dominated government in Prague until suitable guarantees were given to end a virulent anti-American campaign. It was his own "no-appeasement" policy, but tempered on this occasion by a global sense of the Cold War. No one blamed Steinhardt when Stalin staged his brutal coup d'état that destroyed any opposition to the Communist Party in Czechoslovakia in February 1948. This same realistic response to the global challenge of communism marked Steinhardt's final appointment as ambassador to Canada in 1948. Refusing to respond to strident anticommunism calls in Congress, Steinhardt urged that Canada be allowed to work out its own Cold War strategy free from pressure or exhortation. Early in 1950 Steinhardt was killed in a plane crash near Ottawa and was buried in his family mausoleum in New York City. He was fifty-seven years old.

A self-styled professional in diplomacy, Steinhardt prided himself that he had won acceptance by colleagues who had spent a lifetime in diplomacy. This was a fair claim but not the whole story. Intelligence and energy more than qualified him for the post in Moscow, which was the most important and challenging of his career, but temperament was missing. It was ''not so much what you can do in this post,'' one experienced professional in Moscow concluded, ''but what you can stand.'' Steinhardt learned this lesson at some personal cost, and it was an important lesson for ambassadors who went to Moscow in the Cold War period after 1945.

Works by Laurence Steinhardt

Steinhardt's papers containing letters to friends and colleagues are in the Library of Congress. Also, see State Department records.

Works about Laurence Steinhardt

O'Connor, Joseph. ''Laurence A. Steinhardt and American Policy toward the Soviet Union, 1939–1944.'' Ph.D. diss., University of Virginia, 1965.
Stackman, Ralph R. ''Laurence A. Steinhardt, New Deal Diplomat, 1933–1945.'' Ph.D. diss., Michigan State University, 1967.

KEITH EAGLES

ADLAI E. STEVENSON (1900–1965), best known as the

Democratic nominee for president in 1952 and 1956, served as U.S. permanent representative to the United Nations from 1961 to 1965, a period that included the critical days of the Cuban missile crisis.

Stevenson was born in Los Angeles, California, on February 5, 1900. While he was still small, his parents, Helen and Lewis, returned to Bloomington, Illinois, their hometown. His family had long been prominent in Illinois politics. Adlai's grandfather, Adlai E. Stevenson I, had been vice president under Grover Cleveland. Helen's grandfather, Jesse Fell, had published a newspaper in the mid-1800s, had helped found Illinois State University, and had become an early supporter of Abraham Lincoln.

A mediocre student, Stevenson nevertheless attended the prestigious Choate Academy in Wallingford, Connecticut, and later went to Princeton University. In college Stevenson, a likable if unimposing young aristocrat, excelled in extracurricular activities and worked as managing editor of the school newspaper, the *Daily Princetonian*. He graduated from Princeton in 1922. He flunked out of Harvard Law School after two years, but eventually received a law degree from Northwestern University. If Stevenson inherited a taste for politics from his illustrious ancestors, frequent boyhood trips to Europe whetted his interest in international affairs. As a young man, Stevenson probably would have preferred the life of a foreign correspondent to the practice of law. In the summer of 1926 Stevenson made a long and dangerous trip to Russia as a representative of a Chicago newspaper. But he decided on a more conventional career, and the following year he joined a Chicago law firm.

A loyal Democrat, Stevenson admired Woodrow Wilson and supported American participation in the League of Nations. Otherwise there is little evidence of his early foreign policy views or his political leanings. He seemed inclined toward a moderate, if ill-defined, progressivism. In 1930 Stevenson joined the Chicago Council on Foreign Relations, a private organization devoted to promoting the study of international affairs; two years later he became its secretary. He left Chicago briefly as part of the flood of young lawyers descending on Washington in the early days of Franklin Roosevelt's New Deal and stayed in Washington from 1933 to 1934, working first in the Agricultural Adjustment Administration and then briefly in the Federal Alcohol Control Administration. Acquiring a reputation for wit and a polished speaking style, Stevenson was elected president of the Council on Foreign Relations shortly after returning to Chicago. Despite its official nonpartisanship, the council had a definite internationalist bias, favoring an active American role in world affairs. After World War II erupted in Europe, Stevenson supported U.S. aid to Great Britain and became head of the local chapter of the Committee to Defend America by Aiding the Allies, better known as the White Committee for one of its cofounders, Kansas newspaper editor William Allen White. Situated ironically in one of the strongholds of American isolationism, Stevenson worked to mitigate local opposition to Lend-Lease and other administration foreign policy initiatives.

In June 1941 Stevenson accepted a position as special assistant to Secretary of the Navy Frank Knox, the publisher of the *Chicago Daily News*. Stevenson served Knox in a variety of ways: as legal counsel, press secretary, speech writer, and personal surrogate. His duties included routine inspection trips, among which was one long tour of the Pacific theater, and some more sensitive assignments. Stevenson, for example, was one of the first public officials to advocate the desegregation of the navy and the commissioning of blacks as officers, a proposal that Knox allowed his aide to take directly to President Roosevelt.

As the war went on, Stevenson undertook a series of temporary assignments outside the Navy Department. In 1943 he led a survey for the Foreign Economic Administration to assess the needs of liberated, but war-torn, Italy. The following year Stevenson returned to Europe to participate in a study of the effectiveness of close air support and tactical bombing.

Next, the Chicago lawyer joined the poet Archibald MacLeish, then an assistant secretary of state, in a public relations campaign on behalf of the fledgling United Nations. When the San Francisco conference that was to draft the U.N. Charter convened in April 1945, Stevenson handled press relations for the U.S. delegation. San Francisco gave Stevenson his first taste of high-level international politics. It also led to his appointment to the American mission to the U.N. Preparatory Commission, which met in London in the fall of 1945 to organize the first meeting of the U.N. General Assembly and to decide other issues. After a gallstone attack disabled Edward Stettinius, the chief of the American delegation, Stevenson assumed command. He won praise for his leadership, especially his skill in building a consensus behind the selection of Norwegian diplomat Trygve Lie as the first secretary-general of the United Nations. Increasingly skeptical of Soviet intentions, Stevenson nevertheless sought to maintain cordial relations with Russian officials.

In 1947 Stevenson represented the United States as an alternate delegate to the first meeting of the U.N. General Assembly in New York. President Harry Truman reportedly offered Stevenson several full-time, permanent positions, among them a spot as an assistant secretary of state. Stevenson, however, since the 1930s had been longing to run for office, especially an Illinois Senate seat. The Chicago Democratic machine, which dominated party politics in the state, had tagged the noted economist Paul Douglas as its Senate candidate in 1948, but party leaders agreed to support Stevenson for governor. An enthusiastic if inexperienced campaigner, Stevenson exploited his image as an honest, good-government candidate and won a landslide victory over a Republican incumbent whose administration had been plagued by scandal and incompetence.

As governor, Stevenson supported moderate reform. Interested mainly in honest, efficient administration, he appointed trustworthy Republicans as well as faithful Democrats to office. He enjoyed only a few major legislative successes, but he did place the Illinois state police under civil service, he won legislative approval for a major highway-construction program, and he cracked down on illegal gambling. The Illinois governor became one of the first public officials to criticize the anti-Communist extremism that was coming to be symbolized by Senator Joseph R. McCarthy of Wisconsin. In 1951 Stevenson garnered praise from liberals around the country when he vetoed the Broyles Bill, a repressive and badly drafted measure that, among its many provisions, would have required loyalty oaths of state employees and public school teachers. Stevenson suffered two embarrassing defeats as governor. The state legislature blocked his efforts to call a convention to draft a new state constitution and defeated his proposal to create a fair employment practices committee to investigate racial discrimination in the workplace.

Personal problems also marred Stevenson's governorship. In 1928 Stevenson had married a temperamental Chicago socialite named Ellen Borden. The couple had three children—Adlai II, Borden, and John Fell, but Ellen's emotional instability and Stevenson's political ambitions strained their marriage from the start. They finally divorced in 1949. The divorce, a rarity among public figures of the period, triggered rumors of adultery or homosexuality. It pained Stevenson privately and was a substantial political liability for the rest of his career.

With no apparent successor to Truman, the Democratic National Convention drafted Stevenson to run for president against General Dwight D. Eisenhower in 1952. Stevenson subtly encouraged the draft, but refused to seek his party's nomination openly. Stevenson's apparent ambivalence earned him a reputation for indecision that would dog him for years. In reality, Stevenson wanted to run for reelection as governor. He had little desire to oppose Eisenhower, a Republican moderate whose internationalist foreign policy views seemed to mirror Stevenson's. Stevenson hesitated to close the door on the draft movement in part because of the possibility that Eisenhower might lose the Republican nomination to Senator Robert A. Taft of Ohio, a favorite of the Republican Old Guard. Less personable than Eisenhower, Taft, who labored under a reputation as an isolationist, might have been too tempting a target for Stevenson to resist. Meeting in Chicago shortly before the Democrats convened there in the summer of 1952, Republicans handed Eisenhower a narrow victory.

Stevenson, nevertheless, ultimately agreed to accept his party's nomination, and promising "to talk sense" to the American people, he electrified the convention with an eloquent acceptance speech. The war in Korea dominated the fall campaign. Loyal to the administration if not personally close to Truman, Stevenson could only propose to continue the conflict. Saddled with an unpopular war, opposing a military hero, and faced with a public ready for change after twenty years of Democratic rule, Stevenson waged a spirited but uphill campaign. Eisenhower won 55 percent of the popular vote and defeated Stevenson 442 to 89 in the electoral college, but the race transformed Stevenson from a relatively obscure freshman governor into an international figure known for his eloquence, courage, and integrity.

After his first defeat Stevenson made a celebrated world tour, wrote and spoke extensively, remained active in Democratic party politics, and opened a new law office in Chicago. In March 1954 he won acclaim for a speech to a Democratic fund-raiser in Miami in which he took President Eisenhower to task for tolerating the reckless Red-baiting of Joe McCarthy. "A political party divided against itself, half McCarthy and half Eisenhower," Stevenson said, could not govern the nation effectively. Responding for Republicans, Vice President Richard M. Nixon tried to distance the administration from the Wisconsin senator. Stevenson's speech and Nixon's reply added to the growing momentum to silence McCarthy. By the end of the year he was formally censured by his colleagues, virtually ending his political career.

Widely regarded as the leading contender for the Democratic nomination in 1956, Stevenson this time actively sought the presidency, defeating Tennessee Senator Estes Kefauver after bruising primaries in Minnesota, Florida, and California. Once he clinched the nomination, Stevenson took the unusual step of allowing the Democratic convention to select his running mate. The delegates picked Kefauver over Senator John F. Kennedy of Massachusetts and several other contenders.

Stevenson, perhaps exhausted by his battle with Kefauver, seemed to lack a clear focus in his rematch with Eisenhower. The Illinois Democrat did, however, attract attention—much of it unfavorable—with two major policy initiatives. In a September speech to the American Legion Stevenson called for abolition of the draft and for a moratorium on the testing of the hydrogen bomb. He believed that conscription failed to produce recruits with the skills needed by a modern mechanized army. The moratorium was intended to limit both radioactive fallout and the arms race itself. Widely ridiculed for wanting to weaken America's defenses, Stevenson lost even worse in 1956 than he had four year earlier. But the passage of time gave Stevenson a measure of vindication. President John Kennedy signed a nuclear test-ban treaty in 1963, and the volunteer army became a reality during the presidency of Richard M. Nixon.

After his second defeat Stevenson helped organize the Democratic Advisory Council to promote liberal causes within the party and continued to criticize Eisenhower for letting the United States fall behind the Soviets in the battle for prestige and influence in the Third World. The Democrats' titular leader also continued to harbor presidential ambitions. Washington lawyer George Ball, Senator Mike Monroney of Oklahoma, and others attempted to organize a movement to draft Stevenson in 1960. Stevenson, meanwhile, would neither endorse John Kennedy, the clear front-runner, nor enter the race himself. Stevenson's conduct further strained his relationship with the young Massachusetts senator—the two had never been friendly—and probably cost Stevenson whatever chance he had for the job he wanted most: secretary of state in a new Democratic administration.

After Kennedy edged out his Republican opponent, Vice President Nixon, Stevenson reluctantly accepted the lesser position of ambassador to the United Nations. Popular among his fellow delegates, Stevenson proved to be an effective voice for American interests in the world organization. Yet Stevenson disappointed himself and his admirers with his inability to influence U.S. policy. President Kennedy and his inner circle considered Stevenson to be "too soft" as a policymaker and ineffectual as a politician, although the White House also viewed him warily as a potential political rival. Stevenson enjoyed no more rapport with his nominal superior, Secretary of State Dean Rusk. Stevenson dismissed Rusk as a plodding, unimaginative bureaucrat. In fairness to Kennedy and Rusk, for all the rhetorical skill and personal charm that Stevenson brought to his U.N. post, he sometimes neglected his diplomatic homework and did not fight very hard to make his opinions heard within the administration.

The Bay of Pigs debacle in April 1961 demonstrated the limits of Stevenson's influence and the value to the United States of his good name. The White House did not consult Stevenson about its plan to sponsor a Cuban émigré invasion of Fidel Castro's Cuba until after the decision had been made to proceed with the operation. Stevenson disapproved of the attack, but he was forced to defend it before the U.N. Security Council. Castro's forces easily suppressed the invasion. Stevenson nevertheless managed to limit the U.N. response to the disaster to a resolution expressing mild disapproval of the U.S. involvement. He enjoyed similar partial successes elsewhere. When Zaire became independent, the former Belgian Congo quickly collapsed into a Byzantine maze of coups, countercoups, and civil war. Stevenson lobbied hard for administration support for a U.N. peacekeeping force that could at least maintain the territorial integrity of the huge central African nation. He, and the U.N. peacekeepers, succeeded.

Public approval of Stevenson's performance peaked in October 1962 when Stevenson confronted the Soviet ambassador during the Cuban missile crisis. Saying that he was prepared to wait for an explanation until "hell freezes over," Stevenson dramatically presented photographic evidence of Soviet missiles on the island and scored a major propaganda victory for the United States. Within the administration Stevenson advocated a diplomatic solution to the crisis and counseled President Kennedy against rash military action. Stevenson, in fact, saw the crisis as a possible springboard for arms control talks and the neutralization of Cuba. The U.N. ambassador proposed that the United States remove its missiles from Turkey and Italy if the Soviets would withdraw their missiles from Cuba. He also suggested closing the U.S. base at Guantanamo if the Russians would evacuate all their military forces from the Caribbean nation. Kennedy did eventually allow the removal of American Jupiter missiles from Turkey, but he opposed Stevenson's proposals for a broad diplomatic offensive. Fearful of appearing weak, Kennedy also refused to make any formal, public concessions to the Soviet Union. Weeks later, when journalists close to the president published an account of the crisis that quoted an unnamed White House source who claimed that "Adlai wanted a Munich," the reference to

British Prime Minister Neville Chamberlain's effort to appease Adolf Hitler before the state of World War II dealt a damaging blow to Stevenson's prestige.

After Kennedy's assassination in November 1963 Stevenson's already-tenuous position at the United Nations deteriorated further. From the same generation as the new president, Stevenson initially hoped that he could work well with Lyndon B. Johnson. But the Illinois Democrat opposed Johnson's decision to send several thousand American troops to the Dominican Republic to suppress a spurious Communist coup. More important, as Johnson became increasingly preoccupied with the war in Vietnam, the United Nations—and the U.S. ambassador—became increasingly irrelevant to the formation of American foreign policy. Stevenson had serious doubts about Johnson's escalation of the war. He hoped for a diplomatic solution to the conflict and made unsuccessful efforts, through U.N. Secretary-General U Thant, to open negotiations between Washington and Hanoi. By 1965 many of Stevenson's old admirers were encouraging him to resign from the United Nations and speak out openly against the war. Despite his private doubts and the growing pressure, Stevenson remained publicly loyal to Johnson until his death from a heart attack in London on July 14, 1965.

If Stevenson remained a Cold Warrior to the end, his anticommunism was tempered by a commitment to civil liberties and the democratic process at home and to negotiation, international cooperation, and arms control abroad. Stevenson, moreover, felt a genuine concern for the peoples of the Third World and refused to see their countries merely as military battlegrounds for proxy wars between the United States and the Communist bloc. Stevenson will always be known mainly as a domestic politician, but as an influence on American diplomacy, he should probably best be remembered as the intellectual forebear of a younger generation of more dovish liberals—like the antiwar senators Eugene McCarthy and George McGovern—and other critics of the misuse of American military power overseas.

Works by Adlai E. Stevenson

Major Campaign Speeches. New York: Random House, 1953.
Call to Greatness. New York: Harper and Brothers, 1954.
The New America. New York: Harper and Brothers, 1957.
Friends and Enemies: What I Learned in Russia. New York: Harper and Brothers, 1959.
Looking Outward: Years of Crisis at the United Nations. Ed. Robert L. Schiffer and Selma Schiffer. New York: Harper and Row, 1963.
An Ethic for Survival: Adlai Stevenson Speaks on International Affairs, 1936–1965. Ed. Michael H. Prosser. New York: William Morrow and Co., 1969.
The Papers of Adlai E. Stevenson. 8 vols. Ed. Walter Johnson. Boston: Little, Brown and Co., 1972–1979.

Works about Adlai E. Stevenson

Broadwater, Jeff. Adlai Stevenson and American Politics: The Odyssey of a Cold War Liberal. New York: Twayne, 1994.

Martin, John Bartlow. *Adlai Stevenson and the World*. Garden City, NY: Doubleday, 1977.

———. *Adlai Stevenson of Illinois*. Garden City, NY: Doubleday, 1976.

McKeever, Porter. *Adlai Stevenson: His Life and Legacy*. New York: William Morrow and Co., 1989.

Walton, Richard J. *The Remnants of Power: The Tragic Last Years of Adlai Stevenson*. New York: Coward-McCann, 1968.

JEFF BROADWATER

WILLIAM HEALY SULLIVAN (1922–   ) was a career
diplomat who was deeply involved in the formulation of policy during the Vietnam conflict.

A Rhode Island native born on October 12, 1922, Sullivan graduated from Brown University under an accelerated program in 1942. Like most of his cohorts, he entered the military as a junior officer during World War II, serving as a navy lieutenant aboard combat destroyers in various theaters. Having cultivated an early commitment to government service, Sullivan chose to take the Foreign Service examination in 1947 after receiving a graduate degree. A career diplomat, he served in assignments in Washington and Geneva relating specifically to the growing crisis in Indochina before receiving his first ambassadorial appointment to Vientiane in 1964. In 1969 he returned to Foggy Bottom, where he worked as an assistant to Henry Kissinger in the Vietnam peace negotiations. In 1973 he received a second ambassadorial appointment, this time to Manila. In 1977 he accepted his last posting as ambassador to Teheran.

Sullivan's first diplomatic assignment was as third secretary and vice consul in the American legation in Bangkok. His responsibilities included the economic section and later consular matters. In due course he was transferred to Calcutta, where his duties again were largely commercial. In 1950 Sullivan was detailed as political advisor to General Douglas MacArthur in Japan at the time of the outbreak of the Korean War. Sullivan's duties included foreign liaison activities for SCAP (the occupation authority), including dealings with nations involved in the war effort in Korea. He also consulted in the creation of a Japanese foreign affairs establishment and was personally responsible for recommissioning scores of Japanese diplomats. He also negotiated the setting up of embryonic Japanese embassies in foreign nations, a very difficult task to accomplish in some Asian countries given the suffering undergone during wartime occupation. John Foster Dulles, leading the negotiations for a formal peace treaty, placed Sullivan in personal charge of mediation between Japan and South Korea over unresolved issues, such as Koreans living in Japan, property settlements, and restitution. However, these negotiations collapsed over symbolic issues. Sullivan's idea for turning over the administration of Okinawa to the Japanese soon after the end of the occupation also fared poorly. He did assist in the successful conclusion of the mutual security treaty that allowed American forces to remain in Japan, and he joined the Joint U.S.-Japan Committee to oversee the transition from American occupation.

For a time Sullivan left Asian affairs. In late 1952 he became political advisor to the head of the Southern NATO Command in Naples, Italy, consulting on Yugoslavia and the joint occupation of Austria. Soon he became part of the Rome embassy of Ambassador Clare Booth Luce and helped to establish an agreement allowing for the stationing of American forces in Italy. In 1955 he went to The Hague, where he was involved in the continuing confrontation of Holland with Indonesia over West New Guinea. In 1958 he received assignment to Washington in order to work on Southeast Asian affairs in the Far East Bureau, where the principle issue that he faced was how to blunt the advancement of communism in Indochina and Indonesia. In 1960 he planned President Eisenhower's trip to several Asian capitals, which included the infamous cancellation of the leg to Tokyo due to anti-American rioting.

The greatest stroke of luck in Sullivan's career was his selection as the assistant to W. Averell Harriman, a position he held for three years. Then assistant secretary of state and later roving ambassador, in 1961 Harriman led the American delegation in negotiations at Geneva over the independence and neutrality of Laos. Harriman had sent home half his staff so that Sullivan could acquire the necessary seniority to become his deputy. The situation that they faced with Laos was dire. Following the end of status as a French protectorate in 1954, Laos devolved into chaos as reactionary, neutralist, and Communist factions vied for political supremacy. In 1958 a right-wing general assumed control of the country with covert assistance from the CIA. When his government collapsed under pressure from the Communist Pathet Lao, neutralists were able to resume governmental authority briefly in 1960 before they again were ousted in a coup from the political right. Full-scale civil war followed, and the military regime was close to another collapse in 1961 when at the urging of Washington the major powers convened a second Geneva conference to deal specifically with the issue of Laos. For a time when the talks bogged down, Sullivan actually became the acting head of the American delegation. Eventually, after fifteen months of negotiating, a coalition government was set up in Vientiane in July 1962, thereby leaving America's hands free to engage communism in South Vietnam. It was also at this time that Sullivan and Harriman met privately with their North Vietnamese counterparts in order to attempt negotiations over South Vietnam.

For a time thereafter Sullivan was sent to the U.N. General Assembly in order to deal with the issue of mainland Chinese representation, which he successfully prevented from happening with diplomatic maneuvers. He also became involved with efforts to ameliorate the Sino-Indian miniwar over the Kashmir. He and Harriman led a joint Anglo-American mission to New Delhi in order to shore up the Indian government and stabilize the situation. In 1963 he accompanied his patron on a grand but fruitless mission whose aim was to defuse Soviet-American tensions. Next the pair attempted to establish a new economic organization in South America and tried to mediate the Argentinean nationalization of American petroleum holdings. Sullivan was also put in charge of the arrangements for visiting dignitaries to President John F. Kennedy's funeral.

Sullivan became actively involved with the Vietnam War early on. He was part of an interdepartmental team that concluded that there were no strategic targets to bomb in North Vietnam that would influence Hanoi to curtail its war effort; accordingly, bombing targets should be limited and designated farther from major cities. He also worked with the National Security Council (NSC) staff on a potential resolution to be submitted to Congress as legal justification for public debate on war in Vietnam. In 1964 Sullivan was appointed ambassador to Laos. However, when President Johnson selected Maxwell Taylor as ambassador to South Vietnam, Taylor requested that Sullivan be allowed to second him in Saigon, thus delaying Sullivan's arrival in Vientiane. For five months he assisted in attempts by the American embassy to shore up the precarious regime of General Nguyen Khanh, including personally returning the fleeing Khanh to Saigon during one particular coup attempt. He was also the coexecutive of a group known as the Mission Council that was designed to establish coordination between the American advisory effort and the Saigon government, and he provided input on a new Vietnamese constitution. He advocated a more definite American presence in Vietnam as the only way to overcome the lack of will to fight of the Saigon regime.

However, pressing issues also existed for the new ambassador when he finally assumed his duties in Laos in December 1964. The Laotian neutralization arising out of the 1962 Geneva Accords had fallen apart due not only to resumed indigenous political infighting but to violations by the North Vietnamese, who had increased their infiltration into that nation to two divisions along the supply route known as the Ho Chi Minh Trail while exclusively operating another division in northern Laos. In return, the U.S. government had set up a clandestine paramilitary organization, drawn primarily from Hmong hill tribesmen (but also including Thai mercenaries) and headed by leader Vang Pao, to conduct operations against the North Vietnamese. Sullivan still performed his diplomatic duties as ambassador, but more important, he centralized the sole direction of this secret war in himself, a feat accomplished because of the complete trust that the Johnson administration had vested in him. Under his tutelage the Hmong force increased to 40,000 men with an air transport and attack operation of about 150 craft. The actual American role took place through the shadow company known as Air America, which served as the front for the CIA supervisory force in Laos. Sullivan ran the war as a guerrilla operation by maintaining the utmost secrecy, by keeping American ground troops out of the country, and by choosing all the targets and mission objectives from Vientiane. His Hmong and air units would ambush North Vietnamese troops as they withdrew northward during the rainy season, thereby not only preventing infiltration into South Vietnam but also proscribing the North Vietnamese conquest of Laos.

Sullivan had a difficult time containing political squabbles within the Laotian government itself, however. On one occasion he interceded to persuade the head of the Lao air force to end his attack on the general staff. On another occasion he actively undertook to prevent a coup from being successful against the coalition government by organizing sabotage of the national radio network's transmitter link. As the neutralist regime began breaking apart in the mid-1960s, though, Sullivan began to assume a more direct role in the country's politics. He assented to secret bombing within Laos against both the Pathet Lao and the

North Vietnamese army in order to strengthen pro-American forces. The result was that the United States dropped on Laos two million tons of bombs within a decade's time.

In the early part of 1968 Sullivan briefly returned to Washington during the administration's post-Tet reassessment. Sullivan concurred with the decision to deescalate the war, since he believed that General William Westmoreland's strategy of attrition had proven itself a failure. In April, having decided to seek a settlement with Hanoi, Johnson asked Sullivan to resolve a deadlock over the site for peace negotiations with North Vietnam. The request was logical, given Sullivan's past diplomacy involving the North Vietnamese at Geneva and since he had maintained unofficial contact with them over the years. The effort to conduct private meetings between himself and the North Vietnamese ambassador in Laos became a ridiculous game of hide-and-seek from the world press, made more difficult by the fact that the ambassador used a yellow convertible (dubbed "The Yellow Submarine" after a popular song at the time) that the press could easily trace around quaint Vientiane. Sullivan did convince the North Vietnamese to settle on Paris as the site for talks, however, after haggling over a long list of venues.

In May Harriman, who headed the delegation to the Paris talks, asked Sullivan to become part of the team so that he could conduct secret discussions outside of the formal meetings, as had been done at Geneva. However, Sullivan soon became beleaguered by an intestinal infection that forced his removal from the delegation to the naval hospital in Bethesda, Maryland, after a month. Shortly after his recovery he found the Paris negotiations stymied because the North Vietnamese refused to make concessions, and he decided to return to Vientiane.

Passed over for the ambassadorship to Manila toward the end of 1968, Sullivan instead resumed duties in Washington relating to the war in Vietnam when Nixon made him a deputy assistant secretary of state for East Asia. He was head of the State Department's Vietnam Working Group and became part of the Washington Special Action Group that made policy decisions regarding the war. In essence, he had become the liaison between Henry Kissinger's NSC and William Rogers's State Department. In June 1969 Sullivan accompanied President Nixon on his first meeting with President Nguyen Van Thieu at Midway Island. Here the leaders agreed upon the pace of Vietnamization, the turning over of the fighting of the war to South Vietnamese instead of American combat troops, and upon a firm line in the Paris negotiations.

When the national security adviser realized that he needed professional assistance, Sullivan became part of Kissinger's secret talks with Le Duc Tho, one of the few professional diplomats so involved. In a diplomatic charade of famed proportions, they would fly in an American military aircraft bound for Germany to the edge of a runway at a French military base and exit without being observed. They would then transfer to the French president's own craft and hold private talks with their North Vietnamese counterparts in a variety of safe houses owned by the French Communist Party or the CIA, and they were occasionally caught by the overzealous French media. When formal talks resumed in the aftermath of the failed North Vietnamese Easter Offensive, Sullivan was a key player in the final period of negotiating when Kissinger assumed personal charge of the public negotiations and began a whirlwind of shuttles between Washington, Paris, and Saigon. Sullivan interfaced with Hanoi's Vice Foreign Minister Nguyen Co Thach in meetings preparatory to Kissinger-Tho talks that worked out technical protocols. He also briefed foreign ambassadors on the course of the talks and accompanied Kissinger on all his Vietnam-related travels. As well, he stressed to his superior the importance of keeping the Saigon regime in league with the American negotiating effort.

Sullivan and Kissinger tried hard to give the North Vietnamese a chance to prevent the resumption of bombing in December 1972, with personal pleas to North Vietnamese diplomats, but were unable to persuade them to be more accommodative. The bombing was effective in pressing Hanoi to bargain seriously, as Kissinger and Sullivan found out when the team met with their counterparts again in early January. The settlement was achieved in less than a month after the end of the bombing. It allowed for American troops to be withdrawn under honorable conditions, recognition of both the Saigon regime and southern insurrectionists as viable political entities, the exchange of prisoners, and a cease-fire in place. Sullivan accompanied Kissinger when he met with Tho in Hanoi and Paris in the early summer of 1973 for fruitless discussions over North Vietnamese violations of the accords. Sullivan realized, however, that the 1973 agreement had set up well-developed base areas from which the Communists could continue their struggle to overrun South Vietnam.

Sullivan was next named the U.S. ambassador to the Philippines, a post he held from 1973 through 1977. Initially it was meant to be a continuation of his Vietnam assignment. In accordance with an understanding worked out at the time of the Paris Accords, Nixon would designate in short order Sullivan as the first American ambassador to a unified Vietnam. He was supposed to assume this role simultaneously with his principal ambassadorship to Manila, a dual accreditation that is not uncommon. However, Hanoi brazenly violated the Paris agreement, and his credentialing to Vietnam never occurred. He was in the Philippines when the American prisoners of war returned, and he worked out an arrangement to allow former South Vietnamese navy vessels to be turned over to the Filipino navy in 1975.

Notwithstanding the strong and omnipresent American presence in the Philippines, the important issues that Sullivan expected to face in Manila did not materialize. Negotiations on military bases were in suspense, there was no trade agreement worked out to replace one that had lapsed, and President Ferdinand Marcos had continued martial law and his abuses of human rights. Sullivan brought useful skills in dealings with the Marcos regime, though, and kept relations with Marcos friendly. During his tenure U.S. economic and military aid actually rose sharply after Marcos's crackdown. To help Marcos combat the rebellions of the Moros and the New People's Army, Sullivan instituted a new

AID-sponsored program known as the Provincial Development Assistance Project, which detailed American civilian advisors to province chiefs in areas of insurgency, much as had occurred in Laos. In fact, five of the political officers in the Manila embassy had served in Indochina. Despite his buttressing of the Marcos regime, a decade later Sullivan ironically encouraged the U.S. government to align itself with the Philippine opposition after the assassination of Benigno Aquino.

Sullivan was ambassador to Iran from June 1977 through April 1979, the last such posting for him. The Teheran posting had been vacant since Richard Helms's resignation in December 1976. Sullivan stepped in to take over a difficult situation. President Jimmy Carter had selected him because of his experience in dealing with authoritarian governments and forceful personalities. Carter regarded the shah as America's friend to whom nothing was to be denied in terms of American assistance to strengthen his regime, up to and including nuclear power. He supported the shah's reactions to social reform but wanted Sullivan to press for improvement of human rights in Iran.

Sullivan entered a nation on the verge of a dramatic upheaval. Shah Mohammed Reza Pahlavi's control on the nation was slipping. His attempts at reform, alternating with political repression and massive dislocation of rural populations, had alienated key segments in the society. The religious clerics, landed interests, students, reformist-minded parliamentarians, and even Communists constituted a broad-based revolution that was building up rapidly. But it was the Islamic fundamentalism of Ayatollah Khomeini that proved most successful in uniting the masses. Through a mistake the consequences of which were unforeseen at the time, Khomeini had been exiled to Paris, where by the late 1970s he regularly made appeals to his people through broadcasts into Iran.

In reaction to the mounting revolution, the shah and his regime were paralyzed. He eventually refrained from violently confronting his people in the streets. However, Washington leaned toward encouraging the military to put down the civil unrest forcibly. Sullivan disagreed with this policy. He instead recommended that Washington accept the fact of the revolution and steer it toward more moderate ends. Liberalization would be preferable to a military crackdown, he argued, and the United States could not accept responsibility for a bloodbath in Iran. America had to improve its contacts with Iranian moderates (and possibly the radical mullahs) and ease the shah out of power.

Without inherent support, the shah's regime rapidly fell apart when confronted by the angry street mobs in the winter of 1978–1979. The United States abandoned the shah and threw its support behind a parliamentary moderate who wanted to replace the monarchy with a republic but who had little chance of survival in the long run. In accordance with this policy, Sullivan acted under orders to facilitate the departure of the shah from Iran in January 1979. However, frustrated with what it considered Sullivan's ambivalent behavior, the Carter White House continued to unsuccessfully encourage a military option by going around its own ambassador. Despite Sullivan's failure to alter American policy, his prescience was borne out by the fact that the military disintegrated as a factor in the revolution rather quickly. Khomeini soon returned to Iran, and he and his followers assumed control of a radical theocracy when they swept aside the moderate regime that had been installed after the shah's departure.

On February 4, 1979, young Iranian militants attacked the American embassy compound with automatic weapons and succeeded in capturing all one hundred personnel inside. After the intercession of paramilitary forces from the new Iranian government, the Americans were rescued. Sullivan then decided to station a small group of the *mujahadin* inside embassy grounds as a buffer force against future assaults. Sullivan was recalled from Teheran soon thereafter. By the time hostages were again taken on November 4, 1979, no Iranian presence remained inside the compound walls. Sullivan's prudent albeit unorthodox directive had been overturned, with tragic consequences.

Sullivan resigned from diplomatic service in the summer of 1979 to protest the Carter administration's handling of the Iranian revolution. He spent his retirement recounting his career in memoirs and emerging infrequently to testify on matters such as the fate of the Vietnam prisoners of war. His career had spanned a most exacting period in American diplomacy.

Works by William H. Sullivan

"The Road Not Taken." *Foreign Policy* 40 (Fall 1980): 175–86.
Mission to Iran. New York: W. W. Norton, 1981.
Obbligato, 1939–1979: Notes on a Foreign Service Career. New York: W. W. Norton, 1984.

Works about William H. Sullivan

Bain, David. *Sitting in Darkness.* Boston: Houghton Mifflin, 1984.
Bonner, Raymond. *Waltzing with a Dictator.* New York: Times Books, 1987.
Buss, Claude A. *The United States and the Philippines.* Washington, DC: American Enterprise Institute, 1977.
Castle, Timothy N. *At War in the Shadow of Vietnam.* New York: Columbia University Press, 1993.
Rubin, Barry. *Paved with Good Intentions.* New York: Oxford University Press, 1980.
Shawcross, William. *The Shah's Last Ride.* New York: Simon and Schuster, 1988.
Sick, Gary. *All Fall Down: America's Tragic Encounter with Iran.* New York: Random House, 1985.
Stevenson, Charles. *The End of Nowhere.* Boston: Beacon Press, 1972.
Szulc, Tad. *The Illusion of Peace: Foreign Policy in the Nixon Years.* New York: Viking Press, 1978.

KENT G. SIEG

LLEWELLYN E. THOMPSON, JR. (1904–1972),

was a career Foreign Service officer specializing in Soviet affairs who guided U.S. policymakers through some of the most dangerous crises of the Cold War, negotiated the Austrian State Treaty and Trieste Agreement, and helped to lay the groundwork for strategic arms control.

The son of a rancher, Llewellyn Thompson was born in Las Animas, Colorado, on August 24, 1904. Coming from a family of modest means, he worked his way through the University of Colorado, earning an A.B. degree in 1928. Thompson, known to almost everyone as "Tommy," had heard sometime earlier about diplomatic life from a retired consul, and upon graduation he crammed for the Foreign Service exams while working on the side at the accounting firm of Price Waterhouse in Washington.

He entered the Foreign Service in January 1929 and arrived at his first post, Colombo, Ceylon (now Sri Lanka), in August. Like most new Foreign Service officers, Vice Consul Thompson devoted his first tour to consular duties. In March 1933 he transferred to Geneva, where he assisted the U.S. delegation at the International Labor Organization and, in the process, made the acquaintance of Labor Secretary Frances Perkins. In January 1940 Thompson returned to the State Department and a year later took a course at the Army War College.

Thompson's long association with Soviet affairs began in November 1940 when he received a posting to Moscow as second secretary and consul. While the approach of the German army forced most of the diplomatic corps to leave Moscow, Thompson stayed on to care for embassy property and other U.S. interests. He reported on the Soviet chances for survival and took the opportunity to become fluent in Russian. He earned the respect of many Russians for sticking it out in Moscow and received the Medal of Freedom from the U.S. government for his handling of the embassy at risk of capture by the Germans.

Thompson's stay in Moscow increased his admiration for the Russian people, but it did not increase his trust of the Soviet government. On their way from the Potsdam Conference in July 1945, where he was translating, he and Charles Bohlen, another State Department Soviet specialist, agreed that wherever Soviet armies occupied foreign territory, they would attempt to impose an autocratic, Communist system. Both men were already concerned about possible conflict between the United States and the Soviet Union.

In 1944 Thompson moved to London as first secretary. After a relatively quiet tour he received an assignment to the State Department in 1946 as chief of the Division of Eastern European Affairs. In July 1949 he became deputy assistant secretary of state for European affairs, concentrating his efforts on the postwar problems of Eastern Europe. He was already on the department's "fast track" regarding promotion.

Thompson's reserve and devotion to his work had so far prevented romance from playing a large role in his life, but in 1948 he met Jane Goelet from Boston on a voyage to Europe, and they married later that year. His wife later directed the Art in Embassies program.

In 1950 Thompson took the post of counselor of embassy in Rome, where he soon acquired the personal rank of minister, working under Ambassador James C. Dunn. In July 1952 Thompson received appointment as U.S. high commissioner and ambassador to occupied Austria, a post that gave him a chance to utilize his knowledge of the Soviet government. He became the principal actor in two simultaneous negotiations that shaped part of the postwar world, the Austrian State Treaty and the Trieste settlement. In Vienna Thompson was the U.S. representative on the four-member Allied Council, which was technically the sovereign power during the occupation. Due to his diplomatic ability, his knowledge of Russian, and the power of the government he represented, Thompson exercised predominant influence over his British, French, and even Russian colleagues.

The USSR delayed conclusion of a treaty for several years in an apparent effort to use Austrian independence as a bargaining chip to prevent German rearmament and, accordingly, refused to remove its occupation force. In March 1954 the Kremlin relaxed its stand by separating the evacuation of Austria from the question of German rearmament. At last, the Soviets wanted a treaty, and fruitful negotiations became possible. In a hectic finale lasting about two weeks, Thompson took full advantage of the new Soviet desire for progress to force them to scrap most of the limitations they had previously wanted on Austrian independence and to obtain a reasonable settlement of USSR demands for reparations. The commissioners finished their task in mid-May after nearly four hundred negotiating sessions. The result was the independent, neutral Austria that exists today.

During the time Thompson was assigned to Austria, he spent eight months off and on in London, beginning in January 1953, negotiating with the British, the Yugoslavs, and later the Italians over the sovereignty of the Trieste region, the principal port at the head of the Adriatic Sea, which both Italy and Yugoslavia claimed. He found his original instructions too favorable to Italy to be negotiable and the team sent from Washington too large. Thompson amended his instructions with the State Department's reluctant approval and worked one-on-one with the Yugoslav and British negotiators in great secrecy. At the last minute, when almost all problems had been solved, the Italians demanded a small piece of land overlooking Trieste that had been allotted to Yugoslavia. It required a trip to Belgrade by Deputy Under Secretary of State for Political Affairs Robert Murphy to obtain this tiny but crucial concession from Marshal Tito and cinch the agreement.

The dispute ended with the signing of an agreement on October 5, 1954, terminating the military government and turning over to Italy and Yugoslavia the administration of their respective zones. Thompson insisted on secrecy for the entire period of negotiations because he knew that the governments concerned would find it almost impossible to retreat from positions taken in public. Both the Austrian State Treaty and the Trieste Agreement, which Thompson considered to be open covenants secretly arrived at, gained him a considerable reputation as a negotiator.

These foreign policy successes greatly pleased Secretary of State John Foster Dulles, and the Republicans saw to it that they received the attention in the 1956 election campaign. Thompson received the Distinguished Service Award and, in June 1957, the post of ambassador to the Soviet Union.

In Moscow Thompson concentrated on developing as close a relationship as possible with Chairman Nikita Khrushchev and over the years came to know him better than any other American. He was also on cordial terms with Andrei Gromyko, the foreign minister, and became a keen student of the operations of the Soviet government.

Following initial progress made at Geneva in October 1958, discussions over a nuclear test-ban treaty had broken down. President Dwight Eisenhower instructed Thompson to take up the matter again with Khrushchev. Thompson reported back in October 1959 that the Soviet leader would favor such measures as a means of preventing China and Germany from acquiring nuclear weapons. Thus began preparations for the Partial Nuclear Test Ban Treaty that was finally signed in August 1963.

The president also wished Thompson to arrange a summit conference with Khrushchev. This finally took the form of a highly publicized trip by the Russian leader to the United States in 1959. The cordial talks between Eisenhower and Khrushchev gave rise to the phrase "The Spirit of Camp David" to denote a relative relaxation of tensions between the superpowers. Thompson's careful and patient planning contributed much to the success of the trip.

When Vice President Richard Nixon arrived in Moscow in July 1959, he received a cool welcome. Thompson explained to him that the Soviets were angry with the U.S. Congress for passing the Captive Nations Resolution condemning the suppression of human rights by Communist imperialism. Khrushchev, however, offered Nixon the chance at the end of his trip to speak to the Soviet people over television and radio for the first time ever. After Thompson criticized the Nixon draft for its belligerency and orientation toward American domestic politics, the vice president rewrote it, and the speech left a creditable impression.

During this period of relaxed tensions that Thompson had done so much to encourage, the Russian people were delighted at the prospect of a visit from the American president in the spring of 1960, and the media dubbed it the "American Spring." But in early May 1960 a U.S. U-2 spy plane was shot down over the Soviet Union, and the Soviets captured the pilot, Gary Powers, alive. Although Thompson reported at first that the outstanding feature of Khrushchev's reaction was its moderation, he realized fully that the Soviet leader was thoroughly angry over this glaring violation of Soviet airspace. Thompson reported that there was little doubt that Khrushchev hoped that the president would cancel his trip to the Soviet Union and that the Cold War was on again. The Soviet leader became so upset that he even stamped on the ambassador's foot at a reception while berating him for the U-2 incident.

As a consequence of the affair, the May 16, 1960, Paris summit conference between Chairman Khrushchev, President Eisenhower, Prime Minister Harold Macmillan of Great Britain, and President Charles de Gaulle of France, which Thompson had helped to prepare, collapsed. Khrushchev announced at the conference that he could not receive the president in the USSR properly, ending hopes for a presidential spring trip to Russia. However, the fact that the failure did not bring more dire results caused Thompson considerable relief at the time.

In early 1961 Khrushchev began to push the new U.S. president, John F. Kennedy, on the issue of Berlin. In late spring he warned Thompson that if he and Kennedy could not reach agreement on Berlin at the upcoming Vienna summit, he would sign a separate peace treaty with East Germany, which would include Berlin. Thompson replied that if the Communists used force to block access to Berlin, they would be met with force. In succeeding months Thompson advised Kennedy to hold out the prospect of negotiations over Berlin in order to find a formula in which both sides could save face, but the president made no move in that direction.

Thompson also warned that the constant flow of refugees from East Berlin across the boundary to West Berlin would cause the East Germans to seal off the sector boundary, which they subsequently did. He continued to recommend talks with the Soviets to President Kennedy, fearing that a crisis could arise that would carry serious danger of war. Thompson recommended a quiet military buildup in the meantime, to be followed by a diplomatic offensive. President Kennedy did not follow the advice, and the crisis dragged on.

Subsequently Thompson paved the way for the June 1961 Vienna summit during which the status of Berlin was bound to be a major subject. In the briefing before the conference, Thompson advised the president to avoid discussion of ideology with Khrushchev as a useless exercise he could not win. Kennedy disregarded the suggestion in his tumultuous sessions with the Soviet leader, and the Vienna summit ended without agreement on Berlin or a nuclear testban treaty.

Khrushchev did not hold Thompson responsible for the U-2 incident or the period of rocky relations that followed. He drank a toast to Thompson at a social function during the tense days of the Berlin crisis and maintained a friendly relationship. When he learned that the ambassador was scheduled to leave Moscow in July 1962, the Soviet leader made a point of entertaining him grandly at his dacha.

After nearly two years in Moscow under the Kennedy administration, Thompson assumed the position of ambassador-at-large in the State Department beginning in October 1962. He had already received appointment as a career ambassador in 1960, the highest career rank, and became acting deputy under secretary of state for political affairs in June 1964. In terms of substance, the job was the same—chief advisor to the secretary and the president on Soviet affairs.

Back in Washington, Thompson played a critical role in the Cuban missile crisis. In October 1962 the president learned that the Soviet Union was installing ground-to-ground missiles in Cuba. A strong U.S. response was imperative. The initial reaction of many of his advisors was to recommend an attack on the missile sites, but Thompson feared that heavy Russian casualties resulting from an air strike could induce Khrushchev to take counteraction in Berlin or against the U.S. Jupiter missile sites in Turkey, a situation that could escalate. Thompson argued that Khrushchev should have time to reflect and to receive moderate counsel. President Kennedy decided against immediate military action.

In the following tense days it was Thompson who came up with the idea that the president should reply to Khrushchev's first letter, dated October 26, and not to his second, which demanded the pullout of U.S. missiles from Turkey. President Kennedy was doubtful at first, but Thompson argued that the first letter, though vague, contained some positive elements that could be useful in a settlement. He foresaw an agreement in which the missiles would leave Cuba while Khrushchev could claim that he had prevented a U.S. invasion of the island.

Thompson, Secretary of State Dean Rusk, and Under Secretary of State George Ball, as members of Ex-Comm, the president's crisis-management team, prepared a reply to the first letter. Following Thompson's suggestion, Robert Kennedy, attorney general and brother of the president, delivered it to Soviet Ambassador Anatoly Dobrynin after an extensive briefing by Thompson. The ploy succeeded. Both Secretary Rusk and Secretary of Defense Robert McNamara subsequently praised Thompson heartily for his advice, which guided them safely through the crisis.

Thompson was Secretary Rusk's representative on the interdepartmental 303 Committee that reviewed CIA activities. At one point he reported to the secretary that someone at a meeting of the committee had suggested the assassination of Fidel Castro. The two men agreed that the idea should be quashed immediately, and Thompson took steps to that end. The 1975 revelation of a subsequent CIA plot to kill Castro came as a surprise to Secretary Rusk and certainly would have also surprised Llewellyn Thompson.

Thompson was also a participant in the negotiations leading to the 1963 Partial Nuclear Test Ban Treaty, which he had helped initiate in Moscow four years before. In addition, his knowledge of Soviet attitudes became particularly useful to the U.S. delegation at the United Nations in dealing with the Soviet Union and in East-West trade matters.

In spite of growing health problems, Thompson accepted President Lyndon Johnson's offer of a second tour as U.S. ambassador in Moscow, beginning in December 1966. He became immediately involved in planning for Premier Aleksei Kosygin's trip to the United States the following June, which culminated in the meeting of the two leaders at Glassboro, New Jersey.

Upon Thompson's arrival in Moscow, President Johnson instructed him as a matter of priority to explore with the Soviet government the possibility of negotiations limiting antiballistic-missile deployment. The ambassador proposed secret talks to be carried out both in Washington and Moscow. In February he told Kosygin that the United States was prepared to discuss limits on offensive nuclear weapons as well, and by March 1967 many of the preparations were complete. The United States proposed that the opening session take place in Moscow, where McNamara and Rusk could work with the Soviets through Thompson, who enjoyed the confidence of Russians and Americans alike. In spite of Thompson's best efforts, however, the Soviets moved very slowly. At the end of November President Johnson, as a final gesture, instructed Thompson to propose a summit meeting just before Christmas 1967 in Geneva to discuss arms limitation, but he could make no progress. Finally, however, perseverance and patience paid off, and the talks began in Helsinki in November 1969.

At the time of the Six-Day War between Israel and the Arab states, Thompson flew back to Washington as a consultant on possible Soviet reactions. On June 6 he was present in the White House situation room when President Johnson first used the Hot Line, a device suggested by Thompson after the U-2 and Cuban missile incidents illustrated the need to use every possible means in times of crisis to prevent misunderstandings due to faulty communications.

The Vietnam War became a damper on relations during Thompson's second tour in Moscow. It made personal contacts more difficult and slowed progress on important projects like arms control. The ambassador did not have a single serious discussion with Soviet leader Leonid Brezhnev during his entire second posting. At Glassboro the Soviets indicated a willingness to be helpful in working toward a settlement of the Vietnam conflict, and Kosygin actually produced a proposal. President Johnson then made a counterproposal, to which the Russians did not respond. Thereupon Thompson called on Foreign Minister Gromyko, but received a cold shoulder. Nothing ever resulted from the Glassboro initiative.

Thompson left Moscow in January 1969 with the intention of resigning at the change of administrations, but President Richard Nixon appointed him to the U.S. delegation for the strategic arms talks with the Soviet Union (SALT I). He took part in the Helsinki and Vienna sessions in his usual self-effacing but highly effective manner. When more talks took place in the spring of 1971, however, Thompson was too ill to attend.

Back in Washington, Thompson was wary of the Nixon administration's rapprochement with China. He and Bohlen went to see the president on their own initiative to warn him against any attempt to maneuver China against the USSR. They believed that such a move would fatally injure U.S. relations with the Soviets and perhaps endanger world peace. Subsequently Thompson suggested that the U.S. government keep the Soviets informed of its contacts in Warsaw with the Chinese to allay any suspicions that might arise. Nixon appeared to listen sympathetically, but Henry Kissinger, who was his national security adviser, opposed the proposal, and the president sided with him.

Thompson suffered from ulcers for a long time. A glass of milk and a package of graham crackers were almost always visible on his desk. In the last years of his government service his health deteriorated further. He retired in 1971 and died of cancer on February 6, 1972, after a career in which he helped guide the United States through some of the most dangerous years of its existence.

Works about Llewellyn Thompson

Allard, Sven. *Russia and the Austrian State Treaty: A Case Study of Soviet Policy in Europe*. University Park: Pennsylvania State University Press, 1970.

Beschloss, Michael R. *The Crisis Years: Kennedy and Khrushchev, 1960–1963*. New York: Edward Burlingame Books, 1991.

———. *May Day: Eisenhower, Khrushchev, and the U-2 Affair*. New York: Harper and Row, 1986.

Bohlen, Charles E. *Witness to History, 1929–1969*. New York: W. W Norton and Company, 1973.

Campbell, John C., ed. *Successful Negotiation: Trieste, 1954. An Appraisal by the Five Participants*. Princeton: Princeton University Press, 1976.

Johnson, Lyndon B. *The Vantage Point: Perspectives of the Presidency, 1963–1969*. New York: Holt, Rinehart and Winston, 1971.

Newhouse, John. *Cold Dawn: The Story of SALT*. Washington, D.C., and New York: Pergamon-Brassey's International Defense Publishers, 1989.

WILLIAM N. DALE

TERENCE A. TODMAN (1926–   ) was a career diplomat
and six-time U.S. ambassador.

Todman was born on March 13, 1926, in St. Thomas, U.S. Virgin Islands. His mother, Rachel, worked as a laundress and housemaid, while his father, Alphonse, worked as a grocery clerk and occasionally as a stevedore. He graduated salutatorian from his high school and then went on to Polytechnic Institute of Puerto Rico for his B.A. While he was in college, he was drafted, received his officer's training at the Fort Benning Infantry School, and served four years in the U.S. Army, doing a tour of duty in Japan. After his military service was completed, he returned to finish his bachelor's studies in Puerto Rico in 1951 (receiving his degree summa cum laude) and then went to Syracuse University for his master's in public administration, which he received in 1953. These early experiences established in Todman an intense interest in foreign affairs. The cosmopolitan atmosphere of St. Thomas, where various nationalities came in and out of the port city, his experience with different cultures in Puerto Rico, and, most particularly, his service in occupied Japan all combined to point him toward a career in diplomacy. Therefore, even though he received several offers from other U.S. government agencies after taking the Federal Entry Exam in 1952, his sights were set on foreign service, and he took a position with the Department of State. He got off to a not-very-auspicious start when he was told upon reporting to the State Department that his Virgin Islands accent made him unacceptable for U.S. diplomatic work. Todman insisted on an opportunity to prove himself, however, and landed a position in the Office of South Asian Affairs, where he served as assistant desk officer for India until 1954.

Todman's first fifteen years in the Foreign Service were marked by a variety of challenging positions, but also by some degree of personal and professional frustration. From the Office of South Asian Affairs he moved on to an internship with the U.N. Secretariat (1954) and then served as a U.S. representative on the U.N. Trusteeship Council Commission (1954–1957). In response to the vague and tentative promises of the colonial powers to develop plans for the development and eventual independence of their colonies, Todman was able to press through an agreement setting definite intermediate target dates that the colonial nations vowed to meet. In 1957 he received his first overseas assignment, as political/labor officer in New Delhi. In 1960 he moved on to Lebanon for Arabic-language training (finishing the two-year program in eighteen months) and, following his completion of the course, was sent off to Tunis as political officer in 1961. He stayed there until 1964, when he received an assignment as deputy chief of mission to Togo, a job usually considered a stepping-stone to an ambassadorial appointment. Often put in charge of the embassy when the ambassador was absent, Todman got some of his first tastes of crisis, managing U.S. affairs during two attempted coups and one successful revolt in Togo. He also got valuable experience in working person-to-person with the Togolese people. Using monies provided by a discretionary Self-Help Fund in the U.S. embassy, Todman forged valuable connections with the native people, assisting them in building roads, schools, and hospitals. He returned to Washington in 1968 to serve as country director for East Africa.

Despite the generally upward course of his career, Todman also encountered seemingly senseless and frustrating moments in his early years in the Department of State. During his initial training at the Foreign Service Institute in Virginia, he found himself barred from the restaurant that served his white colleagues. Moved to action by Todman's complaints, the State Department eventually leased part of the restaurant and divided it from the segregated part of the establishment. On a professional level, he also encountered the "color bar." Although he was fluent in Spanish, he was told that an assignment to the Latin American Bureau was out of the question, and despite his Arabic-language training, he was never assigned to the Middle East. Both of these areas were considered "off-limits" for African-American appointments, since the consensus was that the nations of these regions would not tolerate African-American diplomats and would see such appointments as affronts. Like the majority of African-American diplomats, Todman therefore spent a good deal of his early career in Africa.

Given all of this, it was little surprise that Todman's first ambassadorial appointment in 1969 was to the African nation of Chad. As would hold true for nearly every one of his six ambassadorial appointments, the assignment to Chad landed Todman in the middle of a crisis situation. The president of Chad, Francois Tombalbaye, had become involved in an increasingly acrimonious war of words with Libyan leader Muammar al-Qaddafi. The latter upped the ante shortly after Todman's arrival by supplying arms to the nomadic Toubous in northern Chad, who thereupon began major attacks against the Tombalbaye government. With the United States unwilling to become involved in the civil war brewing, the French (the former colonial rulers of Chad) were told that they should feel free to give their support to Tombalbaye. This the French did, sending in troops to help put down the rebel attacks. In all of this, Todman had a delicate role to play, having to simultaneously assure the Tombalbaye regime of U.S. support (without real U.S. assistance), convince the French that the United States had no ulterior motives in Chad, and convince his superiors in the State Department that the United States would indeed receive its portion of the credit for relieving the crisis. Todman managed the assignment well, however. The Tombalbaye government survived, and the rebellion, at least in the short run, was stymied. The French, though perhaps never completely allayed in their suspicions of U.S. goals, continued to provide Chad with supplies and aid, and French military forces stayed on for several years. The United States garnered some benefit, as the Chadian government voted with it to block mainland China's entry into the United Nations.

Todman had performed well in Chad and looked forward to his next assignment. Although Tunisia—where his Arabic could be put to better use—was open, he was talked into accepting a very difficult assignment in Guinea. Under the leadership of Sekou Toure, Guinea had steadily adopted a more and more vehemently anti-U.S. attitude. The Soviet Union and other Eastern-bloc nations had developed strong and effective diplomatic relations with the small African nation. The American embassy was, as Todman recalled in an interview some years later, "in the worst shape, psychologically, that I have ever seen." There were almost daily protests against the United States; the U.S. ambassador's residence had been broken into by protesters; and the embassy staff operated under a near state of siege, with people afraid to go outside of the capital city of Conakry. Upon his arrival Todman acted, first, to rebuild morale among the American embassy personnel. Second, and more important, he resolutely decided to open a direct line of communication with President Toure. At his first meeting with the Guinean leader Todman was given the standard anti-American speech and summarily dismissed. Instead of departing, however, Todman insisted on speaking on his own behalf, in part to correct some of the misconceptions the president had manifested in his diatribe. From that point on, President Toure, though initially highly suspicious of the American representative, slowly developed a sense of respect for Todman. The more strident outbursts of anti-Americanism ceased, and Todman was allowed to bring more diplomatic personnel into the country. In addition, Todman was instrumental in helping Guinea reestablish its diplomatic ties to other Western nations, such as the French and the British.

While Todman was in Guinea, he also established close contacts with exiled independence leaders from Guinea-Bissau and the Cape Verde Islands. Foreseeing the coming end of Portuguese colonialism in these nations, Todman, sometimes to the dismay of his superiors in Washington, cultivated friendly relations with the exiles. The net result was that when these nations did achieve their independence in the next few years, the United States was one of the first countries to establish positive diplomatic relations.

Despite Todman's accomplishments in Guinea, life in that nation was difficult. After three years Todman felt that a change was in order and approached the Department of State about a new assignment. Once again he faced a frustrating situation. Despite his training in Arabic, the department still felt that an African-American appointment to that region was problematic. (Indeed, only one African American has ever served as a U.S. ambassador in a Middle Eastern nation— Hugh Smythe in Syria, 1965–1967.) Offered other African posts, Todman rejected them, refusing to be pigeonholed simply because he was black. The department was at something of a loss, but the situation was settled amicably when an opening in Costa Rica appeared. Todman was fluent in Spanish, the original Nixon appointee for Costa Rica had fallen through, the Costa Rican government was anxious for an appointment, and for Todman the appointment meant breaking free of the perception that as an African American he could usefully serve only in Africa. His appointment also marked the first time an African American had been appointed to a Spanish-speaking Latin American nation.

Todman's posting to Costa Rica in 1975 seemed, at first glance, to be much-needed respite from the tensions and turmoil of Guinea. The daily quality of life was certainly much better, and the bitter anti-Americanism that Todman had faced upon his arrival in Guinea was absent in Costa Rica. Nevertheless, in what was to become common to nearly all of Todman's assignments, his arrival in the Latin American republic coincided with a developing crisis. The civil war in neighboring Nicaragua that would eventually lead to the overthrow of the Somoza regime in that nation was beginning to heat up. For Costa Rica, this presented a constant problem, as fighting between the rebel Sandinistas and the Nicaraguan army threatened to spill across the border. Todman's job was two-fold: first, to reassure Costa Rica (which had no army) that the United States would not stand by and see the nation's sovereignty impaired; and second, to make the Somoza government understand that "hot pursuit" of the Sandinistas into Costa Rica would not be permitted. Since he left the post in 1977, however, Todman avoided the more critical situation that developed along the Costa Rican border in the late 1970s and early 1980s.

In addition to the serious border problem, Todman was also confronted by another diplomatic problem, one that sometimes took on comic-opera proportions. Financier Robert Vesco, on the run from criminal charges in the United States, had taken up residence in Costa Rica. Despite repeated U.S. entreaties, Costa Rica had refused every attempt to have the fugitive extradited. Todman's only instructions were to keep the matter before the Costa Rican government, making sure that it understood the U.S. interest in bringing Vesco to trial. Although some U.S. officials suggested that it might be possible to somehow "spirit" Vesco out of the country, Todman never seriously considered such schemes. This did not, however, keep Vesco from believing that Todman was personally set on capturing him and flying him back to justice. The ambassador remembered several occasions on which he found himself in the same location as Vesco and his heavily armed bodyguards. Some tense moments usually ensued, as Vesco seemed to wait for Todman to try and tackle him single-handedly. Eventually, the whole thing blew over, as the U.S. Justice Department decided to drop the extradition attempt.

In 1977 Todman's career took a dramatic turn. The incoming administration of Jimmy Carter approached Todman to inquire whether he would be interested in serving as the new assistant secretary of state for inter-American affairs. Carter and his secretary of state, Cyrus Vance, had made it clear that one of their goals was to increase the number of African Americans serving the Department of State. They also, however, wanted to increase the opportunities for African-American diplomats with years of service. The approach to Todman, therefore, was both a recognition of his long and effective years of work and of the fact that African Americans had been long overlooked for such senior positions.

Todman was hesitant about accepting the position. His only experience in Latin America had been his service in Costa Rica. After long and serious talks with Secretary Vance, however, he came to the conclusion that he could work effectively with the new administration and took the job, becoming the first African American to serve as head of one of the geographical divisions in the Department of State. His selection as assistant secretary coincided with a period of intense activity and, very often, crisis in the relations between the United States and Latin America.

Todman's service as assistant secretary came at a time when the United States was putting a new and sometimes confusing and frustrating accent on human rights as an integral part of the nation's foreign policy. In theory, Todman was in thorough agreement that human rights should play a major role in every major diplomatic undertaking of the United States, yet he was often dismayed by the policy's application. In some cases he believed that in order to punish particularly despotic leaders in Latin America, the United States took actions that actually hurt the oppressed citizenry of the particular nation more than the dictator. In addition, he felt that the policy was applied inconsistently and sometimes arbitrarily, with the United States often blasting a nation for its human rights abuses and then following that up with a request for helping the United States with a particular matter. Finally, Todman was distressed by some members of the Carter administration who talked a good game concerning human rights but were reticent to follow up the words with actions. Overall, though he judged the policy to have had moderate success in Latin America, he believed that more could have been accomplished through a combination of consistent adherence to a clear policy and a greater flexibility in terms of application of the policy, taking into account the very different situations faced in Latin America.

Todman also played a crucial role in the Carter administration's approaches toward Cuba. In face-to-face meetings with Cuban representatives Todman was able to hammer out agreements establishing a maritime boundary and authorizing Cubans to fish in U.S. waters, subject to U.S. control. During a visit to Cuba for negotiations Todman was able to secure the release of some political prisoners and arrange for the return of some U.S. properties. Following up on these successes, Cuba and the United States agreed on establishing Interest Sections in each other's nation.

One of the other pressing issues during Todman's tenure as assistant secretary was the series of negotiations being held with Panama concerning the canal. While Todman did not head the U.S. delegation that negotiated the final agreements, he did play a major role in organizing a public information campaign to inform the American public about the meaning and consequences of what eventually became the Panama Canal Treaties.

Todman's service as assistant secretary came to an end, however, over the issue of Nicaragua. As it became evident that Nicaraguan dictator Anastasio Somoza's position in that nation was becoming more and more untenable, Todman and a group of Carter's advisors became embroiled in numerous differences of opinion as to the proper U.S. policy. Todman believed that the only solution to the turmoil shaking Nicaragua was, first, to establish a formula by which Somoza could leave power in a normal and dignified manner, handing the presidency over to the president of the Nicaraguan Assembly, who would call for elections, and second, to directly face up to the Communist menace posed by the Sandinistas. He felt, however, that many in the Carter administration wished to ''punish'' Somoza for his brutal rule and were reluctant to label the Sandinista rebels as Communists. When he saw that this was a battle he could not win, Todman looked about for other opportunities and left the post of assistant secretary in 1978 to become ambassador to Spain.

The appointment of Todman to Spain represented once again the Carter administration's commitment to expanding the opportunities for African Americans in the diplomatic service. Only six African Americans had been appointed to European posts prior to 1978, and none had been appointed to a major Western European nation. It also turned out to be Todman's longest assignment up to that point, as he remained in Spain for nearly five years.

Todman's arrival in Spain coincided with a period of tumultuous political change and evolution in that nation. The long-time dictator, Francisco Franco, had died just a few years before, and the Spanish nation and people were taking their first halting steps toward democracy. This was not always easily accomplished, and the new American ambassador had to be ready for rapid and sometimes dramatic change. Indeed, while he was in Spain, Todman worked with three different Spanish governments.

One of the most delicate assignments he faced in Spain was the negotiation of a treaty allowing U.S. use of air and naval bases in that nation. The treaty whipped up some anti-American denunciations, especially from the political parties out of power at the time the treaty was finally hammered out. The constantly changing Spanish political scene intruded at that point, as the Socialists came to power before the treaty was actually signed. Working with his superiors in Washington, Todman was able to iron out any possible difficulties, and after some cosmetic changes to the treaty, the document was signed and ratified by both nations. Following up on this success, Todman and the U.S. government worked to gain Spain's entry into NATO, which was also accomplished.

In addition to the changes in the Spanish government, Todman also had to cope with a change in U.S. presidential administrations. The coming to power of the conservative Ronald Reagan initially caused tremendous concern in the new Socialist government in Spain. Conversely, the incoming Reagan administration took a dim view of Spain's leftist regime. Todman's adept handling of the bases treaty issue, as well as his work in setting up a pleasant and productive trip by Secretary of State George Shultz to Madrid, eventually worked to assuage these early suspicions.

In 1983, after nearly five years in Spain, Todman took over the U.S. embassy in Denmark. There was some criticism among African Americans that this move was simply more evidence of the Reagan administration's disinterest in the issue of equal employment opportunity in the Department of State. After all, the argument went, the U.S. embassy in Denmark was much smaller, and so Todman's transfer was essentially a demotion. In fact, Todman had chosen the Denmark assignment from a number of possible opportunities. The post interested him for several reasons. Despite its relatively small size, Denmark was an important player in NATO and European economics. In addition, the post attracted Todman for personal reasons. As a native Virgin Islander, he was fascinated with Danish culture and society.

Despite a generally splendid personal relationship with the Danish people and government, Todman did face some troubling issues. First and foremost was the Danish reluctance to increase its contribution to NATO. In fact, just before Todman's arrival the Danish parliament had voted not to contribute to the deployment of new missiles in Western Europe for NATO forces. While Todman was not able to convince Denmark to reverse its position, he did work strenuously to strengthen both U.S.-Danish ties and the understanding of the Danish people of the need for mutual security.

As in Spain, Todman also faced the question of U.S. military bases in dealing with Denmark. The problem centered around U.S. bases in Greenland. In this case, however, the Greenlanders were not protesting the existence of the bases, but rather the small amount of compensation received by the island in exchange for the use of the large installations. Eventually a new agreement was worked out increasing the money the United States paid to use the bases.

When the Bush administration took office in 1989, Todman, who had served nearly six years in Denmark, was presented with a choice of new assignments. He decided to take on a tough one: Argentina. Todman had visited the nation on several occasions and had always been struck by the awesome potential of the nation. On the other hand, he knew that the United States and Argentina had maintained what amounted to a near-adversarial relationship for years. Todman hoped to change that.

Almost immediately Todman had to cope with a dramatic change in Argentine politics. Just a few days after his arrival in the nation, President Raul Alfonsin announced his resignation, and soon after Carlos Menem was elected as the new president. Although taken by surprise, Todman was optimistic about working with the new Argentine leader, particularly in the area of economic assistance for Argentina. For some years the Argentines had been resentful of what they perceived as the unfair treatment they had received at the hands of both U.S. and international assistance organizations. Conversely, the U.S. agencies and the U.S. representatives in the international organizations had begun to take a harder and harder line with Argentina. Both in Buenos Aires and in Washington Todman worked tirelessly to get the two sides together. He was remarkably successful. In just a short time assistance from the Export-Import Bank, the overseas Private Investment Corporation, the International Bank for Reconstruction and Development, the International Monetary Fund, and the Inter-American Development Bank was pouring into Argentina. One of the substantive results of this new closeness was the decision by Argentina to participate in the Gulf War against Iraq, the only Latin American nation to do so.

In 1993, after nearly forty-two years of service in the Department of State and six ambassadorships, Terence Todman retired with the personal rank of career ambassador, one of only about thirty in U.S. history and the first African American to attain that rank. A singular recognition of his years of service came in November of that year when he was the honored guest at a retirement ceremony held in Statuary Hall in the U.S. Capitol, the first government employee ever to receive such an honor.

Work about Terence A. Todman

Miller, Jake C. *The Black Presence in American Foreign Policy Affairs*. Lanham, MD: University Press of America, 1978.

MICHAEL L. KRENN

VERNON WALTERS (1917–) is a retired lieutenant general

in the U.S. Army, former deputy director of the Central Intelligence Agency, and former U.S. ambassador to the United Nations; he served both as a translator and a negotiator for several U.S. presidents.

Born in New York City on January 3, 1917, Walters spent ten years of his childhood in Europe, where he learned to speak French, Spanish, Italian, and German. On May 2, 1941, he enlisted in the army and was given the billet of truck driver, thus beginning a long and distinguished career in the military. In early 1942 an event occurred that foreshadowed Walters's later involvement in the intelligence community, starting in military intelligence and ending with the CIA. An FBI officer approached him and asked him to infiltrate a group of supposed German spies in the local town. Walters agreed and later received a citation from the FBI. After only a few months in the army he applied for and was accepted into Officer Candidate School and subsequently went to the Military Intelligence Training Center, where the army first recognized his foreign-language proficiency.

Second Lieutenant Walters's first tour took him to North Africa. During this time Walters served as a prisoner-of-war interrogator. He also earned a battlefield promotion for crossing, unarmed, a mined bridge. He then confronted the commanding officer of the Vichy forces who were holding the bridge and succeeded in convincing him to allow the American forces to pass and to join in the fight against Nazi Germany. This event may have been Walters's first diplomatic assignment, as he demonstrated both his linguistic abilities and his ability to negotiate with an adversary under difficult circumstances. After this first tour in Africa he returned to the United States to teach prisoner-of-war interrogation techniques. During this assignment Walters went on his first official diplomatic mission: he accompanied and translated for groups of Portuguese and Brazilian officers who were touring U.S. military installations. At this time Walters had no knowledge of Portuguese apart from being able to recognize the similarities it shared with Spanish, a language in which he was already fluent. Nevertheless, he was selected to serve on these two missions and in doing so added another language to his already-impressive list. At the end of the trip with the Brazilians Walters was invited to visit Brazil. The army agreed to the visit, and Captain Walters gained his first glimpse of a country in which he would spend many years in the future.

Soon after his trip to Brazil Walters returned to the European theater. There he joined General Mark Clark, commander of the Fifth Army, which was operating in western Italy. As Clark's aide, Walters learned an embarrassing lesson while translating for Generals Clark and Charles de Gaulle. Believing that de Gaulle did not speak English, Walters embellished his translations. At the end of the meeting General de Gaulle spoke to Clark in English, demonstrating to

Walters that he had recognized the blunder. While serving in Italy, Walters gained valuable diplomatic experience that would serve him well throughout his career.

During Walters's service in Italy his knowledge of Portuguese involved him again with the Brazilian armed forces. He acted as the combat liaison officer between the Fifth Army and a Brazilian division deployed to Italy. Walters managed the complex task of coordinating combat operations between the two armies, which possessed different equipment, spoke different languages, and employed different tactical doctrines.

After the cessation of hostilities in the European theater, Walters served as the assistant military attaché at the embassy in Rio de Janeiro. As the assistant attaché, his duties included translating for visiting American dignitaries, including General George Marshall, creator of the Marshall Plan; Secretary of Commerce Averell Harriman; and President Truman. Impressed with Walters's performance, Harriman requested that he be reassigned to the newly created headquarters for implementing the European Recovery Program. Walters served as translator for both Harriman and Marshall during their extended diplomatic missions throughout Europe. He established relationships with many of Europe's political and military leaders. Later in his career Walters was able to utilize these experiences when several presidents called upon him to translate for them. Not only would he translate the conversations, but his previous relationships enabled him to more fully understand the meaning of the words he translated.

The outbreak of the Korean War prompted President Truman to appoint Averell Harriman his special assistant. Harriman immediately requested that Walters join his staff. Soon thereafter Walters accompanied Harriman and Truman to Wake Island, where the president confronted General Douglas MacArthur regarding his intentions in prosecuting the war in Korea. Walters's exemplary performance during this period led to his promotion to lieutenant colonel.

In January 1951 General Dwight Eisenhower requested that Walters be assigned to him at the Supreme Headquarters of the Allied Powers in Europe (SHAPE), the headquarters for NATO. Walters served as Eisenhower's interpreter. When Eisenhower moved to the White House in 1953, he continued to utilize Walters's talents. Following his assignment at SHAPE, Walters joined the NATO Standing Group in Washington, D.C. There he performed as a public relations officer and traveled the United States in order to explain to different groups the significance of American involvement in NATO. In this capacity he served a diplomatic role to the American people as well as continuing to serve as President Eisenhower's interpreter.

From the NATO Standing Group Walters was assigned in 1960 to the embassy in Rome as the army attaché. This assignment proved to be relatively quiet for Walters; he regretted leaving Rome because he enjoyed good relations with the Italian armed forces and no major crises disrupted his life. Two years later Walters returned to Rio de Janeiro at the request of Ambassador Lincoln Gordon, who had known Walters while he was assigned to the European Recovery Program headquarters. Gordon requested Walters's service due to the potentially dangerous political situation in Brazil. The ambassador relied upon Walters to keep him informed of any developments in the power struggle between the government and the army. Due to his previous service with the Brazilians in World War II and as assistant attaché in Brazil, Walters had many connections with the Brazilian military. Ironically, these relationships both helped and hampered his assignment; members of Brazil's Communist Party accused Walters of surreptitiously orchestrating events in Brazil as a representative of the U.S. government. Indeed, some scholars continue to believe that the United States encouraged the military to overthrow Brazil's leftist government. However, Walters has denied any knowledge of such activities. In fact, he made a conscious effort to maintain a low profile and to downplay his connections with the Brazilian military. While Walters was in Brazil, he was promoted to the rank of brigadier general. Upon receiving word of Walters's promotion, General George Patton's daughter, Mrs. Ruthe Ellen Totten, presented him with one of her father's stars.

In 1967 Walters learned that he would be transferred to Paris to assume the position of army attaché. With the nation deeply embroiled in the Vietnam War, a sense of duty compelled him to volunteer to serve in Vietnam before going to Paris. As well, he believed that in order to earn the respect of his French counterparts—many of whom had served in Vietnam—he must obtain firsthand knowledge of the ongoing Vietnamese conflict. While he was in Vietnam, he enhanced his knowledge of the military situation by visiting countless units and participating in an air combat assault against a Viet Cong–held village. Although his tour in Vietnam was brief, he left the country more firmly committed to his government's policy and to the American military establishment.

Walters—now a major general—reported to the embassy in Paris, where he continued to perform in a capacity as military liaison and as an interpreter. In addition to his more routine tasks, he began a new phase in his diplomatic career when Henry Kissinger, on behalf of President Richard Nixon, directed him to commence secret negotiations with North Vietnam. Despite the fact that these negotiations never produced anything of substance, Walters performed his mission with admirable results. He managed to establish secret links with the North Vietnamese and succeeded in shuttling Kissinger in and out of France without arousing suspicion in the Central Intelligence Agency, the army, or the embassy. He also successfully kept his activities from the eyes of the press.

Walters also figured prominently in establishing contact with the Chinese in June 1970. These contacts culminated in Nixon's historic visit to Beijing in 1972, which signaled the Sino-American rapprochement. Seven months later Nixon dispatched Walters on a sensitive mission to Spain. He discreetly inquired about Franco's plans regarding the succession of power. Walters subsequently conveyed to Nixon Franco's assurances that a change in leadership would not upset Spain's stability.

Walters gained Nixon's confidence as a result of his performance with regard to the negotiations with North Vietnam and China and his visit with Franco. Nixon rewarded Walters by naming him to the deputy directorship of the Central Intelligence Agency in 1972 after he retired from the army. Apart from his congressional testimony on the CIA's role in the Watergate cover-up, Walters's work at the CIA remains shrouded in secrecy. Four years later, in 1976, he resigned his position at the CIA to pursue his interests in the private sector, namely, lecturing and writing.

Walters's absence from public life did not last long. In 1981 Ronald Reagan named Walters his roving ambassador. From 1981 to 1985 Walters visited over one hundred countries as Reagan's personal emissary. Among his more notable trips was his 1982 visit to Buenos Aires with Secretary of State Alexander Haig in an attempt to avert war between Great Britain and Argentina over the Falklands Islands. In the same year Reagan secretly sent Walters to Cuba to discuss with Fidel Castro Cuba's involvement in the insurgencies in Nicaragua and El Salvador.

In May 1985 President Reagan appointed Walters to succeed Jeane Kirkpatrick as the U.S. ambassador to the United Nations. Convincing François Mitterand to allow American war planes to overfly French territory in response to Libya's connection to the bombing of TWA Flight 840 stands as perhaps his most notable act as ambassador to the United Nations. In fact, when the United States pressed France for overflight permission, Mitterand specifically requested that Walters be sent to Paris for consultations.

To simply say that Vernon Walters was present at some of the important events of the second half of the twentieth century would be to diminish his role as diplomat. Walters's accomplishments as translator for five presidents and his abilities to discreetly and ably conduct sensitive negotiations illustrate his devotion to the service of his country. Furthermore, that his services have been repeatedly requested by American and foreign leaders alike testifies to his prominence as a key figure in American diplomacy during the past fifty years.

Work by Vernon Walters

Silent Missions. Garden City, NY: Doubleday, 1978.

Works about Vernon Walters

Black, Jan Knippers. *United States Penetration of Brazil*. Philadelphia: University of Pennsylvania Press, 1977.

Haig, Alexander M., Jr. *Caveat: Realism, Reagan, and Foreign Policy*. New York: Macmillan, 1984.

Johnson, William. "Gift of Tongues Carried Walters to Senior Posts." *Globe and Mail*, April 1, 1985, 11.

Samuels, Gertrude. "A Talk with Ambassador Walters." *New Leader*, September 19, 1988, 5–8.

Shultz, George P. *Turmoil and Triumph: My Years as Secretary of State*. New York: Maxwell Macmillan International, 1993.

Smist, Frank J., Jr. *Congress Oversees the United States Intelligence Community, 1947–1989*. Knoxville: University of Tennessee Press, 1990.
Wesson, Robert. *The United States and Brazil: Limits of Influence*. New York: Praeger Publishers, 1981.

WILLIAM W. BAIN AND JULIE A. BAIN

CLIFTON REGINALD WHARTON, SR. (1899–1990),

was a career diplomat and the first black American to serve as U.S. minister and ambassador in Europe.

Wharton was born in Baltimore, Maryland, on May 11, 1899. Shortly thereafter his family moved to Boston, where Wharton attended English High School and then went on to Boston University for his LL.B. degree in 1920. In 1923 he earned his LL.M. degree from the same institution.

From 1920 to 1924 he practiced law in Boston. In 1924 he first entered government service, doing a short stint in the Veterans Bureau as an examiner. While doing service with the Massachusetts National Guard during that same year, Wharton was informed that he had been accepted as a law clerk in the Department of State. The circumstances surrounding this appointment are not entirely clear. Wharton was never formally interviewed for the position, and whether or not the Department of State even knew that he was black is not evident. In any event, his appointment was certainly significant, for Wharton was the only black to hold a professional position in the department in 1924; the other blacks in the department were messengers or cleaning people. Only a handful of black Americans worked in the diplomatic service overseas, mostly in Haiti and Liberia.

Wharton's early time in the Department of State was filled with frustration and isolation. He was immediately assigned to a paper-pushing job in the Consular Commercial Office. Left almost completely alone by his white coworkers, Wharton never wavered from his decision to make diplomacy his career. With the passage of the Rogers Act in 1924, which established the new Foreign Service, Wharton saw his opening. As soon as the first Foreign Service examination was given, he became the first black to take and pass the test. He scored well on the written part of the examination and, although somewhat trepidant about facing an all-white oral examination board, he sailed through their questions. On March 20, 1925, he was appointed as a Foreign Service officer (FSO), unclassified, and secretary in the diplomatic service.

Like nearly every other black American who served in the Foreign Service, Wharton began his career in Liberia. The day after his appointment to the Foreign Service, he was made third secretary at the American legation in Monrovia. Although he had expected this thankless assignment, he did not expect the indignities that preceded his move to the post. First, he was not even sent to the Foreign Service School for training, although this was required for all FSOs. According to the department, the haste was due to the pressing need for his services in Liberia. Second, the department made something less than comfortable arrangements for the transportation of Wharton and his wife to his new assignment, booking the two on a cargo ship. Only Wharton's adamant stance on this issue forced the department to make more suitable travel arrangements.

Wharton's early experiences set the tone for the black FSOs who would follow. For twenty-five years he found himself shuffled from one undesirable post
to another. During that time, while other FSOs served in a variety of areas,
Wharton served in only four: Liberia (1925–1930, 1936–1937, 1937–1938,
1941–1942); Las Palmas in the Canary Islands (1930–1936, 1937, 1938–1941);
Tananarive, Madagascar (1942–1945); and Ponta Delgada in the Azores (1945–
1949). (It should be noted that Wharton's frequent returns to Liberia were due
to absences of the U.S. minister from that post at various times. Wharton was
usually called on to keep things functioning.) Wharton was the first black FSO
to serve in Las Palmas, but in Liberia, Madagascar, and the Azores he was
merely following in the footsteps of earlier black appointees. Despite steady
promotions, from FSO-8 to FSO-3 in 1946, Wharton's career—and those of the
handful of black Americans who had joined the Foreign Service since 1925—
seemed to have stalled.

From 1949 on, however, Wharton's career began to take off. Part of the
reason for this was his excellent work up to that point. His service in Madagascar
during the war, in particular, was well praised, not only by American officials
but by British diplomats as well. Another factor working in his favor was his
1946 promotion to FSO-3. Despite the discrimination shown against black FSOs
in terms of assignments, Wharton's senior status made it more and more difficult
to simply shunt him off to one hardship post after another. Finally, a confluence
of domestic and international forces also helped to push Wharton beyond the
traditional black diplomatic postings. In the United States the civil rights movement was gathering steam. In addition to demanding equal employment opportunities in the federal government (where the Department of State, with its
''lily-white'' image, was a favorite target), more and more black Americans
were becoming interested in U.S. foreign relations and insisting on a black voice
in these affairs. Abroad, U.S. segregation and other race problems were giving
the nation a poor reputation, especially among newly independent developing
countries. One solution to these domestic and international problems that the
Truman administration came up with was the appointment of black Americans
to higher-profile positions within the Department of State and Foreign Service.

It was hardly a coincidence that in 1949, when Edward R. Dudley was made
the first black American ambassador in the nation's history, Wharton also received a promotion, breaking out of the Liberia–Azores–Canary Islands–Madagascar cycle of postings. In that year Wharton was sent to Lisbon, Portugal,
as first secretary and consul general. Not only had Wharton been promoted to
a senior position, but he was also the first black ever to serve in the Lisbon
embassy. Far from his days of pushing papers in an insignificant office at the
Department of State, Wharton was soon made supervisory consul general. In
1951 he was promoted to FSO-2.

After a few years in Portugal Wharton again broke the color barrier by becoming the first black ever to serve in the U.S. consulate in Marseilles, France,
once again assuming the position of consul general. Wharton spent nearly five

years at this post, rising to FSO-1 along the way. In 1958, however, the biggest opportunity of his career came about. In that year President Dwight D. Eisenhower offered Wharton the position of U.S. minister to Romania. This was a groundbreaking assignment in many ways. First, Wharton would be the first black career Foreign Service officer to head a U.S. mission. Second, he would be the first black to head a U.S. mission outside of Africa. (The four previous black chiefs of missions had been in Liberia or Guinea.) Finally, and perhaps most strikingly, he would be the first black American to head a U.S. mission in a Communist nation.

It was little wonder that the announcement of Wharton's selection caused quite a stir. *U.S. News and World Report* ran a piece in which it warned Romania to get ready for a "surprise" and applauded the choice as a blow to Communist propaganda about U.S. racism. In black newspapers across the country the selection generally made front-page news and was viewed as a real step forward for black Americans.

Wharton, however, did not simply jump at the opportunity. He first wanted to determine whether his appointment was a "token" selection; if his race was the primary factor, he would rather wait for a position where his diplomatic qualities were the determinants. After a meeting with Deputy Under Secretary for Administration Loy Henderson at which he was assured that race played no role in the appointment, Wharton accepted.

Henderson, an old friend of Wharton's, was no doubt being sincere. There was little doubt that Wharton deserved such a position. He was a thirty-four-year veteran who had honed his diplomatic skills in various posts, excelling at each one. Yet it is hard to imagine that the appointment to a Communist nation, coming in 1958, was simply an example of the Department of State recognizing and rewarding talent and seniority. In the late 1950s the Eisenhower administration was reeling from a series of domestic racial incidents that had seriously damaged U.S. prestige abroad. Some well-publicized lynchings in the South and the uproar over school desegregation, culminating in the standoff in Little Rock, had been seized upon by friend and foe alike to cast the United States as a nation with a serious race problem. Naturally, Communist propagandists had a field day with the issue, directing their message especially to the newly independent nations of Africa and Asia.

The Eisenhower administration had been quick to react, using the United States Information Agency to try to contain the damage and put a different spin on the situation in the United States. It even went so far as to create, as part of the U.S. pavilion at the 1958 World's Fair in Brussels, an exhibit on the problem of segregation in America and how the nation was attempting to solve it. (This exhibit blew up in the administration's face when a group of Southern congressmen complained loudly and angrily about the "anti-South" implications of the show.) It is in this context that Wharton's appointment must be considered.

However, Wharton's appointment was not mere window dressing. By the late

1950s the Eisenhower administration had embarked on a policy of driving a wedge between the Soviet Union and its satellites in Eastern Europe. Romania was one of the targets. Success had been limited. Relations between Romania and the United States had been severely strained since World War II and had gotten progressively worse by the mid-1950s. The United States complained about Romania's human rights abuses and demanded reparations for U.S. properties lost after the Communist takeover of that nation. Romania responded by charging the United States with espionage and refusing admittance of U.S. observers for its 1957 elections. The countermove by the United States was the freezing of Romanian assets in U.S. banks. There matters stood when Wharton assumed his position.

During Wharton's tenure as minister relations between the United States and Romania took a turn for the better. The Romanians were eager for U.S. trade; the United States was eager to try and wean Eastern European nations away from the Soviet Union. The biggest impediments were the reparations claims of the United States and Romania's frozen assets. After long and involved negotiations a settlement was finally reached in early 1960, setting the stage for closer economic relations. Wharton was rewarded for his service by being made career minister in 1959.

With the coming to power of the Democratic administration of John F. Kennedy in 1961, Wharton's career took another upward leap. More so than the Truman and Eisenhower administrations, Kennedy's was interested in the recruitment and promotion of black Americans for U.S. diplomatic service. In looking about for some high-profile appointments immediately after his election, Kennedy quickly hit upon Wharton. With a ministerial appointment already under his belt, there could be no denying Wharton the ultimate award of an ambassadorship. The only question was where to send him.

For years the State Department had debated the issue of sending black U.S. ambassadors to countries other than those in Africa, but prior to 1961 the four black appointees had all served on that continent. In 1961 Kennedy broke that tradition by announcing that Wharton was his choice for U.S. ambassador to Norway. The choice was widely applauded in the U.S. press, and Wharton was quickly confirmed as the first black American to serve as U.S. ambassador to a European nation.

Norway might have seemed an unusual locale for such a groundbreaking appointment. In fact, however, Scandinavia had been discussed for years as a possible European spot for a black appointee, due to the perception of that region's more advanced racial views. (It was not simply coincidence that the second black American to serve as ambassador in Europe, Carl Rowan, was appointed to Finland in 1963.) Moreover, Norway was a good spot for a man with Wharton's experience in European affairs. It was a fairly solid, though sometimes skeptical, ally of the United States, and its border with the Soviet Union meant that communism was an ever-present threat.

Wharton's years in Norway were busy, but relatively calm. Norway was a solid member of NATO, and although its stand against nuclear weapons in the late 1950s and early 1960s disconcerted some U.S. policymakers, it never wavered from the alliance. The United States gently prodded Norway during Wharton's tenure to apply for membership in the European Economic Community, but the failure of Great Britain to win admittance scuttled the opportunity. In addition to his normal work, Wharton also attended the twenty-seventh ministerial meeting of NATO in 1961, served as a delegate to the United Nations, where he assisted on commerce and trade issues, and, coming full circle, was a member of an oral examination board testing Foreign Service hopefuls.

Wharton, having achieved his highest goal and after forty years of service, announced his retirement in 1964. He died on April 25, 1990, in Phoenix, Arizona. Two of his sons, Clifton Wharton, Jr., and William B. Wharton, also served in the Department of State.

Works about Clifton R. Wharton, Sr.

Calkin, Homer L. "A Reminiscence: Being Black in the Foreign Service." *Department of State Newsletter*, February 1978, 25–28.
Miller, Jake C. *The Black Presence in American Foreign Affairs*. Lanham, MD: University Press of America, 1978.

MICHAEL L. KRENN

ANDREW DICKSON WHITE (1832–1918), founder

of Cornell University, cofounder and first president of the American Historical Association, minister to Russia, and twice minister to Germany, witnessed both his home and host country's growth into imperial competitors. His republican convictions and scholarly outlook conduced him to an innocence about and distaste for Bismarckian power politics, but he nevertheless attempted to improve German-American relations. In this effort he followed a number of other Germanophiles such as George Bancroft, John Lothrop, and Bayard Taylor.

Born in Homer, New York, to a businessman/banker and his wife, a daughter of the district's assemblyman, White grew up in a dynamic, public-spirited family. He attended Hobart College and Yale, from which he graduated at age twenty-one. White's educational interests focused mainly on history and literature, and he garnered several student literary prizes. While at Yale he experienced his first bout with a politician's dilemma that caused him to dislike all future political machinations. As editor of the *Yale Literary Magazine*, he needed to please his largely proslavery readership and thus negate his own abolitionist feelings. The inability to express his antislavery ideas left his conscience struggling until he finally had the opportunity to present his views in the commencement address.

This speech lead directly to his first diplomatic appointment. The former governor of Connecticut, Thomas Seymour, impressed with the young man's convictions and eloquent ability to express them, offered White a position with the American legation in St. Petersburg, Russia. Still unsure of his calling and professional ambitions, White performed the duties of an attaché at the American legation in St. Petersburg from 1854 to 1855.

Subsequently he traveled and studied in Europe, where he learned to appreciate the greater independence and rigor in instruction and the decidedly nonsectarian nature of the European university system. After his return to the United States he spent another year at Yale and then married Mary Outwater, with whom he had two daughters and a son. In 1857 he answered the call to move west, where he taught history at the University of Michigan throughout the tumultuous years that witnessed his students going off to fight in the Civil War. According to some of his dedicated students he was an inspiring teacher and great lecturer whose classes, open to the public, drew large crowds.

His European experiences left strong impressions that White felt he should "do something about." He wanted to shape American universities closer to the European model in two important ways: first, in regard to the student's freedom to study independently of classes, and second, by highlighting the importance of science education. Throughout his life he remained dedicated to emphasizing the important influence especially of the German education system on America. This conviction undoubtedly helped in his work as a diplomat there.

His devotion to "truth, justice, rational liberty, and right reason" smacked to many contemporaries as unchristian and irreligious and as tainted by touches of Darwin and Spencer. This struggle of the rightful place of science and religion in the world of education remained a leitmotif throughout White's life, leading him to publish *The Warfare of Science* (1876), *A History of the Warfare of Science with Theology in Christendom* (1896), and *Seven Great Statesmen in the Warfare of Humanity with Unreason* (1910). Collectively these volumes provide White's defense for founding a university under the control of no political party and of no single religious sect. Since White subscribed to the credo that knowledge or truth was independent of any religious affiliation, he dreamed of setting up a state university where such subjects as agriculture and engineering could be taught on an equal footing with such classics as history and theology. His father's death left him money to fulfill this dream.

He thus returned from Michigan to New York just as the state elections had the Republicans searching for a compromise candidate. White was elected state senator. At first he felt unfit for the position because of his lack of familiarity with practical issues. Once he was assigned to chair the Senate's Committee on Education, he felt more at home. He was reelected for a second term and in this position supervised the implementation of the Morrill Act of 1862—the setting aside of a million acres for land-grant colleges. White found in Ezra Cornell, the chairman of the Agriculture Committee, a like-minded colleague with whom he would realize his dream. Together they established a college in Ithaca that had no religious affiliation.

The nonsectarian college, named for Ezra Cornell, was begun at the close of the Civil War, and in 1867 White became its first president, a position he held until 1885. His goals for the college were clear as he visited technical and scientific schools in Europe in order to copy their best features for his new endeavor. He also traveled to western schools to learn about coeducation. Throughout his tenure as president White concerned himself mostly with presenting the university to the outside world, defending its nonsectarian nature, and expanding his friendship with the best and brightest scholars from Europe and America.

The next twenty years were extremely busy for White as he tried to advance the reputation of the college while taking on other assignments such as commissioner to Santo Domingo in 1871 and a two-year stint (from 1879 to 1881) as minister to Germany. His appointments were due in part to Republican Party gratitude for White's service at the various presidential conventions where the New York senator advanced the candidacies of Ulysses Grant (1868 and 1872) and Rutherford Hayes (1876). They were also due to White's belief in the usefulness of personal diplomacy that could outweigh public emotionalism. White was convinced of his own persuasive powers. Moreover, his admiration of the intellectual climate in Germany surely helped his appointment. White was often heard to say that although the United States had English origins, Germany also qualified as a parent because of the great number of American students who studied at Göttingen, Berlin, Heidelberg, and other German universities.

During his tenure as U.S. minister to the German court, White always looked for commonality between the two countries. In commercial relations White, true to his historical training, pointed to the "need for fair and careful collection of the full range of facts regarding important subjects such as railway management, administration of urban politics, and the growth of various competing industries." In overseeing the interests of Americans, White bemoaned the fact that hardly a day passed without some skirmish regarding the rights of "German-Americans in their Fatherland." This was a reference to the mostly young men who escaped Prussian military service by immigrating to the United States and then returned home to gloat over those who had submitted to the rigors of Prussian military duty.

White's tenure also coincided with the appearance of the first serious cracks in the German-American friendship. Yet potential discord figured less prominently in White's own recollections, a two-volume *Autobiography*, which reinforces later criticism that White largely ignored the increasing conflict of interest between the two nations and Bismarck's adroit use of many Americans' love for German things.

In early 1880, for example, the two countries embarked upon a tariff war, the most serious aspect of which was the banning of U.S. pork in Germany. White counseled the State Department against economic retaliation and instead hoped that he could convince the Iron Chancellor to participate in an endeavor to bring "bimetallism" to the international monetary system. White was also conciliatory when the two nations nearly clashed militarily over competing interests in Samoa. It was not until his second tenure as ambassador that White realized how deep-seated the rivalry in Samoa was.

Appointed by President Hayes in 1879, White remained in Germany after James Garfield's election. A few months later he had to explain to his hosts the climate that aroused a disgruntled and deranged office seeker to assassinate Garfield. When Chester Arthur took office, White resigned his post for another mission besides his educational calling as president of Cornell. The diplomat wished for civil service reform, but more important, as part of that reform, a less politicized, improved diplomatic service. White understood that diplomacy was as much presentation as political maneuvering and hoped that he could help define a more professional and financially secure foreign office staff that was less dependent on party favors.

The decade that followed White's return to the United States saw him in various capacities, none of which seemed entirely satisfactory to him. He had not become known for his diplomacy in high politics but rather for his close personal relationship with "men of letters and science" and his promotion of Americans studying abroad. His foremost love still was history teaching, and in 1884 he helped establish the American Historical Association. Throughout these years White was in precarious health, which was further damaged by various troubles at Cornell. In 1885 he relinquished the presidency of this now firmly established institution to his former student Charles Kendall Adams. Declining such appointments as an interstate railway commissionership or candidacy for a congressional seat, White opted to travel in Europe. He extended these travels after his wife died in 1887 and finally returned to his vocation of teaching in 1889 (Stanford made him a nonresident of its faculty).

The Republican Party circulated his name for various offices, including those of secretary of state, vice president, governor, and senator, but in the end White chose for personal reasons an ambassadorship to Russia. In 1890 he had married Helen Magill, a daughter of Swarthmore's president, and had begun a new family. White accepted Benjamin Harrison's offer of an appointment just days after the death of his baby daughter, in a clear effort to leave that personal tragedy behind.

At the court in St. Petersburg White had little meaningful input. His diplomatic tasks were frustrated by the small size of the legation and a limited budget, which he could not augment with private funds. His work was also hampered by his distaste for Russian affairs and his inability to establish meaningful contacts with the more progressive elements in Russia. Instead, he enjoyed the acquaintance of the controversial Constantine Pobedonostzeff, ecclesiastical and civil councilor to the czar, and the writer Leo Tolstoy. He completed his *History of the Warfare of Science with Theology in Christendom* and savored the brilliant festivities at the Winter Palace.

Economic issues (fairness in seal hunting) and human rights issues (improvement of conditions for Russian Jews) dominated his ministerial agenda. Neither assignment was crowned with success. Russian and British diplomats made their own arrangements with regard to exploiting and endangering the seal population in the Bering Straits, and White never went beyond writing dispatches on the discriminatory treatment of Russian Jews. Frustrated with his work and under the threat of a cholera outbreak, White resigned in 1894 and returned to the United States with his wife and a new baby daughter.

The following year President Grover Cleveland named White to the commission charged with finding "the true divisional line between Venezuela and British Guiana." Again White relied on personal encounters and powers of persuasion to have the British accept the boundary line confirmed by the Arbitration Tribunal in Paris.

The 1896 presidential election resulted in a Republican victory, and newly elected William McKinley appointed White to his favorite diplomatic post, minister to Germany. The American legation was upgraded to the most prestigious and influential level, that of embassy. This did not exactly correspond to White's hope for reform of the diplomatic service, since he thought that the ceremonial presentation as ambassador "was an ordeal more picturesque than agreeable," but his title resulted in increased visibility and influence.

This second term as envoy during the McKinley-Roosevelt years differed from his first by the quantity and importance of the German-American issues and the absence of the dominant figure of Chancellor Bismarck. The tariff wars had not subsided, and both the sugar and pork trade still suffered. White considered keeping commercial peace as his foremost obligation. He was much less enthused about solving the lingering questions regarding rule in Samoa. As a protectorate of three nations, Samoa's population was fractionalized, causing a brutal civil war in which Germany supported one contender to the throne while Britain and the United States supported another. The crisis was settled without much input from White when Germany agreed to a division of the island with the United States, while Great Britain was compensated elsewhere. The Americans also retained the important coaling station of Pago Pago, which provided a strategic foothold for expansion into the Pacific and Far East.

Germany missed Bismarck's leadership in foreign affairs and so did White, whose relations with Chancellor Bernhard von Bülow were cordial but never quite as personal. White was a "friendly interpreter" of the "new Germany," which should have made him an ideal candidate to negotiate with Germany on international issues such as the Spanish-American War, the Boxer Rebellion, the independence of Cuba, and, most of all, the handling of America's energetic press. In the eighteen years since his first stay, public opinion in both countries had been shaped by more sensationalistic journalism, and White took great pains to smooth out these misconceptions on the official level.

More often then not, however, White misinterpreted his country's policies as well as Germany's sympathies. He firmly believed in the anti-imperialist nature of the McKinley administration and did not alert his superiors to Germany's clear support for Spain, which almost led to German intervention when Admiral George Dewey took Manila Bay.

White, a staunch supporter of Secretary of State John Hay, watched with interest Hay's policies on China. White had the opportunity to pass to the Germans his superior's Open Door Notes, which he praised as "farseeing, prompt, bold, successful." Yet his diplomatic skills did not speed a German response. The German Empire was the last to send a written acknowledgment and expressed a distaste for the demanded declaration. Moreover, it did not desist from demanding railroad concessions and occupying Kiaochow Peninsula and Tsingtao.

In 1899 the American ambassador interrupted his work in Germany to lead the U.S. delegation at the First Hague Peace Conference. This assignment required different skills since White not only had to deal with foreign powers but also had to face opposition from members of his own delegation. Germany at first blocked the Anglo-American proposal of establishing an arbitration panel but eventually acquiesced in the creation of a permanent court of arbitration. White's ally in the conference was the British delegate Julian Pauncefote, while his fellow American Alfred T. Mahan sided with the German emperor, especially in his opposition to exempting all private property from seizure at sea. Characteristically, White dwelled little on these substantive issues but rather judged a Fourth of July celebration as the most dramatic event of the Hague conference. With White as the main speaker, the commemoration featured a wreath-laying ceremony at the tomb of Hugo Grotius, the father of international law.

Back in the United States for President McKinley's second inauguration, White made many speeches defending the Ohioan from charges of being hostile to Germany. Many German Americans were rightly worried about the two countries' relationship. White had just made it back to Germany when he was informed of yet another presidential assassination. This was a double blow for the almost seventy-year-old White because shortly before McKinley's murder his only son had committed suicide. With these tragedies as backdrop, he delved more intensely into work, defending the new president as a man who had "been brought up to admire and respect Germany." White looked for commonalties and positive points of reference by comparing the German and American leaders. Theodore Roosevelt and Emperor Wilhelm II, he surmised, possessed similar characteristics in their youthful enthusiasm, their commitment to their countries' grandeur, and their fondness for hunting. Yet these similarities only contributed to the increasing difficulties between the two countries, and White's inability to assess the changes diminished his political effectiveness. As White celebrated his seventieth birthday in Berlin, he handed in his resignation.

The last sixteen years of his life were partly enjoyed at Alassio on the Riviera and partly spent in New York and Washington. White kept busy: he wrote his two-volume autobiography, served as a regent of the Smithsonian Institution, and published *Seven Great Statesmen in the Warfare of Humanity with Unreason*. White died in 1918, knowing that the United States had defeated the country with which he had tried so hard to retain an amicable relationship.

Works by Andrew D. White

"The New Germany." *Bulletin of the American Geographical Society*, no. 4 (New York) (1882).

Autobiography of Andrew Dickson White. 2 vols. New York: Century Co., 1905.

Seven Great Statesmen in the Warfare of Humanity with Unreason. New York: Century Co., 1910.

A History of the Warfare of Science with Theology in Christendom. New York: Appleton, [1896] 1919.

Paper Money Inflation in France. (1876 paper, republished in 1913.) Washington, DC: Cato Institute, 1980.

Works about Andrew D. White

Altschuler, Glenn C. *Andrew D. White: Educator, Historian, Diplomat*. Ithaca, NY: Cornell University Press, 1979. Includes extensive bibliography of primary and secondary sources.

Bordin, Ruth. *Andrew Dickson White: Teacher of History*. Ann Arbor: University of Michigan Press, 1958.

Burr, George Lincoln. "Sketch of Andrew D. White." *Popular Science Monthly* 48 (February 1896).
Von Schierbrand, Wolf. "Ambassador White's Work." *North American Review* 175 (November 1902).

VERENA BOTZENHART-VIEHE

ANDREW JACKSON YOUNG, JR. (1932–   ), be-
came the first African American appointed U.S. ambassador to the United Nations, where he pressed the issues of human rights and majority rule in southern Africa.

Young was born in New Orleans, Louisiana, to a family of professionals; his mother was a teacher, and his father, a dentist. This middle-class family lived in a largely white neighborhood; this experience exposed young Andrew to the many facets of racism in the United States. After attending a private high school, Young registered at Howard University in Washington, D.C., at the age of fifteen. During his years at Howard he became acquainted with the teachings of Mahatma Gandhi and the tenets of civil disobedience. He graduated from Howard in 1951 and decided against pursuing the study of dentistry. Instead, he chose to enter Hartford Theological Seminary and was ordained a minister in the United Church of Christ in 1955.

Young began his ministry in Alabama and southwestern Georgia after being denied permission by the Portuguese government to travel to Angola as a missionary. In 1954 he married Jean Childs, and together they became active in the intensified civil rights movement of the 1950s. Young helped found the Southern Christian Leadership Conference (SCLC) with Dr. Martin Luther King, Jr., in 1957. From that point until King's assassination in 1968, Young remained a close advisor of King and an important leader of the civil rights movement. Throughout this period Young participated in all the major protests, conferences, and decisions held by the SCLC. He promoted the use of nonviolent civil disobedience and legislative changes to foster the rights of minorities in the United States. As an advisor to King, Young served as a mediator between the black protesters and the white racist forces seeking to maintain segregation and deny minorities equality. King's frequent arrests often left Young in charge of the daily operations of large-scale protests.

The civil rights movement helped develop Young's positions on racism, education, poverty, and human rights. King's efforts to attain civil and political rights for minorities in the United States remained focused on the use of nonviolent protest to alter the existing social and governmental system. Young concurred with King and offered a voice of moderation as black militancy developed in the late 1960s. The evolutionary approach of King and Young allowed for slow reform. The more revolutionary positions of radical black power groups were rejected by Young, as was the belief in sudden violent change. Young believed that the status of minorities would only be improved by the economic and political empowerment that the civil rights movement sought to foster. The fixed points in his evolutionary ideology centered on his Christian ministry and his belief in the use of civil disobedience and economic pressure to effect change in society.

The assassination of King in 1968 released a torrent of violence from the African-American population. King's death and the ensuing riots damaged the civil rights movement and its efforts at evolutionary change. The earlier successes of the movement in attaining desegregation, voting rights, and new social welfare legislation were not followed by further legislative victories after King's death. Consequently, Young and many other African-American leaders sought to continue the struggle by entering the political arena as candidates. In 1970 Young ran for Congress in Georgia's fifth congressional district against Fletcher Thompson and lost. After the failed attempt he chaired the Atlanta Community Relations Committee and built a constituency in Atlanta. In 1972 he won election to the U.S. Congress and became active in the national politics of the Democratic Party.

Young's association with the Democratic Party and Georgia politics had brought him in contact with Jimmy Carter in 1970. The men became strongly allied during Carter's 1976 presidential election campaign. During the primaries Young stood for the presidential hopeful and encouraged black voters to choose Carter as the Democratic candidate. This effort afforded Carter several key victories in Southern primaries. Young's strong support and delivery of the black vote also provided the necessary margin for Carter's razor-thin victory over incumbent President Gerald Ford. The newly elected president owed Young a great debt, which he attempted to repay by offering Young the position of U.S. ambassador to the United Nations.

Young accepted President Carter's offer amid cries from many African-American activists that Young had been overlooked for a higher-level cabinet appointment. Young, however, saw this as an opportunity to affect U.S. policy and become an international spokesman on the issues of racism, economic disparity, and human rights. Indeed, President Carter and his foreign policy advisors believed that Young could assist in American efforts to secure peaceful change in southern Africa and also promulgate the new American focus on human rights throughout the world. With this mandate, Young traveled immediately in February 1977 to Africa on a fact-finding mission.

Young's mission to Africa focused on meeting many African leaders and discussing the many problem areas of southern Africa. At the time of the mission Angola, Rhodesia (now Zimbabwe), and Namibia were all involved in civil wars that were destabilizing all of southern Africa. Despite the condemnation of all of black Africa and the disapproval of the United States and many of its allies, the systems of white minority rule in Rhodesia and South Africa stood firm. Soviet, Chinese, and Cuban involvement in southern Africa intensified as the political situation deteriorated. In addition to the military and political struggles, Africa suffered from tremendous underdevelopment and economic stagnation. Past American policies had generally neglected sub-Saharan Africa and its many problems. With the Carter administration's approval, Young wanted to involve the United States actively in the solutions.

The development of an active African policy began after Young's fact-finding mission. Young pushed for an aggressive American position on Rhodesia that advocated majority rule and condemnation of Ian Smith's minority government. As a part of this effort, the Carter administration sought the repeal of the Byrd Amendment that had allowed American companies to trade with Rhodesia, especially in chromium, a strategic metal. This trade relation stood in opposition to a U.N. embargo placed on Rhodesia. Young sought the repeal in order to apply more pressure on the Smith government to move toward political reforms. He scored an early victory with the repeal of the Byrd Amendment on March 18, 1977.

Young's position on majority rule gained the support of President Carter and his administration. In May 1977 Carter sent Vice President Walter Mondale to meet South African Prime Minister Johannes Vorster in Vienna. Mondale stated that South Africa must begin implementing reforms with the goal of majority rule. This attack on South Africa's apartheid system bolstered the American image in Africa, although it worsened relations with South Africa, and the repression in that country expanded. Young felt not only that the systems of minority rule in Rhodesia and South Africa were morally wrong, but also that they opened opportunities for Soviet involvement in southern Africa. His thesis held that the establishment of majority rule in both countries would lead to stability and economic growth in the entire region.

The increased importance of Africa stemmed not only from Carter's new human rights policy but also from the strategic issues of oil and minerals. African states produced some 40 percent of American oil imports and maintained large quantities of strategic minerals. Nigeria alone maintained a 20 percent share of American oil imports. Young's position on white minority rule and the need for continued assistance in the development in Africa became an intelligent, as well as morally sound, policy. Young visited Nigeria on his first African tour and found that his message in support of majority rule was very well received. Nigeria actively participated in funding liberation groups in southern Africa and welcomed the new policy. The need for the support of such African states in the United Nations also became evident to policymakers in their efforts throughout the globe. As U.N. ambassador, Young enabled the United States to secure new African friends in the United Nations. As a show of the growing importance of Africa and in appreciation of Nigeria's support for American policies, President Carter visited Nigeria in April 1978, the first time an American president had visited a black African nation.

Young advanced the Carter administration's policy of advocating human rights throughout the world. He condemned the murderous excesses of Idi Amin and supported the 1978 embargo on Ugandan trade that aided the downfall of the Amin government. He also criticized Chilean human rights violations. In a tour of the Caribbean in August 1977 he brought promises of new foreign aid to help foster economic development in Latin America. He offered the American effort to return the Panama Canal to Panama as a token of new American policies toward Latin America that were based on a more equal footing. This equality, however, was tempered with his continued criticism of human rights violations in many Latin American and Caribbean states.

Racism remained a central issue in Young's discussions of Africa. Inequalities created by racist thoughts and actions continued to prevent Africa's economic development and social stability. Having fought for so many years against the barriers built by racism in the United States, Young attempted to highlight the impact of racism on Africa. His focus on racism led him to discount the influence of Communist ideology on the nations of Africa. The appeal of communism to most Africans centered on the doctrine of equality, which racism had denied them. Young believed that the removal of racist governments from Africa would end the appeal of Communist thought. The presence of twenty thousand Cuban troops in Angola in 1977 did not disturb Young in the same way that it bothered many conservative Americans. In an early statement during his tenure as U.N. ambassador, Young discounted the presence of these Cuban troops and stated that they served as an important stabilizing influence in Angola. Though fundamentally accurate, this statement was received poorly by many American leaders who continued to criticize Young's outspoken positions on race, poverty, and majority rule in Africa.

Young's belief that racism stood as the main barrier to African liberation and economic development led him to fall back on his civil rights experiences for solutions. He sought nonviolent methods to create peaceful transitions in the troubled states of southern Africa. His advocacy of economic sanctions and negotiated settlements gained tacit support from many African leaders, but he failed to impress leaders of the various liberation movements. Both Robert Mugabe and Joshua Nkomo, who led the Rhodesian Patriotic Front, which represented the revolutionary black liberation movement, attempted to convey to Young the earlier failures of nonviolent struggle and stressed their total belief in armed struggle. Though they were pleased to have U.S. support for majority rule and an embargo on Rhodesian trade, neither Mugabe nor Nkomo was willing to risk a cease-fire agreement that might benefit Ian Smith's government.

As the Rhodesian civil war dragged on, support for Ian Smith's government grew among conservative congressmen who feared Mugabe's Communist connections. Ultimately, congressional support for sanctions against Rhodesia faded, although the sanctions remained in place until after the transition to majority rule in 1980. Young had urged that the sanctions be maintained and continued to press for a negotiated settlement. Such an agreement was finally arranged by the British government, but by then the United States had fallen out of the negotiating process due to the forced resignation of Ambassador Young in the summer of 1979 and the Iranian hostage crisis, which commenced on November 4, 1979. When in August 1980 Carter welcomed the new prime minister of Zimbabwe, Robert Mugabe, Young attended this happy occasion.

The United States continued its strong attack on South Africa's apartheid system throughout the Carter administration and Young's tenure. Although American pressure remained confined to the areas of economic and diplomatic sanctions, South Africa became more isolated in the world community. However, this isolation did not alter the actions of the Vorster government, which continued its occupation of Namibia, invaded Angola in search of Namibia guerrillas, and continued the creation of black homelands, which the United States refused to recognize. These actions further disturbed Young and other Carter administration officials and led them to support a U.N. arms embargo against South Africa. The United States also banned the export of police equipment and urged U.S. businesses in South Africa to follow American fair labor standards in opposition to apartheid. Young heavily influenced these decisions and created strong support for the continuation of the struggle against minority rule in South Africa.

The success of Young's policies advocating majority rule and supporting human rights depended heavily on the overall focus of the Carter administration on an open, moral foreign policy based on human rights issues. The early achievements of the Carter administration, including normalization with China, the return of the Panama Canal, and the Camp David Accords, boded well for Young's efforts to build the American image in Africa. However, Young's devotion to destroying racism in southern Africa and establishing peaceful states left him vulnerable to attacks from conservative Americans that he failed to understand the Communist threat in Africa. Many of the leaders of African nations espoused Marxist philosophy and accepted aid from the Soviet Union, China, and Cuba. In 1979 a distinct change in the focus of the Carter administration's foreign policy from North-South relations to a renewed focus on East-West relations created difficulties for Young's unqualified support for these African nations. Although Young did not fear Communist penetration of Africa, policymakers like Carter's National Security Adviser Zbigniew Brzezinski worried about continued Communist assistance and the possibility of strategic resources being denied the United States.

Because of these changes in focus, Ambassador Young's influence over African policy began to fade. He had stood for his beliefs and maintained his positions despite the criticism of the white African governments of Ian Smith and John Vorster and that of American conservatives and cold warriors. Young's long career as a civil rights leader attested to the fact that he did not fear speaking out, and he continued to do so while ambassador to the United Nations. Although President Carter had nominated Young for this specific purpose, an incident on July 26, 1979, involving Young's meeting with Zehdilabib Terzi, Palestine Liberation Organization (PLO) observer at the United Nations, led Carter to call for Young's resignation. Young's meeting with Terzi had violated an Israeli-American agreement regarding contacts with the PLO and created tension between the United States and Israel. The failure of Young, the strong voice for Africa, to change his policies and statements while the rest of the Carter administration returned to the paradigms of the Cold War cost him his job.

However, the important connections that Young had made in Africa continued after his resignation. Later in 1979 Young led a trade mission to several African nations, including Nigeria. Throughout the 1980s he maintained his activist stance on majority rule, human rights, and economic development in Africa. As the mayor of Atlanta during the mid-1980s, he sought to continue his support of these causes and to provide the necessary platform for their discussion. Although he no longer directly affected foreign policy, he maintained his positions and attempted to make them known.

The nomination of Young to be U.S. ambassador to the United Nations prefaced a dramatic, if short-lived, change in the foreign policy of the United States. President Carter was the first president to appoint an African American to such a high diplomatic post. Carter chose Young both to reward Young's decisive assistance in the 1976 presidential campaign and to put forward a strong voice on issues affecting Africa. Young's policies of supporting majority rule in southern Africa and human rights and economic development throughout Africa gained the approval of the early Carter administration. The results of these policies projected over many years with the successful negotiation of independent majority rule in Rhodesia in 1979 and the transfer of power to majority rule in South Africa in 1994. Many of Young's diplomatic efforts in southern Africa foundered because of his focus on nonviolent negotiations and legislative action, yet he was able to bring these issues to the forefront of American policy for a brief moment. His efforts aided the solidification of U.S. relations with Nigeria and Zaire at a time when their strategic resources became even more valuable. In each position he held Young strove to proclaim the evils of racism and defeat the policies it fostered. Using the forum of the United Nations and his position in the Carter administration, he spoke against the problems that racism had caused in the United States and Africa as well as worldwide. Young challenged both the white governments of southern Africa and the government of his own nation to see the problems that racism created while he also showed them the benefits of affording the people of the world majority rule and human rights.

Works by Andrew Jackson Young, Jr.

U.S. Policy on Lebanon. Washington, DC: Department of State, Bureau of Public Affairs, 1979.

Law and Policy in the Space Stations' Era. Boston: Nijhoff, 1989.

Coauthor, with Allen V. Banner and Keith W. Hall. *Aerial Reconnaissance for Verification of Arms Limitation Agreements: An Introduction.* New York: United Nations, 1990.

A Way out of No Way: The Spiritual Memoirs of Andrew Young. Nashville: T. Nelson Publishers, 1994.

Works about Andrew Jackson Young, Jr.

Bartlett, C. Jones. *Flawed Triumphs: Andy Young at the United Nations.* Lanham, MD: University Press of America, 1996.

Bryant, Ira B. *Andrew Jackson Young, Mr. Ambassador: United States Ambassador to the United Nations.* Houston: Armstrong Co., 1979.

Gardner, Carl. *Andrew Young: A Biography*. New York: Drake Publishers, 1978.

Newsum, H. E., and Olayiwola Abegunrin. *United States Foreign Policy towards Southern Africa: Andrew Young and Beyond*. London: Macmillan, 1987.

Simpson, Janice Claire. *Andrew Young: A Matter of Choice*. St. Paul: EMC Corp., 1978.

Smith, Gaddis. *Morality, Reason, and Power: American Diplomacy in the Carter Years*. New York: Hill and Wang, 1986.

Stone, Eddie. *Andrew Young: Biography of a Realist*. Los Angeles: Holloway House, 1980.

DANIEL BYRNE

SELECTED BIBLIOGRAPHY

GENERAL REFERENCE WORKS, SELECTED JOURNALS AND DOCUMENTARY SOURCES

Barnes, William, and John Heath Morgan. *The Foreign Service of the United States*. Department of State, Historical Office, Bureau of Public Affairs, 1961.

Bemis, Samuel Flagg, and Robert Ferrell, eds. *The American Secretaries of State and Their Diplomacy*. 18 vols. Cooper Square Publishers, 1927–1972.

Bemis, Samuel Flagg, and Grace Griffin, eds. *Guide to the Diplomatic History of the United States, 1775–1921*. Government Printing Office, 1935.

Council on Foreign Relations. *Documents on American Foreign Relations*. Originally published by the World Peace Foundation. Simon & Schuster, 1938/39–1943/44; Princeton University Press, 1952–1970.

————. *The United States in World Affairs*. Simon and Schuster, 1931–1971.

Diplomatic History. (1977–   ).

Foreign Affairs. (1922–   ).

Foreign Affairs Bibliography. Vol. 1 covers 1919–1932; subsequent volumes cover ten-year periods.

Freidel, Frank, ed. *Harvard Guide to American History*. 2 vols. Belknap Press, 1974.

Hackworth, Green H. *Digest of International Law*. 8 vols. Government Printing Office, 1940–1944.

Historical Abstracts. Part A: Modern History. Abstracts, 1775–1914. American Bibliographical Center, Clio Press, 1977–   .

Journal of American–East Asian Relations. (1992–   ).

Lowrie, Walter, and Matthew St. Clair, eds. *American State Papers, Class I: Foreign Relations*. 6 vols., Government Printing Office, 1832–1859.

Malloy, William, ed. *Treaties, Conventions, International Acts, Protocols, and Agreements between the United States of America and Other Powers, 1776–1937*. 4 vols. Government Printing Office, 1910–1938.

Manning, William, R. ed., *Diplomatic Correspondence of the United States: Canadian Relations, 1784–1860*. 4 vols. Carnegie Endowment for International Peace, 1940–1945.

———. *The Diplomatic Correspondence of the United States. Concerning the Independence of the Latin American Nations*. 7 vols. Oxford University Press, 1925–1926.

Merli, Frank, and Theodore Wilson, eds. *Makers of American Diplomacy*. 2 vols. Scribner's, 1974.

Miller, David Hunter, ed. *Treaties and Other International Acts of the United States of America*. 7 vols. U.S. Department of State, 1931–1948.

Moore, John Bassett. *A Digest of International Law*. 8 vols. Government Printing Office, 1906.

Political Science Abstracts. IFI/Plenum, 1980– .

Richardson, James D., ed. *A Compilation of the Messages and Papers of the Presidents, 1789–1897*. 10 vols. Government Printing Office, 1896–1899.

Trask, David, and Michael Meyer. *A Bibliography of United States–Latin American Relations since 1810*. University of Nebraska Press, 1968.

U.S. Department of State. *American Foreign Policy: Current Documents*. (1956–).

———. *Foreign Affairs Research: A Directory of Governmental Resources*. (1969).

———. *Papers Relating to the Foreign Relations of the United States* (cited as *FRUS*). Various volumes published beginning in 1861.

———. *United States Treaties and Other International Agreements*. (1950–).

Wharton, Francis, ed. *The Revolutionary Diplomatic Correspondence of the United States*. 6 vols. Government Printing Office, 1889.

SELECTED SECONDARY WORKS

Abramson, Rudy. *Spanning the Century: The Life of W. Averell Harriman, 1891–1986*. William Morrow, 1992.

Acheson, Dean. *Fifty Years After*. Overbrook Press, 1961.

———. *Power and Diplomacy*. Harvard University Press, 1958.

———. *Present at the Creation*. Norton, 1969.

Adams, Charles Francis, ed. *Memoirs of John Quincy Adams*. 12 vols. AMS Press, 1970.

Adams, Henry. *History of the United States of America during the Administrations of Jefferson and Madison*. 9 vols. University of Chicago Press, 1967.

———. *John Randolph*. Houghton, Mifflin and Co., 1882.

Adams, Henry M. *Prussian-American Relations, 1775–1871*. Press of Western Reserve University, 1960.

Adler, Cyrus, and Aaron Margalith. *With Firmness in the Right: American Diplomatic Action Affecting Jews*. American Jewish Committee, 1946.

Adler, Selig. *The Isolationist Impulse: Its Twentieth-Century Reaction*. Abelard-Schuman, 1957.

———. *The Uncertain Giant, 1921–1941*. Macmillan, 1965.

Allen, Harry. *Great Britain and the United States: A History of Anglo-American Relations, 1738–1952*. St. Martin's Press, 1955.

Altschuler, Glenn. *Andrew D. White*. Cornell University Press, 1979.

Ambrose, Stephen. *Eisenhower*. 2 vols. Simon and Schuster, 1983, 1984.

Ambrosius, Lloyd. *Wilsonian Statecraft*. Scholarly Resources Books, 1991.
———. *Woodrow Wilson and the American Diplomatic Tradition*. Cambridge University Press, 1987.
Aron, Raymond. *The Imperial Republic*. Prentice-Hall, 1974.
Backer, John. *The Decision to Divide Germany*. Duke University Press, 1978.
———. *Priming the German Economy*. Duke University Press, 1971.
———. *Winds of History*. Van Nostrand Reinhold, 1983.
Bailey, Thomas A. *America Faces Russia*. P. Smith, 1964.
———. *The Art of Diplomacy: The American Experience*. Appleton, Century, and Crofts, 1968.
———. *A Diplomatic History of the American People*. 10th ed. Prentice-Hall, 1980.
Ball, George. *The Past Has Another Pattern*. Norton, 1982.
Barnett, A. Doak. *China and the Major Powers in East Asia*. Brookings Institution, 1977.
Banston, R. P. *Modern Diplomacy*. Longman, 1988.
Beale, Howard K. *Theodore Roosevelt and the Rise of America to World Power*. Johns Hopkins University Press, 1956.
Beam, Jacob. *Multiple Exposure: An American Ambassador's Unique Perspective on East-West Issues*. Norton, 1978.
Beers, Burton. *Vain Endeavor: Robert Lansing's Attempts to End the American-Japanese Rivalry*. Duke University Press, 1962.
Beisner, Robert. *From the Old Diplomacy to the New, 1865–1900*. University of Chicago Press, 1968.
Bell, Coral. *The Reagan Paradox*. Elgan, 1989.
Bemis, Samuel Flagg. *American Foreign Policy and the Blessings of Liberty*. Yale University Press, 1962.
———. *The Diplomacy of the American Revolution*. Indiana University Press, 1957.
———. *Guide to the Diplomatic History of the United States*. Government Printing Office, 1935.
———. *John Quincy Adams and the Foundations of American Foreign Policy*. Knopf, 1973.
———. *The Latin American Policy of the United States*. Harcourt, Brace and Co., 1943.
Bemis, Samuel Flagg, and Robert Ferrell, eds. *The American Secretaries of State and Their Diplomacy*. vol. 15. Cooper Square, 1966.
Bendiner, Elmer. *The Virgin Diplomats*. Knopf, 1976.
Bennett, Edward M. *Franklin D. Roosevelt and the Search for Security: American-Soviet Relations, 1933–1939*. Scholarly Resources, 1985.
———. *Franklin D. Roosevelt and the Search for Victory: American-Soviet Relations, 1939–1945*. Scholarly Resources, 1990.
———. *Recognition of Russia: An American Foreign Policy Dilemma*. Blaisdell, 1970.
Bill, James. *The Eagle and the Lion: The Tragedy of American-Iranian Relations*. Yale University Press, 1988.
Bird, Kai. *The Chairman: John J. McCloy, the Making of the American Establishment*. Simon and Schuster, 1992.
Blair, Clay. *The Forgotten War: America in Korea, 1950–1953*. Time Books, 1987.
Blasier, Cole. *The Hovering Giant: U.S. Responses to Revolutionary Change in Latin America*. University of Pittsburgh Press, 1976.
Blum, Robert M. *Drawing the Line: The Origin of the American Containment Policy in East Asia*. Norton, 1982.

Blumenthal, Henry. *France and the United States: Their Diplomatic Relation, 1789–1914*. University of North Carolina Press, 1970.

———. *Illusion and Reality in Franco-American Diplomacy, 1914–1945*. Louisiana State University Press, 1986.

———. *A Reappraisal of Franco-American Relations, 1830–1871*. Greenwood Press, 1980.

Bohlen, Charles E. *The Transformation of American Foreign Policy*. Norton, 1969.

———. *Witness to History, 1929–1969*. Norton, 1973.

Bolkhovitinov, Nikolai N. *The Beginnings of Russian-American Relations, 1775–1815*. Harvard University Press, 1975.

Boll, Michael. *Cold War in the Balkans*. University Press of Kentucky, 1984.

Borden, William. *The Pacific Alliance*. University of Wisconsin Press, 1984.

Bordin, Ruth. *Andrew Dickson White: Teacher of History*. University of Michigan Press, 1958.

Borg, Dorothy. *American Policy and the Chinese Revolution, 1925–1928*. American Institute of Pacific Relations, Macmillan, 1947.

Borg, Dorothy, and Waldo Heinrichs, eds. *Uncertain Years: Chinese-American Relations, 1947–1950*. Columbia University Press, 1980.

Bourne, Kenneth. *Britain and the Balance of Power in North America, 1815–1908*. Longmans, 1967.

Bowles, Chester. *Ambassador's Report*. Harper, 1954.

———. *American Politics in a Revolutionary World*. Harvard University Press, 1956.

———. *Promises to Keep: My Years in Public Life, 1941–1969*. Harper and Row, 1971.

Bowman, Albert. *The Struggle for Neutrality: Franco-American Diplomacy during the Federalist Era*. University of Tennessee Press, 1974.

Braden, Spruille. *Diplomats and Demagogues*. Arlington House, 1971.

Brands, H. W. *Cold Warriors: Eisenhower's Generation and American Foreign Policy*. Columbia University Press, 1988.

———. *Inside the Cold War: Loy Henderson and the Rise of the American Empire, 1918–1961*. Oxford University Press, 1991.

Brecher, Frank W. *Reluctant Ally*. Greenwood Press, 1991.

Briggs, Ellis. *Anatomy of Diplomacy: The Origin and Execution of American Foreign Policy*. D. McKay Co., 1968.

———. *Farewell to Foggy Bottom*. D. McKay Co., 1964.

Brinkley, Douglas. *Dean Acheson: The Cold War Years, 1953–71*. Yale University Press, 1992.

Broadwater, Jeff. *Adlai Stevenson and American Politics: The Odyssey of a Cold War Liberal*. Twayne, 1994.

———. *Eisenhower and the Anti-Communist Crusade*. University of North Carolina Press, 1992.

Brooks, Philip. *Diplomacy and the Borderlands*. University of California Press, 1939.

Brownell, W., and R. N. Billings. *So Close to Greatness: A Biography of William C. Bullitt*. Macmillan, 1987.

Bryson, Thomas. *American Diplomatic Relations with the Middle East, 1784–1975*. Scarecrow Press, 1977.

Brzezinski, Zbigniew. *Power and Principle*. Farrar, Straus, Giroux, 1983.

Buchanan, George. *My Mission to Russia and other Diplomatic Memories*. Little, Brown and Co., 1923.

Buchanan, James. *James Buchanan's Mission to Russia: 1831–1833*. Arno Press, 1970.

Buckley, William F. *United Nations Journal*. Putnam, 1974.

Buhite, Russell D. *Nelson T. Johnson and American Policy toward China, 1925–1941*. Michigan State University Press, 1968.

———. *Patrick J. Hurley and American Foreign Policy*. Cornell University Press, 1973.

———. *Soviet-American Relations in Asia, 1945–1954*. University of Oklahoma Press, 1981.

Bullitt, William. *The Bullitt Mission to Russia*. Hyperion Press, 1977.

———. *The Great Globe Itself*. C. Scribner's Sons, 1946.

Bundy, William, ed. *Two Hundred Years of American Foreign Policy*. New York University Press, 1977.

Burns, James MacGregor. *Roosevelt: The Soldier of Freedom*. Harcourt, Brace, Jovanovich, 1970.

Burns, Richard Dean. *Guide to American Foreign Relations since 1700*. ABC-Clio, 1983.

Burns, Richard Dean, and Edward M. Bennett, eds. *Diplomats in Crisis: United States–Chinese–Japanese Relations, 1919–1941*. ABC-Clio, 1974.

Buzan, Barry. *People, States, and Fear*. University of North Carolina Press, 1983.

Byrnes, James F. *All in One Lifetime*. Harper, 1958.

———. *Speaking Frankly*. Harper, 1947.

Callcott, Wilfrid. *The Caribbean Policy of the United States, 1890–1920*. Octagon Books, 1942.

Calleo, David. *Beyond American Hegemony*. Basic Books, 1987.

Campbell, Alexander E. *The USA in World Affairs*. Harrar, 1974.

Campbell, Charles. *From Revolution to Rapprochement: The United States and Great Britain, 1783–1900*. Wiley, 1974.

Campbell, Thomas M., and George C. Herring, eds. *The Diaries of Edward R. Stettinius, Jr., 1943–1946*. New Viewpoints, 1975.

Carey, James. *Peru and the United States, 1900–1962*. University of Notre Dame Press, 1964.

Carter, James Earl. *Keeping Faith: Memoirs of a President*. Bantam, 1982.

Chang, Gordon H. *Friends and Enemies: The United States, China, and the Soviet Union, 1948–1972*. Stanford University Press, 1990.

Chester, Edward. *Clash of Titans: Africa and U.S. Foreign Policy*. Orbis Books, 1974.

Child, John. *Unequal Alliance: The Inter-American Military System, 1938–1979*. Westview Press, 1980.

Childs, J. R. *American Foreign Service*. H. Holt, 1948.

———. *Foreign Service Farewell*. University Press of Virginia, 1969.

Claude, Inis. *Swords into Plowshares*. 4th ed. Random House, 1984.

Clay, Lucius D. *Decision in Germany*. Doubleday, 1950.

———. *The Papers of Lucius D. Clay*. Ed. Jean Smith. Indiana University Press, 1974.

Clements, Kendrick. *Woodrow Wilson: World Statesman*. Twayne, 1987.

———, ed. *James F. Byrnes and the Origins of the Cold War*. Carolina Academic Press, 1982.

Clendenen, Clarence, and Peter Duignan. *Americans in Black Africa up to 1865*. Hoover Institution, 1964.

Cline, Howard. *The United States and Mexico*. Rev. ed. Harvard University Press, 1963.

Clubb, Oliver. *The United States and the Sino-Soviet Bloc in Southeast Asia*. Brookings Institution, 1962.

Cockfield, Jamie, ed. *Dollars and Diplomacy: Ambassador David Rowland Francis and the Fall of Tsarism, 1916–17.* Duke University Press, 1981.

Cohen, Theodore. *Remaking Japan: The American Occupation as New Deal.* Ed. Herbert Passin. Free Press, 1987.

Cohen, Warren. *America's Response to China.* Columbia University Press, 1990.

Cole, Wayne S. *Norway and the United States, 1905–1955.* Iowa State University Press, 1989.

———. *Roosevelt and the Isolationists, 1932–1945.* University of Nebraska Press, 1983.

Combs, Jerald A. *American Diplomatic History.* University of California Press, 1983.

Compton, James. *The Swastika and the Eagle: Hitler, the United States, and the Origins of World War II.* Houghton Mifflin, 1967.

Connell-Smith, Gordon. *The Inter-American System.* Oxford University Press, 1966.

———. *The United States and Latin America.* Wiley, 1974.

Costigliola, Frank. *Awkward Dominion: American Political, Economic, and Cultural Relations with Europe, 1919–1933.* Cornell University Press, 1984.

Cotler, Julio, and R. Fagen, eds. *Latin America and the United States.* Stanford University Press, 1974.

Cottam, Richard. *Iran and the United States.* University of Pittsburgh Press, 1988.

Couloumbis, Theodore A., and John O. Iatrides, eds. *Greek-American Relations.* Pella Publishing Co., 1980.

Craig, Gordon, and Felix Gilbert, eds. *The Diplomats: 1919–1939.* Princeton University Press, 1953.

Cresson, W. P. *Francis Dana: A Puritan Diplomat at the Court of Catherine the Great.* Lincoln MacVeagh, The Dial Press, 1930.

Crook, David P. *Diplomacy during the American Civil War.* Wiley, 1985.

———. *The North, the South, and the Powers.* Wiley, 1974.

Crosby, A. *America, Russia, Hemp, and Napoleon.* Ohio State University Press, 1965.

Cumings, Bruce. *Origins of the Korean War.* 2 vols. Princeton University Press, 1981, 1990.

———, ed. *Child of Conflict: The Korean-American Relationship, 1943–1953.* University of Washington Press, 1983.

Curry, Roy. *Woodrow Wilson and Far Eastern Policy, 1913–1921.* Bookman Associates, 1957.

Curtis, George T. *Life of James Buchanan.* Harper E. Brothers, 1883.

Dallek, Robert. *The American Style of Foreign Policy: Cultural Politics and Foreign Affairs.* Knopf, 1983.

———. *Democrat and Diplomat: The Life of William E. Dodd.* Oxford University Press, 1968.

———. *Franklin D. Roosevelt and American Foreign Policy, 1932–1945.* Oxford University Press, 1979.

Dauer, Manning. *The Adams Federalists.* Johns Hopkins University Press, 1953.

Davies, Joseph E. *Mission to Moscow.* Simon and Schuster, 1941.

Davis, Calvin. *The United States and the Second Hague Peace Conference: American Diplomacy and International Organization, 1899–1914.* Duke University Press, 1976.

Deane, John. *The Strange Alliance.* Viking Press, 1947.

DeConde, Alexander. *Entangling Alliance: Politics and Diplomacy under George Washington.* Duke University Press, 1958.

————. *A History of American Foreign Policy*. 2 vols. 3rd ed. Scribner's, 1978.

————. *The Quasi-War*. Scribner's, 1966.

————, ed. *Isolation and Security: Ideas and Interests in Twentieth-Century American Foreign Policy*. Duke University Press, 1957.

Dennett, Tyler. *Americans in Eastern Asia*. Macmillan, 1922.

————. *John Hay*. Dodd, Mead and Co., 1933.

————. *Roosevelt and the Russo-Japanese War*. Doubleday, Pago and Co., 1925.

Dennis, Alfred. *Adventures in American Diplomacy, 1896–1906*. E. P. Dutton, 1928.

DeNovo, John A. *American Interests and Policies in the Middle East, 1900–1939*. University of Minnesota Press, 1963.

De Santis, Hugh. *The Diplomacy of Silence: The American Foreign Service, the Soviet Union, and the Cold War, 1933–1947*. University of Chicago Press, 1980.

Divine, Robert. *Eisenhower and the Cold War*. Oxford University Press, 1981.

————. *The Illusion of Neutrality*. University of Chicago Press, 1962.

————. *The Reluctant Belligerent: American Entry into World War II*. John Wiley, 1965, 1979.

————. *Roosevelt and World War II*. Johns Hopkins University Press, 1969.

————. *Since 1945: Politics and Diplomacy in Recent American History*. 3rd ed. Wiley, 1985.

————, ed. *The Johnson Years*. Vol. 1. University of Texas Press, 1981.

Dobbs, Charles. *Unwanted Symbol: American Foreign Policy, the Cold War, and Korea, 1945–1950*. Kent State University Press, 1981.

Dodd, William E., Jr., and Martha Dodd, eds. *Ambassador Dodd's Diary, 1933–1938*. Harcourt, Brace and Company, 1941.

Doenke, Justus. *Not to the Swift: The Old Isolationists in the Cold War Era*. Bucknell University Press, 1979.

Dowty, Alan. *The Limits of American Isolation: The United States and the Crimean War*. New York University Press, 1971.

Dozer, Donald. *Are We Good Neighbors? Three Decades of Inter-American Relations, 1930–1960*. University of Florida Press, 1959.

Duignan, Peter, and Clarence Clendenen. *The United States and the African Slave Trade, 1619–1862*. Hoover Institution, 1963.

Duignan, Peter, and L. H. Gann. *The United States and Africa in the United Nations*. Cambridge University Press, 1984.

Dull, Jonathan R. *A Diplomatic History of the American Revolution*. Yale University Press, 1985.

————. *Franklin the Diplomat*. American Philosophical Association, 1982.

Dulles, Foster Rhea. *China and America: The Story of Their Relations since 1784*. Princeton University Press, 1946.

Dulles, John Foster. *War or Peace*. Macmillan, 1950; reprint, 1957.

Dumbrell, John. *American Foreign Policy*. St. Martin's, 1997.

————. *The Carter Presidency*. St. Martin's, 1993.

Dunn, Frederick S. *Peace-making and the Settlement with Japan*. Princeton University Press, 1963.

Duroselle, Jean-Baptiste. *France and the United States*. University of Chicago Press, 1978.

Eagles, Keith. *Ambassador Joseph E. Davies and American-Soviet Relations, 1937–1941*. Garland Publishing, 1985.

Edmonds, Robin. *Setting the Mould: The United States and Britain, 1945–1950*. Norton, 1986.

Eisenhower, Dwight D. *Mandate for Change, 1953–1956*. Doubleday, 1963.

———. *Waging Peace: The White House Years, 1956–1961*. Doubleday, 1965.

Ekirch, Arthur. *Ideas, Ideals, and American Diplomacy*. Appleton, Century and Crofts, 1966.

El-Khawas, Mohammed, and Barry Cohen, eds. *The Kissinger Study of Southern Africa*. L. Hill, 1976.

Ellis, L. Ethan. *Republican Foreign Policy, 1921–1933*. Rutgers University Press, 1968.

Emerson, Rupert. *Africa and United States Policy*. Prentice-Hall, 1967.

Esthus, Raymond. *Theodore Roosevelt and Japan*. University of Washington Press, 1966.

Etzold, Thomas. *The Conduct of American Foreign Relations: The Other Side of Diplomacy*. New Viewpoints, 1977.

Fairbank, John K. *China Watch*. Harvard University Press, 1987.

———. *The United States and China*. 4th ed. Harvard University Press, 1979.

Farnsworth, Beatrice. *William C. Bullitt and the Soviet Union*. Indiana University Press, 1967.

Feis, Herbert. *Between War and Peace*. Princeton University Press, 1960.

———. *The Birth of Israel: The Tousled Diplomatic Bed*. Norton, 1969.

———. *Churchill, Roosevelt, Stalin*. Princeton University Press, 1957.

———. *The Road to Pearl Harbor*. Princeton, 1971.

Ferrell, Robert H. *America as a World Power, 1872–1945*. University of South Carolina Press, 1971.

———. *American Diplomacy: A History*. 2nd ed. Norton, 1969.

———. *American Diplomacy in the Great Depression: Hoover-Stimson Foreign Policy, 1929–1933*. Archon Books, 1957.

———. *The American Secretaries of State and Their Diplomacy: Marshall*. vol. 15. Cooper Square Publishers, 1966.

———. *Woodrow Wilson and World War I, 1917–1921*. Harper and Row, 1985.

———, ed. *The Eisenhower Diaries*. Norton, 1981.

———, ed. *Foundations of American Diplomacy, 1775–1872*. University of South Carolina Press, 1968.

Ferris, Norman. *Desperate Diplomacy: William H. Seward's Foreign Policy, 1861*. University of Tennessee Press, 1976.

———. *The Trent Affair*. University of Tennessee Press, 1977.

Field, James. *American and the Mediterranean World, 1776–1882*. Princeton University Press, 1969.

Fifield, Russell. *The Diplomacy of Southeast Asia, 1945–1958*. Harper, 1958.

———. *Woodrow Wilson and the Far East*. Archon Books, 1965.

Filene, Peter. *Americans and the Soviet Experiment, 1917–1933*. Harvard University Press, 1967.

Floto, Inga. *Colonel House in Paris: A Study of American Policy at the Paris Peace Conference 1919*. Princeton University Press, 1980.

Fontaine, Roger. *Brazil and the United States: Toward a Maturing Relationship*. American Enterprise Institute, 1974.

Foot, Rosemary. *The Practice of Power: U.S. Relations with China since 1949*. Oxford University Press, 1995.

————. *The Wrong War: American Policy and the Dimensions of the Korean Conflict, 1950–1953.* Cornell University Press, 1985.

Ford, Gerald. *A Time to Heal.* Harper and Row, 1979.

Forsythe, David. *Human Rights and U.S. Foreign Policy.* University of Florida Press, 1988.

Fossedal, Gregory. *The Democratic Imperative.* Basic Books, 1989.

Foster, John. *Diplomatic Memoirs.* 2 vols. Houghton Mifflin, 1909.

Fox, Annette. *The Politics of Attraction: Four Middle Powers and the United States.* Columbia University Press, 1977.

Francis, David. *Russia from the American Embassy.* C. Scribner's Sons, 1921.

Fredman, Lionel. *The United States Enters the Pacific.* Angus and Robertson, 1969.

Freidel, Frank. *The Splendid Little War.* Little, Brown, 1958.

Frye, Alton. *Nazi Germany and the Western Hemisphere, 1933–1941.* Yale University Press, 1967.

Gaddis, John L. *The Long Peace.* Oxford University Press, 1887.

————. *Russia, the Soviet Union, and the United States.* John Wiley, 1978.

————. *Strategies of Containment.* Oxford University Press, 1982.

————. *The United States and the End of the Cold War.* Oxford University Press, 1992.

————. *The United States and the Origins of the Cold War, 1941–1947.* Columbia University Press, 1972.

Galbraith, John K. *Ambassador's Journal.* Houghton Mifflin, 1969.

Gallagher, Charles. *The United States and North Africa: Morocco, Algeria, and Tunisia.* Harvard University Press, 1963.

Gardner, Lloyd C. *Architects of Illusion: Men and Ideas in American Foreign Policy, 1941–1949.* Quadrangle Books, 1970.

————. *Safe for Democracy.* Oxford University Press, 1984.

Garthoff, Raymond. *Détente and Confrontation.* Brookings Institution, 1985.

————. *The Great Transition: American-Soviet Relations and the End of the Cold War.* Brookings Institution, 1994.

Gatzke, Hans. *Germany and the United States.* Harvard University Press, 1980.

Gelb, Norman. *The Berlin Wall.* Time Books, 1987.

Gelber, Lionel. *The Rise of Anglo-American Friendship.* Oxford University Press, 1938.

Gifford, Prosser, and Wm. Roger Louis, eds. *Decolonization and African Independence: The Transfers of Power, 1960–1980.* Yale University Press, 1988.

————. *The Transfer of Power in Africa: Decolonization, 1940–1960.* Yale University Press, 1982.

Gilbert, Felix. *To the Farewell Address: Ideas of Early American Foreign Policy.* Princeton University Press, 1961.

Gimbel, John. *The American Occupation of Germany.* Stanford University Press, 1968.

————. *The Origins of the Marshall Plan.* Stanford University Press, 1976.

Goetzmann, William. *When the Eagle Screamed: The Romantic Horizon in American Diplomacy, 1800–1860.* Wiley, 1966.

Goldschmidt, Walter, ed. *The United States and Africa.* Praeger Publishers, 1958.

Goode, James. *The United States and Iran, 1946–51.* St. Martin's Press, 1989.

Graber, Doris. *Crisis Diplomacy: A History of U.S. Intervention Policies and Practices.* Public Affairs Press, 1959.

Grabill, Joseph. *Protestant Diplomacy and the Near East: Missionary Influence on American Policy, 1810–1927.* University of Minnesota Press, 1971.

Graebner, Norman. *The Age of Global Power*. Wiley, 1979.
———. *America as a World Power: A Realist Appraisal from Wilson to Reagan*. Scholarly Resources, 1984.
———. *Cold War Diplomacy: 1945–1960*. Van Nostrand, 1962.
———. *Empire on the Pacific*. ABC-Clio 1983.
———. *Foundations of American Foreign Policy: A Realist Appraisal from Franklin to McKinley*. Scholarly Resources, 1985.
———, ed. *Traditions and Values: American Diplomacy, 1865–1945*. University Press of America, 1985.
———, ed. *Traditions and Values: American Diplomacy, 1790–1865*. University Press of America, 1985.
———, ed. *An Uncertain Tradition*. McGraw-Hill, 1961.
Graham, Edward D. *American Ideas of a Special Relationship with China, 1784–1900*. Garland Publishing, 1988.
Green, David. *The Containment of Latin America*. Quadrangle Books, 1971.
Grew, Joseph C. *Ten Years in Japan*. Simon and Schuster, 1944.
———. *Turbulent Era: A Diplomatic Record of Forty Years, 1904–1945*. 2 vols. Houghton Mifflin, 1952.
Grieb, Kenneth. *The Latin American Policy of Warren G. Harding*. Texas Christian University Press, 1976.
Griffin, Charles. *The United States and the Disruption of the Spanish Empire, 1810–1822*. Columbia University Press, 1937.
Griffin, Eldon. *Clippers and Consuls: American Consular and Commercial Relations with Eastern Asia, 1845–1860*. Edwards Bros., 1938.
Griswald, A. W. *The Far Eastern Policy of the United States*. Yale University Press, 1938.
Gromyko, Andrei. *Memoirs*. Doubleday, 1989.
Guhin, Michael. *John Foster Dulles* Columbia University Press, 1972.
Guinsburg, Thomas. *The Pursuit of Isolationism in the United States Senate from Versailles to Pearl Harbor*. Garland Publishing, 1983.
Hagan, Kenneth. *American Gunboat Diplomacy and the Old Navy, 1877–1889*. Greenwood Press, 1973.
Haglund, David. *Latin America and the Transformation of U.S. Strategic Thought, 1936–1940*. University of New Mexico Press, 1984.
Haig, Alexander M., Jr. *Caveat*. Macmillan, 1984.
Halle, Louis J. *The Cold War as History*. Challot and Windus, 1967.
Halliday, Jon, and Bruce Cumings. *Korea: The Unknown War*. Pantheon Books, 1988.
Hance, William, ed. *Southern Africa and the United States*. Columbia University Press, 1968.
Hanrieder, Wolfram. *Germany, America, Europe*. Yale University Press, 1989.
———. *The United States and Western Europe*. Winthrop, 1974.
Harbutt, Fraser. *The Iron Curtain: Churchill, America, and the Origins of the Cold War*. Oxford University Press, 1986.
Harper, John L. *America and the Reconstruction of Italy, 1945–1948*. Cambridge University Press, 1986.
Harriman, W. Averell. *America and Russia in a Changing World*. Doubleday, 1971.
Harriman, W. Averell, and Elie Abel. *Special Envoy to Churchill and Stalin, 1941–1946*. Random House, 1975.

Harrington, Fred. *God, Mammon, and the Japanese: Dr. Horace N. Allen and Korean-American Relations, 1884–1905*. University of Wisconsin Press, 1944.

Harris, George S. *Troubled Alliance: Turkish-American Problems in Historical Perspective, 1945–1971*. American Enterprise Institute, 1972.

Hart, Robert. *The Eccentric Tradition: American Diplomacy in the Far East*. Scribner's, 1976.

Henderson, Loy. *A Question of Trust: The Origins of U.S.-Soviet Diplomatic Relations: The Memoirs of Loy W. Henderson*. Hoover Institution Press, 1986.

Heinrichs, Waldo H., Jr. *American Ambassador: Joseph C. Grew and the Development of the United States Diplomatic Tradition*. Garland Publishing, 1979.

Henkin, Louis. *Foreign Affairs and the Constitution*. Norton, 1972.

Herring, George C. *Aid to Russia, 1941–1946: Strategy, Diplomacy, the Origins of the Cold War*. Columbia University Press, 1973.

———. *America's Longest War: The United States and Vietnam, 1950–1975*. 2nd ed. Knopf, 1986.

Herstein, Robert E. *Roosevelt and Hitler: Prelude to War*. Paragon House, 1989.

Hery, Martin Florian. *215 Days in the Life of an American Diplomat*. School of Foreign Service, Georgetown University, 1981.

———, ed. *The Consular Dimension of Diplomacy*. School of Foreign Service, Georgetown University, 1983.

———, ed. *Diplomacy: The Role of the Wife*. School of Foreign Service, Georgetown University, 1981.

———, ed. *The Modern Ambassador*. School of Foreign Service, Georgetown University, 1983.

Hess, Gary. *America Encounters India, 1941–1947*. Johns Hopkins University Press, 1971.

———. *The United States Emergence as a Southeast Asian Power, 1940–1950*. Columbia University Press, 1987.

———. *Vietnam and the United States: Origins and Legacy of War*. Twayne Publishers, 1990.

Hill, Larry, P. *Emissaries to a Revolution: Woodrow Wilson's Executive Agents in Mexico*. Louisiana State University Press, 1973.

Hixson, Walter. *George F. Kennan: Cold War Iconoclast*. Columbia University Press, 1989.

Hodge, Carl C., and Cathal J. Nolan, eds. *Shepherd of Democracy? America and Germany in the Twentieth Century*. Greenwood Press, 1992.

Hoff-Wilson, Joan. *Ideology and Economics*. University of Missouri Press, 1974.

Hogan, Michael. *The Marshall Plan*. Cambridge University Press, 1987.

Hoopes, Townsend. *The Devil and John Foster Dulles*. Little, Brown, 1973.

Hornbeck, Stanley K. *The Diplomacy of Frustration*. Hoover Institution Press, 1981.

Howe, Russell. *Along the Afric Shore: An Historic Review of Two Centuries of U.S.-African Relations*. Barnes & Noble, 1975.

Hsiao, Gene T., and Michael Witunski, eds. *Sino-American Normalization and Its Policy Implications*. Praeger Publishers, 1983.

Hull, Cordell. *The Memoirs of Cordell Hull*. 2 vols. Macmillan, 1948.

Hunt, Michael H. *Frontier Defense and the Open Door: Manchuria in Chinese-American Relations, 1895–1911*. Yale University Press, 1973.

———. *Ideology and U.S. Foreign Policy*. Yale University Press, 1987.

————. *The Making of a Special Relationship: The United States and China to 1914.* Columbia University Press, 1983.

Huntington, Samuel P. *The Dilemma of American Ideals and Institutions in Foreign Policy.* American Enterprise Institute, 1981.

Hurewitz, Jacob, ed. *Diplomacy in the Near and Middle East: A Documentary Record.* 2 vols. Van Nostrand, 1956.

Hyde, Charles. *International Law Chiefly As Interpreted and Applied by the United States.* 3 vols. 2nd rev. ed. Little, Brown, 1945.

Hyland, William. *The Cold War Is Over.* Time Books/Random House, 1990.

————. *Mortal Rivals.* Random House, 1987.

Iatrides, John O. *Balkan Triangle: Birth and Decline of an Alliance across Ideological Boundaries.* Mouton, 1968.

————. *Revolt in Athens.* Princeton University Press, 1972.

Ilchman, Warren F. *Professional Diplomacy in the United States, 1779–1939.* University of Chicago Press, 1961.

Immerman, Richard, ed. *John Foster Dulles and the Diplomacy of the Cold War.* Princeton University Press, 1990.

Iriye, Akira. *Across the Pacific: An Inner View of American–East Asian Relations.* Harcourt, Brace and World, 1967.

————. *After Imperialism: The Search for a New Order in the Far East, 1921–1931.* Harvard University Press, 1965.

————. *Pacific Estrangement: Japanese and American Expansion, 1897–1911.* Harvard University Press, 1972.

————, ed. *Mutual Images: Essays in American-Japanese Relations.* Harvard University Press, 1975.

Iriye, Akira, and Warren Cohen, eds. *The United States and Japan in the Postwar World.* University Press of Kentucky, 1989.

Irwin, Ray. *The Diplomatic Relations of the United States with the Barbary Powers, 1776–1816.* University of North Carolina Press, 1931.

Isaacson, Walter. *Kissinger: A Biography.* Simon and Schuster, 1992.

Isaacson, Walter, and Evan Thomas. *The Wise Men: Six Friends and the World They Made.* Simon and Schuster, 1986.

Israel, Jerry. *Progressivism and the Open Door: America and China, 1905–1921.* University of Pittsburgh Press, 1971.

Jensen, Kenneth, ed. *Origins of the Cold War: The Novikov, Kennan, and Roberts "Long Telegrams" of 1946.* United States Institute of Peace, 1991.

Johnson, Lyndon B. *The Vantage Point.* Holt, Rinehart and Winston, 1971.

Johnson, Richard A. *The Administration of United States Foreign Policy.* University of Texas Press, 1971.

Jonas, Manfred. *Isolationism in America, 1935–1941.* Cornell University Press, 1966.

Jones, Howard. *To the Webster-Ashburton Treaty: A Study in Anglo-American Relations, 1783–1843.* University of North Carolina Press, 1977.

Jones, Joseph M. *The Fifteen Weeks.* Brace and World, 1955.

Jordan, Donaldson, and Edwin J. Pratt. *Europe and the American Civil War.* Houghton Mifflin, 1931.

Kahin, George McT. *Intervention: How America Became Involved in Vietnam.* Knopf, 1986.

Kamikawa, Hikomatsu. *Japan-American Diplomatic Relations in the Meiji-Taisho Era*. Pan-Pacific Press, 1958.

Kaplan, Lawrence S. *Culture and Diplomacy: The American Experience*. Greenwood Press, 1977.

———. *Entangling Alliances with None: American Foreign Policy in the Age of Jefferson*. Kent State University Press, 1987.

———. *Jefferson and France*. Yale University Press, 1967.

———. *The United States and NATO: The Formative Years*. University Press of Kentucky, 1984.

———, ed. *The American Revolution and "A Candid World."* Kent State University Press, 1977.

Kaufman, Burton. *The Korean War*. Temple University Press, 1986.

Kawai, Kazuo. *Japan's American Interlude*. University of Chicago Press, 1960.

Keenleyside, Hugh, and Gerald Brown. *Canada and the United States*. Knopf, 1929.

Kelly, David. *The Ruling Few: or, The Human Background to Diplomacy*. Hollis and Carter, 1952.

Kennan, George F. *American Diplomacy, 1900–1950*. University of Chicago Press, 1951.

———. *At a Century's Ending: Reflections, 1982–1995*. W. W. Norton, 1996.

———. *The Decline of Bismarck's European Order*. Princeton University Press, 1979.

———. *Memoirs*. 2 vols. Little, Brown, 1967–1972.

———. *Russia and the West under Lenin and Stalin*. Little, Brown, 1961.

———. *Soviet-American Relations, 1917–1920*. 2 vols. Princeton University Press, 1956.

———. *Soviet Foreign Policy, 1917–1941*. Van Nostrand, 1960.

Killen, Linda. *The Russian Bureau: A Case Study in Wilsonian Diplomacy*. University Press of Kentucky, 1983.

Kimball, Warren. *The Juggler: Franklin Roosevelt as Wartime Statesman*. Princeton University Press, 1991.

———. *The Most Unsordict Act*. Johns Hopkins University Press, 1969.

Kirkpatrick, Jeane. *Dictatorships and Double Standards*. Simon and Schuster, 1982.

———. *The Reagan Phenomenon*. American Enterprise Institute, 1983.

Kissinger, Henry A. *Diplomacy*. Simon and Schuster, 1994.

———. *The Troubled Partnership: A Re-appraisal of the Atlantic Alliance*. McGraw-Hill, 1965.

———. *White House Years*. Little, Brown, 1979.

———. *A World Restored*. Grosset and Dunlap, 1964.

———. *Years of Upheaval*. Little, Brown, 1982.

Kitamura, Hiroshi, Ryohei Murata, and Hisahiko Okazaki. *Between Friends: Japanese Diplomats Look at Japan-U.S. Relations*. Trans. Daniel R. Zoll, Nichi-Bei Kankei o toit summeru. Weatherhill, 1985.

Kovrig, Bennett. *The Myth of Liberation: East-Central Europe in U.S. Diplomacy and Politics since 1941*. Johns Hopkins University Press, 1973.

Krenn, Michael. *The Chains of Interdependence: U.S. Policy toward Central America, 1945–1954*. SR Books, 1996.

———. *U.S. Policy toward Economic Nationalism in Latin America, 1917–1929*. M. E. Sharpe, 1990.

Kuehl, Warren F. *Seeking World Order: The United States and International Organization to 1920*. Vanderbilt University Press, 1969.

Kuniholm, Bruce R. *The Origins of the Cold War in the Near East*. Princeton University Press, 1980.

LaFeber, Walter. *America, Russia and the Cold War, 1945–1980*. 4th ed. Knopf, 1985

———. *The New Empire: An Interpretation of American Expansion, 1860–1898*. Cornell University Press, 1963.

Lang, Daniel. *Foreign Policy in the Early Republic*. Louisian State University Press, 1985.

Langer, William L. *The Diplomacy of Imperialism, 1890–1902*. Knopf, 1935, 1950.

Latourette, Kenneth S. *The History of Early Relations between the United States and China, 1784–1844*. Yale University Press, 1917.

Lauren, Paul, ed. *The China Hands' Legacy: Ethics and Diplomacy*. Westview, 1987.

———. *Diplomacy: New Approaches in History, Theory, and Policy*. Free Press, 1979.

———. *Diplomats and Bureaucrats*. Hoover Institution Press, 1976.

———. *Power and Prejudice: The Politics and Diplomacy of Racial Discrimination*. Westview, 2nd ed. 1996.

Lee, Yur-Bok. *Diplomatic Relations between the United States and Korea, 1866–1887*. Humanities Press, 1970.

———. *One Hundred Years of Korean-American Relations*. University of Alabama Press, 1986.

Leffler, Melvyn. *The Elusive Quest: America's Pursuit of European Stability and French Security, 1919–1933*. University of North Carolina Press, 1979.

———. *A Preponderance of Power: National Security, the Truman Administration, and the Cold War*. Stanford University Press, 1992.

Leopold, Richard. *Elihu Root and the Conservative Tradition*. Little, Brown, 1954.

Levin, N. Gordon, Jr. *Woodrow Wilson and World Politics*. Oxford University Press, 1968.

Li, Tien-yi. *Woodrow Wilson's China Policy, 1913–1921*. University of Kansas City Press, 1952.

Lifka, Thomas E. *The Concept "Totalitarianism" and American Foreign Policy, 1933–1949*. 2 vols. Garland Publishing, 1988.

Link, Arthur S. *Wilson the Diplomatist*. Johns Hopkins University Press, 1957.

———. *Woodrow Wilson: Revolution, War, and Peace*. AHM Publishing Corp., 1979.

———, ed. *Woodrow Wilson and a Revolutionary World, 1913–1921*. University of North Carolina Press, 1982.

Logan, Rayford W. *The Diplomatic Relations of the United States with Haiti, 1776–1891*. Kraus Reprint, 1969.

Lowenthal, Abraham F. *The Dominican Intervention*. Johns Hopkins University Press, 1995.

———. *Exporting Democracy: The United States and Latin America*. Johns Hopkins University Press, 1991.

———. *Partners in Conflict: The United States and Latin America*. Johns Hopkins University Press, 1990.

Lowenthal, Francis L., ed. *The Historian and the Diplomat*. Harper and Row, 1967.

Lukas, Richard. *Bitter Legacy: Polish-American Relations in the Wake of World War II*. University Press of Kentucky, 1982.

———. *The Strange Allies: The United States and Poland, 1941–1945*. University of Tennessee Press, 1978.

Lundestad, Geir. *The American Non-Policy towards Eastern Europe, 1943–1947*. Humanities Press, 1975.

Lycan, Gilbert. *Alexander Hamilton and American Foreign Policy*. University of Oklahoma Press, 1970.

Lytle, Mark Hamilton. *The Origins of the Iranian-American Alliance, 1941–1953*. Holmes and Meier, 1987.

MacVeagh, Lincoln. *Ambassador MacVeagh Reports*. Ed. John Iatrides. Princeton University Press, 1980.

Maddux, Thomas. *Years of Estrangement*. University of Florida Press, 1980.

Malik, Hafeez, ed. *Soviet-American Relations with Pakistan, Iran, and Afghanistan*. St. Martin's Press, 1987.

Mamatey, Victor. *The United States and East Central Europe, 1914–1918*. Princeton University Press, 1957.

Manning, William R. *Early Diplomatic Relations between the United States and Mexico*. Johns Hopkins University Press, 1916.

Maresca, John. *To Helsinki—The Conference on Security and Cooperation in Europe, 1973–1975*. Duke University Press, 1985.

Mastny, Vojtech. *Russia's Road to the Cold War*. Columbia University Press, 1979.

Matray, James. *The Reluctant Crusade: American Foreign Policy in Korea, 1941–1950*. University of Hawaii Press, 1985.

Mattox, Henry E. *The Twilight of Amateur Diplomacy: The American Foreign Service and Its Senior Officers in the 1890s*. Kent State University Press, 1989.

May, Ernest. *Imperial Democracy: The Emergence of America as a Great Power*. Harcourt, Brace and World, 1961.

———. *The World War and American Isolation, 1914–1917*. Harvard University Press, 1959.

Mayall, James. *Africa: The Cold War and After*. Elek, 1971.

Mayer, Arno. *Wilson vs. Lenin: Political Origins of the New Diplomacy, 1917–1918*. World Publishing Co., 1964.

———. *Politics and Diplomacy of Peacemaking: Containment and Counterrevolution at Versailles, 1918–1919*. Knopf, 1967.

Mayer, Frank A. *Adenauer and Kennedy: A Study in German-American Relations, 1961–1963*. St. Martin's Press, 1996.

Mayers, David. *The Ambassadors and America's Soviet Policy*. Oxford University Press, 1995.

———. *Cracking the Monolith: U.S. Policy against the Sino-Soviet Alliance, 1949–1955*. Louisiana State University Press, 1986.

———. *George Kennan and the Dilemmas of U.S. Foreign Policy*. Oxford University Press, 1988.

Mayers, David, and Richard A. Melanson. *Reevaluating Eisenhower: American Foreign Policy in the 1950s*. University of Illinois Press, 1987.

McCullough, David. *Truman*. Simon and Schuster, 1992.

McDonald, James G. *My Mission in Israel, 1948–1951*. Simon and Schuster, 1951.

McGeehan, Robert. *The German Rearmament Question: American Diplomacy and European Defense after World War II*. University of Illinois Press, 1971.

McGhee, George. *At the Creation of a New Germany: An Ambassador's Account*. Yale University Press, 1989.

————. *Envoy to the Middle World*. Harper and Row, 1983.

McHenry, Donald. *Micronesia, Trust Betrayed: Altruism vs Self Interest in American Foreign Policy*. Carnegie Endowment for International Peace, 1975.

McKay, Vernon, ed. *African Diplomacy*. Johns Hopkins University Press, 1966.

McKenna, Joseph C. *Diplomatic Protest in Foreign Policy*. Loyola University Press, 1962.

McLellan, David. *Dean Acheson: The State Department Years*. Dodd, Mead and Co., 1976.

McMahon, Robert. *Colonialism and Cold War: The United States and the Struggle for Indonesian Independence, 1945–49*. Cornell University Press, 1981.

Mecham, John Lloyd. *The United States and Inter-American Security, 1889–1960*. University of Texas Press, 1961.

Mee, Charles. *The Marshall Plan*. Simon and Schuster, 1984.

Merk, Frederick. *Manifest Destiny and Mission in American History*. Knopf, 1963.

Miller, Aaron. *Search for Security: Saudi Arabian Oil and American Foreign Policy, 1939–1949*. University of North Carolina Press, 1980.

Milward, Alan S. *The Reconstruction of Western Europe, 1945–1951*. University of California Press, 1984.

Miscamble, Wilson. *George F. Kennan and the Making of American Foreign Policy, 1947–1950*. Princeton University Press, 1992.

Monaghan, Frank. *John Jay*. Bobbs-Merrill, 1935.

Monaghan, Jay. *Diplomat in Carpet Slippers: Abraham Lincoln Deals with Foreign Affairs*. Bobbs-Merrill, 1945.

Moore, John Hammond, ed. *The American Alliance: Australia, New Zealand, and the United States, 1940–1970*. Cassell Australia, 1970.

Morgan, Roger. *New Diplomacy in the Post Cold War World*. St. Martin's Press, 1993.

Morgan, Roger P. *The United States and West Germany, 1945–1973*. Oxford University Press, 1974.

Morris, Richard B. *The Peacemakers: The Great Powers and American Independence*. Harper and Row, 1965.

Mower, A. Glenn. *Human Rights and American Foreign Policy*. Greenwood Press, 1987.

————. *The United States, the United Nations, and Human Rights*. Greenwood Press, 1979.

Munro, Dana. *Intervention and Dollar Diplomacy in the Caribbean, 1900–1921*. Princeton University Press, 1964; Greenwood Press, 1980.

————. *The United States and the Caribbean Area*. World Peace Foundation, 1934.

————. *The United States and the Caribbean Republics, 1921–1933*. Princeton University Press, 1973.

Muravchik, Joshua. *The Uncertain Crusade*. Hamilton Press, 1986.

Murphy, Robert. *Diplomat among Warriors*. Doubleday, 1964.

Nagai, Yonosuke, and Akira Iriye, eds. *The Origins of the Cold War in Asia*. Columbia University Press, 1977.

Nau, Henry R. *The Myth of America's Decline*. Oxford University Press, 1990.

Nelson, Keith. *Victors Divided: America and the Allies in Germany, 1918–1923*. University of California Press, 1975.

Neu, Charles E. *The Troubled Encounter: The United States and Japan*. Wiley, 1975.

————. *An Uncertain Friendship: Theodore Roosevelt and Japan, 1906–1909*. Harvard University Press, 1967.

Neumann, William. *America Encounters Japan: From Perry to MacArthur*. Johns Hopkins University Press, 1963.

———. *Making the Peace, 1941–1945: The Diplomacy of the Wartime Conferences*. Foundation for Foreign Affairs, 1950.

Nevins, Allan. *Henry White: Thirty Years of American Diplomacy*. Harper and Brothers, 1930.

Newsom, David, ed. *Diplomacy and the American Democracy*. Indiana University Press, 1988.

———. *The Diplomacy of Human Rights*. University Press of America, 1986.

———. *Diplomacy under a Foreign Flag: When Nations Break Relations*. St. Martin's Press, 1990.

———. *Private Diplomacy with the Soviet Union*. University Press of America, 1987.

———. *The Public Dimension of Foreign Policy*. Indiana University Press, 1996.

Nicholas, H. G. *The United States and Britain*. University of Chicago Press, 1975.

Nicolson, Harold. *The Congress of Vienna*. Viking, 1946; Harcourt, Brace, Jovanovich, 1974.

———. *Diplomacy*. 3rd ed. Oxford University Press, 1963.

———. *The Evolution of Diplomacy*. Collier Books, 1962.

———. *Peacemaking, 1919*. Grosset and Dunlap, 1965.

Ninkovich, Frank. *The Diplomacy of Ideas: U.S. Foreign Policy and Cultural Relations, 1938–1950*. Cambridge University Press, 1981.

———. *Germany and the United States*. Twayne, 1988.

Nitze, Paul H., with Ann M. Smith and Steven L. Rearden. *From Hiroshima to Glasnost: At the Center of Decision: A Memoir*. Grove Weidenfeld, 1989.

———. *Tension between Opposites*. Maxwell Macmillan, 1993.

Nixon, Richard M. *No More Vietnams*. Arbor House, 1985.

———. *RN: The Memoirs of Richard Nixon*. Grosset and Dunlap, 1978.

Nolan, Cathal J. *Principled Diplomacy: Security and Rights in U.S. Foreign Policy*. Greenwood Press, 1993.

———, ed. *Ethics and Statecraft: The Moral Dimension of International Affairs*. Greenwood Press, 1995.

Nutter, G. Warren. *Kissinger's Grand Design*. American Enterprise Institute, 1975.

Nye, Joseph, Jr. *Bound to Lead*. Basic Books, 1990.

———, ed. *The Making of America's Soviet Policy*. Yale University Press, 1984.

Oeste, George. *John Randolph Clay: America's First Career Diplomat*. University of Pennsylvania Press, 1966.

Offner, Arnold. *American Appeasement: United States Foreign Policy and Germany, 1933–1938*. Belnap Press, 1969.

———. *The Origins of the Second World War: American Foreign Policy and World Politics, 1917–1941*. Praeger Publishers, 1975.

Oksenberg, Michel, and Robert B. Oxnam, eds. *Dragon and Eagle: United States–China Relations: Past and Future*. Basic Books, 1978.

Osborne, John. *White House Watch: The Ford Years*. New Republic Book Co., 1977.

Osgood, Robert E. *Ideals and Self-Interest in America's Foreign Relations*. University of Chicago, 1953.

Ottaway, Marina. *Soviet-American Influence in the Horn of Africa*. Praeger Publishers, 1982.

Ovendale, Ritchie. *The English-Speaking Alliance: Britain, the United States, the Dominions, and the Cold War, 1945–1951*. G. Allen and Unwin, 1985.

Owsley, Frank. *King Cotton Diplomacy*. 2nd ed. rev. University of Chicago, 1959.

Pach, Chester. *Arming the Free World*. University of North Carolina Press, 1991.

Painter, David. *Oil and the American Century*. Johns Hopkins University Press, 1986.

Parkinson, F. *Latin America, the Cold War, and the World Powers, 1945–1973*. Sage Publications, 1974.

Paterson, Thomas. *Meeting the Communist Threat: Truman to Reagan America's Cold War History*. Oxford University Press, 1988.

———, ed. *Kennedy's Quest for Victory*. Oxford University Press, 1989.

Perkins, Bradford. *Castlereagh and Adams: England and the United States, 1812–1823*. University of California Press, 1964.

———. *The First Rapprochement: England and the United States, 1795–1805*. University of California Press, 1955.

———. *The Great Rapprochement: England and the United States, 1895–1914*. Atheneum, 1968.

———. *Prologue to War: England and the United States, 1805–1812*. University of California Press, 1961.

Perkins, Dexter. *Charles Evans Hughes and American Democratic Statesmanship*. Little, Brown, 1956.

———. *Hands Off: A History of the Monroe Doctrine*. Little, Brown, 1941.

———. *The Monroe Doctrine, 1823–1826*. Harvard University Press, 1927.

———. *The Monroe Doctrine, 1826–1867*. Johns Hopkins University Press, 1933.

———. *The Monroe Doctrine, 1867–1907*. Johns Hopkins University Press, 1937.

———. *The United States and the Caribbean*. Rev. ed. Harvard University Press, 1966.

Peterson, Harold. *Argentina and the United States, 1810–1960*. State University of New York Press, 1964.

———. *Diplomat of the Americas: A Biography of William I. Buchanan*. State University of New York Press, 1977.

Pletcher, David. *The Awkward Years: American Foreign Relations under Garfield and Arthur*. University of Missouri Press, 1962.

———. *The Diplomacy of Annexation: Texas, Oregon, and the Mexican War*. University of Missouri Press, 1973.

Plischke, Elmer. *Conduct of American Diplomacy*. Greenwood Press, 1974.

———. *Diplomat in Chief: The President at the Summit*. Praeger Publishers, 1986.

———. *Presidential Diplomacy*. Oceana Publications, 1986.

Pogue, Forrest. *George C. Marshall: Statesman, 1945–1959*. vol 4. Viking, 1963.

Polk, William R. *The United States and the Arab World*. 3rd. ed. Harvard University Press, 1975.

Pollard, Robert. *Economic Security and the Origins of the Cold War, 1945–1950*. Columbia University Press, 1985.

Pond, Elizabeth. *After the Wall*. Priority Press, 1990.

Pratt, Julius. *Challenge and Rejection: The United States and World Leadership, 1900–1921*. Macmillan, 1967.

Pruessen, Ronald. *John Foster Dulles*. Free Press, 1982.

Purifoy, Lewis. *Harry Truman's China Policy*. New Viewpoints, 1976.

Pusey, Merlo J. *Charles Evans Hughes*. 2 vols. Macmillan, 1951.

Quandt, William B. *Decade of Decisions: American Policy toward the Arab-Israeli Conflict, 1967–1976*. University of California Press, 1977.

———. *Peace Process: American Diplomacy and the Arab-Israeli Conflict since 1967*. Brookings Institution, 1993.

Rabel, Roberto. *Between East and West*. Duke University Press, 1988.

Radvanyi, Janos. *Hungary and the Superpowers*. Hoover Institution Press, 1972.

Rappoport, Armin. *Henry L. Stimson and Japan, 1931–33*. University of Chicago Press, 1963.

Reagan, Ronald. *An American Life*. Simon and Schuster, 1990.

Reese, Tevor R. *Australia, New Zealand, and the United States*. Oxford University Press, 1969.

Reitzel, William. *The Mediterranean: Its Role in America's Foreign Policy*. Harcourt, Brace, 1948.

Remini, Robert. *Andrew Jackson and the Course of American Empire, 1767–1821*. Harper and Row, 1977.

———. *Henry Clay: Statesman for the Union*. W. W. Norton, 1991.

Richardson, H. Edward. *Cassius Marcellus Clay*. University Press of Kentucky, 1996.

Richman, John. *The United States and the Soviet Union: The Decision to Recognize*. Camberleigh and Hall, 1980.

Rippy, J. Fred. *Rivalry of the United States and Great Britain over Latin America, 1808–1830*. Octagon Books, 1972.

Robertson, James. *A Kentuckian at the Court of the Tsars: The Ministry of Cassius Marcellus Clay to Russia 1861–1862 and 1863–1869*. Berea College Press, 1935.

Rosati, Jerel. *The Carter Administration's Quest for Global Community*. University of South Carolina Press, 1987.

Rosen, Roman Romanovich, Baron. *Forty Years of Diplomacy*. 2 vols. A.A. Knopf, 1922.

Rotter, Andrew. *The Path to Vietnam: Origins of the American Commitment to Southeast Asia*. Cornell University Press, 1987.

Rubin, Barry. *Secrets of State: The State Department and the Struggle over U.S. Foreign Policy*. Oxford University Press, 1985.

Ruddy, T. Michael. *The Cautious Diplomat: Charles E. Bohlen and the Soviet Union, 1929–1969*. Kent State University Press, 1986.

Russell, Ruth B. *A History of the United Nations Charter: The Role of the United States, 1940–1945*. Brookings Institution, 1958.

———. *The United Nations and United States Security Policy*. Brookings Institution, 1968.

Rutland, Robert. *James Madison and the American Nation, 1751–1836*. Simon and Schuster, 1994.

———. *James Madison: Founding Father*. Collier Macmillan, 1987.

Sapin, Burton. *The Making of United States Foreign Policy*. Brookings Institution, 1966.

Saul, Norman. *Concord and Conflict: The United States and Russia, 1867–1914*. University Press of Kansas, 1996.

———. *Distant Friends: The United States and Russia, 1763–1867*. University Press of Kansas, 1991.

Savelle, Max. *Empires to Nations: Expansion in America, 1713–1824*. University of Minnesota Press, 1974.

———. *The Origins of American Diplomacy: The International History of Angloamerica, 1492–1763*. Macmillan, 1967.

Schaller, Michael. *The American Occupation of Japan*. Oxford University Press, 1985.
———. *Douglas MacArthur*. Oxford University Press, 1989.
———. *The United States and China in the Twentieth Century*. 2nd ed. Oxford University Press, 1990.
———. *The U.S. Crusade in China, 1938–1945*. Columbia University Press, 1979.
Schick, Jack M. *The Berlin Crisis, 1958–1962*. University of Pennsylvania Press, 1971.
Schoenbaum, Thomas. *Waging Peace and War: Dean Rusk in the Truman, Kennedy, and Johnson Years*. Simon and Schuster, 1988.
Scholes, Walter, and Marie Scholes. *The Foreign Policies of the Taft Administration*. University of Missouri Press, 1970.
Schonberger, Howard B. *Aftermath of War: Americans and the Remaking of Japan, 1945–1952*. Kent State University Press, 1989.
Schulzinger, Robert. *Henry Kissinger: Doctor of Diplomacy*. Columbia University Press, 1989.
———. *The Making of the Diplomatic Mind: The Training, Outlook, and Style of United States Foreign Service Officers, 1908–1931*. Wesleyan University Press, 1975.
Schwabe, Klaus. *Woodrow Wilson, Revolutionary Germany, and Peacemaking, 1918–1919*. University of North Carolina Press, 1985.
Schwartz, Thomas Alan. *America's Germany: John J. McCloy and the Federal Republic of Germany*. Harvard University Press, 1991.
Sears, Louis. *Jefferson and the Embargo*. Duke University Press, 1927.
Seymour, Charles. *American Diplomacy During the World War*. Johns Hopkins University Press, 1934.
———. *The Diplomatic Background of the War, 1870–1914*. Yale University Press, 1916.
———. *The Intimate Papers of Colonel House*. 4 vols. Houghton Mifflin, 1926–1928.
Sherwin, Martin. *A World Destroyed: The Atomic Bomb and the Grand Alliance*. Knopf, 1975.
Sherwood, Robert. *Roosevelt and Hopkins*. Rev. ed. Harper, 1950.
Shultz, George P. *Turmoil and Triumph*. Maxwell Macmillan International, 1993.
Silverman, Dan. *Reconstructing Europe after the Great War*. Harvard University Press, 1982.
Smith, Gaddis. *American Diplomacy during the Second World War, 1941–1945*. 2nd ed. Wiley, 1985.
———. *Dean Acheson*. Cooper Square, 1972.
———. *Morality, Reason, and Power*. Hill and Wang, 1986.
Smith, Jean. *Lucius D. Clay*. Henry Holt, 1990.
Smith, Joseph. *Illusions of Conflict: Anglo-American Diplomacy toward Latin America, 1865–1896*. University of Pittsburgh Press, 1979.
———. *The Spanish-American War: Conflict in the Caribbean and the Pacific, 1895–1902*. Longman, 1994.
———. *Unequal Giants: Diplomatic Relations between the United States and Brazil, 1889–1930*. University of Pittsburgh Press, 1991.
Smith, Page. *John Adams*. 2 vols. Doubleday, 1962.
Smith, Robert. *The United States and Revolutionary Nationalism in Mexico, 1916–1932*. University of Chicago Press, 1972.
Smith, Walter Bedell. *My Three Years in Moscow*. Lippincott, 1950.

Snetsinger, John. *Truman, the Jewish Vote, and the Creation of Israel.* Hoover Institution Press, 1974.

Spence, Jonathan. *The China Helpers: Western Advisers in China, 1620–1960.* Bodley Head, 1969.

Spender, Percy. *Exercises in Diplomacy: The ANZUS Treaty and the Colombo Plan.* New York University Press, 1970.

Stagg, J.C.A. *Mr. Madison's War: Politics, Diplomacy, and Warfare in the Early American Republic, 1783–1830.* Princeton University Press, 1983.

Stephanson, Anders. *Kennan and the Art of Foreign Policy.* Harvard University Press, 1989.

———. *Manifest Destiny: American Expansionism and The Empire of Right.* Hill and Wang, 1995.

Steward, Dick. *Trade and Hemisphere: The Good Neighbor Policy and Reciprocal Trade.* University of Missouri Press, 1975.

Stimson, Henry, and McGeorge Bundy. *On Active Service in Peace and War.* Harper, 1948.

Stookey, Robert. *America and the Arab States.* Wiley, 1975.

Stourzh, Gerald. *Benjamin Franklin and American Foreign Policy.* 2nd ed. University of Chicago Press, 1969.

Stuart, Graham. *American Diplomatic and Consular Practice.* 2nd ed. D. Appleton Century Co., 1952.

———. *The Department of State: A History of Its Organization, Procedure and Personnel.* Macmillan, 1949.

Stuart, Reginald. *The Half-way Pacifist: Thomas Jefferson's View of War.* University of Toronto Press, 1978.

———. *War and American Thought from the Revolution to the Monroe Doctrine.* Kent State University Press, 1982.

Stueck, William, Jr. *The Road to Confrontation: American Policy toward China and Korea, 1947–1950.* University of North Carolina Press, 1981.

Talbott, Strobe. *Reagan and Gorbachev.* Vintage, 1987.

———. *The Russians and Reagan.* Vintage, 1984.

Tansill, Charles. *Canadian-American Relations, 1875–1911.* Yale University Press, 1943.

Taubman, William. *Stalin's American Policy.* Norton, 1982.

Thayer, Charles. *Diplomat.* Harper, 1959.

Thompson, John. *Russia, Bolshevism, and the Versailles Peace.* Princeton University Press, 1966.

Thompson, John K., and Stephen Randall. *Canada and the United States: Ambivalent Allies.* University of Georgia Press, 1994.

Thompson, Kenneth W., ed. *Traditions and Values: American Diplomacy, 1945 to the Present.* University Press of America, 1984.

Tilchin, William N. *Theodore Roosevelt and the British Empire: A Study in Presidential Statecraft.* St. Martin's Press, 1997.

Tong, Te-kong. *United States Diplomacy in China, 1844–60.* University of Washington Press, 1964.

Trani, Eugene. *The Treaty of Portsmouth.* University of Kentucky Press, 1969.

Treat, Payson. *Diplomatic Relations between the United States and Japan, 1876–1895.* 2 vols. Stanford University Press, 1932.

————. *Diplomatic Relations between the United States and Japan, 1895–1905*. Stanford University Press, 1938.

————. *Early Diplomatic Relations between the United States and Japan, 1853–1875*. Vol. 1. Johns Hopkins University Press, 1917.

Treverton, Gregory. *America, Germany and the Future of Europe*. Princeton University Press, 1992.

Truman, Harry S. *Memoirs: Year of Decisions*. Doubleday, 1955.

————. *Memoirs: Years of Trial and Hope*. Doubleday, 1956.

Tsou, Tang. *America's Failure in China, 1941–50*. University of Chicago Press, 1963.

Tuchman, Barbara. *Stilwell and the American Experience in China, 1911–45*. Macmillan, 1971.

Tucker, Nancy. *Patterns in the Dust: Chinese-American Relations and the Recognition Controversy, 1949–1950*. Columbia University Press, 1983.

————. *Taiwan, Hong Kong, and the United States, 1945–1992*. Twayne, 1994.

Tucker, Robert W., and David C. Hendrickson. *Empire of Liberty: The Statecraft of Thomas Jefferson*. Oxford University Press, 1990.

————. *The Fall of the First British Empire: Origins of the War of American of Independence*. Johns Hopkins University Press, 1982.

Turner, Stansfield. *Terrorism and Democracy*. Houghton Mifflin, 1991.

Ulam, Adam. *Expansion and Coexistence: Soviet Foreign Policy, 1917–73*. 2nd ed. Praeger Publishers, 1974.

————. *The Rivals: America and Russia since World War II*. Penguin, 1976.

Unterberger, Betty. *American Intervention in the Russian Civil War*. Heath, 1969.

————. *The United States, Revolutionary Russia, and the Rise of Czechoslovakia*. University of North Carolina Press, 1989.

Van Alstyne, R. W. *American Crisis Diplomacy: The Quest for Collective Security, 1918–1952*. Stanford University Press, 1952.

————. *American Diplomacy in Action*. 2nd ed. Stanford University Press, 1947.

————. *The Rising American Empire*. Oxford University Press, 1960.

————. *The United States and East Asia*. Norton, 1973.

Vance, Cyrus. *Hard Choices*. Simon and Schuster, 1983.

Vandenberg, Arthur, Jr., ed. *The Private Papers of Senator Vandenberg*. Houghton Mifflin, 1952.

van Minnen, Cornelis A. *American Diplomats in the Netherlands, 1815–1850*. St. Martin's Press, 1993.

Varg, Paul. *Foreign Polices of the Founding Fathers*. Michigan State University Press, 1963.

————. *The Making of a Myth: The United States and China, 1897–1912*. Greenwood Press, 1968.

————. *Missionaries, Chinese, and Diplomats*. Princeton University Press, 1958.

————. *Open Door Diplomat: The Life of W. W. Rockhill*. University of Illinois Press, 1952.

————. *United States Foreign Relations, 1820–1860*. Michigan State University Press, 1979.

Wall, Irwin. *The United States and the Making of Postwar France, 1945–1954*. Cambridge University Press, 1991.

Walters, Vernon. *Silent Missions*. Doubleday, 1978.

Walton, Richard. *Cold War and Counterrevolution: The Foreign Policy of John F. Kennedy*. Penguin, 1972.

———. *The United States and Latin America*. Seabury Press, 1972.

Walworth, Arthur C. *America's Moment, 1918: American Diplomacy at the End of World War I*. W.W. Norton, 1977.

Ward, Alan. *Ireland and Anglo-American Relations, 1899–1921*. University of Toronto Press, 1969.

Watt, D. Cameron. *Succeeding John Bull: America in Britain's Place, 1900–1975*. Cambridge University Press, 1984.

Watts, Steven. *The Republic Reborn: War and the Making of Liberal America, 1790–1820*. Johns Hopkins University Press, 1987.

Webster, Sir Charles K. *The Art and Practice of Diplomacy*. Barnes and Noble, 1962.

———. *The Congress of Vienna, 1814–1815*. G. Bell and Sons, 1937.

Weeks, William E. *John Quincy Adams and American Global Empire*. University Press of Kentucky, 1992.

Weil, Martin. *A Pretty Good Club: The Founding Fathers of the U.S. Foreign Service*. Norton, 1978.

Weissman, Stephen. *American Foreign Policy in the Congo, 1960–1964*. Cornell University Press, 1974.

Werking, Richard. *The Master Architects: Building the United States Foreign Service, 1890–1913*. University Press of Kentucky, 1977.

West, Rachel. *The Department of State on the Eve of the First World War*. University of Georgia Press, 1978.

Westerfield, H. B. *The Instruments of America's Foreign Policy*. Crowell, 1961.

Whitaker, Arthur. *The United States and Argentina*. Harvard University Press, 1954.

———. *The United States and South America: The Northern Republics*. Harvard University Press, 1948.

———. *The United States and the Independence of Latin America, 1800–1830*. Johns Hopkins University Press, 1941.

———. *The United States and the Southern Cone: Argentina, Chile, and Uruguay*. Harvard University Press, 1976.

Williams, William A. *American-Russian Relations, 1781–1947*. Rinehart, 1952.

———. *The Shaping of American Diplomacy*. 2nd ed. Rand McNally, 1970.

———. *The Tragedy of American Diplomacy*. Dell Publishing Co., 1959.

Wiltz, John. *From Isolation to War, 1931–1941*. Crowell, 1968.

Wittner, Lawrence. *American Intervention in Greece, 1943–1949*. Columbia University Press, 1982.

Wolfe, Robert, ed. *Americans as Proconsuls*. University of Southern Illinois Press, 1984.

Wood, Robert E. *From Marshall Plan to Debt Crisis: Foreign Aid and Development Choices in the World Economy*. University of California Press, 1986.

Woods, Randall Bennett. *A Changing of the Guard: Anglo-American Relations, 1941–1946*. University of North Carolina Press, 1990.

Woods, Randall, and Howard Jones. *Dawning of the Cold War: The United States' Quest for Order*. University of Georgia Press, 1991.

Yergin, Daniel. *Shattered Peace*. Houghton Mifflin, 1977.

Zahnisen, Marvin. *Uncertain Friendship: American-French Diplomatic Relations through the Cold War*. Wiley, 1975.

Zink, Harold. *The United States in Germany, 1944–1955*. Van Nostrand, 1957.

INDEX

Acheson, Dean: 8, 23–24, 25, 122, 141, 151–152, 196, 198, 199, 213–214, 241, 245, 254, 260, 316

Adams, John: 62, 63, 64–65, 66, 67, 108–110, 183–185, 187, 189, 193, 194

Adams, John Quincy: 64–65, 67, 69, 99–101, 102, 176, 177–179, 180

Adelman, Kenneth: 222

Aden: 49–50, 94

Adenauer, Konrad: 58–61, 156–157, 238, 253–256, 257, 260, 261

Afghanistan: 220, 224, 272

Albania: 242

Albright, Madeleine Korbel: 1–6, 291

Algeria: 41

Alliance for Progress: 228–229

alliances. See *Allies, World War I; Allies, World War II; Axis alliance; entangling alliances; League of Armed Neutrality; North Atlantic Treaty Organization (NATO); Southeast Asian Treaty Organization (SEATO); War of Independence; Warsaw Treaty Organization*

Allies, World War I: 36, 127, 173, 277–283

Allies, World War II: 21–22, 137–139, 168, 207, 212, 242–243, 314–317 *passim*, 331–332

Allison, John: 7–11, 316

ambassadorial diplomacy, general character of: 215–216

America First: 195

American Civil War (1861–1865): 17, 147, 234–240, 277–288, 292, 370

American Commission to the Paris Peace Conference: 36–37

American Red Cross: 149

American Revolution. See *War of Independence*

Angola: 310–311, 378–382

Annan, Kofi: 5

Anti-Ballistic Missile (ABM) Treaty: 160

anti-communism. See *communism*

anti-Semitism: 56, 60, 83–84, 152, 212, 289

apartheid: 198, 310–311, 379–382

appeasement: 21–22, 118, 129, 167, 202–203, 204, 214–215, 329, 335

Aquino, Benigno: 272, 343

Arab-Israeli conflict: 42, 44, 46, 95–98, 131, 160–161, 196, 223, 235, 258, 270–

ABOUT THE EDITOR AND CONTRIBUTORS

JULIE A. BAIN has a master's degree from the University of South Carolina and is an independent academic researcher based in South Carolina.

WILLIAM W. BAIN has degrees in political science and international relations from the University of South Carolina and the University of British Columbia and is completing his doctorate in international relations at the University of British Columbia. He has published articles on international relations theory and on U.S. security policy. His dissertation deals with the normative dimensions of statecraft, in particular the legal and moral rights and responsibilities of Great Powers.

EDWARD M. BENNETT is Professor Emeritus at Washington State University, where he taught the history of American foreign relations for thirty-three years. He was a participant in the Reagan/Gorbachev Fifth Protocol gathering of Soviet and American scholars assessing American-Soviet relations in World War II. His major works include editor, *Polycentrism: Growing Dissidence in the Communist Bloc?* (1967); *Recognition of Russia: An American Foreign Policy Dilemma* (1970); coeditor, *Diplomats in Crisis: United States–Chinese–Japanese Relations, 1919–1941* (1974); coauthor, *As the Storm Clouds Gathered: European Perceptions of American Foreign Policy in the 1930s* (1979); *Franklin D. Roosevelt and the Search for Security: American-Soviet Relations, 1933–1939* (1985); and *Franklin D. Roosevelt and the Search for Victory: American-Soviet Relations, 1939–1945* (1990).

ROBERT J. BOOKMILLER received his Ph.D. in foreign affairs from the University of Virginia. He teaches American foreign policy and Middle East politics at Millersville University and Franklin and Marshall College in Lancaster, Pennsylvania. He has published in such journals as *Current History, Journal of Palestine Studies, Middle East Policy*, and *SAIS Review*.

VERENA BOTZENHART-VIEHE is Associate Professor of History and Coordinator of the Humanities Program at Westminster College in Pennsylvania. She has published a number of articles and reviews dealing with American foreign policy and German-American relations and was a contributor to *Statesmen Who Changed the World* (1993).

JEFF BROADWATER teaches American history at Texas Women's University. He previously taught history and political science at Barton College, North Carolina. His books include *Eisenhower and the Anti-Communist Crusade* (1992) and *Adlai Stevenson and American Politics: The Odyssey of a Cold War Liberal* (1994).

DANIEL BYRNE holds degrees in history from the University of Notre Dame and is presently a doctoral candidate in history at Georgetown University, where his research focus is on U.S. diplomatic relations. His dissertation concerns Franco-American relations during the Algerian War of Independence, 1954–1962.

WILLIAM N. DALE graduated summa cum laude and Phi Beta Kappa from Harvard in 1940 and earned a master's in public administration at Harvard in 1942. During World War II he served in the U.S. Navy, after which he joined the Foreign Service. He served, inter alia, on the National Security Council staff, on the Policy Planning Council, as deputy assistant secretary of state, as deputy chief of mission in Tel Aviv, and as ambassador to the Central African Republic. Since his retirement from the Foreign Service he has remained active in the Archeological Institute of America and the United Nations Association of America.

KEITH EAGLES read for his B.A. at Cambridge University and earned his M.A. and Ph.D. at the University of Washington, specializing in American-Soviet relations. He is Associate Professor of History at the University of Waterloo, Canada. Among his major publications is *Ambassador Joseph E. Davies and American-Soviet Relations, 1937–1941* (1985).

CARL CAVANAGH HODGE is Senior Research Fellow with the American Institute for Contemporary German Studies in Washington, D.C. He is also Director of the International Relations Program and College Professor at Okanagan University College in Kelowna, British Columbia. In addition to articles and reviews, he is the author of *The Trammels of Tradition* (1994), a study of European social-ism, and coeditor of *Shepherd of Democracy? America and Germany in the Twentieth Century* (1992). His latest book on American government, entitled *All of the People, All of the Time*, will be published in 1998.

SHIZHANG HU is an Assistant Professor in the Department of History at the University of Wisconsin-Platteville. His publications include *Stanley K. Hornbeck and the Open Door Policy, 1919–1937* (1995). He has also published articles and book reviews in the research areas of Asian studies and Third World studies.

JOHN O. IATRIDES is Professor of International Politics at Southern Connecticut State University. His principal publications include *Balkan Triangle: Birth and Decline of an Alliance across Ideological Boundaries* (1968), *Revolt in Athens: The Greek Communist "Second Round," 1944–1945* (1972), editor, *Ambassador MacVeagh Reports: Greece, 1933–1947* (1980), *Greek-American Relations* (1980), *Greece in the 1940s* (1981), and *Greece at the Crossroads: The Civil War and Its Legacy* (1995).

NORIKO KAWAMURA received her Ph.D. in history from the University of Washington in 1989. She taught at the Virginia Military Institute from 1989 to 1992 and is currently an Assistant Professor in the Department of History at Washington State University. She is completing a major study of Woodrow Wilson's Asian policy, entitled *Odd Associates in World War I: Japanese-American Relations, 1914–1919*.

MICHAEL L. KRENN is an Associate Professor of History at the University of Miami. In addition to articles and reviews on U.S. relations with Latin America, he is the author of *U.S. Policy toward Economic Nationalism in Latin America, 1917–1929* (1990) and *The Chains of Interdependence: U.S. Policy toward Central America, 1945–1954* (1996). His current research deals with black Americans and the Department of State from 1945 to 1969.

ARLENE LAZAROWITZ received her Ph.D. in U.S. political history and foreign policy from the University of California, Los Angeles. She currently teaches at California State University, Long Beach. She has written and published on the Democratic Party in the 1950s, Chester Bowles and foreign aid to India, and Hiram Johnson and the New Deal. She is completing a study of the politics of funding the U.S. Air Force during the early Cold War.

HENRY E. MATTOX is a retired Foreign Service officer. He earned a Ph.D. in American history at the University of North Carolina, Chapel Hill, where he has also taught. He currently teaches in the Department of History at North Carolina State University. In addition to scholarly articles and reviews, among his major works is *The Twilight of Amateur Diplomacy: The American Foreign Service and Its Senior Officers in the 1890s* (1989).

FRANK A. MAYER is the author of *The Opposition Years: Winston S. Churchill and the Conservative Party, 1945–1951* (1992) and *Adenauer and Kennedy: A Study in German-American Relations, 1961–1963* (1996). He is a member of the American Council on Germany and a Fellow in the Consortium of Atlantic Studies.

DAVID MAYERS is Professor of History and Political Science at Boston University. He is the author of *George Kennan and the Dilemmas of U.S. Foreign Policy* (1988), *Cracking the Monolith: U.S. Policy against the Sino-Soviet Alliance, 1949–1955* (1986), and the award-winning *The Ambassadors and America's Soviet Policy* (1995). He coedited *Reevaluating Eisenhower: American Foreign Policy in the 1950s* (1987) and has written numerous scholarly articles and reviews.

CORNELIS A. VAN MINNEN is Executive Director of the Roosevelt Study Centre in Middelburg, the Netherlands. He received his Ph.D. in history from the University of Leiden. He is the author of *American Diplomats in the Netherlands, 1815–1850* (1993) and coeditor of *FDR and His Contemporaries: Foreign Perceptions of an American President* (1992), *Reflections on American Exceptionalism* (1994), and *Aspects of War in American History* (1997).

CHARLES E. NEU is Professor of History at Brown University. He is the author of *An Uncertain Friendship: Theodore Roosevelt and Japan, 1906–1909* (1967) and *The Troubled Encounter: The United States and Japan* (1975) and coeditor of *The Wilson Era: Essays in Honor of Arthur S. Link* (1991). He is completing a biography of Edward M. House.

CATHAL J. NOLAN teaches international relations and political science at Boston University. He previously taught at the University of British Columbia. He has written more than thirty articles and reviews dealing with democratic foreign policy and the normative dimension of international relations. His books include *Principled Diplomacy: Security and Rights in U.S. Foreign Policy* (1993) and *The Longman Guide to World Affairs* (1995), which will be reissued in two foreign-language editions in 1997 and 1998. He also coedited, with Carl C. Hodge, *Shepherd of Democracy? America and Germany in the Twentieth Century* (1992) and edited *Ethics and Statecraft: The Moral Dimension of International Affairs* (1995). He is currently writing a two-volume encyclopedia of world affairs, and completing a book on U.S. diplomatic intervention in Russia entitled *Beyond the Pale: American Diplomacy and Russia's Jews, 1865–1997*.

JODY L. PETERSON is completing her doctoral dissertation in American history at Washington State University and is a specialist in twentieth-century American diplomatic history. She has taught at the University of North Texas, Washington State University, and the University of Idaho. She is currently teaching at Olympic College in Shelton, WA.

MICHAEL J. POLLEY received his Ph.D. from Washington State University in 1984. He is Associate Professor and Chairman of the Department of History at Columbia College in Columbia, Missouri. Among his publications is *A Biography of George F. Kennan: The Education of a Realist* (1990).

NICHOLAS E. SARANTAKES received a B.A. from the University of Texas, an M.A. from the University of Kentucky, and a Ph.D. from the University of Southern California. His research interests are U.S.-Japanese relations in the postwar era. His articles and reviews have appeared in publications such as the *Journal of American–East Asian Relations, Journal of Asian Studies, Journal of Japanese History*, and *Journal of Military History*. He is currently finishing a study of the American occupation of Okinawa and its impact on U.S.-Japanese relations.

KENT G. SIEG received his Ph.D. in history from the University of Colorado in 1993. He specializes in American foreign policy toward the nations of Southeast Asia, a subject on which he has published several articles. He is currently a historian at the U.S. Department of State.

JOSEPH SMITH is Senior Lecturer in History at the University of Exeter, England. Among his books on U.S. diplomatic relations with Latin America are *Illusions of Conflict: Anglo-American Diplomacy toward Latin America, 1865–1896* (1979), *Unequal Giants: Diplomatic Relations between the United States and Brazil, 1889–1930* (1991), and *The Spanish-American War: Conflict in the Caribbean and the Pacific, 1895–1902* (1994).

ROBERT W. SMITH is a Ph.D. candidate in American diplomatic history at the College of William and Mary. His dissertation deals with a key period in early American diplomacy and is entitled ''Keeping the Republic: Ideology and the Diplomacy of John Adams, James Madison, and John Quincy Adams.'' He has presented his research at numerous scholarly conferences and contributed to the American Historical Association's *Guide to Historical Literature*.

TERESA ANN THOMAS is currently Instructor in History at Fitchburg State College in Massachusetts. She completed her Ph.D. dissertation, entitled ''From Orientalism to Professionalism: U.S. Foreign Service Officers in the Middle East since 1947,'' at Clark University, Worcester, Massachusetts in 1996. Her most recent publication is a review of Robert Kaplan's *The Arabists* in *Middle East Journal*.

WILLIAM N. TILCHIN is an Assistant Professor who teaches twentieth-century U.S. foreign relations at Boston University. He has published essays on Theodore Roosevelt's foreign policy, including one in *Statesmen Who Changed the World: A Bio-bibliographical Dictionary of Diplomacy* (Greenwood, 1993). His book *Theodore Roosevelt and the British Empire: A Study in Presidential Statecraft* was published in 1997.

RICHARD D. WIGGERS has degrees in journalism and international history from Carleton University and the University of Ottawa. He is completing his Ph.D. in history at Georgetown University and specializes in U.S. foreign policy. He has published several articles on prisoners' rights in World War II and the Korean War and on international humanitarian law. He also consults on historical research and analysis for the U.S. Business and Industrial Council, Educational Foundation in Washington, D.C.

ALAN T. WOOD is Associate Professor of History and Associate Dean for Academic Affairs at the University of Washington, Bothell. He is the author of *Limits to Autocracy: From Sung Neo-Confucianism to a Doctrine of Political Rights* (1995) and coauthor of the ninth edition of *World Civilizations* (1997). He also writes a newspaper column on Asian and global affairs.

ISBN 0-313-29195-0

90000>

EAN

9 780313 291951

HARDCOVER BAR CODE

Killy